Ethics

FOR THE

INFORMATION

AGE FIFTH EDITION

Ethics

FOR THE

INFORMATION
AGE FIFTH EDITION

Michael J. Quinn

Seattle University

PEARSON

Boston   Columbus   Indianapolis   New York   San Francisco   Upper Saddle River
Amsterdam   Cape Town   Dubai   London   Madrid   Milan   Munich   Paris   Montreal   Toronto
Delhi   Mexico City   Sao Paulo   Sydney   Hong Kong   Seoul   Singapore   Taipei   Tokyo

Vice President and Editorial Director, ECS   Marcia Horton
Editor in Chief   Michael Hirsch
Editorial Assistant   Emma Snider
Vice President Marketing   Patrice Jones
Marketing Manager   Yez Alayan
Marketing Coordinator   Kathryn Ferranti
Vice President and Director of Production   Vince O'Brien
Managing Editor   Jeff Holcomb
Senior Production Project Manager   Marilyn Lloyd
Manufacturing Manager   Nick Sklitsis
Operations Specialist   Lisa McDowell
Text Permissions, assessment   Dana Weightman
Text Permissions, clearance   Danielle Simon/Creative Compliance
Image Permissions   Melody English
Text Designer   Sandra Rigney
Cover Designer   Anthony Gemmellaro
Cover Image   Antenna / Getty Images
Media Editor   Dan Sandin
Full-Service Vendor   Cypress Graphics
Project Management   Paul C. Anagnostopoulos
Interior and Cover Printer/Binder   STP/R. R. Donnelley Harrisonburg

Credits and acknowledgments borrowed from other sources and reproduced, with permission, in this textbook appear on the appropriate page within the text.

This interior of this book was set in Minion and Nofret by Windfall Software using ZzTEX.

Many of the designations by manufacturers and sellers to distinguish their products are claimed as trademarks. Where those designations appear in this book, and the publisher was aware of a trademark claim, the designations have been printed in initial caps or all caps.

Library of Congress Cataloging-in-Publication Data

Quinn, Michael J. (Michael Jay)
    Ethics for the information age / Michael J. Quinn. — 5th ed.
        p.   cm.
    Includes index.
    ISBN 978-0-13-285553-2 — ISBN 0-13-285553-4
    1. Electronic data processing—Moral and ethical aspects.
2. Computers and civilization.   I. Title.
    QA76.9.M65Q56 2013
    303.48′34—dc23   2011049442

16 15 14 13 12—RRD—10 9 8 7 6 5 4 3

ISBN 10: 0-13-285553-4
ISBN 13: 978-0-13-285553-2

Brief Contents

Contents

5   Information Privacy   227

6   **Privacy and the Government**   267

7   Computer and Network Security   315

An Interview with **Matt Bishop**   351

8   Computer Reliability   355

10   Work and Wealth   447

Preface

Computers and high-speed communication networks are transforming our world. These technologies have brought us many benefits, but they have also raised many social and ethical concerns. My view is that we ought to approach every new technology in a thoughtful manner, considering not just its short-term benefits, but also how its long term use will affect our lives. A thoughtful response to information technology requires a basic understanding of its history, an awareness of current information-technology-related issues, and a familiarity with ethics. I have written *Ethics for the Information Age* with these ends in mind.

Ethics for the Information Age is suitable for college students at all levels. The only prerequisite is some experience using computers. The book is appropriate for a stand-alone "computers and society" or "computer ethics" course offered by a computer science, business, or philosophy department. It can also be used as a supplemental textbook in a technical course that devotes some time to social and ethical issues related to computing.

As students discuss controversial issues related to information technology, they have the opportunity to learn from each other and improve their critical thinking skills. The provocative questions raised at the end of every chapter, together with dozens of in-class exercises, provide many opportunities for students to express their viewpoints. My hope is that they will get better at evaluating complex issues and defending their conclusions with facts, sound values, and rational arguments.

WHAT'S NEW IN THE FIFTH EDITION

The most significant changes in the fifth edition are in the chapters dealing with privacy and computer and network security.

I have completely reorganized the material on privacy, dividing what used to be a single chapter into two more manageable chapters. Chapter 5 begins with a philosophical discussion of privacy, moves on to survey various ways in which people disclose information to private organizations, and then presents secondary uses of data and the opt-in versus opt-out debate. Chapter 6 shows how the executive, legislative, and judicial branches of the U.S. government have responded to the competing demands of protecting individual privacy and protecting the common good.

Chapter 7, "Computer and Network Security," has been heavily revised. I have deleted the historical section on hackers and phreaks, replacing stories of what happened in the 1980s with a new section that focuses on twenty-first century hacking incidents and the release of the Firesheep extension to the Firefox Web browser. The section formerly called "Viruses, Worms, and Trojan Horses" has been renamed "Malware," and it has been expanded to cover rootkits, spyware, adware, cross-site scripting, and drive-by downloads. I have eliminated low-level technical details of how various attacks work, focusing instead on their impact. Later in the chapter, I have added new material that underscores the growing significance of cyber attacks by criminal organizations and politically motivated cyber attacks.

The fifth edition references many important recent developments; among them are:

- the role of Twitter and Facebook in the Arab Spring uprisings that led to revolutions in Tunisia and Egypt;
- the security holes of Facebook, Twitter, and Amazon.com exposed by Firesheep;
- the privacy controversy surrounding Facebook Tag Suggestions;
- the Netflix Prize and the perils of releasing large "anonymous" data sets of consumer preferences;
- the release of E-ZPass toll records as evidence in criminal prosecutions and civil lawsuits;
- the protests against law enforcement agencies obtaining six-month-old email messages without a search warrant;
- the invasion of privacy concerns expressed after the introduction of advanced imaging technology scanners at airport security checkpoints;
- organized crime moving into the malicious code industry; and
- politically motivated cyber attacks.

Finally, I have updated facts and figures throughout the book.

ORGANIZATION OF THE BOOK

The book is divided into ten chapters. Chapter 1 has three objectives: to get the reader thinking about the process of technological change; to present a brief history of computing, networking, and information storage and retrieval; and to provide examples of moral problems brought about by the introduction of information technology.

Chapter 2 is an introduction to ethics. It presents eight different theories of ethical decision-making, weighing the pros and cons of each one. Four of these theories—Kantianism, act utilitarianism, rule utilitarianism, and social contract theory—are deemed the most appropriate "tools" for analyzing moral problems in the remaining chapters.

Chapters 3–10 discuss a wide variety of issues related to the introduction of information technology into society. I think of these chapters as forming concentric rings around a particular computer user.

Chapter 3 is the innermost ring, dealing with what can happen when people communicate over the Internet using the Web, email, and Twitter. Issues such as the increase in spam, easy access to pornography, cyberbullying, and Internet addiction raise important questions related to quality of life, free speech, and censorship.

The next ring, Chapter 4, deals with the creation and exchange of intellectual property. It discusses intellectual property rights, legal safeguards for intellectual property, the definition of fair use, digital rights management, abuses of peer-to-peer networks, the rise of the open-source movement, and the legitimacy of intellectual property protection for software.

Chapter 5 focuses on information privacy. What is privacy exactly? Is there a natural right to privacy? How do others learn so much about us? The chapter describes the electronic trail that people leave behind when they use a cell phone, make credit card purchases, open a bank account, go to a physician, or apply for a loan.

Chapter 6 focuses on privacy and the U.S. government. Using Daniel Solove's taxonomy of privacy as our organizing principle, we look at how the government has steered a middle path between the competing interests of personal privacy and public safety. We consider U.S. legislation to restrict information collection and government surveillance; government regulation of private databases and abuses of large government databases; legislation to reduce the dissemination of information and legislation that has had the opposite effect; and finally government actions to prevent the invasion of privacy as well as invasive government actions. Along the way, we discuss the implications of the USA PATRIOT Act and the debate over the REAL ID Act to establish a de facto national identification card.

Chapter 7 focuses on the vulnerabilities of networked computers. A new ethical case study focuses on the release of the Firesheep extension to the Firefox Web browser. The malware section has been heavily revised and now discusses rootkits, spyware, cross-site scripting, and drive-by downloads. A new section, "Cyber Crime and Cyber Attacks," describes how criminal organizations are exploiting human, network, and computer vulnerabilities for monetary gain, as well as how the Internet has become a new battlefield. We conclude with a discussion of the risks associated with online voting.

Computerized system failures have led to lost business, the destruction of property, human suffering, and even death. Chapter 8 describes some notable software system failures, including the story of the Therac-25 radiation therapy system. It also discusses the reliability of computer simulations, the emergence of software engineering as a distinct discipline, and the validity of software warranties.

Chapter 9 is particularly relevant for those readers who plan to take jobs in the computer industry. The chapter presents a professional code related to computing, the Software Engineering Code of Ethics and Professional Practice, followed by an analysis of the code and an introduction to virtue ethics. Several case studies illustrate how to use virtue ethics in conjunction with the Software Engineering Code of Ethics and Professional Practice to evaluate moral problems related to the use of computers. The chapter concludes with an ethical evaluation of whistle blowing, an extreme example of organizational dissent.

Chapter 10 raises a wide variety of issues related to how information technology has impacted work and wealth. Topics include workplace monitoring, telecommuting,

TABLE 1 Mapping between the units of the Social and Professional Issues course in *Computing Curricula 2001* and the chapters in this book.

Unit	Name	Chapter(s)
SP1	History of computing	1
SP2	Social context of computing	1, 3, 10
SP3	Methods and tools of analysis	2–10
SP4	Professional and ethical responsibilities	9
SP5	Risks and liabilities of computer-based systems	8
SP6	Intellectual property	4
SP7	Privacy and civil liberties	5, 6
SP8	Computer crime	3, 7
SP9	Economic issues in computing	10
SP10	Philosophical frameworks	2

and globalization. Does automation increase unemployment? Is there a "digital divide" separating society into "haves" and "have nots?" Is information technology widening the gap between rich and poor? These are just a few of the important questions the chapter addresses.

NOTE TO INSTRUCTORS

In December 2001 a joint task force of the IEEE Computer Society and the Association for Computing Machinery released the final draft of *Computing Curricula 2001* (www.computer.org/education/cc2001/final). The report recommends that every undergraduate computer science degree program incorporate 40 hours of instruction related to social and professional issues related to computing. For those departments that choose to dedicate an entire course to these issues, the report provides a model syllabus for CS 280T, Social and Professional Issues. *Ethics for the Information Age* covers all of the major topics listed in the syllabus. Table 1 shows the mapping between the 10 units of CS 280T and the chapters of this book.

The organization of the book makes it easy to adapt to your particular needs. If your syllabus does not include the history of information technology, you can skip the middle three sections of Chapter 1 and still expose your students to examples motivating the formal study of ethics in Chapter 2. After Chapter 2, you may cover the remaining chapters in any order you choose, because Chapters 3–10 do not depend on each other.

Many departments choose to incorporate discussions of social and ethical issues throughout the undergraduate curriculum. The independence of Chapters 3–10 makes it convenient to use *Ethics for the Information Age* as a supplementary textbook. You can simply assign readings from the chapters most closely related to the course topic.

SUPPLEMENTS

The following supplements are available to qualified instructors on Pearson's Instructor Resource Center. Please contact your local Pearson sales representative, or visit www.pearsonhighered.com/educator to access this material.

- An instructor's manual provides tips for teaching a course in computer ethics. It also contains answers to all of the review questions.
- A test bank contains more than 300 multiple-choice, fill-in-the-blank, and essay questions that you can use for quizzes, midterms, and final examinations.
- A set of PowerPoint lecture slides outlines the material covered in every chapter.

FEEDBACK

Ethics for the Information Age cites hundreds of sources and includes dozens of ethical analyses. Despite my best efforts and those of many reviewers, the book is bound to contain errors. I appreciate getting comments (both positive and negative), corrections, and suggestions from readers. Please send them to quinnm@seattleu.edu or Michael J. Quinn, Seattle University, College of Science and Engineering, 901 12th Avenue, Seattle, WA 98122.

ACKNOWLEDGMENTS

I appreciate the continuing support of a great publications team, beginning with editor Michael Hirsch, and including Emma Snider, Marilyn Lloyd, Kathy Ringrose, Craig Jones, Paul Anagnostopoulos, Jacqui Scarlott, Priscilla Stevens, Richard Camp, and Ted Laux. I thank them and everyone else who helped produce this edition.

I appreciate the contributions of all who participated in the creation of the first four editions or provided useful suggestions for the fifth edition: Paul C. Anagnostopoulos, Valerie Anctil, Beth Anderson, Bob Baddeley, George Beekman, Brian Breck, Sherry Clark, Thomas Dietterich, Roger Eastman, Beverly Fusfield, Robert Greene, Peter Harris, Susan Hartman, Michael Johnson, Marilyn Lloyd, Pat McCutcheon, Beth Paquin, Brandon Quinn, Stuart Quinn, Victoria Quinn, Charley Renn, Lindsey Triebel, and Shauna Weaver.

I am particularly grateful for the feedback of Ramprasad Bala of the University of Massachusetts at Dartmouth, Robert Sloan of the University of Illinois at Chicago, and Eric Manley of Drake University, who carefully read drafts of chapters 5, 6, and 7 and provided me with valuable feedback that led to significant improvements in the presentation.

Reviewers of previous editions include: Phillip Barry, University of Minnesota; Bo Brinkman, Miami University; Diane Cassidy, The University of North Carolina at Charlotte; Madhavi M. Chakrabarty, New Jersey Institute of Technology; John Clark, University of Colorado at Denver; Timothy Colburn, University of Minnesota-Duluth; Lorrie Faith Cranor, Carnegie Mellon University; Lee D. Cornell, Minnesota State University, Mankato; Richard W. Egan, New Jersey Institute of Technology; David Goodall, State

University of New York at Albany; Richard E. Gordon, University of Delaware; Mike Gourley, University of Central Oklahoma; Fritz H. Grupe, University of Nevada, Reno; Ric Heishman, George Mason University; Paulette Kidder, Seattle University; Evelyn Lulis, DePaul University; Tamara A. Maddox, George Mason University; Richard D. Manning, Nova Southeastern University; John G. Messerly, University of Texas at Austin; Joe Oldham, Centre College; Mimi Opkins, California State University, Long Beach; Holly Patterson-McNeill, Lewis-Clark State College; Colin Potts, Georgia Tech; Medha S. Sarkar, Middle Tennessee State University; Michael Scanlan, Oregon State University; Matthew Stockton, Portland Community College; Leon Tabak, Cornell College; Renée Turban, Arizona State University; Scott Vitz, Indiana University–Purdue University Fort Wayne; David Womack, University of Texas at San Antonio; John Wright, Juniata College; and Matthew Zullo, Wake Technical Community College.

Finally, I am indebted to my wife Victoria for her support and encouragement. You are a wonderful helpmate. Thanks for everything.

Michael J. Quinn
Seattle, Washington

We never know how high we are
Till we are called to rise;
And then, if we are true to plan,
Our statures touch the skies.

The heroism we recite
Would be a daily thing,
Did not ourselves the cubits warp
For fear to be a king.

–EMILY DICKINSON, *Aspiration*

I dedicate this book to my children: *Shauna, Brandon,* and *Courtney.*

Know that my love goes with you, wherever your aspirations may lead you.

1

Catalysts for Change

A tourist came in from Orbitville,
parked in the air, and said:

The creatures of this star
are made of metal and glass.

Through the transparent parts
you can see their guts.

Their feet are round and roll
on diagrams of long

measuring tapes, dark
with white lines.

They have four eyes.
The two in back are red.

Sometimes you can see a five-eyed
one, with a red eye turning

on the top of his head.
He must be special–

the others respect him
and go slow

when he passes, winding
among them from behind.

They all hiss as they glide,
like inches, down the marked

tapes. Those soft shapes,
shadowy inside

the hard bodies–are they
their guts or their brains?

–MAY SWENSON, "Southbound on the Freeway"[1]

1.1 Introduction

MOST OF US TAKE TECHNOLOGICAL CHANGE FOR GRANTED. In the past two decades alone, we have witnessed the emergence of exciting new technologies, including cell phones, MP3 players, digital photography, email, and the World Wide Web. There is good reason to say we are living in the Information Age. Never before have so many people had such easy access to information. The two principal catalysts for the Information Age have been low-cost computers and high-speed communication networks (Figure 1.1). Even in a society accustomed to change, the rate at which computers and communication networks have transformed our lives is breathtaking.

In 1950, there were no more than a handful of electronic digital computers in the world. Today we are surrounded by devices containing embedded computers. We rely upon microprocessors to control our heating and cooling systems, microwaves, cell phones, elevators, and a multitude of other devices we use every day. Thanks to

FIGURE 1.1 Low-cost computers and high-speed communication networks make possible the products of the Information Age, such as the Apple iPhone 4. It functions as a phone, email client, Web browser, camera, video recorder, digital compass, and more. (© Sonica83/Dreamstime.com)

microprocessors, our automobiles get better gas mileage and produce less pollution. On the other hand, the days of the do-it-yourself tune-up are gone. It takes a mechanic with computerized diagnostic equipment to work on a modern engine.

In 1990, few people other than college professors used email. Today more than a billion people around the world have email accounts. We consider people without access to email as deprived, even though most of us also complain about the amount of spam we receive.

The World Wide Web was still being designed in 1990; today it contains more than a trillion pages and makes possible extraordinarily valuable information retrieval systems. Even grade school children are expected to gather information from the Web when writing their reports. However, many parents worry that their Web-surfing children may be exposed to pornographic images or other inappropriate material.

May Swenson has vividly described our ambivalent feelings toward technology. In her poem "Southbound on the Freeway," an alien hovers above an expressway and watches the cars move along [1]. The alien notes "soft shapes" inside the automobiles and wonders, "are they their guts or their brains?" It's fair to ask: Do we drive technology, or does technology drive us?

Our relationship with technology is complicated. We create technology and choose to adopt it. However, once we have adopted a technological device, it can change us and how we relate to other people and our environment.

The choice to use a new technology can affect us physically. For example, anecdotal evidence from physicians and physical therapists reveals that the growing popularity of laptop computers is increasing the number of people suffering from wrist, neck, shoulder, and back pain. That's not surprising, given the awkward places many people use laptop computers, such as traditional college lecture halls with cramped seating and tiny writing surfaces. A chiropractor remarks, "Have you seen pictures of kids using computers? They lie on their stomachs on the floor and work on their elbows. That's a prescription for a lifetime of neck pain, back pain, and lower back pain" [2].

Our use of a technology may also affect us mentally. For example, studies with macaque monkeys suggest that when we satisfy our hunger for quick access to information through our use of Web browsers, Twitter, and texting, neurons inside our brains release dopamine, producing a desire to seek out additional information, causing further releases of dopamine, and so on, which is why it can be difficult to break away from these activities [3, 4].

Adopting a technology can change our perceptions, too. For example, more than 90 percent of cell phone users report that having a cell phone makes them feel safer. On the other hand, once people get used to carrying a cell phone, losing the phone may make them feel more vulnerable than they ever did before they began carrying one. A Rutgers University professor asked his students to go without their cell phones for 48 hours. Some students couldn't do it. A female student reported to the student newspaper, "I felt like I was going to get raped if I didn't have my cell phone in my hand." Some parents purchase cell phones for their children so that a child may call a family member

FIGURE 1.2 The Amish carefully evaluate new technologies, choosing those that enhance family and community solidarity. (AP Photo/The Indianapolis Star and News, Mike Fender)

in an emergency. However, parents who provide a cell phone "lifeline" may be implicitly communicating to their children the idea that people in trouble cannot expect help from strangers [5].

The Amish understand that the adoption of a new technology can affect the way people relate to each other (Figure 1.2). Amish bishops meet twice a year to discuss matters of importance to the church, including whether any new technologies should be allowed. Their discussion about a new technology is driven by the question, "Does it bring us together, or draw us apart?" You can visit an "Old Order" Amish home and find a gas barbecue on the front porch, but no telephone inside, because they believe gas barbecues bring people together, while telephones interfere with face-to-face conversations [6].

New technologies are adopted to solve problems, but they often create problems, too. The automobile has given people the ability to travel where they want, when they want to. On the other hand, millions of people spend an hour or more each day stuck in traffic commuting between home and work. Refrigerators make it possible for us to keep food fresh for long periods of time. We save time because we don't have to go grocery shopping every day. Unfortunately, freon leaking from refrigerators has contributed to the depletion of the ozone layer that protects us from harmful ultraviolet rays. New communication technologies have made it possible for us to get access to news and entertainment from around the world. However, the same technologies have enabled major software companies to move thousands of jobs to India, China, and Vietnam, putting downward pressure on the salaries of computer programmers in the United States [7].

We may not be able to prevent a new technology from being invented, but we do have control over whether to adopt it. Nuclear power is a case in point. Nuclear power plants create electricity without producing carbon dioxide emissions, but they also produce radioactive waste products that must be safely stored for 100,000 years. Although nuclear power technology is available, no new nuclear power plants were built in the United States for more than 25 years after the accident at Three Mile Island in 1979 [8].

Finally, we *can* influence the rate at which new technologies are developed. Some societies, such as the United States, have a history of nurturing and exploiting new inventions. Congress has passed intellectual property laws that allow people to make money from their creative work, and the federal income tax structure allows individuals to accumulate great wealth.

Most of us appreciate the many beneficial changes that technology has brought into our lives. In health care alone, computed tomography (CT) and magnetic resonance imaging (MRI) scanners have greatly improved our ability to diagnose major illnesses; new vaccines and pharmaceuticals have eradicated some deadly diseases and brought others under control; and pacemakers, hearing aids, and artificial joints have improved the physical well-being of millions.

To sum up, we adopt a new technology because it promises to solve a problem we are facing, but sometimes its use creates yet another problem. That doesn't mean we should never adopt a new technology, but it does give us a good reason why we should be making informed decisions, weighing the benefits and potential harms associated with the use of new devices. To that end, this book will help you gain a better understanding of contemporary issues related to the use of information technology.

This chapter sets the stage for the remainder of the book. Electronic digital computers and high-performance communication networks are central to contemporary information technology. While the impact of these inventions has been dramatic in the past few decades, their roots go back hundreds of years. Section 1.2 tells the story of the development of computers, showing how they evolved from simple manual calculation aids to complex microprocessors. In Section 1.3 we describe two centuries of progress in networking technology, starting with the semaphore telegraph and culminating in the creation of an email system connecting over a billion users. Section 1.4 shows how information storage and retrieval evolved from the creation of the codex (paginated book) to the invention of the World Wide Web. Finally, Section 1.5 discusses some of the moral issues that have arisen from the deployment of information technology.

1.2 Milestones in Computing

1.2.1 Aids to Manual Calculating

Adding and subtracting are as old as commerce and taxes. Fingers and toes are handy calculation aids, but to manipulate numbers above 20, people need more than their own digits. The tablet, the abacus, and mathematical tables are three important aids to manual calculating [9].

Simply having a tablet to write down the numbers being manipulated is a great help. In ancient times, erasable clay and wax tablets served this purpose. By the late Middle Ages, Europeans often used erasable slates. Paper tablets became common in the nineteenth century, and they are still popular today.

An **abacus** is a computing aid in which a person performs arithmetic operations by sliding counters along rods, wires, or lines. The first abacus was probably developed in the Middle East more than two thousand years ago. In a Chinese, Japanese, or Russian abacus, counters move along rods or wires held in a rectangular frame. Beginning in medieval Europe, merchants performed their calculations by sliding wooden or metal counters along lines drawn in a wooden counting board (Figure 1.3). Eventually the word "counter" came to mean not only the disk being manipulated but also the place in a store where transactions take place [9].

Mathematical tables have been another important aid to manual computing for about two thousand years. A great breakthrough occurred in the early seventeenth century, when John Napier and Johannes Kepler published tables of logarithms. These tables were tremendous time savers to anyone doing complicated math because they allowed them to multiply two numbers by simply adding their logarithms. Many other useful tables were created as well. For example, businesspeople consulted tables to compute interest and convert between currencies. Today, people who compute their income taxes "by hand" make use of tax tables to determine how much they owe.

Even with tablets, abacuses, and mathematical tables, manual calculating is slow, tedious, and error-prone. To make matters worse, mathematical tables prepared centuries ago usually contained errors. That's because somebody had to compute each table entry and somebody had to typeset each entry, and errors could occur in either of these steps. Advances in science, engineering, and business in the post-Renaissance period motivated European inventors to create new devices to make calculations faster and more reliable and to automate the printing of mathematical tables.

1.2.2 Mechanical Calculators

Blaise Pascal had a weak physique but a powerful mind. When he got tired of summing by hand long columns of numbers given him by his father, a French tax collector, he constructed a mechanical calculator to speed the chore. Pascal's calculator, built in 1640, was capable of adding whole numbers containing up to six digits. Inspired by Pascal's invention, the German Gottfried Leibniz constructed a more sophisticated calculator that could add, subtract, multiply, and divide whole numbers. The hand-cranked machine, which he called the Step Reckoner, performed multiplications and divisions through repeated additions and subtractions, respectively. The calculators of Pascal and Leibniz were not reliable, however, and did not enjoy commercial success.

In the nineteenth century, advances in machine tools and mass-production methods, combined with larger markets, made possible the creation of practical calculating machines. Frenchman Charles Thomas de Colmar utilized the stepped drum gear mech-

FIGURE 1.3 This illustration from Gregor Reisch's *Margarita Philosophica*, published in 1503, shows two aids to manual calculating. The person on the left is using a tablet; the person on the right is adding numbers using a counting board, a type of abacus. (© Science Museum Library/Science & Society Picture Library)

anism invented by Leibniz to create the Arithmometer, the first commercially successful calculator. Many insurance companies purchased Arithmometers to help their actuaries compute rate tables more rapidly [9].

Swedish publisher Georg Scheutz was intimately familiar with printing errors associated with the production of mathematical tables. He resolved to build a machine capable of automatically calculating and typesetting table values. Scheutz knew about the earlier work of English mathematician Charles Babbage, who had demonstrated how a machine could compute the values of polynomial functions through the method of differences. Despite promising early results, Babbage's efforts to construct a full-scale Difference Engine had been unsuccessful. In contrast, Georg Scheutz and his son Edvard, who developed their own designs, completed the world's first printing calculator: a machine capable of calculating mathematical tables and typesetting the values onto molds. The Dudley Observatory in Albany, New York, purchased the Scheutz difference engine in 1856. With support from the U.S. Nautical Almanac Office, astronomers used the machine to help them compute the motion of Mars and the refraction of starlight. Difference engines were never widely used; the technology was eclipsed by the emergence of simpler and less expensive calculating machines [9].

America in the late 1800s was a fertile ground for the development of new calculating technologies. This period of American history, commonly known as the Gilded Age, was characterized by rapid industrialization, economic expansion, and a concentration of corporate power. Corporations merged to increase efficiency and profits, but the new, larger corporate organizations had multiple layers of management and multiple locations, and in order for middle- and upper-level managers to monitor and improve performance, they needed access to up-to-date, comprehensive, reliable, and affordable information. All these requirements could not be met by bookkeepers and accountants using pen and paper to sum long columns of transactions by hand [10].

To meet this demand, many entrepreneurs began producing adding and calculating machines. One of these inventors was William Burroughs, a former bank clerk who had spent long days adding columns of figures. Burroughs devised a practical adding machine and offered it for sale. He found himself in a cut-throat market; companies competed fiercely to reduce the size of their machines and make them faster and easier to use. Burroughs distinguished himself from his competitors by putting together first-class manufacturing and marketing organizations, and by the 1890s, the Burroughs Adding Machine Company led the industry. Calculating machines were entrenched in the offices of large American corporations by the turn of the century [10].

The adoption of mechanical calculators led to the "deskilling" and "feminization" of bookkeeping (Figure 1.4). Before the introduction of calculating machines, offices were a male bastion, and men who could rapidly compute sums by hand were at a premium. Calculators leveled the playing field, making people of average ability quite productive. In fact, a 1909 Burroughs study concluded that a clerk using a calculator was six times faster than a clerk adding the same column of figures by hand [11]. As managers introduced mechanical calculators into offices, they replaced male bookkeepers with female bookkeepers and lowered wages. In 1880, only 5.7 percent of bookkeepers, cashiers, and accountants were women, but by 1910, the number of women in these jobs had risen to 38.5 percent [12].

1.2.3 Cash Register

Store owners in the late 1800s faced challenges related to accounting and embezzlement. Keeping accurate sales records was becoming more difficult as smaller stores evolved into "department stores" with several departments and many clerks. Preventing embez-

FIGURE 1.4 Mechanical calculators led to the "deskilling" and "feminization" of book-keeping. This photo shows bookkeepers using Comptometer calculators in 1947. (Princeton University Press)

zlement was tricky when clerks could steal cash simply by not creating receipts for some sales.

While on a European holiday in 1878, Ohio restaurateur James Ritty saw a mechanical counter connected to the propeller shaft of his ship. A year later, he and his brother John used that concept to construct the first cash register, essentially an adding machine capable of expressing values in dollars and cents. Enhancements followed rapidly, and by the early 1900s, the cash register had become an important information processing device (Figure 1.5). Cash registers created printed, itemized receipts for customers, maintained printed logs of transactions, and performed other accounting functions that provided store owners with the detailed sales records they needed.

Cash registers also made embezzlement by clerks more difficult. The bell made it impossible for clerks to sneak money from the cash drawer and helped ensure that every sale was "rung up." Printed logs made it easy for department store owners to compare cash on hand against sales receipts [10].

1.2.4 Punched Card Tabulation

As corporations and governmental organizations grew larger in the late 1800s, they needed to handle greater volumes of information. One of these agencies was the U.S. Bureau of the Census, which collected and analyzed information on tens of millions of residents every decade. Aware of the tedium and errors associated with clerks manually copying and tallying figures, several Census Bureau employees developed mechanical

FIGURE 1.5 An NCR cash register in Miller's Shoe Shine Parlor, Dayton, Ohio (1904). (The NCR Archive at Dayton History)

tabulating machines. Herman Hollerith created the most successful device. Unlike a predecessor, who chose to record information on rolls of paper, Hollerith decided to record information on punched cards. The use of punched cards to store data was a much better approach, because cards could be sorted into groups, allowing the computation of subtotals by categories. Hollerith's equipment proved to be a great success when used in the 1890 census. In contrast to the 1880 census, which had required eight years to complete, the 1890 census was finished in only two years (Figure 1.6).

Other data-intensive organizations found applications for punched cards. Railroads used them to improve their accounting operations and send bills out more frequently. Retail organizations, such as Marshall Field's, used punched cards to perform more sophisticated analyses of information generated by the cash registers at its many stores. The Pennsylvania Steel Company and other heavy industries began to use punched-card technology to do cost accounting on manufacturing processes.

The invention of sorters, tabulators, and other devices to manipulate the data on punched cards created a positive feedback loop. As organizations began using tabulating machines, they thought up new uses of information-processing equipment, stimulating further technological innovations.

International Business Machines (IBM) is the corporate descendant of Hollerith's company. Over a period of several decades, IBM and its principal competitor, Remington Rand, developed sophisticated machines based around punched cards: card punches, card verifiers, card sorters, and card tabulators. Users used these devices

FIGURE 1.6 A U.S. Census Bureau employee uses a Hollerith electric tabulator (1890).
(© Bettmann/CORBIS)

to create **data-processing systems** that received input data, performed one or more calculations, and produced output data. Within these systems, punched cards stored input data, intermediate results, and output data. In the most complicated systems, punched cards also stored the program—the steps of the computational process to be followed. Early systems relied on human operators to carry cards from one machine to the next. Later systems had electrical connections that allowed the output of one machine to be transmitted to the next machine without the use of punched cards or human intervention.

Organizations with large data-processing needs found punched-card tabulators and calculators to be valuable devices, and they continually clamored for new features that would improve the computational capabilities and speed of their systems [10].

These organizations would become a natural market for commercial electronic digital computers.

1.2.5 Precursors of Commercial Computers

Several computing devices developed during and immediately after World War II paved the way for the commercialization of electronic digital computers.

Between 1939 and 1941, Iowa State College professor John Atanasoff and his graduate student Clifford Berry constructed an electronic device for solving systems of linear equations. The Atanasoff-Berry Computer was the first computing device built with vacuum tubes, but it was not programmable.

Dr. John W. Mauchly, a physics professor at the University of Pennsylvania, visited Iowa State College in 1941 to learn more about the Atanasoff-Berry Computer. After he returned to Penn, Mauchly worked with J. Presper Eckert to create a design for an electronic computer to speed the computation of artillery tables for the U.S. Army. They led a team that completed work on the ENIAC (Electronic Numerical Integrator and Computer) in 1946. As it turns out, the war ended before the ENIAC could provide the Army with any ballistics tables, but its speed was truly impressive. A person with a desk calculator could compute a 60-second trajectory in 20 hours. The ENIAC performed the computation in 30 seconds. In other words, the ENIAC was 2,400 times faster than a person with a desk calculator.

The ENIAC had many features of a modern computer. All of its internal components were electronic, and it could be programmed to perform a variety of computations. However, its program was not stored inside memory. Instead, it was "wired in" from the outside. Reprogramming the computer meant removing and reattaching many wires. This process could take many days (Figure 1.7).

Even before the ENIAC was completed, work began on a follow-on system called the EDVAC (Electronic Discrete Variable Automatic Computer). The design of the EDVAC incorporated many improvements over the ENIAC. The most important improvement was that the EDVAC would store the program in primary memory, along with the data manipulated by the program. In 1946, Eckert, Mauchly, and several other computer pioneers gave a series of 48 lectures at the Moore School. While some of the lectures discussed lessons learned from the ENIAC, others focused on the design of its successor, the EDVAC. These lectures influenced the design of future machines built in the United States and the United Kingdom.

During World War II, British engineer F. C. Williams was actively involved in the development of cathode ray tubes (CRTs) used in radar systems. After the war, he decided to put his knowledge to use by figuring out how to use a CRT as a storage device for digital information. In early 1948, a team at the University of Manchester set out to build a small computer that would use a CRT storage device, now called the Williams Tube, to store the program and its data. They called their system the Small-Scale Experimental Machine. The computer successfully executed its first program in 1948. The Small-Scale Experimental Machine was the first operational, fully electronic computer system that had both program and data stored in its memory.

FIGURE 1.7 The ENIAC's first six programmers were women. Every instruction was programmed by connecting several wires into plugboards. (© CORBIS)

1.2.6 First Commercial Computers

In 1951, British corporation Ferranti, Ltd. introduced the Ferranti Mark 1, the world's first commercial computer. The computer was the direct descendant of research computers constructed at the University of Manchester. Ferranti delivered nine computers between 1951–1957, and later Ferranti models boasted a variety of technological breakthroughs, thanks to the company's close association with research undertaken at the University of Manchester and Cambridge University.

After completing work on the ENIAC, Eckert and Mauchly formed their own company to produce a commercial digital computer. The Eckert-Mauchly Computer Corporation signed a preliminary agreement with the National Bureau of Standards (representing the Census Bureau) in 1946 to develop a commercial computer, which they called the UNIVAC, for UNIVersal Automatic Computer. The project experienced huge cost overruns, and by 1950, the Eckert-Mauchly Computer Corporation was on the brink of bankruptcy. Remington Rand bought them out and delivered the UNIVAC I to the U.S. Bureau of the Census in 1951 [13].

In a public relations coup, Remington Rand cooperated with CBS to use a UNIVAC computer to predict the outcome of the 1952 Presidential election (Figure 1.8). The events of election night illustrate the tough decisions people can face when computers produce unexpected results.

FIGURE 1.8 CBS news coverage of the 1952 Presidential election included predictions made by a UNIVAC computer. When the computer predicted Eisenhower would win in a landslide, consternation followed. (Hagley Museum and Library. Accession number 1984.240)

Adlai Stevenson had led Dwight Eisenhower in polls taken before the election, but less than an hour after the polls closed, with just 7 percent of the votes tabulated, the UNIVAC was predicting Dwight Eisenhower would win the election in a landslide. When CBS correspondent Charles Collingwood asked Remington Rand for the computer's prediction, however, he was given the run-around. The computer's engineers were convinced there was a programming error. For one thing, UNIVAC was predicting that Eisenhower would carry several Southern states, and everybody "knew" that Republican Presidential candidates never won in the South. Remington Rand's director of advanced research ordered the engineers to change the programming so the outcome would be closer to what the political pundits expected. An hour later, the reprogrammed computer predicted that Eisenhower would win by only nine electoral votes, and that's what CBS announced. As it turns out, the computer was right and the human "experts" were wrong. Before being reprogrammed, UNIVAC had predicted Eisenhower would win 438 electoral votes to 93 for Stevenson. The official result was a 442–89 victory for Eisenhower [13].

In America in the early 1950s, the word "UNIVAC" was synonymous with "computer." Remington Rand sold a total of 46 UNIVACs to government agencies, such as the U.S. Air Force, the U.S. Army Map Service, the Atomic Energy Commission, and the U.S. Navy, as well as large corporations and public utilities such as General Electric, Metropolian Life, U.S. Steel, Du Pont, Franklin Life Insurance, Westinghouse, Pacific Mutual Life Insurance, Sylvania Electric, and Consolidated Edison.

Office automation leader IBM did not enter the commercial computer market until 1953, and its initial products were inferior to the UNIVAC. However, IBM quickly turned the tables on Remingon Rand, thanks to a larger base of existing customers, a far superior sales and marketing organization, and a much greater investment in research and development. In 1955, IBM held more than half the market, and by the mid-1960s, IBM dominated the computer industry with 65 percent of total sales, compared to 12 percent for number two computer maker Sperry Rand (the successor to Remington Rand) [13].

1.2.7 Programming Languages and Time–Sharing

In the earliest digital computers, every instruction was coded as a long string of 0s and 1s. People immediately began looking for ways to make coding faster and less error-prone. One early improvement was the creation of assembly language, which allowed programmers to work with symbolic representations of the instruction codes. Still, one assembly language instruction was required for every machine instruction. Programmers wanted fewer, higher-level instructions to generate more machine instructions. In 1951, Frances Holberton, one of the six original ENIAC programmers, created a sort-merge generator for the UNIVAC that took a specification of files to be manipulated and automatically produced the machine program to do the sorting and merging. Building on this work, Grace Murray Hopper, also at Remington Rand, developed the A-0 system that automated the process of linking together subroutines to form the complete machine code [14].

Over at IBM, John Backus convinced his superiors of the need for a higher-level programming language for IBM computers. He led the effort to develop the IBM Mathematical Formula Translating System, or FORTRAN. Designed for scientific applications, the first system was completed in 1957. Many skeptics had believed that any "automatic programming" system would generate inefficient machine code compared to hand-coded assembly language, but they were proven wrong: the FORTRAN compiler generated high-quality code. What's more, programmers could write FORTRAN programs 5 to 20 times faster than the equivalent assembly language programs. Most programmers quickly shifted allegiance from assembly language to FORTRAN. Eventually other computer manufacturers developed their own FORTRAN compilers, and FORTRAN became an international standard [15].

Meanwhile, business-oriented programming languages were also being developed by several computer manufacturers. Grace Murray Hopper specified FLOW-MATIC, an English-like programming language for the UNIVAC. Other manufacturers began to develop their own languages. Customers didn't like incompatible languages, because it meant programs written for one brand of computer had to be rewritten before they could be run on another brand of computer. In 1959 an extremely important customer, the U.S. Department of Defense, brought together a committee to develop a common business-oriented programming language that all manufacturers would support. The committee wrote the specification for COBOL. By requiring manufacturers to support COBOL in order to get defense contracts, the U.S. Department of Defense helped ensure its widespread adoption [16].

In the early 1960s, John Kemeny and Thomas Kurtz at Dartmouth College directed teams of undergraduate students who developed a time-sharing system and an easy-to-learn programming language. The Dartmouth Time-Sharing System (DTSS) gave multiple people the ability to edit and run their programs simultaneously, by dividing the computer's time among all the users. Time-sharing made computers accessible to more people because it allowed the cost of owning and operating a computer system to be divided among a large pool of users who purchased the right to connect to the system [17].

The development of BASIC, a simple, easy-to-learn programming language, was another important step toward making computers accessible to a wider audience. Kemeny and Kurtz saw BASIC as a way to teach programming, and soon many other educational instutions began teaching students how to program using Dartmouth BASIC. The language's popularity led computer manufacturers to develop their own versions of BASIC [17].

1.2.8 Transistor and Integrated Circuit

Although the British had radar installations at the beginning of World War II, it became clear during the Battle of Britain that their systems were inadequate. The British and Americans worked together to develop microwave radar systems capable of locating enemy planes more precisely. Microwave radar required higher frequency receivers utilizing semiconductors, and in the process of manufacturing microwave radar systems for the war effort, several American companies, including AT&T, greatly improved their ability to create semiconductors [18].

AT&T was on the lookout for a new technology to replace the vacuum tube. Its long-distance network relied on vacuum tubes to amplify signals, but the tubes required a lot of power, generated a lot of heat, and burned out like lightbulbs. After the war, AT&T put together a team of Bell Labs scientists, led by Bill Shockley, to develop a semiconductor substitute for the vacuum tube. In 1948, Bell Labs announced the invention of such a device, which they called the **transistor** [19].

While most electronics companies ignored the invention of the transistor, Bill Shockley understood its potential. He left Bell Labs and moved to Palo Alto, California, where he founded Shockley Semiconductor in 1956. He hired an exceptional team of engineers and physicists, but many disliked his heavy-handed management style [19].

FIGURE 1.9 The eight founders of Fairchild Semiconductor on the factory floor. Gordon Moore is second from the left and Robert Noyce is on the right. (Wayne Miller/Magnum Photos, Inc.)

In September 1957, eight of Shockley's most talented employees, including Gordon Moore and Robert Noyce, walked out. The group, soon to be known as the "traitorous eight," founded Fairchild Semiconductor (Figure 1.9). By this time transistors were being used in a wide variety of devices, from transistor radios to computers. While transistors were far superior to vacuum tubes, they were still too big for some applications. Fairchild Semiconductor set out to produce a single semiconductor device containing transistors, capacitors, and resistors; in other words, an **integrated circuit**. Another firm, Texas Instruments, was on the same mission. Today, Robert Noyce of Fairchild Semiconductor and Jack Kilby of Texas Instruments are credited for independently inventing the integrated circuit [20].

The Cold War between the United States and the Soviet Union played an important role in advancing integrated circuit technology. American engineers developing the Minuteman II ballistic missile in the early 1960s decided to use integrated circuits to improve the processing speed of its guidance computer. The Minuteman II program was the single largest consumer of integrated circuits in the United States between 1962 and 1965, representing about 20 percent of total sales. During these years companies learned how to make rugged, reliable integrated circuits [9]. They also continued to shrink the components within the integrated circuits, leading to an exponential increase in their power. Gordon Moore noted this trend in a 1965 paper and predicted it would continue.

FIGURE 1.10 Engineers test processors for the System/360 Model 40, a medium-sized IBM mainframe introduced in 1964. (Courtesy of International Business Machines Corporation)

Today, **Moore's Law** refers to the phenomenon of integrated circuits becoming twice as powerful roughly every two years.

1.2.9 IBM System/360

The integrated circuit made possible the construction of much more powerful and reliable computers. The 1960s was the era of mainframe computers, large computers designed to serve the data processing needs of large businesses. Mainframe computers enabled enterprises to centralize all of their data processing applications in a single system. As we have seen, by this time IBM dominated the mainframe market in the United States.

In 1964, IBM announced the System/360, a series of 19 compatible computers with varying levels of computing speed and memory capacity (Figure 1.10). Because the systems were software compatible, a business could upgrade its computer without having to rewrite its application programs. This feature was important, because by the 1960s companies were making much larger investments in software.

1.2.10 Microprocessor

In 1968, Robert Noyce and Gordon Moore left Fairchild Semiconductor to found another semiconductor manufacturing company, which they named Intel. A year later Japanese calculator manufacturer Busicom approached Intel and asked it to design 12 custom chips for use in a new scientific calculator. Intel agreed to provide the chips and assigned responsibility for the project to Marcian "Ted" Hoff. After reviewing the project, Hoff suggested that it was not in Intel's best interests to manufacture a custom chip for every customer. As an alternative, he suggested that Intel create a general-purpose chip that could be programmed to perform a wide variety of tasks. Each customer could program the chip to meet its particular needs. Intel and Busicom agreed to the plan, which reduced the required number of chips for Busicom's calculator from 12 to 4. A year of development by Ted Hoff, Stanley Mazor, and Federico Faggin led to the release of the Intel 4004, the world's first **microprocessor**. Inside the 1/8-inch × 1/6-inch chip were 2,300 transistors, giving the Intel 4004 the same computing power as the ENIAC, which had occupied 3,000 cubic feet.

Microprocessors made it possible to integrate computers into everyday devices. Today we're surrounded by devices containing microprocessors: cell phones, MP3 players, digital cameras, wristwatches, ATM machines, automobiles, microwave ovens, thermostats, traffic lights, and much more. The highest-profile use of microprocessors, however, is in personal computers.

1.2.11 Personal Computer

During the Vietnam conflict in the late 1960s and early 1970s, the area around San Francisco was home to a significant counterculture, including a large number of antiwar and antiestablishment activists. The do-it-yourself idealism of the power-to-the-people movement intersected with advances in computer technology in a variety of ways, including the *Whole Earth Catalog*, the People's Computer Company, and the Homebrew Computer Club [21].

The *Whole Earth Catalog*, first published in 1968, was "sort of like Google in paperback form" [22]—an effort to pull together in a single large volume lists of helpful tools for the creation of a more just and environmentally sensitive society. The definition of "tools" was broad; the catalog's lists included books, classes, garden tools, camping equipment, and (in later issues) early personal computers. "With the *Whole Earth Catalog*, Stewart Brand offered a generation of computer engineers and programmers an alternative vision of technology as a tool for individual and collective transformation" [23].

The People's Computer Company was a not-for-profit corporation dedicated to educating people on how to use computers. One of its activities was publishing a newspaper. The cover of the first issue read: "Computers are mostly used against people instead of for people, used to control people instead of to <u>free</u> them, time to change all that—we need a PEOPLE'S COMPUTER COMPANY" [24]. Typical issues contained programming tips and the source code to programs, particularly educational games written in BASIC. Newspaper publisher Bob Albrecht said, "I was heavily influenced by the *Whole Earth Catalog*. I wanted to give away ideas" [23]. The People's Computer Company also set up the People's Computer Center in a strip mall in Menlo Park. The People's Computer Center allowed people to rent teletype terminals connected to a time-shared computer. A large number of teenagers were drawn to computing through Friday evening game-playing sessions. Many users wrote their own programs, and the center promoted a culture in which computer enthusiasts freely shared software with each other.

In 1975, the Homebrew Computer Club, an outgrowth of the People's Computer Company, became a meeting place for hobbyists interested in building personal computers out of microprocessors. A company in Albuquerque, New Mexico, called MITS had recently begun shipping the Altair 8800 personal computer, and during the first few Homebrew Computer Club meetings, members showed off various enhancements to the Altair 8800. Progress was frustratingly slow, however, due to the lack of a higher-level programming language.

Three months after the establishment of the Homebrew Computer Club, MITS representatives visited Palo Alto to demonstrate the Altair 8800 and the BASIC interpreter created by Paul Allen and Bill Gates, who had a tiny company called Micro-Soft. The audience in the hotel conference room was far larger than expected, and during the overcrowded and chaotic meeting somebody acquired a paper tape containing the source code to Altair BASIC. More than 70 copies of the tape were handed out at the next meeting of the Homebrew Computer Club. After that, free copies of the interpreter proliferated. Some hobbyists felt that the asking price of $500 for the BASIC interpreter was too high, considering that the Altair computer itself cost only $395 as a kit or $495 preassembled [21].

Bill Gates responded by writing "An Open Letter to Hobbyists" that was reprinted in a variety of publications. In the letter he asserted that less than 10 percent of all Altair owners had purchased BASIC, even though far more people than that were using it. According to Gates, the royalties Micro-Soft had received from Altair BASIC made the time spent on the software worth less than $2 an hour. He wrote, "Nothing would please me more than being able to hire ten programmers and deluge the hobby market with good software," but the theft of software created "very little incentive" for his company to release new products [21].

The controversy over Altair BASIC did not slow the pace of innovations. Hobbyists wanted to do more than flip the toggle switches and watch the lights blink on the Altair 8800. Steve Wozniak, a computer engineer at Hewlett-Packard, created a more powerful personal computer that supported keyboard input and television monitor output. Wozniak's goal was to make a machine for himself and to impress other members of the Homebrew Computer Club, but his friend Steve Jobs thought of a few improvements and convinced Wozniak they should go into business (Figure 1.11). They raised $1,300 by selling Job's Volkswagen van and Wozniak's Hewlett-Packard scientific calculator, launching Apple Computer. Although the company sold only 200 Apple I computers, its next product, the Apple II, became one of the most popular personal computers of all time.

FIGURE 1.11 Steve Jobs (right) convinced Steve Wozniak they should go into business selling the personal computer Wozniak designed. They named their company Apple Computer. (© Kimberly White/Corbis)

By the end of the 1970s, many companies, including Apple Computer and Tandy, were producing personal computers. While hundreds of thousands of people bought personal computers for home use, businesses were reluctant to move to the new computer platform. Two significant developments made personal computers more attractive to businesses.

The first development was the computer spreadsheet program. For decades firms have used spreadsheets to perform financial predictions. Manually computing spreadsheets is monotonous and error-prone, since changing a value in a single cell can require updating many other cells. In the fall of 1979, Bob Frankston and Harvard MBA student Dan Bricklin released their program, called VisiCalc, for the Apple II. VisiCalc's labor-saving potential was obvious to businesses. After a slow start, it quickly became one of the most popular application programs for personal computers. Sales of the Apple II computer increased significantly after the introduction of VisiCalc.

The second development was the release of the IBM PC in 1981. The IBM name exuded reliability and respectability, making it easier for companies to make the move to desktop systems for their employees. As the saying went, "Nobody ever got fired for buying from IBM." In contrast to the approach taken by Apple Computer, IBM decided to make its PC an open architecture, meaning the system was built from off-the-shelf parts and other companies could manufacture "clones" with the same functionality. This decision helped to make the IBM PC the dominant personal computer architecture.

The success of IBM-compatible PCs fueled the growth of Microsoft. In 1980, IBM contracted with Microsoft to provide the DOS operating system for the IBM PC. Microsoft let IBM have DOS for practically nothing, but in return IBM gave Microsoft the right to collect royalties from other companies manufacturing PC-compatible computers. Microsoft profited handsomely from this arrangement when PC-compatibles manufactured by other companies gained more than 80 percent of the PC market [25].

1.3 Milestones in Networking

In the early nineteenth century, the United States fell far behind Europe in networking technology. The French had begun constructing a network of telegraph towers in the 1790s, and forty years later there were towers all over the European continent (Figure 1.12). At the top of each tower was a pair of semaphores. Operators raised and lowered the semaphores; each pattern corresponded to a letter or symbol. A message initiated at one tower would be seen by another tower within viewing distance. The receiving tower would then repeat the message for the next tower in the network, and so on. This optical telegraph system could transmit messages at the impressive rate of about 350 miles per hour when the skies were clear.

FIGURE 1.12 A semaphore telegraph tower on the first line from Paris to Lille (1794). (Photo l'Adresse Musée de La Poste, Paris / La Poste)

In 1837, Congress asked for proposals to create a telegraph system between New York and New Orleans. It received one proposal based on proven European technology. Samuel Morse submitted a radically different proposal. He suggested constructing a telegraph system that used electricity to communicate the signals. Let's step back and review some of the key discoveries and inventions that enabled Morse to make his dramatic proposal.

1.3.1 Electricity and Electromagnetism

Amber is a hard, translucent, yellowish brown fossil resin often used to make beads and other ornamental items. About 2,600 years ago the Greeks discovered that if you rub amber, it becomes charged with a force enabling it to attract light objects such as feathers and dried leaves. The Greek word for amber is $\eta\lambda\epsilon\kappa\tau\rho\omega\nu$ (electron). Our word "electric" literally means "to be like amber."

For more than two thousand years amber's ability to attract other materials was seen as a curiosity with no practical value, but in the seventeenth and eighteenth centuries scientists began to study electricity in earnest. Alessandro Volta, a professor of physics at the University of Pavia, made a key breakthrough when he discovered that electricity could be generated chemically. He produced an electric current by submerging two different metals close to each other in an acid. In 1799, Volta used this principle to create the world's first battery. Volta's battery produced an electric charge more than 1,000 times as powerful as that produced by rubbing amber. Scientists soon put this power to practical use.

In 1820, Danish physicist Christian Oersted discovered that an electric current creates a magnetic field. Five years later, British electrician William Sturgeon constructed an electromagnet by coiling wire around a horseshoe-shaped piece of iron. When he ran an electric current through the coil, the iron became magnetized. Sturgeon showed how a single battery was capable of producing a charge strong enough to pick up a nine-pound metal object.

In 1830, American professor Joseph Henry rigged up an experiment that showed how a telegraph machine could work. He strung a mile of wire around the walls of his classroom at the Albany Academy. At one end he placed a battery; at the other end he connected an electromagnet, a pivoting metal bar, and a bell. When Henry connected the battery, the electromagnet attracted the metal bar, causing it to ring the bell. Disconnecting the battery allowed the bar to return to its original position. In this way he could produce a series of rings.

1.3.2 Telegraph

Samuel Morse, a professor of arts and design at New York University, worked on the idea of a telegraph during most of the 1830s, and in 1838, he patented his design of a telegraph machine. The U.S. Congress did not approve Morse's proposal in 1837 to construct a New York–to–New Orleans telegraph system, but it did not fund any of the other proposals, either. Morse persisted with his lobbying, and in 1843, Congress appropriated $30,000 to Morse for the construction of a 40-mile telegraph line between Washington, D.C., and Baltimore, Maryland.

On May 1, 1844, the Whig party convention in Baltimore nominated Henry Clay for President. The telegraph line was only complete to Annapolis Junction at that time. A courier hand-carried a message about Clay's nomination from Baltimore to Annapolis Junction, where it was telegraphed to Washington. This was the first news reported via telegraph. The line officially opened on May 24. Morse, seated in the old Supreme Court chamber inside the U.S. Capitol, sent his partner in Baltimore a verse from the Bible: "What hath God wrought?"

The value of the telegraph was immediately apparent, and the number of telegraph lines quickly increased. By 1846, telegraph lines connected Washington, D.C., Baltimore, Philadelphia, New York, Buffalo, and Boston. In 1850, twenty different companies operated 12,000 miles of telegraph lines. The first transcontinental telegraph line was completed in 1861, putting the Pony Express out of business (Figure 1.13). The telegraph was the sole method of rapid long-distance communication until 1877. By this time the United States was networked by more than 200,000 miles of telegraph wire [26].

The telegraph was a versatile tool, and people kept finding new applications for it. For example, by 1870, fire alarm telegraphs were in use in 75 major cities in the United States. New York City alone had 600 fire alarm telegraphs. When a person pulled the lever of the alarm box, it automatically transmitted a message identifying its location to a fire station. These devices greatly improved the ability of fire departments to dispatch equipment quickly to the correct location [26].

FIGURE 1.13 Pony Express riders lost their jobs when the U.S. transcontinental telegraph line was completed in 1861. (© North Wind Picture Archives / Alamy)

1.3.3 Telephone

Alexander Graham Bell was born in Edinburgh, Scotland, into a family focused on impairments of speech and hearing. His father and grandfather were experts in elocution and the correction of speech. His mother was almost completely deaf. Bell was educated to follow in the same career path as his father and grandfather, and he became a teacher of deaf students. Later, he married a deaf woman.

Bell pursued inventing as a means of achieving financial independence. At first he focused on making improvements to the telegraph. A significant problem with early telegraph systems was that a single wire could transmit only one message at a time. If multiple messages could be sent simultaneously along the same wire, communication delays would be reduced, and the value of the entire system would increase.

Bell's solution to this problem is called a harmonic or musical telegraph. If you imagine hearing Morse code, it's obvious that all of the dots and dashes are the same note played for a shorter or longer period of time. The harmonic telegraph assigned a different note (different sound frequency) to each message. At the receiving end, different receivers could be tuned to respond to different notes, as you can tune your radio to hear only what is broadcast by a particular station.

Bell knew that the human voice is made up of sounds at many different frequencies. From his work on the harmonic telegraph, he speculated that it should be possible to capture and transmit human voice over a wire. He and Thomas A. Watson succeeded in transmitting speech electronically in 1876. Soon after, they commercialized their invention.

Nearly all early telephones were installed in businesses. Leasing a telephone was expensive, and most people focused on its commercial value rather than its social value. However, the number of phones placed in homes increased rapidly in the 1890s, after Bell's first patent expired.

Once telephones were placed in the home, the traditional boundaries between private, family life and public, business life became blurred. People enjoyed being able to conduct business transactions from the privacy of their home, but they also found that a ringing telephone could be an unwelcome interruption [27].

Another consequence of the telephone was that it eroded traditional social hierarchies. An 1897 issue of *Western Electrician* reports that Governor Chauncey Depew of New York was receiving unwanted phone calls from ordinary citizens: "Every time they see anything about him in the newspapers, they call and tell him what a 'fine letter he wrote' or 'what a lovely speech he made,' or ask if this or that report is true; and all this from people who, if they came to his office, would probably never say more than 'Good morning'" [28].

People also worried about the loss of privacy brought about by the telephone. In 1877, *The New York Times* reported that telephone men responsible for operating an early system in Providence, Rhode Island, overheard many confidential conversations. The writer fretted that telephone eavesdropping would make it dangerous for anyone in Providence to accept a nomination for public office [27].

The telephone enabled the creation of the first "online" communities. In rural areas the most common form of phone service was the party line: a single circuit connecting multiple phones to the telephone exchange. Party lines enabled farmers to gather by their phones every evening to talk about the weather and exchange gossip [29].

The power of this new medium was demonstrated in the Bryan/McKinley Presidential election of 1896. For the first time, Presidential election returns were transmitted directly into people's homes. "Thousands sat with their ear glued to the receiver the whole night long, hypnotized by the possibilities unfolding to them for the first time" [30].

The development of cell phone technology in the latter part of the twentieth century made telephone service much more widely available. Telephone service has now been extended to people living in areas never reached by wired telephone service, particularly those living in less developed countries. Today, the number of cell phones in use worldwide exceeds the number of traditional, wired telephones [31].

1.3.4 Typewriter and Teletype

For hundreds of years people dreamed of a device that would allow an individual to produce a document that looked as if it had been typeset, but the dream was not realized until 1867, when Americans Christopher Sholes, Carlos Glidden, and Samuel Soule patented the first typewriter. In late 1873, Remington & Sons Company, famous for guns and sewing machines, produced the first commercial typewriter. It was difficult to use and was not well received; Remington & Co. sold only 5,000 machines in the first five years. However, the typewriter did get the attention of Mark Twain, who used it to produce *Tom Sawyer*, which may have been the world's first typewritten manuscript. By 1890, more reliable typewriters were being produced, and the typewriter became a common piece of office equipment [32].

In 1908, Charles and Howard Krum succeeded in testing an experimental machine that allowed a modified Oliver typewriter to print a message transmitted over a telegraph line. They called their invention the teletype. During the 1920s, news organizations began using teletype machines to transmit stories between distant offices, and Wall Street firms began sending records of stock transactions over teletypes.

1.3.5 Radio

Earlier, we described how the experiments of Oersted, Sturgeon, and Henry led to the development of the electromagnet and the telegraph. The connection between electricity and magnetism remained mysterious, however, until Scottish physicist James Clerk Maxwell published a mathematical theory demonstrating their relationship. This theory predicted the existence of an electromagnetic wave spreading with the velocity of light. It also predicted that light itself was an electromagnetic phenomenon. In 1885, Heinrich Hertz successfully generated electromagnetic waves, proving the correctness of Maxwell's theory.

Guglielmo Marconi put Hertz's discovery to practical use by successfully transmitting radio signals in the hills outside Bologna, Italy, in 1895. Unable to attract the attention of the Italian government, he took his invention to England, where he founded the Marconi Wireless Telegraph Company. The name of the company reflects Marconi's concept of how his invention would be used. To Marconi, radio, or "wireless," was a superior way to transmit telegraph messages.

David Sarnoff emigrated from Russia to the United States with his family when he was nine. When he had completed school, he landed a position with the Marconi Wireless Telegraph Company. In 1912, Sarnoff made a name for himself when he intercepted the first distress signal from the *Titanic* and spent the next three days relaying information about the rescue effort to the rest of the world. Four years later, Sarnoff suggested the use of radio as an entertainment device, writing: "I have in mind a plan of development which would make radio a household utility in the same sense as the piano or phonograph . . . The receiver can be designed in the form of a simple 'Radio Music Box' . . . (which) can be placed in the parlor or living room" [33]. In two decades, Sarnoff's vision had become a reality.

The power of radio as a medium of mass communication was demonstrated on the evening of October 30, 1938 (the night before Halloween). From CBS Radio Studio One in New York, Orson Welles and the Mercury Theater put on a one-hour dramatization of H. G. Wells's *War of the Worlds* (Figure 1.14). To increase suspense, the play was performed as a series of news bulletins interrupting a concert of dance music. These bulletins described events occurring on a farm near Grovers Mill, New Jersey. Many listeners panicked. "People packed the roads, hid in cellars, loaded guns, even wrapped their heads in wet towels as protection from Martian poison gas, oblivious to the fact that they were acting out the role of the panic-stricken public that actually belonged in a radio play" [34].

1.3.6 Television

Broadcasting video over a wire began in 1884 with the invention of an electro-mechanical television by Paul Nipkow, but the first completely electronic television transmission was made in 1927 by Philo Farnsworth. Millions of Americans were formally introduced to the television at the 1939 World's Fair held in New York City, which had as its theme, "The World of Tomorrow." Since an early retail television set cost about as much as an automobile, televisions remained a rarity in American households until the 1950s, when prices fell dramatically.

Television's ability to send a message around the world was demonstrated in July 1969. Hundreds of millions of people watched on live TV as astronaut Neil Armstrong stepped from the lunar module onto the surface of the Moon (Figure 1.15).

Television has created many opportunities for "news junkies" to get their fixes. The major commercial broadcast television networks have been supplemented by Fox, CNN, and other cable news organizations plus a myriad of Web sites. The various organizations compete with each other to be the first to break news stories. Increasingly,

FIGURE 1.14 Orson Welles's radio adaption of *War of the Worlds* on the evening of October 30, 1938, convinced many Americans that Martians were attacking New Jersey. (© Bettmann/CORBIS)

the media have turned to computer technology to help them provide information to the public. Sometimes this has led to embarrassing mistakes, as in the 2000 U.S. Presidential election.

About 7:50 P.M. on the evening of Tuesday, November 7, 2000, before the polls had even closed in the Florida panhandle, the major networks began announcing that Al Gore would be the winner in Florida. Based on the expected result of the Florida election, the networks went on to predict—while people were still voting in the Western states—that Al Gore would be the next President of the United States.

You might be wondering how it is possible to predict the outcome of an election before everyone has voted. In a practice known as exit polling, a company called Voter News Service questions people leaving polling places. It combines the information it collects with early returns to predict the outcome of elections. Since 1988, the television networks have relied upon the Voter News Service to provide them with exit polling results.

FIGURE 1.15 On July 20, 1969, television images of Neil Armstrong walking on the Moon were broadcast to hundreds of millions of viewers around the world. (Courtesy of NASA)

As it turns out, Voter News Service's prediction was wrong. More than a month after the election, after a series of recounts and court decisions, George W. Bush was declared the victor in Florida. With Florida's electoral votes in hand, Bush won the Presidency.

1.3.7 Remote Computing

Working at his kitchen table in 1937, Bell Labs researcher George Stibitz built a binary adder out of telephone relays, batteries, flashlight bulbs, tin strips, and wire. He took his invention back to Bell Labs and enlisted the help of Samuel Williams. Over the next two years they built the Complex Number Calculator, an electromechanical system that would add, subtract, multiply, and divide complex numbers.

Stibitz's next action is what sets him apart from other computer pioneers. He made a teletype machine the input/output device for the Complex Number Calculator. With this innovation, he did not have to be in the same room as the calculator to use it; he could operate it remotely.

In 1940, Stibitz demonstrated remote computing to members of the American Mathematical Society who were meeting at Dartmouth College in New Hampshire. He typed numbers into the teletype, which transmitted the data 250 miles to the calculator in New York City. After the calculator had computed the answer, it transmitted the data back to the teletype, which printed the result.

1.3.8 ARPANET

In reaction to the launch of Sputnik by the Soviet Union in 1957, the Department of Defense created the Advanced Research Projects Agency (ARPA). ARPA funded research and development at prominent universities. The agency's first director, J.C.R. Licklider, imagined a "Galactic Network"—a global computer network that would facilitate the exchange of programs and data.[2] This view of the computer as a device to improve communication was in stark contrast to the mindset of computer manufacturers, which continued to think of computers as number-crunching machines.

Conventional, circuit-switched telephone networks were not a good foundation upon which to build a global computer network (Figure 1.16a). Between 1961 and 1967, three research teams independently came up with an alternative to circuit-switched networks. These teams were led by Donald Davies and Roger Scantlebury at NPL in England, Paul Baran at RAND, and Leonard Kleinrock at MIT. Eventually the new design came to be called a packet-switched network (Figure 1.16b).

In 1967, ARPA initiated the design and construction of the ARPANET. Fear of a nuclear attack led to the crucially important design decision that the network should be decentralized. In other words, the loss of any single computer or communication link would not prevent the rest of the network from working. Every computer on the network would have the ability to make decisions about how message traffic should be routed. Packet-switched networks met this condition; circuit-switched networks did not.

BBN in Boston was responsible for the Interface Message Processor (IMP) that connected a computer to the telephone network. In 1969, BBN delivered its first four IMPs to UCLA, the Stanford Research Institute, the University of California at Santa Barbara, and the University of Utah.

1.3.9 Email

During the earliest years of ARPANET, the networked computers could transfer programs and data only. ARPANET users still relied upon the telephone for personal communications. In March 1972, Ray Tomlinson at BBN wrote the first software enabling email messages to be sent and received by ARPANET computers. A few months later, Lawrence Roberts created the first "killer app" for the network: an email utility that gave individuals the ability to list their email messages, selectively read them, reply to them, forward them to others, and save them. Email quickly became the most popular network application.

Today, email is one of the most important communication technologies on the planet. More than 200 billion email messages are sent each day.

1.3.10 Internet

ARPA researchers anticipated the need to connect the ARPANET with other networks based on different designs. Robert Kahn developed the concept of open architecture networking, which means individual networks could be quite different as long as they shared a common "internetworking architecture." Vinton Cerf and Robert Kahn designed the TCP/IP protocol that would support open architecture networking [36]. TCP

---

2. The primary source document for this description of the evolution of the Internet is *A Brief History of the Internet* by Barry M. Leiner et al. [35].

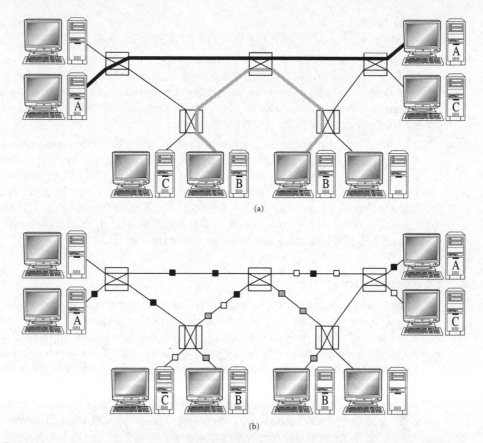

FIGURE 1.16 Comparison of circuit-switched networking and packet-switched networking. (a) In a **circuit-switched network**, a single physical connection is established between the two ends. The physical connection cannot be shared. In this illustration, one circuit links the two computers labeled A, and another circuit links the two computers labeled B. The computers labeled C may not communicate at this time, because no circuit can be established. (b) In a **packet-switched network**, a message is divided up into small bundles of data called packets. Every packet has the address of the computer where it should be routed. If there is more than one path from the message source to the message destination, different message packets may take different routes. Packets from different messages may share the same wire. In this illustration, three pairs of computers (labeled A, B, and C) are communicating simultaneously over a packet-switched network.

(Transmission Control Protocol) is responsible for dividing a message into packets at the sending computer and reassembling the packets at the receiving computer. IP (Internet Protocol) is the set of rules used to route data from computer to computer. The **Internet** is the network of networks that communicate using TCP/IP. You could call January 1, 1983, the birth date of the Internet, because that was the date on which all ARPANET hosts converted to TCP/IP.

1.3.11 NSFNET

The National Science Foundation (NSF) in the United States saw the importance of networking to the academic community. It created a TCP/IP-based network called NSFNET, and it provided grants to universities to join the NSFNET. These grants encouraged broad participation by stipulating that universities would have to make their Internet connections available to all qualified users. The NSFNET consisted of regional networks connected by the NSFNET Backbone.

The NSF encouraged the universities participating in regional networks to reduce their network subscription costs by finding commercial customers for the networks. At the same time, the NSF banned commercial traffic on the NSFNET Backbone. These policies stimulated private companies to create commercial, long-distance Internet connections in the United States. In April 1995, the NSF ceased funding the NSFNET Backbone. Commercial network providers, well established by this time, took over the task of supplying long-distance Internet connections in the United States.

1.3.12 Broadband

The term **broadband** refers to a high-speed Internet connection, such as a cable modem or a DSL modem, that is at least 10 times faster than a dial-up Internet connection. The availability and speed of broadband connections continues to improve as fiber optic networks gradually replace networks based on copper wire. Fiber optic networks support high-capacity international broadband connections, such as those between the United States and India.

Broadband connections make feasible the transfer of large files, such as those containing images, music, and video. The growth of file-swapping among Internet users has paralleled the growth of broadband connections.

Typical broadband speeds vary widely among highly developed countries. The world broadband leaders are South Korea, with an average speed of 14.4 megabits per second, Hong Kong, at 9.2 megabits per second, and Japan, at 8.1 megabits per second. The United States ranks 14th in the world, with an average broadband speed of 5.3 megabits per second [37].

1.4 Milestones in Information Storage and Retrieval

1.4.1 Codex

Two thousand years ago, important information was recorded on papyrus scrolls wrapped around wooden rods. Papyrus had to be stored this way to keep from breaking apart. Even so, the ends of papyrus scrolls tended to fall off.

The development of the codex was a significant advance in information storage and retrieval technology. A codex was made up of rectangular pages sewn together on one side. These pages were made out of sheepskin (parchment) or calfskin (vellum). The codex was superior to papyrus in two ways. First, the codex was much more durable than a papyrus roll. Second, since it was divided into pages, the codex made it much easier for readers to find a particular passage: they could simply flip to the desired page.

Between the second and fourth centuries, the codex gradually replaced the scroll as the most popular method of recording important information. The Church accelerated the transition by insisting that all sacred texts be recorded in codices, to distinguish them from Hebrew scriptures kept on scrolls.

After the fall of the Roman Empire, Irish monks preserved Western culture by copying Greco-Roman and Judeo-Christian texts into codices [38]. Centuries later, most codices were produced using a process of wood engraving. A craftsman would take a block of wood and laboriously chisel away the background for a portion of a page, leaving the letters and illustrations raised. When all the wooden blocks for a page were carved, they would be fastened together. After the surface was inked, a blank page would be printed by pressing the blocks down on the inked surface.

In the late Middle Ages, explorers brought back from China the technology for manufacturing paper in mass quantities. By the fifteenth century, paper gradually began to replace parchment in less expensive European codices.

1.4.2 Gutenberg's Printing Press

In 1436, Johannes Gutenberg began work on a printing press that would imprint pages using movable metal type rather than wood blocks, and in 1455, work was completed on Gutenberg's famous "42 Line Bible." Soon other printers were using the same technology to produce codices. The principal customer of these publishers was the Church. Hence most early publications were religious books and pamphlets.

The printing press proved itself to be a powerful tool for mass communication during the Reformation. Martin Luther did more than nail his 95 theses to the door of a church—he published them. Between 1517 and 1520, more than 300,000 copies of Martin Luther's publications were sold [39]. In the next 50 years, the number of religious tracts produced by Protestant reformers would outnumber those of their Catholic opponents by a factor of 10 to 1.

1.4.3 Newspapers

The printing press made possible the establishment of newspapers. Newspapers provided an important new way for private citizens to get their points of view heard. A free press serves as a powerful counterweight to government and its desire to manage the flow of information. It is not surprising, then, that there is a long history of government censorship or suppression of newspapers.

The first English-language newspaper appeared in Great Britain in the 1600s. Throughout most of the seventeenth century the government controlled the press by licensing approved newspapers and suppressing the rest. However, in 1695, Parliament declined to renew the Licensing Act, paving the way for a free press in England.

In America, newspapers helped to unify the colonies. As colonists read newspapers published in other colonies, they came to realize what values and concerns they shared with other colonists up and down the Atlantic seaboard. In this way newspapers played an important role in swaying American public opinion toward favoring independence from Great Britain.

1.4.4 Hypertext

The July 1945 issue of *The Atlantic Monthly* contained a visionary paper, "As We May Think," written by Vannevar Bush, who had served as Director of the Office of Scientific Research and Development in World War II. In the paper Bush noted, "The world has arrived at an age of cheap complex devices of great reliability; and something is bound to come of it" [40]. He described many ways in which technology can solve important problems. One of the problems he focused on is the problem of information retrieval. He pointed out how difficult it is for scientists to keep up with all the research results that are being published, especially when indexing systems do not lend themselves toward exposing the relationships among documents. Bush noted that the human mind doesn't work by indexing. Instead, our memories are associative. When we think of one thing, other related memories awaken in our minds. He suggested that a machine could simulate, to some degree, the mind's ability to make associations between pieces of information. He gave a description for the Memex, an information retrieval system equipped with "a provision whereby any item may be caused at will to select immediately and automatically another" [40].

Ted Nelson was raised by his grandparents in Greenwich Village, New York. He was a graduate student studying sociology at Harvard when he took his first computer class. There he discovered that "everything everyone was saying about computers was a lie. It was up to me to design the literature of the future" [41]. In 1965, Nelson coined the word **hypertext,** which refers to a linked network of nodes containing information. The links allow readers to visit the nodes in a nonlinear fashion [42]. The proposed system had much in common with Bush's proposal for Memex. In 1967, Nelson proposed the creation of a system called Xanadu, a worldwide network of connected literature. Despite decades of work and a $5 million investment from Autodesk, the system was never completed [41].

1.4.5 Graphical User Interface

Douglas Engelbart grew up on a dairy farm in Oregon. After graduating from high school, he attended Oregon State College, but his electrical engineering studies were interrupted by World War II. While he was stationed in the Philippines, he worked with radar and read "As We May Think" by Vannevar Bush. These two experiences shaped his views about the potential of computing. When his military service ended, he completed his degree at OSC and took a job at Ames Laboratory, but soon began wondering, "How can my career maximize my contribution to mankind?" [43]. Engelbart decided to return to school and completed a Ph.D. in electrical engineering from the University of California at Berkeley in 1955. He joined the Stanford Research Institute, where he set out to use the power of the computer to augment human intellect.

FIGURE 1.17 Douglas Engelbart rehearses for his presentation at the 1968 Fall Joint Computer Conference that is still called "the mother of all demos." (Courtesy of SRI)

In the 1950s and 1960s, people submitted computer jobs in the form of decks of punch cards and often waited hours for them to run. Computer output was typically pages full of numbers that programmers would laboriously examine. Engelbart wondered why people couldn't interact directly with computers and view the output on a CRT, like radar images. He created a research lab called the Augmentation Research Center. This lab developed a hypermedia and groupware system called NLS (oNLine System). Engelbart invented several new input devices, including the computer mouse. In 1968, at the Fall Joint Computer Conference in San Francisco, he gave a 90-minute demonstration of NLS that included a video display divided into windows, email, use of a mouse to direct a cursor, and live videoconferencing with staff members 30 miles away (Figure 1.17). Engelbart's presentation is still called "the mother of all demos." Paul Saffo said, "It was like a UFO landing on the White House lawn." The presentation was so far ahead of its time that some audience members thought it was a hoax [44]. Others thought Engelbart's ideas were completely impractical, noting that he was treating a computer as if it were for his personal use.

Alan Kay saw Engelbart's demo, understood the ramifications of the NLS, and was eager to take the next step. In 1970, he become one of the founding members of Xerox Palo Alto Research Center (PARC), a new facility dedicated to performing research into digital technology. The research team created the Alto, a small minicomputer designed to be used by a single person. The Alto incorporated a bit-mapped display, a keyboard, and a mouse. Kay played a leading role in developing the Alto's graphical user interface that responded to the point, click, and drag operations of a mouse. In order to link together the Altos, the Xerox PARC team also created **Ethernet**, which became a networking standard throughout the computer industry. Ultimately, however, Xerox failed in its attempt to market a commercial personal computer.

In 1979, Apple Computer sold 10 percent of its stock to Xerox. In return, Xerox let Jobs and some Apple engineers visit Xerox PARC and learn more about its research. Jobs returned from the visit committed to building a computer with a graphical user interface. A few years later, Apple released the Lisa, a $10,000 personal computer with a graphical user interface. The price tag was too high, the processor was too slow, and the Lisa was not commercially successful. However, in January 1984, Apple released the Macintosh, a faster, $2,495 computer with a graphical user interface. The Macintosh was an instant hit: Apple sold 300,000 in the first year.

During the 1980s, IBM, VisiCorp, and Microsoft all offered graphical user interfaces for IBM PC-compatible computers, but they could not compare in sophistication to the interface of the Apple Macintosh. Finally, in May 1990, Microsoft released Windows 3.0 for IBM PCs. Consumers eagerly bought 10 million copies of Windows, giving Microsoft a near monopoly in the graphical user interface market that it has maintained ever since.

1.4.6 Single–Computer Hypertext Systems

In 1982, Peter Brown at the University of Kent at Canterbury started a hypertext research project. He named the software Guide. Later, Office Workstations, Ltd. commercialized Guide, releasing versions for both the Apple Macintosh and the IBM PC.

In 1987, Apple Computer released HyperCard, a hypertext system that enabled programmers to create "stacks" of "cards." A card could contain text and images. The HyperCard programmer created links from one card to another with "buttons." Buttons could be visible to the user and labeled, or they could be transparent and associated with an image or an area of the card.

Users typically viewed one card at a time. They jumped from one card to another by using the computer's mouse to move a cursor over a button and then clicking the mouse. The best-selling computer games *Myst* and *Riven* are actually HyperCard stacks.

1.4.7 Networked Hypertext: World Wide Web

Tim Berners-Lee is the son of two mathematicians, both of whom were programmers for the Ferranti Mark 1 computer in the 1950s. From them, Berners-Lee learned that, "in principle, a person could program a computer to do most anything" [45]. He also learned that it is easy to get a computer to keep information in lists or tables, but much more difficult to get it to remember arbitrary relationships.

When Berners-Lee was in high school, his father read some books about the brain; the two of them talked about how a computer might be able to make neural-like connections the way a brain does. This idea stuck with Berners-Lee, and in 1980, while working for CERN in Switzerland, he wrote a program called Enquire that incorporated links between information. Berners-Lee was not familiar with the work of Vannevar Bush, Ted Nelson, or Doug Engelbart, but he was heading in the same direction.

In late 1989, Berners-Lee wrote a memo to a management team at CERN, proposing the development of a networked hypertext system that could be used for documentation purposes. When they didn't respond, he tried again in the spring of 1990. Again, no

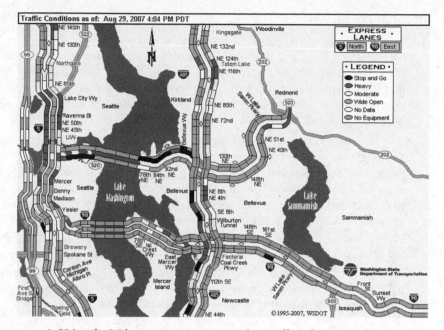

FIGURE 1.18 Using the Web, you can access up-to-date traffic information from many major cities. (Copyright © 2011 by WSDOT. Reprinted with permission.)

response. However, an intriguing new personal computer called the NeXT had just been released. Berners-Lee asked his boss if he could purchase a NeXT to check out its operating system and programming environment. His boss okayed the purchase, then puckishly suggested that maybe Berners-Lee ought to test the system's capabilities by implementing his proposed hypertext system on it [45].

Unlike earlier commercial hypertext systems, Berners-Lee's system allowed links between information stored on different computers connected by a network. Because it is built on top of the TCP/IP protocol, links can connect any two computers on the Internet, even if they have different hardware or are running different operating systems.

A **Web browser** is a program that allows a user to view Web pages and traverse hyperlinks between pages. Berners-Lee completed the first Web browser on the NeXT Computer on Christmas Day, 1990. He called his browser WorldWideWeb. In March 1991, he released the browser to some computer users at CERN.

The first widely used Web browser was Mosaic, developed at the University of Illinois, Urbana-Champaign. Today, the most popular Web browsers are Microsoft's Internet Explorer, Mozilla's Firefox, Google's Chrome, and Apple's Safari. These browsers enable Web surfers to retrieve text, still images, movies, songs, computer programs—in theory, anything that can be digitized. The Web has also become a convenient way for organizations to provide people access to news updates and dynamically changing information (Figure 1.18).

1.4.8 Search Engines

A **search engine** is a program that accepts a list of keywords from a user, searches a database of documents, and returns those documents most closely matching the specified keywords. Today, the term search engine is most frequently used to describe programs that search databases of Web pages. Web search engines are the most powerful information retrieval devices ever invented. The most popular Web search engine, Google, has indexed billions of Web pages.

There are two types of Web search engines. Crawler-based search engines, such as Google and AltaVista, automatically create the database of information about Web pages. In a process similar to Web surfing, programs called spiders follow hyperlinks, eventually visiting millions of different Web pages. Summary information about these pages is collected into massive databases. When you perform a query, the search engine consults its database to find the closest matches.

The second type of Web search engine relies upon humans to build the database of information about various Web pages. People who develop a Web site can submit a summary of their site to the keepers of the search engine. Alternatively, those responsible for the search engine may create their own reviews of Web sites. The advantage of this kind of search engine is that humans can create more accurate summaries of a Web page than a spider program. The disadvantage of this approach is that only a small fraction of the Web can be catalogued. The Open Directory Project falls into this category.

1.5 Information Technology Issues

Information technology (IT) refers to devices used in the creation, storage, manipulation, exchange, and dissemination of data, including text, sound, and images. Computers, telephones, and video cameras are examples of IT. The cost of IT devices continues to fall, while their capabilities continue to increase. As a result, people are making greater use of IT in their everyday lives. Some of these uses create new issues that need to be resolved. In this section, we describe a few of the issues raised by the growth of IT.

The great power of email is that it allows (at least in principle) anyone to send email to anyone else with an email address. Now that just about everyone has an email account, it is easier than ever to contact friends and family. Parents who used to complain because they never got letters from their children at college found out that it was much easier to keep in touch via email. On the other hand, most email traffic is spam: unsolicited, bulk, commercial email. Is spam destroying the value of email?

Thanks to the Web, it is easier than ever to share information with people all over the world. Imagine I live in Canada and post some controversial files on my Web site. Some Americans visit my Web site and download the files, an action that violates U.S. laws. Should I be prevented from posting material that is legal in Canada but illegal in the United States?

For many items of value, making the original copy is expensive, but making copies of the original is inexpensive. For example, an entertainment company may spend hundreds of thousands of dollars to produce a CD, but once a CD has been ripped into MP3 files, the Internet provides a fast and free way to distribute the music. As a result, unauthorized copies of songs, movies, and computer programs are proliferating. Should we continue to give ownership rights to creators of intellectual property, or is it hopeless? If we no longer give ownership rights to creators of intellectual property, will creativity suffer?

If I use a credit card to purchase an item, the credit card company now has information about my spending habits. Who has a right to that information? For example, if I buy a pair of water skis with my credit card, does the credit card company have a right to sell my name, address, and phone number to other companies that may want to sell me related products?

The use of IT has changed the way that banks process loan applications. Rather than using a personal interview to decide my creditworthiness, the bank consults a national credit bureau. What are the advantage and disadvantages of this alternative approach to lending money?

Computers are now embedded in many devices on which we depend, from traffic signals to pacemakers. Software errors have resulted in injury and even death. When bugs result in harm to humans, what should the liability be for the people or corporations that produced the software?

When employees use IT devices in their work, companies can monitor their actions closely. For example, a company can track the number of calls per minute each of its telephone operators is handling. It can document the number of keystrokes per minute of its data entry operators. It can log all of the Web sites its employees visit, and it can read the email they send and receive at work. How does such monitoring affect the workplace? Does it create an unacceptable level of stress among employees?

IT is allowing more people than ever to work from home. What are the advantages and disadvantages of telecommuting?

IT capabilities are leading to changes in the IT industry itself. Silicon Valley used to be the epicenter of the IT industry, but improvements in the speed and reliability of communication networks have led to a more decentralized landscape. New hot spots of innovation include Seattle, Washington (Amazon.com and Microsoft), Austin, Texas (Dell), Armonk, New York (IBM), Walldorf, Germany (SAP), and Bangalore, India (Infosys and Wipro). U.S.-based software companies are doing more development in countries where salaries are much lower, such as India, China, and Vietnam [7]. Will this trend continue? How many software jobs in the United States will be lost to countries where labor is significantly cheaper?

The World Wide Web has provided an unprecedented opportunity for individuals and nongovernmental organizations to have their points of view made available to billions. This could bring about new levels of citizen involvement and democratic reform. On the other hand, some countries are making large portions of the Web unavailable to its citizens. Will the Web prove to be a tool for democracy, or will it be muzzled by repressive regimes?

Summary

We are living in the Information Age, an era characterized by ubiquitous computing and communication devices that have made information much easier to collect, transmit, store, and retrieve. These devices are the culmination of centuries of technological progress.

The first mechanical adding machines date back to the seventeenth century, but real progress in mechanical calculator technology did not occur until the end of the nineteenth century. Advances in machine tools and mass production methods, combined with market demand, made possible the emergence of practical mechanical calculators during the second half of the nineteenth century. During America's Gilded Age, corporations and governmental organizations grew larger and needed to generate and handle greater volumes of information in a shorter amount of time. Calculators, cash registers, and punched-card tabulators were developed to meet these needs. Eventually IBM and Remington Rand began to produce systems capable of performing lengthy calculations. These systems used stacks of punched cards to store input data, output data, intermediate results, and even series of instructions, called programs.

Military-funded research and development projects during World War II, particularly the construction of the ENIAC and the development of microwave radar systems, accelerated the emergence of electronic digital computers in the United States and the United Kingdom. The Small-Scale Experimental Machine constructed at the University of Manchester in England was the first operational, fully electronic digital computer to store both its program and data in memory. Soon after, computers were commercially available.

Higher-level programming languages made it practical for more people to program computers, greatly improved programmer productivity, and allowed organizations to change computer vendors without having to rewrite all their programs. Time-sharing made computers more accessible by allowing the costs of purchasing and operating a computer to be divided among several organizations.

The invention of the transistor and the integrated circuit paved the way for the creation of the microprocessor, or computer on a chip, and the subsequent growth of the personal computer industry. The rapid decline in the cost of manufacturing microprocessors has made possible the use of computers in items as mundane as electric mixers and door locks, as well as solar-powered calculators selling for less than $5, a far cry from the first rudimentary mechanical adders.

Advances in computing technology have been accompanied by equally dramatic improvements in communications networks. Two centuries ago mechanical semaphore telegraph systems could transmit messages at about 350 miles per hour. The discovery of electromagnetism led to the invention of the modern telegraph that could transmit messages at the speed of electricity. Alexander Graham Bell worked on improving the telegraph. He ended up inventing the telephone, which enabled the creation of the first "online" communities. Radio and television made it possible for millions of people around the planet to receive the same message simultaneously. Today's Internet binds hundreds of millions of computers across the globe, creating new opportunities for sending as well as receiving messages.

The codex represented a significant improvement over the scroll as a way of storing information. The codex was more durable than the papyrus scroll, and it was much easier for readers to find a particular passage they were looking for. The availability of paper and printing presses based on movable metal type made it possible for ordinary people to afford codices. Even today, books and magazines are typically produced using this technology.

Vannevar Bush, Ted Nelson, and Douglas Engelbart all envisioned more powerful ways of storing and retrieving information. Bush suggested that a machine be used to mimic the associative memory of the brain. Nelson invented the word "hypertext," meaning a linked network of nodes containing information. Engelbart conceived of a computing system built around a graphical display device. His investigations led to many innovations, including the computer mouse and a video display divided into windows. Engelbart's concepts became practical with the availability of low-cost systems utilizing bit-mapped displays, such as the Apple Macintosh. Single-user hypertext systems were available for the Macintosh a couple of years after its initial release, but the true power of hypertext was revealed when Tim Berners-Lee created the World Wide Web, which allowed links between information stored on different computers. The Web has become a popular and powerful information storage and retrieval mechanism.

© Zits Partnership, KING FEATURES SYNDICATE

What conclusions can we draw from our study of the development of computers, communication networks, and information storage and retrieval devices? First, revolutionary discoveries are rare. Rather, most innovations represent simply the next step in a long staircase of evolutionary changes. Each inventor, or team of inventors, relies upon prior work. In many cases different inventors come up with the same "original" idea at the same time.

A second conclusion we can draw from these stories is that information technology did not begin with the personal computer and the World Wide Web. Many other inventions, including the telegraph, the telephone, the mechanical calculator, the radio, and the television, led to significant social changes when they were adopted.

Nevertheless, in the past two decades the rate of technological change has accelerated, thanks to low-cost computers and high-speed communication networks. The pace of technological progress is so rapid that we may feel hard-pressed to keep up. It's good to reflect on Seymour Papert's observation:

> So we are entering this computer future; but what will it be like? What sort of a world will it be? There is no shortage of experts, futurists, and prophets who are ready to tell us, but they don't agree. The Utopians promise us a new millennium, a wonderful world in which the computer will solve all our problems. The computer critics warn us of the dehumanizing effect of too much exposure to machinery, and of disruption of employment in the workplace and the economy.
>
> Who is right? Well, both are wrong—because they are asking the wrong question. The question is not "What will the computer do to us?" The question is "What will we make of the computer?" The point is not to predict the computer future. The point is to make it. [46]

Review Questions

1. According to the author, why is there good reason to say we are living in the Information Age?

2. What can the Amish teach us about our relationship with technology?

3. Name three aids to manual calculating.

4. Why did commercial mechanical calculators become practical in the nineteenth century?

5. Why did the market for mechanical calculators grow significantly in the late nineteenth century?

6. What factors helped the Burroughs Adding Machine Company to surpass a large number of competitors to become the most successful calculator company by the 1890s?

7. How did the widespread adoption of the mechanical calculator change the office environment?

8. What needs motivated the invention of the cash register?

9. Give four examples of how punched cards were used by large organizations in the early twentieth century.

10. What are the three principal components of a data-processing system?

11. Name three ways the development of radar in World War II stimulated advances in computing.

12. Why did IBM quickly overtake Remington Rand as the leading computer manufacturer in the United States in the 1950s?

13. What was the motivation for the creation of higher-level programming languages? How did the introduction of higher-level programming languages change computing?

14. How did time-sharing give more organizations access to electronic digital computers in the 1960s?

15. In what way did the Cold War accelerate the development of technology needed for the personal computer?

16. What was the principal innovation of the IBM System/360?

17. Can you think of a practical reason why the semaphore telegraph was adopted more rapidly on the continent of Europe than in the British Isles?

18. Give two examples of how the introduction of Morse's telegraph changed life in America.

19. Briefly describe three ways in which society changed by adopting the telephone.

20. What is the difference between a circuit-switched network and a packet-switched network?

21. Why does the Internet have a decentralized structure?

22. How did the National Science Foundation stimulate the creation of commercial, long-distance data networks in the United States?

23. Describe two ways in which the codex represented an improvement over the scroll.

24. What is hypertext?

25. How is a hypertext link similar to a citation in a book? How is it different?

26. Who invented the computer mouse?

27. The Apple Macintosh succeeded in the marketplace, while the Apple Lisa failed. Give two reasons why this happened.

28. In what fundamental way is an Apple HyperCard stack different from the World Wide Web?

29. Berners-Lee decided to build the World Wide Web on top of the TCP/IP protocol. Why did this decision help ensure the success of the Web?

30. What was the first widely used Web browser? Name four popular Web browsers in use today.

31. What is a search engine? Describe the two types of search engines.

32. What is information technology?

33. Name three inventions described in this chapter that were created for a military application.

34. Give four examples from the book of how a social condition influenced the development of a new technology.

35. Give four examples from the book of a social change brought about by the adoption of a new technology.

Discussion Questions

36. Think about the last piece of consumer electronics you purchased. How did you first learn about it? What factors (features, price, ease of use, etc.) did you weigh before you

purchased it? Which of these factors were most influential in your purchase decision? Are you still happy with your purchase?

37. Do you tend to acquire new technological devices before or after the majority of your friends? What are the advantages of being an early adopter of a new technology? What are the advantages of being a late adopter of a new technology?

38. Have you ever gone camping or had another experience where you went for at least a few days without access to a phone, radio, television, or computer? (In other words, there was no communication between you and the outside world.) What did you learn from your experience?

39. Are there any technologies that you wish had never been adopted? If so, which ones?

40. Some say that no technology is inherently good or evil; rather, any technology can be used for either good or evil purposes. Do you share this view?

41. The telephone eroded traditional social hierarchies. Has email had the same effect within colleges and universities? Do students send emails to people they would be uncomfortable talking with personally? Are these emails effective?

42. Is the cell phone changing our views about polite and impolite behavior? For example, is it polite for someone to be talking on their cell phone while ordering a drink at Starbucks?

43. Martin Carnoy writes, "Thanks to a communications and software revolution, we are more 'connected' than ever before—by cell phone, email, and video conferencing—yet more disconnected than in the past from social interaction" [47]. Do you agree?

44. Was it wrong for Altair 8800 owners to use Altair BASIC on their computers without paying Micro-Soft?

45. The story of Altair BASIC highlights a clash between those who see software as something to be developed and freely shared among computer enthusiasts and those who see software development as an entrepreneurial activity. Give some contemporary examples that illustrate these contrasting views of software.

46. More than 90 percent of personal computers run a version of the Microsoft Windows operating system. In what ways is this situation beneficial to computer users? In what ways does this situation harm computer users?

47. Angelo says, "When I'm trying to have a face-to-face conversation with someone, and that person repeatedly interrupts the conversation to answer their cell phone or exchange text messages, they are basically telling me that I'm not worth all of their attention." Do you agree or disagree with Angelo?

In–Class Exercises

48. Use four different search engines (www.altavista.com, www.bing.com, www.google.com, www.yahoo.com) to perform a search on the phrase "Information Technology." Create a table that compares the top 10 Web pages returned by each search engine. Which engines were the most similar?

49. Most smartphones come equipped with cameras. Managers of health clubs are concerned that people in locker rooms may be secretly photographed by other members carrying smartphones.

    Debate the following proposition: "Health clubs should ban all cell phone use within their premises."

50. In the 1984 Presidential election, all the major television networks used computers to predict that Republican Ronald Reagan would defeat Democrat Walter Mondale, even before the polls closed on the West Coast. When they heard this news, some Mondale supporters who had been waiting in line to vote simply went home without voting. This may have influenced the results of some statewide and local elections.

    Debate the following proposition: "In Presidential elections polls should close at the same time everywhere in the United States."

51. Ford, Honda, Mercedes-Benz, Toyota, Volvo, and other automobile manufacturers are currently offering collision mitigation systems on some of their vehicles. A collision mitigation system uses radar to sense when the distance between the car and the vehicle in front of it is rapidly decreasing. The system provides audio and visual warnings to the driver when dangerous situations are detected. It also pretightens the seat belts. If the driver fails to respond, the system brakes the car and tightens the seat belt further to reduce the impact of the collision.

    Debate the following proposition: "Every new car should be equipped with a collision mitigation system."

52. Read about "Star Wars Kid" and "The Bus Uncle" on Wikipedia, then debate the following proposition: "It is wrong to post a photo or video of someone else on the Internet without their permission."

Further Reading

Tim Berners-Lee with Mark Fischetti. *Weaving the Web: The Original Design and Ultimate Destiny of the World Wide Web by Its Inventor*. HarperCollins, New York, NY, 1999.

Martin Campbell-Kelly and William Aspray. *Computer: A History of the Information Machine*. BasicBooks, New York, NY, 1996.

Nicholar Carr. "Is Google Making Us Stupid?" *The Atlantic*, July/August 2008.

Paul Carroll. *Big Blues: The Unmaking of IBM*. Crown Publishers, New York, NY, 1993.

James W. Cortada. *Before the Computer: IBM, NCR, Burroughs, & Remington Rand & the Industry They Created, 1865–1956*. Princeton University Press, Princeton, NJ, 2000.

William H. Dutton, editor, with Malcom Peltu. *Information and Communication Technologies: Visions and Realities*. Oxford University Press, Oxford, England, 1996.

Paul Freiberger and Michael Swaine. *Fire in the Valley: The Making of the Personal Computer*. Osborne/McGraw-Hill, Berkeley, CA, 1984.

Kevin Kelly. "We Are the Web." *Wired* (August 2005).

Barry M. Leiner, Vinton G. Cerf, David D. Clark, Robert E. Kahn, Leonard Kleinrock, Daniel C. Lynch, Jon Postel, Larry G. Roberts, and Stephen Wolff. "A Brief History of the Internet." Internet Society Web site, www.isoc.org/internet/history/brief/shtml, December 10, 2003.

Stephen Manes and Paul Andrews. *Gates: How Microsoft's Mogul Reinvented an Industry—And Made Himself the Richest Man in America*. Doubleday, New York, NY, 1993.

John Markoff. *What the Dormouse Said: How the Sixties Counterculture Shaped the Personal Computer Industry*. Penguin Books, New York, NY, 2005.

Carolyn Marvin. *When Old Technologies Were New: Thinking About Electric Communication in the Late Nineteenth Century*. Oxford University Press, New York, NY, 1988.

John Naughton. *A Brief History of the Future: From Radio Days to Internet Years in a Lifetime*. The Overlook Press, Woodstock, NY, 1999.

Ithiel de Sola Pool, editor. *The Social Impact of the Telephone*. The MIT Press, Cambridge, MA, 1977.

Michael Riordan and Lillian Hoddeson. *Crystal Fire: The Birth of the Information Age*. W. W. Norton & Company, New York, NY, 1997.

David Ritchie. *The Computer Pioneers: The Making of the Modern Computer*. Simon & Schuster, New York, NY, 1986.

Frederick Seitz and Norman G. Einspruch. *Electronic Genie: The Tangled History of Silicon*. University of Illinois Press, Urbana, IL, 1998.

Joel Shurkin. *Engines of the Mind: The Evolution of the Computer from Mainframes to Microprocessors*. W. W. Norton & Company, New York, NY, 1996.

Nancy Stern. *From ENIAC to UNIVAC: An Appraisal of the Eckert-Mauchly Computers*. Digital Press, Bedford, MA, 1981.

Transparency (Web site). www.transparencynow.com.

James Wallace and Jim Erickson. *Hard Drive: Bill Gates and the Making of the Microsoft Empire*. John Wiley & Sons, New York, NY, 1992.

What You Need to Know About (Web site). Inventors section, www.inventors.about.com.

Michael R. Williams. *A History of Computing Technology*. 2nd ed. IEEE Computer Society Press, Washington, DC, 1997.

References

[1]   May Swenson. "Southbound on the Freeway." *The New Yorker*, February 16, 1963.

[2]   Steve Friess. "Laptop Design Can Be a Pain in the Posture." *USA Today*, April 12, 2005.

[3]   Ethan S. Bromberg-Martin and Okihide Hikosaka. "Midbrain Dopamine Neurons Signal Preference for Advance Information about Upcoming Rewards," *Neuron*, Vol. 26, pp. 119–126, July 16, 2009.

[4]   Susan Weinschenk. "100 Things You Should Know about People #8—Dopamine Makes You Addicted to Seeking Information." *What Makes Them Click: Applying Psychology to Understand How People Think, Work, and Relate (blog)*. November 7, 2009. www.whatmakesthemclick.net.

[5]   Christine Rosen. "Our Cell Phones, Ourselves." *The New Atlantis: A Journal of Technology & Society*, Summer 2004.

[6]   Howard Rheingold. "Look Who's Talking." *Wired*, (7.01), January 1999.

[7]   "The New Geography of the IT Industry." *The Economist*, pages 47–49, July 19, 2003.

[8]   D'Arcy Jenish and Catherine Roberts. "Heating Up Nuclear Power." *Maclean's*, 113(24): 19, June 11, 2001.

[9]   Peggy A. Kidwell and Paul E. Ceruzzi. *Landmarks in Digital Computing: A Smithsonian Pictorial History*. Smithsonian Institution Press, Washington, DC, 1994.

[10]   James Cortada. *Before the Computer: IBM, NCR, Burroughs, & Remington Rand & the Industry They Created, 1865–1956*. Princeton University Press, Princeton, NJ, 2000.

[11]   "A Better Day's Work at Less Cost of Time, Work, and Worry to the Man at the Desk: in Three Parts Illustrated," 3d ed. Burroughs Adding Machine Company, Detroit, Michigan, 1909.

[12]   Sharon H. Strom. "'Machines Instead of Clerks': Technology and the Feminization of Bookkeeping, 1910–1950." In *Computer Chips and Paper Clips: Technology and Women's Employment, Volume II: Case Studies and Policy Perspectives*. Edited by Heidi I. Hartmann, Robert E. Kraut, and Louise A. Tilly. The National Academies Press, Washington, DC, 1987.

[13]   Joel Shurkin. *Engines of the Mind: The Evolution of the Computer from Mainframes to Microprocessors*. W.W. Norton & Company, New York, NY, 1996.

[14]   Grace Murray Hopper. "Keynote Address." In *History of Programming Languages*, edited by Richard L. Wexelblat. Academic Press, New York, NY, 1981.

[15]   John Backus. "The History of FORTRAN I, II, and III." In *History of Programming Languages*, edited by Richard L. Wexelblat. Academic Press, New York, NY, 1981.

[16]   Jean E. Sammet. "The Early History of COBOL." In *History of Programming Languages*, edited by Richard L. Wexelblat. Academic Press, New York, NY, 1981.

[17]   Thomas E. Kurtz. "Basic." In *History of Programming Languages*, edited by Richard L. Wexelblat. Academic Press, New York, NY, 1981.

[18]   Robert Buderi. *The Invention that Changed the World: How a Small Group of Radar Pioneers Won the Second World War and Launched a Technological Revolution*. Simon and Schuster, New York, NY, 1996.

[19]   Michael Riordan and Lillian Hoddeson. *Crystal Fire: The Birth of the Information Age*. W. W. Norton & Company, New York, NY, 1997.

[20]   Frederick Seitz and Norman G. Einspruch. *Electronic Genie: The Tangled History of Silicon*. University of Illinois Press, Urbana, IL, 1998.

[21]   John Markoff. *What the Dormouse Said: How the Sixties Counterculture Shaped the Personal Computer Industry*. Penguin Books, New York, NY, 2005.

[22]   Steve Jobs. "You've Got to Find What You Love." Commencement speech, Stanford University, June 12, 2005.

[23]   Fred Turner. *From Counterculture to Cyberculture: Steward Brand, the Whole Earth Network, and the Rise of Digital Utopianism*. University of Chicago Press, Chicago, IL, 2006.

[24]   *The People's Computer Company*, Issue 1, cover, October 1972.

[25]   Paul Carroll. *Big Blues: The Unmaking of IBM*. Crown Publishers, New York, NY, 1993.

[26]   Sidney H. Aronson. "Bell's Electrical Toy." In *The Social Impact of the Telephone*, edited by Ithiel de Sola Pool. The MIT Press, Cambridge, MA, 1977.

[27] Carolyn Marvin. *When Old Technologies Were New: Thinking about Electric Communications in the Late Nineteenth Century*. Oxford University Press, New York, NY, 1988.

[28] "Telephone Cranks." *Western Electrician (Chicago)*, page 37, July 17, 1897.

[29] Ithiel de Sola Pool. Introduction. In *The Social Impact of the Telephone*, edited by Ithiel de Sola Pool. The MIT Press, Cambridge, MA, 1977.

[30] Asa Briggs. "The Pleasure Telephone." In *The Social Impact of the Telephone*, edited by Ithiel de Sola Pool. The MIT Press, Cambridge, MA, 1977.

[31] International Telecommunication Union. "Key Global Telecom Indicators for the World Telecommunication Service Sector." *www.itu.int/ITU-D/ict/statistics*, 2007.

[32] Martin Campbell-Kelly and William Aspray. *Computer: A History of the Information Machine*. BasicBooks, New York, NY, 1996.

[33] "Radio: The Roots of Broadcasting." *Technical Press*. www.tvhandbook.com/History.

[34] "War of the Worlds, Orson Welles, and the Invasion from Mars." *Transparency*. www.transparencynow.com.

[35] Barry M. Leiner, Vinton G. Cerf, David D. Clark, Robert E. Kahn, Leonard Kleinrock, Daniel C. Lynch, Jon Postel, Larry G. Roberts, and Stephen Wolff. *A Brief History of the Internet, Version 3.32*, December 10, 2003. www.isoc.org/internet/history/brief.shtml.

[36] Vinton G. Cerf and Robert E. Kahn. "A Protocol for Packet Network Intercommunication." *IEEE Transactions on Communications*, COM-22(5), May 1974.

[37] "Akamai's 'State of the Internet' Report Enters Fourth Year of Analyzing Global Connectivity, Attack Traffic and Broadband Consumption." Akamai, July 26, 2011. www.akamai.com.

[38] Thomas Cahill. *How the Irish Saved Civilization: The Untold Story of Ireland's Role from the Fall of Rome to the Rise of Medieval Europe*. Anchor Books, New York, NY, 1995.

[39] Elizabeth L. Eisenstein. *The Printing Press as an Agent of Change*. Volume 1. Cambridge University Press, Cambridge, England, 1979.

[40] Vannevar Bush. "As We May Think." *The Atlantic Monthly*, 176(1):101–108, August 1945.

[41] Owen Edwards. "Ted Nelson." *Forbes*, August 25, 1997.

[42] Lauren Wedeles. "Prof. Nelson Talk Analyzes P.R.I.D.E." *Vassar Miscellany News*, February 3, 1965.

[43] T. O'Brien. "The Mouse." *SiliconValley.com*, 2000.

[44] "Internet Pioneers: Doug Engelbart." *ibiblio* (Web site). www.ibiblio.org/pioneers/engelbart.html.

[45] Tim Berners-Lee. *Weaving the Web*. HarperCollins Publishers, New York, NY, 1999.

[46] Seymour Papert. "A Critique of Technocentrism in Thinking About the School of the Future." Technical report, MIT Media Lab, September 1990. Epistemology and Learning Memo No. 2.

[47] Martin Carnoy. *Sustaining the New Economy: Work, Family, and the Community in the Information Age*. Russel Sage Foundation/Harvard University Press, New York, NY/Cambridge, MA, 2000.

Dalton Conley

Dalton Conley is Dean for the Social Sciences, as well as University Professor, at New York University. In 2005, he became the first sociologist (and second social scientist) to win the Alan T. Waterman Award from the National Science Foundation for best young researcher in any field of science, math, or engineering. Conley's research focuses on how socio-economic status is transmitted across generations and on the public policies that affect that process.

He has written six books, including *Elsewhere, U.S.A.: How We Got from the Company Man, Family Dinners and the Age of Affluence to the Home Office, BlackBerry Moms and Economic Anxiety* (2009, New York: Pantheon).

In addition to writing books, he is a frequent contributor to the *New York Times, Los Angeles Times, Salon, Slate, Fortune,* and the *Chronicle of Higher Education.* He also lectures frequently and has appeared on *Today, The O'Reilly Factor, The NewsHour, Fresh Air,* and *20/20.* He has been named one of nine "innovative minds" by *SEED* Magazine.

What do you mean by your term, the "Elsewhere Ethic"?

I argue that whereas once the ethical imperative in American life—as embodied in the culture of individualism—was to "find oneself," that ethic has morphed into one in which we need to "manage one's selves." That is, with constant connectivity and the concomitant decline in solitude, we no longer have the space or opportunity to find a true, single, authentic self. With Facebook, Twitter, email logs, etc., there is hardly a private social space anymore—what sociologist Erving Goffman called the "backstage." Instead, the imperative is to be able to manage these multiple data streams and impulses and avatars in different media of communication.

What are the phenomena that have given rise to the Elsewhere Ethic?

Communications technology, of course, but also rising income inequality and economic anxiety as well as increased work–life tension due to the rapid rise in working mothers (combined with a lack of decline in fathers' work hours that might have compensated).

Are you saying that teenagers texting at the dinner table are just following the lead of adults?

I am saying that the entire culture has shifted and often youth—the so-called digital natives—have been completely reared and socialized within the new normative context. Older folks like myself are caught between the old ethic of individualism and the new fragmented intra-vidualism.

How has social change driven the development of new information technologies, such as cell phones, text messaging, and movie-recommendation software?

A Marxist would say that technology drives social change. Some others might say that technology merely embodies or reacts to social changes. Most of the rest of us social scientists would say that there is a feedback loop. Yes, the Internet revolution and other telecommunications technologies have fundamentally altered the social landscape by, for example, erasing boundaries between home and office, work and leisure, friends and colleagues, public and private. But the development and spread of those technologies is also reactive to social changes such as the increase in two-working-parent families, which, in a sense, necessitate an increased level of connectivity to manage work and home responsibilities. Likewise, rising work hours and inequality have also adopted the work-always ethos of the current epoch, which is both facilitated by and drives demand for ever-faster telecommunications technologies.

Is it possible or even desirable to return to a less-connected lifestyle in which people really give each other their undivided attention?

Desirable is in the eye of the beholder. We can always make a conscious choice to drop out, tune in, and so on. And you can already see a backlash in the popular culture in the form of the slow-food, slow-living movement. However, you can never go home again, as the saying goes, because even if you make efforts to regulate your own attention and usage of technologies, you are doing so on a shifted playing field, fighting intense forces that didn't exist to the same degree in earlier times.

Okay, so there's no going back. What's the best way to move forward?

There are many great aspects of this networked world of "weisure" (a portmanteau that combines work and leisure in this blurred lifestyle). If we are lucky enough to be a member of the Elsewhere Class, we can telecommute when our kids are home sick. We can use our iPhone to locate a farmers market in a strange city in which we find ourselves on a business trip. And work has become more fun for this class. More and more of us find not just our calling—our identity—from our work, many of us also find pleasure and joy in the rhythm of our weisurely lives where we are needed and connected. So my advice is not to pine for a nostalgic past of uninterrupted family dinners and beach vacations. The most successful (and fulfilled) firms and individuals are going to be the ones who bend and blend rather than erect rigid modernist boundaries between the spheres of life. That might mean de-emphasizing "face time" if tasks can get done on Skype. Or it could mean providing on-site day-care. Or laundry rooms and gyms at the office (as Google does). Employees find that more convenient and employers get more productive workers whose other tasks don't get in the way of their work in the knowledge economy.

2

Introduction to Ethics

No man is an island, entire of itself; every man is a piece of the continent, a part of the main. If a clod be washed away by the sea, Europe is the less, as well as if a promontory were, as well as if a manor of thy friend's or of thine own were. Any man's death diminishes me, because I am involved in mankind; and therefore never send to know for whom the bell tolls; it tolls for thee.

–JOHN DONNE, *Meditation XVII*

2.1 Introduction

IMAGINE HOVERING ABOVE THE EARTH in a spacecraft on a cloudless night. Looking down upon our planet, you see beautiful constellations of artificial light (Figure 2.1). The stars in these incandescent galaxies are our communities.

Forming communities allows us to enjoy better lives than if we lived in isolation. Communities facilitate the exchange of goods and services. Instead of each family assuming responsibility for all of its needs, such as food, housing, clothing, education, and health care, individuals can focus on particular activities. Specialization results in higher productivity that increases everyone's quality of life. Communities also make people more secure against external dangers.

There is a price associated with being part of a community. Communities prohibit certain actions and make other actions obligatory. Those who do not conform to these prohibitions and obligations can be punished. Still, the fact that almost everyone *does*

FIGURE 2.1   Looking down on London, England, at night from space.   (Courtesy of NASA)

live in a community is strong evidence that the advantages of community life outweigh the disadvantages.

Responsible community members take the needs and desires of other people into account when they make decisions. They recognize that virtually everybody shares the "core values" of life, happiness, and the ability to accomplish goals. People who respect only their own needs and desires are taking the selfish point of view. Moving to the "ethical point of view" requires a decision that other people and their core values are also worthy of respect [1].

People who take the ethical point of view may still disagree over what is the proper course of action to take in a particular situation. Sometimes the facts of the matters are disputable. At other times, different value judgments arising from competing ethical theories lead people to opposite conclusions. For this reason, it is worthwhile to have a basic understanding of some of the most popular ethical theories. In this chapter, we will describe the difference between morality and ethics, discuss a variety of ethical theories, evaluate their pros and cons, and show how to use the more viable ethical theories to solve moral problems.

2.1.1 Defining Terms

A **society** is an association of people organized under a system of rules designed to advance the good of its members over time [2]. Cooperation among individuals helps promote the common good. However, people in a society also compete with each other;

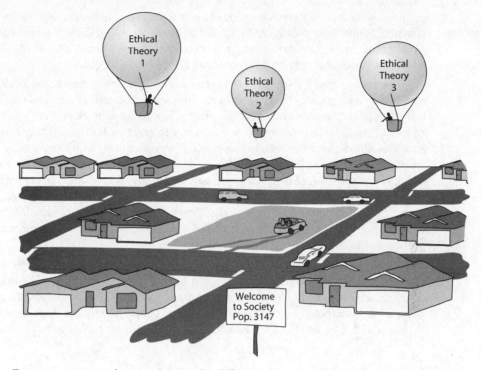

FIGURE 2.2 An analogy explaining the difference between ethics and morality. Imagine society as a town. Morality is the road network within the town. People doing ethics are in balloons floating above the town.

for example, when deciding how to divide limited benefits among themselves. Sometimes the competition is relatively trivial, such as when many people vie for tickets to a movie premiere. At other times the competition is much more significant, such as when two start-up companies seek control of an emerging market. Every society has rules of conduct describing what people ought and ought not to do in various situations. We call these rules **morality**.

A person may simultaneously belong to multiple societies, which can lead to moral dilemmas. For example, what happens when a pacifist (according to the rules of his religion) is drafted to serve in the armed forces (according to the laws of his nation)?

Ethics is the philosophical study of morality, a rational examination into people's moral beliefs and behavior. Consider the following analogy (Figure 2.2). Society is like a town full of people driving cars. Morality is the road network within the town. People ought to keep their cars on the roads. Those who choose to "do ethics" are in balloons floating above the town. From this perspective, an observer can evaluate individual roads (particular moral guidelines) as well as the quality of the entire road network (moral system). The observer can also judge whether individual drivers are staying on the roads (acting morally) or taking shortcuts (acting immorally). Finally, the observer can propose and evaluate various ways of constructing road networks (alternative moral systems). While there may in fact be a definite answer regarding the best way to construct and operate a road network, it may be difficult for the observers to identify and agree upon this answer, because each observer has a different viewpoint.

The study of ethics is particularly important right now. Our society is changing rapidly as it incorporates the latest advances in information technology. Just think about how cell phones, portable digital music players, laptop computers, and the World Wide Web have changed how we spend our time and interact with others! These inventions have brought us many benefits. However, some people selfishly exploit new technologies for personal gain, even if that reduces their overall benefit for the rest of us. Here are two examples. While most of us are happy to have the ability to send email to people all over the world, we are dismayed at the amount of spam—unsolicited bulk email—we receive. Access to the World Wide Web provides libraries with an important new information resource for their patrons, but should children be exposed to pop-up advertisements for pornographic Web sites?

When we encounter new problems such as spam or pornographic Web sites, we need to decide which activities are morally "good," which are morally "neutral," and which are morally "bad." Unfortunately, existing moral guidelines sometimes seem old-fashioned or unclear. If we can't always count on "common wisdom" to help us answer these questions, we need to learn how to work through these problems ourselves.

2.1.2 Four Scenarios

As an initiation into the study of ethics, carefully read each of the following scenarios. After reflection, come up with your own answer to each of the questions.

~ SCENARIO 1

Alexis, a gifted high school student, wants to become a doctor. Because she comes from a poor family, she will need a scholarship in order to attend college. Some of her classes require students to do extra research projects in order to get an A. Her high school has a few older PCs, but there are always long lines of students waiting to use them during the school day. After school, she usually works at a part-time job to help support her family.

One evening Alexis visits the library of a private college a few miles from her family's apartment, and she finds plenty of unused PCs connected to the Internet. She surreptitiously looks over the shoulder of another student to learn a valid login/password combination. Alexis returns to the library several times a week, and by using its PCs and printers she efficiently completes the extra research projects, graduates from high school with straight A's, and gets a full-ride scholarship to attend a prestigious university.

Questions
1. Did Alexis do anything wrong?
2. Who benefited from Alexis's course of action?

3. Who was hurt by Alexis's course of action?

4. Did Alexis have an unfair advantage over her high school classmates?

5. Would any of your answers change if it turns out Alexis did not win a college scholarship after all and is now working at the Burger Barn?

6. Are there better ways Alexis could have accomplished her objective?

7. What additional information, if any, would help you answer the previous questions?   ∽

∽ SCENARIO 2

An organization dedicated to reducing spam tries to get Internet service providers (ISPs) in an East Asian country to stop the spammers by protecting their mail servers. When this effort is unsuccessful, the anti-spam organization puts the addresses of these ISPs on its "black list." Many ISPs in the United States consult the black list and refuse to accept email from the blacklisted ISPs. This action has two results. First, the amount of spam received by the typical email user in the United States drops by 25 percent. Second, tens of thousands of innocent computer users in the East Asian country are unable to send email to friends and business associates in the United States.

Questions

1. Did the anti-spam organization do anything wrong?

2. Did the ISPs that refused to accept email from the blacklisted ISPs do anything wrong?

3. Who benefited from the organization's action?

4. Who was hurt by the organization's action?

5. Could the organization have achieved its goals through a better course of action?

6. What additional information, if any, would help you answer the previous questions?   ∽

∽ SCENARIO 3

In an attempt to deter speeders, the East Dakota State Police (EDSP) installs video cameras on all of its freeway overpasses. The cameras are connected to computers that can reliably detect cars traveling more than five miles per hour above the speed limit. These computers have sophisticated image recognition software that enables them to read license plate numbers and capture high-resolution pictures of vehicle drivers. If the picture of the driver matches the driver's license photo of one of the registered owners of the car, the system issues a speeding ticket to the driver, complete with photo evidence. Six months after the system is put into operation, the number of people speeding on East Dakota freeways is reduced by 90 percent.

The FBI asks the EDSP for real-time access to the information collected by the video cameras. The EDSP complies with this request. Three months later, the FBI uses this information to arrest five members of a terrorist organization.

Questions

1. Did the East Dakota State Police do anything wrong?

2. Who benefited from the actions of the EDSP?

3. Who was harmed by the actions of the EDSP?

4. What other courses of action could the EDSP have taken to achieve its objectives? Examine the advantages and disadvantages of these alternative courses of action.

5. What additional information, if any, would help you answer the previous questions?

∼ Scenario 4

You are the senior software engineer at a start-up company developing an exciting new product that will allow salespeople to generate and email sales quotes and customer invoices from their smartphones.

Your company's sales force has led a major corporation to believe your product will be available next week. Unfortunately, at this point the package still contains quite a few bugs. The leader of the testing group has reported that all of the known bugs appear to be minor, but it will take another month of testing for his team to be confident the product contains no catastrophic errors.

Because of the fierce competition in the smartphone software industry, it is critical that your company be the "first to market." To the best of your knowledge, a well-established company will release a similar product in a few weeks. If its product appears first, your start-up company will probably go out of business.

Questions

1. Should you recommend release of the product next week?

2. Who will benefit if the company follows your recommendation?

3. Who will be harmed if the company follows your recommendation?

4. Do you have an obligation to any group of people that may be affected by your decision?

5. What additional information, if any, would help you answer the previous questions?

Reflect on the process you used in each scenario to come up with your answers. How did you decide if particular actions or decisions were right or wrong? Were your reasons consistent from one case to the next? Did you use the same methodology in more than one scenario? If someone disagreed with you on the answer to one of these questions, how would you try to convince that person that your position makes more sense?

Ethics is the rational, systematic analysis of conduct that can cause benefit or harm to other people. Because ethics is based in reason, people are required to explain *why* they hold the opinions they do. This gives us the opportunity to compare ethical evaluations. When two people reach different conclusions, we can weigh the facts and the reasoning process behind their conclusions to determine the stronger line of thinking.

It's important to note that ethics is focused on the *voluntary, moral* choices people make because they have decided they ought to take one course of action rather than an alternative. Ethics is not concerned about involuntary choices or choices outside the moral realm.

For example, if I am ordering a new car, I may get to choose whether it is red, white, green, or blue. This choice is not in the moral realm, because it does not involve benefit or harm to other people.

Now, suppose I'm driving my new, red car down a city street. A pedestrian, obscured from my view by a parked car, runs out into traffic. In an attempt to miss the pedestrian, I swerve, lose control of my car, and kill another pedestrian walking along the sidewalk. While my action caused harm to another person, this is not an example of ethical decision-making, because my decision was a reflex action rather than a reasoned choice.

However, suppose I did not have full control of the car because I had been driving while intoxicated. In that case the consequences of my voluntary choice to drink alcohol before driving affected another moral being (the innocent pedestrian). Now the problem has entered the realm of ethics.

2.1.3 Overview of Ethical Theories

The formal study of ethics goes back at least 2,400 years, to the Greek philosopher Socrates. Socrates did not put any of his philosophy in writing, but his student Plato did. In Plato's dialogue called the *Crito*, imprisoned Socrates uses ethical reasoning to explain why he ought to face an unjust death penalty rather than take advantage of an opportunity to flee into exile with his family [3].

In the past two millennia, philosophers have proposed many ethical theories. In this chapter, we review some of them. How do we decide if a particular theory is useful? A useful theory allows its proponents to examine moral problems, reach conclusions, and defend these conclusions in front of a skeptical, yet open-minded audience (Figure 2.3).

Suppose you and I are debating a moral problem in front of a nonpartisan crowd. You have concluded that a particular course of action is right, while I believe it is wrong. It is only natural for me to ask you, "Why do you think doing such-and-such is right?" If you are unable to give any logical reasons why your position is correct, you are unlikely to persuade anyone. On the other hand, if you can explain the chain of reasoning that led you to your conclusion, you will be more likely to convince the audience that your position is correct. At the very least you will help reveal where there are disputed facts or values. Therefore, we will reject proposed ethical theories that are not based on reasoning from facts or commonly accepted values.

FIGURE 2.3 A good ethical theory should enable you to make a persuasive, logical argument to a diverse audience.

In the following sections we will consider eight ethical theories—eight frameworks for moral decision-making. We will present the motivation or insight underlying each theory, explain how it can be used to determine whether an action is right or wrong, and give the "case for" and the "case against" the theory. The workable theories will be those that make it possible for a person to present a persuasive, logical argument to a diverse audience of skeptical, yet open-minded people.

The principal sources for these brief introductions to ethical theories are *Ethical Insights: A Brief Introduction, Second Edition* by Douglas Birsch [4] and *The Elements of Moral Philosophy, Fourth Edition* by James Rachels [5]. Consult one or both of these books if you'd like to explore any of these theories in greater depth.

2.2 Subjective Relativism

Relativism is the theory that there are no universal moral norms of right and wrong. According to this theory, different individuals or groups of people can have completely opposite views of a moral problem, and both can be right. Two particular kinds of relativism we'll discuss are subjective relativism and cultural relativism.

Subjective relativism holds that each person decides right and wrong for himself or herself. This notion is captured in the popular expression, "What's right for you may not be right for me."

2.2.1 The Case for Subjective Relativism

1. *Well-meaning and intelligent people can have totally opposite opinions about moral issues.*

   For example, consider the issue of legalized abortion in the United States. There are a significant number of rational people on each side of the issue. Subjective relativists would contend that the reason people cannot reach the same conclusion is that morality is not like gravity; it is not something "out there" that rational people can discover and try to understand. Instead, each of us creates his or her own morality.

2. *Ethical debates are disagreeable and pointless.*

Going back to the example of abortion, the debate in the United States has been going on for more than 30 years. An agreement about whether abortion is right or wrong may never be reached. Nobody is all-knowing. When faced with a difficult moral problem, who is to say which side is correct? If morality is relative, we do not have to try to reconcile opposing views. Both sides are right.

2.2.2 The Case against Subjective Relativism

1. *With subjective relativism the line between doing what you think is right and doing what you want to do is not sharply drawn.*

People are good at rationalizing their bad behavior. Subjective relativism provides an ideal last line of defense for someone whose conduct is being questioned. When pressed to explain a decision or action, a subjective relativist can reply, "Who are *you* to tell *me* what I should and should not do?" If morality means doing whatever you want to do, it doesn't mean much, if it means anything at all.

2. *By allowing each person to decide right and wrong for himself or herself, subjective relativism makes no moral distinction between the actions of different people.*

The fact is that some people have caused millions to suffer, while others have led lives of great service to humanity. Suppose both Adolf Hitler and Mother Teresa spent their entire lives doing what they thought was the right thing to do. Do you want to give both of them credit for living good lives?

A modification of the original formulation of subjective relativism might be: "I can decide what's right for me, as long as my actions don't hurt anybody else." That solves the problem of Adolf Hitler versus Mother Teresa. However, as soon as you introduce the idea that you shouldn't harm others, you must come to an agreement with others about what it means to harm someone. At this point the process is no longer subjective or completely up to the individual. In other words, a statement of the form, "I can decide what's right for me, as long as my actions don't hurt anyone else," is inconsistent with subjective relativism.

3. *Subjective relativism and tolerance are two different things.*

Some people may be attracted to relativism because they believe in tolerance. There is a lot to be said for tolerance. It allows individuals in a pluralistic society like the United States to live in harmony. However, tolerance is not the same thing as subjective relativism. Subjective relativism holds that individuals decide for themselves what is right and what is wrong. If you are a tolerant person, is it okay with you if some people decide they want to be intolerant? What if a person decides that he will only deal fairly with people of his own racial group? Note that any statement of the form, "People ought to be tolerant," is an example of a universal moral **norm**, or rule. Relativism is based on the idea that there are no universal moral norms, so a blanket statement about the need for tolerance is incompatible with subjective relativism.

4. *We should not give legitimacy to an ethical theory that allows people to make decisions based on something other than reason.*

   If individuals decide for themselves what is right and what is wrong, they can reach their conclusions by any means they see fit. They may choose to base their decisions on something other than logic and reason, such as the rolling of dice or the turning of Tarot cards. This path is contrary to using logic and reason.

If your goal is to persuade others that your solutions to actual moral problems are correct, adopting subjective relativism is self-defeating because it is based on the idea that each person decides for himself or herself what is right and what is wrong. According to subjective relativism, nobody's conclusions are any more valid that anyone else's, no matter how these conclusions are drawn. Therefore, we reject subjective relativism as a workable ethical theory.

2.3 Cultural Relativism

If subjective relativism is unworkable, what about different views of right and wrong held by different societies at the same point in time, or those held by the same society at different points in time?

In the modern era, anthropologists have collected evidence of societies with moral codes markedly different from those of the societies of Europe and North America. William Graham Sumner described the evolution of "folkways," which he argues eventually become institutionalized into the moral guidelines of a society:

> The first task of life is to live . . . The struggle to maintain existence was not carried on individually but in groups. Each profited by the other's experience; hence there was concurrence towards that which proved to be the most expedient. All at last adopted the same way for the same purpose; hence the ways turned into customs and became mass phenomena. Instincts were learned in connection with them. In this way folkways arise. The young learn by tradition, imitation, and authority. The folkways, at a time, provide for all the needs of life then and there. They are uniform, universal in the group, imperative, and invariable. As time goes on, the folkways become more and more arbitrary, positive, and imperative. If asked why they act in a certain way in certain cases, primitive people always answer that it is because they and their ancestors always have done so . . . The morality of a group at a time is the sum of the taboos and prescriptions in the folkways by which right conduct is defined . . . 'Good' mores are those which are well adapted to the situation. 'Bad' mores are those which are not so well adapted [6].

Cultural relativism is the ethical theory that the meaning of "right" and "wrong" rests with a society's actual moral guidelines. These guidelines vary from place to place and from time to time.

Charles Hampden-Turner and Fons Trompenaars conducted a modern study that reveals how notions of right and wrong vary widely from one society to another. Here is a dilemma they posed to people from 46 different countries:

> You are riding in a car driven by a close friend. He hits a pedestrian. You know he was going at least 35 miles per hour in an area of the city where the maximum allowed speed is 20 miles per hour. There are no witnesses other than you. His lawyer says that if you testify under oath that he was driving only 20 miles per hour, you will save him from serious consequences.
>
> What right has your friend to expect you to protect him?
>
> • My friend has a definite right as a friend to expect me to testify to the lower speed.
> • He has some right as a friend to expect me to testify to the lower speed.
> • He has no right as a friend to expect me to testify to the lower speed.
>
> What do you think you would do in view of the obligations of a sworn witness and the obligation to your friend?
>
> • Testify that he was going 20 miles per hour.
> • Not testify that he was going 20 miles per hour [7].[1]

About 90 percent of Norwegians would not testify to the lower speed and do not believe that the person's friend has a definite right to expect help. In contrast, only about 10 percent of Yugoslavians feel the same way. About three-quarters of Americans and Canadians agree with the dominant Norwegian view, but Mexicans are fairly evenly divided [7]. Cultural relativists say we ought to pay attention to these differences.

2.3.1 The Case for Cultural Relativism

1. *Different social contexts demand different moral guidelines.*

   It's unrealistic to assume that the same set of moral guidelines can be expected to work for all human societies in every part of the world for all ages. Just think about how our relationship with our environment has changed. For most of the past 10,000 years, human beings have spent most of their time trying to produce enough food to survive. Thanks to science and technology, the human population of the Earth has increased exponentially in the past century. The struggle for survival has shifted away from people to the rest of Nature. Overpopulation has created a host of environmental problems, such as the extinction of many species, the destruction of fisheries in the world's oceans, and the accumulation of greenhouse gases. People must change their ideas about what is acceptable conduct and what is not, or they will destroy the planet.

---

1. From *Building Cross-Cultural Competence: How to Create Wealth From Conflicting Values.* by Charles Hamden-Turner, Fons Trompenaars, and Davis Lewis (ill.). Copyright © 2000 by Yale University Press. Reprinted with permission.

2. *It is arrogant for one society to judge another.*

Anthropologists have documented many important differences among societies with respect to what they consider proper and improper moral conduct. We may have more technology than people in other societies, but we are no more intelligent than they are. It is arrogant for a person living in twenty-first-century America to judge the actions of another person who lived in Peru in the fifteenth century.

2.3.2 The Case against Cultural Relativism

1. *Just because two societies do have different views about right and wrong doesn't imply that they ought to have different views.*

Perhaps one society has good guidelines and another has bad guidelines. Perhaps neither society has good guidelines.

Suppose two societies are suffering from a severe drought. The first society constructs an aqueduct to carry water to the affected cities. The second society makes human sacrifices to appease the rain god. Are both "solutions" equally acceptable? No, they are not. Yet, if we accept cultural relativism, we cannot speak out against this wrongdoing, because no person in one society can make any statements about the morality of another society.

2. *Cultural relativism does not explain how an individual determines the moral guidelines of a particular society.*

Suppose I am new to a society and I understand I am supposed to abide by its moral guidelines. How do I determine what those guidelines are?

One approach would be to poll other people, but this begs the question. Here's why. Suppose I ask other people whether the society considers a particular action to be morally acceptable. I'm not interested in knowing whether they feel personally that the action is right or wrong. I want them to tell me whether the society as a whole thinks the action is moral. That puts the people I poll in the same position I'm in—trying to determine the moral guidelines of a society. How are *they* to know whether the action is right or wrong?

Perhaps the guidelines are summarized in the society's laws, but laws take time to enact. Hence the legal code reflects at best the moral guidelines of the same society at some point in the past, but that's not the same society I am living in today, because the morals of any society change over time. That leads us to our next objection.

3. *Cultural relativism does not explain how to determine right from wrong when there are no cultural norms.*

Sometimes different groups within a society disagree about whether a particular action is right or wrong. This situation often occurs when a new technology emerges. For example, the Internet has made possible massive exchanges of digitized information. Millions of Americans seem to think sharing copyrighted music is okay, but other groups insist this activity is nothing more than stealing. Who is correct?

4. *Cultural relativism does not do a good job of characterizing actions when moral guidelines evolve.*

   Until the 1960s, many southern American states had segregated universities. Today, these universities are integrated. This change in attitudes was accelerated by the actions of a few brave people of color who challenged the status quo and enrolled in universities that had been the exclusive preserve of white students. At the time these students were doing what they "ought not" to have done; they were doing something wrong according to the moral guidelines of the time. By today's standards, they did nothing wrong, and many people view them as heroic figures. Doesn't it make more sense to believe that their actions were the right thing to do all along?

5. *Cultural relativism provides no framework for reconciliation between cultures in conflict.*

   Think about the culture of the Palestinians who have been crowded into refugee camps in the Gaza Strip for the past 50 years. Some of these people are completely committed to an armed struggle against Israel. Meanwhile, some people in Israel believe the Jewish state ought to be larger and are completely committed to the expansion of settlements into the Gaza Strip. The values of each society lead to actions that harm the other, yet cultural relativism says each society's moral guidelines are right. Cultural relativism provides no way out—no way for the two sides to find common ground.

6. *The existence of many acceptable cultural practices does not imply that any cultural practice would be acceptable.*

   Judging *many* options to be acceptable and then reaching the conclusion that *any* option is acceptable is called the **many/any fallacy**. To illustrate this fallacy, consider documentation styles for computer programs. There are many good ways to add comments to a program; that does not mean that any commenting style is good.

   It is false that all possible cultural practices have equal legitimacy. Certain practices must be forbidden and others must be mandated if a society is to survive [1]. This observation leads us directly to our next point.

7. *Societies do, in fact, share certain core values.*

   While a superficial observation of the cultural practices of different societies may lead you to believe they are quite different, a closer examination often reveals similar values underlying these practices. James Rachels argues that all societies, in order to maintain their existence, must have a set of core values [5]. For example, newborn babies are helpless. A society must care for its infants if it wishes to continue on. Hence, a core value of every society is that babies must be cared for. Communities rely upon people being able to believe each other. Hence telling the truth is another core value. Finally, in order to live together, people must not constantly be on guard against attack from their community members. For this reason, a prohibition against murder is a core value of any society.

   The existence of common values among all societies is a powerful response to the contention that different social contexts demand different moral guidelines, which is at the heart of the argument in favor of cultural relativism. Because societies do share certain core values, there is reason to believe we could use these values as a starting point in the creation of a universal ethical theory that would not have the deficiencies of cultural relativism.

8. *Cultural relativism is only indirectly based on reason.*

As Sumner observed, many moral guidelines are a result of tradition. Traditions develop because they meet a need, but once a tradition has been established, people behave in a certain way because it's what they're supposed to do, not because they understand the rationality deeply embedded within the tradition.

Cultural relativism has significant weaknesses as a tool for ethical persuasion. According to cultural relativism, the ethical evaluation of a moral problem made by a person in one society may be meaningless when applied to the same moral problem in another society. Cultural relativism suggests there are no universal moral guidelines. It gives tradition more weight in ethical evaluations than facts and reason. For these reasons, cultural relativism is not a powerful tool for constructing ethical evaluations persuasive to a diverse audience, and we consider it no further.

2.4 Divine Command Theory

The three great religious traditions that arose in the Middle East—Judaism, Christianity, and Islam—teach that a single God is the creator of the universe and that human beings are part of God's creation. Each of these religions has sacred writings containing God's revelation.

Jews, Christians, and Muslims all believe that God inspired the Torah. Here is a selection of verses from Chapter 19 of the third book of the Torah, called Leviticus:

> You shall each revere his mother and his father, and keep My sabbaths. When you reap the harvest of your land, you shall not reap all the way to the edges of your field, or gather the gleanings of your harvest. You shall not pick your vineyard bare, or gather the fallen fruit of your vineyard; you shall leave them for the poor and the stranger. You shall not steal; you shall not deal deceitfully or falsely with one another. You shall not swear falsely by My name. You shall not defraud your neighbor. You shall not commit robbery. The wages of a laborer shall not remain with you until morning. You shall not insult the deaf, or place a stumbling block before the blind. You shall not take vengeance or bear a grudge against your kinsfolk. Love your neighbor as yourself [8].

The **divine command theory** is based on the idea that good actions are those aligned with the will of God and bad actions are those contrary to the will of God. Since the holy books contain God's directions, we can use the holy books as moral decision-making guides. God says we should revere our mothers and fathers, so revering our parents is good. God says do not lie or steal, so lying and stealing are bad (Figure 2.4).

FIGURE 2.4 The divine command theory of ethics is based on two premises: good actions are those actions aligned with the will of God, and God's will has been revealed to us.

It is important to note that the divine command theory is subscribed to by some, but not all, Jews, Christians, and Muslims. Fundamentalists are more likely to consider holy books authentic and authoritative. Most sects within these religious traditions augment holy books with other sources when developing their moral codes.

2.4.1 The Case for the Divine Command Theory

1. *We owe obedience to our Creator.*

   God is the creator of the universe. God created each one of us. We are dependent upon God for our lives. For this reason, we are obligated to follow God's rules.

2. *God is all-good and all-knowing.*

   God loves us and wants the best for us. God is omniscient; we are not. Because God knows better than we do what we must do to be happy, we should align ourselves with the will of God.

3. *God is the ultimate authority.*

   Since most people are religious, they are more likely to submit to God's law than to a law made by people. Our goal is to create a society where everyone obeys the moral laws. Therefore, our moral laws should be based on God's directions to us.

2.4.2 The Case against the Divine Command Theory

1. *There are many holy books, and some of their teachings disagree with each other.*

   There is no single holy book that is recognized by people of all faiths, and it is unrealistic to assume everyone in a society will adopt the same religion. Even among Christians there are different versions of the Bible. The Catholic Bible has six books not found in the Protestant Bible. Some Protestant denominations rely upon the King James version, but others use more modern translations. Every translation has significant differences. Even when people read the same translation, they often interpret the same verse in different ways.

2. *It is unrealistic to assume a multicultural society will adopt a religion-based morality.*

   An obvious example is the United States. In the past two centuries, immigrants representing virtually every race, creed, and culture have made America their home. Some Americans are atheists. When a society is made up of people with different religious beliefs, the society's moral guidelines should emerge from a secular authority, not a religious authority.

3. *Some moral problems are not addressed directly in scripture.*

   For example, there are no verses in the Bible mentioning the Internet. When we discuss moral problems arising from information technology, a proponent of the divine command theory must resort to analogy. At this point the conclusion is based not simply on what appears in the sacred text but also on the insight of the person who invented the analogy. The holy book alone is not sufficient to solve the moral problem.

4. *It is fallacious to equate "the good" with "God."*

   Religious people are likely to agree with the statement "God is good." That does not mean, however, that God and "the good" are exactly the same thing. Trying to equate two related but distinct things is called the **equivalence fallacy**. Instead, the statement "God is good" means there is an objective standard of goodness that God meets perfectly.

   Here's another way to put the question. Is an action good because God commands it, or does God command it because it's good? This is an ancient question: Plato raised it about 2,400 years ago in the Socratic dialogue *Euthyphro*. In this dialogue, Socrates concludes, "The gods love piety because it is pious, and it is not pious because they love it" [9]. In other words, "the good" is something that exists outside of God and was not created by God.

   We can reason our way to the same conclusion. If good means "commanded by God," then good is arbitrary. Why should we praise God for being good if good is whatever God wills? According to this view of the good, it doesn't matter whether God commanded, "Thou shalt not commit adultery," or, "Thou shalt commit adultery." Either way, the command would have been good by definition. If you object that there is no way God would command us to commit adultery because marital fidelity is good and adultery is bad, then you are proving our point: there is a standard of right and wrong separate from God. That means we can talk about the good without talking about God; we can have a non-theological discussion of the good.

5. *The divine command theory is based on obedience, not reason.*

   If good means "willed by God," and if religious texts contain everything we need to know about what God wills, then there is no room left for collecting and analyzing facts. Hence the divine command theory is not based on reaching sound conclusions from premises through logical reasoning. There is no need for a person to question a commandment. The instruction is right because it's commanded by God, period.

   Consider the story of Abraham in the book of Genesis. God commands Abraham to take his only son, Isaac, up on a mountain, kill him, and make of him a burnt offering. Abraham obeys God's command and is ready to kill Isaac with his knife when an angel calls down and tells him not to harm the boy. Because he does not withhold his only son from God, God blesses Abraham [10]. Earlier in Genesis God condemns Cain for killing Abel [11]. How, then, can Abraham's sacrifice of Isaac be considered good? To devout readers, the logic of God's command is irrelevant to this story. Abraham is a good person, a heroic model of faith, because he demonstrated his obedience to the will of God.

   In the divine command theory, moral guidelines are not the result of a logical progression from a set of underlying principles, and this is a significant problem. While you may choose to live your life so that your actions are aligned with God's will, the divine command theory often fails to produce arguments that can persuade skeptical listeners whose religious beliefs are different. Hence, we conclude the divine command theory is not a powerful weapon for ethical debate in a secular society, and we reject it as a workable theory for the purposes of this book.

2.5 Ethical Egoism

In sharp contrast to the divine command theory, which promotes a concern for others with scriptural injunctions such as, "Love your neighbor as yourself," ethical egoism is the philosophy that each person should focus exclusively on his or her self-interest. In other words, according to ethical egoism, the morally right action for a person to take in a particular situation is the action that will provide that person with the maximum long-term benefit.

Many people have become familiar with a version of ethical egoism through the writings of novelist Ayn Rand, who authored *The Fountainhead* and *Atlas Shrugged*. Rand's moral philosophy "holds man's life as the *standard* of value—and *his own life* as the ethical *purpose* of every individual man" [12]. With respect to human relationships, she wrote, "The principle of *trade* is the only rational ethical principle for all human relationships, personal and social, private and public, spiritual and material" [12].

Ethical egoism does not prohibit acting to help someone else, but assisting another is the right thing to do if and only if it is in the helper's own long-term best interest. Here's an example from the writings of Douglas Birsch [4]. Suppose I depend upon a friend to give me a ride to work every day. If my friend's car breaks down and she doesn't have $100 to fix it, I ought to loan her the money. Although I'm out $100 until she pays me back, I'm better off giving her the loan because I'm still able to travel to work and make money. If I don't lend her the money, I'll lose my income. Lending $100 to my friend is the right thing to do because it provides me the maximum overall benefit.

2.5.1 The Case for Ethical Egoism

1. *Ethical egoism is a practical moral philosophy.*

   We are naturally inclined to do what's best for ourselves because each of us has only one life to live, and we want to make the best of it. Unlike other moral codes that ask us to sacrifice our own well-being for the good of other people, ethical egoism recognizes that we should focus on our own well-being.

2. *It's better to let other people take care of themselves.*

   We can't know for sure what is good for someone else. All too often, a "good deed" backfires and actually does more harm than good. Even when people appreciate something done of their behalf, it's not healthy. Dependence upon the charity of others leads to a loss of self-esteem. In contrast, people who accomplish things through their own efforts have higher self-esteem and are able to interact with other successful people as equals.

3. *The community can benefit when individuals put their well-being first.*

   When individuals act in their own self-interest, they often benefit not only themselves but others as well. For example, successful entrepreneurs may make a lot of money for themselves, but they also create jobs that strengthen the economy.

4. *Other moral principles are rooted in the principle of self-interest.*

   Ethical egoism is a rational philosophy. Any rational person will figure out that it doesn't make sense to go around breaking promises, because eventually people will realize that the promise-breaker cannot be trusted, and they will refuse to cooperate with that person. Therefore, it's not in a person's long-term self-interest to break promises. Likewise, it's a bad idea to lie to other people or cheat other people because the long-term consequences of lying and cheating are detrimental to the person doing these things. For this reason, it can be seen that other well-known moral principles are actually rooted in the principle of self-interest.

2.5.2 The Case against Ethical Egoism

1. *An easy moral philosophy may not be the best moral philosophy.*

   The fact that it may be easier to live by a particular moral philosophy is no proof that it is the best moral philosophy to live by. Besides, the statement that ethical egoism aligns with our natural inclination to do what's best for ourselves ignores the fact that people often find it difficult to pass up short-term pleasures (such as partying) in order achieve goals (such as passing the classes needed to earn a college degree) that will most likely result in long-term benefits.

2. *We do, in fact, know a lot about what is good for someone else.*

As we noted at the beginning of the chapter, practically everyone shares the "core values" of life, happiness, and the ability to accomplish goals. It's not that hard to figure out what would help another. The question is: How are we going to respond to that person's need? Charity usually doesn't lead to dependence; rather, it gives someone the opportunity to become more independent. Consider, for example, how a scholarship can provide a bright high school student from a poor family with a path to a university degree, a well-paying job, and self-sufficiency.

3. *A self-interested focus can lead to blatantly immoral behavior.*

Here is a true story related by James Rachels [13]. An affluent doctor in a small Southern town in the 1970s was visited by a poor, uneducated African-American woman, who had a variety of minor complaints. The doctor quickly determined that the woman was suffering from malnutrition. He knew that she worked a variety of menial jobs, but earned very little money to support herself or her children. After spending no more than five minutes with her, and doing nothing for her, the doctor told her the charge would be $25. The woman had only $12 to her name, so the doctor took the $12 as payment, leaving the woman with no money to buy food. There were no negative consequences to the doctor as a result of his action. According to the theory of ethical egoism, the doctor did the right thing: he was only supposed to take his own interest into account, and receiving $12 from the woman was to his advantage. This answer, however, is incorrect; what the doctor did was morally reprehensible.

4. *Other moral principles are superior to the principle of self-interest.*

Suppose you have the opportunity to save a drowning person at the cost of getting one of your shirtsleeves wet [4]. According to the theory of ethical egoism, saving a life is the right thing to do if and only if that action will provide you with the maximum benefit. Possible benefits from saving a drowning person include earning that person's undying gratitude and gaining favorable publicity. But isn't this a backwards and degrading way of evaluating the action? Doesn't it make a lot more sense to consider the action in light of the value of a human life? If you have the opportunity to save a human life with no signficant negative consequences to yourself, you should do it, even if your action is not rewarded. That proves the principle of preserving life is superior to the principle of self-interest.

5. *People who take the good of others into account live happier lives.*

In the Framingham Heart Study, which followed 5,000 individuals over a 20-year period, scientists discovered that happiness spreads through close relationship with family members, friends, and neighbors [14]. In order to create and maintain close relationships with other people, it is necessary to consider what is good for them.

Ethical egoism does not respect the ethical point of view: it does not recognize that in order to reap the benefits of living in community, individuals must consider the good of other community members. For this reason we reject ethical egoism as a workable ethical theory.

2.6 Kantianism

Kantianism is the name given to the ethical theory of the German philosopher Immanuel Kant (1724–1804). Kant spent his entire life in or near Königsberg in East Prussia, where he was a professor at the university. Kant believed that people's actions ought to be guided by moral laws, and that these moral laws were universal. He held that in order to apply to all rational beings, any supreme principle of morality must itself be based on reason. While many of the moral laws Kant describes can also be found in the Bible, Kant's methodology allows these laws to be derived through a reasoning process. A Kantian is able to go beyond simply stating *that* an action is right or wrong by citing chapter and verse; a Kantian can explain *why* it is right or wrong.

2.6.1 Good Will and the Categorical Imperative

Kant begins his inquiry by asking, "What is always good without qualification?" Many things, such as intelligence and courage, can be good, but they can also be used in a way that is harmful. For example, a group of gangsters may use intelligence and courage to rob a bank. Kant's conclusion is that the only thing in the world that can be called good without qualification is *a good will*. People with good will often accomplish good deeds, but producing beneficial outcomes is not what makes a good will good. A good will is good in and of itself. Even if a person's best efforts at doing good should fall short and cause harm, the good will behind the efforts is still good. Since a good will is the only thing that is universally good, the proper function of reason is to cultivate a will that is good in itself.

Most of us have probably had many experiences when we've been torn between *what we want to do* and *what we ought to do*. According to Kant, what we want to do is of no importance. Our focus should be on what we ought to do. Our sense of "ought to" is called **dutifulness** [15]. A dutiful person feels compelled to act in a certain way out of respect for some moral rule. Our will, then, should be grounded in a conception of moral rules. The moral value of an action depends upon the underlying moral rule. It is critical, therefore, that we be able to determine if our actions are grounded in an appropriate moral rule.

What makes a moral rule appropriate? To enable us to answer this question, Kant proposes the Categorical Imperative.

~

CATEGORICAL IMPERATIVE (FIRST FORMULATION)

Act only from moral rules that you can at the same time will to be universal moral laws.

~

To illustrate the Categorical Imperative, Kant poses the problem of an individual in a difficult situation who must decide if he will make a promise with the intention of later breaking it. The translation of this moral rule could be: "A person may make a false promise when that is the only way to escape a difficult situation."

To evaluate this moral rule, we universalize it. What would happen if everybody in extreme circumstances made false promises? If that were the case, nobody would believe promises, and it would be impossible for our individual in distress to make a promise that anyone believed. The moral rule self-destructs when we try to make it a universal law. Therefore, it is wrong for a person in distress to make a promise with the intention of breaking it.

It is important to see that Kant is *not* arguing that the consequences of everybody breaking promises would be to undermine interpersonal relationships, increase violence, and make people miserable, and that is why we cannot imagine turning our hypothetical moral rule into a universal law. Rather, Kant is saying that simply willing that our moral rule become a universal law produces a logical contradiction.

Let's see how. Suppose I am the person who can escape from a difficult situation by making a promise I intend to break later on. On the one hand, it is my will that I be able to make a promise that is believed. After all, that's what promises are for. If my promise isn't believed, I won't be able to get out of the difficult situation I am in. But when I universalize the moral rule, I am willing that everybody be able to break promises. If that were a reality, then promises would not be believable, which means there would be no such thing as a promise [16]. If there were no such thing as a promise, I would not be able to make a promise to get myself out of a difficult situation. Trying to universalize our proposed moral rule leads to a contradiction.

Here's another way to see why the proposed action is wrong. In order for my false promise to be believed, I want everyone *except* myself to be truthful all the time. Because there is a contradiction between what I wish to do and how I expect others in a similar situation to act, I know that what I am considering doing is wrong.

Kant also presents a second formulation of the Categorical Imperative, which many find easier to work with.

~

CATEGORICAL IMPERATIVE (SECOND FORMULATION)

Act so that you always treat both yourself and other people as ends in themselves, and never only as a means to an end.

~

Figure 2.5 The second formulation of the Categorical Imperative states that it is wrong for one person to use himself or another person solely as a means to an end.

To use popular terminology, the second formulation of the Categorical Imperative says it is wrong for one person to "use" another (Figure 2.5). Instead, every interaction with other people must respect them as rational beings.

Here is an example that illustrates how we can apply the second formulation. Suppose I manage a semiconductor fabrication plant for a large corporation. The plant manufactures integrated circuits on 8-inch wafers. I know that in one year the corporation is going to shut down the plant and move all of its production to other sites capable of producing 12-inch wafers. In the meantime, I need new employees to work in the clean room. Many of the best applicants are from out of state. I am afraid that if they knew the plant was going to shut down next year, they would not want to go through the hassle and expense of moving to this area. If that happens, I'll have to hire less-qualified local workers. Should I disclose this information to the job applicants?

According to the second formulation of the Categorical Imperative, I have an obligation to inform the applicants, since I know this information is likely to influence their decision. If I deny them this information, I am treating them as a means to an end (a way to get wafers produced), not as ends in themselves (rational beings).

2.6.2 Evaluating a Scenario Using Kantianism

~ Scenario

Carla is a single mother who is working hard to complete her college education while taking care of her daughter. Carla has a full-time job and is taking two evening courses per semester. If she can pass both courses this semester, she will graduate. She knows her child will benefit if she can spend more time at home.

One of her required classes is modern European history. In addition to the midterm and final examinations, the professor assigns four lengthy reports, which is far more than the usual amount of work required for a single class. Students must submit all four reports in order to pass the class.

Carla earns an "A" on each of her first three reports. At the end of the term, she is required to put in a lot of overtime where she works. She simply does not have time to research and write the final report. Carla uses the Web to identify a company that sells term papers. She purchases a report from the company and submits it as her own work.

Was Carla's action morally justifiable?

Analysis

Many times it is easier to use the second formulation of the Categorical Imperative to analyze a moral problem from a Kantian point of view, so that's where we begin. By submitting another person's work as her own, Carla treated her professor as a means to an end. She deceived her professor with the goal of getting credit for someone else's work. It was wrong for Carla to treat the professor as a grade-generating machine rather than a rational agent with whom she could have communicated her unusual circumstances.

We can also look at this problem using the first formulation of the Categorical Imperative. Carla wants to be able to get credit for turning in a report she has purchased. A proposed moral rule might be: "I may claim academic credit for a report written by someone else." However, if everyone followed this rule, reports would cease to be credible indicators of the students' knowledge, and professors would not give academic credit for reports. Her proposed moral rule is self-defeating. Therefore, it is wrong for Carla to purchase a report and turn it in as her own work.

Commentary

Note that the Kantian analysis of the moral problem focuses on the will behind the action. It asks the question: "What was Carla trying to do when she submitted under her own name a term paper written by someone else?" The analysis ignores extenuating circumstances that non-Kantians may cite to justify her action.   ∽

2.6.3 The Case for Kantianism

1. *Kantianism is rational.*

   Kantianism is based on the premise that rational beings can use logic to explain the "why" behind their solutions to ethical problems.

2. *Kantianism produces universal moral guidelines.*

   Kantianism aligns with the intuition of many people that the same morality ought to apply to all people for all of history. These guidelines allow us to make clear moral judgments. For example, one such judgment might be: "Sacrificing living human beings to appease the gods is wrong." It is wrong in North America in the twenty-first century, and it was wrong in South America in the fifteenth century.

3. *All persons are treated as moral equals.*

A popular belief is that "all people are created equal." Because it holds that people in similar situations should be treated in similar ways, Kantianism provides an ethical framework to combat discrimination.

2.6.4 The Case against Kantianism

1. *Sometimes no single rule fully characterizes an action.*

Kant holds that every action is motivated from a rule. The appropriate rule depends upon how we characterize the action. Once we know the rule, we can test its value using the Categorical Imperative. What happens when no single rule fully explains the situation? Douglas Birsch gives this example: Suppose I'm considering stealing food from a grocery store to feed my starving children [4]. How should I characterize this action? Am I stealing? Am I caring for my children? Am I trying to save the lives of innocent people? Until I characterize my action, I cannot determine the rule and test it against the Categorical Imperative. Yet no single one of these ways of characterizing the action seems to capture the ethical problem in its fullness.

2. *Sometimes there is no way to resolve a conflict between rules.*

One way to address the previous problem is to allow multiple rules to be relevant to a particular action. In the previous example, we might say that the relevant rules are (1) You should not steal, and (2) You should try to save the lives of innocent persons. Now the question becomes: If we have a conflict between two rules, which one should we follow?

Kant distinguished between **perfect duties**, duties we are obliged to fulfill in each instance, and **imperfect duties**, duties we are obliged to fulfill in general but not in every instance. For example, you have a perfect duty to tell the truth. That means you must always tell the truth without exception. On the other hand, you have an imperfect duty to develop your talents. If you happen to have a talent for music, you ought to find a way to develop it, but you do not have to take up every instrument in the orchestra.

If we have a conflict between a perfect duty and an imperfect duty, the perfect duty must prevail. Returning to our example, we have a perfect duty not to steal. In contrast, we have only an imperfect duty to help others. Therefore, according to Kant, it is wrong to steal bread to feed my starving children.

In this case we were fortunate because the conflict was between a perfect duty and an imperfect duty. In those cases where there is a conflict between perfect duties, Kantianism does not provide us a way to choose between them.

3. *Kantianism allows no exceptions to perfect duties.*

Common sense tells us that sometimes we ought to "bend" the rules a bit if we want to get along with other people. For example, suppose your mother asks you if you like her new haircut, and you think it is the ugliest haircut you have ever seen. What should you say? Common sense dictates that there is no point in criticizing your mother's hair. She certainly isn't going to get her hair un-cut, no matter what you say. If you compliment her, she will be happy, and if you criticize her looks, she will be angry and hurt. She expects you to say something complimentary, even if you don't mean it. There just seems to be no downside to lying. Yet a Kantian would argue that lying is always wrong because we have a perfect duty to tell the truth. Many people hold that any ethical theory so unbending is not going to be useful for solving "real world" problems.

While these objections point out weaknesses with Kantianism, the theory does support moral decision-making based on logical reasoning from facts and commonly held values. It is culture neutral and treats all humans as equals. Hence, it meets our criteria for a workable ethical theory, and we will use it as a way of evaluating moral problems in the rest of the book.

2.7 Act Utilitarianism

2.7.1 Principle of Utility

The English philosophers Jeremy Bentham (1748–1832) and John Stuart Mill (1806–1873) proposed a theory that is in sharp contrast to Kantianism. According to Bentham and Mill, an action is good if it benefits someone; an action is bad if it harms someone. Their ethical theory, called **utilitarianism,** is based upon the Principle of Utility, also called the Greatest Happiness Principle.

~

PRINCIPLE OF UTILITY (GREATEST HAPPINESS PRINCIPLE)

An action is right (or wrong) to the extent that it increases (or decreases) the total happiness of the affected parties.

~

Utility is the tendency of an object to produce happiness or prevent unhappiness for an individual or a community. Depending on the circumstances, you may think of "happiness" as advantage, benefit, good, or pleasure, and "unhappiness" as disadvantage, cost, evil, or pain.

We can use the Principle of Utility as a yardstick to judge all actions in the moral realm. To evaluate the morality of an action, we must determine, for each affected person, the increase or decrease in that person's happiness, and then add up all of these values to reach a grand total. If the total is positive (meaning the total increase in happiness is greater than the total decrease in happiness), the action is moral; if the total is negative (meaning the total decrease in happiness is greater than the total increase in happiness), the action is immoral. The Principle of Utility is illustrated in Figure 2.6.

Note that the morality of an action has nothing to do with the attitude behind the action. Bentham writes: "There is no such thing as any sort of motive that is in itself a bad one. If [motives] are good or bad, it is only on account of their effects" [17]. We call

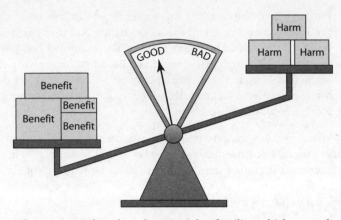

FIGURE 2.6 Utilitarianism is based on the Principle of Utility, which states that an action is good (or bad) to the extent that it increases (or decreases) the total happiness of the affected parties.

utilitarianism a **consequentialist** theory, because the focus is on the consequences of an action.

Act utilitarianism is the ethical theory that an action is good if its net effect (over all affected beings) is to produce more happiness than unhappiness. Suppose we measure pleasure as a positive number and pain as a negative number. To make a moral evaluation of an action, we simply add up, over all affected beings, the change in their happiness. If the sum is positive, the action is good. If the sum is negative, the action is bad.

Did you notice that I used the word "beings" rather than "persons" in the previous paragraph? An important decision an act utilitarian must make is determining which beings are considered to be morally significant. Bentham noted that at one time only adult white males were considered morally significant beings. Bentham felt that any being that can experience pain and pleasure ought to be seen as morally significant. Certainly women and people of color are morally significant beings by this definition, but in addition all mammals (and perhaps other animals) are morally significant beings, because they, too, can experience pain and pleasure. Of course, as the number of morally significant beings increases, the difficulty of evaluating the consequences of an action also increases. It means, for example, that the environmental impacts of decisions must often be included when performing the utilitarian calculus.

2.7.2 Evaluating a Scenario Using Act Utilitarianism

∾ SCENARIO

A state is considering replacing a curvy stretch of highway that passes along the outskirts of a large city. Would building the highway be a good action?

Analysis

To perform the analysis of this problem, we must determine who is affected and the effects of the highway construction on them. Our analysis is in terms of dollars and cents. For this reason we'll use the terms "benefit" and "cost" instead of "happiness" and "unhappiness."

About 150 houses lie on or very near the proposed path of the new, straighter section of highway. Using its power of eminent domain, the state can condemn these properties. It would cost the state $20 million to provide fair compensation to the homeowners. Constructing the new highway, which is three miles long, would cost the taxpayers of the state another $10 million. Suppose the environmental impact of the new highway in terms of lost habitat for morally significant animal species is valued at $1 million.

Every weekday, 15,000 cars are expected to travel on this section of highway, which is one mile shorter than the curvy highway it replaces. Assuming it costs 40 cents per mile to operate a motor vehicle, construction of the new highway will save drivers $6,000 per weekday in operating costs. The highway has an expected operating lifetime of 25 years. Over a 25-year period, the expected total savings to drivers will be $39 million.

We'll assume the highway project will have no positive or negative effects on any other people. Since the overall cost of the new highway is $31 million and the benefit of the new highway is $39 million, building the highway would be a good action.

Commentary

Performing the benefit/cost (or happiness/unhappiness) calculations is crucial to the utilitarian approach, yet it can be controversial. In our example, we translated everything into dollars and cents. Was that reasonable? Neighborhoods are the site of many important relationships. We did not assign a value to the harm the proposed highway would do to these neighborhoods. There is a good chance that many of the homeowners will be angry about being forced out of their houses, even if they are paid a fair price for their properties. How do we put a dollar value on their emotional distress? On the other hand, we can't add apples and oranges. Translating everything into dollars and cents is one way to put everything into common units.   ∽

Bentham acknowledged that a complete analysis must look beyond simple benefits and harms. Not all benefits have equal weight. To measure them, he proposed seven attributes that can be used to increase or decrease the weight of a particular pleasure or pain:

- *intensity:* magnitude of the experience
- *duration:* how long the experience lasts
- *certainty:* probability it will actually happen
- *propinquity:* how close the experience is in space and time
- *fecundity:* its ability to produce more experiences of the same kind

- *purity:* extent to which pleasure is not diluted by pain, or vice versa
- *extent:* number of people affected

As you can see, performing a complete calculation for a particular moral problem can be a daunting prospect!

2.7.3 The Case for Act Utilitarianism

1. *It focuses on happiness.*

   By relying upon the Greatest Happiness Principle as the yardstick for measuring moral behavior, utilitarianism fits the intuition of many people that the purpose of life is to be happy.

2. *It is down-to-earth.*

   The utilitarian calculus provides a straightforward way to determine whether a particular action is good or bad: simply sum up the anticipated positive and negative consequences resulting from an action. For this reason, it is a good way for a diverse group of people to come to a collective decision about a controversial topic.

   For example, suppose your state needs to build a new prison because the number of prisoners is growing. Everybody understands the prison must be built somewhere in the state, but nobody wants the prison in their neighborhood. A panel of trusted citizens considers a variety of siting options and, after a series of public hearings to gather evidence, weighs the pluses and minuses of each location. At the end of the process, the panel recommends the site with the highest total net good. While some will be unhappy at the prospect of a prison being built near their homes, an open and impartial process can speed their acceptance of the decision.

3. *It is comprehensive.*

   Act utilitarianism allows the moral agent to take into account all the elements of a particular situation. Recall the problem of having to decide what to say about your mother's haircut? Since telling the truth would cause more emotional distress to all parties involved than lying, deciding what the right thing to do would be a "no brainer" using the utilitarian calculus.

2.7.4 The Case against Act Utilitarianism

1. *When performing the utilitarian calculus, it is not clear where to draw the line, yet where we draw the line can change the outcome of our evaluation.*

   In order to perform our calculation of total net happiness produced by an action, we must determine whom to include in our calculation and how far into the future to consider the consequences. In our highway example, we counted the people who lost their homes and the people who would travel the new highway in the next 25 years. The proposed highway may cut neighborhoods in two, making it more difficult for some children to get to school, but we did not factor in consequences for neighbors. The highway may cause people to change their commutes, increasing traffic congestion in other parts of town, but we did not count those people either. The highway may be in existence more than 25 years, but we didn't look beyond that date. We cannot include all morally relevant beings for all time into the future. We must draw the line somewhere. Deciding where to draw the line can be a difficult problem.

2. *It is not practical to put so much energy into every moral decision.*

   Correctly performing the utilitarian calculus requires a great deal of time and effort. It seems unrealistic that everyone would go to so much trouble every time they were faced with a moral problem.

   A response to this criticism is that act utilitarians are free to come up with moral "rules of thumb." For example, a moral rule of thumb might be: "It is wrong to lie." In most situations it will be obvious this is the right thing to do, even without performing the complete utilitarian calculus. However, an act utilitarian always reserves the right to go against the rule of thumb if particular circumstances should warrant it. In these cases, the act utilitarian will perform a detailed analysis of the consequences to determine the best course of action.

3. *Act utilitarianism ignores our innate sense of duty.*

   Utilitarianism seems to be at odds with how ordinary people make moral decisions. People often act out of a sense of duty or obligation, yet the act utilitarian theory gives no weight to these notions. Instead, all that matters are the consequences of the action.

   W. D. Ross gives the following example [18]. Suppose I've made a promise to A. If I keep my word, I will perform an action that produces 1,000 units of good for him. If I break my promise, I will be able to perform an action that produces 1,001 units of good for B. According to act utilitarianism, I ought to break my promise to A and produce 1,001 units of good for B. Yet most people would say the right thing for me to do is keep my word.

   Note that it does no good for an act utilitarian to come back and say that the hard feelings caused by breaking my word to A will have a negative impact on total happiness of $-N$ units, because all I have to do is change the scenario so that breaking my promise to A enables me to produce $1,001 + N$ units of good for B. We've arrived at the same result: breaking my promise results in 1 more unit of good than keeping my word. The real issue is that utilitarianism forces us to reduce all consequences to a positive or negative number. "Doing the right thing" has a value that is difficult to quantify.

4. *We cannot predict with certainty the consequences of an action.*

   In doing the utilitarian calculus, we can identify possible consequences of an action, but we may misjudge the certainty, intensity, and duration of these consequences. The action may have other, unforeseen consequences that we forget to include in our calculation. These errors may cause us to choose the wrong course of action.

5. *Act utilitarianism is susceptible to the problem of moral luck.*

As we noted in the previous point, sometimes actions have unforeseen consequences. Is it right for the moral worth of an action to depend solely on its consequences when these consequences are not fully under the control of the moral agent? This is called the **problem of moral luck.**

Suppose I hear that one of my aunts is in the hospital, and I send her a bouquet of flowers. After the bouquet is delivered, she suffers a violent allergic reaction to one of the exotic flowers in the floral arrangement, extending her stay in the hospital. My gift gave my aunt a bad case of hives and a much larger hospital bill. Since my action had far more negative consequences than positive consequences, an act utilitarian would say my action was bad. Yet many people would say I did something good. For this reason, some philosophers prefer a theory in which the moral agent has complete control over the factors determining the moral worth of an action.

Two additional arguments have been raised against utilitarianism in general. We'll save these arguments for the end of the section on rule utilitarianism.

While it is not perfect, act utilitarianism is an objective, rational ethical theory that allows a person to explain why a particular action is right or wrong. It joins Kantianism on our list of workable ethical theories we can use to evaluate moral problems.

2.8 Rule Utilitarianism

2.8.1 Basis of Rule Utilitarianism

The weaknesses of act utilitarianism have led some philosophers to develop another ethical theory based on the Principle of Utility. This theory is called rule utilitarianism. Some philosophers have concluded that John Stuart Mill was actually a rule utilitarian, but others disagree.

Rule utilitarianism is the ethical theory that holds that we ought to adopt those moral rules which, if followed by everyone, will lead to the greatest increase in total happiness. Hence, a rule utilitarian applies the Principle of Utility to moral rules, while an act utilitarian applies the Principle of Utility to individual moral actions.

Both rule utilitarianism and Kantianism are focused on rules, and the rules these two ethical theories derive may have significant overlap. However, the two ethical theories derive moral rules in completely different ways. A rule utilitarian chooses to follow a moral rule because its universal adoption would result in the greatest happiness. A Kantian follows a moral rule because it is in accord with the Categorical Imperative: all human beings are to be treated as ends in themselves, not merely as means to an end. In other words, the rule utilitarian is looking at the consequences of the action, while the Kantian is looking at the will motivating the action.

2.8.2 Evaluating a Scenario Using Rule Utilitarianism

∽ SCENARIO

A worm is a self-contained program that spreads through a computer network by taking advantage of security holes in the computers connected to the network. In August 2003, the Blaster worm infected many computers running the Windows 2000, Windows NT, and Windows XP operating systems. The Blaster worm caused computers it infected to reboot every few minutes.

Soon, another worm was exploiting the same security hole in Windows to spread through the Internet. However, the purpose of the new worm, named Nachi, was benevolent. Since Nachi took advantage of the same security hole as Blaster, it could not infect computers that were immune to the Blaster worm. Once Nachi gained access to a computer with the security hole, it located and destroyed copies of the Blaster worm. It also automatically downloaded from Microsoft a patch to the operating system software that would fix the security problem. Finally, it used the computer as a launching pad to seek out other Windows PCs with the security hole.

Was the action of the person who released the Nachi worm morally right or wrong?

Analysis

To analyze this moral problem from a rule utilitarian point of view, we must think of an appropriate moral rule and determine if its universal adoption would increase the happiness of the affected parties. In this case, an appropriate moral rule might be: "If I can write and release a helpful worm that improves the security of the computers it infects, I should do so."

What would be the benefits if everyone followed the proposed moral rule? Many people do not keep their computers up to date with the latest patches to the operating system. They would benefit from a worm that automatically removed their network vulnerabilities.

What harm would be caused by the universal adoption of the rule? If everyone followed this rule, the appearance of every new harmful worm would be followed by the release of many other worms designed to eradicate the harmful worm. Worms make networks less usable by creating a lot of extra network traffic. For example, the Nachi worm disabled networks of Diebold ATM machines at two financial institutions [19]. The universal adoption of the moral rule would reduce the usefulness of the Internet while the various "helpful" worms were circulating.

Another negative consequence would be potential harm done to computers by the supposedly helpful worms. Even worms designed to be benevolent may contain bugs. If many people are releasing worms, there is a good chance some of the worms may accidentally harm data or programs on the computers they infect.

A third harmful consequence would be the extra work placed on system administrators. When system administrators detect a new worm, it is not immediately obvious whether the worm is harmful or beneficial. Hence the prudent response of system administrators is to combat every new worm that attacks their computers. If the proposed moral rule were adopted, more worms would be released, forcing system administrators to spend more of their time fighting worms [20].

In conclusion, the harms caused by the universal adoption of this moral rule appear to outweigh the benefits. Therefore, the action of the person who released the Nachi worm is morally wrong.   ∽

2.8.3 The Case for Rule Utilitarianism

1. *Not every moral decision requires performing the utilitarian calculus.*

   A person who relies on rules of behavior does not have to spend a lot of time and effort analyzing every particular moral action in order to determine if it is right or wrong.

2. *Exceptional situations do not overthrow moral rules.*

   Remember the problem of choosing between keeping a promise to A and producing 1,000 units of good for A, or breaking the promise to A and producing 1,001 units of good for B? A rule utilitarian would not be trapped on the horns of this dilemma. A rule utilitarian would reason that the long-term consequences of everyone keeping their promises produce more good than giving everyone the liberty to break their promises, so in this situation a rule utilitarian would conclude the right thing to do is keep the promise to A.

3. *Rule utilitarianism solves the problem of moral luck.*

   Since it is interested in the typical result of an action, the highly unusual result does not affect the goodness of an action. A rule utilitarian would conclude that sending flowers to people in the hospital is a good action.

4. *Rule utilitarianism avoids the problem of egocentrism.*

   A weakness of act utilitarianism is that it creates the temptation to perform an ego-centric analysis. By asking, "Is it okay for me to do this?" an act utilitarian may conclude the action is acceptable by consciously or unconsciously inflating the personal benefits and/or deflating the anticipated harms to others. In contrast, a rule utilitarian must ask the question, "Is it okay for everyone in a similar circumstance to do this?" The person who answers the latter question is more likely to place appropriate weights on the benefits and harms of the action.

5. *It appeals to a wide cross section of society.*

   Bernard Gert points out that utilitarianism is "paradoxically, the kind of moral theory usually held by people who claim that they have no moral theory. Their view is often expressed in phrases like the following: 'It is all right to do anything as long as no one gets hurt,' 'It is the actual consequences that count, not some silly rules,' or 'What is important is that things turn out for the best, not how one goes about making that happen.' On the moral system, it is not the consequences of the particular violation that are decisive in determining its justifiability, but rather the consequences of such a violation being publicly allowed" [21]. In other words, an action is justifiable if allowing that action would, as a rule, bring about greater net happiness than forbidding that action.

2.8.4 The Case against Utilitarianism in General

As we have just seen, rule utilitarianism seems to solve several problems associated with act utilitarianism. However, two criticisms have been leveled at utilitarian theories in general. These problems are shared by both act utilitarianism and rule utilitarianism.

1. *Utilitarianism forces us to use a single scale or measure to evaluate completely different kinds of consequences.*

   In order to perform the utilitarian calculus, all consequences must be put into the same units. Otherwise, we cannot add them up. For example, if we are going to determine the total amount of happiness resulting from the construction of a new highway, many of the costs and benefits (such as construction costs and the gas expenses of car drivers) are easily expressed in dollars. Other costs and benefits are intangible, but we must express them in terms of dollars in order to find the total amount of happiness created or destroyed as a result of the project. Suppose a sociologist informs the state that if it condemns 150 homes, it is likely to cause 15 divorces among the families being displaced. How do we assign a dollar value to that unfortunate consequence? In certain circumstances utilitarians must quantify the value of a human life. How can the value of a human life be reduced to an amount of money?

2. *Utilitarianism ignores the problem of an unjust distribution of good consequences.*

   The second, and far more significant, criticism of utilitarianism is that the utilitarian calculus is solely interested in the total amount of happiness produced. Suppose one course of action results in every member of a society receiving 100 units of good, while another course of action results in half the members of society receiving 201 units of good each, with the other half receiving nothing. According to the calculus of utility, the second course of action is superior because the total amount of good is higher. That doesn't seem right to many people.

   A possible response to this criticism is that our goal should be to promote the greatest good of the greatest number. In fact, that is how utilitarianism is often described. A person subscribing to this philosophy might say that we ought to use two principles to guide our conduct: (1) we should act so that the greatest amount of good is produced, and (2) we should distribute the good as widely as possible. The first of these principles is the Principle of Utility, but the second is a principle of distributive justice. In other words, "act so as to promote the greatest good of the greatest number" is not pure utilitarianism. The proposed philosophy is not internally consistent, because there are times when the two principles will conflict. In order to be useful, the theory also needs a procedure to resolve conflicts between the two principles. We'll talk more about the principle of distributive justice in the next section.

The criticisms leveled at utilitarianism point out circumstances in which it seems to produce the "wrong" answer to a moral problem. However, rule utilitarianism treats all persons as equals and provides its adherents with the ability to give the reasons why a particular action is right or wrong. Hence, we consider it a third workable theory for evaluating moral problems, joining Kantianism and act utilitarianism.

2.9 Social Contract Theory

In the spring of 2003, a coalition of military forces led by the United States invaded Iraq and removed the government of Saddam Hussein. When the police disappeared, thousands of Baghdad residents looted government ministries [22]. Sidewalk arms merchants did a thriving business selling AK-47 assault rifles to homeowners needing protection against thieves. Are Iraqis much different from residents of other countries, or should we view the events in Baghdad as the typical response of people to a lack of governmental authority and control?

2.9.1 The Social Contract

Philosopher Thomas Hobbes (1603–1679) lived during the English civil war and saw firsthand the terrible consequences of social anarchy. In his book *Leviathan*, he argues that without rules and a means of enforcing them, people would not bother to create anything of value, because nobody could be sure of keeping what they created. Instead, people would be consumed with taking what they needed and defending themselves against the attacks of others. They would live in "continuall feare, and danger of violent death," and the life of man would be "solitary, poore, nasty, brutish, and short" [23].

To avoid this miserable condition, which Hobbes calls the *state of nature*, rational people understand that cooperation is essential. However, cooperation is possible only when people mutually agree to follow certain guidelines. Hence, moral rules are "simply the rules that are necessary if we are to gain the benefits of social living" [5]. Hobbes argues that everybody living in a civilized society has implicitly agreed to two things: (1) the establishment of such a set of moral rules to govern relations among citizens, and (2) a government capable of enforcing these rules. He calls this arrangement the **social contract.**

The Franco-Swiss philosopher Jean-Jacques Rousseau (1712–1778) continued the evolution of social contract theory. In his book *The Social Contract,* he writes, "Since no man has any natural authority over his fellows, and since force alone bestows no right, all legitimate authority among men must be based on covenants" [24]. Rousseau states that the critical problem facing society is finding a form of association that guarantees everybody their safety and property, yet enables each person to remain free. The answer, according to Rousseau, is for everybody to give themselves and their rights to the whole community. The community will determine the rules for its members, and each of its members will be obliged to obey the rules. What prevents the community from enacting bad rules is that no one is above the rules. Since everyone is in the same situation, no community members will want to put unfair burdens on others because that would mean putting unfair burdens on themselves.

While everyone might agree to this in theory, it's easy for a single person to rationalize selfish behavior. How do we prevent individuals from shirking their duties to the group? Suppose Bill owes the government $10,000 in taxes, but he discovers a way to cheat on his taxes so that he only has to pay $8,000. Bill thinks to himself, "The government gets billions of dollars a year in taxes. So to the government another $2,000 is just a drop in the bucket. But to me, $2,000 is a lot of money." What restrains Bill from acting selfishly is the knowledge that if he is caught, he will be punished. In order for the social contract to function, society must provide not only a system of laws, but a system of enforcing the laws as well.

According to Rousseau, living in a civil society gives a person's actions a moral quality they would not have if that person lived in a state of nature. "It is only then, when the voice of duty has taken the place of physical impulse, and right that of desire, that man, who has hitherto thought only of himself, finds himself compelled to act on other principles, and to consult his reason rather than study his inclinations" [24].

James Rachels summarizes these ideas in an elegant definition of social contract theory:

SOCIAL CONTRACT THEORY

"Morality consists in the set of rules, governing how people are to treat one another, that rational people will agree to accept, for their mutual benefit, on the condition that others follow those rules as well" [5].

Both social contract theory and Kantianism are based on the idea that there are universal moral rules that can be derived through a rational process. However, there is a subtle, but important difference in how we decide what makes a moral rule ethical. Kantianism has the notion that it is right for me to act according to a moral rule if the rule can be universalized. Social contract theory holds that it is right for me to act according to a moral rule if rational people would collectively accept it as binding because of its benefits to the community.

Hobbes, Locke, and many other philosophers of the seventeenth and eighteenth centuries held that all morally significant beings have certain rights, such as the right to life, liberty, and property. Some modern philosophers would add other rights to this list, such as the right to privacy.

There is a close correspondence between rights and duties. If you have the right to life, then others have the duty or obligation not to kill you. If you have a right to free health care when you are ill, then others have the duty to make sure you receive it. Rights can be classified according to the duties they put on others. A **negative right** is a right that another can guarantee by leaving you alone to exercise your right. For example, the right of free expression is a negative right. In order for you to have that right, all others have to do is not interfere with you when you express yourself. A **positive right** is a right that obligates others to do something on your behalf. The right to a free education is a positive right. In order for you to have that right, the rest of society must allocate resources so that you may attend school.

Another way to view rights is to consider whether they are absolute or limited. An **absolute right** is a right that is guaranteed without exception. Negative rights, such as the right to life, are usually considered absolute rights. A **limited right** is a right that may be restricted based on the circumstances. Typically, positive rights are considered to be limited rights. For example, American states guarantee their citizens the right to an education. However, because states do not have unlimited budgets, they typically provide a free education for everyone up through the 12th grade but require people to pay for at least some of the costs of their higher education.

Proponents of social contract theory evaluate moral problems from the point of view of moral rights. Kant argued that rights follow from duties. Hence, Kantians evaluate moral problems from duties or obligations.

2.9.2 Rawls's Theory of Justice

One of the criticisms of utilitarianism is that the utilitarian calculus is solely interested in the total amount of happiness produced. From a purely utilitarian standpoint, an unequal distribution of a certain amount of utility is better than an equal distribution of a lesser amount of utility.

Social contract theory recognizes the harm that a concentration of wealth and power can cause. According to Rousseau, "the social state is advantageous to men only when all possess something and none has too much" [24]. John Rawls (1921–2002), who did much to revive interest in social contract theory in the twentieth century, proposed two principles of justice that extend the definition of the social contract to include a principle dealing with unequal distributions of wealth and power.

∼

John Rawls's Principles of Justice

1. Each person may claim a "fully adequate" number of basic rights and liberties, such as freedom of thought and speech, freedom of association, the right to be safe from harm, and the right to own property, so long as these claims are consistent with everyone else having a claim to the same rights and liberties.

2. Any social and economic inequalities must satisfy two conditions: first, they are associated with positions in society that everyone has a fair and equal opportunity to assume; and second, they are "to be to the greatest benefit of the least-advantaged members of society (the **difference principle**)" [25].

∼

Rawls's first principle of justice, illustrated in Figure 2.7, is quite close to our original definition of social contract theory, except that it is stated from the point of view of rights and liberties rather than moral rules. The second principle of justice, however, focuses

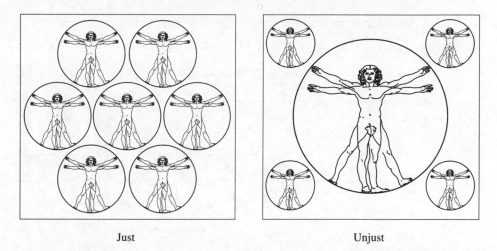

Just   Unjust

FIGURE 2.7 Rawls's first principle of justice states that each person may have a "fully adequate" number of rights and liberties as long as they are consistent with everyone else having the same rights and liberties.

on the question of social and economic inequalities. It is hard to imagine a society in which every person has equal standing. For example, it is unrealistic to expect every person to be involved in every civic decision. Instead, we elect representatives who vote in our place and officials who act on our behalf. Likewise, it is hard to imagine everybody in a society having equal wealth. If we allow people to hold private property, we should expect that some people will acquire more than others. According to Rawls, social and economic inequalities are acceptable if they meet two conditions.

First, every person in the society should have an equal chance to assume a position of higher social or economic standing. That means that two people born with equal intelligence, equal talents, and equal motivation to use them wisely should have the same probability of reaching an advantaged position, regardless of the social or economic class to which they were born. For example, the fact that someone's last name is Bush or Kennedy should not give that person a greater probability of being elected President of the United States than any other American born with equal intelligence, talent, and determination.

The second condition, called the difference principle, states that social and economic inequalities must be justified. The only way to justify a social or economic inequality is to show that its overall effect is to provide the most benefit to the least advantaged. The purpose of this principle is to help maintain a society composed of free *and equal* citizens. An example of the difference principle in action is a graduated income tax system in which people with higher incomes pay a higher percentage of their income in taxes (Figure 2.8). An example of a violation of the difference principle would be a military draft system in which poor people had a higher probability of being drafted than wealthy people.

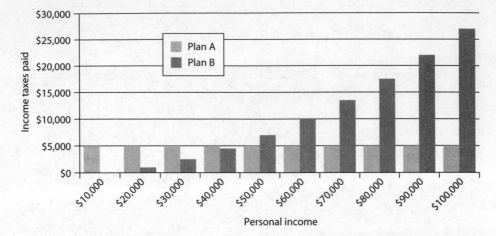

FIGURE 2.8 Suppose both of these income tax structures will produce the same income to the government. Under Plan A, every citizen pays $5,000; under Plan B, the amount each citizen pays depends upon his or her income. Plan B does not treat every citizen equally, but the inequality is justified under Rawls's difference principle because it is of greatest benefit to the most disadvantaged.

2.9.3 Evaluating a Scenario Using Social Contract Theory

∽ SCENARIO

Bill, the owner of a chain of DVD rental stores in a major metropolitan area, uses a computer to keep track of the DVDs rented by each customer. Using this information, he is able to construct profiles of the customers. For example, a customer who rents a large number of Disney titles is likely to have children. Bill sells these profiles to mail order companies. The customers begin receiving many unsolicited mail order catalogs. Some of the customers are happy to receive these catalogs and make use of them to order products. Others are unhappy at the increase in the amount of "junk mail" they are receiving.

Analysis

To analyze this scenario using social contract theory, we think about the rights of the rational agents involved. In this case, the rational agents are Bill, his customers, and the mail order companies. The morality of Bill's actions revolve around the question of whether he violated the privacy rights of his customers. If someone rents a DVD from one of Bill's stores, both the customer and Bill have information about the transaction. Are their rights to this information equal? If both the customer and Bill have equal rights to this information, then you may conclude there is nothing wrong with him selling this information to a mail order company. On the other hand, if customers have the right to expect transactions to be confidential, you may conclude that Bill was wrong to sell this information without gaining the permission of the customer.   ∽

2.9.4 The Case for Social Contract Theory

1. *It is framed in the language of rights.*

   The cultures of many modern countries, particularly Western-style democracies, promote individualism. For people raised in these cultures, the concept of individual rights is powerful and attractive.

2. *It explains why rational people act out of self-interest in the absence of a common agreement.*

   Suppose we are living in a city experiencing a gasoline shortage. If every car owner uses public transportation two days a week, there will be enough gasoline to go around. I need to decide if I will take the bus two days a week.

   Suppose no other car owners ride the bus two days a week. If I decide to ride the bus, I will have to put up with the inconvenience and the city will still run out of gas. Alternatively, I can do what everybody else is doing and continue driving my car until the gasoline supply is exhausted. Since the city will run out of gas either way, I experience less inconvenience by continuing to drive my car every day.

   On the other hand, suppose all the other car owners decide to ride the bus two days a week. If I decide to ride the bus, I will have plenty of company, which is good, but I will still have to adjust my work schedule to fit the bus schedule, waste time waiting at the bus stop, and so on. Alternatively, I can continue to drive my car. That will be more convenient for me. The amount of gasoline my car consumes is insignificant compared to the needs of the city, and the city will not run out of gasoline. Since the city will not run out of gas either way, I experience less inconvenience by continuing to drive my car every day.

   To summarize, if no one else rides the bus, it's better for me if I drive my car. If everyone else rides the bus, it's better for me if I drive my car. I have used logic to conclude that I should continue to drive my car. *Unfortunately, everyone else in the town logically reaches the same conclusion!* As a result, the city runs out of gasoline.

   The reason we all decided to act selfishly was because we did not have a common agreement. If all of us agreed that everyone should ride the bus two days a week, and those who did not would be punished, then logic would have led people to choose to use public transportation.

   Social contract theory is based on the idea that morality is the result of an implicit agreement among rational beings who understand that there is a tension between self-interest and the common good. The common good is best realized when everyone cooperates. Cooperation occurs when those acting selfishly suffer negative consequences.

3. *It provides a clear ethical analysis of some important moral issues regarding the relationship between people and government.*

   For example, social contract theory provides a logical explanation of why it is morally acceptable to punish someone for a crime. You might ask, "If everyone has a right to liberty, how can we put in prison someone who has committed a crime?" The social contract is based on the notion that everyone benefits when everyone bears the burden of following certain rules. Knowledge that those who do not follow the rules will be punished restrains individuals from selfishly flouting their obligations. People will have this knowledge only if society punishes those who commit crimes.

Another example is the problem of civil disobedience. Social contract theory provides a straightforward explanation of why civil disobedience can be the morally right decision.

Consider the lunch counter sit-ins of the 1960s. On February 1, 1960, four African-American students from North Carolina A&T walked into the Woolworth's store on South Elm Street in Greensboro, sat down at a whites-only lunch counter, and asked for service. When they were denied service, they refused to leave, sitting at their stools until the store closed. Two days later, 85 students participated in the "sit-in" at Woolworth's. All of these students were breaking segregation laws, but according to social contract theory, their actions could be considered morally justified. As we have said, the social contract is based on the idea that everyone receives certain benefits in return for bearing certain burdens. The segregation laws were designed to give people of color greater burdens and fewer benefits than white people. Therefore, they were unjust.

2.9.5 The Case against Social Contract Theory

1. *None of us signed the social contract.*

   The social contract is not a real contract. Since none of us have actually agreed to the obligations of the citizens of our society, why should we be bound to them?

   Defenders of social contract theory point out that the social contract is a theoretical notion that is supposed to explain the rational process through which communities adopt moral guidelines. As John Rawls puts it, social contract agreements are *hypothetical* and *nonhistorical*. They are hypothetical in the sense that they are what reasonable people "could, or would, agree to, not what they have agreed to" [25]. They are nonhistorical because they "do not suppose the agreement has ever, or indeed ever could actually be entered into" [25]. Furthermore, even if it could be entered into, that would make no difference. The reason it would make no difference is because the moral guidelines are supposed to be the result of analysis (facts and values plus logical reasoning), not history. Social contract theory is *not* cultural relativism in disguise.

2. *Some actions can be characterized in multiple ways.*

   This is a problem social contract theory shares with Kantianism. Some situations are complicated and can be described in more than one way. Our characterization of a situation can affect the rules or rights we determine to be relevant to our analysis.

3. *Social contract theory does not explain how to solve a moral problem when the analysis reveals conflicting rights.*

This is another problem social contract theory shares with Kantianism. Consider the knotty moral problem of abortion, in which the mother's right to privacy is pitted against the fetus's right to life. As long as each of these rights is embraced by one side in the controversy, the issue cannot be resolved. What typically happens in debates is that advocates on one side of the issue "solve" the problem by discounting or denying the right invoked by their adversaries.

4. *Social contract theory may be unjust to those people who are incapable of upholding their side of the contract.*

Social contract theory provides every person with certain rights in return for that person bearing certain burdens. When a person does not follow the moral rules, he or she is punished. What about human beings who, through no fault of their own, are unable to follow the moral rules?

A response to this objection is that there is a difference between someone who deliberately chooses to break a moral rule and someone who is incapable of understanding a rule. Society must distinguish between these two groups of people. People who deliberately break moral rules should be punished, but people who cannot understand a rule must be cared for.

However, this response overlooks the fact that distinguishing between these two groups of people can be difficult. For example, how should we treat drug addicts who steal to feed their addiction? Some countries treat them as criminals and put them in a prison. Other countries treat them as mentally ill people and put them in a hospital.

These criticisms demonstrate some of the weaknesses of social contract theory. Nevertheless, social contract theory is logical and analytical. It allows people to explain why a particular action is moral or immoral. According to our criteria, it is a workable ethical theory, joining Kantianism, act utilitarianism, and rule utilitarianism.

2.10 Comparing Workable Ethical Theories

The divine command theory, ethical egoism, Kantianism, act utilitarianism, rule utilitarianism, and social contract theory share the viewpoint that moral good and moral precepts are objective. In other words, morality has an existence outside the human mind. For this reason we say these theories are examples of **objectivism**.

What distinguishes ethical egoism, Kantianism, utilitarianism, and social contract theory from the divine command theory is the assumption that ethical decision-making is a rational process by which people can discover objective moral principles with the use of logical reasoning based on facts and commonly held values. Kantianism, utilitarianism, and social contract theory explicitly take other people into consideration when defining what makes an action morally correct, which sets these theories apart from ethical egoism. Of all the theories we have considered, we conclude that Kantianism, act utilitarianism, rule utilitarianism, and social contract theory are the most workable.

An act utilitarian considers the consequences of the action, computing the total change in utility to determine if an action is right or wrong. The other three workable theories are rule-based. According to Kantianism, rule utilitarianism, and social contract theory, an action is morally right if it is in accord with a correct moral rule.

Each of the rule-based theories has a different way of determining if a moral rule is correct. A Kantian relies upon the Categorical Imperative. A rule utilitarian considers what the long-term consequences of everyone following the rule would be for the total good. An adherent of social contract theory considers whether rational people would agree to accept the rule, for everyone's mutual benefit, provided that everyone else agreed to follow the rule as well.

These differences among the theories are presented graphically in Figure 2.9.

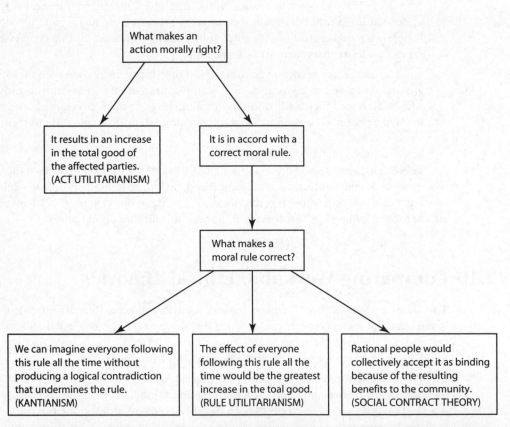

FIGURE 2.9 Comparison of four workable ethical theories. All of these theories explicitly take people other than the decision-maker into consideration, assume that moral good and moral precepts are objective, and rely upon reasoning from facts and commonly held values.

2.11 Morality of Breaking the Law

What is moral and what is legal are not identical. Certain actions may be wrong, even if there are no laws forbidding these actions. For example, most American states do not have laws prohibiting texting while driving, but people are still morally responsible for traffic accidents they cause because they are distracted by texting. What about the opposite situation? Is it possible that an action may be the right thing to do, even if it is illegal?

In our discussion of social contract theory, we discussed the morality of civil disobedience, and we concluded that the lunch counter sit-ins were morally acceptable because the segregation laws being violated were unjust. Here we are considering a different situation. We are assuming the law is just and there are no overriding moral concerns. When this is the case, is it possible that an illegal action may be the right action?

Let's analyze this question from the point of view of our four workable ethical theories. To ground our analysis, we will consider a particular illegal action: violating a licensing agreement by copying a CD containing copyrighted music and giving it to a friend.[2]

2.11.1 Social Contract Theory Perspective

Social contract theory is based on the assumption that everyone in society ought to bear certain burdens in order to receive certain benefits. The legal system is instituted to guarantee that people's rights are protected. It guarantees people will not choose their selfish interests over the common good. For this reason we have a *prima facie* obligation to obey the law (Figure 2.10). That means, everything else being equal, we should be law-abiding. In return, our own legal rights will be respected. Our obligation to obey the law should only be broken if we are compelled to follow a higher-order moral obligation.

From the point of view of social contract theory, then, it is wrong to give a friend a copy of a CD containing copyrighted music, because that action violates the legal rights of the person or organization owning the copyright, and the desire to do something nice for a friend is not an overriding moral concern.

2.11.2 Kantian Perspective

According to the Categorical Imperative, we should act only from moral rules that we can at the same time will to be universal moral laws. Suppose I think the current copyright laws are unjust because they unfairly favor the producers of intellectual property rather than the consumers. I could propose the following rule: "I may ignore a law that I believe to be unjust."

---

2. This action is illegal in the United States and many other countries, but it is not illegal in every country.

FIGURE 2.10 According to social contract theory, we have a *prima facie* obligation to obey the law.

What happens when we universalize this rule? If everyone acted according to this rule—ignoring laws they felt to be unjust—then the authority of the legislature to create laws would be fatally undermined. Yet the goal of the legislature is to create laws that ensure we live in a just society. Hence, there is a logical contradiction, because I cannot both will that there be justice (by ignoring what I consider to be an unjust law) and will that there be no justice (by denying the legislature the authority it needs to create a just society).

Another line of Kantian reasoning leads us to the same conclusion. If I copy a CD containing copyrighted material, I am violating the legal rights of the person who owns the copyright. No matter how good my intended use of the CD, I am using the copyright owner if I make a copy without his or her permission. This violates the second formulation of the Categorical Imperative. Therefore, it is wrong to copy the CD.

2.11.3 Rule Utilitarian Perspective

What would be the consequences of people ignoring laws they felt to be unjust? A beneficial consequence is the happiness of the people who are doing what they please rather than obeying the law. There are, however, far more harmful consequences. First, the people directly affected by lawless actions will be harmed. Second, people in general would have less respect for the law. Third, assuming increased lawlessness puts an additional burden on the criminal justice system, society as a whole would have to pay for having additional police officers, prosecutors, judges, and prisons. Hence, from a rule utilitarian viewpoint, breaking the law is wrong.

2.11.4 Act Utilitarian Perspective

We will do an act utilitarian analysis to show it is possible to conceive of situations where the benefits of breaking a law are greater than the harms. Suppose I purchase a music CD. I play it, and I think it is great. A friend of mine is in a terrible automobile accident. While he recovers, he will need to stay quiet for a month. I know he has no money to spend on music. In fact, people are doing fundraisers simply to help his family pay the medical bills. I don't have money to contribute to a fundraiser, but I think of another way I could help him out. I give my friend a copy of the CD. He is grateful for having a diversion during his time of bed rest.

What are the consequences of my action? As far as I can tell, there is no lost sale, because even if I had not given my friend a copy of the CD, he would not have bought it. In fact, giving a copy of the CD to my friend may actually increase the sales of the CD if my friend likes it and recommends it to other people who do have money to spend on CDs. I am not likely to be prosecuted for what I did. Therefore, there will be no impact on the legal system. No extra police detectives, prosecutors, or judges will need to be hired as a result of my action. The principal harm I have done is to have violated the legal rights of the owner of the copyright. The benefits are that my friend is thrilled to have something to do during his recovery and I am happy to have been able to do something to help him out during his time of need. Overall, the benefits appear to outweigh the harms.

Our analysis has concluded that copying a CD is morally acceptable in this particular and admittedly rather extreme situation, but it would be a logical fallacy to conclude from this analysis that all instances of CD copying are morally acceptable according to act utilitarianism.

2.11.5 Conclusion

There is nothing intrinsically immoral about copying a CD. However, our society has chosen to enact laws that grant intellectual property rights to people who do creative work and distribute it on CDs. From the viewpoint of Kantianism, rule utilitarianism, and social contract theory, breaking the law is wrong unless there is a strong overriding moral obligation. Copying a disc to save a few dollars or help a friend does not fall into that category. Copying a CD containing copyrighted music is immoral *because* it is illegal.

From an act utilitarian viewpoint, it is possible to come up with an exceptional circumstance where making a copy of a copyrighted CD is the right action. However, it would be wrong to extrapolate from this particular case and conclude that an act utilitarian analysis would determine all instances of CD copying to be morally acceptable.

Summary

We live together in communities for our mutual benefit. Every society has guidelines indicating what people are supposed to do in various circumstances. We call these guidelines morality. Ethics, also called moral philosophy, is a rational examination into people's moral beliefs and behaviors. In this chapter, we have considered a variety of ethical theories with the purpose of identifying those that will be of most use to us as we consider the effects of information technology on society.

Relativistic theories are based on the idea that people *invent* morality. A relativist claims there are no universal moral principles. Subjective relativism is the theory that morality is an individual creation. Cultural relativism is the idea that each society determines its own morality. If morality is invented, and no set of moral guidelines is any better than another, then there are no objective criteria that can be used to determine if one set of guidelines is better than another. Under these circumstances, the study of ethics is extremely difficult, if not impossible. For this reason we shall not make use of relativistic theories.

In contrast, objectivism is based on the idea that morality has an existence outside the human mind. It is the responsibility of people to *discover* morality. An objectivist claims there are certain universal moral principles that are true for all people, regardless of their historical or cultural situation. All of the remaining ethical theories we considered fall into this category.

The divine command theory is based on the idea that God has provided us with moral guidelines designed to promote our well-being. These guidelines are to be followed because they reflect the will of God, not because we understand them. Because this theory does not rationally derive moral guidelines from facts and commonly held values, we reject it as a useful ethical theory.

According to ethical egoism, the right thing for a person to do in any situation is the action that will benefit him or her the most. Because ethical egoism formally excludes giving weight to the benefits to other people or the community as a whole when making decisions, it is incompatible with our assumption that other people and their core values should be considered.

Another objectivist theory, Kantianism, is focused on dutifulness. If we are dutiful, we will feel compelled to act in certain ways out of respect for moral rules. A moral rule is appropriate if it is consistent with the Categorical Imperative. Kant provides two formulations of the Categorical Imperative. The first is: "Act only from moral rules that you can at the same time will to be universal laws." The second is: "Act so that you always treat both yourself and other people as ends in themselves, and never solely as a means to an end." While both Kantianism and the divine command theory hold that actions should be motivated by the desire to obey universal moral rules, Kantianism holds that rational beings can discover these rules without relying upon divine inspiration. Kantianism is considered a non-consequentialist theory because the morality of an action is determined by evaluating the moral rule upon which the will to act is grounded rather than the action's consequences.

Utilitarianism, developed by Jeremy Bentham and John Stuart Mill, is based upon the Principle of Utility, also called the Greatest Happiness Principle. According to this principle, an action is right (or wrong) to the extent that it increases (or decreases) the total happiness of the affected parties. Utilitarianism is called a consequentialist theory, because its focus is on the consequences of an action. Act utilitarianism is the theory that an action is good if its net effect (over all affected beings) is to produce more happiness than unhappiness. An action is bad if its net effect is to produce more unhappiness than happiness. Rule utilitarianism is the ethical theory that holds that we ought to adopt those moral rules which, if followed by everyone, will lead to the greatest increase in total happiness. In other words, rule utilitarianism applies the Principle of Utility to moral rules, while act utilitarianism applies the Principle of Utility to individual moral actions. Both of these theories hold that rational beings can perform the analysis needed to determine if a moral action or moral rule is good or evil.

The final ethical theory we considered was social contract theory, identified with Thomas Hobbes, John Locke, Jean-Jacques Rousseau, and John Rawls. Social contract theory holds that "morality consists in the set of rules, governing how people are to treat one another, that rational people will agree to accept, for their mutual benefit, on the condition that others follow those rules as well" [5]. Rawls proposed two principles of justice that are designed to maintain society over time as an association of free and equal citizens. Like Kantianism and both forms of utilitarianism, social contract theory is based on the premise that there are universal, objective moral rules that can be discovered through rational analysis.

Our survey identified four practical ethical theories: Kantianism, act utilitarianism, rule utilitarianism, and social contract theory. We used these theories to analyze the question, "Is it morally acceptable to break the law?" According to social contract theory, Kantianism, and rule utilitarianism, the answer to this question is, "Probably not." It is wrong to break the law unless there is an overriding moral concern. From an act utilitarian perspective, it is possible to devise an obscure situation in which the benefits of breaking the law outweigh the harms. However, act utilitarianism cannot be used to justify a general disregard for obeying the law.

Our discussion of the strengths and weaknesses of Kantianism, utilitarianism, and social contract theory revealed that each of these theories contains a valuable insight. According to Kant, interactions with other people should respect them as rational beings, and it is wrong for one person to treat someone else only as a means to an end. Utilitarians understand that it's helpful to consider the consequences of an action when deciding whether it is right or wrong. Social contract theory focuses on the individual and collective benefits of a common agreement that promotes certain rights, such as the right to life, liberty, and property.

In the chapters that follow, we'll use Kantianism, act utilitarianism, rule utilitarianism, and social contract theory to evaluate a variety of problems arising from the introduction of information technology into society. Every analysis will be based on one of the theories, so that you may come to a better understanding of how to apply each theory to different situations.

In practice, however, there is no reason why you cannot consider duties *and* rights *and* consequences when making moral decisions. (For an example of this approach, read the interview with James Moor at the end of this chapter.) You will, however, encounter many problems for which it is impossible to respect everyone's rights absolutely and also maximize the total beneficial consequences. Instead, one of these considerations will have to take priority. Pondering the situations described in the rest of this book and discussing them with others will help you learn more about your personal values and what it means for you to be a person of good character, setting the stage for the introduction of virtue ethics in Chapter 9.

Review Questions

1. Define in your own words what "the ethical point of view" means.
2. Define morality and ethics in your own words.
3. What is the difference between morality and ethics?
4. What is the difference between relativism and objectivism?
5. What are the advantages of using an ethical theory in which all humans are treated equally and guidelines are developed through a process of logical reasoning?
6. Two people are debating the morality of a particular action. Person A explains why he believes the action is wrong. Person B disagrees with Person A. Her response to him is, "That's your opinion." Person B has not made a strong ethical argument. Why not?
7. What do we mean when we say an ethical theory is rational?
8. What is the many/any fallacy? Invent your own example of this fallacy.
9. What is the equivalence fallacy? Invent your own example of this fallacy.
10. Come up with your own example of a moral rule that would violate the Categorical Imperative.
11. What is plagiarism? Describe four different ways that a person can commit plagiarism. (See Appendix A.)
12. What is the difference between plagiarism and misuse of sources?
13. What is the difference between a consequentialist theory and a non-consequentialist theory?
14. Give three examples of a situation in which your action would be primarily motivated by a sense of duty or obligation. Give three examples of a situation in which your action would be primarily motivated by its expected consequences.
15. What is the problem of moral luck?
16. Why do businesses and governments often use utilitarian thinking to determine the proper course of action?
17. What is the difference principle?
18. Is social contract theory as first presented a consequentialist theory or a non-consequentialist theory? Is social contract theory as articulated in Rawls's two principles of justice a consequentialist theory or a non-consequentialist theory?
19. Describe similarities and differences between subjective relativism and ethical egoism.
20. Describe similarities and differences between divine command theory and Kantianism.

21. Describe similarities and differences between subjective relativism and act utilitarianism.

22. Describe similarities and differences between Kantianism and rule utilitarianism.

23. Describe similarities and differences between act utilitarianism and rule utilitarianism.

24. Describe similarities and differences between cultural relativism and social contract theory.

25. Describe similarities and differences between Kantianism and social contract theory.

26. Evaluate the four scenarios presented in Section 2.1 from a Kantian perspective.

27. Evaluate the four scenarios presented in Section 2.1 from an act utilitarian perspective.

28. Evaluate the four scenarios presented in Section 2.1 from a rule utilitarian perspective.

29. Evaluate the four scenarios presented in Section 2.1 from the perspective of social contract theory.

Discussion Questions

30. If everyone agreed to take the ethical point of view by respecting others and their core values, would there be any need for a rigorous study of ethics?

31. If you had to choose only one of the ethical theories presented in this chapter and use it for all of your personal ethical decision-making, which theory would you choose? Why? How would you respond to the arguments raised against the theory you have chosen?

32. Most ethical theories agree on a large number of moral guidelines. For example, it is nearly universally held that it is wrong to steal. What difference, then, does it make whether someone subscribes to the divine command theory, Kantianism, utilitarianism, or one of the other ethical theories? (Hint: Think about which theories are more persuasive when they lead to different conclusions about the right thing to do.)

33. Suppose a spaceship lands in your neighborhood. Friendly aliens emerge and invite humans to enter the galactic community. You learn that this race of aliens has colonized virtually the entire galaxy; Earth is one of the few inhabitable planets to host a different intelligent species. The aliens seem to be remarkably open-minded. They ask you to outline the ethical theory that should guide the interactions between our two species. Which ethical theory would you describe? Why?

34. According to the Golden Rule, you should do unto others as you would want them to do unto you. Is the Categorical Imperative simply the Golden Rule in disguise?

35. The Silver Rule states, "Do not do unto others what you do not want them to do unto you." Which ethical theory presented in this chapter is closest to the Silver Rule?

36. Are there any ethical theories described in this chapter that would allow someone to use the argument, "Everybody is doing it," to show that an activity is not wrong?

37. How well does Moor's theory of "just consequentialism" (described in the interview at the end of this chapter) solve the problems associated with Kantianism and rule utilitarianism?

38. Can moral decisions be made on a purely rational, algorithmic basis, or are there limits to rationality in moral decision-making?

39. What are some examples of contemporary information technology issues for which our society's moral guidelines seem to be nonexistent or unclear? (Hint: Think about issues that are generating a lot of media coverage or lawsuits.)

40. People give a variety of reasons for copying a music CD from a friend instead of buying it [27]. Refute each of the reasons given below using one of the viable theories described in this chapter. (You don't have to use the same theory each time.)

    a. I don't have enough money to buy it.
    b. The retail price is too high. The company is gouging customers.
    c. Since I wouldn't have bought it anyway, the company didn't lose a sale.
    d. I'm giving my friend the opportunity to do a good deed.
    e. Everyone else is doing it. Why should I be the only person to buy it when everyone else is getting it for free?
    f. This is a drop in the bucket compared to Chinese pirates who sell billions of dollars worth of copied music.
    g. This is insignificant compared to the billions of dollars worth of music being exchanged over the Internet.

41. Students in a history class are asked to take a quiz posted on the course Web site. The instructor has explained the following rules to the students: First, they are supposed to do their own work. Second, they are free to consult their lecture notes and the textbook while taking the quiz. Third, in order to get credit for the quiz, they must correctly answer at least 80 percent of the questions. If they do not get a score of 80 percent, they may retake the quiz as many times as they wish.

    Mary and John are both taking the quiz. They are sitting next to each other in the computer room. John asks Mary for help in answering one of the questions. He says, "What's the difference if you tell me the answer, I look it up in the book, or I find out from the computer that my answer is wrong and retake the quiz? In any case, I'll end up getting credit for the right answer." Mary tells John the correct answer to the question.

    Discuss the morality of Mary's decision.

42. Suppose a society holds that it is wrong for one individual to eavesdrop on the telephone conversations of another citizen. Should that society also prohibit the government from listening in on its citizens' telephone conversations?

In-Class Exercises

43. In Plato's dialogue *The Republic*, Glaucon argues that people do not voluntarily do what is right [28]. According to Glaucon, anyone who has the means to do something unjust and get away with it will do so. Glaucon illustrates his point by telling the story of Gyges.

    Gyges, a shepherd, discovers a magic ring. He accidentally discovers that wearing this ring renders him invisible. He uses the power of the ring to seduce the queen, kill the king, and take over the kingdom.

Divide the class into two groups (pro and con) to debate the following proposition: Whenever people have the opportunity to act unjustly without any fear of getting caught or anyone thinking the worse of them, they do so.

44. For one of the following issues divide the class into two groups (pro and con) to argue whether the right should be considered a legitimate positive right by our society:

    a. The right to a higher education
    b. The right to housing
    c. The right to health care
    d. The right of a Presidential candidate to receive time on television

45. Is the right to life a negative right or a positive right? In other words, when we say someone has the right to life, are we simply saying we have an obligation not to harm that person, or are we saying we have an obligation to provide that person what he or she needs in order to live, such as food and shelter?

    Divide the class into two groups. One group should argue that the right to life is a negative right; the other should argue that the right to life is a positive right.

46. Divide the class into two groups (pro and con) to debate this proposition: The citizens of a representative democracy are morally responsible for the actions of their government.

47. Divide the class into two groups (pro and con) to debate this proposition: The moral guidelines for individuals should apply to interactions among nation-states.

Further Reading

Douglas Birsch. *Ethical Insights: A Brief Introduction*. 2nd ed. McGraw-Hill, New York, NY, 2002.

Brian Hansen. "Combating Plagiarism: Is the Internet Causing More Students to Copy?" *The CQ Researcher*, September 19, 2003 (entire issue).

Oliver A. Johnson. *Ethics: Selections from Classical and Contemporary Writers*. 8th ed. Harcourt Brace, Fort Worth, TX, 1999.

Immanuel Kant. *Foundations of the Metaphysics of Morals and What Is Enlightenment?* Translated, with an introduction, by Lewis White Beck. Prentice Hall, Upper Saddle River, NJ, 1997.

John Stuart Mill, *On Liberty and Utilitarianism*. with an introduction by Alan M. Dershowitz. Bantam Books, New York, NY, 1993.

Plato. *Gorgias*. Translated, with an introduction, by Walter Hamilton. Penguin Books, Harmondsworth, England, 1960.

James Rachels. *The Elements of Moral Philosophy*. 4th ed. McGraw-Hill, New York, NY, 2003.

Jean-Jacques Rousseau. *The Social Contract*. Penguin Books, London, England, 1968.

Christopher Shea. "Rule Breaker." *The Chronicle of Higher Education*, June 12, 2011. chronicle.com.

References

[1] James H. Moor. "Reason, Relativity, and Responsibility in Computer Ethics. In *Readings in CyberEthics*. 2nd ed. Edited by Richard A. Spinello and Herman T. Tavani. Jones and Bartlett, Sudbury, MA, 2004.

[2] John Rawls. *A Theory of Justice, Revised Edition*. The Belknap Press of Harvard University Press, Cambridge, MA, 1999.

[3] Plato. *Portrait of Socrates: Being the Apology, Crito and Phaedo of Plato in an English Translation*. Translated by Sir R. W. Livingstone. Clarendon Press, Oxford, England, 1961.

[4] Douglas Birsch. *Ethical Insights: A Brief Introduction*. 2nd ed. McGraw-Hill, Boston, MA, 2002.

[5] James Rachels. *The Elements of Moral Philosophy*. 4th ed. McGraw-Hill, Boston, MA, 2003.

[6] William Graham Sumner. *Folkways: A Study of the Sociological Importance of Usages, Manners, Customs, Mores, and Morals*. Ginn and Company, Boston, MA, 1934.

[7] Charles M. Hampden-Turner and Fons Trompenaars. *Building Cross-Cultural Competence: How to Create Wealth from Conflicting Values*. Yale University Press, New Haven, CT, 2000.

[8] *The Torah: A Modern Commentary*. Union of American Hebrew Congregations, New York, NY, 1981.

[9] Plato. *Plato's Euthyphro: with Introduction and Notes and Pseudo-Platonica*. Arno Press, New York, NY, 1976.

[10] *The Holy Bible, New Revised Standard Version*. Genesis, Chapter 22. Oxford University Press, Oxford, England, 1995.

[11] *The Holy Bible, New Revised Standard Version*. Genesis, Chapter 4. Oxford University Press, Oxford, England, 1995.

[12] Ayn Rand. "The Objectivist Ethics." In *The Virtue of Selfishness*. Signet Books, New York, NY. 1964.

[13] James Rachels. "Two Arguments Against Ethical Egoism." *Philosophia*, Vol. 4, Nos. 2–3, pp. 297–314, April–July 1974.

[14] James H. Fowler and Nicholar A. Christakis. "Dynamic Spread of Happiness in a Large Social Network: Longitudinal Analysis Over 20 Years in the Framingham Heart Study." *British Medical Journal*, December 4, 2008.

[15] Lewis White Beck. "Translator's Introduction." In *Foundations of the Metaphysics of Morals*. 2nd ed. Library of Liberal Arts / Prentice Hall, Upper Saddle River, NJ, 1997.

[16] William K. Frankena. *Ethics*. 2nd ed. Prentice Hall, Englewood Cliffs, NJ, 1973.

[17] Jeremy Bentham. *An Introduction to the Principles of Morals and Legislation*. Oxford, 1823.

[18] W. D. Ross. *The Right and the Good*. 2nd ed. Oxford University Press, Oxford, England, 2003.

[19] Kevin Poulsen. "Nachi Worm Infected Diebold ATMs." *The Register*, November 25, 2003. www.theregister.co.uk.

[20] Florence Olsen. "Attacks Threaten Computer Networks as Students Arrive for the Fall Semester." *The Chronicle of Higher Education*, September 5, 2003.

[21] Bernard Gert. "Common Morality and Computing." In *Readings in CyberEthics*. 2nd ed. Edited by Richard A. Spinello and Herman T. Tavani. Jones and Bartlett, Sudbury, MA, 2004.

[22] John Daniszewski and Tony Perry. "War with Iraq; U.S. in Control; Baghdad in U.S. Hands; Symbols of Regime Fall As Troops Take Control." *The Los Angeles Times*, April 10, 2003.

[23] Thomas Hobbes. *Leviathan*. Penguin Books, London, England, 1985.

[24] Jean-Jacques Rousseau. *The Social Contract*. Translated by Maurice Cranston. Penguin Books, London, England, 1968.

[25] John Rawls. *Justice as Fairness: A Restatement*. The Belknap Press of Harvard University Press, Cambridge, MA, 2001.

[26] Terry Winograd. "Computers, Ethics, and Social Responsibility." In *Computers, Ethics & Social Values*. Edited by Deborah G. Johnson and Helen Nissenbaum. Prentice Hall, Englewood Cliffs, NJ, 2005.

[27] Sara Baase. *A Gift of Fire*. 2nd ed. Prentice Hall, Upper Saddle River, NJ, 2003.

[28] Plato. *The Republic of Plato*. Translated by F. M. Cornford. Oxford University Press, London, England, 1941.

James Moor

James Moor is the Daniel P. Stone Professor in Intellectual and Moral Philosophy at Dartmouth College. He is also the Editor-in-Chief of the philosophical journal *Minds and Machines*, and he has served as President of the International Society for Ethics and Information Technology.

Professor Moor has written extensively on computer ethics, the philosophy of artificial intelligence, the philosophy of mind, the philosophy of science, and logic. His publications include "Why we Need Better Ethics for Emerging Technologies," *Ethics and Information Technology*, Vol. 7, No. 3 (2005) pp. 111–119. He and Terrell Bynum co-edited *The Digital Phoenix: How Computers Are Changing Philosophy* (Oxford: Basil Blackwell Publishers, 1998 and revised edition 2000) and *Cyberphilosophy: The Intersection of Computing and Philosophy* (Oxford: Basic Blackwell Publishers, 2002).

In 2003, Dr. Moor received the Making a Difference Award from the Association for Computing Machinery's Special Interest Group on Computers and Society. In 2006, he received the Barwise Prize for his work in philosophy and computing from the American Philosophical Association. He holds a Ph.D. in History and Philosophy of Science from Indiana University.

What stimulated your interest in studying the philosophy of technology?

My interest developed initially through a fascination with computing. The philosophy of computing is a combination of logic, epistemology, metaphysics, and value theory—the complete philosophical package wrapped up in a very practical and influential technological form. Who wouldn't be interested in that? Many standard philosophical issues are brought to life in a computer setting. Consider a simple example: In the *Republic*, Plato tells a story about the Ring of Gyges in which a shepherd finds a ring that, when he wears it and turns it, makes him invisible. Being a clever but rather unethical shepherd, he uses the power of the ring to take over the kingdom, including killing the king and marrying the queen. Through this story Plato raises a deep and important philosophical question: Why be just if one can get away with being unjust? Today the Internet offers each of us our own ring of Gyges. Agents on the Internet can be largely invisible. The question for us, echoing Plato, is why be just while using the Internet if one can get away with being unjust?

What distinguishes ethical problems in computing from ethical problems in other fields?

Some have argued that the ethical problems in the field are unique. This is difficult to show, because the problems involving computing usually connect with our ordinary ethical problems in some way. Nevertheless, what makes the field of computer ethics special and important, though probably not unique, is the technology itself–the computer. Computers are logically malleable machines in that they can be shaped to do any task that one can design, train, or evolve them to do. Computers are universal tools, and this explains why they are so commonplace and culturally transforming. Because they are used in so many ways, new situations continually arise for which we do not have clear policies to guide actions. The use of computing creates policy vacuums. For instance, when wireless technology first appeared, there were questions about whether one should be allowed to access someone else's wireless system, e.g., when driving down the street. Should such access be considered trespassing? Ethical rights and duties of novel situations are not always clear. Because computers are universal tools and can be applied in so many diverse ways, they tend to create many more policy vacuums than other technologies. This is one respect in which the ethical problems in computing are different from other fields at least in degree if not in kind. This makes computer ethics an extraordinarily important discipline for all of us.

How has information technology affected the field of ethics in the past two decades?

Twenty years ago, I had to search newspapers and magazines to find stories on computer/information ethics. Such stories were uncommon. Now many such stories appear daily. They are so common that the fact that computing is involved is unremarkable. Stories about body parts being sold on eBay or identity theft over the Internet or spam legislation all presuppose computing, but computing has so permeated our culture that it is not something uncommon, but something almost everybody uses. In a sense, much of ethics has become computer ethics!

Why do you believe it is helpful to view computer ethics issues in terms of policies?

When we act ethically, we are acting such that anyone in a similar situation would be allowed to do the same kind of action. I am not allowed to have my own set of ethical policies that allow me to do things that others in a relevantly similar situation cannot do. Ethical policies are public policies. An act utilitarian, by contrast, would consider each situation individually. On this view, cheating would not only be justified but required if the individual doing the cheating benefited and others were not harmed because they did not know about it. This seems to me to be a paradigm of unethical behavior, and hence, I advocate a public policy approach. If cheating is allowed for some, then everyone should be allowed to cheat in similar situations.

Rather than using "policies" I could use "rules." But ethical rules are sometimes regarded as binding without exceptions. A system of exceptionless rules will never work as an ethical theory, for rules can conflict and sometimes exceptions must be made because of extraordinary consequences. One might be justified in lying to save a life, for example. I prefer using the word "policy" because I want to suggest modification may be necessary in cases of conflict or in extraordinary circumstance. Notice that the policies involving exceptions must themselves be treated as public policy. If it is justifiable for someone to lie to save a life, it will be justified for others to lie to save a life in similar circumstances.

Please explain the process of resolving an ethical issue using your theory of "just consequentialism."

The view is somewhat like rule utilitarianism and somewhat like Kantian ethics, but differs crucially from both of them. Rule utilitarians wish to maximize the good, but typically without concern for justice. Just consequentialism does not require maximization of the good, which is in general unknowable, and does not sanction unjust policies simply because they have good consequences. Kant's theory requires us to act only on those maxims that we can will to be a universal law. But Kant's theory does not allow for exceptions. Kant thought one ought never lie. Moreover, the typical Kantian test question of what would happen if everyone did a certain kind of action is not the right question, for this test rules out far too much, e.g., becoming a computer programmer (what if everyone were to become a computer programmer?). For just consequentialism, the test question is what would happen if everyone were *allowed* to do a certain kind of action. We need to consider both the consequences and the justice of our public policies.

In ethics we are concerned about rights and duties, and consequences of actions. Just consequentialism is a mixed system in that it is part deontological and part consequential. Rights and duties can be challenged if they are unfair or cause significant harm, but usually are properly taken as normative guides. One's rights as a citizen and one's duties as a parent are examples. In evaluating consequences we need to consider values that all people share, because we want to develop a policy that we can impartially publicly advocate. Everyone in similar circumstances should be allowed to follow it. At least some of these universal values to be considered will be happiness, life, ability, security, knowledge, freedom, opportunity, and resources. Notice that these are core goods that any sane human wants regardless of which society the human is in.

In the ethical decision process, step one is to consider a set of policies for acting in the kind of situation under consideration. Step two is to consider the relevant duties, rights, and consequences involved with each policy. Step three is to decide whether the policy can be impartially advocated as a public policy, i.e., anyone should be allowed to act in a similar way in similar circumstances. Many policies may be readily acceptable. Many may be easily rejected. And some may be in dispute, as people may weigh the relevant values differently or disagree about the factual outcomes.

In general, rights and duties will carry prima facie weight in ethical decision making, and in general cannot be overridden lightly. But if the consequences of following certain rights and duties are bad enough, then overriding them may be acceptable as long as this kind of exception can be an acceptable public policy. In controversial cases, there will be rational disagreements. Just consequentialism does not require complete agreement on every issue. Note that we have disagreements in ordinary non-ethical decision making as well. But just consequentialism does guide us in determining where and why the disagreements occur so that further discussion and resolution may be possible.

You have also studied the field of artificial intelligence from a philosophical point of view. Do you believe it is possible to create a truly intelligent machine capable of ethical decision-making? If so, how far are we from making such a machine a reality?

Nobody has shown that it is impossible, but I think we are very far away from such a possibility. The problem may have less to do with ethics than with epistemology. Computers (expert systems) some-times possess considerable knowledge about special topics, but they lack common-sense knowledge. Without even the ability to understand simple things that any normal child can grasp, computers will not be able to make considered ethical decisions in any robust sense.

Can an inanimate object have intrinsic moral worth, or is the value of an object strictly determined by its utility to one or more humans?

I take values or moral worth to be a judgment based on standards. The standards that count for us are human. We judge other objects using our standards. This may go beyond utility, however, as we might judge a non-useful object to be aesthetically pleasing. Our human standards might be challenged sometime in the future if robots developed consciousness or if we become cyborgs with a different set of standards. Stay tuned.

3

Networked Communications

Lo, soul, seest thou not God's purpose from the first?
The earth to be spann'd, connected by network,
The races, neighbors, to marry and be given in marriage,
The oceans to be cross'd, the distant brought near,
The lands to be welded together.

—WALT WHITMAN, *Passage to India*

3.1 Introduction

During government meetings in Washington, D.C., it's common for those sitting around the conference table to bow their heads. They're not praying—they're using their smartphones. "You'll have half the participants [texting] each other as a submeeting, with a running commentary on the primary meeting," reports Philippe Reines, a senior advisor to Secretary of State Hillary Clinton [1].

Musician Ken Stringfellow of The Posies uses the Web to interact with his fans. "I log in to Facebook, and in like 30 seconds, I have like 50 people in my chat windows. And I answer their questions: 'Oh, yeah, you wanna get that record? I've got a couple of those in stock.' That kind of stuff" [2].

According to the Pew Research Center, more American adults get their news from the Internet than from newspapers. In a 2008 survey, 40% of adults said they get most of their news from the Internet, compared to 35% who said they rely upon newspapers as their primary source [3].

The Internet has opened up new opportunities for politicians to attract donations. During his successful run for the Presidency in 2008, Barack Obama raised $500 million from three million donors who contributed over the Internet [4]. A grassroots movement supporting longshot Presidential candidate Ron Paul raised $4 million for him in a single day in 2007 [5].

These stories illustrate how networked communications have become integrated into our lives. Using these networks can be a double-edged sword, however. The Internet and the telephone system efficiently support our desire to interact with other people and accomplish a wide variety of everyday tasks. On other hand, some people use these technologies to lower the quality of our lives through such activities as trying to sell us products we don't want to buy, harassing us, or luring us into wasting our time with frivolous or counterproductive activities.

In this chapter, we explore moral issues associated with our use of the Internet and the telephone system. We begin by focusing on email, the most popular Internet application. After describing how email is routed, we discuss how the increase in unsolicited bulk email, or spam, has degraded the quality of email service.

The World Wide Web has proven to be the most popular way of organizing information on the Internet, and millions of people are using the Web-based social networking service Twitter to communicate with each other. Some governments are threatened by the way in which the Internet has made it so easy for people to access information and communicate with each other. We discuss the different kinds of censorship, the challenges posed to censorship by the Internet, and the morality of censorship.

Next we turn to the issue of freedom of expression. We explore its history in England and the United States, and examine how it became enshrined as the First Amendment to the United States Constitution. While the First Amendment protects freedom of expression, it is not an absolute right. The U.S. Supreme Court has ruled that personal freedom of expression must be balanced against the public good.

To ground our discussion of freedom of expression, we focus on the issue of children and inappropriate content. We discuss how Web filters work, and we summarize the Child Internet Protection Act, which requires Web filters to be installed in public libraries receiving federal funds. We use our set of workable ethical theories to evaluate the morality of this law. At the end of this section, we describe a relatively new phenomenon called sexting, in which children use cell phones to send sexually provocative images of themselves. Sexting provides a good example of how technology has created what James Moor would call a policy vacuum: a situation in which society has not yet determined what should be allowed, what should be forbidden, and what the legal consequences of forbidden actions should be.

The Internet provides new ways to commit fraud and deceive people. Identity thieves are using email and Web sites to capture credit card numbers and other personal information. Pedophiles have used chat rooms to arrange meetings with children. Police have responded to the pedophile threat with "sting" operations, which are themselves morally questionable. Web surfers must be aware that the Web contains a great deal of low-quality information. We describe one way in which search engines attempt to direct Web surfers to higher-quality sites.

Some people have used the Internet and/or the telephone network to bully other people. We describe a couple famous instances of cyberbullying and discuss the controversy that has arisen over proposed legislation to ban cyberbullying.

The widespread availability of the Internet has increased the number of people who spend 40 or more hours a week online. Some psychologists claim there are a vast number of Internet addicts. Others say these fears are overblown. In the last section of this chapter we discuss this issue and evaluate the problem of excessive Internet use from an ethical point of view.

3.2 Email and Spam

3.2.1 How Email Works

Email refers to messages embedded in files transferred from one computer to another via a telecommunications system. An **email address** uniquely indicates a virtual mailbox in cyberspace. Every email address has two parts. The first part (before the @ sign) identifies the individual user. The second part (after the @ sign) identifies the domain name. If you are a college student, your college may provide you with an email account, in which case some or all of your domain name is the domain name of your college. Another way to get an email account is through an Internet service provider (ISP). Each ISP has its own domain name.

Suppose you want to send an email to your friend Alyssa Allbright (login name AA) at East Dakota State University (domain name edsu.edu). You compose the message, indicate the recipient is AA@edsu.edu, and send the message. Your mail server uses the domain name system (DNS) to look up edsu.edu and find its Internet Protocol (IP) address. This address uniquely identifies a mail server at East Dakota State University. Next, if your email message to Alyssa is more than a few lines long, it is broken up into two or more pieces, called **packets.** At the front of each packet is the IP address of East Dakota State University.

There is a good chance that your mail server is not directly connected to Alyssa's mail server. The Internet contains thousands of interconnected routers that cooperate to get IP packets to their destination (Figure 3.1). Your server sends the packets to a router that is on the path to East Dakota State. It forwards the packets to the next router on the path, and so on, until the packets arrive at Alyssa's mail server. Her mail server reassembles the packets into an email message and puts it in her mailbox.

3.2.2 The Spam Epidemic

The growth of email has been phenomenal—well over a billion people now have email accounts [6]. Every day about 300 billion email messages are sent. Unfortunately, a significant percentage of this traffic consists of unsolicited bulk email, or **spam.**

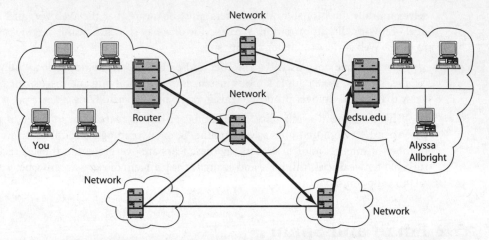

FIGURE 3.1 The Internet connects thousands of local area networks (LANs). Routers pass email and other messages from one LAN to another. Usually there are multiple possible routes.

Why is spam called spam? Brad Templeton, Chairman of the Board of the Electronic Frontier Foundation, traces the term back to the SPAM sketch from *The Final Rip Off* by Monty Python's Flying Circus, in which a group of Vikings drown out a cafe conversation by loudly and obnoxiously repeating the word "spam" [7]. In a similar way, legitimate email messages can get "drowned out" by spam.

The rise of spam corresponds with the transformation of the Internet from a non-commercial academic and research enterprise into a commercial global network. Early spam messages provoked Internet users and generated big headlines. For example, in 1994 Phoenix lawyers Laurence Canter and Martha Siegel sent an email advertising their immigration services to more than 9,000 electronic newsgroups. Canter and Siegel received tens of thousands of responses from outraged newsgroup users who did not appreciate seeing an off-topic, commercial message. *The New York Times* reported the incident with the headline, "An Ad (Gasp!) in Cyberspace." Canter and Siegel were undeterred. Their ad was successful in bringing them new clients. "We will definitely advertise on the Web again," Canter said. "I'm sure other businesses will be advertising on the network in the very near future" [8].

As recently as 2000, spam accounted for only about 8 percent of all email. It was still viewed as a problem for individuals managing their mailboxes. By 2009, about 90 percent of all emails were spam (Figure 3.2) [9]. Today, spam consumes a large percentage of the Internet's bandwidth and huge amounts of storage space on mail servers and individual computers. The cost to businesses is estimated at billions of dollars per year in wasted productivity.

The volume of spam is increasing because spam is effective. The principal advantage of spam is its low cost compared to other forms of advertising. For between $500 and $2,000, a company can send an advertisement to a million different email addresses.

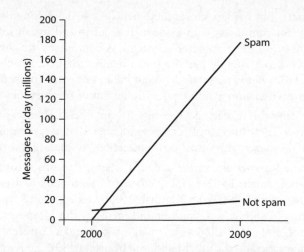

FIGURE 3.2 The increase in spam between 2000 and 2009. In 2000, spam accounted for 8 percent of all email. By 2009, the volume of email had increased 20-fold, and about 90 percent of email messages were spam.

Sending the same advertisement to a million addresses using the U.S. Postal Service costs at least $40,000 for the mailing list and $190,000 for bulk-rate postage. And that doesn't include the cost of the brochures! In other words, an email advertisement is more than 100 times cheaper than a traditional flyer sent out in the mail. The cost is so low that a company can make money even if only one in 100,000 recipients of the spam actually buys the product or service [10].

Where do spammers get email lists with millions of addresses? The Internet provides a variety sources of email addresses that can be harvested and sold to spammers. For example, email addresses often appear in Web sites, in chat-room conversations, and newsgroups. Some computer viruses gather email addresses stored in the address books of PCs and transmit these addresses to spammers.

Another way to garner email addresses is through dictionary attacks (also called directory harvest attacks). Spammers bombard Internet service providers with millions of emails containing made-up addresses, such as AdamA@isprovider.com, AdamB@isprovider.com, AdamC@isprovider.com, and so on. Of course, most of these emails will bounce back, because the addresses are no good. However, if an email *doesn't* bounce, the spammer knows there is a user with that email address and adds it to its mailing list.

Sometimes people voluntarily reveal their email address. Have you ever entered a contest on the Web? There is a good chance the fine print on the entry form said you agree to receive "occasional offers of products you might find valuable" from the company's marketing partners; in other words, spam [10]. Sign-ups for email lists often contain this fine print, too.

How can spammers send out so many email messages? About 90 percent of spam is sent out by bot herders: people who are able to take control of huge networks of computers. Bot herders create these networks by launching programs that search the Internet for computers with inadequate security and install software robot programs, called bots, on these vulnerable systems. A computer with the bot program installed on it is called a zombie because it can be directed by a remote computer to perform certain tasks. Bot herders can send out billions of email messages every day by dividing the address lists among hundreds of thousands of zombies they control [11].

To deal with this deluge, ISPs install spam filters to block spam from reaching users' mailboxes. These filters look for a large number of messages coming from the same email address, messages with suspicious subject lines, or messages with spam-like content.

Some Internet users have added "challenge-response" software to weed out spam that is not caught by their ISPs. When you send your first email message to one of these users, you'll receive an automated reply, asking you to type in the words or letters appearing in an image. If you respond correctly, the computer knows you're a human, not a bot, and it will allow your email message and all future messages to be delivered. Spam messages, on the other hand, will be blocked [9].

3.2.3 Need for Social–Technical Solutions

As we saw in Chapter 1, new technologies sometimes cause new social situations to emerge. The spam epidemic is an example of this phenomenon. The Internet allows people to send email messages for virtually no cost. Because a spammer's profits increase as the number of sent messages increases, every spammer has an incentive to send as many messages as possible.

The spam problem arose because the Internet and email technology developed without taking social expectations into account. The design of the Internet allows sophisticated users to disguise their own email addresses. Spammers take advantage of this loophole to send out millions of messages, knowing that unhappy recipients will not be able to respond. This is contrary to a fundamental social expectation: fairness. In order to be fair, communications should be two-way, not one-way [12].

3.2.4 Case Study: Ann the Acme Accountant

Ann is an accountant at Acme Corporation, a medium-sized firm with 50 employees. All of the employees work in the same building, and Ann knows all of them on a first-name basis. In fact, Ann distributes paychecks to Acme's employees at the end of every month.

Ann's daughter is a Girl Scout. During the annual Girl Scout cookie sale, Ann sent an email to all of the other Acme employees, inviting them to stop by her desk during a break and place orders. (There is no company rule prohibiting the use of the email system for personal emails.) Nine of the recipients were happy to get Ann's email, and they ordered an average of four boxes of cookies, but the other 40 recipients did not appreciate having to take the time to read and delete an unwanted message; half of them complained to a co-worker about Ann's action.

Did Ann do anything wrong?

KANTIAN ANALYSIS

According to the second formulation of the Categorical Imperative, we should always respect the autonomy of other people, treating them as ends in themselves and never only as the means to an end. The story provides evidence that Ann was not simply "using" her co-workers as the means to her end of making money for the Girl Scouts. She didn't misrepresent what she was doing. She didn't force anyone to buy the cookies or even read the entire email; employees not interested in Girl Scout cookies could simply delete Ann's message as soon as they read the subject line. Some people who received the email freely chose to buy some cookies. Therefore, what Ann did wasn't strictly wrong.

On the other hand, if Ann had found a way for those people interested in hearing about the Girl Scout cookie drive to "opt in" to her announcement, those people not interested in purchasing Girl Scout cookies would not have been bothered by her email. An "opt in" approach would have been better because it would have shown more respect for the autonomy of Ann's co-workers.

ACT UTILITARIAN ANALYSIS

We will do our evaluation in terms of dollars and cents, quantifying the benefits and costs of Ann's action. Let's begin with the benefits. A box of cookies costs $4 and provides $3 of profit to the Girl Scouts. Someone who buys a box of Girl Scout cookies understands it is a fundraising activity and is happy with what he receives for $4. Since the cost of $4 is matched with $4 of benefit, they cancel each other out in our analysis, and we do not have to worry about this factor any more. The average employee who participated in the sale purchased four boxes of cookies. Nine employees participated, which means Ann sold 36 boxes of cookies and provided $108 of benefit to the Girl Scouts.

Now let's look at the harms. The principal harm is going to be the time wasted by Acme's employees. Ann took orders and made deliveries during coffee or lunch breaks, rather than on company time, so our focus is on the 40 employees who did not appreciate getting Ann's solicitation. It's reasonable to assume that they spent an average of 15 seconds reading and deleting the message. That adds up to 10 minutes of lost productivity.

Half of the employees spent 5 minutes complaining about what Ann did with a co-worker. You can imagine the typical conversation. "What makes her so special?" "How does she get away with this kind of thing?" "If I did this for my kid, I'd get in trouble." Taking both the employee's time and the co-worker's time into account, Acme loses 10 minutes of productivity for each conversation. Multiplying 10 minutes by 20 conversations gives us 200 minutes.

The total time wasted equals 210 minutes or 3.5 hours. Assume the average Acme employee makes $20 per hour. The cost of the lost productivity is 3.5 hours times $20 per hour or $70.

The benefit of $108 exceeds the cost of $70, so we may conclude that Ann's action was good. We should note, however, that all of the benefit went to the Girls Scouts and all of the cost was borne by Acme Corporation. It would be perfectly reasonable if the owners of Acme Corporation concluded that this kind of activity was not in the best interests of the company and created a new policy forbidding the use of company email for cookie drives and other fundraisers.

RULE UTILITARIAN ANALYSIS

What would be the consequences if everyone used the company email system to solicit donations to their favorite causes? All the employees would receive many more messages unrelated to business. There would be plenty of grumbling among employees, lowering morale. Reading and deleting these solicitations would waste people's time, a definite harm. It's unlikely that any one cause would do well if everyone was trying to raise money for his or her own charity. There is a good chance the owner would become aware of this problem, and a logical response would be to ban employees from sending out this kind of solicitation. Because the harms are much greater than the benefits, it is wrong to use the company email system to solicit donations to a charity.

SOCIAL CONTRACT THEORY ANALYSIS

Acme Corporation does not have a prohibition against using the company's email system for personal business. You could say that by sending out her email solicitation, Ann was exercising her right to free speech. Of course, she did it in a way that many people might find obnoxious, because even if they did not choose to read her entire message, they had to take the time to scan the subject line and delete it. Unlike spammers, however, Ann did not disguise her identity as the sender, thereby providing unhappy recipients with the opportunity to respond to her email and voice their disapproval of her solicitation. If many of the 40 people who did not appreciate receiving her email sent a reply communicating their displeasure, then Ann got a taste of her own medicine by having to wade through a bunch of unwanted email messages, and she may choose a better method of advertising the Girls Scout cookie drive next year. From a social contract theory point of view, Ann did nothing wrong.

SUMMARY

Although the analyses of Ann's action from the perspectives of these four ethical theories reached different conclusions, it is clear she could have taken another course of action that would have been much less controversial. Since Ann has only 49 co-workers, it would not have been too difficult for her to find out who wanted to be notified the next time Girl Scouts were selling cookies. She could have put a sign-up sheet on her desk or the company bulletin board, for example. By notifying only those people who signed up, Ann's emails would have been solicited and personal. She could still take advantage of the efficiency of the email system without anyone objecting that she was "using" co-workers or contributing to lost productivity, meaning there would be much less chance of the company instituting a policy forbidding the use of its email system for fundraising activities.

3.3 The World Wide Web

3.3.1 Attributes of the Web

In the past decade the World Wide Web has become the world's most important information storage and retrieval technology. Its creator, Tim Berners-Lee, initially proposed the Web as a documentation system for CERN, the Swiss research center for particle physics, but the creation of easy-to-use Web browsers made the Web accessible to "ordinary" computer users as well [13]. The Web is a hypertext system: a flexible database of information that allows Web pages to be linked to each other in arbitrary fashion.

In Chapter 1 we examined the history of technological innovations that led to the creation of the Web. Here we focus on the attributes that have enabled the Web to become a global tool for information exchange.

1. *It is decentralized.*

   An individual or organization can add new information to the Web without asking for permission from a central authority.

2. *Every object on the Web has a unique address.*

   Any object can link to any other object by referencing its address. A Web object's address is called a **URL** (Uniform Resource Locator).

3. *It is based on the Internet.*

   Building on the Internet makes the Web accessible to people using a wide variety of different computers, such as Macintoshes, Windows systems, or Unix workstations.

The decentralized nature of the Web is one reason why it has grown so rapidly. It also makes the Web more difficult to control. Sometimes the lack of control is viewed as a good thing. For example, the existence of the Web makes it more difficult for an authoritarian government to control the flow of information. On the other hand, the lack of control is sometimes viewed as a weakness. An example of this is when parents attempt to shield their children from Web pages with violent or pornographic content.

3.3.2 How We Use the Web

Web browsers, with their point-and-click navigation and file transfer capabilities, have made the Internet accessible to people with little or no formal computer training. Today, millions of people use the Web for a wide variety of purposes. Here are just a few examples of how people are using the Web.

1. *We shop.*

   The Web enables us to view and order merchandise from the comfort of our homes. Forrester Research predicts that products purchased online in the United States will grow from 6 percent of all retail sales in 2009 to 8 percent in 2014 [14].

2. *We socialize.*

The Web has become a popular way for friends to keep in touch with each other. The most popular social network is Facebook, with more than 750 million active users in August 2011.

3. *We contribute content.*

A **wiki** is a Web site that allows multiple people to contribute and edit its content. The most famous wiki is Wikipedia, an online encyclopedia. Relying on the submissions of hundreds of thousands of volunteers, Wikipedia has become by far the largest encyclopedia in the world. More than three dozen languages are represented by at least 100,000 articles, but by far the most popular language is English, with more than 3.5 million articles written as of 2011. However, critics wonder about the quality of a reference work that allows anyone with a Web browser to contribute [15].

Other Web sites allow people to upload videos, photos, podcasts, or other digital content. Flickr members can post photos to share with family, friends, or the general public. Reddit combines posting of digital content with an evaluation feature. The most popular submissions rise to the top and are displayed more prominently.

4. *We blog.*

A **blog** (short for "Web log") is a personal journal or diary kept on the Web. Used as a verb, the word blog means to maintain such a journal. Blogs may contain plain text, images, audio clips, or video clips [16].

Some commentators use the term **Web 2.0** to refer to a change in the way people use the Web. Social networking services, wikis, Flickr, Reddit, and blogs illustrate that many people are now using the Web not simply to download content, but to build communities and upload and share content they have created.

5. *We learn.*

In 2001, the Massachusetts Institute of Technology launched its OpenCourseWare program, which has put about 2,000 courses online. Now more than 200 universities from around the globe are partnering with M.I.T. to share course materials on the OpenCourseWare site. These materials are meant to support the independent-learning community rather than replace a traditional university degree [17].

6. *We explore our roots.*

In the past, genealogists interested in accessing American immigration and census records had the choice between mailing in their requests and waiting for them to be processed or visiting the National Archives and examining the documents by hand. Now that the National Archives has put more than 50 million historical records online, the same searches can be performed remotely—and much more quickly—over the Internet (Figure 3.3) [18].

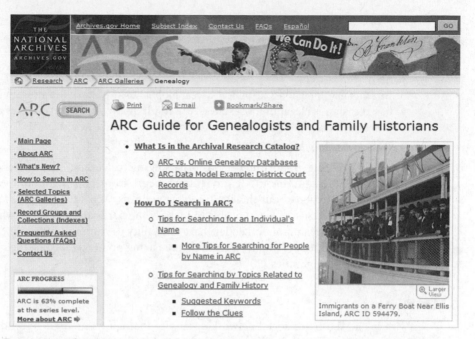

FIGURE 3.3 The U.S. National Archives and Records Administration has simplified the work of genealogists by putting millions of records online.

7. *We enter virtual worlds.*

An **online game** is a game played on a computer network that supports the simultaneous participation of multiple players. A **persistent online game** is an online game in which each player assumes the role of a character in a virtual world and the attributes of the character and the world persist beyond a single gaming session. The most popular persistent online game is *World of Warcraft*, with more than ten million monthly subscribers worldwide [19]. At times, the number of simultaneous players in China alone has reached one million [20].

Another hub of persistent online gaming is South Korea. Cybercafés (called **PC bangs** in South Korea) have large-screen monitors enabling spectators to watch the gameplay, which is full of virtual violence and mayhem. Some children spend up to 10 hours a day playing games, hoping to turn professional. Kim Hyun Soo, chairman of the Net Addiction Treatment Center, complains that "young people are losing their ability to relate to each other, except through games" [21]. We'll discuss the topic of Internet addiction in Section 3.8.

The phenomenon of global online gaming has created a real economy based on virtual worlds. Some people are making a living playing persistent online games. Chinese "gold farmers" who work 12 hours a day, 7 days a week can earn $3,000 a year killing monsters, harvesting virtual gold coins and artifacts, creating powerful avatars, and selling them over the Internet [22].

8. *We pay our taxes.*

Millions of Americans now file their federal income taxes through the Internal Revenue Service's Web site [23].

9. *We gamble.*

Internet gambling is a $20-billion-a-year global business [24]. Running an Internet-based casino is illegal in most states. As a result, many American emigrés are operating gambling Web sites from the Caribbean or Central America [25].

10. *We take humanitarian action.*

Kiva is Web site supporting person-to-person micro-lending. Kiva works with microfinance institutions to identify entrepreneurs from poor communities, and it posts information about these entrepreneurs on its Web site. People who wish to make an interest-free loan are able to identify the particular person to whom they would like to lend money. Lenders have the ability to communicate with the entrepreneurs and see the impact their loans are having on the recipients, their families, and their communities [26].

3.3.3 Twitter

Twitter is a Web-based social networking service that allows its users to send out text messages known as **tweets**. Tweets are limited to 140 characters because that's the maximum length of a cell phone text message. The service is popular because people who want their friends to know what they are doing find it more convenient to post a single tweet than to type a bunch of text messages. Many people also use Twitter as a blogging tool; they make their tweets public so that anyone can read them. Other Twitter members never post tweets, but they sign up to follow the tweets posted by other people they are interested in.

More than 200 million people use Twitter, making it one of the most popular Web services in the world [27]. Users posted 7,196 tweets per second at the conclusion of the exciting World Cup final soccer match between the United States and Japan in 2011 [28].

BUSINESS PROMOTION

When carpenter Curtis Kimball started a part-time business running a crème brûlée cart in San Francisco, he used Twitter to let people know the cart's location and the flavors of the day. Before long, he had attracted 5,400 followers. Business became so good he quit his day job in order to keep up with demand. Many tiny businesses with no money for advertising rely upon Twitter as their only marketing tool [29].

ARAB SPRING UPRISINGS

Twitter and Facebook played a highly visible role in the "Arab Spring" demonstrations in 2011 that led to revolutions in Tunisia and Egypt, a civil war in Libya, and protests in many other Arab countries. In the midst of the protests in Cairo that led to the resignation of President Hosni Murbarak, one protester tweeted: "We use Facebook to schedule the protests, Twitter to coordinate, and YouTube to tell the world" [30]. Arab news organization Al Jazeera has created a "Twitter Dashboard" indicating the level of tweeting activity in many Arab nations where there has been unrest [31].

Scholars of the Arab Spring uprisings point to an interesting phenomenon: People started using online social networks such as Twitter in order to keep up with their friends, but these interactions caused them to become politicized. Through these networks, bloggers met new people, became exposed to new ideas, and developed an interest in human rights [32].

Others think the role of social media in catalyzing social change has been overblown. They argue that social networks like Twitter and Facebook are great at building networks of people with weak connections to each other, but high-risk activism requires strong ties among the members of a hierarchical organization [33].

3.3.4 Too Much Governmental Control or Too Little?

The University of Toronto, Harvard Law School, the University of Cambridge, and Oxford University formed the OpenNet Initiative to research Internet filtering and surveillance around the world [34]. Their research has revealed that the level of filtering by governments has increased rapidly in the past few years. Governments limit access to the Internet in a variety of ways.

One approach is to make the Internet virtually inaccessible. The governments of Burma (Myanmar), Cuba, and North Korea make it difficult for ordinary citizens to use the Internet to communicate with the rest of the world [35, 36, 37].

In other countries, Internet access is easier, but still carefully controlled. Saudi Arabians gained access to the Internet in 1999, after the government installed a centralized control center outside Riyadh. Virtually all Internet traffic flows through this control center, which blocks pornography sites, gambling sites, and many other pages deemed to be offensive to Islam or the government of Saudi Arabia [38]. Blocked sites and pages are from such diverse categories as Christian evangelism, women's health and sexuality issues, music and movies, gay rights, Middle Eastern politics, and information about ways to circumvent Web filtering.

The Chinese government has blocked access to the Internet during times of social unrest. For example, in July 2009, China responded to ethnic riots in the autonomous region of Xinjiang by turning off Internet service to the entire region for ten months [39, 40].

China has also built one of the world's most sophisticated Web filtering systems [41]. The Great Firewall of China prevents Chinese citizens from accessing certain Internet content by blocking messages coming from blacklisted sites. The government employs human censors to identify sites that should be blacklisted [42]. Among the Web sites blacklisted by the government include those containing pornography, those associated with the Dalai Lama or the Falun Gong, those referring to the 1989 military crackdown, and those run by certain news organizations, such as Voice of America and

BBC News. Before the 2008 Summer Olympics, the International Olympic Committee assured journalists that they would have unfettered access to the Internet during their stay in Beijing, but once the journalists arrived in Beijing, they discovered that many sites were blocked. The International Olympic Committee admitted that it had agreed to allow to be blocked sensitive sites "not considered Games related" [43].

Some contend that blogs and nongovernmental Web sites are eroding the Chinese government's ability to restrict the communications of its citizens [42], but the government has not given up. The government continues to shut down Web sites and censor blogs that it finds contrary to the interests of the state. In May 2009, the government told all PC makers that they would need to install Web-content filtering software on all PCs sold in China beginning July 1, 2009. The software, called Green Dam/Youth Escort, is designed to prevent a Web browser from displaying Web pages from blacklisted sites. As the government updated its list of banned sites, computers would automatically download the updated lists. The proposal did not sit well with many Chinese citizens, who protested the decision on blogs and social networking sites. They argued that although the government claimed the software would be used only to block access to pornographic Web sites, its real use would be to block politically sensitive sites. Computer experts critized the Green Dam/Youth Escort software for making personal computers vulnerable to intrusions from hackers. At the end of June 2009, the Chinese government declared that it was delaying—but not cancelling—the requirement that all new PCs come equipped with Green Dam/Youth Escort software [44, 45, 46]. In August 2009, the government retreated further, stating that while public computers in schools and Internet cafes must run Green Dam/Youth Escort, its use among private computer owners would be voluntary [47].

Meanwhile, Western nations have different standards about what is acceptable and what is not. For example, Germany forbids access to any neo-Nazi Web site, but Web surfers in the United States can access many such sites.

Political satire and pornography are easily available through American ISPs. Americans are used to political satire, but many citizens are concerned about the corrupting influence of pornography, particularly with respect to minors. Since 1996 the U.S. Congress has passed three laws aimed at restricting access of children to sexually explicit materials on the Web: the Communications Decency Act, the Child Online Protection Act, and the Children's Internet Protection Act. The first two laws were ruled unconstitutional by the U.S. Supreme Court; the third was upheld by the Supreme Court in June 2003.

3.4 Censorship

Censorship is the attempt to suppress or regulate public access to material considered offensive or harmful. Historically, most censorship has been exercised by governments and religious institutions. For example, Roman censors banished the poets Ovid and Juvenal for their writings. During the Middle Ages the Inquisition suppressed the publication of many books, including the work of Galileo Galilei.

Censorship became a much more complicated issue with the invention of the printing press. The printing press broke the virtual monopoly held by governments and religious institutions on distributing material to a large audience, and the increase in printed material increased the number of literate people. For the first time, private individuals could broadcast their ideas to others on a wide scale.

In Western democracies, the gradual separation of church and state has left the government as the sole institution responsible for censorship. In other parts of the world, such as the Middle East, religious institutions continue to play a significant role in determining which material should be accessible to the public.

3.4.1 Direct Censorship

Direct censorship has three forms: government monopolization, prepublication review, and licensing and registration.

The first form of direct censorship is government monopolization. In the former Soviet Union, for example, the government owned all the television stations, radio stations, and newspapers. Private organizations could not even own a photocopy machine. Government monopolization is an effective way to suppress the flow of information. Modern computer and communication technology makes government monopolization much more difficult than it has been in the past.

Prepublication review is the second form of direct censorship. This form of censorship is essential for material the government wishes to keep secret, such as information about its nuclear weapons program. Most governments have laws restricting the publication of information that would harm the national security. In addition, autocratic governments typically block publication of material deemed injurious to the reputations of their rulers.

The third form of direct censorship is licensing and registration. This form of censorship is typically used to control media with limited bandwidth. For example, there are a limited number of radio and television stations that can be accommodated on the electromagnetic spectrum. Hence a radio or television station must obtain a license to broadcast at a particular frequency. Licensing invites censorship. For example, the U.S. Federal Communications Commission has banned the use of certain four-letter words. This led to a challenge that went all the way to the U.S. Supreme Court, as we will see in Section 3.5.3.

3.4.2 Self–Censorship

Perhaps the most common form of censorship is self-censorship: a group deciding for itself not to publish material. In some countries a publisher may censor itself in order to avoid persecution. For example, after U.S.-led forces toppled the regime of Saddam Hussein in April 2003, CNN's chief news executive Eason Jordan admitted that CNN had suppressed negative information about the actions of the Iraqi government for more than a decade in order to keep CNN's Baghdad bureau open and protect Iraqi employees of CNN [48].

In other countries, publishers may want to maintain good relations with government officials. Publications compete with each other for access to information. Often this information is available only from government sources. Publishers know that if they offend the government, their reporters may not be given access to as much information as reporters for rival publications, putting them at a competitive disadvantage. This knowledge can lead a "free" press to censor itself.

Publishers have adopted ratings systems as a way of helping people decide if they (or their children) should access particular offerings. For example, television stations in the United States broadcast shows with "mature content" late in the evening. Voluntary rating systems help people decide if they (or their children) will see a movie, watch a television show, or listen to a CD.

The Web does not have a universally accepted ratings system. Some Web sites practice a form of labeling. For example, the home page may warn the user that the site contains nudity and require the user to click on an "I agree" button to enter the site. However, other sites have no such warnings. People who stumble onto these sites are immediately confronted with images and text they may find offensive.

3.4.3 Challenges Posed by the Internet

Five characteristics of the Internet make censorship more difficult:

1. *Unlike traditional one-to-many broadcast media, the Internet supports many-to-many communications.*

   While it is relatively easy for a government to shut down a newspaper or a radio station, it is very difficult for a government to prevent an idea from being published on the Internet, where millions of people have the ability to post Web pages.

2. *The Internet is dynamic.*

   Millions of new computers are being connected to the Internet each year.

3. *The Internet is huge.*

   There is simply no way for a team of human censors to keep track of everything that is posted on the Web. While automated tools are available, they are fallible. Hence, any attempt to control access to material stored on the Internet cannot be 100 percent effective.

4. *The Internet is global.*

   National governments have limited authority to restrict activities happening outside their borders.

5. *It is hard to distinguish between children and adults on the Internet.*

   How can an "adult" Web site verify the age of someone attempting to enter the site?

3.4.4 Ethical Perspectives on Censorship

KANT'S VIEWS ON CENSORSHIP

As a thinker in the tradition of the Enlightenment, Kant's motto was, "Have courage to use your own reason" [49]. Kant asks the rhetorical question, "Why don't people think for themselves?" and answers it: "Laziness and cowardice are the reasons why so great a portion of mankind, after nature has long since discharged them from external direction, nevertheless remain under lifelong tutelage, and why it is so easy for others to set themselves up as their guardians. It is so easy not to be of age. If I have a book which understands for me, a pastor who has a conscience for me, a physician who decides my diet, and so forth, I need not trouble myself. I need not think, if I can only pay—others will readily undertake the irksome work for me" [49].

The Enlightenment was a reaction to the institutional control over thought held by the aristocracy and the Church. Kant believed he was living in a time in which the obstacles preventing people from exercising their own reason were being removed. He opposed censorship as a backward step.

MILL'S VIEWS ON CENSORSHIP

John Stuart Mill also championed freedom of expression. He gave four reasons why freedom of opinion, and freedom of expression of opinion, were necessary.

First, none of us is infallible. All of us are capable of error. If we prevent someone from voicing their opinion, we may actually be silencing the voice of truth.

Second, while the opinion expressed by someone may be erroneous, it may yet contain a kernel of truth. In general, the majority opinion is not the whole truth. We ought to let all opinions be voiced so that all parts of the truth are heard.

Third, even if the majority opinion should happen to be the whole truth, it is in the clash of ideas that this truth is rationally tested and validated. The whole truth left untested is simply a prejudice.

Fourth, an opinion that has been tested in the fire of a free and open discourse is more likely to have a "vital effect on the character and conduct" [50].

Therefore, Mill, like Kant, fundamentally supported the free exchange of ideas with the conviction that good ideas would prevail over bad ones. Applying their philosophy to the World Wide Web, it seems they would support the free exchange of opinions and oppose any kind of government censorship of opinions.

MILL'S PRINCIPLE OF HARM

However, a lack of government censorship can also lead to harm. Under what circumstances should the government intervene? Mill proposed the principle of harm as a way of deciding when an institution should intervene in the conduct of an individual.

PRINCIPLE OF HARM

"The only ground on which intervention is justified is to prevent harm to others; the individual's own good is not a sufficient condition" [50].

In other words, the government should not get involved in the private activities of individuals, even if the individuals are doing something to harm themselves. Only if individuals' activities are harming other people should the government step in.

The principle of harm can be used to explain the position of most Western democratic governments with respect to censoring pornographic material depicting adults. Some ethicists conclude it is not wrong for adults to view pornography depicting adults. Others hold that this activity is immoral. If the activity is immoral, it is more certain the harm is being done to the individual consumer; less certain is how much harm is being done to other people. Hence, the principle of harm can be used as an argument why the government should not be trying to prevent adults from using pornography depicting adults.

3.5 Freedom of Expression

In the United States, freedom of expression is one of the most cherished—and most controversial—rights. In this section, we explain the history behind the adoption of the First Amendment to the United States Constitution. We also explore why the freedom of expression has not been treated as an absolute right.

3.5.1 History

At the time of the American Revolution, any criticism of government was seen as a threat to public order and could result in fines and/or imprisonment. Restrictions on freedom of speech in England date back to 1275 and a law called De Scandalis Magnatum. According to this law, a person could be imprisoned for spreading stories about the King that could have the effect of weakening the loyalty of his subjects. The scope of the law became much broader through numerous revisions over the next two centuries. Eventually it encompassed seditious words and words spoken against a wide variety of government officials, including justices [51].

The De Scandalis Magnatum was administered by the Court of Star Chamber, or "Star Chamber" for short. The Star Chamber reported directly to the King, and it did not have to obey traditional rules of evidence. Rulings of the Star Chamber demonstrated that a person could be convicted for making a verbal insult or for something written in a private letter. The Star Chamber was abolished in 1641, but the law continued to be enforced through Common Law Courts [51].

At the end of the eighteenth century, freedom of the press in England and its colonies meant freedom to print without a license. In other words, there were no **prior restraints** on publication. People could publish what they pleased. However, those who published material found to be seditious or libelous would face severe consequences [51].

The law against libel simply considered if the material printed was harmful; arguing that the information was true was not relevant to the proceedings and could not be used in a publisher's defense. Between 1760 and the end of the American Revolution, about 50 people were successfully prosecuted for libel. To prevent such prosecutions from continuing, most states adopted bills of rights after gaining independence from England [51].

In May 1787, delegates from the thirteen states gathered in Philadelphia to revise the Articles of Confederation. Soon they were drafting a completely new Constitution. Delegate George Mason, author of the Virginia Declaration of Rights, strongly opposed the proposed Constitution because it contained no declaration of the rights of the citizens. Patrick Henry and other political leaders shared Mason's objections [51].

While the proposed Constitution was ratified by all thirteen states, most state legislatures adopted the Constitution with the expectation that Congress would offer amendments addressing the human rights concerns brought up by the opponents of the Constitution. During the first Congress, James Madison proposed 12 such amendments. All 12 of these amendments were sent to the states for ratification. Of these 12 amendments, 10 were quickly ratified. Today, these 10 amendments are commonly known as the Bill of Rights. The first of these amendments, the one Madison considered most essential, was the one guaranteeing freedom of speech and freedom of the press [51].

~

FIRST AMENDMENT TO THE UNITED STATES CONSTITUTION

Congress shall make no law respecting an establishment of religion, or prohibiting the free exercise thereof; or abridging the freedom of speech, or of the press; or the right of the people peaceably to assemble, and to petition the government for a redress of grievances.

~

3.5.2 Freedom of Expression Not an Absolute Right

The primary purpose of the First Amendment's free speech guarantee is political. Free speech allows an open discussion of public issues. It helps make government responsive to the will of the people [52].

However, the First Amendment right to free expression is not limited to political speech. Nonpolitical speech is also covered (Figure 3.4). There are good reasons for protecting nonpolitical as well as political speech. First, it is sometimes hard to draw the line between the two. Asking a judge to make the distinction turns it into a political decision. Second, society can benefit from nonpolitical as well as political speech. Hence, the free speech guarantee of the First Amendment also promotes scientific and artistic expression. For the same reason, the definition of "speech" encompasses more than words. Protected "speech" includes art and certain kinds of conduct, such as burning an American flag [53].

Decisions by the U.S. Supreme Court have made clear that freedom of expression is not an absolute right. Instead, the private right to freedom of expression must be balanced against the public good. Those who abuse this freedom and harm the public may be punished. For example, protection is not given to "libel, reckless or calculated lies, slander, misrepresentation, perjury, false advertising, obscenity and profanity, solicitation of crime, and personal abuse or 'fighting' words," because these actions do not serve the ends of the First Amendment [52].

FIGURE 3.4 Jeremy Jaynes was convicted under Virginia law for sending millions of spam messages. His conviction was overturned by the Supreme Court of Virginia because the anti-spam law was too broad and also prohibited the anonymous transmission of unsolicited bulk emails "containing political, religious or other speech protected by the First Amendment to the United States Constitution" [54]. (AP Photo/Loudoun County Sheriff's office)

Various restrictions on freedom of speech are justified because of the greater public good that results. For example, U.S. law prohibits cigarette advertising on television because cigarette smoking has detrimental effects on public health. Some cities use zoning laws to concentrate adult bookstores in a single part of town because the presence of adult bookstores lowers property values and increases crime.

3.5.3 *FCC v. Pacifica Foundation et al.*

To illustrate limits to First Amendment protections, we consider the decision of the U.S. Supreme Court in the case of *Federal Communications Commission v. Pacifica Foundation et al.*

In 1973, George Carlin recorded a performance made in front of a live audience in California. One track on the resulting record is a 12-minute monologue called "Filthy Words." In the monologue Carlin lists seven words that "you couldn't say on the public, ah, airwaves, um, the ones you definitely wouldn't say, ever" [55]. The audience laughs as

Carlin spends the rest of the monologue creating colloquialisms from the list of banned words.

On the afternoon of October 30, 1973, counterculture radio station WBAI in New York aired "Filthy Words" after warning listeners the monologue contained "sensitive language which might be regarded as offensive to some" [56]. A few weeks after the broadcast, the Federal Communications Commission (FCC) received a complaint from a man who had heard the broadcast on his car radio in the presence of his son. In response to this complaint, the FCC issued a declaratory order and informed Pacifica Foundation (the operator of WBAI) that the order would be placed in the station's license file. The FCC warned Pacifica Foundation that further complaints could lead to sanctions.

Pacifica sued the FCC, and the resulting legal battle reached the U.S. Supreme Court. In 1978, the Supreme Court ruled, in a 5–4 decision, that the FCC did not violate the First Amendment [56]. The majority opinion states, "[O]f all forms of communication, it is broadcasting that has received the most limited First Amendment protection." There are two reasons why broadcasters have less protection than book sellers or theater owners:

1. *"Broadcast media have a uniquely pervasive presence in the lives of all Americans."*

   Offensive, indecent material is broadcast into the privacy of citizens' homes. Since people can change stations or turn their radios on or off at any time, prior warnings cannot completely protect people from being exposed to offensive material. While someone may turn off the radio after hearing something indecent, that does not undo a harm that has already occurred.

2. *"Broadcasting is uniquely accessible to children, even those too young to read."*

   In contrast, restricting children's access to offensive or indecent material is possible in bookstores and movie theaters.

The majority emphasized that its ruling was a narrow one and that the context of the broadcast was all-important. The time of day at which the broadcast occurred (2 p.m.) was an important consideration, because that affected the composition of the listening audience.

3.5.4 Case Study: Kate's Blog

Kate is a journalism major who maintains a popular blog focusing on campus life. Kate attends a private birthday party in someone's apartment for her friend Jerry, a college student active in the Whig Party on campus. Someone gives Jerry a Tory Party T-shirt as a gag gift, and Jerry puts it on. Kate uses her cell phone to get a picture of Jerry wearing the T-shirt when he is looking the other way. She posts the photo on her blog without asking him permission. In the blog she identifies Jerry and explains the context in which the photo was taken.

The story is read by many people both on and off campus. The next day, Jerry confronts Kate, yells at her for posting the photo, and demands that she remove it from her Web site. Kate complies with Jerry's request by removing the photo, and the two of them remain friends. As a result of the incident, Jerry becomes more popular on campus, and the number of people who read Kate's blog increases.

Was it wrong for Kate to post the picture of Jerry on her blog without first getting his permission?

KANTIAN ANALYSIS

By uploading Jerry's photo to her blog without first asking his permission, Kate didn't respect Jerry's autonomy. Instead, she treated him as a means to her end of increasing the readership of her Web site. Therefore, her action was wrong according to the second formulation of the Categorical Imperative.

SOCIAL CONTRACT THEORY ANALYSIS

The birthday party was held in the apartment of one of Jerry's friends. In this private setting and among friends Jerry had a legitimate expectation that what happened during the party would not be broadcast to the world. By secretly taking a photo of Jerry doing something out of character and posting that photo on her blog, Kate violated Jerry's right to privacy. For this reason Kate's action was wrong.

ACT UTILITARIAN ANALYSIS

We need to determine the positive and negative consequences of Kate's action on the two people involved. Kate increased the popularity of her blog, which is precisely the positive outcome she wanted. Jerry's anger at Kate shows that he was hurt and upset by what she did, but after he confronted her, she removed the photo from her Web site and they reconciled. Therefore, while the intensity of this negative consequence to Jerry was intense, its duration was brief. As a result of the posting, Jerry became more popular on campus, a very good thing for someone active in campus politics. Jerry had Kate to thank for this boost in his popularity, further quenching the unhappiness he initially felt when he learned what she had done. We conclude that the short-term consequences for both Kate and Jerry were positive.

The long-term consequences are difficult to determine. It is possible that the photo could land in the wrong hands and be used to discredit Jerry some day in the future, but this would depend on many factors. Jerry is currently politically active. Is he going to stay active in Whig politics after he graduates from college? The photo was only on the Web for a day. Did anyone download it? If so, what is the chance that some day the photo will fall into the hands of someone who wants to make Jerry look bad?

An important part of a utilitarian analysis is looking at the certainty of each consequence: in other words, the probability that it will happen. The short-term consequences of Kate's action are certainly positive for both Kate and Jerry. The long-term negative consequences, if any, are not certain at all. We conclude Kate did nothing wrong by posting Jerry's photo on her blog.

RULE UTILITARIAN ANALYSIS

Let's consider what would happen if everyone were constantly taking photos of everyone they bumped into and posting them on the Web. There would be some positive consequences. It would be easier for people to see what their friends were up to. People might be more reluctant to engage in illegal activities if they thought photo or video evidence might appear on the Web. There would also be a variety of negative consequences. Once people started to feel as if they were always being photographed, they would become self-conscious, making it more difficult for them to simply be themselves. People would be less free to take off their public persona and express their true feelings. Inevitably people would post photos that caused hard feelings and led to strained relationships. Ultimately, the negative consequences seem to be more weighty than the positive consequences, and we conclude Kate's action was wrong.

SUMMARY

The analyses from the perspectives of Kantianism, social contract theory, and rule utilitarianism all conclude it was wrong for Kate to post the photo without asking Jerry's permission, though each analysis uses a different line of reasoning to reach that conclusion. Kate imagined (correctly, as it turns out) that Jerry would be angry if she took a photo of him wearing the Tory Party T-shirt, and that is why she took the photo when he wasn't looking. Kate figured it would be better to beg for forgiveness than ask for permission, but what she did was cut Jerry out of a decision that affected both of them. This is no way to treat anybody, much less a friend. Kate would have been better off trying to persuade Jerry that putting the photo on her blog would be to their mutual advantage, posting the image only after obtaining his consent.

3.6 Children and Inappropriate Content

Many parents and guardians believe they ought to protect their children from exposure to pornographic and violent materials. A few years ago, the center of concern was the Web, and a large software industry sprang up to provide browsers with the ability to block inappropriate images. Now, camera-equipped cell phones are becoming commonplace, and some parents are being forced to confront the unpleasant reality that their children have emailed sexually provocative images of themselves to friends or even strangers.

3.6.1 Web Filters

A **Web filter** is a piece of software that prevents certain Web pages from being displayed by your browser. While you are running your browser, the filter runs as a background process, checking every page your browser attempts to load. If the filter determines that the page is objectionable, it prevents the browser from displaying it.

Filters can be installed on individual computers, or an ISP may provide filtering services for its customers. Programs designed to be installed on individual computers, such as Cyber Sentinel, eBlaster, and Spector PRO, can be set up to email parents as soon as they detect an inappropriate Web page [57]. America Online's filtering service is called AOL Guardian. It enables parents to set the level of filtering on their children's accounts. It also allows parents to look at logs showing the pages their children have visited.

Typical filters use two different methods to determine if a page should be blocked. The first method is to check the URL of the page against a "blacklist" of objectionable sites. If the Web page comes from a blacklisted site, it is not displayed. The second method is to look for combinations of letters or words that may indicate a site has objectionable content.

Neither of these methods is foolproof. The Web contains millions of pages containing pornography, and new sites continue to be created at a high rate, so any blacklist of pornographic sites will be incomplete by definition. Some filters sponsored by conservative groups have blacklisted sites associated with liberal political causes, such as those sponsored by the National Organization of Women and gay and lesbian groups. The algorithms used to identify objectionable words and phrases can cause Web filters to block out legitimate Web pages.

CALVIN AND HOBBES © 1990 Watterson. Dist. By UNIVERSAL UCLICK.
Reprinted with permission. All rights reserved.

3.6.2 Child Internet Protection Act

In March 2003, the Supreme Court weighed testimony in the case of *United States v. American Library Association*. The question: Can the government require libraries to install antipornography filters in return for receiving federal funds for Internet access?

More than 14 million people access the Internet through public library computers. About one-sixth of the libraries in the United States have already installed filtering software on at least some of their computers. The Child Internet Protection Act requires that libraries receiving federal funds to provide Internet access to its patrons must prevent children from getting access to visual depictions of obscenity and child pornography. The law allows adults who desire access to a blocked page to ask a librarian to remove the filter.

In his testimony before the Supreme Court, Solicitor General Theodore Olson argued that since libraries don't offer patrons X-rated magazines or movies, they should not be obliged to give them access to pornography over the Internet.

Paul Smith, representing the American Library Association and the American Civil Liberties Union, argued that in their attempt to screen out pornography, filters block tens of thousands of inoffensive pages. He added that requiring adults to leave the workstation, find a librarian, and ask for the filter to be turned off would be disruptive to their research and would stigmatize them.

In June 2003, the U.S. Supreme Court upheld CIPA, ruling 6–3 that anti-pornography filters do not violate First Amendment guarantees [58]. Chief Justice William Rehnquist wrote, "A public library does not acquire Internet terminals in order to create a public forum for Web publishers to express themselves, any more than it collects books in order to provide a public forum for the authors of books to speak . . . Most libraries already exclude pornography from their print collections because they deem it inappropriate for inclusion" [59].

3.6.3 Ethical Evaluations of CIPA

In this section, we evaluate CIPA from the perspectives of Kantianism, act utilitarianism, and social contract theory.

KANTIAN EVALUATION

We have already covered Kant's philosophical position against censorship. He optimistically believed that allowing people to use their own reason would lead to society's gradual enlightenment. In this case, however, the focus is narrower. Rather than talking about censorship in general, let's look at CIPA in particular.

The goal of CIPA is to protect children from the harm caused by exposure to pornography. The way the goal is being implemented is through Web filters. Studies have demonstrated that Web filters do not block all pornographic material, but do block some nonpornographic Web pages. Some nonpornographic information posted on the Web will not be easily accessible at libraries implementing government-mandated Web filters. The people posting this information did not consent to their ideas being blocked. Hence, the decision to require the use of Web filters treats the creators of non-offensive but blocked Web pages solely as means to the end of restricting children's access to pornographic materials. This analysis leads us to conclude that CIPA is wrong.

ACT UTILITARIAN EVALUATION

Our second evaluation of CIPA is from an act utilitarian point of view. What are the consequences of passing CIPA?

1. While not all children access the Web in public libraries, and while Web filtering software is imperfect, it is probable that enacting CIPA will result in fewer children being exposed to pornography, which is good.

2. Because Web filters are imperfect, people will be unable to access some legitimate Web sites. As a result, Web browsers in libraries will be less useful as research tools, a harmful consequence.

3. Adult patrons who ask for filters to be removed may be stigmatized (rightfully or not) as people who want to view pornography, a harm to them.

4. Some blocked sites may be associated with minority political views, reducing freedom of thought and expression, which is harmful.

Whenever we perform the utilitarian calculus and find some benefits and some harms, we must decide how to weigh them. This is a good time to think about utilitarian philosopher Jeremy Bentham's seven attributes. In particular, how many people are in each affected group? What is the probability the good or bad event will actually happen? How soon is the event likely to occur? How intense will the experience be? To what extent is the pain not diluted by pleasure, or vice versa? How long will it last? How likely is the experience to lead to a similar experience? Actually performing the calculus for CIPA is up to each person's judgment. Different people could reach opposite conclusions about whether enacting CIPA is the right thing for the U.S. government to do.

SOCIAL CONTRACT THEORY EVALUATION

In social contract theory, morally binding rules are those rules mutually agreed to in order to allow social living [60]. Freedom of thought and expression is prized. According to John Rawls, "liberty of conscience is to be limited only when there is a reasonable expectation that not doing so will damage the public order which the government should maintain" [61].

It would be difficult to gain consensus around the idea that the private viewing of pornography makes social living no longer possible. For this reason, the private use of pornography is considered to be outside the social contract and nobody else's business. However, when we think about the availability of pornography in public libraries, the issue gets thornier.

Some argue that allowing people to view pornography in a public place demeans women, denying them dignity as equal persons [62]. On the other hand, we know that filtering software is imperfect. In the past it has been used to promote a conservative political agenda by blocking sites associated with other viewpoints [63, 64]. Hence it reduces the free exchange of ideas, limiting the freedoms of thought and expression. For some adults, public libraries represent their only opportunity to access the Web for no cost. In order to be treated as free and equal citizens, they should have the same Web access as people who have Internet access from their homes. If Web filters are in place, their access is not equal because they must ask for permission to have the filters disabled. Finally, while most people would agree that children should not be exposed to pornographic material, it would be harder to convince reasonable people that social living would no longer be possible if children happened to see pornography in a library.

Our analysis from the point of view of social contract theory has produced arguments both supporting and opposing the Children's Internet Protection Act. However, installing filters does not seem to be necessary to preserve the public order. For this reason, the issue is outside the social contract and freedom of conscience should be given precedence.

3.6.4 Sexting

Sexting refers to sending sexually suggestive text messages or emails containing nude or nearly nude photographs [65]. In a 2009 survey of 655 American teenagers conducted by Cox Communications, 9 percent said they had sent a sext at least once, 17 percent said they had received a sext at least once, and 3 percent said they had forwarded a sext at least once. Of the teens who had sent sexts, 11 percent admitted to having sent a sext to someone they didn't know. Interestingly, when those who had sent sexts were asked if a photo they had sent was ever forwarded to someone they didn't want to see it, only 2 percent said "yes," but when the same group of people was asked if their friends ever had photos forwarded to people they didn't want to see it, 30 percent answered "yes" [65].

Although sexting is a relatively recent phenomenon, there are already plenty of stories in the mainstream media about the serious impact it is having on people's lives. Here are three recent stories.

Ohio high school student Jesse Logan sent nude pictures of herself to her boyfriend. When they broke up, the ex-boyfriend distributed the photos to other girls in her high school. Jesse endured months of harassment from her high school classmates and began skipping classes on a daily basis. After attending the funeral of another classmate who committed suicide, Jesse went home and hanged herself [66].

After Phillip Alpert got into an argument with his 16-year-old girlfriend, he emailed a nude photo of her to dozens of her friends and family members. "It was a stupid thing I did because I was upset and tired and it was the middle of the night and I was an immature kid," Alpert said upon reflection. The Orlando, Florida, police arrested Alpert, who had just turned 18, charging him with sending child pornography, a felony. It didn't matter that Alpert's girlfriend was 16, that they had dated for two-and-a-half years, and that she was the one who had originally sent the photo to him. Alpert was sentenced to five years probation and required to register with the state of Florida as a sex offender. He will remain a registered sex offender until he is 43 years old [67].

Ting-Yi Oei, a 59-year-old assistant principal at Freedom High School in South Riding, Virgina, was asked to investigate rumors that students were distributing nude photographs on their cell phones. His investigation led to a 16-year-old boy, who admitted to having a provocative photo on his cell phone. The photo showed the torso of a 17-year-old girl wearing panties, with her arms mostly covering her breasts. Oei showed the image to the principal, who told him to keep a copy on his computer as evidence. Two weeks later, the same boy got in trouble again, and Oei suspended him for two weeks. When Oei met with the boy's mother, he told her about the earlier photo incident. The boy's mother was upset that Oei hadn't immediately told her about the photo, and she demanded that Oei revoke her son's suspension. When Oei refused, the mother went to the police and told them about the photo. Sheriff's investigators came to the school and found the photo of the girl on Oei's computer. County prosecutor James Plowman gave Oei an ultimatum: resign or face felony charges for possession of child pornography. Plowman's assistant told the press, "We just feel very strongly that this is not someone who should be in the Loudoun County school system." Oei refused to resign, and in August 2008, a grand jury indicted him for possession of child pornography. The school district removed him from his position as vice principal and reassigned him to a job at a testing center. Oei had to take out a second mortgage on his house to pay legal expenses. In April 2009, Loudoun Circuit Court Judge Thomas Horne dismissed the charges, noting that nudity alone is not sufficient to categorize an image of a minor as child pornography. Though never convicted, Oei ended up deeply in debt and with a tarnished reputation, unsure if he would ever return to his former position at the high school [68].

There appears to be a widespread sentiment that child pornography laws should not be used to prosecute teenagers who are caught sexting. In 2009, legislation was introduced in a number of state legislatures that would make sexting among teenagers a misdemeanor [69].

3.7 Breaking Trust on the Internet

3.7.1 Identity Theft

Dorothy Denning defines **identity theft** as "the misuse of another person's identity, such as name, Social Security number, driver's license, credit card numbers, and bank account numbers. The objective is to take actions permitted to the owner of the identity, such as withdraw funds, transfer money, charge purchases, get access to information, or issue documents and letters under the victim's identity" [70].

The leading form of identity theft in United States is credit card fraud. Identity thieves either take out a new credit card in someone else's name or commandeer an existing account [71]. By changing the billing address of existing accounts, a thief can run up large debts before the victim becomes aware of the problem. These activities can blemish the target's credit history. As a result, victims of identity theft may have applications for credit cards, mortgage loans, and even employment denied. If the impostor shows false credentials to the police, the victim may even be saddled with a false criminal record or outstanding arrest warrants.

Financial institutions contribute to the problem of identity theft by making it easy for people to open up new accounts. Since information brokers on the Web are selling driver's license numbers, Social Security numbers, and credit card information, it's easy for an identity thief to gather a great deal of information about another person. Assuming another person's identity is made simpler by banks allowing people to open accounts online [72].

The number of Americans victimized by identity theft decreased from about 11 million in 2009 to 8 million in 2010, but the average loss increased from $387 to $631 [73]. Fortunately, United States law says that a consumer's liability for losses due to credit card fraud are limited to $50 if reported promptly. Most victims end up paying nothing out-of-pocket because their banks and credit card companies offer zero-liability fraud protection [73]. However, victims of identity theft typically spend more than 30 hours resolving the problem [73].

Most cases of identity theft are not the result of someone using computers to break into a database containing information about a target. Instead, identity thieves are much more likely to use low-tech methods to gain access to the personal information they need. A 2008 survey of identity theft victims revealed that in 43 percent of the cases, the theft was the result of a lost or stolen wallet, credit card, checkbook, or another physical document [74]. Some identity thieves engage in **dumpster diving**—looking for personal information in garbage cans or recycling bins. Old bills, bank statements, and credit card statements contain a wealth of personal information, including names, addresses, and account numbers. Another simple way to get information is through **shoulder surfing**—looking over the shoulders of people filling out forms.

In 19 percent of the cases surveyed in 2008, someone at a business obtained a credit card number when the owner was making a purchase [74]. Waiters or store clerks match each legal swipe through a cash register with an illegal swipe through a **skimmer**, a small, battery-powered credit card reader. Identity theft rings use numbers collected this way to manufacture counterfeit credit cards.

Surprisingly, 14 percent of the cases of identity theft identified in 2010 were "friendly thefts" in which family members, friends, or in-house employees made purchases without the account-holder's consent [73].

Still, a significant number of people are victims of identity theft through their online activities. Gathering financial information via spam is called **phishing** (pronounced "fishing"). Thieves send out spam messages designed to look like they originated from PayPal, eBay, or another well-known Internet-active business. Through these messages they hope to con unsuspecting recipients into connecting with authentic-looking Web sites and revealing their credit card numbers or other personal information.

For example, a victim might receive an email message purportedly from PayPal, asking the person to go to the PayPal Web site to confirm a transaction. The email message contains a hypertext link. When the victim clicks on the link, he is connected to the counterfeit PayPal site. Phishing, spyware, and other online methods resulted in more than a million cases of identity theft in the United States in 2008 [74].

The stereotypical victim of identity theft is an elderly person who isn't computer savvy, but the facts speak otherwise. The average age of a victim of identity theft is 40. Many victims are experienced computer users who have become comfortable typing in their credit card information while online [75].

The Identity Theft and Assumption Act of 1998 makes identity theft a federal crime. In 2004, Congress passed the Identity Theft Penalty Enhancement Act, which lengthened prison sentences for identity thieves [76]. A variety of law enforcement agencies investigate alleged violations of this law: the U.S. Secret Service, the FBI, the U.S. Postal Inspection Service, and the Office of the Inspector General of the Social Security Administration [77]. Unfortunately, the probability that a particular case of identity theft will result in an arrest is about 1 in 700 [78].

3.7.2 Chat–Room Predators

Instant messaging is a real-time communication between two or more people supported by computers and a telecommunications system. A **chat room** is similar to instant messaging, except that it supports discussions among many people. A large number of organizations sponsor chat rooms dedicated to a wide variety of topics. For example, in July 2009, America Online's "Chats" page listed hundreds of chat rooms divided into 30 general categories, including Arts and Entertainment, Black Voices, Friends & Flirts, GLBT, Latino, Life, Places, Politics, Romance, and Town Square.

The popularity of instant messaging varies from country to country. According to Nielsen/NetRatings, the number of people who used instant messaging between January 2002 and March 2002 varied from 13 percent of all Internet users in Denmark to 43 percent in Spain [79]. Participation in chat rooms also varies from country to country. According to the same survey, the number of people with Internet accounts who participated in a chat room between January and March 2002 varied from 16 percent in the United Kingdom to 41 percent in Brazil. Conservatively estimating average use of instant messaging or chat rooms at 25 percent, the number of people worldwide who use this technology at least occasionally is about 150 million.

In 1995, Katie Tarbox, a 13-year-old swimmer from New Canaan, Connecticut, met a man in an AOL chat room [80]. He said his name was Mark and his age was 23. His grammar and vocabulary were good, and he made her feel special. Katie agreed to meet Mark at a hotel in Texas, where her swim team was competing. Soon after she entered his hotel room, he molested her. "Mark" turned out to be 41-year-old Francis Kufrovich from Calabasas, California, a man with a history of preying on children. In March 1998, Kufrovich was the first person in the United States to be sentenced for Internet pedophilia. After pleading guilty, he served 18 months in prison.

In 1999, the FBI investigated 1,500 crimes in which an alleged pedophile crossed a state line to meet and molest a child met through an Internet chat room [80]. Many say the problem is growing. Parry Aftab, executive director of Cyber Angels, says, "I know that I can go into a chat room as a 12-year-old and not say anything, and be hit on and asked if I'm a virgin within two minutes" [80]. In New York a 42-year-old man was sentenced to 150 years in prison after being convicted of kidnapping a 15-year-old girl and raping her repeatedly over the course of a week. He met the girl in a chat room [81].

Police have begun entering chat rooms posing as young girls to lure pedophiles [82]. During a three-week-long sting operation in Spokane, Washington, a police detective posed as a 13-year-old girl in a chat room. In early March 2003, police arrested a 22-year-old man on charges of attempted second-degree rape of a child. Inside his car the officers found handcuffs, a large folding knife, and a condom. The suspect was still on parole for an earlier conviction for fourth-degree assault with sexual motivation. Police sergeant Joe Petersen asked, "What happens had it been a real girl?" [81]. Chat-room sting operations are leading to many arrests all over the United States [83, 84, 85, 86, 87, 88].

3.7.3 Ethical Evaluations of Police "Sting" Operations

Is it morally right for police detectives to entrap pedophiles by posing as children in chat rooms and agreeing to meet with them?

UTILITARIAN ANALYSIS

Let's consider the various consequences of such a sting operation. A person allegedly interested in having sex with an underage minor is arrested and charged with attempted child rape. Suppose the person is found guilty and must serve time in prison. The direct effects of the sting operation are the denial of one person's freedom (a harm) and an increase in public safety (a benefit). Since the entire public is safer and only a single person is harmed, this is a net good.

The sting operation also has indirect effects. Publicity about the sting operation may deter other chat-room pedophiles. This, too, is a beneficial result. It is harder to gauge how knowledge of sting operations influences innocent citizens. First, it may reduce citizens' trust in the police. Many people believe that if they are doing nothing wrong, they have nothing to fear. Others may become less inclined to provide information to the police when requested. Second, sting operations can affect everyone's chat-room experiences. They demonstrate that people are not always who they claim to be. This knowledge may make people less vulnerable to being taken advantage of, but it may also reduce the amount of trust people have in others. Sting operations prove that supposedly private chat-room conversations can actually be made public. If chat-room conversations lack honesty and privacy, people will be less willing to engage in serious conversations. As a result, chat rooms lose some of their utility as communication devices. How much weight you give to the various consequences of police sting operations in chat rooms determines whether the net consequences are positive or negative.

KANTIAN ANALYSIS

A Kantian focuses on the will leading to the action rather than the results of the action. The police are responsible for maintaining public safety. Pedophiles endanger innocent children. Therefore, it is the duty of police to try to prevent pedophiles from accomplishing what they intend to do. The will of the police detective is to put a pedophile in prison. This seems straightforward enough.

If we dig a level deeper, however, we run into trouble. In order to put a pedophile in prison, the police must identify this person. Since a pedophile is unlikely to confess on the spot if asked a question by a police officer, the police lay a trap. In other words, the will of the police detective is to deceive a pedophile in order to catch him. To a Kantian, lying is wrong, no matter how noble the objective. By collecting evidence of chat-room conversations, the police detective also violates the presumed privacy of chat rooms. These actions of the police detective affect not only the alleged pedophile, but also every innocent person in the chat room. In other words, detectives are using every chat-room occupant as a means to their end of identifying and arresting the pedophile. While police officers have a duty to protect the public safety, it is wrong for them to break other moral laws in order to accomplish this purpose. From a Kantian point of view, the sting operation is morally wrong.

SOCIAL CONTRACT THEORY ANALYSIS

An adherent of social contract theory could argue that in order to benefit everyone, there are certain moral rules that people in chat rooms ought to follow. For example, people ought to be honest, and conversations ought to be kept confidential. By misrepresenting identity and/or intentions, the pedophile has broken a moral rule and ought to be punished. In conducting sting operations, however, police detectives also misrepresent their identities and record everything typed by suspected pedophiles. The upholders of the law have broken the rules, too. Furthermore, we have the presumption of innocence until proof of guilt. What if the police detective, through miscommunication or bad judgment, actually entraps someone who is not a pedophile? In this case, the innocent chat-room users have not broken any rules. They were simply in the wrong place at the wrong time. Yet society, represented by the police detective, did not provide the benefits chat-room users expect to receive (honest communications and privacy). In short, there is a conflict between society's need to punish a wrongdoer and its expectation that everyone (including the agents of the government) will abide by its moral rules.

SUMMARY OF ETHICAL ANALYSES

To summarize our ethical evaluation of police sting operations, the actions of the police seem immoral from a Kantian point of view. Evaluations using the other ethical theories do not yield a clear-cut endorsement or condemnation of the stings. While the goals of the police are laudable, they accomplish their goals by deceiving other chat-room users and revealing details of conversations thought to be private. Sting operations are more likely to be viewed as morally acceptable by someone who is more focused on the results of an action than the methods used; in other words, a consequentialist.

3.7.4 False Information

The Web is a more open communication medium than newspapers, radio stations, or television stations. Individuals or groups whose points of view may never be published in a newspaper or broadcast on a television or radio show may create an attractive Web site. The ease with which people may get information out via the Web is one of the reasons the Web contains billions of pages. However, the fact that no one has to review a Web page before it is published means the quality of information available on the Web varies widely.

You can find many Web sites devoted to the American manned space program. You can also find many Web sites that provide evidence the moon landings were a hoax by NASA. Many Web sites describe the Holocaust committed by the Nazis before and during World War II. Other sites explain why the Holocaust could not have happened.

Disputes about commonly held assumptions did not begin with the Web. Some television networks and newspapers are well known for giving a forum to people who question information provided through government agencies. Twice in 2001, the Fox TV network aired a program called "Conspiracy Theory: Did We Land on the Moon?" The program concludes NASA faked the moon landing in the Nevada desert. Supermarket tabloids are notorious for their provocative, misleading headlines. Experienced consumers take into account the source of the information. Most people would agree that *60 Minutes* on CBS is a more reliable source of information than *Conspiracy Theory* on Fox. Similarly, people expect information they find in *The New York Times* to be more reliable than the stories they read in a tabloid.

In traditional publishing, various mechanisms are put in place to improve the quality of the final product. For example, before Addison-Wesley published the first edition of this book, an editor sent draft copies of the manuscript to a dozen reviewers who checked it for errors, omissions, or misleading statements. The author revised the manuscript to respond to the reviewers' suggestions. After the author submitted a revised manuscript, a copy editor made final changes to improve the readability of the text, and a proofreader corrected typographical errors.

Web pages, on the other hand, can be published without any review. As you're undoubtedly well aware, the quality of Web pages varies dramatically. Fortunately, search engines can help people identify those Web pages that are most relevant and of the highest quality. Let's take a look at how the Google search engine does this.

The Google search engine keeps a database of many billions of Web pages. A software algorithm ranks the quality of these pages. The algorithm invokes a kind of voting mechanism. If Web page A links to Web page B, then page B gets a vote. However, all votes do not have the same weight. If Web page A is itself getting a lot of votes, then page A's link to page B gives its vote more weight than a link to B from an unpopular page.

When a user makes a query to Google, the search engine first finds the pages that closely match the query. It then considers their quality (as measured by the voting algorithm) to determine how to rank the relevant pages.

3.7.5 Cyberbullying

In November 2002, Ghyslain Raza, a chubby high school student living in Quebec, Canada, borrowed a videotape and used one of the high school's video cameras to film himself swinging a golf ball retriever like a light saber, à la Darth Maul in *Star Wars Episode I*. A few months later, the owner of the videotape discovered the content and shared it with some friends. After one of them digitized the scene and made it available on the Internet, millions of people downloaded the file in the first two weeks [90]. Ghyslain was nicknamed "the Star Wars kid," endured prolonged harassment from other students, and eventually dropped out of school [91]. By 2006, the video had been viewed more than 900 million times [92].

Cyberbullying is the use of the Internet or the phone system to inflict psychological harm on another person. Frequently, a group of persons gangs up to cyberbully the victim. Examples of cyberbullying include:

- Repeatedly texting or emailing hurtful messages to another person
- Spreading lies about another person
- Tricking someone into revealing highly personal information
- "Outing" or revealing someone's secrets online
- Posting embarrassing photographs or videos of other people without their consent
- Impersonating someone else online in order to damage that person's reputation
- Threatening or creating significant fear in another person

Surveys have revealed that cyberbullying is common among teenagers. Cox Communications surveyed 655 American teenagers in 2009, and 19 percent reported that they had been cyberbullied online, via cell phone, or through both media. Ten percent of the teenagers admitted to cyberbullying someone else. When asked why they had cyberbullied someone else, the most common responses were, "They deserved it" and, "To get back at someone" [65].

In some instances cyberbullying has led to the suicide of the victim, as in the case of 13-year-old Megan Meier. According to her mother, "Megan had a lifelong struggle with weight and self-esteem" [93]. She had talked about suicide in third grade, and ever since then she had been seeing a therapist [93]. Megan's spirits soared when she met a 16-year-old boy named Josh Evans on MySpace. They flirted online for four weeks but never met in person. Then Josh seemed to sour on their relationship. One day he let her know that he didn't know if he wanted to be friends with her anymore. The next day he posted [93, 94]:

```
You are a bad person and everybody hates you.
Have a shitty rest of your life.
The world would be a better place without you.
```

When Megan angrily responded to this post, others ganged up on her: "Megan Meier is a slut. Megan Meier is fat." [93]. Later that afternoon, Megan hanged herself in her bedroom.

Eventually, the community learned that "Josh Evans" did not exist. The MySpace account had been created just a couple of houses away from the Meier home by 18-year-old Ashley Grills, 13-year-old Sarah Drew, and Lori Drew, Sarah's mother. Sarah had had a falling out with Megan, and Ashley suggested creating the MySpace account to find out what Megan might be saying about Sarah. Lori Drew had approved the plan. Most of the messages from "Josh" had been written by Sarah or Ashley, but Lori Drew had been aware of what they were doing [95].

The county's district attorney declined to prosecute Lori Drew because there was no Missouri law against cyberbullying [96]. The FBI investigated the case, however, and in 2008, federal prosecutors charged Drew with four felony counts under the Computer Fraud and Abuse Act for violating the MySpace terms of service. A jury found her not guilty of these crimes but did convict her of three misdemeanors [97]. In 2009, a U.S. district judge overturned these convictions, stating that criminal charges should not have been brought against Drew for breaking a contract with an Internet service provider [98].

In April 2009, the Megan Meier Cyberbullying Prevention Act was introduced in the U.S. House of Representatives. The purpose of the proposed law was to "impose criminal penalties on anyone who transmits in interstate or foreign commerce a communication intended to coerce, intimate, harass, or cause substantial emotional distress to another person, using electronic means to support severe, repeated, and hostile behavior" [99]. Some civil libertarians objected to the proposed legislation, arguing that it would take away free speech rights guaranteed under the First Amendment to the U.S. Constitution. The law did not win approval by the House of Representatives.

3.8 Internet Addiction

3.8.1 Is Internet Addiction Real?

Using an Internet-enabled computer can be a lot of fun—the number of different things you can do online is staggering. Some psychologists warn about the dangers of Internet addiction. Are these fears justified?

In 1976, long before most computers were networked, Joseph Weizenbaum pointed out what attracts computer programmers to their machines: feelings of freedom and power. Because programmers deal with bits instead of physical objects, they are largely free to create whatever they can imagine, and computers execute their instructions without hesitation. The resulting thrill causes some programmers to have a "compulsion to program." In Weizenbaum's words:

> [B]right young men of disheveled appearance, often with sunken glowing eyes, can be seen sitting at computer consoles, their arms tensed and waiting to fire their fingers, already poised to strike, at the buttons and keys on which their attention seems to be as riveted as a gambler's on the rolling dice . . . They work until they nearly drop, twenty, thirty hours at a time. Their food, if they arrange it, is brought to them: coffee, Cokes, sandwiches. If possible, they sleep on cots near the computer. But only for a few hours—then back to the console or the printouts. Their rumpled clothes, their unwashed and unshaven faces, and their uncombed hair all testify that they are oblivious to their bodies and to the world in which they move. They exist, at least when so engaged, only through and for the computers [89].

Weizenbaum's observation is echoed by Maressa Orzack, who states, "Computer addiction is real . . . As an impulse control disorder, computer addiction resembles pathological gambling" [100].

The traditional definition of addiction is the persistent, compulsive use of a chemical substance, or drug, despite knowledge of its harmful long-term consequences [101]. Today, however, Orzack and some other psychologists and psychiatrists have extended the definition of addiction to include any persistent, compulsive behavior that the addict recognizes to be harmful. According to their broader definition of addiction, people can be addicted to gambling, food, sex, long-distance running, and other activities, including computer-related activities [102].

Some people spend between 40 and 80 hours per week on the Internet, with individual sessions lasting up to 20 hours [103, 104]. Spending so much time online can have a wide variety of harmful consequences. Fatigue from sleep deprivation can lead to unsatisfactory performance at school or at work. Physical ailments include carpal tunnel syndrome, back strain, and eyestrain. Too many hours in front of a computer can weaken or destroy relationships with friends and family members [103]. In a few cases, people have died after prolonged sessions sitting in front of a computer.

Kimberly Young has created a test for Internet addiction. Using the diagnosis of pathological gambling in the *Diagnostic and Statistical Manual of Mental Disorders* as her starting point, Young has produced an eight-question screening instrument, which I reproduce verbatim [105]:[1]

1. Do you feel preoccupied with the Internet (think about previous online activity or anticipate next online session)?

2. Do you feel the need to use the Internet with increasing amounts of time in order to achieve satisfaction?

3. Have you repeatedly made unsuccessful efforts to control, cut back, or stop Internet use?

4. Do you feel restless, moody, depressed, or irritable when attempting to cut down or stop Internet use?

5. Do you stay online longer than originally intended?

6. Have you jeopardized or risked the loss of significant relationship, job, educational or career opportunity because of the Internet?

7. Have you lied to family members, therapist, or others to conceal the extent of involvement with the Internet?

8. Do you use the Internet as a way of escaping from problems or of relieving a dysphoric mood (e.g., feelings of helplessness, guilt, anxiety, depression)?

Young considers patients who answer "yes" to five or more of these questions to be addicted to the Internet, unless "their behavior could not be better accounted for by a Manic Episode" [103].

Young's use of the phrase "Internet addiction" and her questionnaire are controversial. John Charlton points out that computer use, unlike drug use, is generally considered to be a positive activity. In addition, while drug addiction leads to an increase in criminal activity, the same level of societal harm is unlikely to occur even if the Internet is overused by some people. Charlton performed his own study of computer users and has concluded that Young's checklist approach is likely to overestimate the number of people addicted to the Internet. According to Charlton, some "people who are classified as computer-dependent or computer-addicted might often be more accurately said to be highly computer-engaged" [106].

Mark Griffiths holds a position similar to Charlton, stating that "to date there is very little empirical evidence that computing activities (i.e., Internet use, hacking, programming) are addictive" [104]. Richard Ries argues that it would be more accurate to call excessive use of the Internet a compulsion [107].

However, others share Young's perspective. Stanton Peele maintains that "people become addicted to experiences" [102]. In his broader view of addiction, non-drug experiences can be addictive. Peele has developed a model of addiction that extends "to all areas of repetitive, compulsive behavior" [102].

---

1. "Internet Addiction: The Emergence of a New Clinical Disorder," by Kimberly S. Young from CYBERPSYCHOLOGY AND BEHAVIOR. Copyright © 1998 by Mary Ann Liebert, Inc. Publishers. Reprinted with permission.

Our concern in this section is excessive Internet use that causes harm. The dispute over terminology is not important to our discussion. We will use the term "Internet addiction" rather than "Internet compulsion," since the former term appears to be more widely used by the press.

3.8.2 Contributing Factors

According to Peele, social, situational, and individual factors can increase a person's susceptibility to addiction. For example, peer groups play an important role in determining how individuals use alcohol and other drugs. People in stressful situations are more likely to become addicted, as are those who lack social support and intimacy, and those who have limited opportunities for "rewarding, productive activity" [102]. Individual factors that make a person more susceptible to addiction include a tendency to pursue an activity to excess, a lack of achievement, a fear of failure, and feelings of alienation.

Young's studies have led her to "believe that behaviors related to the Internet have the same ability to provide emotional relief, mental escape, and ways to avoid problems as do alcohol, drugs, food, or gambling" [103]. She notes that the typical Internet addict is addicted to a single application.

3.8.3 Ethical Evaluation of Internet Addiction

People who use the Internet excessively can harm themselves and others for whom they are responsible. For this reason, excessive Internet use is a moral issue.

Kantianism, utilitarianism, and social contract theory all share the Enlightenment view that individuals, as rational beings, have the capacity and the obligation to use their critical judgment to govern their lives [108]. Kant held that addiction is a vice, because it's wrong to allow your bodily desires to dominate your mind [109]. Mill maintained that some pleasures are more valuable than others and that people have the obligation to help each other "distinguish the better from the worse" [50].

Ultimately, people are responsible for the choices they make. Even if an addict is "hooked," the addict is responsible for choosing to engage in the activity the first time. This view assumes that people are capable of controlling their compulsions. According to Jeffrey Reiman, vices are "dispositions that undermine the sovereignty of practical reason. Dispositions, like habits, are hard but not impossible to overcome, and undermining something weakens it without necessarily destroying it entirely" [108].

Reiman's view is supported by Peele, who believes addicts can choose to recover from their addictions. "People recover to the extent that they (1) believe an addiction is hurting them and wish to overcome it, (2) feel enough efficacy to manage their withdrawal and life without the addiction, and (3) find sufficient alternative rewards to make life without the addiction worthwhile" [102].

While our analysis to this point has concluded that individual addicts are morally responsible for their addictions, it's also possible for a society to bear collective moral responsibility for the addictions of some of its members. We have already discussed how social conditions can increase a person's susceptibility to addiction, and Peele states an addict will not recover unless life without the addiction has sufficient rewards.

Addiction is wrong because it means voluntarily surrendering the sovereignty of your reason by engaging in a compulsion that has short-term benefits but harms the quality of your life in the long term. However, if somebody is living in a hopeless situation where any reasonable person would conclude there are no long-term prospects for a good life, then what is lost by giving in to the compulsion? Reiman believes that this is the case for many American inner-city drug addicts. "They face awful circumstances that are unjust, unnecessary, and remediable, and yet that the society refuses to remedy. Addiction is for such individuals a bad course of action made tolerable by comparison to the intolerable conditions they face. In that face, I think that moral responsibility for their strong addictions . . . passes to the larger society" [108].

Of course, the circumstances facing a typical suburban Internet addict are radically different from those facing a typical inner-city drug addict. For this reason, it is tempting to dismiss the notion that society could in any way be responsible for the Internet addiction of some of its members. However, some people use the Internet as a way to escape into their own world, because in the "real world" they suffer from social isolation [104]. Perhaps we should reflect on whether any of our actions or inactions make certain members of our community feel excluded.

Summary

The Internet and the telephone system are powerful and flexible tools that support a wide variety of social interactions. In this chapter, we have explored text messaging, email, chat rooms, and the Web. All of these technologies have had both positive and negative impacts on society.

Twenty years ago, relatively few people had email accounts. Back then, email advertising was virtually unheard of. Email users did not have to delete large numbers of unwanted messages from their mailboxes. On the other hand, email was not too useful outside work, because most people didn't have it.

Today, well over a billion people have an email account. Most anyone you'd like to communicate with has an email address. However, the large number of email users has attracted the attention of direct marketing firms. In the past few years the volume of unsolicited bulk email (spam) has risen dramatically. Many believe the presence of spam has harmed the email system, and a variety of steps have been taken to filter out spam messages before they reach users.

The Web contains over one trillion pages. It contains images of sublime beauty and shocking cruelty, uplifting poetry and expletive-ridden hate speech, well-organized encyclopedias and figments of paranoid imaginations. In short, it is a reflection of the best and the worst of humanity. Web-based social networking sites such as Facebook and Twitter have attracted hundreds of millions of users and created new communication paradigms. Some point to the use of Facebook and Twitter by participants in the Arab

Spring uprising as evidence that these tools can be powerful agents for social change, while others think the impact of these tools has been overblown.

Governments have responded to the idea-sharing potential of the Web and social networking sites in a variety of ways. The most repressive governments have simply made the Internet inaccessible to their people. Other governments have instituted controls that prevent certain sites from being accessed. Most governments allow their citizens nearly universal access to Web sites and Web-based applications.

In the United States, there have been numerous efforts to make pornography inaccessible to children via the Web. The U.S. Congress passed three laws attempting to make pornography less accessible to children via the Web. All of these laws raised objections from civil libertarians, who called them an infringement on free speech rights. The U.S. Supreme Court ruled the first two laws unconstitutional; it upheld the third.

Given the amount of legislation that has been passed to protect children from pornography, it is ironic that many teenagers have become a source of suggestive images. The legal system has not yet caught up with sexting: the use of email or cell phones to send messages containing photos of nude or partially nude people. Child pornography laws were written with pedophiles in mind. What is the proper response to minors who are sexting photos of themselves?

The Internet provides new ways for people to be misled. For example, chat rooms are a popular way for groups of like-minded people to come together to discuss a topic of mutual interest. Unfortunately, sexual predators have used chat rooms as a tool to contact children. In response, police have begun to set up "sting" operations to snare these predators. While sting operations may catch sexual predators, they also change the climate of chat rooms.

The Internet has facilitated e-commerce. Many people are comfortable purchasing items over the Internet. Submitting a credit card number and other identifying information is part of this process. In this environment, the problem of identity theft is a serious concern. Every year, millions of people are conned into revealing their credit card numbers to scam artists who use this information to get cash advances or purchase goods using someone else's identity.

The Web provides a remarkably simple way for people to post and access information. People looking for answers can often get more information, and get it much more quickly, by retrieving what they want from the Web instead of searching printed encyclopedias, books, journals, and newspapers. Ordinary people can also use the Web to broadcast their ideas around the globe. There are many advantages to this information-rich environment. Unfortunately, because anybody can post information on the Web, incorrect information is mixed in with correct information. Web users cannot believe everything they read on the Web. Web search engines incorporate algorithms that attempt to steer people toward higher-quality sites.

The Internet and the telephone system have provided a new way for people to intimidate or humiliate others. After Megan Meier was cyberbullied, she took her own life. The adult involved in the cyberbullying was not prosecuted by local authorities because there were no state laws against cyberbullying. Efforts to create a national cyberbullying law in the United States drew objections from civil libertarians, who feared that it would greatly restrict freedom of expression, and the law was not passed.

A wide variety of enticing activities are available online, and some people exhibit a compulsion to spend extraordinarily long hours connected to the Internet. Numerous commentators have compared compulsive computer users to compulsive gamblers. Whether or not a compulsive online activity is a true addiction, excessive computer use can have harmful consequences. According to Kantianism, utilitarianism, and social contract theory, people must take responsibility for the voluntary choices they make, including the decision to go online. However, we should also remember that social and cultural factors can make people more susceptible to addictions.

Review Questions

1. What is the Internet?

2. Explain the meaning of the two parts of an email address.

3. Describe how email is transmitted from the sender to the recipient.

4. What is spam?

5. What does a spam filter do?

6. What is a URL?

7. What is a wiki?

8. What is a blog?

9. What is a PC bang?

10. Describe five uses of the Web not covered in the text.

11. Define censorship in your own words.

12. Summarize the different forms of direct censorship.

13. According to the U.S. Supreme Court, why do broadcasters have the most limited First Amendment rights?

14. What characteristics of the Internet make censorship difficult?

15. What is a Web filter?

16. What is sexting?

17. What is the leading form of identity theft in the United States?

18. What is phishing?

19. Define cyberbullying in your own words.

20. How does the idea of "Internet addiction" stretch the traditional concept of addiction?

21. What is the Enlightenment view regarding responsibility for addiction?

Discussion Questions

22. Why is texting more popular than making phone calls?

23. Should nonprofit organizations be regulated the same way as for-profit organizations with respect to their use of unsolicited bulk email?

24. Why is "cold calling" considered to be an acceptable sales practice, but spamming isn't?

25. Suppose a fee (an electronic version of a postage stamp) was required in order to send an email message. How would this change the behavior of email users? Suppose the fee was one cent. Do you think this would solve the problem of spam?

26. Internet service providers monitor their chat rooms and expel users who violate their codes of conduct. For example, users can be kicked off for insulting a person or a group of people based on their race, religion, or sexual orientation. Is it wrong for an ISP to expel someone for hate speech?

27. Suppose you are the director of an ISP that serves the email needs of 10,000 customers. You receive dozens of complaints from them every week about the amount of spam they are receiving. Meanwhile, American spammers are hacking into computers in Jamborea (an East Asian country) and using them to mail spam back to the United States. You estimate that at least 99 percent of email originating from Jamborea is spam. A few of the messages, however, are probably legitimate emails. Should you do anything to restrict the flow of email messages from Jamborea to your customers?

28. Stockbrokers are now required to save all their instant messaging communications. Is having a record of everything you type good or bad? Do you think this requirement will change the behavior of brokers?

29. There is a thriving "real world" market for gold, artifacts, and avatars from virtual worlds such as *World of Warcraft*. In effect, rich Westerners are offshoring game-playing to China. Do you find this image disturbing?

30. What are the benefits and harms of Internet censorship?

31. Should citizens of democratic nations help people in authoritarian nations get around the Web censorship of their repressive governments?

32. Should people publishing accusations against others on their blogs or MySpace pages be held responsible if they disseminate false information?

33. Should a college or university have the right to suspend its students who brag about breaking its rules on their Facebook or MySpace pages?

34. Discuss similarities and differences between the Web and each of these other ways that we communicate: the telephone system, physical mail, bookstores, movie theaters, newspapers, broadcast and cable TV. Should governments ignore the Web, or should they regulate it somehow? If governments should regulate the Web, should the regulations be similar to the regulations for one of the aforementioned communication systems, or should they be unique in significant ways?

35. The convenience of Wikipedia makes it a popular reference for students. After several instances in which students cited incorrect information, however, the history department at Middlebury College prohibited references to Wikipedia articles in papers or exams.

Did the Middlebury history department go too far? What is the proper role, if any, for Wikipedia in academic research?

36. Should bloggers be given the same rights as newspaper, magazine, or television journalists?

37. Should children be prevented from accessing some Web sites? Who should be responsible for the actions of children surfing the Web?

38. A female employee of a high-tech company receives on average 40 spam messages per day. About one-quarter of them are advertising pornographic Web sites and have photographs of naked women. All of these emails pass through the company's email server. The woman sues the company for sexual harassment, saying that the company tolerates an atmosphere that is degrading to women. Is the company responsible for the pornographic spam reaching the computers of its employees?

39. You are in charge of the computers at a large, inner-city library. Most of the people who live in the neighborhood do not have a computer at home. They go to the library when they want to access the Internet. About two-thirds of the people surfing the Web on the library's computers are adults.

    You have been requested to install filtering software that would block Web sites containing various kinds of material deemed inappropriate for children. You have observed this software in action and know that it also blocks many sites that adults might legitimately want to visit. How should you respond to the request to install filtering software?

40. Are there any circumstances under which sexting is morally acceptable?

41. What is the age at which a parent or guardian should provide a child with a cell phone? Should younger children be provided with cell phones having fewer features?

42. Discuss the morality of Google's page-ranking algorithm. Does it systematically exclude Web pages containing opinions held only by a small segment of the population? Should every opinion on the Web be given equal consideration?

43. What is the longest amount of time you have ever spent in a single session in front of a computer? What were you doing?

44. The income of companies providing persistent online games depends on the number of subscribers they attract. Since consumers have a choice of many products, each company is motivated to create the best possible experience for its customers. Role-playing adventures have no set length. When playing one of these games, it's easy to spend more time on the computer than originally planned. Some subscribers cause harm to themselves and others by spending too much time playing these games. Should the designers of persistent online games bear some moral responsibility for this problem?

45. A school district forbids students from using their cell phones on school buses, but many students ignore this rule. A frustrated bus driver installs a cell phone jammer on his bus. When the jammer is turned on, cell phones within 40 feet stop working. (The use of jammers is against the law.) The bus driver says, "The kids think they are sneaky by hiding low in their seats and using their phones. Now the kids can't figure out why their phones don't work, but can't ask because they will get in trouble! It's fun to watch them try to get a signal" [110].

    Discuss the morality of the bus driver's use of the jammer.

46. According to some commentators, Facebook and Twitter played a vital role in the Arab Spring uprising because they made it possible for activists to organize large protests in a short amount of time. Others argue that Facebook and Twitter were simply tools used by activists and that genuine social grievances led to the revolutions in Tunisia and Egypt. What is your view?

47. After popular uprisings in Tunisia and Egypt in 2011, the United States government said it would spend $30 million to fund the development of new services and technologies designed to allow activists in other countries to get around Internet restrictions imposed by their governments.

    Announcing this initiative, Secretary of State Hillary Clinton said, "We are convinced that an open Internet fosters long-term peace, progress and prosperity. The reverse is also true. An Internet that is closed and fractured, where different governments can block activity or change the rules on a whim—where speech is censored or punished, and privacy does not exist—that is an Internet that can cut off opportunities for peace and progress and discourage innovation and entrepreneurship" [111].

    Should the U.S. government provide activists in other countries the tools to get around Internet restrictions imposed by authoritarian governments?

48. In July 2011, activists shut down a San Francisco subway station as a way of protesting the death of a drunk man shot by a Bay Area Rapid Transit (BART) police officer [112]. A month later, the subway system blocked cell phone service at several stations in an effort to prevent another protest. According to BART officials, protesters had said they "would use mobile devices to coordinate their disruptive activities and communicate about the location and number of BART Police" [113]. The agency said, "A civil disturbance during commute times at busy downtown San Francisco stations could lead to platform overcrowding and unsafe conditions for BART customers, employees and demonstrators" [113].

    Was BART justified in blocking cell phone service?

In-Class Exercises

49. Divide the class into groups. Each group should come up with a variant of the case study "Ann the Acme Accountant," in which both a Kantian evaluation and an act utilitarian evaluation would conclude Ann did something wrong.

50. Divide the class into groups. Each group should come up with a variant of the case study "Kate's Blog," in which the analysis from the perspective of social contract theory would conclude Kate did nothing wrong, but an act utilitarian evaluation would conclude Kate did something wrong.

51. Divide the class into teams representing each of the following groups:
    - Small, struggling business
    - Large, established corporation
    - Internet service provider
    - Consumer

    Discuss the value of direct email versus other forms of advertising, such as direct mail, television advertising, radio advertising, the Yellow Pages, and setting up a Web site.

52. A company uses pop-up advertising to market its software product, which blocks pop-ups from appearing when someone is surfing the Web. Debate the morality of the company's marketing strategy.

53. Ad-blocking software attachments to Web browsers enable a Web surfer to visit Web sites without having to view the pop-up advertisements associated with these Web pages. Debate this proposition: "People who use ad-blocking software are violating an implicit 'social contract' with companies that use advertising revenues as a means of providing free access to Web pages."

54. In 2000, the Estonian parliament passed a law declaring Internet access to be a fundamental human right of its citizens. Divide the class into two groups (pro and con) to debate the following proposition: Internet access should be a fundamental human right, along with the such other fundamental human rights as the right to life and the right to free speech.

55. How do you determine the credibility of information you get from the Web? Does the source of the information make any difference to you? If so, how would you rank the reliability of each of the following sources of Web pages? Does the type of information you're seeking affect your ranking?
   - Establishment newspaper
   - Counterculture newspaper
   - Television network
   - Corporation
   - Nonprofit organization
   - Individual

56. Martin Dula has suggested that parents should not provide their children with phones capable of taking photos and videos because these phones tempt children to participate in sexting [67].

   Debate the following proposition: Parents and legal guardians should not allow their children under the age of 18 to own cell phones capable of taking, transmitting, or receiving photographs or videos.

Further Reading

Chris Anderson and Michael Wolff. "The Web Is Dead. Long Live the Internet." *Wired*, September 2010. www.wired.com.

Anand Giridharadas. "Where a Cellphone Is Still Cutting Edge." *The New York Times*, April 9, 2010. www.nytimes.com.

Malcolm Gladwell. "Small Change: Why the Revolution Will Not Be Tweeted." *The New Yorker*, October 4, 2010.

Aldous Huxley. *Brave New World*. Harper Perennial Modern Classics, 2006. (Originally published in 1932.)

Steven Levy. "How Early Twitter Decisions Led to Anthony Weiner's Dickish Demise." *Wired Epicenter*, June 13, 2011. www.wired.com/epicenter/.

Steven Levy. "Mob Rule! How Users Took Over Twitter." *Wired*, November 2009. www.wired.com.

Gary Wolf. "The Tragedy of Craigslist." *Wired*, September 2009. www.wired.com.

Allen Salkin. "Party On, But No Tweets." *The New York Times*, August 9, 2009. www.nytimes.com.

Cass R. Sunstein. *Democracy and the Problem of Free Speech.* The Free Press, New York, NY, 1993.

Brian Whitworth and Elizabeth Whitworth. "Spam and the Social-Technical Gap." *Computer* 37(10):38–45, October 2004.

References

[1]   Alex Williams. "Mind Your BlackBerry or Mind Your Manners," *The New York Times*, June 22, 2009. www.nytimes.com.

[2]   Neda Ulaby. "The Posies: How Do Bands Make Money Now?" *National Public Radio: All Things Considered (radio show)*, July 29, 2009. www.npr.org.

[3]   "Internet Overtakes Newspapers as News Outlet." Pew Research Center for the People & the Press, December 23, 2008. pewresearch.org.

[4]   Jose Antonio Vargas. "Obama Raised Half a Billion Online." *WashingtonPost.com*, November 20, 2008.

[5]   "Paul Sets One-day GOP Fundraising Record." *MSNBC*, November 6, 2007. www.msnbc.msn.com.

[6]   "The Radicati Group, Inc, Releases Q2 2008 Market Numbers Update," June 18, 2009. www.radicati.com.

[7]   Brad Templeton. "Origin of the Term 'Spam' to Mean Net Abuse," July 8, 2005. www.templetons.com/brad/spamterm.html.

[8]   Peter H. Lewis. "An Ad (Gasp!) in Cyberspace." *The New York Times*, April 19, 1994.

[9]   "Filters Getting Better at Blocking Spam." *The Boston Globe*, May 12, 2009.

[10] Saul Hansell. "Internet Is Losing Ground in Battle against Spam." *The New York Times*, April 22, 2003.

[11] Joe Stewart. "Top Spam Botnets Exposed." April 8, 2008. www.secureworks.com/research/threats/topbotnets.

[12] Brian Whitworth and Elizabeth Whitworth. "Spam and the Social-Technical Gap." *Computer* 37(10):38–45, October 2004.

[13] Tim Berners-Lee. *Weaving the Web*. HarperCollins Publishers, New York, NY, 1999.

[14] Erick Schonfeld. "Forrester Forecast: Online Retail Sales Will Grow to $250 Billion by 2014." *Tech Crunch*, March 8, 2010. techcrunch.com.

[15] Daniel H. Pink. "The Book Stops Here." *Wired*, page 125, March 2005.

[16] Paul Festa. "Dialing for Bloggers." *The New York Times*, February 25, 2003.

[17] Rebecca Kern. "Free Online Course Offerings Grow in Abundance and Popularity." *U.S. News and World Report*, February 12, 2010. www.usnews.com.

[18] Associated Press. "50 Million Historical Documents Posted on Web." *CNN.com*, April 5, 2003.

[19]   "World of Warcraft Reaches New Milestone: 10 Million Subscribers." Blizzard Entertainment, January 22, 2008. eu.blizzard.com.

[20]   Tim Ingham. "CHINA: Warcraft Hits One Million Unique Users." *MCV*, April 14, 2008. www.mcvuk.com.

[21]   Jimmy Yap. "Power Up!" *Internet Magazine*, February 2003.

[22]   David Barboza. "Ogre to Slay? Outsource It to China." *The New York Times*, December 9, 2005.

[23]   Associated Press. "IRS Online Filing Tops 2M Users." *The New York Times*, March 25, 2003.

[24]   "Internet Gambling Yield Passes US$20bn: Online Gambling Shows Resilience in Face of Recession." *Reuters*, March 9, 2009. www.reuters.com.

[25]   Bob Tedeschi. "Gambling Sites Adjust to Scrutiny." *The New York Times*, March 31, 2003.

[26]   www.kiva.org.

[27]   Maggie Shiels. "Twitter Co-founder Jack Dorsey Rejoins Company." *BBC News*, March 28, 2011. www.bbc.co.uk.

[28]   Emma Barnett. "Twitter Record Broken During the Women's World Cup Final." *The Telegraph* (London, England). www.telegraph.co.uk.

[29]   Claire Cain Miller. "Mom-and-Pop Operators Turn to Social Media." *The New York Times*, July 23, 2009.

[30]   Philip N. Howard. "The Arab Spring's Cascading Effects." *Miller-McCune*. www.miller-mccune.com.

[31]   "Region in Turmoil." *Al Jazeera*. Accessed August 8, 2011. blogs.aljazeera.net/twitter-dashboard.

[32]   William Saletan. "Springtime for Twitter." *Slate*, July 18, 2011. www.slate.com.

[33]   Malcolm Gladwell. "Small Change: Why the Revolution Will Not Be Tweeted." *The New Yorker*, October 4, 2011.

[34]   "About Filtering." August 1, 2007. opennet.net/about-filtering.

[35]   Privacy International. "Silenced—Burma." September 21, 2003. www.privacyinternational.org.

[36]   Stephen Gibbs. "Cuba Law Tightens Internet Access." *BBC News*, January 24, 2004.

[37]   Rebecca MacKinnon. "Chinese Cell Phone Breaches North Korean Hermit Kingdom." *YaleGlobal Online*, January 17, 2005.

[38]   Jonathan Zittrain and Benjamin Edelman. "Documentation of Internet Filtering in Saudi Arabia." Technical report, Harvard Law School, Cambridge, MA, September 12, 2002.

[39]   Rebekah Heacock. "China Shuts Down Internet in Xinjiang Region after Riots." *OpenNet Initiative*, July 6, 2009. opennet.org.

[40]   Asher Moses. "Censoring Mobiles and the Net: How the West Is Clamping Down." *The Sydney Morning Herald*, August 15, 2011. www.smh.com.au.

[41]   "Internet Filtering in China." OpenNet Initiative, June 15, 2009. opennet.net.

[42]   Oliver August. "Staring Down the Censors." *Wired*, November, 2007.

[43]   "IOC Agrees to Internet Blocking at the Games." *The New York Times*, July 30, 2008.

[44]   Andrew Jacobs. "China Requires Censorship Software on New PCs." *The New York Times*, June 9, 2009.

[45]   Edward Wong. "China Orders Patches to Planned Web Filter." *The New York Times*, June 16, 2009.

[46]   Anurag Viswanath. "Green Dam on the Back Burner." *Business Standard (India)*, August 2, 2009. www.business-standard.com.

[47]   Matthew Taylor. "China Drops Green Dam Web Filtering System." *The Guardian*, August 13, 2009. www.guardian.co.uk.

[48]   Eason Jordan. "The News We Kept to Ourselves." *The New York Times*, April 11, 2003.

[49]   Immanuel Kant. "What Is Enlightenment?" In *Foundations of the Metaphysics of Morals*, Upper Saddle River, NJ, 1997. Library of Liberal Arts.

[50]   John Stuart Mill. "On Liberty." In *On Liberty and Utilitarianism*. Bantam Books, New York, NY, 1993.

[51]   Edward G. Hudon. *Freedom of Speech and Press in America*. Public Affairs Press, Washington, DC, 1963.

[52]   Francis Canavan. *Freedom of Expression: Purpose as Limit*. Carolina Academic Press, Durham, NC, 1984.

[53]   Cass R. Sunstein. *Democracy and the Problem of Free Speech*. The Free Press, New York, NY, 1993.

[54]   G. Steven Agee. *Jeremy Jaynes v. Commonwealth of Virginia*. Court of Appeals of Virginia, Record No. 062388, September 12, 2008.

[55]   George Carlin. "Filthy Words." In *Occupation: Foole*. Atlantic Records, 1973.

[56]   Supreme Court of the United States. *Federal Communications Commission v. Pacifica Foundation et al.*, 1978. 438 U.S. 726.

[57]   "Spying on Kids' Internet Use." *CBS News*, February 2003.

[58]   Associated Press. "Justices Uphold Use of Internet Filters in Public Libraries." *NYTimes.com*, June 23, 2003.

[59]   Jeffrey Kosseff. "Libraries Should Bar Web Porn, Court Rules." *The Oregonian (Portland, Oregon)*, June 24, 2003.

[60]   James Rachels. *The Elements of Moral Philosophy*. 4th ed. McGraw-Hill, Boston, MA, 2003.

[61]   John Rawls. *A Theory of Justice, Revised Edition*. The Belknap Press of Harvard University Press, Cambridge, MA, 1999.

[62]   Lorenne Clark. "Sexual Equality and the Problem of an Adequate Moral Theory: The Poverty of Liberalism." In *Contemporary Moral Issues*, McGraw-Hill Ryerson, Toronto, 1997.

[63]   Langdon Winner. "Electronically Implanted 'Values'." *Technology Review*, 100(2), February/March 1997.

[64]   Doug Johnson. "Internet Filters: Censorship by Any Other Name?" *Emergency Librarian*, 25(5), May/June 1998.

[65]   "Teen Online & Wireless Safety Survey: Cyberbullying, Sexting, and Parental Controls." Cox Communications, May 2009.

[66]   Mike Celizic. "Her Teen Committed Suicide over 'Sexting.' " *TodayShow.com*, March 6, 2009. www.msnbc.msn.com.

[67]   Martin Dula. "Sexting: the Convergence of Two Revolutions." *Pop Culture History (blog)*. June 25, 2009. www.greathistory.com.

[68]   Kim Zetter. "'Sexting' Hysteria Falsely Brands Educator as Child Pornographer." *Wired*, April 3, 2009. www.wired.com.

[69]   "2009 Legislation Related to 'Sexting.'" National Conference of State Legislatures, July 27, 2009. www.ncsl.org.

[70]   Dorothy E. Denning. *Information Warfare and Security*. Addison-Wesley, Boston, MA, 1999.

[71]   States News Service. "FTC Testifies on Identify Theft, Impact on Seniors." July 18, 2002.

[72]   Matt Richtel. "Financial Institutions May Facilitate Identity Theft." *NYTimes.com*, August 12, 2002.

[73]   Javelin Strategy & Research. "2011 Identity Fraud Survey Report: Consumer Version." February 2011. www.javelinstrategy.com.

[74]   Javelin Strategy & Research. "2009 Identity Fraud Survey Report: Consumer Version." February 2009. www.javelinstrategy.com.

[75]   Jason Gertzen. "Protect Your Finances from Online Fraudsters, Experts Warn." *The Milwaukee Journal Sentinel (Wisconsin)*, December 8, 2003.

[76]   David McGuire. "Bush Signs Identity Theft Bill." *WashingtonPost.com*, July 15, 2004.

[77]   Federal Trade Commission. "Take Charge: Fighting Back Against Identity Theft," February 2005. www.ftc.gov/bcp/conline.pubs.

[78]   Gartner, Inc. "Gartner Says Identity Theft Is Up Nearly 80 Percent," July 21, 2003.

[79]   "Nielsen/NetRatings Finds E-mail Is the Dominant Online Activity Worldwide." *Nielsen/NetRatings*, May 9, 2002. www.nielsen-netratings.com.

[80]   Lynn Burke. "Memoir of a Pedophile's Victim." *Wired News*, April 26, 2000. www.wired.com.

[81]   Thomas Clouse. "Man Accused of Seeking Sex with 13-Year-Old Girl; Police Say Internet Sting Caught Suspect Who Had Handcuffs, Knife." *Spokane Spokesman-Review*, March 5, 2003.

[82]   Shaila K. Dewan. "Who's 14, 'Kewl' and Flirty Online? A 39-Year-Old Detective, and He Knows His Bra Size." *The New York Times*, April 7, 2003.

[83]   "Police Say Arkansas Man Made an Online Deal to Buy a Little Girl for Sex." *ZDNet UK*, September 3, 1999. news.zdnet.co.uk.

[84]   "Chat Room Cops Nab Possible Predator." *Tech TV Inc.*, May 17, 2002. www.techtv.com.

[85]   Paige Akin. "Man Arrested in Undercover Cyber Sex Sting." *Richmond Times Dispatch (Virginia)*, March 8, 2003.

[86]   Suzannah Gonzales. "Sex Case May Lead to More Charges." *St. Petersburg Times (Florida)*, March 14, 2003.

[87]   Jennifer Sinco Kelleher. "Arrests in Sex Chats with 'Girls.'" *Newsday*, March 15, 2003.

[88]   Amy Klein. "Cops in the Chat Room; Detectives Play Teenagers to Bait Sexual Predators." *The Record (Bergen County, NJ)*, April 6, 2003.

[89]   Joseph Weizenbaum. *Computer Power and Human Reason: From Judgment to Calculation*. W. H. Freeman and Company, San Francisco, CA, 1976.

[90]   Andy Baio. "Finding the Star Wars Kid." *Waxy.org*, May 13, 2003. waxy.org.

[91]   Tu Thanh Ha. "Parents File Lawsuit over Star Wars Video." *The Globe and Mail*, Toronto, Ontario, Canada, July 23, 2003.

[92]   "Star Wars Kid Is Top Viral Video." *BBC News*, November 27, 2006. www.bbc.co.uk.

[93]   Steve Pokin. "'MySpace' Hoax Ends with Suicide of Dardenne Prairie Teen." *Suburban Journals*, November 11, 2007. suburbanjournals.stltoday.com.

[94]   "Parents Want Jail Time for MySpace Hoax Mom." November 29, 2007. abcnews.go .com.

[95]   Kim Zetter. "Government's Star Witness Stumbles: MySpace Hoax Was Her Idea, Not Drew's." November 20, 2008. www.wired.com.

[96]   "Missouri Begins Prosecuting Under Cyberbullying Law." *Fox News*, December 20, 2008. www.foxnews.com.

[97]   Kim Zetter. "Lori Drew Not Guilty of Felonies in Landmark Cyberbullying Trial." November 26, 2008. www.wired.com.

[98]   Kim Zetter. "Judge Acquits Lori Drew in Cyberbullying Case, Overrules Jury." www .wired.com.

[99]   Congressional Research Service. "H.R. 1966: Megan Meier Cyberbullying Prevention Act (Summary)." April 2, 2009. www.govtrack.us.

[100] "Computer Addiction: Is It Real or Virtual?" *Harvard Mental Health Letter*, 15(7), January 1999.

[101] *Merriam-Webster's Collegiate Dictionary, Tenth Edition*. Merriam-Webster, Springfield, MA, 1994.

[102] Stanton Peele. *The Meaning of Addiction: Compulsive Experience and Its Interpretation.* Lexington Books, Lexington, MA, 1985

[103] Kimberly S. Young. "Internet Addiction: Symptoms, Evaluation, and Treatment." *Innovations in Clinical Practice*, volume 17, edited by L. VandeCreek and T. L. Jackson. Professional Resource Press, Sarasota, FL, 1999.

[104] Mark Griffiths. "Does Internet and Computer 'Addiction' Exist? Some Case Study Evidence." *CyberPsychology and Behavior*, 3(2), 2000.

[105] Kimberly S. Young. "Internet Addiction: The Emergence of a New Clinical Disorder." *CyberPsychology and Behavior*, 1(3), 1998.

[106] John P. Charlton. "A Factor-Analysis Investigation of Computer 'Addiction' and Engagement." *British Journal of Psychology*, 99(3), August 2002.

[107] Aydrea Walden. "Center Helps Those Hooked on Internet." *The Seattle (WA) Times*, February 5, 2002.

[108] Jeffrey Reiman. *Critical Moral Liberalism: Theory and Practice*. Rowman & Littlefield Publishers, Lanham, MD, 1997.

[109] Immanuel Kant. *Lectures on Ethics*. Cambridge University Press, 2001.

[110] Matt Richtel. "Devices Enforce Silence of Cellphones, Illegally." *The New York Times*, November 4, 2007. www.nytimes.com.

[111] U.S. Department of State. "Internet Freedom." Fact sheet, February 15, 2011. www .state.gov.

[112] "Protesters Angry about Police Shooting Shut Down S.F. Subway Stop." *CNN*, July 12, 2011. www.cnn.com.

[113] "S.F. Subway System Admits Cutting Cellphone Service to Stop Planned Protest." *CNN*, August 13, 2011. news.blocks.cnn.com.

Michael Liebhold

Mike Liebhold is a Senior Researcher at the Institute for the Future focusing on the mobile and abundant computation, immersive media, and Geospatial Web foundations for context-aware and ubiquitous computing. Previously, Mike was a Visiting Researcher at Intel Labs, working on a pattern language based on Semantic Web frameworks for ubiquitous computing. Before that, during the late 1990s, Mike worked on startups building large-scale international public IT services and IP networks for rural and remote regions and for GPS-enhanced precision agriculture, a complete IT architecture for schools in Shandong Province, China, satellite networks in India, Europe, and Latin America, and was the Principal Investigator for a National Science Foundation project to bring Internet2 broadband IP networks to seventy rural low-income communities in the United States.

Mike is a frequent speaker on the topic of the Geospatial Web and has authored a number of papers, including one recently published in a special edition of the IEEE *Journal on Pervasive Computing*, "Data Management in the World-Wide Sensor Web."

You've said the Apple iPhone represents one of the most important inflection points in the history of technology. What makes the iPhone so significant?

I've been working in technology since 1977. My iPhone is the most profoundly impressive device that I've ever been around. What it represents is a mobile computer that everyone can afford. It's a device that can compute. It can give you Web access to all kinds of media information. It's a global library. And that's the way to think about the Web—as a global library for humanity. It supports rich video and audio, so you can actually imagine a spoken interactive interface to the global library that would let you gain access to information without being literate. It has position sensing. The device knows where it is, so very, very precise contextual information can become available to people.

Our forecast is that between 2015 and 2020 every human on Earth will be able to afford a device that's equivalent to an iPhone. Now that's not to say that the cost of network and data connectivity is going to drop commensurately, but over time there will be improved and lower cost networks for every human on Earth. And so I think we're at the dawning of a new wave of global literacy and connectivity.

In your answer you alluded to computers being able to provide information to people based on their location. How is geographical information being introduced into the Web?

The Geospatial Web has four components. The first is Web information that is identified by URL and its location: by latitude and longitude and increasingly by elevation. We now have Web standards that allow you to publish a piece of information by location that's viewable in a variety of Web browsers. The second component is a collection of Web-enabled maps of many, many varieties. Environmental maps, infrastructure maps, commercial maps, historical maps, cultural maps—many, many types of free and malleable maps are coming online. When I say malleable, I mean you can import the data that work with the map. The third component is real-time sensor data, such as temperature data, humidity data, and video feeds from cameras. Finally, the component of the Geospatial Web that's not quite here yet is embedded information. I've seen a computer chip that's as tiny as a mote of dust that has a CPU, a memory and a radio. There's a group at Carnegie Mellon that's made a Web server that's about as big as your fingernail on your little finger. So you can begin to imagine the physical things and physical places that are going to incorporate data.

What are people going to do with all this information?

There's a thought exercise that I do regularly, and I encourage people to think of it this way. I imagine I can see the invisible information. As I walk by a tree I pretend I can see a label that identifies not only the species of the tree but whether it's been watered or pruned lately—its maintenance record. I look at a building, and I imagine I can see the architectural drawings behind the facade. As I look at a historical building, I imagine I can see the tags that describe the historical significance of the place. As I see someone down the street I imagine they've got a digital cloak on and that they're a game player in a physical space. As I walk by a restaurant or a store I can see a listing of the things that are in the store. As I walk down the street I can see traffic indicators—arrows pointing the direction for me.

And in fact these things are all practical now. It's now possible for the viewfinder in your phone to be a Web browser, so you can hold up the viewfinder of your phone and see data attached to a place. Many applications are already available for the iPhone and Android, and there are more to come. There are restaurant menus that you can see as you walk down the street. There are applications that show you the health risk or danger of a place. There are applications that show you if it's safe to park your car. There are applications that guide you to real estate listings, and on and on and on.

You've been talking about using computers to augment reality, to give people more information about where they are and what they are looking at in the real world. What about the tens of millions of people who use computers to escape to virtual worlds through games like World of Warcraft or Halo?

I have to say that *World of Warcraft* and many, many other games are coming. Point-and-shoot video games are immensely popular among young men. So, yes, we do see that in their homes people are going to put on glasses and enjoy all kinds of immersive 3-D experiences, games, virtual travel, and lots and lots of other kinds of things. That's fairly legitimate, but I don't think people are going to be gone or lost any more than they are watching television today. People will get up and go outside. The world is an exciting place.

On the other hand, if I "travel" in a virtual world I don't have to worry about the long lines at airport security or the big crowd waiting to see David in Florence.

Telepresence might attract a lot of people, and it's going to help global literacy. There will be very, very compelling experiences with 3-D, and I think people are going to have a lot richer understanding of the world. But telepresence will never equal walking on the streets of Rome.

Tell me more about how people will use telepresence to enhance their lives in the "real world."

We see really remarkable things happening with applications like Skype videoconferencing. Distant relatives turn on Skype and leave it on all day because it's essentially free. I heard a story about two elderly sisters who use Skype voice calls. They turn it on, sit down, knit, chat, feed the cat, and enjoy each other's companionship. I met a guy who bought a flat screen television for his parents in France. They put it in their dining area, and he's got one in his kitchen. So when he sits down to have brunch on Sunday mornings his parents have dinner in France. And they can just leave it on and have a family meal together.

I think this is another great trend. I think that modern technology is actually bringing families and friends closer together instead of alienating or isolating people.

CHAPTER

4

Intellectual Property

Friends share all things.

—PYTHAGORAS

Today's pirates operate not on the high seas but on the Internet.

—RECORDING INDUSTRY ASSOCIATION OF AMERICA

4.1 Introduction

At a Bowling for Soup concert, the band made up a song onstage. Singer Jaret Reddick says, "That thing was on YouTube before I even got back home from the show" [1]. Do entertainers have the right to control who sees and hears a performance of their music?

About 40% of software installed on personal computers worldwide and about 80% of software in China was obtained illegally [2]. Is it fair for some people to pay full price for software when so many others are getting the same programs for little or no money?

Half of teenage Internet users in America admit to downloading music files [3]. The Recording Industry Association of America (RIAA) responds by identifying file-sharers and sending each of them a letter warning of an impending lawsuit, but giving the file-sharer the opportunity to settle out of court, usually by paying between $3,000 and $5,000 [4]. Boston University graduate student Joel Tenenbaum refused to settle out of court, was found guilty of violating copyright law by downloading and sharing 30 songs, and ordered by the jury to pay record companies $675,000 [5]. Meanwhile, the

FIGURE 4.1 The Electronic Frontier Foundation is advocating a reform of the copyright laws in the United States. (Advertisement from the Electronic Frontier Foundation. Copyright © 2011 by Electric Frontier Foundation (Creative Commons). Reprinted with permission.)

Electronic Frontier Foundation runs a "Let the Music Play" campaign (Figure 4.1) to convince Americans they should put pressure on Congress to change copyright laws [6].

As a society we benefit from access to high-quality music, movies, computer programs, and other products of the human intellect. The value of these intellectual properties is much higher than the cost of the media on which they are distributed, tempting people to make unauthorized copies. When this happens, producers of intellectual property do not receive all of the payments the law says they are entitled to. The legal system has responded by giving more rights to the creators of intellectual property. Are these changes in the best interests of our society, or are our politicians catering to special interest groups?

In this chapter, we discuss how information technology is affecting our notions of intellectual property. We consider what makes intellectual property different from tangible property and how governments have created a variety of mechanisms to guarantee intellectual property rights. We examine what has been considered "fair use" of intellectual property created by others, and how new copy-protection technologies are eroding the notions of fair use. Meanwhile, peer-to-peer networks are making it easier than ever for consumers to get access to music and movies without purchasing them. We look at what the entertainment industry is doing to fight free access to copyrighted material. We also explore the evolution of intellectual property protection for computer software and the rise of the open-source movement, which advocates the distribution of source code to programs. Finally, we take a look at one organization's efforts to make it easier for artists, musicians, and writers to use the Internet as a vehicle for stimulating creativity and enhancing collaboration.

4.2 Intellectual Property Rights

4.2.1 What Is Intellectual Property?

Intellectual property is any unique product of the human intellect that has commercial value [7]. Examples of intellectual property are books, songs, movies, paintings, inventions, chemical formulas, and computer programs.

It is important to distinguish between intellectual property and its physical manifestation in some medium. If a poet composes a new poem, for example, the poem itself is the intellectual property, not the piece of paper on which the poem is printed.

In most of the world there is a widely accepted notion that people have the right to own property. Does this right extend to intellectual property as well? To answer this question, we need to examine the philosophical justification for a natural right to property.

4.2.2 Property Rights

The English philosopher John Locke (1632–1704) developed an influential theory of property rights. In *The Second Treatise of Government*, Locke makes the following case for a natural right to property. First, people have a right to property in their own person. Nobody has a right to the person of anybody else. Second, people have a right to their own labor. The work that people perform should be to their own benefit. Third, people have a right to those things that they have removed from nature through their own labor [8].

For example, suppose you are living in a village, in the middle of woods that are held in common. One day you walk into the woods, chop down a tree, saw it into logs, and split the logs into firewood (Figure 4.2). Before you cut down the tree, everyone had a common right to it. By the time you have finished splitting the logs, you have mixed your labor with the wood, and at that point, it has become your property. Whether you burn the wood in your stove, sell it to someone else, pile it up for the winter, or give it away, the choice of what to do with the wood is yours.

FIGURE 4.2 According to John Locke, people have a natural right to the things they have removed from nature through their own labor.

Locke uses the same reasoning to explain how a person can gain the right to a piece of land. Taking a parcel out of the state of nature by clearing the trees, tilling the soil, and planting and harvesting crops gives people who performed these labors the right to call the land their property.

To Locke, this definition of property makes sense as long as two conditions hold. First, no person claims more property than he or she can use. In the case of harvesting a natural resource, it is wrong for someone to take so much that some of it is wasted. For example, people should not appropriate more land than they can tend. Second, when people remove something from the common state in order to make it their own property, there is still plenty left over for others to claim through their labor. If the woods are full of trees, I can chop a tree into firewood without denying you or anyone else the opportunity to do the same thing.

Locke's description of a natural right to property is most useful at explaining how virtually unlimited resources are initially appropriated. It is not as useful in situations where there are few or no resources left for appropriation.

4.2.3 Extending the Argument to Intellectual Property

Is there a natural right to intellectual property?

We can try to demonstrate such a right exists by extending Locke's theory of property rights to intellectual property. However, since Locke was talking about the ownership of physical objects and we are talking about the ownership of ideas, we must resort to an analogy. We'll compare creating a piece of intellectual property to making a belt buckle [9]. In order to make a belt buckle, a person must mine ore, smelt it down, and cast it. To write a play, a playwright "mines" words from the English language, "smelts" them into stirring prose, and "casts" them into a finished play.

Attempting to treat intellectual property the same as ordinary property leads to certain paradoxes, as Michael Scanlan has observed [9]. We will consider two of Scanlan's scenarios illustrating problems that arise when we extend Locke's natural rights argument to intellectual property.

∾ Scenario A, Act 1

After a day of rehearsals at the Globe Theatre, William Shakespeare decides to have supper at a pub across the street. The pub is full of gossip about royal intrigue in Denmark. After his second pint of beer, Shakespeare is visited by the muse, and in an astonishing burst of energy, he writes *Hamlet* in one fell swoop.

∾

If we apply Locke's theory of property to this situation, clearly Shakespeare has the right to own *Hamlet*. He mixed his labor with the raw resources of the English language and produced a play. Remember, we're not talking about the piece of paper upon which the words of the play are written. We're talking about the sequence of words comprising the play. The paper is simply a way of conveying them.

What should Shakespeare get from his ownership of *Hamlet*? Here are two ideas (you can probably think of more): He should have the right to decide who will perform the play. He should have the right to require others who are performing the play to pay him a fee.

So far, so good. But let's hear the end of the story.

∾ Scenario A, Act 2

On the very same night, Ben Jonson, at a pub on the opposite side of London, hears the same gossip, is struck by the same muse, and writes *Hamlet*—exactly the same play!

∾

Ben Jonson has mixed his intellectual labor with the English language to produce a play. According to Locke's theory of natural rights to property, he ought to own it. Is it possible for both Ben Jonson and William Shakespeare to own the same play (Figure 4.3)? No, not as we have defined ownership rights. It is impossible for both of them to have the exclusive right to decide who will perform the play. Both of them cannot have an exclusive claim to royalties collected when *Hamlet* is performed. We've uncovered a paradox: two people labored independently and produced only a single artifact.

We ended up with this paradox because our analogy is imperfect. If two people go to the same iron mine, dig ore, smelt it, and cast it into belt buckles, there are two belt buckles, one for each person. Even if the belt buckles look identical, they are distinct, and we can give each person ownership of one of them. This is not the case with *Hamlet*. Even though Jonson and Shakespeare worked independently, there is only one *Hamlet*: the sequence of words that constitute the play. Whether we give one person complete ownership or divide the ownership among the two men, both cannot get full ownership of the play, which is what they ought to have if the analogy were perfect. Therefore, the

"To be or not to be,
that is the question"

Figure 4.3 Suppose both Ben Jonson and William Shakespeare simultaneously write down *Hamlet*. Who owns it?

uniqueness of intellectual properties is the first way in which they differ from physical objects.

A second paradox has to do with the copying of intellectual property. Consider a slightly different version of our story.

∼ Scenario B

One evening William Shakespeare stays up all night in a pub writing *Hamlet* while Ben Jonson goes to a party. The next morning Shakespeare returns to the Globe Theatre, but he carelessly leaves a copy of *Hamlet* in the pub. Jonson stops by for a pint, sees the manuscript, transcribes it, and walks out the door with a copy of the play in his possession, leaving the original copy where it was.   ∼

Did Jonson steal *Hamlet*? Shakespeare still has his physical copy of the play, but he has lost exclusive control over who will read, perform, or hear the play. If you want to call this stealing, then stealing in the sense of intellectual property is quite different from stealing a physical object. When you steal someone's car, they can't drive it any more. When you steal someone's joke, both of you can tell it.

Certainly any creator of a piece of intellectual property has the right to keep his ideas a secret. After Shakespeare wrote *Hamlet*, he could have locked it in a trunk to prevent others from seeing it. Ben Jonson would not have the right to break into Shakespeare's trunk to get access to the play. Hence we can argue that there is a natural right to keep an idea confidential. Unfortunately, this is a weak right, because Shakespeare cannot perform the play while he is keeping it confidential. He must give up the confidentiality in order to put his creation to good use.

We began this section with the follwing question: Is there a natural right to intellectual property? We have found no right other than the weak right to keep an idea confidential. In our quest for stronger rights, we have uncovered two important differences between tangible property and intellectual property. First, every intellectual property is one-of-a-kind. Second, copying a piece of intellectual property is different from stealing a physical object.

4.2.4 Benefits of Intellectual Property Protection

New ideas in the form of inventions and artistic works can improve the quality of life for the members of a society. Some people are altruistic and will gladly share their creative energies. For example, Benjamin Franklin (1706–1790) invented many useful items, including an improved wood stove, the lightning rod, the odometer, and bifocals. He did not patent any of them. Franklin said, "As we enjoy great advantages from the invention of others, we should be glad of an opportunity to serve others by any invention of ours; and this we should do freely and generously" [10]. However, most people find the allure of wealth to be a strong inducement for laboring long hours in the hope of creating something useful. So even if there are no natural rights to intellectual property, a society may choose to grant intellectual property rights to people because of the beneficial consequences.

The authors of the Constitution of the United States recognized the benefits society reaps by encouraging creativity. Article I, Section 8, of the U.S. Constitution gives Congress the power to "promote the Progress of Science and useful Arts by securing for limited Times to Authors and Inventors the exclusive Right to their respective Writings and Discoveries."

If a person has the right to control the distribution and use of a piece of intellectual property, there are many opportunities for that person to make money. For example, suppose you build a better mousetrap and the government given you ownership of this design. You may choose to manufacture the mousetrap yourself. Anyone who wants the better mousetrap must buy it from you, because no other mousetrap manufacturer has the right to copy your design. Alternatively, you may choose to license your design to other manufacturers, who will pay you for the right to build mousetraps according to your design.

On the other hand, it is possible for you to be rewarded for your creativity without the new device ever reaching the public. Suppose you sell an exclusive license for your better mousetrap to the company that dominates the mousetrap market. The company chooses not to manufacture the new mousetrap because—for whatever reason—it can make more money selling the existing technology. In this situation you and the company benefit, but society is deprived access to the new, improved technology.

4.2.5 Limits to Intellectual Property Protection

Society benefits the most when inventions are in the public domain and anyone can take advantage of them. Going back to the mousetrap example, we would like everyone in society who needs a mousetrap to get the best possible trap. If someone invents a superior mousetrap, the maximum benefit would result if all mousetrap manufacturers were able to use the better design. On the other hand, if the inventor of the superior mousetrap did not have any expectation of profiting from her new design, she may not have bothered to invent it. Hence there is a tension between the need to reward the creators of intellectual property by giving them exclusive rights to their ideas and the need to disseminate these ideas as widely as possible.

The way the Congress has traditionally addressed this tension is through a compromise. It has granted authors and inventors exclusive rights to their writings and discoveries, but only for a limited period of time. (Note: Rights to a piece of intellectual property produced by an employee in the normal course of his or her duties belong to the employer.) At the end of that time period, the intellectual property enters the public domain. While creators have control over the distribution of their properties, use of the properties is more expensive, and the creators are rewarded. After properties enter the public domain, using them becomes less expensive, and everyone has the opportunity to produce derivative works from them.

Consider a community orchestra that wishes to perform a piece of classical music. It may purchase a piece of music from the public domain for far less money than it cost simply to rent the same piece of music while it was still protected by copyright (Table 4.1).

The question is: What is a reasonable length of time to grant authors and inventors exclusive rights to their creative works? Supreme Court Justice Stephen Breyer [12], Kembrew McLeod [13], and Lawrence Lessig [14] have used "Happy Birthday to You" as evidence that copyright protections are excessive.

"Happy Birthday to You" is the most popular song in the world. Have you ever wondered why you almost never hear it sung on television? The reason is that the music

TABLE 4.1 Once a piece of classical music enters the public domain, it may be purchased for much less than it cost simply to rent the same piece of music for two performances when it was still under copyright protection. These prices assume the orchestra has an annual budget of $150,000 or less [11]. (Table from "Letter to The Honorable Senator Spencer Abraham," by Randolph P. Luck from LUCK'S MUSIC LIBRARY. Copyright © 1996 by Randolph P. Luck. Reprinted with permission.)

Artist	Work	Previous Rental Fee	Year Became Public Domain	Purchase Price
Ravel	Daphnis et Chloe Suite no. 1	$450.00	1987	$155.00
Ravel	Mother Goose Suite	540.00	1988	70.00
Ravel	Daphnis et Chloe Suite no. 2	540.00	1989	265.00
Griffes	The White Peacock	335.00	1993	42.00
Puccini	O Mio Babbino Caro	252.00	1994	26.00
Respighi	Fountains of Rome	441.00	1994	140.00
Ravel	Le Tombeau de Couperin	510.00	1995	86.00
Respighi	Ancient Aires and Dances Suite no. 1	441.00	1996	85.00
Elgar	Cello Concerto	550.00	1997	140.00
Holst	The Planets	815.00	1997	300.00
Ravel	Alborada Del Gracioso	360.00	1999	105.00

publisher Clayton F. Summy Company (now a subsidiary of TimeWarner) copyrighted the song in 1935, and television networks must pay TimeWarner to air it. TimeWarner collects about $2 million in royalties each year for public performances of "Happy Birthday to You" [15]. Under the Copyright Term Extension Act of 1998, the song will remain copyrighted until at least 2030!

More recently, George Washington University law professor Robert Brauneis has objected that "Happy Birthday to You" should not be used as an example of the "overly generous protection of copyright law." In a meticulously researched article, he concludes that the song "is almost certainly no longer under copyright, due to a lack of evidence about who wrote the words; defective copyright notice; and a failure to file a proper renewal application" [16]. However, to this date no one has challenged TimeWarner's copyright in court.

4.3 Protecting Intellectual Property

While the U.S. Constitution gives Congress the right to grant authors and inventors exclusive rights to their creations, it does not elaborate on how these rights will be protected. Today, there are four different ways in which individuals and organizations protect their intellectual property: trade secrets, patents, copyrights, and trademarks/service marks.

4.3.1 Trade Secrets

A **trade secret** is a confidential piece of intellectual property that provides a company with a competitive advantage. Examples of trade secrets include formulas, processes, proprietary designs, strategic plans, customer lists, and other collections of information. The right of a company to protect its trade secrets is widely recognized by governments around the world. In order to maintain its rights to a trade secret, a company must take active measures to keep it from being discovered. For example, companies typically require employees with access to a trade secret to execute a confidentiality agreement.

A famous trade secret is the formula for Coca-Cola syrup. The formula, known inside the company as "Merchandise 7X," is locked in a bank vault in Atlanta, Georgia. Only a few people within the company know the entire formula, and they have signed nondisclosure agreements. The task of making the syrup is divided among different groups of employees. Each group makes only one part of the final mixture, so that nobody in these groups learns the complete recipe.

An advantage of trade secrets is that they do not expire. A company never has to disclose a trade secret. Coca-Cola has kept its formula secret for more than 100 years.

The value of trade secrets is in their confidentiality. Hence trade secrets are not an appropriate way to protect many forms of intellectual property. For example, it would make no sense for a company to make a movie a trade secret, because a company can only profit from a movie by allowing it to be viewed, which would make it no longer confidential. On the other hand, it would be appropriate for a company to make the *idea* for a movie a trade secret. Art Buchwald pitched Paramount Pictures a story called *King for a Day*, about an African prince who visits the United States. After the studio produced the movie *Coming to America*, starring Eddie Murphy, Buchwald successfully sued the studio for breach of contract, because he had made the studio sign a confidentiality agreement before he gave them the plot [17].

While it is illegal to steal a trade secret, there are other ways in which the confidentiality may be broken. "Reverse engineering" is one way in which a competing firm can legally gain access to information contained in a trade secret. If another company can purchase a can of Coca-Cola and figure out the formula, it is free to manufacture a soft drink that looks and tastes just like Coke.

Another way in which a competing firm can gain access to information contained in another company's trade secret is by hiring its employees. While a firm can require its employees to sign confidentiality agreements, it cannot erase the memories of an employee who starts working for a competing firm. Hence some "leakage" of confidential information may be inevitable when employees move from one company to another.

4.3.2 Trademarks and Service Marks

A **trademark** is a word, symbol, picture, sound, or color used by a business to identify goods. A **service mark** is a mark identifying a service [18].

By granting a trademark or service mark, a government gives a company the right to use it and the right to prevent other companies from using it. Through the use of a trademark, a company can establish a "brand name." Society benefits from branding because branding allows consumers to have more confidence in the quality of the products they purchase.

When a company is the first to market a distinctive product, it runs the risk that its brand name will become a common noun used to describe any similar product. When this happens, the company may lose its right to exclusive use of the brand name. Some trademarks that have become generic are "yo yo," "aspirin," "escalator," "thermos," and "brassiere."

Companies strive to ensure their marks are used as adjectives rather than nouns or verbs. One way they do this is through advertising (Figure 4.4). Kimberly-Clark's advertisements refer to "Kleenex *brand* facial tissue." Remember Johnson & Johnson's jingle, "I am stuck on Band-Aid *brand* 'cause Band-Aid's stuck on me"?

Another way companies protect their trademarks is by contacting those who are misusing them. For example, Adobe has responded to Web posts about "photoshopping images" by posting this follow-up message: "The Photoshop trademark must never be used as a common verb or as a noun. The Photoshop trademark should always be capitalized and should never be used in possessive form, or as a slang term" [19].

4.3.3 Patents

A **patent** is a way the U.S. government provides an inventor with an exclusive right to a piece of intellectual property. A patent is quite different from a trade secret because a

If a trademark is misused it could come undone.

If you didn't know zipper was a trademark, don't worry, it's not. But it used to be. It was lost because people misused the name. And the same could happen to ours, Xerox. Please help us ensure it doesn't. Use Xerox only as an adjective to identify our products and services, such as Xerox copiers, not a verb, "to Xerox," or a noun, "Xeroxes." Something to keep in mind that will help us keep it together.

xerox.com   Ready For Real Business **xerox**

FIGURE 4.4 Xerox Corporation ran this advertisement as part of its campaign to protect its trademark. (Screenshot by Xerox. Copyright © 2012 by Xerox Corporation. All rights reserved. Reprinted with permission.)

patent is a public document that provides a detailed description of the invention. The owner of the patent can prevent others from making, using, or selling the invention for the lifetime of the patent, which is currently 20 years. After the patent expires, anyone has the right to make use of its ideas.

POLAROID V. KODAK

Dr. Edwin Land invented "instant" photography. The company he founded, Polaroid Corporation, had ten patents protecting the invention of film that developed in 60 seconds. Polaroid did not license these patents to other firms, and for many years it was the only company to sell cameras and film allowing photographs to be developed in a minute.

When Kodak introduced its first instant camera in 1976, Polaroid sued Kodak [20]. In 1985 a court ruled that Kodak had infringed on seven of Polaroid's original ten patents; six years later Kodak paid Polaroid a $925 million settlement [21, 22].

SPARC INTERNATIONAL

Sometimes companies see an advantage in licensing their inventions. After Sun Microsystems invented the SPARC architecture, it wanted to maximize the number of SPARC-compliant computers being manufactured. For this reason, Sun transferred ownership of the SPARC specifications to an independent, nonprofit organization called SPARC International. SPARC International has licensed SPARC technology to a variety of other firms. In 2008, the list of companies manufacturing SPARC-based systems included Epoka Group A/S, Fujitsu, Itronix, Nature Worldwide Technology Corporation

(NatureTech), Rave Computer Association, Inc., Sun Microsystems, Inc., Themis Computer, and Toshiba Corporation.

4.3.4 Copyrights

A **copyright** is how the U.S. government provides authors with certain rights to original works that they have written. The owner of a copyright has five principal rights:

1. The right to reproduce the copyrighted work
2. The right to distribute copies of the work to the public
3. The right to display copies of the work in public
4. The right to perform the work in public
5. The right to produce new works derived from the copyrighted work

Copyright owners have the right to authorize others to exercise these five rights with respect to their works. The owner of a copyright to a play may sell a license to a high school drama club that wishes to perform it. After a radio station broadcasts a song, it must pay the songwriter(s) and the composer(s) through a performance rights organization such as ASCAP, BMI, or SESAC.

Copyright owners have the right to prevent others from infringing on their rights to control the reproduction, distribution, display, performance, and production of works derived from their copyrighted work.

By permission of John Deering and Creators Syndicate, Inc.

Several important industries in the United States, including the movie industry, music industry, software industry, and book publishing, rely upon copyright law for protection. "Copyright industries" account for over 6 percent of the United States gross domestic product, with about $900 billion in sales. About 5.5 million U.S. citizens work in these industries, which are growing at a much faster rate than the rest of the U.S. economy. With foreign sales and exports of $126 billion, copyright industries were the leading export sector in the United States in 2007 [23].

In this section, we examine court cases and legislation that have helped define the limits of copyright in the United States.

GERSHWIN PUBLISHING CORPORATION V. COLUMBIA ARTISTS MANAGEMENT, INC.

Columbia Artists Management, Inc. (CAMI) managed concert artists, and it sponsored hundreds of local, nonprofit community concert associations that arranged concert series featuring CAMI artists. CAMI helped the associations prepare budgets, select artists, and sell tickets. CAMI printed the programs and sold them to the community concert associations. In addition, all musicians performing at these concerts paid CAMI a portion of their fees.

On January 9, 1965, the CAMI-sponsored Port Washington (NY) Community Concert Association put on a concert that included Gershwin's "Bess, You Is My Woman Now" without obtaining copyright clearance from Gerwshwin Publishing Corporation. The American Society of Composers, Authors, and Publishers (ASCAP) sued CAMI for the copyright infringement.

CAMI argued that it was not responsible for the copyright infringement, since the concert was put on by the Port Washington Community Concert Association. However, the U.S. District Court for the Southern District of New York ruled that CAMI could be held liable because it was aware that the community concert associations it supported were not obtaining proper copyright clearances. In 1971, the U.S. Court of Appeals for the Second Circuit upheld the ruling of the district court [24].

BASIC BOOKS V. KINKO'S GRAPHICS CORPORATION

In the 1980s, Kinko's Graphics Corporation engaged in what it called the "Professor Publishing" business. It distributed brochures to university professors asking them to provide lists of readings they planned to use in their courses. Kinko's used these lists to produce packets of reading materials for students taking these classes. The packets typically contained chapters from books. In 1991, the U.S. District Court for the Southern District of New York ruled that when Kinko's produced these packets it infringed upon the copyrights held by the publishers. The judge ordered Kinko's to pay statutory damages of $510,000 to the plaintiffs, a group of eight book publishers [25]. Kinko's subsequently got out of the Professor Publishing business.

DAVEY JONES LOCKER

Richard Kenadek ran a computer bulletin board system (BBS) called Davey Jones Locker. Subscribers paid $99 a year for access to the BBS, which contained copies of more than 200 commercial programs. In 1994, Kenadek was indicted for infringing on the copyrights of the owners of the software. He pleaded guilty and was sentenced to six months' home confinement and two years' probation [26].

NO ELECTRONIC THEFT ACT

Another incident in 1994 led to further legislation protecting copyrights. David LaMacchia, an MIT student, posted copyrighted software on a public bulletin board he created on a university computer. According to prosecutors, bulletin board users downloaded more than a million dollars' worth of software in less than two months. However, the prosecutors were forced to drop charges against LaMaccia because he had made the programs available for free. Since he had not profited from his actions, he had not violated copyright law. To close this legal loophole, Congress passed the No Electronic Theft Act of 1997, which made it a criminal offense *simply to reproduce or distribute* more than $1,000 worth of copyrighted material in a six-month period.

COPYRIGHT CREEP

As a result of the Sonny Bono Copyright Term Extension Act of 1998, works created and published before January 1, 1978, are protected for 95 years. Works created on or after January 1, 1978, are protected for the author's lifetime plus 70 years after the author's death. If the work is a work made for hire, the length of protection is 95 years from the date of publication or 120 years from the date of creation, whichever is less.

According to Siva Vaidhyanathan, "in the early republic and the first century of American legal history, copyright was a Madisonian compromise, a necessary evil, a limited, artificial monopoly, not to be granted or expanded lightly" [27]. Over time, however, Congress has gradually increased both the term of copyright protection and the kind of intellectual properties that are protected by copyright (Figure 4.5). One reason

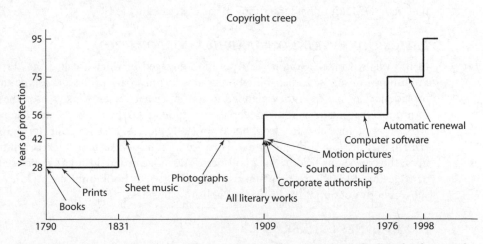

FIGURE 4.5 Since the first Copyright Act was passed in 1790, both the length of copyright protection and the kinds of intellectual property that can be copyrighted have grown dramatically.

has been the desire to have international copyright agreements. In order to complete these agreements, Congress has had to reconcile American copyright law with European law, which in general has had much stronger protections for the producers of intellectual property [27]. Another reason for "copyright creep" has been the introduction of new technologies such as photography, audio recording, and video recording.

For example, since 1831, music publishers have been able to copyright sheet music and collect royalties from musicians performing this music in public. In 1899, Melville Clark introduced the Apollo player piano, which played songs recorded on rolls of heavy paper. Apollo manufactured and sold piano rolls of copyrighted songs. White-Smith Music Company sued Apollo for infringing on its copyrights. In 1908, the Supreme Court ruled that Apollo had not infringed on White-Smith Music's copyrights. The court suggested that Congress ought to change copyright law if it wanted owners of copyrights to have control over recordings such as piano rolls and phonograph records. Congress responded by revising the Copyright Act in 1909. The new copyright law recognized that player piano rolls and phonograph records could be copyrighted.

Some people believe the expansion of the scope of copyright protection has shifted the balance of private versus public rights too far toward the copyright holders. They say it is no coincidence that copyright terms were extended just before Mickey Mouse was to enter the public domain. The Walt Disney Corporation lobbied Congress to pass the Sonny Bono Copyright Term Extension Act (CTEA) of 1998, protecting its profits derived from Mickey Mouse, Donald Duck, and its other famous characters [28]. Some critics suggest that since Walt Disney made a great deal of money on *Snow White and the Seven Dwarfs, Cinderella, Pinocchio, The Hunchback of Notre Dame, Alice in Wonderland,* and *The Jungle Book*, all based on stories taken from the public domain, it's only fair that at some point Walt Disney characters become part of the public domain, available for others to use in new creative works [29].

Eric Eldred, who digitizes old books and makes them freely available over the Web, led a group of petitioners who challenged the CTEA. They argued that the U.S. Constitution gives Congress the power to grant exclusive rights to authors for "limited times," and that the writers of the Constitution expected copyright durations to be short. By extending the terms of existing copyrights 11 times in 40 years, they said, Congress had exceeded its Constitutional power [30].

The government and groups representing the entertainment industry, including The Walt Disney Co., the Motion Picture Association of America, and the Recording Industry Association of America, argued that Congress does have the Constitutional authority to extend the terms of existing copyrights [31].

In a 7–2 decision the U.S. Supreme Court ruled in favor of the government and the entertainment industry, stating that the petitioners did not demonstrate how the CTEA had crossed "a constitutionally significant threshold." In the opinion of the Court, "Those earlier Acts did not create perpetual copyrights, and neither does the CTEA" [32].

In 2004, the Royal Society of Arts in London commissioned an international group of artists, scientists, and lawyers to create a statement regarding intellectual property laws. The group wrote the Adelphi Charter on Creativity Innovation and Intellectual Property. Within the Charter is the following statement: "The expansion in the law's breadth, score, and term over the last 30 years has resulted in an intellectual property regime which is radically out of line with modern technological, economic and social trends. This threatens the chain of creativity and innovation on which we and future generations depend" [33]. The Charter proposes a set of public-interest tests that governments should apply before approving further changes to intellectual property laws. It remains to be seen whether the Adelphi Charter will influence the global debate on intellectual property.

4.4 Fair Use

The right given to a copyright owner to reproduce a work is a limited right. Under some circumstances, called **fair use,** it is legal to reproduce a copyrighted work without the permission of the copyright holder. Examples of fair use include citing short excerpts from copyrighted works for the purpose of teaching, scholarship, research, criticism, commentary, and news reporting.

The United States Copyright Act does not precisely list the kinds of copying that are fair use. Instead, what is considered to be fair use has been determined by the judicial system. The courts have relied upon Section 107 of the Copyright Act, which lists four factors that need to be considered [34]:

1. *What is the purpose and character of the use?*

    An educational use is more likely to be permissible than a commercial use.

2. *What is the nature of the work being copied?*

    Use of nonfiction is more likely to be permissible than use of fiction. Published works are preferred over unpublished works.

3. *How much of the copyrighted work is being used?*

    Brief excerpts are more likely to be permissible than entire chapters.

4. *How will this use affect the market for the copyrighted work?*

    Use of out-of-print material is more likely to be permissible than use of a readily available work. A spontaneously chosen selection is better than an assigned reading in the course syllabus.

In the previous section on copyright we discussed the case against Kinko's. A number of factors led the judge to conclude that the reproductions made by Kinko's Professor Publishing business were not fair use. Kinko's is a commercial enterprise; it started the Professor Publishing business to make a profit. It copied significant portions of books to create the course reading packets. Some of the books were still in print; hence, Kinko's negatively affected the market for the copyrighted work. Finally, the readings were not spontaneously chosen. Kinko's had time to contact publishers and gain permission to reproduce the materials, perhaps by paying a licensing fee.

Let's consider two scenarios in which copyrighted works are duplicated and determine if they made fair use of the material. These scenarios are closely modeled after situations presented on the Web site of CETUS, the Consortium for Educational Technology in University Systems (www.cetus.org).

∼ Fair use Example #1

A professor puts a few journal articles on reserve in the library and makes them assigned reading for the class. Some students in the class complain that they cannot get access to the articles because other students always seem to have them checked out. The professor scans them and posts them on his Web site. The professor gives the students in the class the password they need to access the articles.   ∼

The first factor to consider is the purpose of the use. In this case the purpose is strictly educational. This factor weighs in favor of fair use.

The second factor is the nature of the work being copied. The journal articles are nonfiction. Again this weighs in favor of fair use.

The third factor is the amount of material being copied. The fact that the professor is copying entire articles rather than brief excerpts weighs against a ruling of fair use.

The fourth factor is the effect the copying will have on the market for journal sales. If the journal issues containing these articles are no longer for sale, then the professor's actions cannot affect the market. The professor took care to prevent people outside the class from accessing the articles. Overall, this factor appears to weigh in favor of fair use.

Three of the four factors weigh in favor of fair use. The professor's actions probably constitute fair use of the copyrighted material.

∼ Fair use Example #2

An art professor takes slide photographs of a number of paintings reproduced in a book about Renaissance artists. She uses the slides in her class lectures.   ∼

The first factor to consider is the purpose of the copying. The professor's purpose is strictly educational. Hence, the first factor weighs in favor of fair use.

The second factor is the type of material being copied. The material is art. Hence, this factor weighs against a ruling of fair use.

The third factor is the amount of material copied. In this case, the professor is displaying copies of the paintings in their entirety. Fair use almost never allows a work to be copied in its entirety. Note that even if the original painting is in the public domain, the photograph of the painting appearing in the art book is probably copyrighted.

The final factor is the effect the copying will have on the market. The determination of this factor would depend on how many images the professor took from any one book and whether the publisher is in the business of selling slides of individual images appearing in its book.

Overall, this professor's actions are less likely to be considered fair use than the actions of the professor in the first scenario.

4.4.1 *Sony v. Universal City Studios*

In 1975, Sony introduced its Betamax system, the first consumer VCR. People used these systems to record television shows for viewing later, a practice called **time shifting**. Some customers recorded entire movies onto videotape.

A year later, Universal City Studios and Walt Disney Productions sued Sony, saying it was responsible for copyright infringements performed by those who had purchased VCRs. The movie studios sought monetary damages from Sony and an injunction against the manufacturing and marketing of VCRs. The legal battle went all the way to the U.S. Supreme Court. The Supreme Court evaluated the case in light of the four fair use factors.

The first factor is the intended purpose of the copying. Since the purpose is private, not commercial, time shifting should be seen as fair use with respect to the first factor.

The second factor is the nature of the copied work. Consumers who are time shifting are copying creative work. This would tend to weigh against a ruling of fair use.

The third factor is the amount of material copied. Since a consumer copies the entire work, this weighs against a ruling of fair use.

The final factor is the effect time shifting will have on the market for the work. The Court determined that the studios were unable to demonstrate that time shifting had eroded the commercial value of their copyrights. The movie studios receive large fees from television stations in return for allowing their movies to be broadcast. Television stations can pay these large fees to the studios because they receive income from advertisers. Advertising rates depend upon the size of the audience; the larger the audience, the more a television station can charge an advertiser to broadcast a commercial. Time shifting allows people who would not ordinarily be able to watch a show to view it later. Hence, it can be argued that VCRs actually increase the size of the audience, and since audience size determines the fees studios receive to have their movies broadcast on television, it is not at all clear whether the copying of these programs harms the studios.

The Supreme Court ruled, in a 5–4 decision, that time shifting television programs is a fair use of the copyrighted materials [35]. It said that the private, noncommercial use of copyrighted materials ought to be presumed fair use unless it could be shown that the copyright holder would be likely to suffer economic harm from the consumer's actions (Figure 4.6). Importantly, the Court also noted that the Sony Betamax VCR could be used to copy both copyrighted and noncopyrighted material, and that Sony should not be held accountable if some of the people who buy a VCR choose to use it to infringe on copyrights.

4.4.2 Digital Recording Technology

In the not-so-distant past, music publishers distributed content on vinyl records, and some purchasers made backup copies on cassette tapes. The copying process introduced

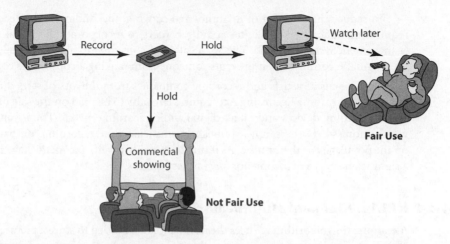

FIGURE 4.6 The Supreme Court ruled that videotaping television broadcasts for private viewing at a later time is fair use of the copyrighted material. This practice is called time shifting. Using videotaped material for a commercial purpose is not considered fair use.

hiss and distortions that significantly degraded the quality of the music. Trying to make a copy from a copy resulted in a nearly worthless tape. Music publishers focused on suing major violators of copyright law (those producing thousands of tapes) and ignored people who made a few copies of albums for their friends [36].

Digital technologies disrupted the status quo. The first of these technologies was the compact disc (CD). Initially, the introduction of CDs was a huge boon for the music publishing industry. The per-unit production cost of CDs was lower than vinyl albums or tapes, but their sound quality was higher, meaning companies could charge more for them. As a result, their profits swelled.

Someone with a digital recording device can copy a CD perfectly because it encodes music digitally—as a stream of ones and zeroes. When consumers didn't have access to digital recording devices, that wasn't a problem, but in the mid-1980s, Sony began selling digital audio tape (DAT) recorders in Japan and Europe. The Recording Industry Association of America opposed the introduction of DAT recorders in the United States on the grounds that giving consumers the ability to make unlimited numbers of perfect copies would destroy the recording industry. On the other side were Sony, Phillips, and other electronics companies that wanted to sell these devices to consumers.

4.4.3 Audio Home Recording Act of 1992

The Audio Home Recording Act represents a compromise between the desires of the recording industry, the electronics industry, and consumers. The Act protects the right of consumers to make copies of analog or digital recordings for personal, noncommercial use. For example, a consumer may copy a recording to put in another music player, to give to another family member, or to use as a backup.

To reduce the problem of unauthorized copying, the Audio Home Recording Act requires manufacturers of digital audio recorders to incorporate the Serial Copyright Management System (SCMS). The SCMS allows a consumer to make a digital copy from the original recording, but it prevents someone from making a copy of the copy.

To compensate artists and recording companies from the loss of sales due to copying, the Audio Home Recording Act requires a royalty to be paid on the sale of all digital audio recording devices and blank digital audio recording media. The royalties are divided among songwriters, music publishers, musicians, and recording companies, based on the popularity of their music. As it turns out, these royalty payments have never been a significant source of income for any of these groups.

4.4.4 *RIAA v. Diamond Multimedia Systems Inc.*

A **compression algorithm** reduces the number of bits needed to store a picture or sound. The most popular compression algorithm for music is MP3, which was developed by a team of European scientists. An MP3 music file is typically less than 10 percent the size of the original file, but it is difficult to hear the difference between the original and the compressed versions. The availability of MP3 encoders and decoders in the mid-1990s helped speed the development of portable music players.

Diamond Multimedia Systems introduced the Rio MP3 portable music player in 1998. About the size of an audio cassette, the Rio stored an hour of digitized music. The Recording Industry Association of America (RIAA) asked for an injunction preventing Diamond Multimedia Systems from manufacturing and distributing the Rio. The RIAA alleged that the Rio did not meet the requirements for the Audio Home Recording Act of 1992 because it did not employ the Serial Copyright Management System to prevent unauthorized copying of copyrighted material.

The U.S. Court of Appeals, Ninth Circuit, upheld the ruling of a lower court that the Rio was not a digital audio recording device as defined by the Audio Home Recording Act. It denied the injunction on these technical grounds. In addition, the Court affirmed that **space shifting**, or copying a recording in order to make it portable, is fair use and entirely consistent with copyright law (Figure 4.7).

4.4.5 *Kelly v. Arriba Soft Corporation*

Leslie Kelly was a photographer who maintained a Web site containing many of his copyrighted photos. Arriba Soft Corporation created an Internet-based search engine that responded to user queries by displaying thumbnail images. Arriba Soft created the thumbnail images by copying images from other Web sites. When Kelly discovered that the Arriba Soft search engine was displaying thumbnail images of his photographs, he sued Arriba Software for copyright infringement.

The U.S. Court of Appeals, Ninth Circuit, upheld the ruling of a lower court that Arriba Soft's use of the images was a fair use of the work [37]. Two factors heavily favored Arriba Soft's claim of fair use. First, the character and purpose of Arriba Soft's use of the images was "significantly transformative" [37]. Kelly's original images were

Fair Use | Not Fair Use

Your stereo | Your friend's stereo

Backup | Copy | Original | Copy

Copy

Your portable player

FIGURE 4.7 Space shifting is the creation of a copy for backup purposes or for use in a portable device, and it is considered fair use. Making a copy for a friend is not considered fair use.

artistic creations designed to provide the viewer with an aesthetic experience. Arriba Soft's use of the thumbnails was to create a searchable index that would make it easier for people to find images on the Internet. The thumbnail images had such low resolution that enlarging them resulted in a blurry image with little aesthetic appeal. Second, Arriba Soft's use of Kelly's images did not harm the value of the original images or the market for these images. If anything, the search engine's display of Kelly's images "would guide users to Kelly's web site rather than away from it," increasing the demand for his photographs [37].

4.4.6 Google Books

In December 2004, Google announced a plan to scan millions of books held by Harvard University, the University of Michigan, the New York Public Library, Oxford University, and Stanford University, creating a database containing the words contained in all of these books [38]. This database is much more powerful than traditional library card catalogs because it allows users to search for words or phrases appearing anywhere in the cataloged books. The system responds to a user query by returning the books that match the query most closely. If the book is in the public domain, the user can view and download a PDF file containing the scanned images of the book's pages. If the book is still under copyright, the user can see a few sentences from the book that show the search term in context, and the search engine provides links to libraries holding the book and online bookstores selling the book.

In September 2005, the Authors Guild filed a lawsuit in the U.S. District Court for the Southern District of New York, claiming that "by reproducing for itself a copy of those works that are not in the public domain, Google is engaging in massive copyright infringement" [39]. A month later, a group of five major publishers sued Google for copyright infringement. The publishers claimed that Google was infringing their rights under the Copyright Act because Google's intent was "purely commercial" and in order to create its database, Google was systematically copying entire books still protected by copyright [40].

Three years later, Google reached an out-of-court settlement with the Authors Guild and the Association of American Publishers. A joint public FAQ from the Authors Guild, the Association of American Publishers, and Google stated that the agreement would enable them "to do more together than copyright owners or Google could have done alone or through a court ruling" [41]. According to the three parties, the settlement would result in five important benefits:

1. Readers in the United States would have much easier access to millions of copyrighted books, including millions of books that are out-of-print, by allowing readers to search through them and preview them online.

2. The market for copyrighted books in the United States would grow by offering Google Books users the opportunity to purchase online access to them.

3. People would gain online access to out-of-print books at designated computers in U.S. public libraries and university libraries.

4. U.S. colleges and universities would have the opportunity to purchase subscriptions that would enable their students to gain online access to the collections of some of the world's greatest libraries.

5. Authors and publishers would receive payments earned from the online access of their books, fees paid when people printed pages from their books, and advertising revenues.

As part of the settlement, Google agreed to pay $125 million to resolve legal claims made by authors and publishers, cover their legal fees, and establish the Book Rights Registry. By registering their works with the Book Rights Registry, copyright holders would be able to receive payments received from institutional subscriptions, book sales, and advertising revenues.

The out-of-court settlement was controversial [42]. According to some, Google should not have made a deal with the plaintiffs. They felt Google's use of the copyrighted material was a fair use, based on the precedent of *Kelly v. Arriba Soft Corporation*, and if Google had gone to trial and been found not guilty, the public would have been able to access these books at lower rates. Others criticized the settlement because they thought it gave Google a virtual monopoly over **orphaned works**: copyrighted books for which the copyright owner cannot be located. The Electronic Frontier Foundation expressed concerns about the potential chilling effect of Google tracking the pages that people are viewing.

In March 2011, the U.S. District Court for the Southern District of New York rejected the proposed settlement. The judge ruled that the agreement "would give Google a significant advantage over competitors, rewarding it for engaging in wholesale copying of copyrighted works without permission" [43]. In particular, the judge objected to the part of the agreement that would have given Google liberal rights over orphaned works; according to the judge, a process for making use of orphaned books should be established by Congress, not a federal judge. Meanwhile, Google now has scanned more than 15 million books, even though most of them are still under copyright [44].

4.5 New Restrictions on Use

CDs and DVDs store sounds and images in digital form. When information is stored digitally, anyone with the right equipment can make perfect copies. China is the principal source of counterfeit CDs and DVDs (Figure 4.8) [45].

The increase in the number of people with broadband Internet connections has stimulated digital copying. Although a patient person with an ordinary dial-up connection to the Internet can download large files, connections that are dozens of times faster make file sharing much more practical. As more people got DSL or cable access to the Internet, the number of downloads soared [46]. Broadband connections have also made video sharing much more popular. As a result, the music industry is in real trouble. Total revenue from music sales and licensing in the United States dropped from $14.6 billion in 1999 to $6.3 billion in 2009 [47].

Governments and recording companies have responded to the threat of illegal copying of copyrighted materials by introducing new legal and technological restrictions on copying. Sometimes that makes it impossible for consumers to make copies even for purposes that are considered fair use, such as making a backup. Larry Kenswil of

FIGURE 4.8 Counterfeit CDs are destroyed in Thailand. (© Reuters/CORBIS)

Universal Music Group says, "What we really want to do is not to stop copying, simply to stop redistributing. But the technology available doesn't distinguish between the two" [36].

4.5.1 Digital Millennium Copyright Act

The Digital Millennium Copyright Act (DMCA), passed by Congress in 1998, was the first major revision of United States copyright law since 1976. The primary purpose of the DMCA was to bring the United States into compliance with international copyright agreements it had signed [34]. Provisions in the DMCA significantly curtail fair use of copyrighted material. The DMCA makes it illegal for consumers to circumvent encryption schemes placed on digital media, and it is illegal to sell (or even discuss online) a software program designed to circumvent copy controls [48].

Online service providers that misuse copyrighted materials face severe penalties [48]. That means, for example, a university that knows students are exchanging MP3 files on the campus network and does nothing to stop them can be sued [49].

The DMCA extends the copyright protection to music broadcast over the Internet. It requires royalty payments to be made to copyright holders of music played over the Internet since October 1998. For example, a college Internet radio station would pay the larger of an annual fee of $500 or $0.0002 per listener per song for every song that it plays. Radio stations are having a hard time determining how much they owe, because most of them have not kept track of how many online listeners they have or the number of songs they have played [50].

4.5.2 Digital Rights Management

Digital rights management (DRM) can refer to any of a variety of actions owners of intellectual property may take to protect their rights. As Christopher May puts it, "All DRM technologies are aimed at tracking and controlling the use of content once it has entered the market" [51]. DRM technologies may be incorporated into a computer's operating system, a program, or a piece of hardware.

One approach to DRM is to encrypt the digital content so that only authorized users can access it. Another approach is to place a digital mark on the content so that a device accessing the content can identify the content as copy-protected.

4.5.3 Secure Digital Music Initiative

The Secure Digital Music Initiative (SDMI) was an effort to create copy-protected CDs and secure digital music downloads that would play only on SDMI-compliant devices. About 200 entertainment and technology companies joined the consortium, which worked for three years to develop "digital watermarks" that would make unauthorized copying of audio files impossible. The SDMI was unsuccessful for three reasons. First, before any copy-protection technologies could be put in place, the number of music files being copied on the Internet mushroomed. Second, some of the sponsors of the

SDMI—consumer electronics companies—started making a lot of money selling devices that became more attractive to customers as access to free MP3 files got easier. Their sales could be hurt by restrictions on copying. Third, the digital watermarking scheme was cracked [52].

In September 2000, SDMI issued a "Hack SDMI" challenge. It released some digitally watermarked audio files and offered a $10,000 prize to the first person to crack them. Princeton computer science professor Edward Felten and eight colleagues picked up the gauntlet. Three weeks later, the team had successfully read the audio files. The team declined to accept the cash prize. Instead, it wrote a paper describing how it broke the encryption scheme. It prepared to present a paper at the Fourth Annual Information Hiding Workshop at Carnegie-Mellon University in April 2001 [53]. At this point, the Recording Industry Association of America sent Dr. Felten a letter stating, "Any disclosure of information gained from participating in the public challenge would be outside the scope of activities permitted by the agreement and could subject you and your research team to actions under the Digital Millennium Copyright Act" [54]. Fearing litigation, Dr. Felten agreed to withdraw the paper from the conference. However, that did not prevent the information from being leaked. Even before the conference, copies of the research paper and the letter from the RIAA were placed on a freedom-of-speech Web site [54]. Four months later Felten's group published the paper [55].

4.5.4 Sony BMG Music Entertainment Rootkit

In the summer and fall of 2005, Sony BMG Music Entertainment shipped millions of audio CDs with Extended Copy Protection, a DRM system. Extended Copy Protection prevented users from ripping audio tracks into MP3 format or making more than three backup copies of the CD. It also monitored the user's listening habits and reported back to Sony via the Internet. Extended Copy Protection did this by secretly installing a "rootkit" on Windows computers when the CD was played for the first time. A **rootkit** is a way of hiding files and processes from users; rootkits are commonly associated with computer hackers. The installation of the rootkit also compromised the security of the user's computer, making it vulnerable to "Trojan horse" programs (see Chapter 6) [56].

A computer expert discovered the Sony rootkit on his computer and publicized its existence, resulting in a huge public outcry and a class action lawsuit. Without admitting any wrongdoing, Sony BMG agreed to the following:

- Cease production of CDs with Extended Copy Protection
- Provide financial incentives to retailers to return unsold audio CDs with Extended Copy Protection
- Make freely available the software patch needed to uninstall the rootkit
- Allow customers to exchange CDs with Extended Copy Protection for identical CDs with no DRM
- Give consumers $7.50 or three free album downloads for every CD with Extended Copy Protection they exchange [57]

4.5.5 Encrypting DVDs

A DVD (Digital Versatile Disc) is capable of storing a full-length motion picture. DVDs are smaller than videotapes and have higher video and audio fidelity. People can view DVDs on DVD players attached to home entertainment systems; they can also watch DVDs on Windows and Macintosh computers equipped with DVD players.

To prevent unauthorized viewing of DVD movies, the contents of the discs are encrypted using a scheme called the Content Scramble System (CSS), developed by Matsushita and Toshiba. DVD players and DVD drives inside PCs and Macintoshes have a licensed copy of CSS including the decryption keys [58].

In 1999, 16-year-old Norwegian Jon Johansen wrote a computer program called DeCSS that decoded the CSS encryption scheme. DeCSS enabled him to view DVD movies on a computer running the Linux operating system, which was not supported by CSS. Johansen distributed the program to others via the Internet.

2600 Magazine published the code and provided links to it. Eight major motion picture studios successfully sued the publisher of *2600 Magazine* for violating the Digital Millennium Copyright Act [59]. In November 2001, a federal appeals court upheld the ruling. The appeals court ruled that while a computer code is "speech," the code enjoys only limited First Amendment protection because its purpose is more "functional" than "expressive." The court held that the publisher's right to post the code on the Internet was outweighed by the potential harm the program could do in the form of increasing the illegal copying of digitally encoded motion pictures [60].

Jon Johansen was also brought to trial in Norway for creating and distributing DeCSS, but in January 2003, an Oslo City Court acquitted Johansen. The court ruled he had the right to access information on a DVD that he had purchased. It noted the program Johansen developed to decrypt DVDs could be used for both legal and illegal purposes [59].

4.5.6 Foiling HD–DVD Encryption

IBM, Intel, Microsoft, Panasonic, Sony, Toshiba, The Walt Disney Company, and Warner Brothers cofounded an organization that created the Advanced Access Content System (AACS) for encrypting high-definition DVDs (HD-DVDs). The purpose of the AACS is to prevent the unauthorized copying and viewing of HD-DVDs.

In January 2007, this 32-character AACS encryption key was posted on Digg.com, a social news Web site:

```
09 F9 11 02 9D 74 E3 5B D8 41 56 C5 63 56 88 C0
```

In theory, consumers could use this key to play HD-DVDs on their Linux computers or rip movies to their computer hard drives, but the post did not link to a program that could actually do either of these things. The AACS parent organization immediately contacted Digg, claiming the post violated its intellectual property rights and ordering Digg to purge the key from its site. Tiny Digg, with only a few employees, deleted the offending story and closed the account of the person who submitted it. Some other

Digg users had reproduced the story or mentioned the key in comments. Digg closed the accounts of these users and deleted their posts, too. Digg CEO Jay Adelson explained the company's decision this way: "Whether you agree or disagree with the policies of the intellectual property holders and consortiums, in order for Digg to survive, it must abide by the law" [61].

The reaction of "diggers"—regular Digg users—to these actions was swift and unambiguous. In the words of some bloggers, "an Internet riot" ensued. Thousands of diggers reposted the key in a variety of imaginative ways and "dugg" each other's stories. Soon every front-page story had the encryption key in its headline. At the end of the day, the Digg administrators backed down. Digg's founder and chief architect said, "You've made it clear. You'd rather see Digg go down fighting than bow down to a bigger company. If we lose, then what the hell, at least we died trying" [61].

In response to the release on the Web of this key, the AACS organization expired the compromised key, requiring owners of HD DVD and Blu-ray players to go online and fetch a replacement key [62]. A month later, a story revealing the new "secret" processing key was posted on Digg [63].

4.5.7 Criticisms of Digital Rights Management

The introduction of DRM technologies has been controversial. Here are some criticisms that have been raised against DRM.

Many experts suggest that any technological "fix" to the problem of copyright abuse is bound to fail. As we have seen in the previous examples, all prior attempts to create encryption or anti-copying schemes have been abandoned or circumvented.

Others argue that DRM undermines the well-established principle of fair use. Under DRM, a consumer may not be able to make a private copy of a DRM-protected work without making an extra payment, even if he has the right to do so under traditional fair use standards. Selena Kim writes:

> In the analogue world, people go ahead and use the work if they believe themselves entitled to do so. It is only if users are sued for infringement that they invoke the relevant copyright exceptions as defence. In a digital world encapsulated by access control and embedded with copy control, a potential user of a work may have to ask for permission twice: once to access a work, and again to copy an excerpt. The exception to copyright is not being put forward as a defence; it is put forward to show entitlement to use the work. [64]

DRM restrictions sometimes prevent libraries from reformatting materials to make them more accessible to persons with disabilities. In addition, DRM protections, unlike copyrights, never expire [65].

Finally, some DRM schemes prevent people from anonymously accessing content. Microsoft's Windows Media Player has an embedded globally unique identifier (GUID). The Media Player keeps track of all the content the user views. When the Media Player contacts Microsoft's central server to obtain titles, it can upload information about the user's viewing habits.

4.5.8 Online Music Stores Drop Digital Rights Management

When Apple began selling music through the iTunes Music Store in 2003, all of the songs were protected with a DRM scheme called FairPlay. FairPlay blocked users from freely exchanging music they had purchased by preventing songs from being played on more than five computers or being copied onto CDs more than seven times. FairPlay had two other "features" that were strong incentives for consumers to stick with the Apple brand: music purchased from the iTunes store couldn't be played on portable devices other than the Apple iPod, and DRM-protected music purchased from other online retailers couldn't be played on the iPod [66].

Consumers complained about the restrictions associated with DRM, and eventually music retailers responded. In 2007, EMI announced it would begin offering all of its songs without DRM through the iTunes Store for $1.29, 30 cents more than the previous price [67]. A year later, Amazon became the first online music store to reach an agreement with all four major labels to sell music free of DRM restrictions [68]. Apple followed suit in 2009 with an announcement that it, too, had reached an agreement with all the major music labels to sell music without DRM restrictions [69].

4.6 Peer–to–Peer Networks

On the Internet, the adjective **peer-to-peer** refers to a transient network allowing computers running the same networking program to connect with each other and access files stored on each other's hard drives (Figure 4.9). Peer-to-peer networks stimulate the

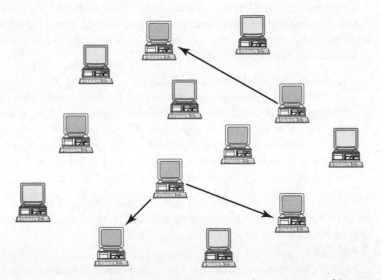

FIGURE 4.9 Some of the computers on the Internet run the same networking program to form a peer-to-peer network. The network supports multiple simultaneous file transfers. The files may contain digitized music, images, computer software, or other content.

exchange of data in three ways. First, they give each user access to data stored in many other computers. Second, they support simultaneous file transfers among arbitrary pairs of computers. Third, they allow users to identify those systems that will be able to deliver the desired data more rapidly, perhaps because they have a faster Internet connection or are fewer routing hops away.

4.6.1 Napster

Napster, which began operation in 1999, was a peer-to-peer network that facilitated the exchange of music files. In December 1999, the RIAA sued Napster for copyright infringement, asking for damages of $100,000 each time a Napster user copied a copyrighted song. In June 2000, the RIAA asked for a preliminary injunction to block Napster from trading any copyrighted content from major record labels. In February 2001, a federal appeals court ruled that Napster must stop its users from trading copyrighted material. Napster put in place file-filtering software that was 99 percent effective in blocking the transfer of copyrighted material. In June 2001, a district court judge ruled that unless Napster could block 100 percent of attempted transfers of copyrighted material, it must disable file transfers. This court order effectively killed Napster, which went offline in July 2001 and officially shut down in September 2002 [70, 71, 72]. The following year, Napster reemerged as an online subscription music service and music store.

4.6.2 FastTrack

FastTrack is a second-generation peer-to-peer network technology developed by Scandinavians Niklas Zennistrõm and Janus Friis. Because of its decentralized design, a FastTrack network may be more difficult to shut down than Napster [73, 74].

Figure 4.10 illustrates the differences between the Napster and FastTrack implementations of peer-to-peer file sharing. Napster relied upon a central computer to maintain a global index of all files available for sharing. The existence of this central index made it easy to eliminate the distribution of copyrighted files via Napster.

In contrast, FastTrack distributes the index of available files among a large number of "supernodes." Any computer with a high-speed Internet connection running FastTrack has the potential to become a supernode. The use of multiple supernodes makes searching for content slower, but it also makes it much more difficult for legal authorities to shut down the file-sharing network.

Popular peer-to-peer networks Kazaa and Grokster use the FastTrack technology. Morpheus, operated by StreamCast, is based on a different file-sharing technology called Neonet [75].

4.6.3 BitTorrent

For a computer with a broadband connection to the Internet, downloading a file from the network is about ten times faster than uploading a file to the network. A problem with FastTrack and other peer-to-peer networking protocols is that when one peer computer shares a file with another peer computer, the file is transferred at the slower, upload

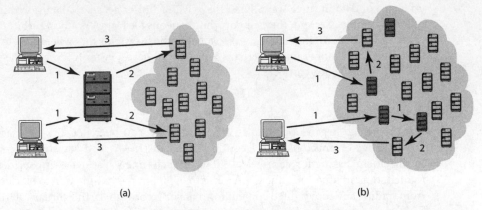

(a)   (b)

Figure 4.10 Comparison of the Napster and FastTrack implementations of peer-to-peer file sharing. (a) In Napster, a central server maintains the index of all files available for sharing. Retrieving a file is a three-step process: (1) making the request to the central server, (2) establishing a peer-to-peer connection between the sending and receiving computers, and (3) transferring the file. (b) In FastTrack, the index of available files is distributed among many "supernodes." Each supernode has information about files available for sharing on "nearby" computers. Different users connect with different supernodes.

speed rather than the faster, download speed. To solve this problem, Bram Cohen developed BitTorrent [76].

BitTorrent divides a file into pieces about a quarter megabyte in length. Different pieces of a file can be downloaded simultaneously from different computers, avoiding the uploading bottleneck (Figure 4.11). As soon as a user has a piece of a file, the user can share this piece with other users. Since BitTorrent gives a priority for downloads to those users who allow uploading from their machines, users tend to be generous. As a result, downloading speeds increase as more peers get a copy of the file. Put another way, downloading speeds increase with the popularity of a title.

With its markedly higher downloading rates, BitTorrent has made practical the exchange of files hundreds of megabytes long. People are using BitTorrent to download copies of computer programs, television shows, and movies. Linspire, a Linux operating system developer, reduces demand on its servers (and saves money) by using BitTorrent to distribute its software [77]. BitTorrent was also the vehicle by which *Revenge of the Sith* became available on the Internet before it appeared in movie theaters [78].

4.6.4 RIAA Lawsuits

In April 2003, the RIAA warned Grokster and Kazaa users that they could face legal penalties for swapping files containing copyrighted music. The message read, in part:

> It appears that you are offering copyrighted music to others from your computer. . . . When you break the law, you risk legal penalties. There is a simple way to avoid that risk: DON'T STEAL MUSIC, either by offering it to others to copy or

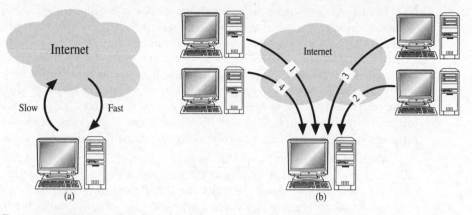

FIGURE 4.11 (a) Broadband Internet connections provide higher speeds for downloading than for uploading. (b) BitTorrent reduces downloading times by enabling a computer to download different pieces of a file simultaneously from many different peers.

downloading it on a 'file-sharing' system like this. When you offer music on these systems, you are not anonymous and you can easily be identified [79].

The RIAA identified the IP addresses of the most active Kazaa supernodes, leading it to the ISPs of users who have stored large numbers of copyrighted files on their computers. Under the terms of the Digital Millennium Copyright Act, the RIAA subpoenaed Verizon, asking it to identify the names of customers suspected of running these Kazaa supernodes. Verizon resisted responding to the subpoenas, claiming that responding to the subpoenas would violate the privacy of its customers. In June 2003, a judge in Washington, D.C., ruled that Verizon had to release the names of these customers [80].

In September 2003, the RIAA sued 261 individuals for distributing copyrighted music over the Internet [81]. A month later, the RIAA sent letters to 204 people who had downloaded at least 1,000 music files, giving them an opportunity to settle before being sued by the RIAA [82].

In December 2003, the RIAA suffered a setback when the U.S. Court of Appeals for the District of Columbia Circuit ruled that Verizon did not have to respond to the subpoenas of the RIAA and identify its customers [83]. Still, there is some evidence the RIAA lawsuits have reduced illegal file-swapping across the Internet. A survey from ComScore reported activity on Kazaa declined by 15 percent between November 2002 and November 2003 [84]. The Pew Internet & American Life Project reported that the percentage of Internet users who say they download music dropped from 32% in October 2002 to 22% in January 2005, and more than half of the January 2005 downloaders said that they purchased their music from an online service, such as iTunes. However, the report cautioned that because of the stigma associated with illegal downloading, fewer people may be willing to admit they do it. Interestingly, about half of music downloaders said they have gotten music from email, instant messages, or someone else's MP3 player or iPod [85].

The RIAA's campaign to impose severe penalties on file-sharers has been successful in the courtroom, but huge jury judgments against file sharers have been overruled by judges. In June 2009, a federal jury in Minnesota ordered Jammie Thomas-Rassert, a single mother of four, to pay $1.92 million—$80,000 a song—for violating the copyrights of 24 songs [86]. (The RIAA accused her of making 1,700 songs available on Kazaa, but they only tried to prove 24 copyright infringements.) In July 2011, Judge Michael Davis reduced the damage award against Thomas-Rassett to $54,000. Judge Davis called the original award "appalling," and said it was "so severe and oppressive as to be wholly disproportioned to the offense and obviously unreasonable" [91].

Another verdict went the RIAA's way in July 2009. The RIAA had accused Joel Tenenbaum of copyright infringement for using Kazaa to share 31 music files. The jury awarded the music companies $675,000, or $22,500 per song [5]. In July 2010, Judge Nancy Gertner reduced the jury's award to $67,500. In her ruling, Judge Gertner wrote: "[T]here is substantial evidence indicating that Congress did not contemplate that the Copyright Act's broad statutory damages provision would be applied to college students like Tenenbaum who file-shared without any pecuniary gain. . . There is no question that this reduced award is still severe, even harsh. It not only adequately compensates the plaintiffs for the relatively minor harm that Tenenbaum caused them; it sends a strong message that those who exploit peer-to-peer networks to unlawfully download and distribute copyrighted works run the risk of incurring substantial damages awards" [90].

During these trials the RIAA did not prove that people had actually downloaded songs from the defendants' computers. Instead, they contended that simply making the music files available to others was a violation of copyright law. In other words, making it possible for someone to download a music file from you means you've violated copyright law, even if no one ever does it. In April 2008, a federal court judge in New York agreed with the position of the RIAA, but judges in Massachusetts and Arizona reached the opposite conclusion, holding that simply making music files available for copying is not copyright infringement [87, 88, 89].

4.6.5 *MGM v. Grokster*

A group of movie studios, recording companies, music publishers, and songwriters sued Grokster and StreamCast for the copyright infringements of their users. The plaintiffs (henceforth referred to as MGM) sought damages and an injunction against the defendants.

During the discovery phase of the litigation, the following facts were revealed:

- The defendants' networks were used to transfer billions of files every month.
- About 90 percent of the files available on Grokster's FastTrack network were copyrighted.
- Grokster and StreamCast promoted their networks to investors and potential customers as replacements for Napster.

- An internal StreamCast document revealed that StreamCast's executives wanted to have more copyrighted songs available on their network than on competing networks.

- Grokster sent its users a newsletter touting its ability to deliver popular copyrighted songs.

- Grokster and StreamCast provided technical support to users who were having difficulty locating or playing copyrighted content.

A U.S. District Court granted Grokster and StreamCast a summary judgment; that is, it made its decision without a trial based on the facts and evidence collected. According to the judge, "[T]he defendants distribute and support software, the users of which can and do choose to employ it for both lawful and unlawful ends. Grokster and StreamCast are not significantly different from companies that sell home video recorders or copy machines, both of which can be and are used to infringe copyrights" [92]. The judge referred to *Sony v. Universal City Studios*, the Supreme Court's 1984 ruling on the legality of Sony's Betamax VCR. MGM appealed to the U.S. Court of Appeals for the Ninth Circuit, which upheld the ruling.

After another appeal, the U.S. Supreme Court *unanimously* reversed the decision of the lower courts in June 2005. Justice Souter wrote: "The question is under what circumstances the distributor of a product capable of both lawful and unlawful use is liable for acts of copyright infringement by third parties using the software. We hold that one who distributes a device with the object of promoting its use to infringe copyright, as shown by clear expression or other affirmative steps taken to foster infringement, is liable for the resulting acts of infringement by third parties" [93].

The Supreme Court made clear it was not reversing the Sony Betamax decision. Instead, it ruled that the "safe harbor" provided to Sony did not apply to Grokster and StreamCast. The Sony Betamax VCR was primarily used for time-shifting television shows, which the Court found to be a fair use. There was no evidence Sony had done anything to increase sales of its VCRs by promoting illegal uses. Therefore, Sony could not be found liable simply for selling VCRs.

The situation for Grokster and StreamCast was quite different. Both companies gave away their software, but made money by streaming advertisements to users. Advertising rates are higher when the number of users is greater. Hence, both companies wanted to increase their user base. They realized the way to do this was to make sure their networks had the content people are interested in downloading. The opinion notes dryly, "Users seeking Top 40 songs, for example, or the latest release by Modest Mouse, are certain to be far more numerous than those seeking a free Decameron, and Grokster and StreamCast translated that demand into dollars . . . [T]he unlawful objective is unmistakable" [93].

According to the Supreme Court, the Ninth Circuit Court of Appeals erred when it cited *Sony v. Universal City Studios*. The more relevant precedent was *Gershwin Publishing Corporation v. Columbia Artists Management, Inc.* The Supreme Court remanded the case to the Court of Appeals, suggesting that a summary judgment in favor of MGM would be in order. Grokster shut down its peer-to-peer network in November 2005 and paid $50 million to "movie studios, record labels and music publishers" [94].

4.6.6 Legal Action Against The Pirate Bay

The Pirate Bay, based in Stockholm, Sweden, is one of the biggest file-sharing Web sites in the world, with an estimated 25 million users [95]. People use The Pirate Bay to search for songs, movies, TV shows, or computer programs they can download for free. These items of intellectual property are broken into BitTorrent fragments stored in thousands of different computers scattered across the globe. Established in 2003, The Pirate Bay has been called "the most visible member of a burgeoning international anti-copyright—or pro-piracy—movement" [96].

The movie industry pressured the Swedish government to do something about The Pirate Bay, and in 2006, Swedish police raided its offices and confiscated 186 servers, but the site was offline for only three days [96, 97]. After the site was reactivated, the number of people accessing it increased significantly, perhaps because of the international publicity The Pirate Bay received as a result of the raid [96].

In 2008, the International Federation of the Phonographic Industry sued four individuals connected with The Pirate Bay for making available 33 copyrighted works: 20 songs, nine films, and four computer games [95]. The defendants argued that The Pirate Bay is simply a search engine and does not host any copyrighted content [98]. In April 2009, a District Court in Stockholm found Carl Lundström, Fredrik Neij, Peter Sunde, and Gottfrid Svartholm Warg guilty of aiding and abetting copyright infringement. All four were sentenced to one year in prison, and altogether were fined 30 million Swedish kronor (about $3.6 million). In November 2010, an appeals court in Sweden upheld the convictions, but shortened the sentences and increased the fine to 46 million kronor ($6.5 million) [99].

Meanwhile, The Pirate Bay Web site is still operational and enormously popular. On August 15, 2011, Alexa.com ranked thepiratebay.org as the 88th most popular Web site in the world, higher than such well-known sites as NYTimes.com, Myspace.com, and Netflix.com.

4.6.7 Legal Music Services on the Internet

Subscription music-streaming services, such as Napster, Rhapsody, and Spotify, are an alternative to illegal file-swapping. These services charge a monthly fee for legal access to millions of songs. Depending upon the plan, subscribers may or not pay extra to download songs. However, a common feature with subscription services is that they all have a form of digital rights management: subscribers who drop their subscription lose the ability to play the songs they've downloaded.

Another model is the online music store, in which you pay to download music without digital rights management. Three leading online music stores are Amazon MP3, eMusic, and Apple's iTunes Store. The iTunes Store is easily the biggest player in the legal online music business. In 2008, the iTunes Store surpassed Wal-Mart to become the top music retailer in the United States, with over 50 million customers, a catalog of more than six million songs, and cumulative sales of more than four billion songs [100]. Digital music sales continue to climb, and Forrester Research has predicted that in 2012 revenues from sales of digital music will finally surpass CD sales [101].

Still, illegal downloading remains far more popular than legal music services. According to the International Federation of the Phonographic Industry, 1.4 billion songs were purchased and downloaded worldwide in 2008, compared to about 40 billion songs illegally exchanged through file-sharing services [102].

4.7 Protections for Software

The two primary sources for the information in this section are the BitLaw Web site (www.bitlaw.com), created by Daniel A. Tysver of the law firm Beck & Tysver, and *Legal Protection of Digital Information* by Lee Hollaar [103].

In the early days of the computer industry, there was no strong demand for intellectual property protection for software. Most commercial software was produced by the same companies manufacturing computer hardware. They sold complete systems to customers, and the licensing agreements covered use of the software as well as the hardware. Interest in copyrighting software grew with the emergence of an independent software industry in the 1960s.

4.7.1 Software Copyrights

The first software copyrights were applied for in 1964. The Copyright Office allowed the submitted computer programs to be registered, reasoning that a computer program is like a "how-to" book. The Copyright Act of 1976 explicitly recognizes that software can be copyrighted.

When a piece of software gets copyright protection, what exactly is copyrighted? First, copyright protects the expression of an idea, not the idea itself. For example, suppose you develop a program for a relational database management system. You may be able to copyright your implementation of a relational database management system, but you cannot copyright the concept of using relational databases to store information.

Second, copyright usually protects the object (executable) program, not the source program. Typically, the source code to a program is confidential, in other words, a trade secret of the enterprise that developed it. The company only distributes the object program to its customers. The copyright also protects the screen displays produced by the program as it executes. This is particularly valuable for the developers of video games.

4.7.2 Violations of Software Copyrights

The holder of a copyright has a right to control the distribution of the copyrighted material. Obviously, this includes making copies of the program. The definition of what it means to make a copy of a program is broad. Suppose you purchase a program stored on a CD. If you transfer a copy of the program from the CD to a hard disk, you are making a copy of it. If you execute the program, it is copied from the hard disk of the computer into its random access memory (RAM). This, too, is considered making a copy of the program. The standard licensing agreement that comes with a piece of commercial software allows the purchaser of the product to do both of the above-mentioned copying operations.

However, doing any of the following actions without authorization of the copyright holder is a violation of copyright law:

1. Copying a program onto a CD to give or sell to someone else
2. Preloading a program onto the hard disk of a computer being sold
3. Distributing a program over the Internet

Another kind of copyright violation can occur when a company attempts to create software that competes with an existing product. Two court cases illustrate a copyright infringement and fair use of another company's product.

APPLE COMPUTER, INC. V. FRANKLIN COMPUTER CORP.

In the early 1980s, Franklin Computer Corp. manufactured the Franklin ACE to compete with the Apple II. The Franklin ACE was Apple II compatible, meaning that programs sold for the Apple II would run on the Franklin ACE without modification. In order to ensure compatibility, the Franklin ACE contained operating systems functions directly copied from a ROM on the Apple II. Apple Computer sued Franklin for infringing on its copyright. The U.S. Court of Appeals for the Third Circuit ruled in favor of Apple Computer, establishing that object programs are copyrightable.

SEGA V. ACCOLADE

Video game–maker Accolade wanted to port some of its games to the Sega Genesis console. Sega did not make available a technical specification for the Genesis console, so Accolade disassembled the object code of a Sega game in order to determine how to interface a video game with the game console. Sega sued Accolade for infringing on its copyright. In 1992, the U.S. Court of Appeals for the Ninth Circuit ruled in favor of Accolade, judging that Accolade's actions constituted fair use of the software. It noted that Accolade had no other way of discerning the hardware interface and that the public would benefit from additional video games being available on the Genesis console.

4.7.3 Software Patents

Until the early 1980s, the U.S. Patent and Trademark Office refused to grant patents for computer software. Its position was that a computer program is a mathematical algorithm, not a process or a machine.

However, a U.S. Supreme Court decision in 1981 forced the Patent and Trademark Office to begin considering software patents. In the case of *Diamond v. Diehr*, the Supreme Court ruled that an invention related to curing rubber could be patented. Even though the company's principal innovation was the use of a computer to control the heating of the rubber, the invention was a new process for rubber molding, and hence, patentable.

Further court rulings compelled the Patent and Trademark Office to begin issuing patents for a much broader range of software. In 1992, the Court of Appeals for the Federal Circuit considered a patent application from a company that had developed a computerized monitoring device that analyzed signals from an electrocardiograph to determine whether a heart attack victim was at a risk of a dangerous arrhythmia. The court ruled that the software was patentable because the numbers being manipulated by the computer program represented concrete values in the real world. Further court rulings reinforced the idea that computer software and data structures could be patented in the United States [104].

Since then, hundreds of thousands of software patents have been granted [105]. Microsoft alone files about 3,000 patent applications every year [106]. Companies generate revenue by licensing their software patents to other companies. It's also common for several technology companies to hold patents that cover different, but essential components of a commercial product. By signing an agreement to cross-license each other's patents, all of the companies are free to bring their own versions of the product to market.

Given the value of software patents, it's not surprising that a secondary market for them has arisen. For example, when a company holding patents goes bankrupt, its patents are sold to another company [107]. Some companies specialize in holding patents and licensing the rights to use these patents. Patent-holding companies aggressively use the courts to enforce their patent rights; these companies are sometimes referred to as patent trolls. Because defending against a patent infringement lawsuit can easily exceed $1 million, companies that get sued have a strong motivation to simply settle out of court, putting patent trolls "in a position to negotiate licensing fees that are grossly out of alignment with their contribution to the alleged infringer's product or services" [108].

In 1992, inventor Thomas Campana and lawyer Donald Stout formed New Technologies Products (NTP), a patent-holding company. The purpose of the company was never to make anything, but to protect valuable intellectual property. About half of the company's 50 patents were originally held by Telefind Corporation, which went out of business. In 2000, NTP sent letters to several companies, warning them that they were infringing on NTP wireless email patents, and inviting them to negotiate licensing rights. One of these letters went to Research In Motion (RIM), maker of the BlackBerry, but RIM did not respond to the letter. The next year NTP sued RIM for patent infringement. Instead of settling out of court for a few million dollars, RIM took the case to trial and lost. After more unsuccessful legal maneuvering, RIM in 2006 agreed to pay NTP $612.5 million to settle the patent infringement dispute [109, 110].

Critics of software patents argue that too many software patents have been granted. A problem faced by patent examiners in the Patent and Trademark Office is knowing what the existing technical knowledge (prior art) in computer programming is. Patent examiners typically look at patents already issued to determine prior art. This works fine for other kinds of inventions, but it doesn't work well for software patents, because a significant amount of software was written before software patents were first granted.

The consequence is that patent examiners issue many "bad patents"—patents that would not have been issued if the examiner knew about all of the prior art. The Patent Office has also been criticized for granting patents for trivial inventions that would be obvious to any skilled computer programmer.

As a consequence of the extremely large number of software patents, the large number of bad patents, and the number of obvious software inventions that are patented, any company releasing a new product that includes software runs a significant risk of being sued for infringing a software patent owned by someone else. Large corporations are resorting to building stockpiles of their own patents, so that if they are sued for infringing another company's patent, they can retaliate with their own patent infringement counter-suit. The use of software patents as legal weapons is a perversion of their original purpose [111].

Some opponents of the current software patent system maintain that patent protection is inappropriate for software, which is less expensive to produce and has a much shorter useful life than other patentable properties, such as new pharmaceutical drugs. Jeff Bezos, CEO of Amazon.com, has suggested that software patents should have a lifespan of only three to five years [112].

4.7.4 Safe Software Development

An organization must be careful not to violate the copyrights held by its competitors. Even unconscious copying can have serious consequences. Years after hearing the song "He's So Fine," George Harrison wrote "My Sweet Lord." The owner of "He's So Fine" sued Harrison for copyright infringement and prevailed after a lengthy legal battle. Unconscious copying is a real concern in the software industry because programmers frequently move from one firm to another.

Suppose a company needs to develop a software product that duplicates the functionality of a competitor's product without violating the competitor's copyright. For example, in the 1980s, companies developing IBM-compatible computers needed to develop their own implementations of the BIOS (Basic Input/Output System). A "clean room" software development strategy helps ensure a company's software program does not duplicate any code in another company's product.

In this strategy, two independent teams work on the project. The first team is responsible for determining how the competitor's program works. It may access the program's source code, if it is available. If it cannot get access to the source, it may disassemble the object code of the competitor's product. It also reads the product's user manuals and technical documentation. The first team produces a technical specification for the software product. The specification simply states how the product is supposed to function. It says nothing about how to implement the functionality.

The second team is isolated from the first team. Members of this team have never seen any code or documentation from the competitor's product. It relies solely on the technical specification to develop, code, and debug the software meeting the specification. By isolating the code developers from the competitor's product, the company developing the competing product can demonstrate that its employees have not copied code, even unconsciously.

4.8 Open–Source Software

In the early years of commercial computing, there was no independent software industry. Computer manufacturers such as IBM produced both the hardware and the software needed for the system to be usable. Well into the 1960s, software distributions included the source code. Customers who wanted to fix bugs in the programs or add new features could do so by modifying the source code and generating a new executable version of the program.

In the 1970s, the number of computer applications expanded, and organizations recognized the increasing value of software. To protect their investments in software development, most companies decided to make their programs proprietary (owned).

Today, companies developing proprietary software tightly control the distribution of their intellectual property. Typically, they do this by treating source code as a trade secret and distributing only the object code, which is not in human-readable form. In addition, they do not sell the object code. Instead, when people "purchase" the program, what they are actually buying is a license allowing them to run the program. Their rights to do other things with the code, such as make backup copies, are limited.

4.8.1 Consequences of Proprietary Software

Governments have given ownership rights to those who produce computer software because of the perceived beneficial consequences. A key benefit is the ability to profit from the licensing of the software. The assumption is that people will work harder and be more creative if they must compete with others to produce the best product. Those who produce the best products will have the opportunity to make money from them.

While most people point to the benefits of a system encouraging the development of proprietary software, some people have noted the harms caused by such a system. A well-known critic of proprietary software is Richard Stallman. According to Stallman, granting intellectual property rights to creators of computer software has numerous harmful consequences:

- The copyright system was designed for an era in which it was difficult to create copies. Digital technology has made copying trivial. In order to enforce copyrights in the digital age, increasingly harsh measures are being taken. These measures infringe on our liberties.

- The purpose of the copyright system is to promote progress, not to make authors wealthy. Copyrights are not promoting progress in the computer software field.

- It is wrong to allow someone to "own" a piece of intellectual property. Granting someone this ownership forces the users of a piece of intellectual property to choose between respecting ownership rights and helping their friends. When this happens, the correct action is clear. If a friend asks you for a copy of a proprietary program, you would be wrong to refuse your friend. "Cooperation is more important than copyright" [113].

The **open-source movement** is the philosophical position that source code to software ought to be freely distributed and that people should be encouraged to examine and improve each other's code. The open-source software movement promotes a cooperative model of software development.

4.8.2 "Open Source" Definition

Open source is an alternative way of distributing software. Licenses for open-source programs have the following key characteristics (there are others) [114]:

1. There are no restrictions preventing others from selling or giving away the software.
2. The source code to the program must be included in the distribution or easily available by other means (such as downloadable from the Internet).
3. There are no restrictions preventing people from modifying the source code, and derived works can be distributed according to the same license terms as the original program.
4. There are no restrictions regarding how people can use the software.
5. These rights apply to everyone receiving redistributions of the software without the need for additional licensing agreements.
6. The license cannot put restrictions on other software that is part of the same distribution. For example, a program's open-source license cannot require all of the other programs on the CD to be open source.

Note that there is nothing in these guidelines that says an open-source program must be given away for free. While people may freely exchange open-source programs, a company has the right to sell an open-source program. However, a company cannot stop others from selling it either. In order for a company to be successful selling open-source software that people can find for free on the Internet, it must add some additional value to the software. Perhaps it packages the software so that it is particularly easy to install. It may provide great manuals, or it may provide support after the sale.

The Open Source Initiative (www.opensource.org) is a nonprofit corporation that promotes a common definition of open source. In July 2005, its Web site listed the names of 58 software licenses that met its definition of open source.

4.8.3 Beneficial Consequences of Open–Source Software

Advocates of open-source software describe five beneficial consequences of open-source licensing.

The first benefit of open source is that it gives everyone using a program the opportunity to improve it. People can fix bugs, add enhancements, or adapt the program for entirely new uses. Software evolves more quickly when more people are working on it.

Rapid evolution of open-source software leads to the second benefit: new versions of open-source programs appear much more frequently than new versions of commercial programs. Users of open-source programs do not have to wait as long for bug fixes and patches [115].

A third benefit of open source is that it eliminates the tension between obeying copyright law and helping others. Suppose you legally purchased a traditional license to use a program, and your friend asks you for a copy. You must choose between helping your friend and conforming to the license agreement. If the program had an open-source license, you would be free to distribute copies of it to anyone who wanted it.

The fourth benefit is that open-source programs are the property of the entire user community, not just a single vendor. If a vendor selling a proprietary program decides not to invest in further improvements to it, the user community is stuck. In contrast, a user community with access to the source code to a program may continue its development indefinitely [115].

The fifth benefit of open source is that it shifts the focus from manufacturing to service, which can result in customers getting better support for their software [115]. If source code were distributed freely, companies would make money by providing support, and the companies that provided the best support would be rewarded in the marketplace [116].

4.8.4 Examples of Open-Source Software

Open-source software is a key part of the Internet's infrastructure, and an increasing number of open-source applications are reaching the desktop. Here are a few examples of highly successful programs distributed under open-source licenses:

- BIND provides DNS (domain name service) for the entire Internet.
- Apache runs about half of the world's Web servers.
- The most widely used program for moving email about the Internet is the open-source program sendmail.
- The Android operating system is the world's best-selling smartphone platform [117].
- Firefox is the most popular Web browser in Europe and the second most popular browser worldwide [118].
- OpenOffice.org is an office application suite supporting word processing, spreadsheets, databases, and presentations (Figure 4.12).
- Perl is the most popular Web programming language.
- Other popular open-source programming languages and tools are Python, Ruby, TCL/TK, PHP, and Zope.
- Programmers have long recognized the high quality of the GNU compilers for C, C++, Objective-C, Fortran, Java, and Ada.

FIGURE 4.12 OpenOffice.org is an open-source office application suite that competes with the commercial product Microsoft Office. (Screenshot from OpenOffice.org, a registered trademark of Apache Software Foundation. Copyright © 2012 by Apache Software Foundation. Reprinted with permission.)

Surveys indicate that the quality and dependability of open-source software is about the same as the quality of commercial software [119].

4.8.5 The GNU Project and Linux

The GNU Project and Linux are important success stories in the history of the open-source movement. Richard Stallman began the GNU Project in 1984. (GNU is pronounced "guh-new" with the accent on the second syllable. It's a tradition among hackers to invent recursive acronyms; GNU stands for "GNU's Not Unix.") The goal of the GNU Project was ambitious: to develop a complete Unix-like operating system consisting entirely of open-source software.

In order to be fully functional, a modern operating system must include text editors, command processors, assemblers, compilers, debuggers, device drivers, mail servers, and many other programs. During the late 1980s, Stallman and others developed most of the necessary components. The GNU Project also benefited from open-source software previously developed by others, notably Donald Knuth's TeX typesetting system and MIT's X Window System. Most of the software developed as part of the GNU Project is distributed under the GNU Public License, an example of an open-source license. (For technical reasons some programs have been distributed as open-source software under other licenses.)

In 1991, Linus Torvalds began work on a Unix-like kernel he named Linux. (The kernel is the software at the very heart of an operating system.) He released version 1.0 of the kernel in 1994. Because the other major components of a Unix-like operating system had already been created through the GNU Project, Torvalds was able to combine all of the software into a complete, open-source, Unix-like operating system. To the obvious chagrin of Stallman, Linux has become the commonly accepted name for the open-source operating system based on the Linux kernel. (Stallman urges people to refer to the entire system as GNU/Linux [120].)

4.8.6 Impact of Open-Source Software

Andrew Leonard summarized the impact of Linux this way: "Linux is subversive. Who could have thought even five years ago that a world-class operating system could coalesce as if by magic out of part-time hacking by several thousand developers scattered all over the planet, connected only by the tenuous strands of the Internet?" [116].

As a reliable open-source alternative to Unix, Linux is putting price pressure on companies selling proprietary versions of Unix. Many corporations, including Morgan Stanley, Credit Suisse First Boston, Pixar, and the E*Trade Group, have replaced Sun file servers with less expensive "Lintel" boxes—servers running the Linux operating system on Intel-compatible CPUs [121]. A 2004 survey of 140 large North American firms by Forrester Research revealed that slightly more than half of them were using Linux for "mission-critical" applications, and slightly more than half of them were running new applications on Linux [122]. However, another Forrester Research survey resulted in the conclusion that despite the shift toward purchasing Linux servers, large companies would continue to maintain servers running proprietary operating systems [123].

Linux is also putting pressure on Microsoft and Apple, which sell proprietary operating systems for desktop computers. The cost of commodity, off-the-shelf hardware has gotten so low that the cost of a proprietary operating system is a significant portion of the selling price of low-end systems. Retailers such as Wal-Mart have begun offering Linux-equipped PCs for about $300.

While more than 90 percent of the personal computers on people's desktops run Microsoft operating systems, Microsoft is clearly worried about losing market share to Linux. In the summer of 2002, Microsoft sent an email message to senior managers urging them to hold on to government and large institutional accounts at all costs. If a negotiation to renew a licensing agreement looked hopeless, managers were authorized to draw from a special fund enabling them to offer the Microsoft software at large discounts, or even for free. "Under NO circumstances lose against Linux," the memo instructed [124].

4.8.7 Critique of the Open-Source Software Movement

The open-source movement has many detractors. They have raised the following criticisms of the open-source model of software development.

First, if a particular open-source project does not attract a critical mass of developers, the overall quality of the software can be poor [115].

Second, without an "owner," there is always the possibility that different groups of users will independently make enhancements to a software product that are incompatible with each other. The source code to a single program may fork into a multitude of irreconcilable versions. (In reality, this possibility hasn't materialized. Code forking would fragment the developer community, which is bad for everyone. Hence there are incentives to keep a single version of the source code. About 99 percent of Linux distributions have the same source code [115].)

Third, open-source software as a whole tends to have a relatively weak graphical user interface, making it harder to use than commercial software products. This is one explanation why to this point open-source systems have made greater inroads as servers than as desktop systems [115].

Fourth, open source is a poor mechanism for stimulating innovation. Currently, corporations invest billions of dollars developing new software products. By removing the financial reward for creating new software, companies will sharply curtail or even eliminate research and development. They will no longer be a fountain of new programs. The open-source movement has proven it is able to produce alternatives to proprietary programs (for example, StarOffice instead of Microsoft Office), but it has not demonstrated its ability to innovate completely new products.

4.9 Legitimacy of Intellectual Property Protection for Software

Licenses for proprietary software usually forbid you from making copies of the software to give or sell to someone else. These licenses are legal agreements. If you violate the license, you are breaking the law. In this section, we are *not* discussing the morality of breaking the law. Rather, we are considering whether as a society we ought to give the producers of software the right to prevent others from copying the software they produce. In other words, should we give copyright and/or patent protection to software?

Rights-based and consequentialist arguments have been given for granting intellectual property protection to those who create software. Let's review and test the strength of these arguments. To simplify the discussion, we'll assume that a piece of software is written by a person. In reality, most software is created by teams, and the company employing the team owns the rights to the software the team produces. However, the logic is the same whether the software creator is an individual or a corporation.

4.9.1 Rights–Based Analysis

Not everyone can write good computer programs, and programming is hard work. Programmers who write useful programs that are widely used by others should be rewarded for their labor. That means they should own the programs they write. Ownership implies control. If somebody creates a piece of software, he or she has the right to decide who gets to use it. Software owners ought to be able to charge others for using their programs. Everybody ought to respect these intellectual property rights.

This line of reasoning is a variation of Locke's natural rights argument we discussed at the beginning of the chapter. It is based on the Lockean notion that mixing your labor with something gives you an ownership right in it.

Here are two criticisms of the "just deserts"[1] argument. First, why does mixing your labor with something mean that you own it? Doesn't it make just as much sense to believe that if you mix your labor with something you lose your labor? Robert Nozick gives this example: If you own a can of tomato juice and pour it in the ocean, mixing the tomato juice with the salt water, you do not own the ocean. Instead, you have lost your can of tomato juice. Certainly it would be unjust if someone else could claim ownership of something you labored to produce, but if there were no notion of property ownership, and everybody understood when they mixed their labor with something they lost their labor, it would be just.

Of course, we do live in a society that has the notion of ownership of tangible property. How can we justify giving a farmer the right to the crop he labors to produce while failing to give a programmer the right to the accounting program he produces for the benefit of the farmer?

Still, if we do want to give ownership rights to those who produce intellectual property, we run into the problems we discussed at the beginning of the chapter. The second criticism of the "just deserts" argument is that Locke's natural rights argument does not hold up well when extended to the realm of intellectual property. There are two crucial differences between intellectual property and tangible property. Each piece of intellectual property is unique, and copying intellectual property is different from stealing something physical.

4.9.2 Utilitarian Analysis

A second argument in favor of providing intellectual property protection for software producers is based on consequences. Failing to provide this protection would have net harmful consequences. The argument goes like this [125]: When software is copied, it reduces software purchases. If less software is purchased, less money will flow to the producers of software. As a result, less new software will be produced. As a whole, new software titles benefit society. When the number of new titles drops, society is harmed. Therefore, when software is copied, society is harmed. Copying software is wrong.

You can view this argument as a chain of consequences (Figure 4.13). Copying software causes software sales to drop, which causes the software industry to decline, which causes fewer products to be released, which causes society to be harmed. Logically,

---

1. Pronounced with the accent on the second syllable. Think of the related word "deserve."

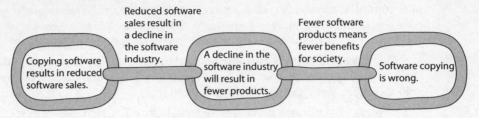

Figure 4.13 The chain of reasoning of a consequentialist argument for why copying software is bad. (Beth Anderson)

all of the links in the chain must be strong in order for the argument to be convincing. We will look at each of the links in turn, and we'll see that none of them are strong.

The first claim is that copying software results in reduced sales of software. When talking about software piracy, the computer industry cites the dollar value of the copied software as if each instance of copying represents a lost sale. Obviously this is an exaggeration. Not everyone who gets a free copy of a computer game has the money or the desire to purchase the game for $50. In fact, sometimes software copying may lead to a sale. A person may not have been interested in buying a particular program. After trying it out for free, the person may decide it is so useful she is willing to buy a copy of the program in order to get access to all of the documentation, the technical support line, or another service provided to registered users of the program. It is fair to say that copying software sometimes results in reduced sales of software, but it is not always the case. Hence, it is incorrect to make a universal statement.

The second claim is that reduced sales of software will result in a decline in the software industry. An argument against this claim is the continued success of Microsoft, despite the fact that software counterfeiting is prevalent in some countries. A better argument against the claim is that it makes a strong cause-and-effect connection between the creation of software and financial remuneration. However, the open-source movement demonstrates many people are willing to create software without being rewarded financially. Some people write programs because they find it fun. Others are motivated by the desire to gain a good reputation by writing a program many people find useful. Advocates of open-source software, including Richard Stallman, suggest that the best way to stimulate innovation is to allow a free exchange of ideas and source code. From this point of view, allowing software producers to control the distribution of their code stifles, rather than promotes, innovation in the software industry.

Finally, the second claim assumes that software customers are solely responsible for the health of the software industry. In reality, other groups want to ensure that there are plenty of new software titles released. Intel, for example, makes its money from selling CPU chips. Every year the chips are faster. If a person owns a computer fast enough to run his current programs, he has little motivation to upgrade the hardware. However, if that same person purchases a new program that requires additional CPU cycles, he may be motivated to upgrade his computer. Hence it is in Intel's interest to encourage the development of ever more computationally intensive computer programs. Software customers are not solely responsible for promoting the growth of the software industry.

The third claim is that new software packages benefit society. This is a difficult claim to prove. Certainly some programs would benefit society more than others. Hence, it's not the number of different programs that matters, it's what they can be used for. The utility of new software titles must be weighed against the utility of letting people give away copies of programs that would help their friends.

4.9.3 Conclusion

We have examined two arguments for why society ought to provide intellectual property protection to software creators. The first argument is based on the notion of just deserts. It is a variation of the natural rights argument we discussed at the beginning of the chapter. This argument is weak; it rests on the faulty assumption that a natural right to own property extends cleanly to intellectual property.

The second argument is based on consequences. It holds that denying intellectual property protection for software would have harmful consequences. It relies upon a chain of cause-and-effect relationships: copying leads to a loss of revenue, which leads to a decline in software production, which harms society. The strength of each of the links in the chain is debatable; taken as a whole, the argument is not strong.

Our conclusion is that the arguments for granting intellectual property protection for software are not strong. Nevertheless, our society *has* granted copyright protection to owners of computer programs. If you violate a licensing agreement by copying a CD containing a computer program and giving it to a friend, you are breaking the law. As we discovered in Chapter 2, from the viewpoint of Kantianism, rule utilitarianism, and social contract theory, breaking the law is wrong unless there is a strong overriding moral obligation.

4.10 Creative Commons

As we saw earlier in this chapter, some believe strong intellectual property protection stimulates creativity by dangling the prospect of financial reward in front of artists and inventors. Others believe that creativity is suppressed in such an environment. They argue that people are more creative when they are free to build on the work of others. Consider music, for example. It's not just rap musicians who sample the works of others to create new songs. Listen to the classical piece *Appalachian Spring* by Aaron Copland and you'll find that he used the Shaker hymn "Simple Gifts."

Information technology has created an environment in which an unprecedented amount of creativity could be unleashed. Never before has it been so inexpensive to record and mix music, combine photographs and computer-generated images, or tape and edit movies. Wouldn't it be great to take what others have done and add your own talents to produce even better works of art for everyone's enjoyment? Quoting the movie

Get Creative on the Creative Commons Web site: "Collaboration across space and time. Creative co-authorship with people you've never met. Standing on the shoulders of your peers. It's what the Internet is all about" [126].

Strong intellectual property protection, however, stands in the way of this vision. Under current U.S. copyright law, works of intellectual property are copyrighted the moment they are made, even if the creator does not attach a copyright symbol © to the work. Since copyright is implicit, permission is required before use. The current system discourages people from building on the work of others.

Imagine the difficulty an art professor has trying to put together a Web site of images for an online course! She needs to request permission for every image she wishes to display on the Web site. Suppose there are three suitable images of Michelangelo's *Pieta*. It may be impossible for her to tell in advance which, if any, of the photographers would be willing to let her use the image. It would be better if there were an official way for a photographer to say, "It's fine if you use this photograph, as long as you give me credit for taking it."

Stanford law professor Lawrence Lessig realized there was a need for a system that would allow producers of intellectual property to indicate to the world the rights they wanted to keep. Lessig asks us to think about instances of the **commons**, a "resource to which anyone within the relevant community has a right without obtaining the permission of anyone else" [127]. Examples of the commons include public streets, parks, beaches, the theory of relativity, and the works of Shakespeare. Lessig says that "there is a benefit to resources held in common and the Internet is the best evidence of that benefit . . . [T]he Internet forms an *innovation commons*" [127]. The reason Lessig calls the Internet an innovation commons is because its control is decentralized: one person can introduce a new application or new content without getting anyone else's permission.

Lessig joined with Hal Abelson, James Boyle, Eric Eldred, and Eric Saltzman to found the nonprofit corporation Creative Commons in 2001. Creative Commons provides standard copyright licenses free of charge. Every license comes in three forms: human-readable, lawyer-readable, and computer-readable. With a Creative Commons license, you can retain the copyright while allowing some uses of your intellectual property under certain circumstances. Because you have published the circumstances under which your work may be used, others do not have to ask for permission before using your work [126].

How does the system work? Suppose you have taken a photograph and wish to post it on your Web site accompanied by a Creative Commons license. You visit the Creative Commons Web site (www.creativecommons.org), which allows you to choose between six different licenses, depending upon your responses to two questions (quoted verbatim):

- Allow commercial uses of your work?
  - Yes
  - No

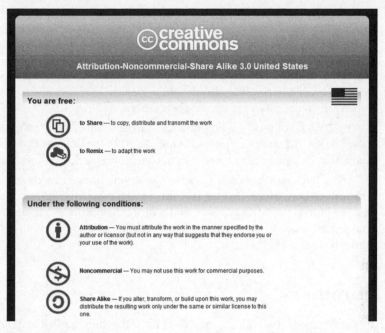

FIGURE 4.14 A portion of the human-readable summary of a Creative Commons license as it appears to a Web site visitor. (Screenshot from Creative Commons. Copyright © 2011 by Creative Commons. Reprinted with permission.)

- Allow modifications of your work?
  - Yes
  - Yes, as long as others share alike
  - No

After you answer these two questions, the Web site creates HTML code containing the appropriate Creative Commons license. You can copy the HTML code and paste it into the appropriate Web page along with your photograph. Visitors to your Web site will be able to see a human-readable summary of the license you have chosen (Figure 4.14).

Commercial artists may choose to use Creative Commons licenses to increase exposure to their work. For example, suppose you take a great photograph of the Golden Gate Bridge. You post it on your Web site with a Creative Commons license indicating the photograph may be used for noncommercial purposes as long as the user gives attribution to you. People from around the world think the image is stunning, and they copy it to their own personal Web sites, giving you credit for the photo. A travel agent in a foreign country sees the image and wants to put it on a travel poster. Since this is a commercial purpose, she must gain your permission before using the image. At that time you can negotiate a fair price for its use. Without the widespread distribution of the image through a Creative Commons license, the travel agent might never have seen it.

The computer-readable versions of the licenses are designed to make it easier for search engines to identify content based upon the particular criteria. For example, a history professor might use a search engine hoping to find an image of the Coliseum in Rome that he could include on his Web site. His purpose is noncommercial, and he is happy to credit the photographer, but he does not want to have to pay to display the image or write a letter asking for the photographer's permission. A search engine could return only those images that meet these criteria.

By 2008, about 130 million different pieces of intellectual property had been distributed using Creative Commons licenses. In 2009, the Creative Commons Attribution-Share Alike license became the principal content license for Wikipedia.

John Buckman has used Creative Commons licenses to create an online record label called Magnatune [128]. Magnatune puts complete albums online for potential customers to preview. Customers who wish to download an album or purchase a CD choose how much they wish to pay for it (between $5 and $18), with half of the proceeds going to the artists [129].

Summary

Intellectual property is any unique product of the human intellect that has commercial value. Because our society values property rights, simply calling products of the intellect "intellectual property" creates a bias toward ownership. Some believe the creators of intellectual property have a natural right to own what they create. However, paradoxes occur when we try to extend John Locke's theory of property rights to intellectual property. As we saw in our hypothetical scenarios involving William Shakespeare and Ben Jonson, intellectual property has two characteristics that make it significantly different from ordinary property. First, each creation is unique. That creates a problem when two people independently create the same work. Second, ideas are copied, not stolen. When I take your idea, you still have it. These paradoxes illustrate that Locke's natural rights argument for property does not extend to intellectual property. We conclude there are no strong arguments for a natural right to intellectual property.

Nevertheless, our society recognizes the value of intellectual property creation. In order to stimulate creativity in the arts and sciences, governments have decided to grant limited ownership rights in intellectual property to its creators. In the United States, there are four different ways in which individuals and organizations can protect their intellectual property: trade secrets, patents, copyrights, and trademarks/service marks.

A trade secret is a confidential piece of intellectual property that provides a company with a competitive advantage. The formula for Coca-Cola is a famous trade secret. A company may keep a trade secret confidential indefinitely.

A trademark is a word, symbol, picture, sound, or color used by a business to identify goods. A service mark is a mark identifying a service. Xerox is a well-known trademark identifying a brand of photocopy machine. Companies protect their marks to ensure they are used as adjectives rather than common nouns.

A patent gives an inventor the exclusive right to an invention for a period of 20 years. A patent is a public document, and after the patent expires, anyone has the right to make use of its ideas.

A copyright provides authors with certain rights to original works they have written: reproduction, distribution, public display, performance, and production of derivative works. Books, movies, sheet music, songs, and computer software are all protected by copyright. Industries producing products protected by copyright account for 6 percent of the U.S. economy, with about $900 billion in sales. Over time, both the length of copyright protection and the kinds of intellectual property that can be copyrighted have increased significantly. Works created today are protected for the author's lifetime plus 70 years.

The rights given copyright holders are limited. The fair use doctrine allows certain uses of copyrighted works without asking the copyright holder for permission. To determine whether a particular use is fair use, courts consider the purpose of the use (commercial versus noncommercial), the nature of the work being copied (fiction versus nonfiction), how much of the copyrighted work is being used, and how the use will affect the market for the copyrighted work. Two court cases legitimized time shifting— recording a TV program for viewing later—and space shifting—copying a recording to make it portable.

The introduction of digital technology and the Internet have brought intellectual property issues to the forefront. Representing audio and video content digitally means anyone with the right equipment can make perfect copies. Internet technology enables these copies to be widely disseminated. Recording companies have responded by putting new restrictions on copying, even though sometimes these restrictions make it impossible for consumers to make copies that were previously considered fair use. Many digital rights management strategies have been abandoned or circumvented. Recording companies have begun to soften their stance toward digital rights management, as evidenced by the fact that consumers may now purchase DRM-free music from Amazon and the Apple iTunes Store.

Peer-to-peer networks enable people to swap files around the world. Many of these files contain copyrighted songs, TV shows, or movies. Napster facilitated the exchange of music files until it was sued by the Recording Industry Association of America (RIAA). A judge shut down Napster after Napster indicated it could not block 100 percent of attempted transfers of copyrighted material. However, other free file-sharing services such as Grokster and StreamCast took Napster's place. A diverse group of movie studios, recording companies, music publishers, and songwriters sued Grokster and StreamCast. The U.S. Supreme Court ruled that Grokster and StreamCast could be held liable for the copyright infringements of their users since they had actively promoted these activities. Grokster shut down its peer-to-peer network and paid $50 million to copyright holders. Despite these legal victories by the entertainment industry, popular Web sites such as The Pirate Bay continue to facilitate the exchange the copyrighted materials on peer-to-peer networks. Meanwhile, the RIAA has sued or demanded out-of-court settlements from individuals who allegedly have distributed large numbers of copyrighted songs via the Internet. These legal actions have reduced the percentage of Internet users who illegally download music, or at least the percentage of Internet users who are willing to admit to doing it.

Until the mid-1960s, there was no intellectual property protection for computer software other than trade secrets. Now, both copyrights and patents are used to protect software. The case of Apple Computer versus Franklin Computer demonstrates that object code as well as source code is protected by copyright. The area of software patents is highly controversial. There are a large number of bad software patents, and many software patents have been issued for obvious inventions. Large corporations are stockpiling software patents, so that if they are sued for infringing another company's patent, they can retaliate with their own patent infringement counter-suit.

The open-source movement is an alternative to the more conventional proprietary model of software development. A great deal of the software that keeps the Internet running is open-source software. Linux is a popular operating system for servers. In addition, many low-cost netbook computers are also using the Linux operating system. The Android operating system is the most popular platform for smartphones. Popular open-source desktop applications are Firefox and OpenOffice.org.

We examined the question, "Should we give intellectual property protection to software?" There are both rights-based and utilitarian arguments why we ought to give intellectual property protection to software. The first argument is based on the notion of just deserts. It relies upon a natural right to intellectual property, which as we have seen is a weak right at best. The second argument is based on a chain of consequences: copying leads to a loss of revenue, which leads to a decline in software production, which harms society. Taken as a whole, the second argument is not strong. In short, we concluded the arguments for providing intellectual property protection to software are weak.

The story of the GNU Project and Linux demonstrate how thousands of volunteers can work together to produce high-quality, industrial-strength software. Today, millions of people have access to personal computers, digital cameras, digital recording devices, and the Internet.

Why can't the success of GNU/Linux be replicated in the arts? Imagine a culture that encouraged the production of new creative works from existing works, a culture in which songs would rapidly evolve, different versions of movies were exchanged and compared, and hypertext novels accumulated links to fan sites. Today's intellectual property laws make it difficult to achieve this vision in the entertainment field. Little can be done with a copyrighted work without first asking for permission, a labor-intensive process that puts a drag on innovation. Creative Commons is an effort to streamline the process by allowing copyright holders to indicate up front the conditions under which they are willing to let other people use their work.

Review Questions

1. What is intellectual property? Give ten examples of intellectual property.
2. Summarize John Locke's explanation why there is a natural right to property.

3. What paradoxes arise when we attempt to extend a natural right to property into the realm of intellectual property?

4. What are the ways in which an individual or firm may protect intellectual property in the United States?

5. What is the difference between a trademark and a trade secret?

6. What are the relative advantages and disadvantages of patents versus trade secrets?

7. When referring to copyrighted materials, what is meant by the term "fair use"?

8. Explain how advances in information technology have made it easier for consumers to violate copyright law.

9. How has the Digital Millennium Copyright Act affected fair use of copyrighted material by consumers?

10. What does the term "digital rights management" mean? Describe three different technologies that have been used or proposed for digital rights management.

11. What is a peer-to-peer network?

12. What property makes the peer-to-peer network FastTrack more difficult to shut down than Napster?

13. How does BitTorrent provide an order-of-magnitude increase in downloading speed, compared to Kazaa and Grokster?

14. The U.S. Supreme Court ruled that Sony was not responsible for the copyright infringements of Betamax customers, but Grokster and StreamCast were responsible for the copyright infringements of those who used their peer-to-peer networks. Explain the differences in the two situations that led the Supreme Court to reach opposite conclusions.

15. Why are patents considered an unreliable way of protecting intellectual property rights in software?

16. Suppose company A wants to develop a program that duplicates the functionality of a program made by company B. Describe how company A may do this without violating the copyrights held by company B.

17. When describing a software license, what does the phrase "open source" mean?

18. How has Linux affected the market for proprietary software?

19. Suppose your band has recorded a song and posted it as an MP3 file on your Web site. How can you allow people to download your music for noncommercial purposes while retaining your copyright on the song?

Discussion Questions

20. Benjamin Franklin created many useful inventions without any desire to receive financial reward. Is intellectual property protection needed in order to promote innovation?

21. Any original piece of intellectual property you have created, such as a poem, term paper, or photograph, is automatically copyrighted, even if you did not label it with a copyright notice. Think about your most valuable piece of intellectual property. Describe in detail the ownership rights you would like to claim on it.

22. If the Google Books out-of-court settlement is approved, people will be able to access millions of out-of-print books and read them online. Do you think the fact that Google will have the ability to monitor online page viewing will have a chilling effect on what people read?

23. Discuss the morality of posting the 32-character encryption key for HD-DVDs on Digg.com; the morality of terminating the poster's account; and the morality of re-posting the encryption key.

24. How does the debate over digital music illuminate the differences among ethics, morality, and law?

25. Is the concept of digital rights management doomed to failure?

26. What does the U.S. Supreme Court decision in *MGM v. Grokster* mean for the development of future peer-to-peer network technologies?

27. The current legal system allows both proprietary software and open-source software to be distributed. What are the pros and cons of maintaining the status quo?

28. Examine the analyses of Section 4.9 regarding the legitimacy of providing intellectual property protection for software. Do these arguments apply equally well to the question of providing intellectual property protection for music? Why or why not?

29. Should copyright laws protect musical compositions? Should copyright laws protect recordings of musical performances?

30. Which is more likely to be effective in protecting intellectual property in digital media such as CDs and DVDs: tougher copyright laws or new technologies incorporating more sophisticated anti-copying measures? Or is it hopeless to try to protect intellectual property in digital media?

In-Class Exercises

31. A plane makes an emergency crash landing on a deserted tropical island. Two dozen survivors must fend for themselves until help arrives. All of them are from large cities, and none of them has camping experience. The survivors find it impossible to gather enough food, and everyone begins losing weight. One person spends a lot of time by himself and figures out how to catch fish. He brings fish back to camp. Others ask him to teach them how to catch fish. He refuses, but offers to share the fish he has caught with the other passengers as long as they take care of the other camp chores, such as hauling fresh water, gathering firewood, and cooking.

    Debate the morality of the bargain proposed by the fisherman. One group should explain why the fisherman's position is morally wrong. The other group should explain why the fisherman's position is morally acceptable.

32. Survey ten of your peers. How many own an iPod? How many own another company's portable digital music player? How many tracks were purchased from an online store? How many tracks were ripped from a CD the person owns? How many tracks were gotten for free?

33. Research your university's policy on bandwidth abuse and file sharing. What kinds of activities are explicitly forbidden? Is the policy sensible?

Further Reading

Justin Hughes. "The Philosophy of Intellectual Property." *The Georgetown Law Review*, 77, pp. 287–366, 1988.

Lawrence Lessig. *The Future of Ideas: The Fate of the Commons in a Connected World*. Random House, New York, NY, 2001.

Charles C. Mann. "Who Will Own Your Next Good Idea?" *Atlantic Monthly*, September 1998.

Michael C. McFarland. "Intellectual Property, Information, and the Common Good." In *Readings in CyberEthics*, edited by Richard A. Spinello and Herman T. Tavani. Jones and Bartlett, Boston, MA, 2001, pp. 252–262.

Eric S. Raymond. *The Cathedral & the Bazaar: Musings on Linux and Open Source by an Accidental Revolutionary*. O'Reilly & Associates, Sebastopol, CA, 1999.

Paula Samuelson. "Good News and Bad News on the Intellectual Property Front." *Communications of the ACM*, 42(3), pp. 19–24, 1999.

Richard M. Stallman. *Free Software, Free Society: Selected Essays of Richard M. Stallman*. Edited by Joshua Gay. GNU Press, Boston, MA, 2002.

Siva Vaidhyanathan. *Copyrights and Copywrongs: The Rise of Intellectual Property and How It Threatens Creativity*. New York University Press, New York, NY, 2001.

Shelly Warwick. "Is Copyright Ethical? An Examination of the Theories, Laws, and Practices Regarding the Private Ownership of Intellectual Work in the United States." In *Readings in CyberEthics*, edited by Richard A. Spinello and Herman T. Tavani. Jones and Bartlett, Boston, MA, 2001, pp. 263–279.

References

[1]   "Cell Phones Taking Center Stage at Concerts." Posted May 16, 2008. www.redorbit.com.

[2]   "Sixth Annual BSA-IDC Global Software 08 Piracy Study." Business Software Alliance and IDC, May 2009. www.bsa.org.

[3]   Amanda Lenhart and Mary Madden. "Teen Content Creators and Consumers." *Pew Internet & American Life Project*, November 2, 2005. www.pewinternet.org.

[4]   Thomas Mennecke. "RIAA Announces New Campus Lawsuit Strategy." *Slyck News*, February 27, 2007. www.slyck.com.

[5]   Denise Lavoie. "Joel Tenenbaum: Jury Awards $675,000 in Boston Music Downloading Case." *HuffingtonPost*, July 31, 2009. www.huffingtonpost.com.

[6]   Adamson Rust. "'RIAA Hit by 'EFFing' Music Campaign." *The Inquirer IT*, June 30, 2003.

[7]   The University of Texas at Arlington, Office of Technology Transfer. "Intellectual Properties." www.uta.edu/tto/ip-defs.htm.

[8]   John Locke. *Two Treatises of Government*. Cambridge University Press, Cambridge, England, 1988.

[9]   Michael Scanlan. "Locke and Intellectual Property Rights." Technical report, Oregon State University, Philosophy Department, 2003.

[10]   Edmund S. Morgan. *Benjamin Franklin*. Yale University Press, New Haven, CT, 2002.

[11]   Randolph P. Luck. "Letter to The Honorable Senator Spencer Abraham." Luck's Music Library, June 28, 1996.

[12]   Justice Breyer, dissenting. Supreme Court of the United States. No. 01-618. *Eric Eldred, et al., v. John D. Ashcroft*. January 15, 2003.

[13]   Kembrew McLeod. *Freedom of Expression(R): Overzealous Copyright Bozos and Other Enemies of Creativity*. Doubleday, New York, NY. 2005.

[14]   Lawrence Lessig. "The Same Old Song." *Wired*, July 2005.

[15]   snopes.com. "Happy Birthday, We'll Sue." *Urban Legends Reference Pages*, April 27, 2007. www.snopes.com.

[16]   Robert Brauneis. "Copyright and the World's Most Popular Song." GWU Legal Studies Research Paper No. 1111624. George Washington University Law School, March 21, 2008.

[17]   Neill A. Levy. "The Rights and Wrongs of Copyright." *CINAHLnews*, 15(1), Spring 1996.

[18]   www.freeadvice.com. "What Is a Trademark?"

[19]   www.adobe.com/misc/trade.html. "Permissions and Trademark Guidelines."

[20]   John Case. "Snapshots in Legal Drama: Polaroid Inventor vs. Kodak." *The Christian Science Monitor*, October 21, 1981.

[21]   David E. Sanger. "Kodak Infringed on Polaroid Patents." *The New York Times*, September 14, 1985.

[22]   Lawrence Edelman. "Kodak Pays Polaroid $925m; Part of a Surprise Out-of-Court Settlement Ends 15-Year Legal Hassle." *The Boston Globe*, July 16, 1991.

[23]   International Intellectual Property Alliance, Washington, DC. "Copyright Industries in the U.S. Economy: the 2003-2007 Report." 2009. www.iipa.com.

[24]   United States Court of Appeals for the Second Circuit. *Gershwin Publishing Corporation, Plaintiff-Appelle, v. Columbia Artists Management, Inc., Defendant-Appellant, and Community Concerts, Inc., Defendant*, May 24, 1971. 443 F.2d 1159.

[25]   United States District Court for the Southern District of New York. *Basic Books, Inc. v. Kinko's Graphics Corporation*, March 28, 1991. 758 F. Supp. 1522.

[26]   "Millbury Man Pleads Guilty in 'Davey Jones' Computer Case." *Worcester (MA) Telegram & Gazette*, December 16, 1994.

[27]   Siva Vaidhyanathan. *Copyrights and Copywrongs: The Rise of Intellectual Property and How It Threatens Creativity*. New York University Press, New York, NY, 2001.

[28]   Suzanne Fields. "Free Mickey Mouse (and Robert Frost)." *Jewish World Review*, January 24, 2003.

[29]   Chris Sprigman. "The Mouse that Ate the Public Domain: Disney, the Copyright Term Extension Act, and Eldred v. Ashcroft." FindLaw Legal News and Commentary, March 5, 2002. writ.news.findlaw.com.

[30]   "Brief for Petitioners." Supreme Court of the United States. *Eric Eldred, et al., v. John D. Ashcroft, in his official capacity as Attorney General*. 2002.

[31] "Eldred v. Ashcroft: A Primer." *WashingtonPost.com*, January 15, 2003.

[32] Supreme Court of the United States. *Eldred et al. v. Ashcroft, Attorney General*, January 15, 2003. 239 F.3d 372, affirmed.

[33] *The Adelphi Charter on Creativity, Innovation and Intellectual Property*. www.adelphi charter.org, 2007.

[34] Kathleen Amen, Tish Keogh, and Necia Wolff. "Digital Copyright." *Computers in Libraries*, May 2002.

[35] Supreme Court of the United States. *Sony Corporation of American et al. v. Universal City Studios, Inc., et al.*, January 17, 1984. 464 U.S. 417.

[36] "The Copyright Wars." *IEEE Spectrum*, pages 21–23, May 2003.

[37] Leslie A. Kelly v. Arriba Soft Corporation. United States Court of Appeals for the Ninth Circuit. July 7, 2003.

[38] "About Google Books." Accessed August 13, 2009. http://books.google.com/intl/en/googlebooks/about.html.

[39] *The Authors Guild et al. v. Google Inc.* U.S. District Court, Southern District of New York, September 20, 2005.

[40] *The McGraw-Hill Companies et al. v. Google Inc.* U.S. District Court, Southern District of New York, October 19, 2005.

[41] "Authors, Publishers, and Google Reach Landmark Settlement." Google Press Center, October 28, 2008. www.google.com.

[42] Erik Sherman. "Google Book Deal in DOJ Sights." *BNet (blog)*, June 11, 2009. www.bnet.com.

[43] United States District Court, Southern District of New York. *The Authors Guild et al. v. Google Inc.*, March 22, 2011. 05 Civ. 8136 (DC).

[44] David Kravets. "Google Books Settlement Rejected." *Threat Level*, March 22, 2011. www.wired.com.

[45] Hong Kong Trade Development Council. "EDU Reports Increase in Counterfeit and Pirated Goods; Mainland China Still Found to Be Main Source." May 30, 2008. www.hktdc.com.

[46] Steven Andersen. "How Piracy, Culture and High-Tech Hackers Brought the Recording Indsutry to Its Knees." *Corporate Legal Times*, November 2002.

[47] David Goldman. "Music's Lost Decade: Sales Cut in Half." *CNNMoney*, February 3, 2010. money.cnn.com.

[48] Royal Van Horn. "The Digital Millenium Copyright Act and Other Egregious Laws." *Phi Delta Kappan*, November 2002.

[49] Kelly McCollum and Peter Schmidt. "How Forcefully Should Universities Enforce Copyright Law on Audio Files?" *The Chronicle of Higher Education*, November 11, 1999.

[50] Dan Carnevale. "Some College Radio Stations Struggle to Determine Webcasting Payments." *The Chronicle of Higher Education*, November 11, 2002.

[51] Christopher May. *First Monday*, 8(11), November 2003.

[52] Ron Harris. "Where's SDMI? Digital Music Protection Effort Flames Out." *Associated Press*, April 29, 2002.

[53] Kevin Coughlin. "Cyber Music Makers Seek to Gag Code-Breakers." *Newhouse News Service*, April 24, 2001.

[54]   John Markoff. "Scientists Drop Plan to Present Music-Copying Study That Record Industry Opposed." *The New York Times*, April 27, 2001.

[55]   "A Speed Bump vs. Music Copying; Master Cryptographer—and Code Cracker— Edward Felten Says Technology Isn't the Answer to Digital Copyright Violations." *Business Week Online*, January 9, 2002.

[56]   "FAQ: Sony's 'Rootkit' CDs." *CNet News*, November 21, 2005. news.cnet.com.

[57]   "Sony BMG Settlement FAQ." Electronic Frontier Foundation. www.eff.org/IP/DRM/ Sony-BMG.

[58]   Richard A. Spinello and Herman T. Tavani. "Notes on the DeCSS Trial." In *Readings in CyberEthics*, edited by Richard A. Spinello and Herman T. Tavani. Jones and Bartlett, Sudbury, MA, 2001.

[59]   Gillian Law. "Defendant Acquitted in DVD Hacking Case." *IDG News Service*, January 7, 2003. www.pcworld.com.

[60]   Donna Euben. "Talkin' 'bout a Revolution? Technology and the Law." *Academe*, May/June 2002.

[61]   Heather Havenstein. "Revolt Against Digg Tests Users Content Model." *Computerworld*, 41:19, May 7, 2007.

[62]   "AACS LA Announces Security Updates (Updated URLs)." Advanced Access Content System. www.aacsla.com/press/.

[63]   "455FE10422CA29C4933F95052B792AB2 = AACS Processing Key." Digg Web site. www.digg.com.

[64]   S. Kim. "The Reinforcement of International Copyright for the Digital Age." *Intellectual Property Journal*, 16:93–122, 2003.

[65]   Tom Espiner. "British Library Calls for Digital Copyright Action." *CNet News*, September 25, 2006. news.cnet.com.

[66]   Ali Matin. "Digital Rights Management (DRM) in Online Music Stores: DRM-Encumbered Music Downloads' Inevitable Demise as a Result of the Negative Effects of Heavy-handed Copyright Law." *Entertainment Law Review, Volume 28*. Loyola Law School, Los Angeles, CA, 2008.

[67]   Michael Arrington. "EMI, Apple to Sell DRM-Free Music for $1.29/song." *TechCrunch .com*, April 2, 2007.

[68]   Jacqui Cheng. "Amazon Rounds Out DRM-free Music Offering with Sony BMG." *Ars Technica*, January 10, 2008. arstechnica.com.

[69]   "iTunes Store and DRM-free Music: What You Need to Know." *MacWorld*, January 7, 2009. www.macworld.com.

[70]   Danielle Roy. "Napster Timeline." *IDG News Service, Boston Bureau*, April 2, 2001.

[71]   Nathan Ruegger. "Napster Withers Away, but Peer-to-Peer Legacy Remains." *The Dartmouth*, October 3, 2002.

[72]   Ron Harris. "Bankruptcy Judge Blocks Sale of Napster to Bertelsmann." *Associated Press*, September 4, 2002.

[73]   "How to Pay the Piper." *The Economist*, May 1, 2003.

[74]   "FastTrack." *Wikipedia*, July 1, 2005.

[75]   John Borland. "Super-Powered Peer to Peer." *CNet News*, October 6, 2004, news.cnet .com.

[76]   Clive Thompson. "The BitTorrent Effect." *Wired*, page 150, January 2005.

[77]   Krysten Crawford. "BitTorrent as Friend, Not Foe." *CNN.com*, April 30, 2005.

[78]   "Authorities Strike Back at 'Star Wars' Pirates." *Associated Press*, May 25, 2005.

[79]   Reuters. "Music Industry Sends Warnings to Song Swappers." *NYTimes.com*, April 29, 2003.

[80]   Phil Hardy. "Verizon Agrees to Give the RIAA the Names of Four Subscribers Alleged to be File-Sharing Copyrighted Works." *Music & Copyright*, June 11, 2003.

[81]   Sara Calabro. "RIAA Lawsuits—Music Industry Mistakes Its Lawsuits for a PR Maneuver." *PR Week*, September 22, 2003.

[82]   Phil Hardy. "Media Reaction to RIAA's New Round of Lawsuits Less Hostile but Grassroots Oppposition Grows." *Music & Copyright*, October 29, 2003.

[83]   John Schwartz. "Record Industry May Not Subpoena Online Providers." *NYTimes.com*, December 19, 2003.

[84]   Kevin Fitchard. "Verizon Gains Upper Hand in RIAA Subpoena Ruling." *Telephony*, January 12, 2004.

[85]   Mary Madden and Lee Rainie. "Music and Video Downloading Moves beyond P2P." *Pew Internet & American Life Project.* Report, March 23, 2005. www.pewinternet.org/reports.

[86]   Mike Harvey. "Single-mother Digital Pirate Jammie Thomas-Rasset Must Pay $80,000 per Song." *The Sunday Times*, June 19, 2009. www.thesundaytimes.co.uk.

[87]   Fred von Lohmann. "Offering to Distribute = Distribution, Says Court in Elektra v. Barker." *Electronic Freedom Foundation*, April 1, 2008. www.eff.org.

[88]   Fred von Lohmann. "Making Available Is Not Distribution, Says Court in London-Shire v. Doe." *Electronic Frontier Foundation*, April 2, 2008. www.eff.org.

[89]   Fred von Lohmann. "Big Victory in Atlantic v. Howell: Court Rejects RIAA 'Making Available' Theory." *Electronic Frontier Foundation*, April 29, 2008. www.eff.org.

[90]   United States District Court for the District of Massachusetts. *Sony BMG Music Entertainment; Warner Bros. Records Inc.; Atlantic Recording Corp.; Arista Records LLC; and UMG Recordings, Inc. v. Joel Tenenbaum*, July 9, 2010. 07cv11446-NG.

[91]   United States District Court, District of Minnesota. *Capitol Records, Inc., et al., v. Jammie Thomas-Rasset*, July 22, 2011. 06-1497 (MJD/LIB).

[92]   John Borland. "Judge: File-Swapping Tools Are Legal." *CNet News*, April 25, 2003, news.cnet.com.

[93]   Supreme Court of the United States. *Metro-Goldwyn-Mayer Studios Inc. et al. v. Grokster, Ltd., et al.*, June 27, 2005. 545 U.S.

[94]   John Borland. "Last Waltz for Grokster." *CNet News*, November 7, 2005. news.cnet.com.

[95]   Jenny Stiernstedt, Astrid E. Johansson, and Fredrik Söderling. Translated by Oliver Grassman. "The Pirate Bay Sentenced to One Year in Prison." *Kultur & Nöje (Sweden)*, April 17, 2009. www.dn.se.

[96]   David Sarno. "The Internet Sure Loves Its Outlaws." *Los Angeles Times*, April 29, 2007.

[97]   "Police Cleared of Wrongdoing in Pirate Bay Raid." *The Local (Sweden)*, April 2, 2007. www.thelocal.se.

[98]   Nate Anderson. "Pirate Bay on IFPI Lawsuit: Labels Can 'Go Screw Themselves.'" *Ars Technica*, April 1, 2008. arstechnica.com.

[99] Associated Press. "Swedish Court Upholds Convictions in File-Sharing Case." *The New York Times*, November 26, 2010. www.nytimes.com.

[100] "iTunes Store Top Music Retailer in the US." Apple (press release), April 3, 2008. www .apple.com.

[101] Mike Melanson. "Report: Digital Music Sales Will Surpass CDs in 2012." *Read-WriteWeb*, January 14, 2010. www.readwriteweb.com.

[102] "IFPI Digital Music Report 2009." International Federation of the Phonographic Industry, January 16, 2009. www.ifpi.org.

[103] Lee A. Hollaar. *Legal Protection of Digital Information*. The Bureau of National Affairs, Washington, DC, 2002.

[104] Daniel A. Tysver. "The History of Software Patents: From Benson and Diehr to State Street and Bilski." *Bitlaw*, accessed August 14, 2011. www.bitlaw.com.

[105] Rob Tiller. "The PTO Addresses Bilski and Software Patents." *Opensource.com*, September 30, 2010. opensource.com.

[106] "Microsoft Patent Portfolio Tops IT Industry Scorecards." Microsoft News Center, January 28, 2008. www.microsoft.com.

[107] Michael Kanellos. "Patent Auctions: Lawyer's Dream or Way of the Future?" *ZDNet News*, March 3, 2006. web.archive.org.

[108] Matthew Sag and Kurt Rohde. "Patent Reform and Differential Policy." Northwestern Law & Econ Research Paper No. 925722, August 21, 2006. papers.ssrn.com.

[109] Barrie McKenna, Paul Waldie, and Simon Avery. "Patently Absurd." *The Global and Mail*, February 21, 2006. www.theglobeandmail.com.

[110] Rob Kelley. "BlackBerry Maker, NTP Ink $612 million Settlement." *CNNMoney*, March 3, 2006. money.cnn.com.

[111] Larry Downes. "The Bilski Case and the Future of Software Patents." The Center for Internet and Society, November 11, 2009. cyberlaw.stanford.edu.

[112] Jeff Bezos. "An Open Letter from Jeff Bezos on the Subject of Patents." About Amazon.com, March 2000. web.archive.org.

[113] Richard P. Stallman. "Why Software Should Not Have Owners." *GNU Project Web Server*, June 17, 2003. www.gnu.org/philosophy/why-free.html.

[114] *The Open Source Definition*, 2003. www.opensource.org/docs/definition.php.

[115] Carolyn A. Kenwood. "A Business Case Study of Open Source Software." Technical report, The MITRE Corporation, Bedford, MA, July 2001.

[116] Andrew Leonard. "Let My Software Go!" *Salon.com*, April 14, 1998.

[117] Tarmo Virki and Sinead Carew. "Google Topples Nokia from Smartphones Top Spot." *Reuters*, January 31, 2011. uk.reuters.com.

[118] Tarmo Virki. "Firefox 3 Becomes Top Browser in Europe." *Reuters*, March 31, 2009. www.reuters.com.

[119] Stephen Shankland. "Study Lauds Open-Source Code Quality." *CNet News*, February 19, 2003, news.cnet.com.

[120] Richard P. Stallman. "Linux and the GNU Project." *GNU Project Web Server*, December 14, 2002. www.gnu.org/gnu/linux-and-gnu.html.

[121] Gary Rivlin. "McNealy's Last Stand." *Wired*, July 2003.

[122] Brad Day, Laura Koetzle, and Carey Schwaber. "Linux Crosses into Mission-Critical Apps." Technical report, Forrester Research, April 26, 2004. www.forrester.com.

[123] Brad Day, Frank E. Gillett, and Richard Fichera. "Firms Plan to Maintain Windows, Add Linux OS." Technical report, Forrester Research, June 18, 2004. www.forrester .com.

[124] Thomas Fuller. "How Microsoft Warded Off Rival." *International Herald Tribune*, May 15, 2003.

[125] Helen Nissenbaum. "Should I Copy My Neighbor's Software?" In *Computers, Ethics, & Social Values*, edited by Deborah G. Johnson and Helen Nissenbaum. Prentice Hall, Englewood Cliffs, NJ, 1995.

[126] Creative Commons, Stanford Law School. *Get Creative (movie)*. www.creativecom mons.org.

[127] Lawrence Lessig. *The Future of Ideas: The Fate of the Commons in a Connected World*. Random House, New York, NY, 2001.

[128] Ariana Eunjung Cha. "Creative Commons Is Rewriting Rules of Copyright." *Washington Post*, March 15, 2005.

[129] "What Is 'Open Music'?" *Magnatune (Web site)*, July 7, 2005.

June Besek

June Besek is the Executive Director of the Kernochan Center for Law, Media and the Arts and a Lecturer in Law at Columbia Law School in New York City, where she teaches Current Issues in Copyright and a seminar that focuses on the rights of individual authors and artists. Previously she was a partner in a New York City law firm where she specialized in copyright law. She is a former chair of the Copyright Division of the American Bar Association's Intellectual Property Law Section. She is a frequent speaker on copyright issues and the author of many articles on copyright law, particularly as it relates to new technologies.

I read that Bob Dylan, Charlie Daniels, Loretta Lynn, Don Henley from the Eagles, and other recording artists have notified the U.S. Copyright Office that they intend to exercise their termination rights and recover the copyrights to their music. What are termination rights?

Section 203 of the Copyright Act gives authors or their heirs the right to terminate any grant of copyrights like a license or assignment 35 years after the grant was made. That particular termination right applies only to grants made by the author on or after January 1, 1978. When I say "authors," I mean any kind of creators: book authors, composers, sound recording artists, and so on. The effect of termination is that all of the rights that were transferred or licensed under the grant revert back to the authors or their heirs.

Why do we have termination rights?

The point of termination is that authors and artists often have very little bargaining power when they negotiate contracts, and frequently neither the author nor the publisher has any realistic idea of how popular or how lucrative their work might become. So this termination provision lets an author renegotiate the agreement or even take the work to a new publisher and maybe get more money or perhaps more control over how the work is marketed.

Why is this specifically an issue in the sound-recording context?

Federal copyright law didn't protect sound recordings until 1972, and then there was a major revision of the copyright law that went into effect six years later in 1978. A lot of the recordings created under the old law were done as "works made for hire," and therefore under the law the grants weren't eligible for termination. The work-made-for-hire rules were changed in 1978, but there haven't yet been any terminations under the revised copyright law, so the effect of the revised work-made-for-hire rules on artists' ability to terminate is uncertain. So that's why this is a new issue.

Must recording artists give notice to reclaim ownership?

Yes, in order to reclaim their rights they have to give notice. If you signed a grant the first day of the new Copyright Act, January 1, 1978, the earliest you could terminate would be January 1, 2013. In order to terminate, you have to serve a notice on the party whose grant you're terminating, and you have to file it in the Copyright Office. That notice can be served anywhere from ten years out to two years out. So if you wanted to terminate at the beginning of 2013, you could have served that notice as early as the beginning of 2003 and as late as the beginning of 2011. But there's a five-year window for terminating. So if you didn't serve the notice in 2011, you can't terminate in 2013, but you have until January 1, 2018, to actually terminate the grant.

It's important to note that even if you terminate the grant to a copyright, you can't cut off the rights to derivative works that have already been made. Suppose the record company licensed your recording to be used in some sort of combination recording, where one track is run over the other to create a new recording. If that was done with authorization, you can't cut off the rights to that. It could still be marketed, and you would continue to be paid for it. But you can prevent new derivative works from being made from your recording.

Is there any reason why sound-recording artists wouldn't want to reclaim copyright ownership of their work?

Some recording artists own the label. If they own their own label, then they wouldn't have any particular interest in termination. If they're very happy with their relationship with their label, maybe they wouldn't want to terminate. A lot of people wouldn't want to be the test case, so they might kind of drag their heels until they see what's happening with other people.

What's the problem with being the test case?

Litigation is very, very expensive. You could spend as much in litigation as you could ever hope to gain on your recordings. So the people who are the test cases will likely be the artists who are making a fair amount of money from their older recordings and are willing to spend money and time and effort to get out from under their record company.

Which side do you think has the stronger argument?

This is a very complicated issue. It all revolves around whether or not these works are works made for hire, because you can terminate the copyright grant if the work was created in your individual capacity, but you can't terminate if it is a work made for hire.

There are two ways a work can be a work made for hire. One is if it was created by an employee in the course of his or her employment. That usually will not be the case with sound recordings. For the most part, the artists are not employees of the label. But the other way it can be a work made for hire is if it's a specially commissioned work. For a commissioned work to be a work made for hire, there has to be an agreement signed by both parties that the work will be work made for hire, and the work has to fall within one of nine specified categories of works. If it doesn't fit into one of these categories, it doesn't matter what you said in your agreement, it's not a work made for hire.

Most of these categories aren't ones that sound recordings would likely fall into. But there are three categories that sound recordings might fit into: a contribution to a collective work, part of a motion picture or other audiovisual work, or a compilation. Most of the time the label's money is going to be on contribution to a collective work. They'll say, "We have a signed agreement, and we hired you recording artists to create your sound recording as part of a collective work—specifically, an album. Therefore, it is a work made for hire, and you are not entitled under the law to terminate it."

It's not clear to me whether the labels will succeed. I think these cases are going to be very fact-based. So to answer your question, I think it's going to depend upon the circumstances under which the sound recording was created. If the sound recording was created and marketed as a single, then I don't think you have a contribution to a collective work. Also, some courts have held that a work-made-for-hire agreement must be signed before the song is recorded. So if the case were to go to one of those courts, then the success of the artist could depend on when the contract was signed. And there are some other more complicated arguments that might be made with regard to whether a particular recording is a work made for hire. But everybody is going to be watching those first cases very, very carefully.

Does it matter that artists typically get an advance for making an album, but then they end up having to pay all the costs of producing the album, and that has to come out of their future royalties?

That's very relevant because it suggests that they're not employees, they're outside contractors. But because the statute allows in some cases for outside contractors to create works made for hire, I don't think the fact that the artists have to pick up these expenses necessarily indicates that it's a not a work for hire. It more likely depends on whether you can shoehorn the particular recording into one of these commissioned-work categories.

As I mentioned, the cases are somewhat fact-based. That means the label may win in one case and the artist in another because the facts are different. For example, there are sound recordings that were created as a contribution to a motion picture or another audiovisual work. That's one of the categories, and if that's the case then it will be a work for hire assuming there was a signed agreement. But most sound recordings were not created that way, so even if one case comes out one way, it doesn't mean they all will.

Are the stakes in this so high that the losing party would want to keep appealing all the way to the U.S. Supreme Court?

Probably. I would be surprised if this would get resolved before you get to that level. If the record labels are not successful in claiming that these are works made for hire, it definitely will diminish an important income stream. So I don't think they will just accept a negative decision. This is true of the artists as well.

5 Information Privacy

Count not him among your friends who will retail your privacies to the world.

—PUBLILIUS SYRUS (100 BCE)

5.1 Introduction

DO YOU WANT TO KNOW WHERE I LIVE? If you visit the Whitepages.com Web site and type my phone number into the Reverse Phone field, it returns a page giving my name and address. Click on the address, and you'll soon see a map of the neighborhood around my house.

Spend a few seconds more, and you can learn a lot about my standard of living. Go to Zillow.com and enter the address that you just learned from whitepages.com. Zillow dutifully returns the estimated value of my house, based on public records that document its size, its assessed value, and information about recent sales of other homes in my neighborhood. Click on the "Street View" tab, and you'll see a photo of my house taken from Google's camera-equipped car as it passed down my street.

If you become a friend of one of my friends on Facebook, you can get even more glimpses into my personal life by viewing photos of me that other people have posted and tagged. You can see me lounging by a swimming pool at a family reunion, un-wrapping a Christmas present, and walking my daughter Shauna down the aisle on her wedding day.

Scott McNealy, former CEO of Sun Microsystems, caused quite a stir when he said: "You have zero privacy anyway. Get over it" [1]. Why did his statement provoke such a strong reaction? You can't deny that computers, databases, and the Internet have made it easier than ever to get lots of information about total strangers. Still, many of us would like to think that we can keep some things private. Is it possible to maintain privacy in the Information Age?

NON SEQUITUR © 2005 Wiley Ink, Inc. Dist. By UNIVERSAL UCLICK.
Reprinted with permission. All rights reserved.

In this chapter, we focus on privacy issues related to the introduction of information technology. We begin by taking a philosophical look at privacy. What is privacy exactly? Do we have a natural right to privacy distinct from other rights, such as the right to property and the right to liberty? What about our need to know enough about others so that we can trust them? How do we handle conflicts between the right to privacy and the right to free expression?

We then survey some of the ways that we leave an "electronic trail" of information behind us as we go about our daily lives. Both private organizations and governments construct databases documenting our activities.

Finally, we take a look at data mining, an important tool for building profiles of individuals and communities. Companies use data mining to improve service and target product marketing to the right consumers. Sometimes they push on the borders of personal privacy a little too hard; we will look at a few examples of where companies have had to retreat because of a consumer backlash.

5.2 Perspectives on Privacy

5.2.1 Defining Privacy

Philosophers struggle to define privacy. Discussions about privacy revolve around the notion of *access*, where access means either physical proximity to a person or knowledge about that person. There is a tug of war between the desires, rights, and responsibilities of a person who wants to restrict access to himself, and the desires, rights, and responsibilities of outsiders to gain access.

From the point of view of an individual seeking to restrict access, privacy is a "zone of inaccessibility" that surrounds a person [2]. You have privacy to the extent that you can control who is allowed into your zone of inaccessibility. For example, you exercise your privacy when you lock the door behind you when using the toilet. You also exercise your privacy when you choose not to tell the clerk at the health club your Social Security number. However, privacy is not the same thing as being alone. Two people can have a private relationship. It might be a physical relationship, in which each person lets the other person become physically close while excluding others, or it might be an intellectual relationship, in which they exchange letters containing private thoughts.

When we look at privacy from the point of view of outsiders seeking access, the discussion revolves around where to draw the line between what is private and what is public (known to all). Stepping over this line and violating someone's privacy is an affront to that person's dignity [3]. You violate someone's privacy when you treat him or her as a means to an end. Put another way, some things ought not to be known. Suppose a friend invites you to see a cool movie trailer available on the Web. You follow him into the computer lab. He sits down at an available computer and begins to type in his login name and password. While it is his responsibility to keep his password confidential, it is also generally accepted that you ought to avert your eyes when someone is typing in their password. Another person's password is not something that you should know.

On the other hand, society can be harmed if individuals have too much privacy. Suppose a group of wealthy people of the same racial, ethnic, and religious background forms a private club. The members of the club share information with each other that is not available to the general public. If the club facilitates business deals among its members, it may give them an unfair advantage over others in the community who are just as capable of fulfilling the contracts. In this way, privacy can encourage social and economic inequities, and the public at large may benefit if the group had less privacy (or its membership were more diverse).

Here is another example of a public/private conflict, but this one focuses on the privacy of an individual. Most of us distinguish between a person's "private life" (what they do at home) and their "public life" (what they do at work). In general, we may agree that people have the right to keep outsiders from knowing what they do away from work. However, suppose a journalist learns that a wealthy candidate for high public office has lost millions of dollars gambling in Las Vegas. Does the public interest outweigh the politician's desire for privacy in this case?

In summary, privacy is a social arrangement that allows individuals to have some level of control over who is able to gain access to their physical selves and their personal information.

5.2.2 Harms and Benefits of Privacy

HARMS OF PRIVACY

Giving people privacy can result in harm to society. Some people take advantage of privacy to plan and carry out illegal or immoral activities. Most wrongdoing takes place under the cover of privacy [4].

Other suggest that increasing privacy has caused unhappiness by putting too great a burden on the nuclear family to care for all of its members. In the past, people received moral support not just from their immediate family, but also from other relatives and neighbors. Today, by contrast, families are expected to solve their own problems, which puts a great strain on some individuals [5].

On a related note, family violence leads to much pain and suffering in our society. Often, outsiders do not even acknowledge that a family is dysfunctional until one of its members is seriously injured. One reason dysfunctional families can maintain the pretense of normality as long as they do is because our culture respects the privacy of each family [6].

Humans are social beings. Most of us seek some engagement with others. The poor, the mentally ill, and others living on the fringes of society may have no problem maintaining a "zone of inaccessibility," because nobody is paying any attention to them. For outcasts, privacy may be a curse, not a blessing.

BENEFITS OF PRIVACY

Socialization and individuation are both necessary steps for a person to reach maturity. Privacy is necessary for a person to blossom as an individual [7].

Privacy is the way in which a social group recognizes and communicates to the individual that he is responsible for his development as a unique person, a separate moral agent [8]. Privacy is a recognition of each person's true freedom [9].

Privacy is valuable because it lets us be ourselves. Consider the following example. Imagine you are in a park playing with your child. How would your behavior be different if you knew someone was carefully watching you, perhaps even videotaping you, so that he or she could tell others about your parenting skills? You might well become self-conscious about your behavior. Few people would be able to carry on without any change to their emotional state or physical actions [10].

On a similar note, privacy lets us remove our public persona [11]. Imagine a businessman who is having a hard time with one of his company's important clients. At work, he must be polite to the client and scrupulously avoid saying anything negative about the client in front of any coworkers, lest he demoralize them, or even worse, lose his job. In the privacy of his home, he can "blow off steam" by confiding in his wife, who lends him a sympathetic ear and helps motivate him to get through the tough time at work. If people did not have privacy, they would have to wear their public face at all times, which could be damaging to their psychological health.

Privacy can foster intellectual activities. It allows us to shut out the rest of the world so that we can focus our thoughts without interruption, be creative, and grow spiritually [12, 13, 14].

Some maintain that privacy is the only way in which people can develop relationships involving respect, love, friendship, and trust. You can think of privacy as "moral capital" [15]. People use this capital to build intimate relationships. Taking away people's privacy means taking away their moral capital. Without moral capital, they have no means to develop close personal relationships.

In order to have different kinds of social relationships with different people, we need to have some kind of control over who knows what about us [16]. You can imagine everyone having a "ladder" of privacy [10]. At the top of the ladder is the person we share the most information with. For many people, this person is their spouse. As we work our way down the ladder, we encounter people we would share progressively less information with. Here is an example of what someone's ladder of privacy might look like:

spouse

priest/minister/rabbi

brothers and sisters

parents

children

friends

in-laws

coworkers

neighbors

marketers

employers

government

news media

ex-spouses

potential rivals/enemies

Others are critical of suggestions that tie intimacy too closely to sharing information [8]. A woman might tell her psychoanalyst things she would not even reveal to her husband, but that does not imply that she experiences deeper intimacy with her psychoanalyst than with her husband. Intimacy is not just about sharing information; it's also about caring. The mutual caring that characterizes a healthy marriage results in a greater level of intimacy than can be gained simply by sharing personal information.

SUMMARY

To summarize our discussion, allowing people to have some privacy has a variety of beneficial effects. Granting people privacy is one way that society recognizes them as adults and indicates they are responsible for their own moral behavior. Privacy helps people to develop as individuals and to truly be themselves. It provides people the opportunity to shut out the world, be more creative, and develop spiritually. It allows each of us to create different kinds of relationships with different people.

Privacy also has numerous harmful effects. It provides people with a way of covering up actions that are immoral or illegal. If a society sends a message that certain kinds of information must be kept private, some people caught in abusive or dysfunctional relationships may feel trapped and unable to ask others for help.

Weighing these benefits and harms, we conclude that granting people at least some privacy is better than denying people any privacy at all. That leads us to our next question: Is privacy a natural right, like the right to life?

5.2.3 Is There a Natural Right to Privacy?

Most of us agree that every person has certain natural rights, such as the right to life, the right to liberty, and the right to own property. Many people also talk about our right to privacy. Is this a natural right as well?

PRIVACY RIGHTS EVOLVE FROM PROPERTY RIGHTS

Our belief in a right to privacy may have grown out of our property rights [7]. Historically, Europeans have viewed the home as a sanctuary. The English common law tradition has been that "a man's home is his castle." No one—not even the King—can enter without permission, unless there is probable cause of criminal activity.

In 1765, the British Parliament passed the Quartering Act, which required American colonies to provide British soldiers with accommodations in taverns, inns, and unoccupied buildings. After the Boston Tea Party of 1773, the British Parliament attempted to restore order in the colonies by passing the Coercive Acts. One of these acts amended the Quartering Act to allow the billeting of soldiers in private homes, breaking the centuries-old common law tradition and infuriating many colonists. It's not surprising, then, that Americans restored the principle of home as sanctuary in the Bill of Rights.

⁓

THIRD AMENDMENT TO THE UNITED STATES CONSTITUTION

No Soldier shall, in time of peace be quartered in any house, without the consent of the Owner, nor in time of war, but in a manner to be prescribed by law.

⁓

In certain villages in the Basque region of Spain, each house is named after the person who originally constructed it. Villagers refer to people by their house names, even if the family living in the house has no relation to the family originally dwelling there.

These examples show a strong link between a person and his property. From this viewpoint, privacy is seen in terms of control over personal territory, and privacy rights evolve out of property rights.

WARREN AND BRANDEIS: CLEARLY PEOPLE HAVE A RIGHT TO PRIVACY

We can see this evolution laid out in a highly influential paper, published in 1890, by Samuel Warren and Louis Brandeis. Samuel Warren was a Harvard-educated lawyer who became a businessman when he inherited a paper manufacturing business. His wife was the daughter of a U.S. Senator and a leading socialite in Boston. Her parties attracted the upper-crust of Boston society. They also attracted the attention of the *Saturday Evening Gazette*, a tabloid that delighted in shocking its readers with lurid details about the lives of the Boston Brahmins.[1] Fuming at the paper's coverage of his daughter's wedding, Warren enlisted the aid of Harvard classmate Louis Brandeis, a highly successful Boston attorney (and future U.S. Supreme Court justice). Together, Warren and Brandeis published an article in the *Harvard Law Review* called "The Right to Privacy" [17]. In their highly influential paper, Warren and Brandeis argue that political, social, and economic changes demand recognition for new kinds of legal rights. In particular, they write that it is clear that people in modern society have a right to privacy and that this right ought to be respected. To make their case, they focus on—you guessed it—abuses of newspapers.

According to Warren and Brandeis:

The press is overstepping in every direction the obvious bounds of propriety and of decency. Gossip is no longer the resource of the idle and of the vicious, but has become a trade, which is pursued with industry as well as effrontery. To satisfy the prurient taste the details of sexual relations are spread broadcast in the columns of the daily papers . . . The intensity and complexity of life, attendant upon advancing civilization, have rendered necessary some retreat from the world, and man, under the refining influence of culture, has become more sensitive to publicity, so that solitude and privacy have become more essential to the individual; but modern enterprise and invention have, through invasions upon his privacy, subjected him to mental pain and distress, far greater than could be inflicted by mere bodily injury. [17]

Meanwhile, Warren and Brandeis argue, there are no adequate legal remedies available to the victims. Laws against libel and slander are not sufficient because they do not address the situation where malicious, but true, stories about someone are circulated. Laws addressing property rights also fall short because they assume people have control over the ways in which information about themselves is revealed. However, cameras and

---

1. To learn more about the Boston Brahmins, consult Wikipedia (www.wikipedia.org).

FIGURE 5.1 Warren and Brandeis argued that the legal system should protect people's "right to be left alone." (PhamousFotos / Splash News/Newscom)

other devices are capable of capturing information about a person without that person's consent (Figure 5.1).

Warren and Brandeis pointed out that the right to privacy had already been recognized by French law. They urged the American legal system to recognize the right to privacy, which they called "the right to be let alone" [17]. Their reasoning was highly influential. Though it took decades, the right to privacy is now recognized in courts across America [18].

THOMSON: EVERY "PRIVACY RIGHT" VIOLATION IS A VIOLATION OF ANOTHER RIGHT

Judith Jarvis Thomson has a completely different view about a right to privacy. She writes: "Perhaps the most striking thing about the right to privacy is that nobody seems to have any very clear idea what it is" [19]. Thomson points out problems with defining privacy as "the right to be let alone," as Warren and Brandeis have done. In some respects, this definition of privacy is too narrow. Suppose the police use an X-ray device and supersensitive microphones to monitor the movements and conversations of Smith in his home. The police have not touched Smith or even come close to him. He has no knowledge they are monitoring him. The police have let Smith alone, yet people who believe in a right to privacy would surely argue that they have violated Smith's privacy. In other respects, the definition of privacy as "the right to be let alone" is too broad. If I hit Jones on the head with a brick, I have not let him alone, but it is not his right of privacy I have violated—it is his right to be secure in his own person.

Thomson argues that whenever the right to privacy is violated, another right is violated as well. For example, suppose a man owns a pornographic picture. He doesn't want anyone else to know he owns it, so he keeps it in a wall safe. He only takes it out of his safe when he has taken pains to prevent others from looking into his home. Suppose we use an X-ray machine to look into his home safe and view the picture. We have violated his privacy, but we have also violated one of his property rights—the right to decide who (if anybody) will see the picture.

Here is another example. Suppose a Saudi Arabian woman wishes to keep her face covered for religious reasons. When she goes out in public, she puts a veil over her face. If I should walk up and pull away her veil to see her face, I have violated her privacy. But I have also violated one of her rights over her person—to decide who should touch her.

According to Thomson, there are a cluster of rights associated with privacy, just as there are a cluster of rights associated with property and a cluster of rights associated with our physical self. In Thomson's view, every violation of a privacy right is also a violation of a right in some other cluster. Since this is the case, there is no need to define privacy precisely or to decide exactly where to draw the line between violations of privacy and acceptable conduct.

AUTONOMOUS MORAL AGENTS NEED SOME PRIVACY

Thomson is not alone in disputing that privacy is a natural right. Many philosophers think privacy principles should be based on the more fundamental principle that each person is worthy of respect [9]. We give each other privacy because we recognize privacy is needed if people are to be autonomous moral agents able to develop healthy personal relationships and act as free citizens in a democratic society.

Jeffrey Reiman supports this view when he writes:

> The right to privacy protects the individual's interest in becoming, being, and re-maining a person. It is thus a right which *all* human individuals possess—even those in solitary confinement. It does not assert a right never to be seen even on a crowded street. It is sufficient that I can control whether and by whom my body is experienced in some significant places and that I have the real possibility of repair-ing to those places. It is a right which protects my capacity to enter into intimate relations, not because it protects my reserve of generally withheld information, but because it enables me to make the commitment that underlies caring as *my* com-mitment uniquely conveyed by *my* thoughts and witnessed by *my* actions. [8]

Note Reiman's fairly restricted view of privacy. He carefully points out areas where privacy is necessary. He does not argue that privacy is a natural right, nor does he suggest that a person has complete control over what is held private.

CONCLUSION: PRIVACY IS A PRUDENTIAL RIGHT

In conclusion, philosophers disagree whether there is a natural right to privacy, but most commentators can agree that privacy is a *prudential right*. That means rational agents would agree to recognize some privacy rights, because granting these rights is to the benefit of society [20].

5.2.4 Privacy and Trust

While many people complain about threats to privacy, it is clear upon reflection that we have more privacy than our ancestors did [21]. Only a couple of centuries ago, our society was agrarian. People lived with their extended families in small homes. The nearest community center was the village, where everyone knew everyone else and people took a keen interest in each other's business. Organized religion played an important role in everyday life. In this kind of society, there was a strong pressure to conform [11]. There was greater emphasis on the community and lesser emphasis on the individual.

Modern culture fosters much greater privacy. Prosperity, the single-family home, the automobile, television, and computers have contributed to our privacy. The single-family home gives us physical separation from other people. The automobile allows us to travel alone instead of on a bus or train in the presence of others. The television brings entertainment to us inside the comfort of our homes, taking us out of the neighborhood movie theater. With a computer and an Internet connection, we can access information at home rather than visit the public library [10]. These are just a few examples of ways in which modern conveniences allow us to spend time by ourselves or in the company of a few family members or friends.

In the past, young people typically lived at home with their parents until they were married. Today, many young unmarried adults live autonomously. This lifestyle provides them with previously unthought-of freedom and privacy [21].

The consequence of all this privacy is that we live among strangers. Many people know little more about their neighbors than their names (if that). Yet, when we live in a society with others, we must be able to trust them to some extent. How do we know that the taxi driver will get us where we want to go without hurting us or overcharging us? How do parents know that their children's teachers are not child molesters? How does the bank know that if it loans someone money, it will be repaid?

In order to trust others, we must rely on their reputations. This was easier in the past, when people didn't move around so much and everyone knew everyone else's history. Today, society must get information out of people to establish reputations. One way of getting information from a person is through an **ordeal,** such as a lie detector test or a drug test. The other way to learn more about individuals is to issue (and request) **credentials,** such as a driver's license, key, employee badge, credit card, or college degree [21].

5.2.5 Case Study

Jim and Nancy Sullivan are the proud parents of a baby girl. Nancy was on maternity leave, but now she has returned to her full-time job, and they have hired a nanny, after interviewing her and calling a couple of her references. Jim and Nancy's friends tell them horror stories about abusive nannies, and they recommend a software program called LiveSecurityWatch that would let them monitor what's happening at home from a remote computer. Jim and Nancy purchase LiveSecurityWatch and install it on a laptop computer placed in the family room. With the system in place, Jim and Nancy can use their workplace computers to see and hear how the nanny interacts with their baby. The nanny has no idea that the Sullivan's computer is being used as a surveillance system.

Is it wrong for Jim and Nancy Sullivan to secretly monitor the behavior of their baby's nanny?

RULE UTILITARIAN EVALUATION

If all parents monitored their nannies or child care providers and took actions when warranted, such as firing nannies who did not perform well, it is unlikely such monitoring would remain a secret for long. Under these circumstances, nannies would be much more careful to be on their best behavior. This would potentially have the long-term effects of reducing the instances of child abuse and increasing the peace of mind of parents. On the other hand, the harms of the monitoring would be significant in terms of increasing the stress and reducing the job satisfaction of nannies and child care providers. After all, who wants to be monitored constantly? These negative aspects of the job could lead to an increased turnover rate of nannies. Less experienced nannies might well provide lower quality care to the babies they tend. The harms of having all parents monitoring their nannies or child care providers appear to be greater than the benefits. Hence, we conclude it is wrong for the Sullivans to secretly monitor their nanny.

SOCIAL CONTRACT THEORY EVALUATION

Social contract theory emphasizes the adoption of rules that rational people would agree to accept because they are to everyone's mutual benefit, as long as everyone else follows the rules as well. As we discussed earlier in this section, privacy is a prudential right. It is reasonable for society to give privacy to people in their own homes, and it is also reasonable for family members within each home to give each other some privacy as well. The nanny wouldn't expect her interactions with the baby in a park or a grocery store to be private, but it is reasonable for her to expect privacy when taking care of the baby inside the Sullivans's home. Hence, the Sullivans' decision to secretly monitor the nanny was wrong because it violated her right to privacy.

KANTIAN EVALUATION

Let's consider the morality of acting according to the rule: "An employer may secretly monitor the work of an employee who works with vulnerable people." To evaluate the rule using the first formulation of the Categorical Imperative, we universalize it. What would happen if every employer secretly monitored the work of employees who worked with vulnerable people? If that were the case, then employees who worked with vulnerable populations would have no expectation of privacy, and it would be impossible for employers to secretly monitor their work. Hence, the proposed rule is self-defeating, and it would be wrong to act according to this rule.

We can also evaluate this situation using the second formulation of the Categorical Imperative. As parents, the Sullivans are responsible for the well-being of their baby. In order to be more confident that their baby is safe in the care of the nanny, they choose to secretly observe the behavior of the nanny. The observation is the means to their desired end of having their baby well cared for. The nanny naturally assumes that her interactions with the baby in the Sullivan residence are private. By not disclosing to the nanny the fact that she is being watched remotely, the Sullivans have treated the nanny as a means to an end. Hence, the action of the Sullivans is wrong.

SUMMARY

From the points of view of rule utilitarianism, social contract theory, and Kantianism, we have concluded that it is wrong for the Sullivans to secretly monitor how well their nanny takes care of their baby.

Does this mean that the Sullivans must throw up their hands and simply hope for the best with regard to the quality of their child's care? No. They do have several morally acceptable options that do not involve deceit. They could conduct a more comprehensive interview of the nanny, they could more thoroughly check the nanny's references, or one of them could spend a day or two a home observing the nanny from a distance as she interacted with the baby. The Sullivans could also be candid with the nanny; they could inform her that they would like to install software on their laptop computer that allows them to see and hear what is happening in the apartment. That course of action would respect the autonomy of the nanny and give her the freedom to agree to the monitoring, negotiate a different arrangement, or quit.

5.3 Information Disclosures

As we go about our lives, we leave behind an electronic trail of our activities, thanks to computerized databases. Some events result in the creation of public records. A **public record** contains information about an incident or action reported to a government agency for the purpose of informing the public [22]. Examples of public records are birth certificates, marriage licenses, motor vehicle records, criminal records, deeds to property, and the salaries of state employees (including your professor, if you are studying at a public institution). Making government records public is one way to hold government agencies accountable for their actions and help ensure that all citizens are being treated fairly.

When public records were written on paper and kept in county courthouse basements, they were relatively hard to retrieve. Computerized databases and the Internet have made accessing many public records quick and inexpensive, and there are a lot of good purposes to which we can put all that information. Before a school hires a teacher, it can check the candidate's criminal record to ensure there are no convictions for child abuse. Before a transit system hires a bus driver, it can check the applicant's driving record. Before moving to a new city, you can check out the crime rate of the neighborhood you're interested in.

Other uses of public records may not be as laudable. Thanks to information technology, it easier than ever to learn a lot about someone's wealth. For most people, their home is their principal asset. As we've already mentioned, you can visit Zillow.com, type in the address of someone's house, and quickly learn Zillow's estimate of the house's worth, based on information about the size of the house (a public record), the selling price of the house (a public record), and recent sales of similar houses in the neighbor-hood (also public records).

Private organizations, too, maintain extensive records of our activities. Databases store information about the purchases we make with our credit cards, the groceries we buy at a discount with our loyalty cards, the DVDs we rent, the calls we make with our cell phones, and much more. The companies collecting this information use it to bill us. They also can use this information to serve us better. For example, Amazon uses information about book purchases to build profiles of its customers. With a customer profile, Amazon can recommend other books the customer may be interested in buying. On the other hand, companies may share information about our purchases with other companies that then send us junk mail for products we have no interest in buying.

Often people voluntarily disclose information to private organizations. Product reg-istration forms and contest entries often ask consumers to reveal a great deal of personal information. I once received a product preference survey from Proctor & Gamble; it said, in part:

> Your opinions matter to us. That's why we've selected you to participate in one of the most important consumer research surveys we'll do this year. Whether or not you have completed one of our surveys in the past, you can help us continue to create the products that meet your needs. Simply answer the following questions, provide your name and address and mail it back to us. That way, we will be able to contact you if there are any special offers that might be of interest to you.

The questionnaire asked about my family's use of nasal inhalants, coffee, peanut butter, orange juice, laundry detergent, fabric softener, household cleaner, deodorant, tooth-paste, detergents, skin care and hair care products, cosmetics, mouthwash, diapers, laxatives, and disposable briefs. It provided a list of 60 leisure activities, ranging from various sports to travel to gambling, and asked me to choose the three activities most important to my family. It also asked my date of birth, the sex and age of everyone living in my home, my occupation, the credit cards we used, and our annual family income. If I had returned the questionnaire (which I didn't), Proctor & Gamble would have been free to use this information any way it wished.

Many of us voluntarily share information about our activities by posting messages and uploading photos to social network sites like Facebook. These sites make it easy to communicate with many friends and acquantances at once, but this information can be put to other purposes as well [23]. Social Intelligence Corporation provides employers with background checks on potential employees by searching the Internet for posts and photos by the job candidates that reveal negative activities specified by the employer, such as "racist remarks or activities, sexually explicit photos or videos, and illegal activity such as drug use" [24].

Recall the perspective that privacy is a "zone of inaccessability." Using this defini-tion, we can say that our personal information is private to the extent that we can control who has access to it. In some settings we expect to have much more control over our per-sonal information than in other venues. For example, we have much more control over who takes our picture when we're at home than when we're at a football game. Hence, our expectations about the privacy of our personal information depend on the situation. In this rest of this section, we survey a variety of ways in which private organizations collect and use personal information, starting with situations in which most of us would assume to have less privacy, and finishing with situations in which we would expect to have much more privacy.

5.3.1 Facebook Tags

In the Facebook social network, a **tag** is a label identifying a person in a photo. When you post a photo to Facebook, you can tag the people in the photo who are on your list of Facebook friends. In a similar way, any of your Facebook friends can tag you in photos they post to the site.

People tag photos in Facebook an average of 100 million times per day [25]. In December 2010, Facebook introduced a new time-saving feature called Tag Suggestions. When a Facebook user adds a new photo, Facebook uses facial recognition software to suggest the name of the friend appearing in the photo.

In June 2011, the Electronic Privacy Information Center (EPIC) filed a complaint about Facebook Tag Suggestions with the Federal Trade Commission [26]. EPIC claimed that in order to develop its facial recognition technology, Facebook gathered facial data from users' photos without their consent. Others raised the concern that the introduction of an automatic tagging feature would increase the chance that photos would be improperly tagged, which could cause a problem if the photos were not complimentary [27].

5.3.2 Enhanced 911 Services

All cell phone providers in the United States are required by law to be able to track the locations of active cell phone users to within 100 meters. The safety benefit of this capability is obvious. Emergency response teams can reach people in distress who have dialed 911, even if they are unable to speak or do not know exactly where they are.

The ability to identify the location of active cell phone users has other benefits. For example, it makes it easier for cell phone companies to identify where signal strength is weak and coverage needs to be improved.

The downside of enhanced 911 service is a potential loss of privacy. Because it is possible to track the location of active cell phone users, what happens if information is sold or shared? Suppose you call your employer and tell him you are too sick to come into work. Your boss is suspicious, since this is the third Friday this winter you've called in sick. Your employer pays your cell phone provider and discovers that you made your call from a ski resort [28].

5.3.3 Rewards or Loyalty Programs

Rewards or loyalty programs for shoppers have been around for more than 100 years. Your grandparents may remember using S&H Green Stamps, the most popular rewards program in the United States from the 1950s through the 1970s. Shoppers would collect Green Stamps with purchases, paste them into booklets, and redeem the booklets by shopping in the Sperry and Hutchinson catalog for household items.

Today, many shoppers take advantage of rewards programs sponsored by grocery stores. Card-carrying members of the store's "club" save money on many of their purchases, either through coupons or instant discounts at the cash register. The most significant difference between the Green Stamps program and a contemporary shopper's club is that today's rewards programs are run by computers that record every purchase. Companies can use information about the buying habits of particular customers to provide them with individualized service.

For example, ShopRite grocery stores have computerized shopping carts. The shopping cart has a card reader and an LCD screen. Customers identify themselves by swiping their loyalty card through the card reader. A computer taps into a database with the customer's buying history and uses this information to guide the customer to frequently purchased products. As the cart passes through the aisles, pop-up ads display items the computer predicts the customer may be interested in purchasing [29].

Critics of grocery club cards say that the problem is not that card users pay less for their groceries, but that those who don't use cards pay more. They give examples of club-member prices being equivalent to the regular product price at stores without customer loyalty programs [30].

Some consumers respond to the potential loss of privacy by giving phony personal information when they apply for these cards. Others take it a step further by regularly exchanging their cards with those held by other people [31].

5.3.4 Body Scanners

(This section describes scanners designed to take a person's measurements. Advanced imaging technology scanners used at airport security checkpoints are discussed in Section 6.11.2.)

Looking good is important to many, if not most, of us. Computer technology is making it possible for us to save time shopping and find clothes that fit us better (Figure 5.2).

In some stores in the United Kingdom, you can enter a booth, strip to your undergarments, and be scanned by a computer, which produces a three-dimensional model of your body. The computer uses this information to recommend which pairs of jeans ought to fit you the best. You can then sit in front of a computer screen and preview what various pairs of jeans will look like on you. When you have narrowed down your search to a few particular brands and sizes, you can actually try on the jeans.

Body scans are also being used to produce custom-made clothing. At Brooks Brothers stores in the United States, customers who have been scanned can purchase suits tailored to their particular physiques [32].

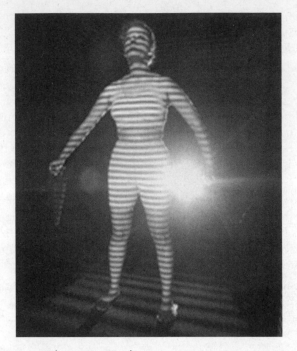

FIGURE 5.2 A computer takes a customer's measurements. (AP Photo/Richard Drew)

5.3.5 RFID Tags

Imagine getting up in the morning, walking into the bathroom, and seeing a message on the medicine cabinet's computer screen warning you that your bottle of aspirin is close to its expiration date. Later that day, you are shopping for a new pair of pants. As you try them on, a screen in the dressing room displays other pieces of clothing that would complement your selection.

These scenarios are possible today thanks to a technology called RFID, short for radio frequency identification. An RFID is a tiny wireless transmitter. Manufacturers are replacing bar codes with RFIDs, because they give more information about the product and are easier to scan. An RFID can contain specific information about the particular item to which it is attached (or embedded), and a scanner can read an RFID from six feet away. When barcodes are replaced by RFIDs, check-outs are quicker and companies track their inventory more accurately (Figure 5.3).

However, because RFIDs are not turned off when an item is purchased, the new technology has raised privacy concerns. Imagine a workplace full of RFID scanners. A scanner in your cubicle enables a monitoring system to associate you with the tags in your clothes. Another scanner picks up your presence at the water cooler. The next thing you know, your boss has called you in for a heart-to-heart talk about how many breaks you're taking. Some privacy advocates say consumers should have a way to remove or disable RFIDs in the products they purchase [33, 34].

FIGURE 5.3 Employees take inventory more quickly and make fewer errors when items are marked with RFID tags. (© Marc F. Henning / Alamy)

5.3.6 Implanted Chips

In Taiwan, every domesticated dog must contain a microchip implant identifying its owner and residence [35]. The microchip, about the size of a grain of rice, is implanted into the dog's ear using a syringe. When a dog gets lost, the authorities can easily retrieve the address and return the pet to its owner.

Verichip Corporation created an RFID tag approved for use in humans. The company claimed than 2,000 people worldwide had a Verichip implant. The most common reason for getting an implanted RFID chip was to allow doctors to learn about the medical conditions of unconscious patients [36]. However, in some trendy European nightclubs, patrons have used their implanted RFID chips as in-house "debit cards" for purchasing food and drinks [37]. After some highly publicized incidents of abducted or missing children, the media have reported parents ruminating on the idea of implanting microchip tracking devices in their kids [38, 39].

5.3.7 OnStar

OnStar Corporation manufactures a communication system incorporated into an automobile's rear-view mirror. OnStar provides emergency, security, navigation, and diagnostics services to its subscribers. For example, a driver who runs out of gas can push the Blue OnStar button to initiate a conversation with an OnStar representative. The driver does not have to know his or her exact location, because the system automatically sends the GPS location of the automobile to OnStar, which can send help. The driver does not always need to initiate the communication with OnStar representatives. For example, whenever the airbags deploy on an OnStar-equipped vehicle, the system automatically communicates the location of the vehicle to an OnStar center, which can initiate a 911 call.

The capabilities of the OnStar system were dramatically revealed in in Visalia, California, in October 2009, when a man with a sawed-off shotgun ordered two occupants of a 2009 Chevrolet Tahoe to get out of their vehicle. He took their money and drove off in the SUV. After the police got the victim's permission to track down the stolen vehicle, OnStar provided the police with its current location. When police cars began to tail the Tahoe, its driver sped up. At this point the OnStar service center issued a command to the SUV that electronically disabled the gas pedal, causing the Tahoe to gradually slow to a halt, and allowing the police to apprehend the carjacker. Visalia Police Chief Colleen Mestas complimented the new technology for preventing a potentially dangerous high-speed car chase [40].

Because OnStar has the ability to track the location of OnStar-equipped vehicles and listen to conversations happening within them, some privacy advocates have expressed concerns about possible abuses that could occur if this information were shared with law enforcement agencies. For example, suppose the police were looking for suspects in an unsolved crime. Should they have the right to gather information from OnStar about all OnStar-equipped vehicles that were in the area at the time of the crime?

In an hour-long Web chat on the General Motors FastLane site in November 2009, OnStar's Jane Speelman responded to these concerns. According to Speelman, OnStar does not continuously monitor the location of OnStar-equipped vehicles, OnStar does not provide information about the speed of vehicles to law enforcement agencies, and OnStar representatives cannot listen to conversations inside a vehicle without alerting the vehicle's occupants [41].

5.3.8 Automobile "Black Boxes"

You probably know about airplane flight data recorders, also called "black boxes," which provide information useful in postcrash investigations. Did you know that modern automobiles also come equipped with a "black box"? A microprocessor attached to the car's airbag records information about the speed of the car, the amount of pressure being put on the brake pedal, and whether the seat belts are connected. After a collision, investigators can retrieve the microprocessor from the automobile and view data collected in the five seconds before the accident [42].

5.3.9 Medical Records

The change from paper-based to electronic medical records has the potential to lower the costs and improve the quality of medical care by making it quicker and cheaper for information about patients to be shared among nurses, physicians, and other caregivers. The U.S. government has been promoting the conversion to electronic medical records as one way to rein in the rapid increases in health care costs.

However, once an individual's entire medical history is consolidated in a database accessible by many, it can be more difficult to control how that information is disseminated, with potentially significant consequences. An employer may choose to pass over a job candidate whose medical history indicates he may be expensive to insure [43]. A woman who has successfully completed a treatment program for drug addiction may be discriminated against if information about her former drug use is revealed.

In November 2003, Florida state law enforcement officials seized the medical records of radio commentator Rush Limbaugh, as part of an investigation to determine whether Limbaugh had illegally obtained prescription pain medications from several doctors. The American Civil Liberties Union filed a friend-of-the-court brief in partial support of Limbaugh, arguing that law enforcement officials acted improperly in obtaining a warrant that allowed them to seize *all* of Limbaugh's medical records, not just those relevant to the criminal investigation [44].

5.3.10 Digital Video Recorders

TiVo, Inc. is a well-known manufacturer of digital video recorders. TiVo provides a service that allows its subscribers to more easily record programs they are interested in watching later. For example, with a single command a subscriber can instruct the TiVo to record every episode of a TV series. TiVo collects detailed information about the viewing habits of its users. Because the system monitors the activities of the users second by second, its data are more valuable than that provided by other services. For example, TiVo's records show that 66 percent of the ads shown during primetime on broadcast networks are skipped [45].

5.3.11 Cookies and Flash Cookies

A **cookie** is a file placed on your computer's hard drive by a Web server. The file contains information about your visits to a Web site. Cookies can contain login names and passwords, product preferences, and the contents of virtual "shopping carts." Web sites use cookies to provide you with personalized services, such as custom Web pages. Instead of asking you to type in the same information multiple times, a Web site can retrieve that information from a cookie. Most Web sites do not ask for permission before creating a cookie on your hard drive. You can configure your Web browser to alert you when a cookie is being placed on your computer, or you can set your Web browser to refuse to accept any cookies. However, some Web sites cannot be accessed by browsers that block cookies.

In recent years, Web sites have begun using another kind of cookie called a **flash cookie**, which is a file placed on your computer's hard drive by a Web server running the Adobe Flash Player. Two attributes of flash cookies have raised privacy concerns. First, a flash cookie can hold 25 times as much information as a browser cookie. Second, flash cookies are not controlled by the browser's privacy controls. Some Web sites take advantage of this loophole and use flash cookies as a way of backing up ordinary cookies. That way, if you delete the browser cookie associated with a Web site, it can be "respawned" from the flash cookie. A survey by researchers at the University of California, Berkeley revealed that more than half of the 100 most popular Web sites used flash cookies, but only four of them mentioned flash cookies in their privacy policies [47].

5.4 Data Mining

In the previous section, we surveyed a few of the many ways that companies collect information on people's daily activities. In this section, we look at how this information has itself become a commodity that companies buy and sell in order to provide more personalized services to their existing customers and to target potential customers more accurately.

5.4.1 Data Mining Defined

Before you use a grocery store's loyalty card, you have to spend some time filling out an application that asks for a lot of personal information, such as your name, address, and phone number. After the store has processed your application, using your loyalty card is easy. You just swipe your card or type in your phone number, and the register recognizes you as a customer and gives you the appropriate discounts on your food purchases. At the same time, information about your purchases is entered into a database.

A record in a database records a single transaction, such as a particular item you purchased at the grocery store. A database record is like a single snapshot of a person. It tells you something about the person, but in isolation, its value is limited. **Data mining** is the process of searching through many records in one or more databases looking for patterns or relationships. Data mining is a way to generate new information by combining facts found in multiple transactions, and it can also be a way to predict future events. By drawing upon large numbers of records, data mining allows an organization to build an accurate profile of an individual from a myriad of snapshots.

Companies can use data mining in order to create more personal relationships with their customers [48].

GOOGLE'S PERSONALIZED SEARCH

When information is put to another purpose, that is called a **secondary use** of the data. A simple example of secondary use of data is Google's personalized search feature. Google keeps track of your search queries and the Web pages you have clicked. When you type in a new query, it can use this information to infer what you are interested in and return pages more likely to be what you are seeking. For example, the word "bass" has multiple meanings, but if you have a history of queries and page clicks related to fishing, but not music, that can help the search engine return the most appropriate pages.

Google is able to personalize search results whether or not you have a Google account. If you are signed in to Google, the search engine examines your Web history to personalize the search results. This information is held indefinitely, unless you delete your Web history. If you are not signed in, Google creates a cookie linked to your computer's browser, and it stores records of all queries associated with that cookie, as well as results that have been clicked, for up to 180 days [49].

COLLABORATIVE FILTERING

Collaborative filtering algorithms draw upon information about the preferences of a large number of people to predict what an individual may enjoy. An organization performing collaborative filtering may determine people's preferences explicitly, through rankings, or implicitly, by tracking their purchases. The filtering algorithm looks for patterns in the data. Perhaps many people who purchase peanut butter also purchase jam. If a new customer buys a jar of peanut butter, the software may instruct the register to print out a discount coupon for a particular brand of jam along with the sales receipt. Collaborative filtering software is also used by online retailers and movie sites to make recommendations [50].

5.4.2 Opt–in Versus Opt–out Policies

We have just examined a few secondary uses of data: ways in which a company that collects information about its customers' activities can use this information to provide its customers with a more personalized service. It only makes sense that if several companies pooled the information they had on the same person, they could construct a more complete electronic profile that would lead to new insights into products or services that person might wish to purchase. Do companies have the right to buy and sell information about their customers' transactions, or should the person buying a product or service have the right to control the information about that transaction?

Consider the following hypothetical example. Dr. Knowitall, a computer science professor, takes his broken computer to the Computer Shop so that 18-year-old Andy can fix it for him. Dr. Knowitall is embarrassed that he can't fix the computer himself, and he doesn't want anybody to find out that he must pay someone to fix it. Dr. Knowitall certainly isn't going to tell anyone, but does he have the right to prevent Andy from telling anyone? Or maybe Andy wants to keep the transaction a secret, because he's embarrassed it took him so long to fix the computer and he doesn't want anyone to find out he was in over his head. Does Andy have the right to keep Dr. Knowitall from talking about it?

It seems that neither person can claim the right to control information about this transaction. Since information about the transaction becomes public information if either party discloses it, keeping the transaction private is more difficult (hence, more valuable) than making it public.

If Dr. Knowitall wants to keep the transaction private, he should be willing to pay for it. He may tell Andy, "I'll give you an extra 20 bucks if you promise you won't tell anybody that you fixed my computer." At this point, Dr. Knowitall has purchased control over the information about this transaction. Andy is obliged to keep his mouth shut, not because of Dr. Knowitall's right to privacy, but because of his right to expect the agreement will be upheld.

What rules should govern the sharing of information collected by organizations selling products or services? Two fundamentally different policies are called opt-in and opt-out.

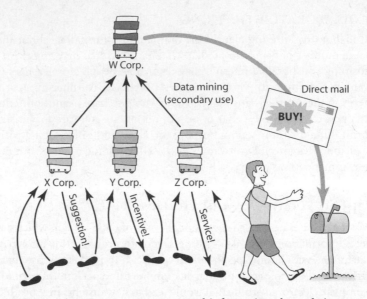

FIGURE 5.4 Companies use computers to record information about their customers and their buying habits. They analyze this information to suggest additional purchases, provide incentives, and deliver better service. They may also sell this information to other companies. By combining information from various sources, a company can build sophisticated profiles of individuals and target its direct mail advertising to those people most likely to be interested in its products.

The **opt-in** policy requires the consumer to explicitly give permission for the organization to share the information with another organization. Opt-in policies are preferred by privacy advocates.

The **opt-out** policy requires the consumer to explicitly forbid an organization from sharing information with other organizations. Direct marketing associations prefer the opt-out policy, because opt-in is a barrier for new businesses. New businesses do not have the resources to go out and collect all the information they need to target their mailings to the correct individuals. In an opt-out environment, most people will not go through the effort required to actually remove themselves from mailing lists. Hence, it is easier for new businesses to get access to the mailing lists they need to succeed [51]. Another argument for opt-out is that companies have the right to control information about the transactions they have made. Information is a valuable commodity. An opt-in policy takes this commodity away from companies.

At this time opt-out policies are far more common than opt-in policies. *Information about customers has itself become a commodity.* Organizations sell or exchange information with other organizations (Figure 5.4). This is a common way for organizations to gather large databases of information they can mine.

For example, a company selling time-share condominiums purchases from a hotel chain the names and addresses of people who have vacationed in a resort area in the past two years. From another organization, it purchases a database that gives the approximate annual household income of a family, based on that family's nine-digit ZIP code. Combining these lists allows the time-share agency to target people most likely to have both the interest and the financial resources to purchase a share of a vacation condominium. It uses direct mail to send brochures to these people.

5.4.3 Examples of Data Mining

CREDIT REPORTS

Credit reports are a great example of how information about customers has itself become a commodity. A credit bureau is a company that keeps track of an individual's assets, debts, and history of paying bills and repaying loans, using this information to determine the creditworthiness of that person. Credit bureaus sell credit reports to banks, credit card companies, and other potential lenders.

Thanks to the national credit bureau system, you can get a credit card from a bank or store with which you have never done business. When you want to borrow money to purchase a home, you don't have to go to your local bank. You can get the money from a bank across the country that trusts you to repay the loan because of your positive credit report. Competition among banks leads to lower interest rates, a definite advantage for consumers.

Of course, if you have a poor record of paying bills on time and repaying loans, your credit score will be low. People with low credit scores have a harder time getting loans and pay higher interest rates on the loans they do get.

A poor credit report can come back to haunt people in ways they might not have anticipated. Many employers conduct a credit check late in the job interview process, as a way of double-checking a candidate before making a job offer. A credit report received by an employer doesn't give the applicant's credit score, but it does list the applicant's debts. Critics of the use of credit reports when making hiring decisions have stated that these reports can cause employers to shy away from minorities and those who are currently out of work. "I think the assumption that is made is, if somebody is behind on their bills, then it tells something about their integrity or responsibility, but in many cases that assumption is flawed," said Sarah Crawford of the Lawyers' Committee for Civil Rights Under Law [52].

MICROTARGETING

Since 2004, direct marketing based on data mining has become part of U.S. Presidential campaigns [53]. In a technique called **microtargeting**, a campaign combines data about voter registration, voting frequency, and contributions with consumer data and information available from a Geographical Information System to gain insights into which candidate the voter is likely to favor. The campaign then uses direct mailings, email, text messages, or home visits to encourage likely supporters to vote.

CONNECTING THE DOTS

Data mining can be surprisingly powerful. Suppose a government agency managing tollbooths sells information records of the following form:

⟨transponder number⟩ ⟨date⟩ ⟨time⟩ ⟨location⟩ ⟨charge⟩

The agency does not reveal the names of the owners of the cars, so it believes it is protecting their anonymity. However, many people have an account set up so that their tollbooth payments are automatically charged to their credit cards. If a credit card company buys these records from the tollbooth agency, it can match the date, time, and amount of the tollbooth payments with the date, time, and charge on its credit cards to determine the identity of the person driving a vehicle with a particular transponder number. Once this has been done, the credit card company can figure out which customers are driving the most miles and are likely to purchase new cars more frequently. It can then sell this information to banks interested in soliciting automobile loan applications [28].

5.4.4 Organizations Push the Boundaries

Advances in information technology have led to a drop in the cost of acquiring information. Meanwhile, the value of information continues to rise, as organizations refine their data mining techniques. The result of these trends is that organizations have an incentive to acquire more information, making it more difficult for individuals to protect their privacy [20]. Still, people can and do fight back when they feel an organization has gone too far.

MARKETPLACE: HOUSEHOLDS

Lotus Development Corporation spent $8 million developing a CD with information on 120 million people, along with software that would help the purchaser produce mailing lists based on various criteria, such as household income. Lotus hoped to sell the CD, which it called "Marketplace: Households," to small businesses. When consumers found out about the CD, they complained loudly and vigorously, with more than 30,000 letters, phone calls, and emails. Lotus dropped plans to sell the CD [54].

FACEBOOK BEACON

In November 2007, Facebook announced Beacon, "a core element of the Facebook Ads system for connecting businesses with users and targeting advertising to the audiences they want" [55]. Beacon promised to be an important way for Facebook to earn advertising revenue. Fandango, eBay, and 42 other online businesses paid Facebook to do "word-of-mouth" advertising of their products and services through Beacon. For example, after a Facebook user bought movie tickets on Fandango, Fandango would send this information to Facebook so that Facebook could broadcast it to that user's friends.

Beacon was based on an opt-out policy, meaning that it was in effect unless a user explicitly asked to be excluded. That decision was good for Facebook because advertising revenue depends on the size of the audience. However, the decision to make the system opt-out upset many Facebook users, who were unaware of Beacon until it revealed information they thought was private. For example, after Sean Lane purchased what was supposed to be a surprise Christmas gift, the following news headline was broadcast to his wife and more than 700 other people in his Facebook network: "Sean Lane bought 14K White Gold 1/5 ct Diamond Eternity Flower Ring from overstock.com" [56].

Beacon soon attracted strong criticism from a variety of sources. A spokesman for MoveOn.org said, "Sites like Facebook are revolutionizing how we communicate with one another and organize around issues together in a 21st century democracy. The question is: Will corporate advertisers get to write the rules of the Internet or will these new social networks protect our basic rights, like privacy?"[56]. MoveOn.org created an online group calling for Beacon to require an explicit opt-in from users, and it attracted the support of more than 50,000 Facebook users. A few weeks later, Facebook decided to switch to an opt-in policy for Beacon. "I'm not proud of the way we've handled this situation, and I know we can do better," said Mark Zuckerberg, the CEO of Facebook [57].

NETFLIX PRIZE

Netflix is a popular subscription service for movies and television shows. An important feature of Netflix is its movie recommendation service. After a subscriber has rated several movies, Netflix uses a collaborative filtering algorithm to predict how well the subscriber will like other movies in its collection. It then recommends to the subscriber movies the subscriber is likely to enjoy.

In 2006, Netflix offered a $1 million prize to any group that could come up with a collaborative filtering algorithm that was at least 10 percent better than Netflix's own algorithm at predicting user ratings for movies. Netflix released more than 100 million movie ratings from nearly half a million customers, stripped of private information in an attempt to make the records anonymous. Each movie rating consisted of four pieces of information—subscriber, movie, date of grade, and grade—where each subscriber was represented by an integer.

However, a group of researchers at the University of Texas-Austin demonstrated how it was possible, with just a little information about movies seen by an individual, to identify the movie rating records associated with that person, revealing potentially sensitive information, such as their political leanings or sexual orientation [58]. The revelation that the release of "anonymous" movie ratings information could compromise the privacy of Netflix subscribers led to a complaint by the U.S. Federal Trade Commission and a lawsuit. On March 12, 2010, Netflix announced that it was canceling a Netflix Prize sequel [59].

5.4.5 Social Network Analysis

A promising new area in data mining is the incorporation of information collected from social networks. Here are a few examples of how organizations have used social network analysis to meet their objectives [60]:

FIGURE 5.5 Some police departments are monitoring Facebook and Twitter to identify locations of big parties and deploy officers accordingly. (© Allen Sullivan/ZUMA Press/Newscom)

- In ultracompetitive cell phone markets, it's crucial that companies keep their subscribers from defecting to rival firms. Bharti Airtel, India's largest cell phone company, uses software to analyze phone records and identify "influencers," those subscribers most like to be able to persuade their friends and family members to follow them when they switch carriers. It then offers the influencers special promotions to keep them loyal. How can Bharti Airtel identify influencers from their phone records? They are the ones whose calls are quickly returned, who call other people late at night more frequently, and who get more calls on Friday afternoons when parties are often organized.

- Police in Richmond, Virginia, monitor Facebook and Twitter messages to determine where parties are happening. Data mining software identifies the party locations mentioned most frequently. By deploying officers more strategically on big party nights, the department saves about $15,000 on overtime pay, and the community has seen a big drop in criminal activity (Figure 5.5).

- Banks are combining data collected from social networks with credit card statements and other information to evaluate the riskiness of loans. For example, someone applying for a loan to start a new business may be a bad risk if the proposed business has no connection with their social network, educational background, travel history, or previous business dealings.

Summary

This chapter has focused on privacy issues brought to the forefront by the introduction of information technology. The issues of privacy and intellectual property are similar in the sense that both issues relate to how information ought to be controlled. Modern information technology makes it much easier to collect and transmit information, whether it be a song or a Social Security number. Information has become a valuable commodity.

Privacy can be seen as a balancing act between the desires of the individual and the needs of society. The individual seeks to restrict access. Society must decide where to draw the line between what ought to be private and what should be public. While privacy has both costs and benefits, the benefits of providing people at least some privacy exceed the costs. Philosophers disagree whether people have a natural right to privacy, but most of them agree it is a prudential right. We choose to give each other some privacy for our mutual good.

There is a tension between privacy and trust. We desire privacy, but we also want others to trust us. That means we have to reveal personal information to others.

Sometimes we are required to disclose information that is shared with everyone. A public record is a piece of information collected by a government agency. Certain activities, such as getting arrested, buying a house, and having a child result in the creation of a public record.

Quite often we participate in activities that result in private organizations collecting information about us. Data mining is a way for organizations to create a complex profile of a person from a large collection of individual facts. Companies use data mining to direct advertising to the most promising customers. Data mining is possible because organizations handling transactions have the right to sell information about these transactions to other organizations.

Whether to provide customers with better service, increase their revenues, or both, companies frequently push the boundaries of what consumers are willing to tolerate. Every few years, a company is forced to withdraw a new service because consumers loudly voice privacy concerns. In the face of consumer protests, Lotus pulled its Marketplace: Households product from the market, Facebook changed its Beacon feature from opt-out to opt-in, and Netflix canceled its second Netflix Prize competition.

Review Questions

1. How is Whitepages.com able to produce a map to a person's home, given only that person's phone number?
2. Is privacy a negative right or a positive right?
3. What right is guaranteed by the Third Amendment to the U.S. Constitution?
4. What does it mean when we say that privacy is a prudential right?

5. Give three examples of ways in which an inhabitant of New York City in 2003 has more privacy than an inhabitant of New York City in 1903.

6. What is a public record?

7. List five pieces of information about a person that are public records.

8. Provide an example (not already given in the book) of a situation where people must disclose personal information to a private organization in order to get something they want.

9. What objections were raised to Facebook's introduction of the Tag Suggestions feature?

10. Why does enhanced 911 service raise new concerns about privacy?

11. How do companies use loyalty cards to improve their sales?

12. What privacy concerns have been raised with the increasing use of RFID tags?

13. How are RFID tags being used to return pets to owners?

14. What safety and security features are provided by the OnStar system?

15. What are the advantages of consolidating a patient's medical records into a single database accessible by many? What are the risks associated with this consolidation?

16. In what way do digital video recorders provide viewers with less privacy than videotape recorders?

17. How could "cookies" created by a Web server affect a computer user's privacy?

18. What is data mining?

19. What are we referring to when we talk about a secondary use of data?

20. What is collaborative filtering? Who uses it?

21. How are some political campaigns using data mining?

22. Explain the difference between an opt-in policy and an opt-out policy.

23. What about Facebook Beacon made it so unpopular with Facebook users?

24. Give three examples of how data mining is being used on information collected from social networks.

Discussion Questions

25. Do you agree with Scott McNealy's statement that people have "zero privacy" and should just get over it?

26. If people value privacy so much, why do they put so much personal information on their Facebook pages and in their blogs?

27. M.I.T. computer science professor Harold Abelson has said, "In today's online world, what your mother told you is true, only more so: people really can judge you by your friends" [61]. Have you ever been upset or embarrassed by what your friends posted on Facebook? Are you concerned that people are going to judge you based on what your friends are posting?

28. Warren and Brandeis argued that it is a violation of a person's privacy to take their photograph without their consent.

    a. Do you agree with their position? Why or why not?

    b. If someone takes your photo, should you just assume it's going to be posted on the Web?

29. What is the difference between privacy and anonymity?

30. Canadian science fiction author Robert Sawyer argues that we need privacy because we have "silly laws" that attempt to make people feel ashamed for indulging in certain harmless activities. He suggests that if there were no privacy, people would insist these laws be overturned [62]. Do you agree with Sawyer's position? Why or why not?

31. Do you agree with the author that it is more difficult to know whom to trust in modern society than it was in a small village of a few centuries ago? Why or why not?

32. Critics of grocery club cards give examples of card-member prices being equal to the regular product price at stores without customer loyalty programs. In other words, customers who want to get food at the regular price must use the card. Customers pay extra if they don't want to use the card. Is it fair for a store to charge us more if we don't want to use its loyalty card? Explain your reasoning.

33. Some consumers give phony personal information when they apply for rewards or loyalty cards at stores. Others take it a step further by regularly exchanging their cards with those held by other people. Are these people doing anything wrong? Why or why not?

34. If you voluntarily have your body scanned at a department store, who should own that information, you or the store? Should the store have the right to sell your body measurements to other businesses? Explain your reasoning.

35. TiVo keeps detailed information about the television viewing habits of customers who subscribe to its service.

    a. Should your television viewing habits be private information?

    b. Do you care if anyone else knows what television shows or pay-per-view movies you have watched in the past year?

    c. Do voters have the right to know the viewing habits of people running for elected office?

36. You are sitting on a jury. A driver of a car has been charged with manslaughter for killing a pedestrian. The prosecution presents evidence collected from the automobile's "black box" that indicates the car was traveling at 45 miles per hour before the accident. The defense presents four eyewitnesses to the accident, all of whom testify that the car could not have been going faster than 30 miles per hour. Are you more inclined to believe the eyewitnesses or the data collected from the "black box"?

37. Enhanced 911 service allows cell phone companies to track the locations of active cell phone users within 100 meters.

    a. Who should have access to location information collected by cell phone companies?

    b. How long should this information be kept?

    c. If this information could be used to help you establish an alibi, would you want the cell phone company to be able to release it to the police?

    d. How would you feel about the cell phone company releasing compromising information about your whereabouts to the police?

    e. Should the police be able to get from the cell phone company the names of all subscribers using their phones close to a crime scene around the time of the crime?

38. Should parents implant microchips in their children to make them easier to identify in case they are lost or kidnapped? Why or why not?

39. Before offering a job candidate a position, some potential employers do a criminal background check of the candidate. What are the pros and cons of this policy?

40. You are setting up an account at a local store that rents outdoor equipment (tents, backpacks, ski gear, etc.). The clerk asks you to fill out the application form completely. One of the fields asks for your Social Security number. You leave that field blank. The clerk refuses to accept your application without the field filled in. You ask to speak to the manager, and the clerk says the manager is not available. Would it be wrong in this situation to fill in a fake Social Security number?

41. A company discovers that some of its proprietary information has been revealed in Internet chat rooms. The disclosure of this information results in a substantial drop in the price of the company's shares. The company provides Internet service providers with the screen names of the people who posted the confidential information. It asks the ISPs to disclose the actual identities of these people. Should the ISPs comply with this request? Explain your reasoning. (This scenario is adapted from an actual event [63].)

42. Music files downloaded from Apple's iTunes Store have the purchaser's name and email address embedded in them [64]. Conceivably, Apple could use this information to learn how much file sharing goes on (e.g., it could find out that a month after Ann purchases a song there are 10 computers that have a copy of Ann's music file).

    By including personal information in music files it sells, has Apple violated the privacy rights of its customers?

43. On March 31, 2011, CNN reported that Google was planning to introduce a face-recognition feature into Google Goggles that would allow cell phone users to take someone's picture and then instantly connect with that person's profile on a social network. The next day Google demanded a retraction from CNN, stating, "As we've said for over a year, we won't add face recognition to Goggles unless we can figure out a strong privacy model for it" [65]. What are the privacy implications of adding a face-recognition feature into Google Goggles? In your opinion, what would be the features of "a strong privacy model" for this feature?

44. What special responsibilities do computer professionals have with respect to understanding and protecting the privacy rights of their fellow citizens?

In–class Exercises

45. What does your "ladder of privacy" look like? How does it compare to those of your classmates?

46. Give an example of a piece of information that a person should not have to reveal to anyone else. Give an example of a piece of information that society should be able to demand that a person reveal.

47. Divide the class into two groups. The first group should come up with evidence supporting the proposition "We live in a global village." The second group should come up with evidence supporting the proposition "We live in a world of strangers."

48. When you purchase a product or service using a credit card, the merchant has information linking you to the transaction. Divide the class into two groups (pro and con) to debate the proposition that merchants should be required to follow an opt-in policy. Such a policy would require the consumer to explicitly give permission before a merchant could share information about that consumer with another organization.

49. While the cost of automobile insurance varies from person to person, based on the driving record of each individual, health insurance premiums are typically uniform across groups of people, such as all of the employees of a company. However, a majority of health care costs are incurred by a minority of the population.

   Today, it is possible to take a blood sample from a person and to extract a genetic profile that will reveal that person's disposition to certain diseases. Debate the proposition that health insurance rates should be tailored to reflect each individual's propensity to illness.

50. Joe Herzenberg was a historian and politician, as well as the first openly gay elected official in North Carolina. After he died in 2007, his papers, including correspondence, photographs, diaries, and other materials, were donated to the Southern Historical Collection (SHC). Herzenberg kept a record of his personal and professional accomplishments and struggles in a series of diaries spanning more than 50 years. In the diaries, "Herzenberg documents his sexual encounters and alludes to his friends' sexual relationships and illegal activities" [66].

   "Most SHC collections are unrestricted for both research and duplication in the SHC's search room. In that relatively controlled environment, [the SHC transfers] the responsibilities for the use of sensitive materials to the researcher" [66]. SHC librarians must decide whether they should digitize the contents of Joe Herzenberg's diaries and make them available on the Web.

   Debate the following proposition: The SHC librarians should not digitize the contents of Joe Herzenberg's diaries until everyone mentioned in the diaries has either given permission or died.

Further Reading and Viewing

Robby Bryant and Bryan Horling. "Personalized Search." *Google*, December 4, 2009. www
.youtube.com.

Poppy Harlow. "My Private Life Revealed on the Web." *CNNMoney Reports*, May 26, 2011.
money.cnn.com/video/.

Ellen Frankel Paul, Fred D. Miller, Jr., and Jeffrey Paul, editors. *The Right to Privacy*. Cambridge University Press, Cambridge, England, 2000.

Evan Ratliff, "Shedding Your Identity in the Digital Age." *Wired*, December 2009.

Jeffrey Rosen. "The Web Means the End of Forgetting." *The New York Times*, July 21, 2010.
www.nytimes.com.

Ferdinand David Schoeman, editor. *Philosophical Dimensions of Privacy: An Anthology*. Cambridge University Press, Cambridge, England, 1984.

Charles J. Sykes. *The End of Privacy*. St. Martin's Press, New York, NY, 1999.

References

[1] Polly Sprenger. "Sun on Privacy: 'Get Over It.' " *Wired*, January 26, 1999. www.wired .com.

[2] Edmund F. Byrne. "Privacy." In *Encyclopedia of Applied Ethics*, volume 3, pages 649–659. Academic Press, 1998.

[3] Edward J. Bloustein. "Privacy as an Aspect of Human Dignity: An Answer to Dean Prossera." In *Philosophical Dimensions of Privacy: An Anthology*, edited by Ferdinand David Schoeman, pages 156–202, Cambridge University Press, Cambridge, England, 1984.

[4] Ferdinand Schoeman. "Privacy: Philosophical Dimensions of the Literature." In *Philosophical Dimensions of Privacy: An Anthology*, edited by Ferdinand David Schoeman, pages 1–33, Cambridge University Press, Cambridge, England, 1984.

[5] Edmund Ronald Leach. *A Runaway World?* British Broadcasting Corporation, London, England, 1967.

[6] Marie Hartwell-Walker. "Why Dysfunctional Families Stay That Way." *Amherst Bulletin*, January 28, 1994.

[7] Morton H. Levine. "Privacy in the Tradition of the Western World." In *Privacy: A Vanishing Value?* edited by William C. Bier, S.J., pages 3–21. Fordham University Press, New York, NY, 1980.

[8] Jeffrey H. Reiman. "Privacy, Intimacy, and Personhood." *Philosophy & Public Affairs*, 6(1):26–44, 1976. Reprinted in *Philosophical Dimensions of Privacy: An Anthology*, edited by Ferdinand David Schoenan, Cambridge University Press, Cambridge, England, 1984.

[9] Stanley I. Benn. "Privacy, Freedom, and Respect for Persons." In *Philosophical Dimensions of Privacy: An Anthology*, edited by Ferdinand David Schoeman, pages 223–244, Cambridge University Press, Cambridge, England, 1984.

[10] Charles J. Sykes. *The End of Privacy*. St. Martin's Press, New York, NY, 1999.

[11] Gini Graham Scott. *Mind Your Own Business: The Battle for Personal Privacy*. Insight Books / Plenum Press, New York, NY, 1995.

[12] Constance T. Fischer. "Privacy and Human Development." In *Privacy: A Vanishing Value?* edited by William C. Bier, S.J., pages 37–45. Fordham University Press, New York, NY, 1980.

[13] Robert C. Neville. "Various Meanings of Privacy: A Philosophical Analysis." In *Privacy: A Vanishing Value?* edited by William C. Bier, S.J., pages 22–33. Fordham University Press, New York, NY, 1980.

[14] Joseph G. Keegan, S.J. "Privacy and Spiritual Growth." In *Privacy: A Vanishing Value?* edited by William C. Bier, S.J., pages 67–87. Fordham University Press, New York, NY, 1980.

[15]   Charles Fried. "Privacy: A Moral Analysis." *Yale Law Review*, 77:475–493, 1968. Reprinted in *Philosophical Dimensions of Privacy: An Anthology*, edited by Ferdinand David Schoeman, Cambridge University Press, Cambridge, England, 1984.

[16]   James Rachels. "Why Privacy Is Important." *Philosophy & Public Affairs*, 4(4):323–333, 1975. Reprinted in *Philosophical Dimensions of Privacy: An Anthology*, edited by Ferdinand David Shoeman, Cambridge University Press, Cambridge, England, 1984.

[17]   Samuel D. Warren and Louis D. Brandeis. "The Right to Privacy." *Harvard Law Review*, 4(5), December 15, 1890.

[18]   William L. Prosser. "Privacy: A Legal Analysis." *California Law Review*, 48:338–423, 1960. Reprinted in *Philosophical Dimensions of Privacy: An Anthology*, edited by Ferdinand David Shoeman, Cambridge University Press, Cambridge, England, 1984.

[19]   Judith Jarvis Thomson. "The Right to Privacy." *Philosophy & Public Affairs*, 4(4):295–314, 1975. Reprinted in *Philosophical Dimensions of Privacy: An Anthology*, edited by Ferdinand David Schoeman, Cambridge University Press, Cambridge, England, 1984.

[20]   Alexander Rosenberg. "Privacy as a Matter of Taste and Right." In *The Right to Privacy*, edited by Ellen Frankel, Jr., Fred D. Miller, and Jeffrey Paul, pages 68–90. Cambridge University Press, Cambridge, England, 2000.

[21]   Steven L. Nock. *The Costs of Privacy: Surveillance and Reputation in America*. Aldine de Gruyter, New York, NY, 1993.

[22]   Michael L. Sankey and Peter J. Weber, editors. *Public Records Online: The National Guide to Private & Government Online Sources of Public Records*. 4th ed. Facts on Demand Press, Tempe, AZ, 2003.

[23]   Ben Popken. "New Service Adds Your Drunken Facebook Photos to Employer Background Checks, For Up To Seven Years," *The Consumerist*, June 21, 2011. www .consumerist.com.

[24]   www.socialintelligencehr.com/home.

[25]   Justin Mitchell. "Making Photo Tagging Easier," *The Facebook Blog*, December 15, 2010. blog.facebook.com.

[26]   The Federal Trade Commission. "EPIC Complaint In re Facebook and the Facial Identification of Users," June 10, 2011.

[27]   Rachel King. "Facebook Photo Tag Suggestions: What's So Bad about Them Anyway?" *Between the Lines, ZDNet*, June 9, 2011. www.zdnet.com.

[28]   Jay Warrior, Eric McHenry, and Kenneth McGee. "They Know Where You Are." *IEEE Spectrum*, pages 20–25, July 2003.

[29]   Elizabeth Montalbano. "Microsoft Helps Put Ads on Computerized Shopping Carts." *IDG News*, January 16, 2008. www.pcworld.com.

[30]   John Vanderlippe. "Supermarket Cards: An Overview of the Pricing Issues." *Consumers Against Supermarket Privacy Invasion and Numbering*, 2003. www.nocards.org/overview.

[31]   Elizabeth Weise. "Identity Swapping Makes Privacy Relative." *USA Today*, June 6, 2000.

[32]   Amy Tsao. "So, We'll Take It In . . . " *Retail Traffic*, May 1, 2003.

[33]   Charles J. Murray. "Privacy Concerns Mount over Retail Use of RFID Technology." *Electronic Engineering Times*, (1298), December 1, 2003.

[34]   Meg McGinty. "RFID: Is This Game of Tag Fair Play?" *Communications of the ACM*, 47(1):15–18, January 2004.

[35]   "Owners of Dogs Lacking Implants Face Fines." *The China Post*, September 1, 2000.

[36]   Amal Graafstra. "How Radio-Frequency Identification and I Got Personal." *IEEE Spectrum*, March 2007.

[37]   Duncan Graham-Rowe. "Clubbers Choose Chip Implants to Jump Queues." *NewScientist*, May 21, 2004. www.newscientist.com.

[38]   "Parents Look to Microchip Children." *CNN.com/World*, September 3, 2002. archives.cnn.com.

[39]   Lylah M. Alphonse. "In the Parenthood." *Boston.com Moms*, June 9, 2010. www.boston.com.

[40]   Tom Krisher. "OnStar Halts Stolen SUV in Visalia Police Chase." *BakersfieldNow.com*, Bakersfield, California, October 19, 2009.

[41]   "OnStar Takes on Conspiracy Theorists." *Edmunds InsideLine*, November 13, 2009. www.insideline.com.

[42]   Ian Austen. "Your Brake Pads May Have Something to Say (by E-mail)." *NYtimes.com*, March 27, 2003.

[43]   Editorial. "Your E-Health Records." *The New York Times*, January 31, 2009.

[44]   American Civil Liberties Union. "Seizure of Rush Limbaugh's Medical Records Violates Florida's Constitutional Right of Privacy, ACLU Tells Court" (press release), February 17, 2004. www.aclu.org.

[45]   "TiVo: Viewers Skip Fewer 'Relevant Ads.'" *Adweek*, July 30, 2008. www.adweek.com.

[46]   Amy Harmon. "TiVo Plans to Sell Information on Customers' Viewing Habits." *NYTimes.com*, June 2, 2003.

[47]   Ashkan Soltani, Shannon Canty, Quentin Mayo, Lauren Thomas, and Chris Jay Hoofnagle. "Flash Cookies and Privacy." University of California, Berkeley - School of Law, Berkeley Center for Law & Technology, August 10, 2009.

[48]   L. A. Lorek. "Data Mining Extracts Online Gold; Stores Collect Information about Web Customers to Target Future Sales Pitches." *San Antonio Express-News*, December 15, 2002.

[49]   "Personalized Search: Basics." Google Web site, accessed September 2, 2011. www.google.com/support.

[50]   "United We Find." *The Economist*, March 10, 2005.

[51]   Carolyn Hirschman. "Congress Sticks Its Nose into Online Privacy." *Telephony*, 241(7), August 13, 2001.

[52]   Katie Leslie and Marcus K. Gamer. "Poor Credit Prevents Some from Scoring a Job." *Chicago Tribune*, November 12, 2010. articles.chicagotribune.com.

[53]   Jeanne Cummings. "Rove's Patented Strategies Will Endure." *Politico*, August 13, 2007. www.politico.com.

[54]   Ann Cavoukian and Don Tapscott. *Who Knows: Safeguarding Your Privacy in a Networked World*. McGraw-Hill, New York, NY, 1996.

[55]   Facebook. "Leading Websites Offer Facebook Beacon for Social Distribution" (press release). November 6, 2007. www.facebook.com.

[56]   Ellen Nakashima. "Feeling Betrayed, Facebook Users Force Site to Honor Their Privacy." *The Washington Post*, November 30, 2007.

[57]   Farhad Manjoo. "Facebook Finally Lets Users Turn Off Privacy-invading Ads." *Salon.com*, December 6, 2007.

[58]   Arvind Narayanan and Vitaly Shmatikov. "Robust De-anonymization of Large Sparse Datasets." *2008 IEEE Symposium on Security and Privacy*.

[59]   Neil Hunt. "NetFlix Prize Update." *The Official Netflix Blog*, March 12, 2010. blog .netflix.com.

[60]   "Untangling the Social Web." *The Economist Technology Quarterly*, September 4, 2010, pp. 16–17.

[61]   Steve Lohr. "How Privacy Vanishes Online." *The New York Times*, March 16, 2010.

[62]   Robert J. Sawyer. "Privacy: Who Needs It?: We're Better Off without It, Argues Canada's Leading Sci-Fi Writer." *Maclean's (Toronto Edition)*, page 44, October 7, 2002.

[63]   Stewart Deck. "Legal Thumbs-Up for Raytheon Employee Suit; Privacy Groups Chilled by ISP Subpoenas." *Computerworld*, April 12, 1999.

[64]   Ken Fisher. "Apple Hides Account Info in DRM-free Music, Too." *Ars Technica*, May 30, 2007. http://arstechnica.com.

[65]   Jared Newman. "Google Won't Release Awesome Facial Recognition App." *Today@ PCWorld*. April 1, 2011.

[66]   Laura Clark Brown. "Third-Party-Privacy-Case-Studies." *Southern Historical Collection 2009 Symposia Wiki.* http://shc2009symposia.pbworks.com.

Michael Zimmer

Michael Zimmer, PhD, is an assistant professor in the School of Information Studies at the University of Wisconsin–Milwaukee, and co–director of the Center for Information Policy Research. With a background in new media and Internet studies, the philosophy of technology, and information policy and ethics, Zimmer's research focuses on the ethical dimensions of new media and information technologies, with particular interest in privacy, social media, internet research ethics, and ethical design.

Zimmer serves on numerous advisory boards, including the Washington, D.C.–based Future of Privacy Forum policy think tank, and the NSF–sponsored Values–in–Design Council. He is on the editorial advisory boards of the scholarly journals *Internet Research* and the *International Review of Information Ethics,* and is co–editor of *The Information Society* book series for MIT Press. He has participated in various public interest activities, and provided expert advice and consultation for projects at the American Library Association, the New York Public Library, Google, and Microsoft.

You've become known for your critique of the "Tastes, Ties, and Time" (T3) research project. Please give us an overview of the T3 project.

The explosive popularity of online social networking platforms such as MySpace, Twitter, and Facebook has attracted attention from a variety of researchers and disciplines. However, most studies rely on external surveys of social networking participants, ethnographies of smaller subsets of subjects, or the analysis of limited profile information extracted from what subjects chose to make visible. As a result, the available data can often be tainted due to self-reporting biases and errors, have minimal representativeness of the entire population, or fail to reflect the true depth and complexity of the information and connections that flow across social networking sites.

Recognizing the data limitations faced by typical sociological studies of online social network dynamics, a group of researchers from Harvard University and the University of California, Los Angeles set out to construct a more robust dataset that would fully leverage the rich data available on social networking websites. Given its popularity, the researchers chose the social network site Facebook as their data source, and located a university that allowed them to download the Facebook profiles of every member of the freshman class. This was repeated annually until the study population graduated, providing 4 years of data about this collegiate social network. Each student's official housing records were also obtained from the university, allowing the researchers to compare Internet-based connections and real-world proximity.

The resulting dataset is quite unique: it was collected without relying on participant self-reporting, it represents nearly an entire real-world social network of college students, includes valuable demographic, cultural, and relational information about the subjects, and provides four years of data for robust longitudinal study.

The sociologists didn't reveal the name of the college where they had collected the data. How did you determine that the subjects were Harvard College students?

When the researchers released the dataset, it was noted, "all the data is cleaned so you cannot connect anyone to an identity". This assertion caught my attention, since this dataset potentially includes personal and sensitive information about the students, and attempts to completely anonymize large datasets have fallen short in the past (such as the AOL search data released in 2006, and the NetFlix dataset in 2008). So, I decided to investigate.

I downloaded the publicly available codebook of the dataset (gaining access to the data itself required approval by the researchers), and also started examining various articles and public comments made about the research project. An examination of the codebook revealed the source was a private, co-educational institution, whose class of 2009 initially had 1640 students in it. Elsewhere, the source was described as a "New England" school. A search through an online college database revealed only seven private, co-ed colleges in New England states (Connecticut, Maine, Massachusetts, New Hampshire, Rhode Island, Vermont) with total undergraduate populations between 5000 and 7500 students (a likely range if there were 1640 in the 2006 freshman class): Tufts University, Suffolk University, Yale University, University of Hartford, Quinnipiac University, Brown University, and Harvard College.

The codebook also listed the majors represented in the dataset, which included very unique descriptors, such as Near Eastern Languages and Civilizations, Studies of Women, Gender and Sexuality, and Organismic and Evolutionary Biology. A quick search revealed that only Harvard provides these degree programs. The identification of Harvard College was further confirmed after analysis of a June 2008 video presentation by one of the researchers, where he noted that "midway through the freshman year, students have to pick between 1 and 7 best friends" that they will essentially live with for the rest of their undergraduate career. This describes the unique method for determining undergraduate housing at Harvard: all freshmen who complete the fall term enter into a lottery, where they can designate a "blocking group" of between 2 and 8 students with whom they would like be housed in close proximity. I was able to confirm this, again, through a simple web search.

The announcement of this likely identification of the source of the T3 dataset did not prompt a public reply by the research team, but within a week of the discovery, the dataset was pulled from the publicly available repository.

Why does it matter that you were able to determine the subjects of the T3 study were Harvard students?

There are two primary concerns. First, there is the issue of possibly being able to identify particular subjects in the dataset. The researchers took care to remove obvious identifiable data (names, email addresses, etc), but now that the source of the dataset has been determined, it might be easier to identify unique individuals. For example, the codebook reveals that there is only one person in the dataset from each of the states of Delaware, Louisiana, Mississippi, Montana, and Wyoming. Some time in front of a search engine might reveal the identity of that one student that the state of Delaware sent to Harvard in 2006. Once we've identified that student, we can now connect her with her personal data elements in the dataset. In short, the privacy of the subjects in the database is at risk.

My other concern is actually greater: that the researchers felt their methodology was sufficient. There were a number of good-faith steps taken by the research team, but each fell short. The research team has defended itself by noting it only gathered Facebook information that was already publicly accessible. However, the team utilized Harvard graduate students to access and retrieve the profile data. At the time of the study, it was possible for Facebook users to restrict access to their profiles to only people within their home university. Thus, it is entirely possible that the research team had privileged access to a profile by virtue of being within the Harvard network, while the general public would have been locked out by the user's privacy settings. Researchers must avoid such cavalier positions: just because something happens to be accessible on a social media site does not mean that it is free for the taking, no questions asked.

Is it reasonable for anyone to expect that the information they post online will be kept as private as information shared verbally among a few confidants?

This is an important issue. It is easy for a researcher to simply say "if it is publicly available, then I can take it"; but that simple statement doesn't necessarily fit within the broader tenets of research ethics. Our concern should be with the subject: what was the intention of that post? Whom did they think would see it? Did they understand it is visible to everyone? Did the default settings of the platform change since it was originally posted (consider how Facebook has suddenly made people's "likes" publicly viewable, when previously they could be hidden)?

I don't mean to suggest that it is never acceptable to mine these websites for research data, but simply we must take great care to consider the context and expectations. It is not simply a matter of "already public".

What is your fundamental objection to the research methodology used in the T3 study?

Fundamentally, my concern is centered on the fact that even well-intended researchers—and their Institutional Research Board (IRB)—failed to fully understand the implications of their methodology. Like many, they seemed to be holding onto the traditional dichotomy of "public vs. private" information, assuming that because someone posted something on a (possibly) public social media profile page, that it is free for the taking without consent or concern over the poster's original intentions or expectations. I'm concerned that as more powerful tools to automate this kind of scraping of social media platforms are developed, and more research—both from highly experienced scholars and novice undergrads—takes place, this kind of potential breach of privacy and anonymity will become more common.

If the researchers had been more careful and had succeeded in their goal of making the data set truly anonymous, would you still have criticized their study?

Better protecting the source of the data would have helped, and it appears that the researchers have rewritten the original codebook to remove the very unique names of the majors, and also make the geographic origin of the subjects more generic. Despite these improvements, the methodological concerns persist, and I likely would have still expressed concern over the need for informed consent before scraping the students' Facebook data.

Are you saying that social scientists engaged in research projects should be required to get written permission from subjects before gathering information those subjects have posted on social networks?

This is a complicated issue, and it certainly isn't possible to get written consent from all subjects in every case. Each research project should be considered separately, and reviewed by an IRB and related experts. I do feel that the intents of the subjects should be strongly weighed in the decision-making process. I suspect few people with public Twitter feeds ever expected their 140-character utterances—typically lost in a sea of thousands of Tweets every moment—would be archived by the Library of Congress for research purposes. These are the kinds of scenarios that should force us as a research community to think about what is the most ethical approach to social media-based research projects.

CHAPTER

6

Privacy and the Government

A system that fails to respect its citizens' right to privacy fails to respect the citizens themselves.

—Richard Nixon, "Radio Address about the American Right of Privacy,"
February 23, 1974

6.1 Introduction

In 2005, a senior at UMass Dartmouth was collecting materials for a research paper on communism he was writing for one of his history classes. The campus library did not have a copy of Mao Tse-Tung's "Little Red Book," so he filled out an interlibrary loan request, giving his name, address, phone number, and Social Security number. A couple of months later, two agents of the Department of Homeland Security visited him. They told him the book is on a "watch list." The student's interlibrary loan request, combined with the fact that he had spent significant time abroad, apparently triggered the visit. His professor said, "I shudder to think of all the students I've had monitoring al-Qaeda Web sites, what the government must think of that" [1].

On the morning of July 18, 1989, actress Rebecca Schaeffer opened the door to her apartment and was shot to death by obsessed fan Robert Bardo. Bardo got Schaeffer's home address from a private investigator who purchased her driver's license information from the California Department of Motor Vehicles [2]. In response to this murder, the U.S. Congress passed the Driver's Privacy Protection Act in 1994. The law prohibits states from revealing certain personal information provided by drivers in order to obtain licenses. *It also requires states to provide this information to the federal government.*

After seven-year-old Megan Kanka of New Jersey was abducted, raped, and murdered by a neighbor who had a criminal record as a pedophile, Congress passed a law requiring that local police release information about registered sex offenders living in the community. Today, there are more than half a million registered sex offenders in the United States. Some experts say police are overwhelmed by the number of offenders they need to monitor; the experts question the value of laws that require persons convicted of relatively minor offenses to be registered along with those who have committed terrible crimes [3].

Since the terrorist attacks of September 11, 2001, concerns about national security have risen significantly, at the expense of privacy rights. A 2006 poll revealed that a majority of Americans support "expanded camera surveillance on streets and in public places" (70 percent), "law enforcement monitoring of Internet discussions in chat rooms and other forums" (62 percent), "closer monitoring of banking and credit card transactions, to trace funding sources" (61 percent), and even "expanded government monitoring of cell phones and email, to intercept communications" (52 percent). Remarkably, one-third of those polled agreed that "this use of investigative powers by the president should be done under his executive authority without needing Congressional authorization" [4]. In post-9/11 America, President Nixon's abuses of presidential power seem like ancient history.

In this chapter, we consider the impact that federal, state, and local governments in the United States have had on the information privacy of those living in America. We will survey legislation designed to protect the information privacy of individuals as well as legislation allowing law enforcement agencies to collect information about individuals in an effort to prevent criminal or terrorist activities. We will also look at famous examples from American history in which governmental agencies engaged in illegal or unconstitutional activities under the banner of protecting public safety and/or national security.

To organize our presentation, we will use the taxonomy of privacy proposed by Daniel Solove [5].[1] Solove groups privacy-related activities into four categories:

1. *Information collection* refers to activities that gather personal information. We will discuss issues related to information collection by the government in Sections 6.2 through 6.6.

2. *Information processing* refers to activities that store, manipulate, and use personal information that has been collected. Sections 6.7 through 6.9 will focus on the information processing category.

3. *Information dissemination* refers to activities that spread personal information. Section 6.10 will provide examples of laws designed to restrict information dissemination by private organizations, as well as legal ways in which information held by the government can be disseminated.

---

1. Reproduced by permission of the publisher from *Understanding Privacy* by Daniel J. Solove, p. 103, Cambridge, MA: Harvard University Press, Copyright © 2008 by the President and Fellows of Harvard College.

4. *Invasion* refers to activities that intrude upon a person's daily life, interrupt a person's solitude, or interfere with someone's decision-making. In Section 6.11 we will survey government actions to limit intrusion by other organizations, as well as government programs that can be seen as intrusive.

We will consider each of these categories in turn, examining how federal, state, and local governments in the United States have drawn the line between the often-competing interests of protecting personal privacy and promoting the common good. The next five sections will focus on the *information collection* category of Solove's taxonomy.

6.2   U.S. Legislation Restricting Information Collection

This section gives three examples of federal legislation that limits the amount of information private entities can collect from individuals.

6.2.1   Employee Polygraph Protection Act

The Employee Polygraph Protection Act of 1988 (EPPA) prohibits most private employers from using lie detector tests under most situations. An employer may not require or even request a job applicant or employee to take a lie detector test, and an employee who refuses to take a lie detector test cannot suffer any retaliation.

The law has several important exceptions. Pharmaceutical companies and security firms may administer polygraph tests to job applicants in certain job categories. Employers who have suffered an economic loss, such as theft, may administer polygraph tests to employees whom they reasonably suspect were involved. Most significantly, EPPA does not apply to federal, state, and local governments.

6.2.2   Children's Online Privacy Protection Act

The Children's Online Privacy Protection Act (COPPA), which went into effect in 2000, is designed to reduce the amount of public information gathered from children using the Internet. According to COPPA, online services must obtain parental consent before collecting any information from children 12 years old and younger.

6.2.3   Genetic Information Nondiscrimination Act

The Genetic Information Nondiscrimination Act of 2008 is designed to prevent discrimination in the areas of medical benefits and employment based on genetic information. It prohibits health insurance companies and health plan administrators from requesting genetic information from individuals or their family members, and it forbids them from using genetic information when making decisions about coverage, rates, or preexisting conditions. It also prohibits most employers from taking genetic information into account when making hiring, firing, promotion, or any other decisions related to the terms of employment. The law does not extend these non-discrimination protections to life insurance, disability insurance, or long-term care insurance, and it does not apply to employers with fewer than 15 employees [6].

6.3 Information Collection by the Government

In the previous section, we considered ways in which the federal government has restricted the amount of information that private organizations can collect about individuals. In this section, we look at ways in which the federal government itself has collected vast amounts of sensitive information about its citizens.

6.3.1 Census Records

In order to ensure each state has fair representation in the House of Representatives, the United States Constitution requires the government to perform a census every ten years.

The first census of 1790 had six questions. It asked for the name of the head of the household and the number of persons in each of the following categories: free white males at least 16 years old; free white males under 16 years old; free white females; all other free persons (by sex and color); and slaves.

As time passed, the number of questions asked during the census increased. The 1820 census determined the number of people engaged in agriculture, commerce, and manufacturing. The 1840 census had questions regarding school attendance, illiteracy, and occupations. In 1850, census takers began asking questions about taxes, schools, crime, wages, and property values.

The 1940 census is notable because for the first time statistical sampling was put to extensive use. A random sample of the population, about 5 percent of those surveyed, received a longer form with more questions. The use of sampling enabled the Census Bureau to produce detailed demographic profiles without substantially increasing the amount of data it needed to process.

Today, the Census Bureau only uses a single, short form when conducting the decennial census. It gathers more detailed information on a continuous basis through the American Community Survey. This program mails a questionnaire with more than 50 questions to 3 million addresses per year. Questions include:

- What is this person's ancestry or ethnic origin?
- Does this person speak a language other than English at home?
- How many times has this person been married?
- How did this person usually get to work last week?
- Which fuel is used most for heating this house, apartment, or mobile home?

According to federal law, the Census Bureau is supposed to keep confidential the information it collects. However, in times of national emergency, the Census Bureau has revealed its information to other agencies. During World War I, the Census Bureau provided the names and addresses of young men to the military, which was searching

FIGURE 6.1 After the Japanese attack on Pearl Harbor, the Army used information illegally obtained from the Census Bureau to round up Japanese-Americans. (National Archives. file #210-G-3B-414)

for draft resistors. After the Japanese attack on Pearl Harbor, the Census Bureau provided the Justice Department with information from the 1940 census about the general location of Japanese-Americans. The Army used this information to round up Japanese-Americans and send them to internment camps (Figure 6.1).

6.3.2 Internal Revenue Service Records

The United States enacted a national income tax in 1862 to help pay for expenses related to the Civil War. In 1872, the income tax was repealed. Congress resurrected the national income tax in 1894, but a year later the Supreme Court ruled it unconstitutional. The 16th Amendment to the Constitution, ratified by the states in 1913, gives the United States government the power to collect an income tax. A national income tax has been in place ever since. The Internal Revenue Service (IRS) now collects more than $2 trillion a year in taxes.

Your income tax form may reveal a tremendous amount of personal information about your income, your assets, the organizations to which you give charitable contributions, your medical expenses, and much more.

6.3.3 FBI National Crime Information Center 2000

The FBI National Crime Information Center 2000 (NCIC) is a collection of databases supporting the activities of federal, state, and local law-enforcement agencies in the United States, the United States Virgin Islands, Puerto Rico, and Canada [7]. Its predecessor, the National Crime Information Center, was established by the FBI in January 1967 under the direction of J. Edgar Hoover.

When it was first activated, the NCIC consisted of about 95,000 records in five databases: stolen automobiles, stolen license plates, stolen or missing guns, other stolen items, and missing persons. Today, NCIC databases contain more than 39 million records. The databases have been expanded to include such categories as wanted persons, criminal histories, people incarcerated in federal prisons, convicted sex offenders, unidentified persons, people believed to be a threat to the President, foreign fugitives, violent gang members, and suspected terrorists. More than 80,000 law enforcement agencies have access to these data files. The NCIC processes about five million requests for information each day, with an average response time of less than one second.

The FBI points to the following successes of the NCIC:

- Investigating the assassination of Dr. Martin Luther King, Jr., the NCIC provided the FBI with the information it needed to link a fingerprint on the murder weapon to James Earl Ray.

- In 1992, the NCIC led to the apprehension of 81,750 "wanted" persons, 113,293 arrests, the location of 39,268 missing juveniles and 8,549 missing adults, and the retrieval of 110,681 stolen cars.

- About an hour after the April 19, 1995, bombing of the Alfred P. Murrah Federal Building in Oklahoma City, Oklahoma state trooper Charles Hanger pulled over a Mercury Marquis with no license plates. Seeing a gun in the back seat of the car, Hanger arrested the driver—Timothy McVeigh—on the charge of transporting a loaded firearm in a motor vehicle. He took McVeigh to the county jail, and the arrest was duly entered into the NCIC database. Two days later, when federal agents ran McVeigh's name through the NCIC, they saw Hanger's arrest record. FBI agents reached the jail just before McVeigh was released (Figure 6.2). McVeigh was subsequently convicted of the bombing.

Critics of the National Crime Information Center point out ways in which the existence of the NCIC has led to privacy violations of innocent people:

- Erroneous records can lead law enforcement agencies to arrest innocent persons.

- Innocent people have been arrested because their name is the same as someone listed in the arrest warrants database.

- The FBI has used the NCIC to keep records about people not suspected of any crime, such as opponents of the Vietnam War.

- Corrupt employees of law enforcement organizations with access to the NCIC have sold information to private investigators and altered or deleted records.

FIGURE 6.2 The National Crime Information Center facilitated the arrest of Timothy McVeigh for the 1995 bombing of the Federal Building in Oklahoma City. (© Bob E. Daemmrich/Sygma/Corbis)

- People with access to the NCIC have illegally used it to search for criminal records on acquaintances or to screen potential employees, such as babysitters.

6.3.4 OneDOJ Database

The OneDOJ database, managed by the U.S. Department of Justice, provides state and local police officers access to information supplied by five federal law enforcement agencies: the FBI, the Drug Enforcement Agency, the Bureau of Alcohol, Tobacco, Firearms, and Explosives, the U.S. Marshals Service, and the Bureau of Prisons. The database, called OneDOJ, stores incident reports, interrogation summaries, and other information not presently available through the National Crime Information Center. At the end of 2006, the OneDOJ database already contained more than 1 million records.

Critics of the OneDOJ database point out that it gives local police officers access to information about people who have not been arrested or charged with any crime. Barry

Steinhardt, of the American Civil Liberties Union said, "Raw police files or FBI reports can never be verified and can never be corrected. . . The idea that the whole system is going to be full of inaccurate information is just chilling" [8].

6.3.5 Closed–circuit Television Cameras

The use of closed-circuit television cameras for video surveillance in the United States began in western New York in 1968. The small town of Olean installed a surveillance camera along its main business street in an effort to reduce crime. Within a year, more than 160 police chiefs from around the country visited Olean to learn more about their system [9]. Today, there are an estimated 30 million surveillance cameras operating in the United States [10].

The number of surveillance cameras keeps increasing (Figure 6.3). New York City is spending $201 million to install 3,000 closed-circuit security cameras in lower Manhattan. These surveillance cameras are connected to computer systems with sophisticated image-scanning software that can sound alarms if someone leaves an unattended package. The cameras are part of a larger network of sensors that also includes license plate readers and radiation detectors [11].

FIGURE 6.3 The number of surveillance cameras keeps increasing, but critics say they are not effective in preventing crimes. (© xiao-ming/iStockphoto.com)

The New York Civil Liberties Union has expressed opposition to the large increase in security cameras, saying they represent a violation of privacy and will not prevent terrorist attacks. The Associate Legal Director of the NYCLU, Christopher Dunn, said "Our main concern is that it's unlike most police activity, which is focused on people who are suspected of unlawful activity. In fact, 99.9 percent of people who are captured in the system are just going to be people walking around, going about their business" [11].

Some critics point to Great Britain as proof that surveillance cameras cannot guarantee public safety. Britain has long led the world in the deployment of closed-circuit television cameras to conduct surveillance. There are 4.2 million surveillance cameras in Britain, one for every 14 people. It has been estimated that the average Briton is caught on camera an average of 300 times per day [12]. Still, the presence of all these cameras did not prevent the suicide bombings in the London subway system in 2005 [13]. Some experts have reached the conclusion that closed-circuit television cameras are "largely ineffective" for crime prevention [14].

6.4 Covert Government Surveillance

We now turn to ways in which the United States government has collected information in order to detect and apprehend suspected criminals or to improve national security. Because the individuals being observed are suspected of wrongdoing, they are not alerted or asked for permission before the surveillance begins.

Does covert surveillance violate any of the rights of a citizen? The most relevant statement in the U.S. Constitution is the Fourth Amendment:

~

FOURTH AMENDMENT TO THE UNITED STATES CONSTITUTION

The right of the people to be secure in their persons, houses, papers, and effects, against unreasonable searches and seizures, shall not be violated, and no Warrants shall issue, but upon probable cause, supported by Oath or affirmation, and particularly describing the place to be searched, and the persons or things to be seized.

~

Before the American Revolution, English agents in pursuit of smugglers made use of *writs of assistance*, which gave them authority to enter any house or building and seize any prohibited goods they could find. This activity drew the ire of the colonists. It is not surprising, then, that a prohibition against unreasonable searches and seizures appears in the Bill of Rights.

The position of the U.S. Supreme Court with respect to covert electronic surveillance has changed over time. Let's see how the Supreme Court's position evolved.

6.4.1 Wiretaps and Bugs

Wiretapping refers to the interception of a telephone conversation. (The term is somewhat anachronistic, because many telephone conversations are no longer transmitted over wires.) Wiretapping has been taking place ever since the 1890s, when telephones became commonly used. The State of New York made wiretapping a felony in 1892, but the police in New York City ignored the law and continued the practice of wiretapping. Until 1920, the New York City police listened to conversations between lawyers and clients, doctors and patients, and priests and penitents. On several occasions the police even tapped the trunk lines into hotels and listened to the telephone conversations of all the hotel guests [15].

OLMSTEAD V. UNITED STATES

Wiretapping was a popular tool for catching bootleggers during Prohibition (1919–1933). The most famous case involved Roy Olmstead, who ran a $2-million-a-year bootlegging business in Seattle, Washington. Without a warrant, federal agents tapped Olmstead's phone and collected enough evidence to convict him. Although wiretapping was illegal under Washington law, the state court allowed evidence obtained through the wiretapping to be admitted. Olmstead appealed all the way to the U.S. Supreme Court. His lawyer argued that the police had violated Olmstead's right to privacy by listening in on his telephone conversations. He also argued that the evidence should be thrown out because it was obtained without a search warrant [15, 16].

In a 5–4 decision, the Supreme Court ruled in *Olmstead v. United States* that the Fourth Amendment protected tangible assets alone. The federal agents did not "search" a physical place; they did not "seize" a physical item. Hence the Fourth Amendment's provision against warrantless search and seizure did not apply. Justice Louis Brandeis (mentioned in Section 5.2.3) was one of the four judges siding with Olmstead. In his dissenting opinion, Brandeis argued that the protections afforded by the Bill of Rights ought to extend to electronic communications as well. He wrote:

> Whenever a telephone line is tapped, the privacy of the persons at both ends of the line is invaded, and all conversations between them upon any subject, and although proper, confidential, and privileged, may be overheard. Moreover, the tapping of one man's telephone line involves the tapping of the telephone of every other person whom he may call, or who may call him. As a means of espionage, writs of assistance and general warrants are but puny instruments of tyranny and oppression when compared with wiretapping. [17]

CONGRESS MAKES WIRETAPPING ILLEGAL

The public and the press were critical of the Supreme Court decision. Since the Court had ruled that wiretapping was constitutional, those interested in prohibiting wiretapping focused their efforts on the legislative branch. In 1934, the U.S. Congress passed the Federal Communications Act, which (among other things) made it illegal to intercept and reveal wire communications. Three years later, the Supreme Court used the Federal Communications Act to reverse its position on warrantless wiretaps. In *Nardone v.*

United States, the Court ruled that evidence obtained by federal agents from warrantless wiretaps was inadmissible in court. In another decision, *Weiss v. United States*, it ruled that the prohibition on wiretapping applied to intrastate as well as interstate telephone calls. Subsequently, the attorney general announced that the FBI would cease wiretapping [15, 16].

FBI CONTINUES SECRET WIRETAPPING

After World War II broke out in Europe, FBI Director J. Edgar Hoover pressed to have the ban on wiretapping withdrawn (Figure 6.4). The position of the Department of Justice was that the Federal Communications Act simply prohibited intercepting *and* revealing telephone conversations. In the Justice Department's view, it was permissible to intercept conversations as long as they were not revealed to an agency outside the federal government. President Roosevelt agreed to let the FBI resume wiretapping in cases involving national security, though he asked that the wiretaps be kept to a minimum and limited as much as possible to aliens [15].

Because it knew evidence obtained through wiretapping was inadmissible in court, the FBI began maintaining two sets of files: the official files that contained legally obtained evidence, and confidential files containing evidence obtained from wiretaps and other confidential sources. In case of a trial, only the official file would be released to the court [15].

The FBI was supposed to get permission from the Department of Justice before installing a wiretap, but in practice it did not always work that way. During his 48-year reign as Director of the FBI, J. Edgar Hoover routinely engaged in political surveillance,

FIGURE 6.4 Under the leadership of J. Edgar Hoover, the FBI engaged in illegal wiretapping. (© Bettmann/CORBIS)

tapping the telephones of senators, congressmen, and Supreme Court justices. The information the FBI collected on these figures had great political value, even if the recordings revealed no criminal activity. There is evidence Hoover used information gathered during this surveillance to discredit congressmen who were trying to limit the power of the FBI [15].

CHARLES KATZ V. UNITED STATES

A **bug** is a hidden microphone used for surveillance. In a series of decisions, the U.S. Supreme Court gradually came to an understanding that citizens should also be protected from all electronic surveillance conducted without warrants, including bugs. The key decision was rendered in 1967. Charles Katz used a public telephone to place bets. The FBI placed a bug on the outside of the telephone booth to record Katz's telephone conversations. With this evidence, Katz was convicted of illegal gambling. The Justice Department argued that since it placed the microphone on the outside of the telephone booth, it did not intrude into the space occupied by Katz [15]. In *Charles Katz v. United States*, the Supreme Court ruled in favor of Katz. Justice Potter Stewart wrote that "the Fourth Amendment protects people, not places" [18]. Katz entered the phone booth with the reasonable expectation that his conversation would not be heard, and what a person "seeks to preserve as private, even in an area accessible to the public, may be constitutionally protected" [18].

6.4.2 Operation Shamrock

During World War II, the U.S. government censored all messages entering and leaving the country, meaning U.S. intelligence agencies had access to all telegram traffic. At the end of the war, the censorship bureaucracy was shut down, and the Signal Security Agency (predecessor to the National Security Agency) wanted to find a new way to get access to telegram traffic. It contacted Western Union Telegraph Company, ITT Communications, and RCA Communications, and asked them to allow it to make photographic copies of all foreign government telegram traffic that entered, left, or transited the United States. In other words, the Signal Security Agency asked these companies to break federal law in the interests of national security. All three companies agreed to the request. The Signal Security Agency gave this intelligence-gathering operation the name "Shamrock."

When the National Security Agency (NSA) was formed in 1952, it inherited Operation Shamrock. The sophistication of the surveillance operation took a giant leap forward in the 1960s, when the telegram companies converted to computers. Now the contents of telegrams could be transmitted electronically to the NSA, and the NSA could use computers to search for key words and phrases.

In 1961, Robert Kennedy became the new attorney general of the United States, and he immediately focused his attention on organized crime. Discovering that information about mobsters was scattered piecemeal among the FBI, IRS, Securities and Exchange Commission (SEC), and other agencies, he convened a meeting in which investigators from all of these agencies could exchange information. The Justice Department gave the names of hundreds of alleged crime figures to the NSA, asking that these figures be put on its "watch list." Intelligence gathered by the NSA contributed to several prosecutions.

Also during the Kennedy administration, the FBI asked the NSA to put on its watch list the names of U.S. citizens and companies doing business with Cuba. The NSA sent information gathered from intercepted telegrams and international telephone calls back to the FBI.

During the Vietnam War, the Johnson and Nixon administrations hypothesized that foreign governments were controlling or influencing the activities of American groups opposed to the war. They asked the NSA to put the names of war protesters on its watch list. Some of the people placed on the watch list included the Reverend Dr. Martin Luther King, Jr., the Reverend Ralph Abernathy, Black Panther leader Eldrige Cleaver, pediatrician Dr. Benjamin Spock, folk singer Joan Baez, and actress Jane Fonda.

In 1969, President Nixon established the White House Task Force on Heroin Suppression. The NSA soon became an active participant in the war on drugs, monitoring the phone calls of people put on its drug watch list. Intelligence gathered by the NSA led to convictions for drug-related crimes.

Facing hostile Congressional and press scrutiny, the NSA called an end to Operation Shamrock in May 1975 [19].

6.4.3 Carnivore Surveillance System

The FBI developed the Carnivore system in the late 1990s to monitor Internet traffic, including email messages. The system itself consisted of a Windows PC and packet-sniffing software capable of identifying and recording packets originating from or directed to a particular IP address. Armed with a search warrant, the FBI would set up its Carnivore system at the suspect's Internet service provider [20].

In 2000, the Justice Department demanded that Earthlink, an Internet service provider, allow the FBI to use Carnivore without a warrant. Earthlink filed a legal challenge questioning the FBI's authority to do this under the Electronic Communications Privacy Act, but a U.S. District Court ruled against Earthlink [21, 22].

Between 1998 and 2000, the FBI used the Carnivore system about 25 times. In late 2001, the FBI stopped using Carnivore, replacing it with commercial software capable of performing the same function [23].

6.4.4 Covert Activities after 9/11

The September 11, 2001, attacks on the World Trade Center and the Pentagon spawned new, secret intelligence-gathering operations within the United States. The same question emerged after each activity became public knowledge: Is it constitutional?

NSA WIRETAPPING

Early in 2002, the Central Intelligence Agency captured several top al-Qaeda members, along with their personal computers and cell phones. The CIA recovered telephone numbers from these devices and provided them to the NSA. The NSA was eager to eavesdrop on these telephone numbers, hoping to gather information that could be used to disrupt future terrorist attacks. President Bush signed a presidential order allowing the NSA to eavesdrop on international telephone calls and international emails initiated by people living inside the United States, without first obtaining a search warrant [24].

The list of persons being monitored gradually expanded, as the NSA followed connections from the original list of telephone numbers. At any one time, the NSA eavesdropped on up to 500 people inside the United States, including American citizens, permanent residents, and foreigners. The NSA also monitored another 5,000 to 7,000 people living outside the United States at any one time [24].

Sources told *The New York Times* that the surveillance program had foiled at least two al-Qaeda plots: Ohio truck driver Iyman Faris's plan to "bring down the Brooklyn Bridge with blowtorches" and another scheme to bomb British pubs and train stations. Civil libertarians and some members of Congress objected to the program, arguing that warrantless wiretapping of American citizens violated the Fourth Amendment to the U.S. Constitution [24].

In March 2010, Vaughn Walker, the chief judge of the Federal District Court in San Francisco, ruled that the NSA's warrantless wiretapping program was illegal [25]. As of July 2011, Judge Walker's decision is still under appeal by the Obama administration.

TALON DATABASE

The U.S. Department of Defense created the Threat and Local Observation Notices (TALON) database in 2003. The purpose of the database was to collect reports of suspicious activities or terrorist threats near military bases. These reports were submitted by military personnel or civilians and then assessed by Department of Defense experts as either "credible" or "not credible."

In December 2005, NBC News reported that the database contained reports on anti-war protests occurring far from military bases [26]. In July 2006, the Servicemembers Legal Defense Network reported that the TALON database contained emails from students at Southern Connecticut State University, the State University of New York at Albany, the University of California at Berkeley, and William Paterson University of New Jersey who were planning protests against on-campus military recruiting [27].

The Department of Defense removed many of these reports from TALON after conducting an in-house review that concluded the database should only contain information related to terrorist activity. The American Civil Liberties Union asked Congress to take steps "to ensure that Americans may once again exercise their First Amendment rights without fear that they will be tracked in a government database of suspicious activities" [28]. In April 2007, the new Under Secretary of Defense for Intelligence recommended that the TALON program be terminated [29]. The TALON database was shut down on September 17, 2007 [30].

6.5 U.S. Legislation Authorizing Wiretapping

As we have seen, the Federal Communications Act of 1934 made wiretapping illegal, and by 1967 the U.S. Supreme Court had closed the door to wiretapping and bugging performed without a warrant (court order). After the Katz decision, police were left without any electronic surveillance tools in their fight against crime.

Meanwhile, the United States was in the middle of the Vietnam War. In 1968, the country was rocked by violent antiwar demonstrations and the assassinations of Martin Luther King, Jr., and Robert F. Kennedy. Law-enforcement agencies pressured Congress to allow wiretapping under some circumstances.

6.5.1 Title III

Congress responded by passing Title III of the Omnibus Crime Control and Safe Streets Act of 1968. Title III allows a police agency that has obtained a court order to tap a phone for up to 30 days [15].

The government continued to argue that in cases of national security, agencies should be able to tap phones without a warrant. In 1972, the Supreme Court rejected this argument when it ruled that the Fourth Amendment forbids warrantless wiretapping, even in cases of national security [15].

6.5.2 Electronic Communications Privacy Act

Congress updated the wiretapping law in 1986 with the passage of the Electronic Communications Privacy Act (ECPA). The ECPA allows police to attach two kinds of surveillance devices to a suspect's phone line. If the suspect makes a phone call, a **pen register** displays the number being dialed. If the suspect gets a phone call, a **trap-and-trace device** displays the caller's phone number. While a court order is needed to approve the installation of pen registers and trap-and-trace devices, prosecutors do not need to demonstrate probable cause, and the approval is virtually automatic.

The ECPA also allows police to conduct **roving wiretaps**—wiretaps that move from phone to phone—if they can demonstrate the suspect is attempting to avoid surveillance by using many different phones [15].

6.5.3 Stored Communications Act

The Stored Communications Act, part of the Electronic Communications Privacy Act, has significant privacy implications related to the collection of email messages. Under this law, the government does not need a search warrant to obtain from an Internet service provider email messages more than 180 days old. In other words, when a computer user allows an Internet service provider to store his or her email messages, the user is giving up the expectation of privacy of that information [31].

In the past, it had been understood that the government needed a court order to gain access to emails under 180 days old, but in 2010, the government asked Yahoo to turn over emails under 180 days old that had already been read by the recipient [32]. Yahoo challenged this request in federal court, supported by Google, the Electronic Frontier Foundation, and the Center for Democracy & Technology, and the government withdrew its demand for the emails.

Nearly 50 companies and privacy rights organizations, including AOL, the American Civil Liberties Union, the American Library Association, AT&T, Consumer Action, the Electronic Frontier Foundation, Facebook, Google, IBM, Intel, and Microsoft, have joined forces to form an organization called Digital Due Process, which is lobbying Congress to update the Electronic Communications Protection Act. In the past, Internet service providers simply transmitted email messages from senders to recipients. Today, most Internet service providers provide convenient, long-term storage of their customers' emails, and millions of customers take advantage of this service to hold their messages indefinitely. With the advent of cloud computing, companies such as Amazon, Google, and Microsoft are storing sensitive documents and other materials that in the past would have been held on personal computers. The view of the Digital Due Process coalition is that the government should not be able to obtain an email message, document, or photo from an Internet or cloud service provider without a proper search warrant [33].

6.5.4 Communications Assistance for Law Enforcement Act

The implementation of digital phone networks interfered with the wiretapping ability of the FBI and other organizations. In response to these technological changes, Congress passed the Communications Assistance for Law Enforcement Act of 1994 (CALEA), also known as the Digital Telephony Act. This law required networking equipment used by phone companies be designed or modified so that law-enforcement agencies can trace calls, listen in on telephone calls, and intercept email messages. CALEA thereby ensured that court-ordered wiretapping would still be possible even as new digital technologies were introduced.

CALEA left unanswered many important details about the kind of information the FBI would be able to extract from digital phone calls. The precise requirements were to be worked out between the FBI and industry representatives. The FBI asked for many capabilities, including the ability to intercept digits typed by the caller after the phone call was placed. This feature would let it catch credit card numbers and bank account numbers, for example. In 1999, the FCC finally issued the guidelines, which included this capability and five more requested by the FBI [34]. Privacy-rights organizations argued these capabilities went beyond the authorization of CALEA [35]. Telecommunications companies claimed that implementing these capabilities would cost them billions [36]. Nevertheless, in August 2005, the FCC gave voice over Internet Protocol (VoIP) and certain other broadband providers 18 months to modify their systems as necessary so that law enforcement agencies could wiretap calls made using their services [37]. The Electronic Frontier Foundation and other groups challenged the FCC decision in court, blocking the implementation of the order. Since then, the Department of Justice has pursued a legislative solution, asking Congress to revise CALEA and explicitly authorize the wiretapping of online communications, but to date, no legislation has been passed [38].

6.6   USA PATRIOT Act

On the morning of September 11, 2001, terrorists hijacked four passenger airliners in the United States and turned them into flying bombs. Two of the planes flew into New York's World Trade Center, a third hit the Pentagon, and the fourth crashed in a field in Pennsylvania. Soon after these attacks, which resulted in about 3,000 deaths and the destruction of the twin towers of the World Trade Center, the United States Congress passed the Uniting and Strengthening America by Providing Appropriate Tools Required to Intercept and Obstruct Terrorism (USA PATRIOT) Act of 2001, henceforth referred to as the Patriot Act [39]. The Patriot Act has raised many questions about the extent to which government agencies should be able to collect information about individuals in the United States without first obtaining a search warrant.

6.6.1   Provisions of the Patriot Act

The Patriot Act amended many existing laws. Its provisions fall into four principal categories:

1. Providing federal law enforcement and intelligence officials with greater authority to monitor communications
2. Giving the Secretary of the Treasury greater powers to regulate banks, preventing them from being used to launder foreign money
3. Making it more difficult for terrorists to enter the United States
4. Defining new crimes and penalties for terrorist activity

We focus on those provisions of the Patriot Act that most directly affect the privacy of persons living inside the United States.

The Patriot Act expands the kinds of information that law enforcement officials can gather with pen registers and trap-and-trace devices. It allows police to use pen registers on the Internet to track email addresses and URLs. The law does not require they demonstrate probable cause. To obtain a warrant, police simply certify that the information to be gained is relevant to an ongoing criminal investigation.

Law enforcement agencies seeking to install a wiretap or a pen register/trap-and-trace device have always been required to get a court order from a judge with jurisdiction over the location where the device was to be installed. The Patriot Act extends the jurisdiction of court-ordered wiretaps to the entire country. A judge in New York can authorize the installation of a device in California, for example. The act also allows the nationwide application of court-ordered search warrants for terrorist-related investigations.

The Patriot Act broadened the number of circumstances under which roving surveillance can take place. Previously, roving surveillance could only be done for the purpose of law enforcement, and the agency had to demonstrate to the court that the person under investigation actually used the device to be monitored. The Patriot Act allows roving surveillance to be performed for the purpose of intelligence, and the government does not have to prove that the person under investigation actually uses the device to be tapped. Additionally, it does not require that the law enforcement agency report back to the authorizing judge regarding the number of devices monitored and the results of the monitoring.

Under the Patriot Act, law enforcement officials wishing to intercept communications to and from a person who has illegally gained access to a computer system do not need a court order if they have the permission of the owner of the computer system.

The Patriot Act allows courts to authorize law enforcement officers to search a person's premises without first serving a search warrant when there is "reasonable cause to believe that providing immediate notification of the execution of the warrant may have an adverse affect." Officers may seize property that "constitutes evidence of a criminal offense in violation of the laws of the United States," even if that offense is unrelated to terrorism.

6.6.2 National Security Letters

The Patriot Act expanded the use of National Security Letters, making it easier for the FBI to collect Internet, business, medical, educational, library, and church/mosque/synagogue records. To obtain a search warrant authorizing the collection of records about an individual, the FBI merely needs to issue a National Security Letter stating that the records are related to an ongoing investigation. (The Patriot Act does specifically prohibit the FBI from investigating citizens solely on the basis of activities protected by the First Amendment.) A typical National Security Letter contains a gag order that forbids the letter's recipient from disclosing receipt of the letter. National Security Letters are controversial because, unlike warrants, they do not require the approval of a judge. That means there is no need for the FBI to show probable cause. Between 2003 and 2006, the FBI issued 192,499 National Security Letters [40].

National Security Letters have prompted several legal challenges by the American Civil Liberties Union (ACLU). One of these cases involved the Library Connection, a consortium of 26 libraries in Connecticut. In July 2005, the FBI sent a National Security Letter to the Library Connection, demanding records of a patron who had used a particular computer. This happened while Congress was debating reauthorization of the Patriot Act, and an important point in the debate was whether the FBI had actually attempted to use the Patriot Act to get information from libraries. The ACLU sought an emergency court order that would have allowed representatives of the Library Connection to tell Congress that they had received a National Security Letter. In September 2005, a district court judge in Connecticut ruled that the National Security Letter's gag order violated the First Amendment to the U.S. Constitution, but the executive branch continued to enforce it. In April 2006, six weeks after Congress had reauthorized the Patriot Act, the FBI dropped the gag order and its demand for the information. The ACLU hailed the government's decision as a victory "not just for librarians but for all Americans who value their privacy" [41].

6.6.3 Responses to the Patriot Act

Critics of the Patriot Act warn that its provisions give too many powers to the federal government. Despite language in the Patriot Act to the contrary, civil libertarians are concerned that law enforcement agencies may use their new powers to reduce the rights of law-abiding Americans, particularly those rights expressed in the First and Fourth Amendments to the United States Constitution.

First Amendment rights center around the freedom of speech and the free exercise of religion. We have seen that in the past, the FBI and the NSA used illegal wiretaps to investigate people who had expressed unpopular political views. In November 2003, the ACLU reported that public apprehension about the Patriot Act had led to a significant drop in attendance and donations at mosques [42].

Critics maintain that other provisions of the Patriot Act undermine the right against unreasonable searches and seizures guaranteed by the Fourth Amendment:

- By revealing the URLs of Web sites visited by a suspect, a pen register is a much more powerful surveillance tool on the Internet than it is on a telephone network. The Patriot Act allows police to install Internet pen registers without demonstrating probable cause that the suspect is engaged in a criminal activity.

- Court orders authorizing roving surveillance do not "particularly describe the place to be searched."

- It allows law enforcement agencies, under certain circumstances, to search homes and seize evidence without first serving a search warrant.

- It allows the FBI to obtain—without showing probable cause—a warrant authorizing the seizure of business, medical, educational, and library records of suspects.

The Council of the American Library Association passed a resolution on the Patriot Act in January 2003. The resolution affirms every person's rights to inquiry and free expression. It "urges librarians everywhere to defend and support user privacy and free and open access to knowledge and information," and it "urges libraries to adopt and implement patron privacy and record retention policies" that minimize the collection of records about the activities of individual patrons [43]. More than four hundred cities and several states have also passed anti–Patriot Act resolutions [44].

Tribune Media Services TMS Reprints

The federal government issues 50,000 National Security Letters every year [45]. Google is an obvious organization for law enforcement agencies to contact, given the significant amount of information it collects from individuals who use its search engine. In December 2009, Google's CEO Eric Schmidt told CNBC, "If you have something that you don't want anyone to know, maybe you shouldn't be doing it in the first place." Schmidt admitted Google is obliged to release personal data to law enforcement agencies, saying, "[T]he reality is that search engines—including Google—do retain this information for some time and it's important, for example, that we are all subject in the United States to the Patriot Act and it is possible that all that information could be made available to the authorities" [46].

6.6.4 Successes and Failures

According to Tom Ridge, former Secretary of the Department of Homeland Security, the Patriot Act has helped the government in its fight against terrorism by allowing greater information sharing among law enforcement and intelligence agencies, and by giving law enforcement agencies new investigative tools—"many of which have been used for years to catch mafia dons and drug kingpins" [47]. Terrorism investigations have led to charges being brought against 361 individuals in the United States. Of these, 191 have been convicted or pled guilty, including shoe-bomber Richard Reid, and John Walker Lindh, who fought with the Taliban in Afghanistan. More than 500 individuals linked to the September 11th attacks have been removed from the United States. Terrorist cells in Buffalo, Seattle, Tampa, and Portland (the "Portland Seven")[2] have been broken up [47].

Unfortunately, a few innocent bystanders have been affected by the war against terrorism. A notable example is Brandon Mayfield.

During the morning rush hour on March 11, 2004, ten bombs exploded on four commuter trains in Madrid, Spain, killing 191 people and wounding more than 2,000 others. The Spanish government retrieved a partial fingerprint from a bag of detonators, and the FBI linked the fingerprint to Brandon Mayfield, an attorney in Portland, Oregon [48].

Without revealing their search warrant, FBI agents secretly entered Mayfield's home multiple times, making copies of documents and computer hard drives, collecting ten DNA samples, removing six cigarette butts for DNA analysis, and taking 355 digital photographs. The FBI also put Mayfield under electronic surveillance [49]. On May 6, 2004, the FBI arrested Mayfield as a material witness and detained him for two weeks. After the Spanish government announced that it had matched the fingerprints to Ouhnane Daoud, an Algerian national living in Spain, a judge ordered that Mayfield be released. The FBI publicly apologized for the fingerprint misidentification [48].

Mayfield said his detention was "an abuse of the judicial process" that "shouldn't happen to anybody" [48]. He said, "I personally was subject to lockdown, strip searches, sleep deprivation, unsanitary living conditions, shackles and chains, threats, physical pain, and humiliation" [50]. The only evidence against Mayfield was a partial fingerprint match that even the Spanish police found dubious. Mayfield had not left the United States in more than a decade, and he had no connections with any terrorist organizations. Some civil rights groups suggest Mayfield was targeted by the FBI because of his religious beliefs. The affidavit that the FBI used to get an arrest warrant pointed out that Mayfield "had converted to Islam, is married to an Egyptian-born woman, and had once briefly represented a member of the Portland Seven in a child-custody case" [51]. Mayfield sued the U.S. government for continuing to investigate him after the Spanish police had eliminated him as a suspect, and in November 2006, the government issued a formal apology and agreed to pay him $2 million [50].

6.6.5 Patriot Act Renewal

Most of the provisions of the Patriot Act have now been made permanent, but three provisions of particular concern to civil liberties groups must be renewed periodically—the provisions permitting the use of roving wiretaps, the surveillance of "lone wolf" suspects not linked to terrorist groups, and the seizure of business, medical, educational, and library records without showing probable cause. In May 2011, President Obama signed into law a four-year extension of these provisions [52].

---

2. The "Portland Seven" included six American Muslim men accused of attempting to travel to Afghanistan to fight with the Taliban.

6.7 Regulation of Public and Private Databases

In this section, we switch our focus to the information processing category of Solove's taxonomy of privacy. (Our coverage of issues related to information processing and the government will continue through Section 6.9.)

Once organizations have collected information, they can manipulate and use it in a variety of ways, and some of these uses have privacy implications. We begin by describing the social conditions that led to the creation of the Code of Fair Information Practices and the passage of the Privacy Act of 1974. We then move on to further legislation that regulates databases managed by private organizations.

6.7.1 Code of Fair Information Practices

In 1965, the Director of the Budget commissioned a consulting committee, composed largely of economists, to look at problems caused by the decentralization of statistical data across many federal agencies. The Census Bureau, the Bureau of Labor Statistics, the Statistical Reporting Service, and the Economic Research Service of the Department of Agriculture maintained independent computer databases, making it impossible for economists and other social scientists to combine information about individuals. Carl Kaysen, the chair of the committe, wrote:

> It is becoming increasingly difficult to make informed and intelligent policy decisions on such questions in the area of poverty as welfare payments, family allowances, and the like, simply because we lack sufficient "dis-aggregated" information—breakdowns by the many relevant social and economic variables—that is both wide in coverage and readily usable. The information the Government does have is scattered among a dozen agencies, collected on a variety of not necessarily consistent bases, and not really accessible to any single group of policy-makers or research analysts. A test of the proposition, for example, that poor performance in school and poor prospects of social mobility are directly related to family size would require data combining information on at least family size and composition, family income, regional location, city size, school performance, and post-school occupational history over a period of years in a way that is simply not now possible, even though the separate items of information were all fed into some part of the Federal statistical system at some time. [53]

After Kaysen's committee recommended the creation of a National Data Center, there was an immediate outcry from citizens and legislators expressing concerns about possible abuses of a massive, centralized government database containing detailed information about millions of Americans. The U.S. House of Representatives created a Special Subcommittee on Invasion of Privacy, which held hearings about these issues [54].

In the early 1970s, Elliot Richardson, the Secretary of the U.S. Department of Health, Education, and Welfare, convened a group to recommend policies for the development of government databases that would protect the privacy of American citizens. The Secretary's Advisory Committee of Automated Personal Data Systems, Records,

Computers, and the Rights of Citizens produced a report for Congress, which included the following "bill of rights" for the Information Age [55]:

~

CODE OF FAIR INFORMATION PRACTICES

1. There must be no personal data record–keeping systems whose very existence is secret.

2. There must be a way for a person to find out what information about the person is in a record and how it is used.

3. There must be a way for a person to prevent information about the person that was obtained for one purpose from being used or made available for other purposes without the person's consent.

4. There must be a way for a person to correct or amend a record of identifiable information about the person.

5. Any organization creating, maintaining, using, or disseminating records of identifiable personal data must assure the reliability of the data for their intended use and must take precautions to prevent misuses of the data.

~

At about the same time that the Richardson Committee was established in the United States, similar efforts were underway in Europe. In fact, a year before the Richardson Committee issued the report containing the Code of Fair Information Practices, a Committee on Privacy in the United Kingdom released its own report containing many of the same principles. Sweden passed privacy laws consistent with the fair information practices in 1973, and later that decade, the Federal Republic of Germany and France followed suit [56].

6.7.2 Privacy Act of 1974

The Privacy Act of 1974 represents Congress's codification of these principles described in the Code of Fair Information Practices. While the Privacy Act does allow individuals in some cases to get access to federal files containing information about them, in other respects it has fallen short of the desires of privacy advocates. In particular, they say the Privacy Act has not been effective in reducing the flow of personal information into governmental databases, preventing agencies from sharing information with each other, or preventing unauthorized access to the data. They claim agencies have been unresponsive to outside attempts to bring them into alignment with the provisions of the Privacy Act. The Privacy Act has the following principal limitations [57]:

1. *The Privacy Act applies only to government databases.*

   Far more information is held in private databases, which are excluded. This is an enormous loophole, because government agencies can purchase information from private organizations that have the data they want.

2. *The Privacy Act only covers records indexed by a personal identifier.*

Records about individuals that are not indexed by name or another identifying number are excluded. For example, a former IRS agent tried to gain access to a file containing derogatory information about himself, but the judge ruled he did not have a right to see the file, since it was indexed under the name of another IRS employee.

3. *No one in the federal government is in charge of enforcing the provisions of the Privacy Act.*

    Federal agencies have taken it upon themselves to determine which databases they can exempt. The IRS has exempted its database containing the names of taxpayers it is investigating. The Department of Justice has announced that the FBI does not have to ensure the reliability of the data in its NCIC databases.

4. *The Privacy Act allows one agency to share records with another agency as long as they are for a "routine use."*

    Each agency is able to decide for itself what "routine use" means. The Department of Justice has encouraged agencies to define "routine use" as broadly as possible.

Although the Privacy Act applies only to government databases, Congress has passed legislation regulating how some private institutions manage databases containing sensitive information about individuals, and these laws put into effect many of the principles of the Code of Fair Information Practices. In the remainder of this section, we survey some of the most influential of these laws.

6.7.3 Fair Credit Reporting Act

Credit bureaus and other consumer reporting agencies maintain information on your bill-paying record, whether you've been sued or arrested, and if you've filed for bankruptcy. They sell reports to other organizations that are trying to determine the credit-worthiness of consumers who are applying for credit, applying for a job, or trying to rent an apartment. The Fair Credit Reporting Act, passed in 1970 and revised in 1996, was designed to promote the accuracy and privacy of information used by credit bureaus and other consumer reporting agencies to produce consumer reports. It also ensures that negative information does not haunt a consumer for a lifetime.

The three major credit bureaus are Equifax, Experian, and Trans Union. According to the Fair Credit Reporting Act, these credit bureaus may keep negative information about a consumer for a maximum of seven years. There are several exceptions to this rule. The two most important are that information about criminal convictions may be kept indefinitely, and bankruptcy information may be held for 10 years.

6.7.4 Fair and Accurate Credit Transactions Act

The Fair and Accurate Credit Transactions Act of 2004 requires the three major credit bureaus to provide consumers a free copy of their credit report every 12 months. Consumers can use this opportunity to detect and correct errors in their credit reports. The bureaus do not issue the reports automatically; consumers must take the initiative and request them from AnnualCreditReport.com.

The law also has provisions to reduce identity theft. It requires the truncation of account numbers on credit card receipts, and it establishes the National Fraud Alert System. Victims of identity theft may put a fraud alert on their credit files, warning credit card issuers that they must take "reasonable steps" to verify the requestor's identity before granting credit.

6.7.5 Financial Services Modernization Act

The Financial Services Modernization Act (also called the Gramm-Leach-Bliley Act of 1999) contains dozens of provisions related to how financial institutions do business. One of the major provisions of the law allows the creation of "financial supermarkets" offering banking, insurance, and brokerage services.

The law also contains some privacy-related provisions. It requires financial institutions to disclose their privacy policies to their customers. When a customer establishes an account, and at least once per year thereafter, the institution must let the customer know the kinds of information it collects and how it uses that information. These notices must contain an opt-out clause that explains to customers how they can request that their confidential information not be revealed to other companies. The law requires financial institutions to develop policies that will prevent unauthorized access of their customers' confidential information [58].

6.8 Data Mining by the Government

Data mining is the process of searching through one or more databases looking for patterns or relationships among the data. In this section, we continue our coverage of the information processing category of Solove's taxonomy by surveying a few well-known data-mining projects run by government agencies.

6.8.1 Internal Revenue Service Audits

To identify taxpayers who have paid less in taxes than they owe, the Internal Revenue Service (IRS) uses computer matching and data mining strategies. First, it matches information on the tax form with information provided by employers and financial institutions. This is a straightforward way to detect unreported income.

Second, the IRS audits a couple of million tax returns every year. Its goal is to select the most promising returns—those containing errors resulting in underpayment of taxes. The IRS uses a computerized system called the discriminant function (DIF) to score every tax return. The DIF score is an indicator of how many irregularities there are on a tax form, compared to carefully constructed profiles of correct tax returns. About 60 percent of tax returns audited by the IRS are selected due to their high DIF scores.

6.8.2 Syndromic Surveillance Systems

Another application of data mining by the government is protecting society from imminent dangers.

A syndromic surveillance system is a computerized system that analyzes 911 calls, visits to the emergency room, school absenteeism, purchases of prescription drugs, and Internet searches to find patterns that might indicate the onset of an epidemic, an environmental problem leading to illnesses, or bioterrorism.

In the fall of 2002, a syndromic surveillance system in New York City detected a surge in people seeking treatment for vomiting and diarrhea. These symptoms were the first signs of an outbreak of a Norwalk-type virus. The alert generated by the system allowed city officials to warn doctors about the outbreak and advise them to be particularly careful about handling the highly contagious body fluids of their affected patients [59].

6.8.3 Telecommunications Records Database

Shortly after September 11, 2001, several major telecommunications providers began turning over the phone call records of tens of millions of Americans to the National Security Agency, without a court order. The NSA was not monitoring or recording the actual conversations; instead, it was analyzing calling patterns in order to detect potential terrorist networks. [60].

After *USA Today* revealed the existence of the database in May 2006, more than a dozen class-action lawsuits were filed against the telecommunications companies. In August 2006, a federal judge in Detroit ruled the program to be illegal and unconstitutional, violating several statutes as well as the First and Fourth Amendments to the U.S. Constitution [61]. In July 2007, the U.S. Court of Appeals for the Sixth Circuit overturned the ruling on the grounds that the plaintiffs did not have standing to bring the suit forward. In other words, the plaintiffs had not produced any evidence that they personally were victims of warrantless wiretapping.

6.9 National Identification Card

A great deal can be learned about an individual when information collected at different places and times is combined. In order to combine information from two records, the records must share a common key. A name cannot be used as a common key, because more than one person can have the same name, but if every individual had a unique identification number *and* that identification number appeared in every database record referring to that individual, then all of these records could theoretically be combined into a massive "electronic dossier" documenting that person's life. In this section, we survey the debate around the establishment of a national identification card in the United States.

6.9.1 History and Role of the Social Security Number

The Social Security Act of 1935 established two social insurance programs in the United States: a federal system of old-age benefits to retired persons, and a federal-state system of unemployment insurance. Before the system could be implemented, employers and workers needed to become registered. The Social Security Board contracted with the U.S. Postal Service to distribute applications for Social Security cards. The post office collected the forms, typed the Social Security cards, and returned them to the applicants. In this way, over 35 million Social Security cards were issued in 1936–1937 [62].

The U.S. government initially stated that Social Security numbers (SSNs) would be used solely by the Social Security Administration, and not as a national identification card. In fact, from 1946 to 1972, the Social Security Administration put the following legend on the bottom of the cards it issued: "FOR SOCIAL SECURITY PURPOSES—NOT FOR IDENTIFICATION." However, use of the SSN has gradually increased. President Roosevelt ordered, in 1943, that federal agencies use SSNs as identifiers in new federal databases. In 1961, the Internal Revenue Service began using the SSN as the taxpayer identification number. Because banks report interest to the IRS, people must provide their SSN when they open a bank account. The SSN is typically requested on applications for credit cards. Motor vehicle departments and some other state agencies received permission to use SSNs as identification numbers in 1976. Many universities use the SSN as an identification number for faculty and students. The IRS now requires parents to provide the SSNs of their children over one year old on income tax forms in order to claim them as dependents. For this reason, children now get a SSN soon after they are born. Many private organizations ask people to provide SSNs for identification. The SSN has become a de facto national identification number in the United States.

Unfortunately, the SSN has serious defects that make it a poor identification number. The first problem with SSNs is that they are not unique. When Social Security cards were first issued by post offices, different post offices accidentally assigned the same SSN to different people. In 1938, wallet manufacturer E. H. Ferree included sample Social Security cards in one of its products. More than 40,000 people purchasing the wallets from Woolworth stores thought the cards were real and used the sample card's number as their SSN [63].

A second defect of SSNs is that they are rarely checked. Millions of Social Security cards have been issued to applicants without verifying that the information provided by the applicants is correct. Many, if not most, organizations asking for a SSN do not actually require the applicant to show a card, making it easy for criminals to supply fake SSNs.

A third defect of SSNs is that they have no error-detecting capability, such as a check digit at the end of the number. A check digit enables computer systems to detect common data entry errors, such as getting one digit wrong or transposing two adjacent digits. If someone makes one of these mistakes, the data-entry program can detect the error and ask the person to retype the number. In the case of SSNs, if a person accidentally types in the wrong number, there is a high likelihood that it is a valid SSN (albeit one assigned to a different person). Hence, it is easy to contaminate databases with records containing incorrect SSNs [64]. Similarly, without check digits or another error-detection mechanism, there is no simple way for a system to catch people who are simply making up a phony SSN.

6.9.2 Debate over a National ID Card

The events of September 11, 2001, resurrected the debate over the introduction of a national identification card for Americans.

Proponents of a national identification card point out numerous benefits to its adoption:

1. *A national identification card would be more reliable than existing forms of identification.*

   Social Security cards and driver's licenses are too easy to forge. A modern card could incorporate a photograph as well as a thumbprint or other biometric data.

2. *A national identification card could reduce illegal immigration.*

   Requiring employers to check a tamper-proof, forgery-proof national identification card would prevent illegal aliens from working in the United States. If illegal aliens couldn't get work, they wouldn't enter the United States in the first place.

3. *A national identification card would reduce crime.*

   Currently it's too easy for criminals to mask their true identity. A tamper-proof national identification card would allow police to positively identify the people they apprehend.

4. *National identification cards do not undermine democracy.*

   Many democratic countries already use national ID cards, including Belgium, France, Germany, Greece, Luxembourg, Portugal, and Spain.

Opponents of a national identification card suggest these harms may result from its adoption:

1. *A national identification card does not guarantee that the apparent identity of an individual is that person's actual identity.*

   Driver's licenses and passports are supposed to be unique identifiers, but there are many criminals who produce fake driver's licenses and passports. Even a hard-to-forge identification card system may be compromised by insiders. For example, a ring of motor vehicle department employees in Virginia was caught selling fake driver's licenses [65].

2. *It is impossible to create a biometric-based national identification card that is 100 percent accurate.*

   All known systems suffer from false positives (erroneously reporting that the person does not match the ID) and false negatives (failing to report that the person and ID do not match). Biometric-based systems may still be beaten by determined, technology-savvy criminals [65].

3. *There is no evidence that institution of a national ID card actually leads to a reduction in crime.*

   In fact, the principal problem faced by police is not the inability to make positive identifications of suspects, but the inability to obtain evidence needed for a successful prosecution.

4. *A national identification card makes it simpler for government agencies to perform data mining on the activities of its citizens.*

   According to Peter Neumann and Lauren Weinstein, "The opportunities for overzealous surveillance and serious privacy abuses are almost limitless, as are opportunities for masquerading, identity theft, and draconian social engineering on a grand scale . . . The road to an Orwellian police state of universal tracking, but actually *reduced* security, could well be paved with hundreds of millions of such [national identification] cards" [65].

5. *While most people may feel they have nothing to fear from a national identification card system, since they are law-abiding citizens, even law-abiding people are subject to fraud and the indiscretions and errors of others.*

   Suppose a teacher, a doctor, or someone else in a position of authority creates a file containing misleading or erroneous information. Files created by people in positions of authority can be difficult to remove [66].

   In a society with decentralized record-keeping, old school or medical records are less likely to be accessed. The harm caused by inaccurate records is reduced. If all records are centralized around national identification numbers, files containing inaccurate or misleading information could haunt individuals for the rest of their lives.

6.9.3 The REAL ID Act

In May 2005, President George W. Bush signed the REAL ID Act, which would significantly change driver's licenses in the United States. To date, this law has not been put into effect. The motivation for passing the REAL ID Act was to make driver's licenses a more reliable form of identification. Critics, however, say the act would create a de facto national ID card in the United States.

The REAL ID Act requires that every state issue new driver's licenses. These licenses will be needed in order to open a bank account, fly on a commercial airplane, enter a federal building, or receive a government service, such as a Social Security check. The law makes it more difficult for impostors to get driver's licenses, by requiring applicants to supply four different kinds of documentation and requiring state employees to verify these documents using federal databases. Because the driver's license contains a biometric identifier, it is supposed to be a stronger credential than current licenses [67].

Although each state is responsible for issuing new driver's licenses to its own citizens, these licenses must meet federal standards. The license must include the person's full legal name, date of birth, gender, driver's license number, digital photograph, legal address, and signature. All data on the license must be in machine-readable form. The license must have physical security features designed to prevent tampering, counterfeiting, or duplication [68]. The federal government estimates the total cost of implementing REAL ID nationwide to be more than $23 billion—or more than $100 per driver's license.

Supporters of the measure say making the driver's license a more reliable identifier will have numerous benefits. Law enforcement is easier when police can be more certain that a driver's license correctly identifies the individual carrying it. Society is better off when parents ducking child support and criminals on the run cannot change their identities by crossing a state border and getting a new driver's license under a different name [69].

Some critics fear having machine-readable information on driver's licenses will aggravate problems with identity theft. Each state is required to share all this information with every other state and the federal government. American Civil Liberties Union lawyer Timothy Sparapani said, "We will have all this information in one electronic format, in one linked file, and we're giving access to tens of thousands of state DMV employees and federal agents" [70].

Proponents of the bill say such fears are unjustified. They suggest that the personal information actually available on the new driver's license is relatively insignificant compared with all the other personal information circulating around cyberspace [69].

The Department of Homeland Security pushed back the deadline for implementing the new driver's licenses from 2008 to 2013, but at this point it appears doubtful that the new deadline will be met. California and North Carolina have taken active steps to implement new driver's licenses meeting the specifications of REAL ID, but sixteen states have passed laws prohibiting its implementation, and eight other states have passed measures expressing some form of opposition to the new driver's license standard [71].

6.10 Information Dissemination

We now consider the information dissemination category of Solove's taxonomy. After we survey three federal laws that restrict the dissemination of personal information that organizations have collected, we discuss the Freedom of Information Act, designed to promote open government by allowing news organizations and private citizens to access records maintained by federal agencies. We also explore how information collected by the government for one purpose—collecting tolls—is being used as evidence of people's whereabouts in both criminal and civil cases.

6.10.1 Legislation to Restrict Information Dissemination

FAMILY EDUCATION RIGHTS AND PRIVACY ACT

The Family Education Rights and Privacy Act (FERPA) provides students 18 years of age and older the right to review their educational records and to request changes to records that contain erroneous information. Students also have the right to prevent information in these records from being released without their permission, except under certain

FIGURE 6.5 Judge Robert Bork, a nominee to the U.S. Supreme Court, had to endure the publication of his video rental records by the *Washington City Paper*. (AP Photo/Charles Tasnadi)

circumstances. For students under the age of 18, these rights are held by their parents or guardians. FERPA applies to all educational institutions that receive funds from the U.S. Department of Education.

VIDEO PRIVACY PROTECTION ACT

In 1988, President Ronald Reagan nominated Judge Robert Bork to the U.S. Supreme Court (Figure 6.5). Bork was a noted conservative, and his nomination was controversial. A Washington, D.C., video store provided a list of Bork's video rental records to a reporter for the *Washington City Paper*, which published the list. While the intention of the paper was most likely to embarrass Bork, it also had the effect of prompting Congress to pass the Video Privacy Protection Act of 1988. According to this law, videotape service providers cannot disclose rental records without the written consent of the customer. In addition, rental stores must destroy personally identifiable information about rentals within a year of the date when this information is no longer needed for the purpose for which it was collected.

HEALTH INSURANCE PORTABILITY AND ACCOUNTABILITY ACT

As part of the Health Insurance Portability and Accountability Act of 1996, Congress directed the Department of Health and Human Services (HHS) to come up with guidelines for protecting the privacy of patients. These guidelines went into effect in April

2003. They limit how doctors, hospitals, pharmacies, and insurance companies can use medical information collected from patients.

The regulations attempt to limit the exchange of information among health care providers to that information necessary to care for the patient. They forbid health care providers from releasing information to life insurance companies, banks, or other businesses without specific signed authorization from the person being treated. Health care providers must provide their patients with a notice describing how they use the information they gather. Patients have the right to see their medical records and to request corrections to errors they find in those records [72].

6.10.2 Examples of Information Dissemination

We now give two examples of ways in which information held by the government can be released to the public.

FREEDOM OF INFORMATION ACT

The Freedom of Information Act is a law designed to ensure that the public has access to U.S. government records. Signed into law by President Johnson in 1966, it applies only to the executive branch of the Federal government, not the legislative or judicial branches. The Act carries a presumption that the government will release the requested records. If an agency does not disclose records, it must explain why the information is being withheld.

There are nine exemptions in the Freedom of Information Act, spelling out those situations in which the government may legitimately withhold information. For example, a document may be withheld if it has been classified as secret for national defense or foreign policy reasons. The Government may withhold the release of documents containing trade secrets or confidential commercial or financial information. Another exemption deals with documents related to law enforcement investigations.

TOLL BOOTH RECORDS USED IN COURT

E-ZPass is an automatic toll-collection system used on most toll roads, bridges, and tunnels between Illinois and Maine. Drivers who have installed an E-ZPass tag (an RFID transponder) in their vehicles are able to pass through toll booths without stopping to pay an attendant. Instead, an E-ZPass reader installed in the automated toll lane gets information from the tags of the cars that pass through and deducts the appropriate toll from each driver's account.

The New York State Department of Transportation has installed tag readers at locations other than toll booths in order to track the progress of individual vehicles. In this way, the system can provide helpful information to other drivers by displaying on electronic signs above the turnpike the estimated time to reach popular destinations. According to the NYSDOT, the system encrypts information from individual tags, deletes the information as soon as the vehicle passes the last reader, and never makes information about individual cars available to the department [73].

However, states do maintain records of when cars pass through toll booths, and most of the states in the E-ZPass network provide information in response to court orders in criminal and civil cases. A well-known example is the case of Melanie McGuire, a New Jersey nurse suspected of murdering her husband and throwing his dismembered corpse into Chesapeake Bay. To help prove their case against McGuire, prosecutors used E-ZPass records to reconstruct her movements. E-ZPass records are also playing a role in divorce cases by providing evidence of infidelity. Pennsylvania divorce lawyer Lynne Gold-Bikin explained how E-ZPass helped her show that a client's husband had been unfaithful: "He claimed he was in a business meeting in Pennsylvania. And I had records to show he went to New Jersey that night" [74].

6.11 Invasion

We now turn to the last category in Solove's taxonomy of privacy: invasion. This category refers to activities that intrude upon someone's everyday life, either by interrupting his solitude or interfering with his decision-making. We begin this section by giving examples of government actions to prevent invasion and then move on to survey some government actions that can be seen as invasive.

6.11.1 Government Actions to Prevent Invasion

TELEMARKETING

After being sworn in as Chairman of the Federal Trade Commission (FTC) in 2001, Timothy Muris looked for an action that the FTC could take to protect the privacy of Americans. It did not take long for the FTC to focus on telemarketing. A large segment of the American population views dinner-time phone calls from telemarketers as an annoying invasion of privacy. In fact, Harris Interactive concluded that telemarketing is the reason why the number of Americans who feel it is "extremely important" to not be disturbed at home rose from 49 percent in 1994 to 62 percent in 2003 [75]. Responding to this desire for greater privacy, the FTC created the National Do Not Call Registry (www.donotcall.gov), a free service that allows people who do not wish to receive telemarketing calls to register their phone numbers. The public reacted enthusiastically to the availability of the Do Not Call Registry by registering more than 50 million phone numbers before it even took effect in October 2003 [76, 77].

The Do Not Call Registry has not eliminated 100 percent of unwanted solicitations. The regulations exempt political organizations, charities, and organizations conducting telephone surveys. Even if your phone number has been registered, you may still receive phone calls from companies with which you have done business in the past eighteen months. Still, the Registry is expected to keep most telemarketers from calling people who do not wish to be solicited. The creation of the Registry is a good example of how privacy is seen as a prudential right: the benefit of shielding people from telemarketers is judged to be greater than the harm caused by putting limits on telephone advertising.

LOUD TELEVISION COMMERCIALS

Since the 1960s, television watchers have complained to the Federal Communications Commission (FCC) about loud commercials. The Commercial Advertisement Loudness Mitigation Act (CALM Act), signed into law by President Obama in December 2010, required the Federal Communications Commission to ensure that television commercials are played at the same volume as the programs they are interrupting. The sponsor of the bill, Representative Anna Eshoo of California, said, "Consumers have been asking for a solution to this problem for decades, and today they finally have it . . . It's a simple fix to a huge nuisance" [78].

6.11.2 Invasive Government Actions

Early in Chapter 5, we described privacy as a "zone of inaccessibility." People have information privacy to the extent that they have some control over who has access to their personal information. In quite a few modern situations, people may have very little control; they must cede access to their personal information if they wish to use the service provided. If the loss of control is accompanied by a loss of tranquility or interferes with someone's freedom of decision-making, that is a privacy invasion, according to Solove. Here, we provide two examples of government actions that could be viewed as invasive.

REQUIRING IDENTIFICATION FOR PSEUDOEPHEDRINE PURCHASES

In an effort to curb the illegal production of methamphetamine ("meth"), federal and state governments have passed laws limiting access to products containing pseudoephedrine, which is used in the manufacture of methamphetamine. The Combat Methamphetamine Epidemic Act limits the quantity of pseudoephedrine that an individual can purchase in a month. Whether the laws have been effective is a matter of debate. In most states, original Sudafed is still sold behind the counter to adults, but they must show an identification card and fill out a sales log with their name, address, and signature. Two states, Oregon and Mississippi, require a prescription to acquire a product containing pseudoephedrine.

ADVANCED IMAGING TECHNOLOGY SCANNERS

In an effort to provide enhanced passenger security at airports, the Transportation Security Administration began deploying advanced imaging technology (AIT) scanners in 2007. Some AIT scanners use backscatter x-rays to produce a detailed image of the passenger's body, and other scanners use millimeter waves. The TSA began testing AIT systems at Phoenix's Sky Harbor International Airport in 2007 [79]. When the first AIT system was deployed, passengers who failed the primary security screening could choose between the x-ray scan and a traditional pat-down search. In June 2011, the Transportation Security Administration announced that had already deployed 500 AIT units and would deploy an additional 500 units, enabling it to use this technology to screen 60 percent of all airline passengers in the United States [80].

Some people were offended at the images produced by AIT scanners, which reveal "all anatomical features" (Figure 6.6) [81]. Lawyers for the American Civil Liberties

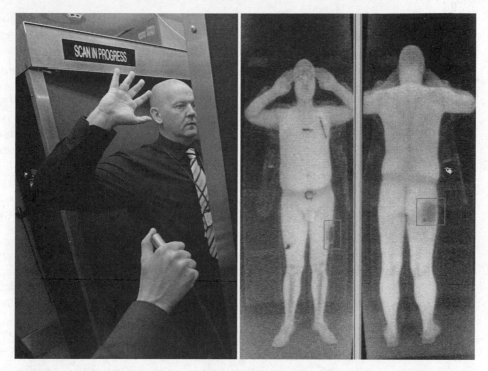

FIGURE 6.6 When the first advanced imaging technology scanners were deployed in American airports, they revealed anatomical features in great detail. (© PAUL ELLIS/AFP/Getty Images/Newscom)

Union called the AIT scan a "virtual strip-search" [82]. In July 2010, the Electronic Privacy Information Center filed a lawsuit to suspend the deployment of AIT systems, pending further review. EPIC called the program "unlawful, invasive, and ineffective," arguing that it violated the Privacy Act, the Religious Freedom Restoration Act, and the Fourth Amendment to the U.S. Constitution [83].

In February 2011, the Transportation Security Administration announced that it was about to begin testing new software on its advanced imaging technology machines that would eliminate passenger-specific images. TSA Administrator John Pistole said that the new system "auto-detects potential threat items and indicates their location on a generic outline of a person" [84].

Summary

It's only natural that people want government to leave them alone, but they also expect government to keep them safe and secure through effective policing and a strong national defense. Frequently, the Constitutional guarantees in the Bill of Rights come into conflict with the desires of law enforcement agencies to gather information that can help them apprehend criminals. Through legislation, administrative policies, and court decisions, the three branches of American government have been engaged in the attempt to find the right balance between competing concerns.

In this chapter, we have looked at the role that federal, state, and local governments have played in protecting and eroding the information privacy of individual citizens. We organized our presentation using the taxonomy of privacy proposed by Daniel Solove, which divides the field into four categories: information collection, information processing, information dissemination, and invasion. We reviewed legislation and administrative policies that have protected the information privacy of individuals by restricting how organizations can collect, process, and disseminate information, as well as limit the extent to which they can intrude into people's daily lives.

We also looked at ways in which governments have promoted public safety and security by collecting, processing, and disseminating personal information and intruding into people's lives.

We surveyed many governmental activities related to information collection. The federal government maintains extensive databases containing a vast amount of information about individual Americans, and from time to time information in these databases has been misused. The government also collects information through overt and covert surveillance.

After the terrorist attacks of September 11, 2001, concerns about individual privacy took a back seat to concerns about national security, and signficant changes occurred in the government's activities related to information collection, information processing, and invasion. The USA PATRIOT Act amended many laws and enhanced the ability of law enforcement agencies to gather information about suspected terrorists and criminals. The National Security Agency acquired records of domestic phone calls from telecommunications companies and performed data mining in an attempt to find calling patterns indicating the presence of terrorist networks. The Transportation Security Administration installed highly intrusive advanced imaging technology scanners at airport security checkpoints.

The Social Security Number is an important identifier in the United States, but its has many flaws. The U.S. Congress passed the REAL ID Act that created a new standard for driver's licenses. They would probably become the most trusted form of identification in the United States, a de facto national identification card. Interestingly, 24 states have opposed the new requirements, and at this point it is unclear whether the national standard will actually go into effect.

Review Questions

1. What are the four categories in Daniel Solove's taxonomy of privacy? Come up with your own examples of activities conducted by government agencies falling into each of these categories.

2. How does the Employee Polygraph Protection Act help job applicants and company employees maintain their privacy? What is the most significant loophole in the Employee Polygraph Protection Act?

3. What is the purpose of the Children's Online Privacy Protection Act?

4. What are the two principal purposes of the Genetic Information Nondiscrimination Act?

5. Give two examples of the Census Bureau illegally revealing census data to other federal agencies.

6. Name two notable successes claimed by the National Crime Information Center.

7. What is the purpose of the OneDOJ database? What are its weaknesses, according to the critics of this database?

8. Which country leads the world in the deployment of closed-circuit television cameras?

9. Provide an example of overt surveillance by a government agency in the United States.

10. Provide two examples of covert surveillance by the U.S. government.

11. What right is guaranteed by the Fourth Amendment to the U.S. Constitution?

12. Why was the U.S. Supreme Court decision in *Nardone v. United States* so important?

13. What was the key ruling of the U.S. Supreme Court in the case of *Weiss v. United States*?

14. How did the decision of the U.S. Supreme Court in the case of *Katz v. United States* change the concept of privacy?

15. How did Operation Shamrock begin? What abuses arose from the continuation of Operation Shamrock?

16. What was the purpose of the Carnivore system?

17. Why did the National Security Agency begin its secret wiretapping program?

18. Why did the TALON database spark controversy?

19. What is a pen register?

20. What is a trap-and-trace device?

21. What is a roving wiretap?

22. What are the implications of the Stored Communication Act for all those who let an Internet service provider handle their email?

23. What are the three most controversial provisions of the USA PATRIOT Act?

24. Why has the expansion in the use of National Security Letters raised privacy concerns?

25. Briefly summarize in your own words the five tenets of the Code of Fair Information Practices.

26. Robert Bellair has said, "The Privacy Act, it turns out, is no protection at all. You can drive a truck through the Privacy Act" [57]. Explain why Bellair and other privacy advocates feel the Privacy Act of 1974 is a weak piece of legislation.

27. The Fair Credit Report Act says that information which may negatively affect an individual's credit rating must be removed after seven years. What are two exceptions to this guideline?

28. How does the Fair and Accurate Credit Transactions Act help consumers verify the accuracy of their credit reports?

29. Summarize the major provisions of the Financial Services Modernization Act.

30. Give two examples of data mining programs run by governments.

31. What are the problems with using the Social Security number as an identification number?

32. Give two arguments in favor of a national identification card for the United States. Give two arguments against creating a national identification card.

33. What are the rights provided by the Family Education Rights and Privacy Act?

34. How does the Video Privacy Protection Act enhance privacy?

35. Describe the privacy protections resulting from the Health Insurance Portability and Accountability Act.

36. What is the purpose of the Freedom of Information Act?

37. Name two important exemptions in the Freedom of Information Act that allow the government to withhold information.

38. Give an example of how information gathered by the E-ZPass system has been used for a purpose other than collecting tolls.

39. How did the Federal Trade Commission reduce unwanted telemarketing?

40. What is the purpose of the CALM Act?

41. Why have federal and state governments passed laws limiting access to cold products containing pseudoephedrine?

42. Why have privacy groups objected to the installation of advanced imaging technology scanners at airport security checkpoints? How has the Transportation Security Administration responded to these objections?

Discussion Questions

43. Florida, Missouri, Ohio, and Oklahoma have passed laws that require lifetime monitoring of some convicted sex offenders after they have been released from prison. The offenders must wear electronic ankle bracelets and stay close to small GPS transmitters, which can be carried on a belt or in a purse. Computers monitor the GPS signals and alert law enforcement officials if the offenders venture too close to a school or other off-limits area. Police interested in the whereabouts of a monitored person can see his location, traveling direction, and speed plotted on a map [85].

    Do these laws represent an unacceptable weakening of personal privacy, or are they sensible public safety measures? Should they be repealed? Should people convicted of other crimes also be monitored for life? Would there be less crime if everyone in society were monitored?

44. Think about what you do when you get up in the morning. How would you act differently if you knew you were being watched? Would you feel uncomfortable? Do you think you would get used to being watched?

45. Discuss these responses to the revelation that telecommunications companies provided domestic phone call records to the National Security Agency [86].

    President George Bush: "Al-Qaeda is our enemy, and we want to know their plans."

    Senator Patrick Leahy of Vermont: "Are you telling me tens of millions of Americans are involved with al-Qaeda?"

    Senator Jon Kyl of Arizona: "We are in a war, and we have got to collect intelligence on the enemy."

    Senator Chuck Grassley of Iowa: "Why are the telephone companies not protecting their customers? They have a social responsibility to people who do business with them to protect our privacy as long as there isn't some suspicion that we're a terrorist or a criminal or something."

46. When asked about Google releasing personal information to law enforcement agencies, Google's CEO Eric Schmidt told CNBC: "If you have something that you don't want anyone to know, maybe you shouldn't be doing it in the first place" [46]. Discuss Mr. Schmidt's perspective.

47. Was the U.S. government's $2 million settlement with Brandon Mayfield reasonable and just?

48. In order to combat the counterfeiting of currency, the U.S. Secret Service convinced several color laser printer manufacturers to add a secret code to every printed page. The code is invisible to the human eye but can be seen under a microscope. When decrypted, it reveals the serial number of the printer and the time and date the page was printed [87].

    By agreeing to secretly insert the codes, did the printer manufacturers violate the privacy rights of their customers?

49. What special responsibilities do computer professionals have with respect to understanding and protecting the privacy rights of their fellow citizens?

In-class Exercises

50. The Code of Fair Information Practices applies only to government databases. Divide the class into two groups to debate the advantages and disadvantages of extending the Code of Fair Information Practices to private databases managed by corporations.

51. A database containing the DNA information of every citizen of a country could be a valuable resource to medical researchers. It could also help police solve crimes. Divide the class into two groups (pro and con) to debate the following proposition: It would be in the best interests of society if the government constructed a DNA database of every resident and made the database available to medical researchers and police agencies.

52. Divide the class into two groups (pro and con) to debate the proposition that every citizen of the United States ought to carry a national identification card.

53. Debate the following proposition: By creating the Threat and Local Observation Notices (TALON) database, which enabled citizens to report on each other's activities, the U.S. government effectively reduced freedom of speech.

Further Reading and Viewing

James Bamford. *The Puzzle Palace: A Report on America's Most Secret Agency*. Penguin Books, New York, NY, 1983.

Maria Bartiromo. "Inside the Mind of Google." *CNBC Video*, February 9, 2010. video.cnbc.com.

Whitfield Diffie and Susan Landau. *Privacy on the Line: The Politics of Wiretapping and Encryption*. The MIT Press, Cambridge, MA, 1998.

Digital Due Process: Modernizing Surveillance Laws for the Internet Age (Web site) digitaldueprocess.org.

Steven L. Nock. *The Costs of Privacy: Surveillance and Reputation in America*. Aldine de Gruyter, New York, NY, 1993.

George Orwell. *1984*. Knopf, New York, NY, 1992.

Priscilla M. Regan. *Legislating Privacy*. The University of North Carolina Press, Chapel Hill, NC, 1995.

References

[1]   Aaron Nicodemus. "Agents' Visit Chills UMass Dartmouth Senior." *The Standard-Times (MA)*, December 20, 2005.

[2]   Jamie Prime. "Privacy vs. Openness." *Quill*, 82(8), October 1994.

[3]   Marisol Bello. "Questions Arise on Monitoring of Sex Offenders." *USA Today*, September 1, 2009. www.usatoday.com.

[4]   "Majority of Americans Support Increased Surveillance, Poll Shows." *The Wall Street Journal*, August 17, 2006.

[5]   Daniel J. Solove. *Understanding Privacy*. Harvard University Press, Cambridge, MA, 2008.

[6]   Department of Health and Human Services, USA. "GINA: The Genetic Information Nondiscrimination Act of 2008: Information for Researchers and Health Care Professionals," April 6, 2009. www.genome.gov.

[7]   Stephanie L. Hitt. "NCIC 2000." *FBI Law Enforcement Bulletin*, 69(7), July 2000.

[8]   Dan Eggen. "Justice Dept. Database Stirs Privacy Fears." *The Washington Post*, December 26, 2006.

[9]   John T. Eberth. "Nation's First Surveillance Cameras Were Installed in Olean." *Olean Times Herald*, October 5, 2008. www.oleantimesherald.com.

[10]   James Vlahos. "Surveillance Society: New High-Tech Cameras Are Watching You." *Popular Mechanics*.

[11]   "Cameras to Catch Terrorists Triple in New York with Bomb Plots," Chris Dolmetsch, www.bloomberg.com, November 13, 2010.

[12]   Jamie Roth. "Bloomberg in London to Study Security System." WABC local news, May 11, 2010. abclocal.go.com/wabc/.

[13]   Jennifer Lee. "Study Questions Whether Cameras Cut Crime," *The New York Times*, March 3, 2009.

[14]   M. Angela Sasse. "Privacy and Security: Not Seeing the Crime for the Cameras?" *Communications of the ACM*, February 2010, pp. 22–25.

[15]   Whitfield Diffie and Susan Landau. *Privacy on the Line: The Politics of Wiretapping and Encryption*. The MIT Press, Cambridge, MA, 1998.

[16]   Priscilla M. Regan. *Legislating Privacy*. The University of North Carolina Press, Chapel Hill, NC, 1995.

[17]   Supreme Court of the United States. *Dissenting Opinion in* Olmstead v. United States, 1928. 277 U.S. 438.

[18]   Supreme Court of the United States. *Katz v. United States*, 1967. 389 U.S. 347.

[19]   James Bamford. *The Puzzle Palace: A Report on America's Most Secret Agency*. Penguin Books, New York, NY, 1983.

[20]   Heinz Tschabitscher. "How Carnivore Email Surveillance Worked." email.about.com.

[21]   Holly E. Ventura, J. Mitchell Miller, and Mathieu Deflem. "Governmentality and the War on Terror: FBI Project Carnivore and the Diffusion of Disciplinary Power." *Critical Criminology* 13(1): 55–70, January 2005.

[22]   U.S. District Court, Central District of California, Western Division. "In the Matter of the Application of the United States of America for an Order Authorizing the Installation of a Pen Register and Trap and Trace Device." Criminal No. 99-2713M, February 4, 2000.

[23]   Kevin Poulsen. "FBI Retires Its Carnivore." *SecurityFocus*, January 14, 2005. www .securityfocus.com.

[24]   James Risen and Eric Lichtblau. "Bush Lets U.S. Spy on Callers without Courts." *The New York Times*, December 16, 2005.

[25]   Charlie Savage and James Risen. "N.S.A. Wiretaps Were Unlawful, U.S. Judge Rules." *The New York Times*, April 1, 2010.

[26]   Lisa Myers, Douglas Pasternak, Rich Gardella and the NBC Investigative Unit. "Is the Pentagon Spying on Americans?" MSNBC.com, December 14, 2005.

[27]   Samantha Henig. "Pentagon Surveillance of Student Groups Extended to Scrutinizing E-Mail." *The Chronicle of Higher Education*, July 21, 2006.

[28]   American Civil Liberties Union. "No Real Threat: The Pentagon's Secret Database on Peaceful Protest." www.aclu.org, January 17, 2007.

[29]   Siobhan Gorman. "Intelligence Policies Shift: Pentagon Spy Chief Rolling Back Some of Rumsfeld's Strategies." *Baltimore Sun*, May 26, 2007.

[30]   Nate Anderson. "US to Shutter DoD TALON Database As It Works on Replacement." *Ars Technica*, August 21, 2007. www.arstechnica.com.

[31]   Orin S. Kerr. "The Case for the Third-Party Doctrine." *Michigan Law Review*, Volume 107, 2009.

[32]   David Kravets. "Yahoo, Feds Battle over E-Mail Privacy." *Threat Level: Privacy, Crime and Security Online*. April 14, 2010. www.wired.com.

[33]   Ryan Singel. "Google, Microsoft Push Feds to Fix Privacy Laws." *Threat Level: Privacy, Crime and Security Online*. March 30, 2010. www.wired.com.

[34]   Nancy Gohring. "FCC Inflates CALEA." *Telephony*, 237(10), September 6, 1999.

[35]   Charlotte Twight. "Conning Congress." *Independent Review*, 6(2), Fall 2001.

[36]   Kirk Laughlin. "A Wounded CALEA Is Shuttled Back to the FCC." *America's Network*, 104(15), October 1, 2000.

[37]   Federal Communications Commission. "FCC Requires Certain Broadband and VoIP Providers to Accommodate Wiretaps," August 5, 2005. www.fcc.gov.

[38]   Charlie Savage. "As Online Communications Stymie Wiretaps, Lawmakers Debate Solutions." *The New York Times*, February 17, 2011.

[39]   "USA Patriot Act: Major Provisions of the 2001 Antiterrorism Law." *Congressional Digest*, 82(4), April 2003.

[40]   Pete Yost. "FBI Access to E-mail, Web Data Raises Privacy Fear." Associated Press, July 30, 2010. seattletimes.nwsource.com.

[41]   American Civil Liberties Union. "With Help of ACLU, Connecticut Library Group Successfully Keeps Patron Records Private." Press Release, June 26, 2006. www.aclu.org.

[42]   American Civil Liberties Union, New York, NY. "PATRIOT Act Fears Are Stifling Free Speech, ACLU Says in Challenge to Law," November 11, 2003. www.aclu.org.

[43]   American Library Association. "Resolution on the USA PATRIOT Act and Related Measures That Infringe on the Rights of Library Users," January 29, 2003. 2002–2003 CD #20.1, 2003 ALA Midwinter Meeting. www.ala.org.

[44]   Bill of Rights Defense Committee (Web site). Accessed September 2, 2011. www.bordc.org.

[45]   Bob Garfield. "Subpoenas ane Online Service Providers." *On the Media*, January 21, 2011. www.onthemedia.org.

[46]   Cade Metz. "Google Chief: Only Miscreants Worry about Net Privacy." *The Register*, December 7, 2009. www.theregister.co.uk.

[47]   Tom Ridge. "Using the PATRIOT Act to Fight Terrorism." *Congressional Digest*, pages 266–268, November 2004.

[48]   Ben Jacklet and Todd Murphy. "Now Free, Attorney Brandon Mayfield Turns Furious." *Washington Report on Middle East Affairs*, 23(6), July/August 2004.

[49]   Dan Eggen. "Flawed FBI Probe of Bombing Used a Search Warrant." *The Washington Post*, April 7, 2005.

[50]   Eric Lichtblau. "U.S. Will Pay $2 Million to Lawyer Wrongly Jailed." *The New York Times*, November 30, 2006. www.localnewsdaily.com.

[51]   Andrew Murr, Michael Isikoff, Eric Pape, and Mike Elkin. "The Wrong Man." *Newsweek*, 143(23), June 7, 2004.

[52]   Jim Abrams. "Patriot Act Extension Signed by Obama." Associated Press, May 27, 2011. www.huffingtonpost.com.

[53]   Carl Kaysen. "Data Banks and Dossiers." *The Public Interest*, Spring 1967, pp. 52–60.

[54]   G. Russell Pipe. "Privacy: Establishing Restrictions on Government Inquiry." *The American University Law Review*, Vol. 18, 1969, pp. 516–551.

[55]   U.S. Department of Health, Education and Welfare. *Secretary's Advisory Committee of Automated Personal Data Systems, Records, Computers, and the Rights of Citizens*, 1973.

[56] Robert Gellman. "Fair Information Practices: A Basic History." July 15, 2011. bobgellman.com.

[57] William Petrocelli. *Low Profile: How to Avoid the Privacy Invaders*. McGraw-Hill, New York, NY, 1981.

[58] Privacy Rights Clearinghouse. "Fact Sheet 24: Protecting Financial Privacy," July 14, 2005. www.privacyrights.org.

[59] Richard Peŕez-Peña. "An Early Warning System for Diseases in New York." *NYTimes.com*, April 4, 2003.

[60] Leslie Cauley. "NSA Has Massive Database of Americans' Phone Calls." *USA Today*, May 11, 2006.

[61] Wayne Rash. "Federal Court Finds NSA Wiretaps Unconstitutional." *eWeek.com*, August 18, 2006. www.eweek.com.

[62] Social Security Administration, USA. "A Brief History of Social Security," August 2000.

[63] Social Security Administration, USA. "Social Security Cards Issued by Woolworth." www.ssa.gov/history/ssn/misused.html.

[64] Office of Inspector General, Department of Health and Human Services, USA. "Extent of Social Security Number Discrepancies," January 1990. OAI-06-89-01120.

[65] Peter G. Neumann and Lauren Weinstein. "Risks of National Identity Cards." *Communications of the ACM*, page 176, December 2001.

[66] Richard Turner. Letter to the editor. *The Times (London)*, September 7, 2001.

[67] Declan McCullagh. FAQ: How Real ID will affect you. *The New York Times*, May 6, 2005.

[68] National Conference of State Legislatures. "REAL ID Act of 2005 Driver's License Title Summary" 2007. www.ncsl.org

[69] Dennis Bailey. "Debating Barry Steinhardt's UNREAL ID," August 7, 2005. www.opensocietyparadox.com.

[70] Joseph Menn. "Federal ID Act May Be Flawed." *The Los Angeles Times*, May 31, 2005.

[71] Declan McCullagh. "Homeland Security Bows to Real ID Outcry." *Privacy Inc.*, March 5, 2011. news.cnet.com.

[72] Department of Health and Human Services, USA. "Protecting the Privacy of Patients' Health Information," April 14, 2003. www.hhs.gov/news.

[73] New York State Department of Transportation. "NYSDOT Announces Travel Time Signs in Staten Island." Press Release, July 10, 2007. www.nysdot.gov.

[74] Chris Newmarker. "E-ZPass Records Out Cheaters in Divorce Court." Associated Press, August 10, 2007. www.msnbc.com.

[75] Humphrey Taylor. "Most People Are 'Privacy Pragmatists' Who, While Concerned About Privacy, Will Sometimes Trade It Off for Other Benefits." HarrisInteractive, March 19, 2003. The Harris Poll #17.

[76] James Toedtman. "Court Unblocks Do Not Call Registry in Latest Ruling." *Sun-Sentinel (Fort Lauderdale, FL)*, October 8, 2003.

[77] Heather Fleming Phillips. "Consumers Can Thank Do-Not-Underestimate FTC Chairman for Do-Not-Call Peace." *San Jose (CA) Mercury News*, January 2, 2004.

[78] Chris Foresman. "CALM Act Passed, Will Quiet Loud TV Commercials within a Year." *Ars Technica*, December 2, 2010. www.arstechnica.com.

[79]   Ginger D. Richardson. "Revealing X-ray Machine Set to Scan Sky Harbor Flyers." *The Arizona Republic*, February 23, 2007. www.azcentral.com/arizonarepublic.

[80]   *Statement of John S. Pistole, Administrator, Transportation Security Administration, U.S. Department of Homeland Security, Before the United States House of Representatives, Committee on Homeland Security, Subcommittee on Transportation Security*, June 2, 2011. www.tsa.gov.

[81]   Melissa Cheung. "New Airport X-Ray Too Revealing?" CBS News, February 11, 2009. www.cbsnews.com.

[82]   Paul Giblin and Eric Lipton. "New Airport X-Rays Scan Bodies, Not Just Bags." *The New York Times*, February 24, 2007.

[83]   Electronic Privacy Information Center. "Whole Body Imaging Technology and Body Scanners ('Backscatter' X-Ray and Millimeter Wave Screening)" (web site), accessed July 9, 2011. epic.org/privacy/airtravel/backscatter/.

[84]   Transportation Security Administration. "TSA Begins Testing New Advanced Imaging Technology Software." Press Release, February 1, 2011.

[85]   David A. Lieb. "States Move on Sex Offender GPS Tracking." *Associated Press*, July 30, 2005.

[86]   Susan Page. "NSA Secret Database Report Triggers Fierce Debate in Washington." *USA Today*, May 11, 2006.

[87]   John P. Mello Jr. "Codes Make Printers Stool Pigeons." *E-Commerce Times*, October 18, 2005. www.ecommercetimes.com.

Jerry Berman

Jerry Berman is the founder and Chairman of the Board of Directors of the Center for Democracy and Technology (CDT). CDT is a Washington, D.C.–based Internet public policy organization founded in December 1994. CDT plays a leading role in free speech, privacy, Internet governance, and architecture issues affecting democracy and civil liberties on the global Internet. Mr. Berman has written widely on Internet and civil liberties issues, and often appears in print and television media. He has testified before the U.S. Congress on Internet policy and civil liberties issues.

Prior to founding the Center for Democracy and Technology, Mr. Berman was Director of the Electronic Frontier Foundation. From 1978–1988, Mr. Berman was Chief Legislative Counsel at the ACLU and founder and director of ACLU Projects on Privacy and Information Technology. Mr. Berman received his BA, MA, and LLB from the University of California, Berkeley.

How did you get involved in Internet law?

When I worked on civil liberties and privacy at the ACLU in the early 1980s, the prevailing view was computer databases and the rise of the computer state posed a major threat to privacy. This is true. But at the same time there was the beginning of the use of the computer as a communications device, and the start of data networks for communications purposes—the beginnings of the Internet. While recognizing the threat to privacy, I saw that the Internet had the potential to facilitate and broaden First Amendment speech.

In many ways, my colleagues and I have been involved in trying to frame the law and to define privacy, free speech, and how the Internet is governed. We're trying to sort out the "constitution" for this new social space. By analogy, the Internet business community wants to make sure there's a "commerce clause" to encourage robust commercial transactions over the Internet. We agree with that, but also see the need for a "bill of rights" to protect speech, privacy, and other democratic values. We have had some successes, but the work is very much in progress.

The Internet is a more powerful communication medium than newspapers or television, because it allows everyone with an Internet connection to express their views. How can the Internet be anything but democratic?

Like any other technology, the Internet can be regulated. Other countries are exercising considerable control over what ISPs can connect to and what can reside on a server. Even a well-intentioned Congress attempting to protect intellectual property to reduce theft of music and movies could mandate technological changes to computers that make it difficult to use the computer in an open, interconnected way. So one way the Internet can be less than democratic is from bad laws and bad policy.

Another threat is from bad actors provoking bad law. Hackers, people stealing music, using spyware, and engaging in online fraud can provoke policy responses that may have the unintended consequence of undermining the openness of the Internet. We're seeing this now in legitimate efforts to combat spam, spyware, and piracy. We need appropriate laws which combat these harms without harming the openness of the Net. Finding the right solutions is what CDT is about.

One of the great challenges is that given the freedom to connect and communicate that everyone has on the Internet, there is a corollary concept of responsibility. Unless there are shared ethics that respect property, privacy, pluralism, diversity, and the rule of law, the Internet will never realize its potential.

Responding to public pressure, the U.S. Congress passed the Communications Decency Act to restrict access of children to sexually explicit materials on the Web. Why did you organize a legal challenge to the CDA?

In enacting the CDA over our objections, Congress attempted to treat the Internet the same way as other broadcast mass media (TV, radio). The first filed challenge to the CDA, *ACLU v. Reno*, was designed to persuade the courts that if you restrict speech for children, you also necessarily restrict adults' free-speech rights, because the definition of indecency covers Constitutionally protected speech for adults. If ISPs had to block all indecent content for children, that content would not reach adults who are entitled to it, because adults and children are all on the same Internet network.

We filed a second challenge to the CDA, and eventually the ACLU suit and the CDT suit were joined and argued together. CDT brought together a broad coalition of Internet technology companies, news organizations, and librarians to educate the courts that the Internet was architecturally different from broadcast media. Traditional media is a one-to-many [communication] and the Internet is a many-to-many communication, much like print. It was also critical to explain that the Internet is a global medium: it isn't effective to censor speech in the U.S. if it's also available on the Internet from outside the U.S. It is impossible for ISPs to prevent content flowing from sources they do not control, and any ISP censorship would violate Constitutional rights. The architecture of the Internet leads to different analysis and different policy solutions to both protect free speech and protect children from inappropriate content. The lawyers for our coalition argued the case in the Supreme Court on behalf of all the plaintiffs and made the case for user control and user empowerment. The only effective way to deal with unwanted content is for parents and other users (rather than the government) to voluntarily employ available filtering tools and parental controls offered by ISPs and other vendors.

In issues of Constitutionally protected speech, the courts seek to determine if Congress has chosen the least restrictive means for achieving their public purpose. We were able to show that blocking content at the provider end is neither effective nor the least restrictive means for protecting children from inappropriate content. Voluntary filtering is a less restrictive means because it allows users to decide what comes into their homes and, given the global nature of the Internet, gives them the most effective means to do that.

Should an ordinary American citizen's Web site enjoy the same Constitutional protections as The New York Times?

On the Internet everyone can be publishers. And if they're holding themselves out as publishers, they have the same credentials as *The New York Times*, since no one's handing out credentials on the Internet. The Supreme Court heard the Communications Decency Act (CDA) challenge and ruled that the Internet communicator enjoys the maximum protection afforded under the First Amendment. Like the print media, the Internet is not subject to equal time, to the fairness doctrine, or various spectrum allocations. The whole technology of the Internet and the ability of anyone to be a publisher suggests the Internet publisher should, if anything, enjoy greater protection than *The New York Times*. For example, if a newspaper libels someone with false charges, it may require a lawsuit to restore a reputation. On the Internet, anyone can answer back in the blogosphere and reputations are often quickly restored. Thus Courts may narrow the scope of libel suits when the Internet is concerned in favor of more robust debate and "give and take" on the Internet.

Why should a person who has committed no crime be concerned about electronic information gathering and data mining by government agencies?

These databases contain vast amounts of information on all of us, including very personal information—our medical histories, financial transactions, what we purchase, and what we read. Under our concept of privacy, people who have done nothing wrong should have every expectation that the government is not viewing, collecting, or analyzing information about them. So asking "Why should I worry if I have nothing to hide?" is the wrong formulation. The question should be "Since I have done nothing wrong, why should the government be investigating me?"

The government can look at records that pertain to a suspected terrorist. Yet with data mining, the government may have no articulable suspicion pointing at anyone, but simply mines personal data from airlines, banks, and commercial entities to look at patterns of behavior that might indicate someone may be a terrorist, is associated with a terrorist, knows a terrorist, or is engaged in a behavior that may fit a pattern that the government thinks applies to terrorists. These types of data mining and data analysis can result in significant false positives—innocent people get caught up in investigations— and this can have consequences. First, just being investigated can be an intrusion into privacy. Second, consequences flow from fitting a pattern—you may be denied the right to get on a plane or be passed over for employment because you lived in an apartment building at the same time as a tenant with the same name as a terrorist's.

Privacy advocates argue that the government needs to have an articulable reason to collect or analyze personal information: the government should need a court order from a judge and should show why they believe a data mining project is likely to result in identifying suspected or potential terrorists. We do need to realize the government has almost *carte blanche* to conduct these investigations because they have significant authority under current law to engage in data mining exercises. There are very few privacy protections under the Constitution or statutes pertaining to these vast databases of personal information. We need stronger privacy laws to deal with data mining.

CHAPTER

7 Computer and Network Security

A ship in harbor is safe, but that's not what ships are for.

—JOHN SHEDD

7.1 Introduction

THE CONFICKER WORM HAS INFECTED MILLIONS OF WINDOWS COMPUTERS. Is your PC one of them? You can click on a link from the home page of the Conficker Working Group (www.confickerworkinggroup.org) to find out.

Do you ever go to a coffee shop and use its open wireless network to surf the Web? Did you know freely available software gives any nearby computer user the ability to break into the accounts of people accessing Web sites through password-free wireless networks?

In the movie *Live Free or Die Hard*, a terrorist organization hacks into a variety of computer and communication systems to seize control of traffic lights, natural gas pipelines, and electrical power grids. Are such episodes purely the stuff of Hollywood fiction, or could they really happen?

Millions of people use computers and the Internet to send and receive email, access bank accounts, purchase goods and services, and keep track of personal information, making the security of these systems an important issue. Malicious software can enter computers in a variety of ways. Once active, these programs can steal personal information, destroy files, disrupt industrial processes, and launch attacks on financial systems, supporting criminal enterprises and politically motivated attacks on corporations and governments around the world.

This chapter focuses on threats to computer and network security. We will begin our survey with examples of individuals using cunning or skill to gain unauthorized access into computer systems.

7.2 Hacking

7.2.1 Hackers, Past and Present

Today, people associate the word "hacking" with computers, but it didn't start out that way. In its original meaning, a **hacker** is an explorer, a risk taker, someone who is trying to make a system do something it has never done before. Hackers in this sense of the word abounded at MIT's Tech Model Railroad Club in the 1950s and 1960s. The Club constructed and continuously improved an enormous HO-scale model train layout. Members of the Signals and Power Subcommittee built an elaborate electronic switching system to control the movement of the trains. Wearing chino pants, short-sleeved shirts, and pocket protectors, the most dedicated members would drink vast quantities of Coca-Cola and stay up all night to improve the system. To them, a "hack" was a newly constructed piece of equipment that not only served a useful purpose, but also demonstrated its creator's technical virtuosity. Calling someone a hacker was a sign of respect; hackers wore the label with pride.

In 1959, after taking a newly created course in computer programming, some of the hackers shifted their attention from model trains to electronic computers [1]. The term hacker came to mean a "person who delights in having an intimate undertanding of the internal workings of a system, computers and networks in particular" [2].

In the 1983 movie *WarGames*, a teenager breaks into a military computer and nearly causes a nuclear Armageddon. After seeing the movie, a lot of teenagers were excited at the thought that they could prowl cyberspace with a home computer and a modem. A few of them became highly proficient at breaking into government and corporate computer networks. These actions helped change the everyday meaning of the word "hacker."

Today, hackers are people who gain unauthorized access to computers and computer networks. An example of this use of the word is a story in *Computerworld* describing how hackers broke into the Web site of *USA Today* on July 11, 2002, and inserted fabricated news stories [3].

Typically, you need a login name and password to access a computer system. Sometimes a hacker can guess a valid login name/password combination, particularly when system administrators allow users to choose short passwords or passwords that appear in a dictionary.

Three other low-tech techniques for obtaining login names and passwords are eavesdropping, dumpster diving, and social engineering. Eavesdropping, such as simply looking over the shoulder of a legitimate computer user to learn his login name and password, is a common way that hackers gain access to computers. **Dumpster diving** means looking through garbage for interesting bits of information. Companies typically do not put a fence around their dumpsters. In midnight rummaging sessions hackers have found user manuals, phone numbers, login names, and passwords. **Social engineering** refers to the manipulation of a person inside the organization to gain access to confidential information. Social engineering is easier in large organizations where people do not know each other very well. For example, a hacker may identify a system administrator and call that person, pretending to be the supervisor of his supervisor and demanding to know why he can't access a particular machine. In this situation, a cowed system administrator, eager to please his boss's boss, may be talked into revealing or resetting a password [4].

7.2.2 Penalties for Hacking

Under U.S. law, the maximum penalties for hacking are severe. The Computer Fraud and Abuse Act criminalizes a wide variety of hacker-related activities, including:

- Transmitting code (such as a virus or worm) that causes damage to a computer system
- Accessing without authorization any computer connected to the Internet, *even if no files are examined, changed, or copied*
- Transmitting classified government information
- Trafficking in computer passwords
- Computer fraud
- Computer extortion

The maximum penalty imposed for violating the Computer Fraud and Abuse Act is 20 years in prison and a $250,000 fine.

Another federal statute related to computer hacking is the Electronic Communications Privacy Act. This law makes it illegal to intercept telephone conversations, email, or any other data transmissions. It also makes it a crime to access stored email messages without authorization.

The use of the Internet to commit fraud or transmit funds can be prosecuted under the Wire Fraud Act and/or the National Stolen Property Act. Adopting the identity of another person to carry out an illegal activity is a violation of the Identity Theft and Assumption Deterrence Act.

7.2.3 Selected Hacking Incidents

Despite potentially severe penalties for convicted hackers, computer systems continue to be compromised by outsiders. Many break-ins are orchestrated by organized groups with a high degree of expertise, but others are committed by solo hackers who exploit a security weakness.

In 2003, a hacker broke into computers at the University of Kansas and copied the personal files of 1,450 foreign students. The files contained names, Social Security numbers, passport numbers, countries of origin, and birthdates. The University of Kansas had collected the information in one place in order to comply with a Patriot Act requirement that it report the information to the Immigration and Naturalization Service [5]. In a similar incident two years later, an intruder broke into a University of Nevada, Las Vegas computer containing personal information on 5,000 foreign students [6].

In March 2005, someone discovered a security flaw in the online-admissions software produced by ApplyYourself and used by six business schools. The discoverer posted instructions on a *Business Week* online forum explaining how business school applicants could circumvent the software security system and take a look at the status of their applications. It took ApplyYourself only nine hours to fix the flaw, but in the interim period hundreds of eager applicants had exploited the bug and peeked at their files. A week later, Carnegie Mellon University, Harvard University, and the Massachusetts Institute of Technology announced that they would not admit any of the applicants who had accessed their computer systems without authorization [7].

7.2.4 Case Study: Firesheep

Only a small fraction of the information transported by the Internet is encrypted; everything else is sent "in the clear" using the HyperText Transport Protocol (HTTP). Encrypting everything would make Internet communications slower and more expensive, which is why most Web sites use encryption only when communicating the most sensitive information, such as user names, passwords, and credit card numbers. You can tell when a Web site is encrypting the communication because the start of the address in the Web browser is "https://" (meaning secure HyperText Transport Protocol).

The widespread use of WiFi to connect to the Internet has exposed a vulnerability caused by Internet packets being sent in the clear. A WiFi network uses radio signals to communicate between devices. If the wireless access point is not using encryption, it's easy for devices within range to snoop on the network traffic. (Encryption is the process of protecting information by transforming it into a form that cannot be understood by anyone who does not possess the key; i.e., the means of reversing the process and recreating the original information.)

Sidejacking is the hijacking of an open Web session by the capturing of a user's cookie, giving the attacker the same privileges as the user on that website. Ecommerce Web sites typically use encryption to protect the user name and password people provide when logging in, but they do not encrypt the cookie that the Web browser sends to the user to continue the session. Sidejacking is possible on unencrypted wireless networks because another device on the wireless network can "hear" the cookie being transmitted from the Web site back to the user's computer. Even though the Internet security community has known and complained about the sidejacking vulnerabilty for years, ecommerce Web sites did not change their practices.

On October 24, 2010, Eric Butler released an extension to the Firefox browser called Firesheep. Firesheep makes it easy for a Firefox user to sidejack open Web sessions. The user starts the Firefox browswer, connects to an open WiFi network, and clicks on a button called "Start Capturing." When someone using the network visits an insecure Web site that Firesheep knows about, the user's name and photo are displayed in a sidebar, along with the name of the Web site he is connected to, such as Amazon, Facebook, or Twitter. By double-clicking on the photo, the attacker becomes logged in as that user on that Web site and is able to do the same things that the legitimate user is able to do, such as post status messages and purchase products.

Butler released Firesheep as free, open source software for Mac OS X and Windows. He wrote: "Websites have a responsibility to protect the people who depend on their services. They've been ignoring this responsibility for too long, and it's time for everyone to demand a more secure web. My hope is that Firesheep will help the users win" [8].

The Firesheep extension was downloaded more than 500,000 times in its first week of availability, and it attracted a great deal of media attention [9]. The typical story warned social network users about the dangers of using unencrypted wireless public networks and criticized the social network companies for not providing more security [10, 11, 12, 13].

Responding to criticism for providing a tool that makes it easy for ordinary computer users perform sidejacking, Butler wrote: "The attack that Firesheep demonstrates is easy to do using tools that have been available for years. Criminals already knew this, and I reject the notion that something like Firesheep turns otherwise innocent people evil" [14].

Three months after Butler released Firesheep, Facebook made the following announcement:

> Starting today we'll provide you with the ability to experience Facebook entirely over HTTPS. You should consider enabling this option if you frequently use Facebook from public Internet access points found at coffee shops, airports, libraries or schools. The option will exist as part of our advanced security features, which you can find in the "Account Security" section of the Account Settings page. [15]

In March 2011, Twitter announced it was offering an "Always use HTTPS" option [16].

ETHICAL EVALUATION

We begin by evaluating Butler's action from a utilitarian point of view. The release of Firesheep led the media to focus on the risks associated with the use of Web sites from unsecured wireless networks, and a few months later Facebook and Twitter made their Web sites more secure. There continues to be strong pressure for other Web services to follow suit. These are tremendous benefits for everyone who accesses the Web at a public Internet access point without encryption.

Butler is right when he predicted that Firesheep would not turn people into criminals. Even though half a million people downloaded Firesheep in the first week, there is no evidence of a big increase in identity theft or even malicious pranks. The harms caused by Firesheep appear to be minimal. Because the release of Firesheep caused great benefits and negligible harm, we conclude it was a good action from a utilitarian point of view.

Now let's look at this situation from a Kantian point of view. To begin with, accessing someone else's user account is an invasion of that person's privacy and is wrong. Butler clearly agrees with this perspective because he refers to people who sidejack accounts as "evil." Butler's goal was to pressure Facebook, Twitter, Amazon, and other Web sites to adopt proper security measures to protect their users. He saw the best way to achieve this end was to release a tool that would bring to light a well-known security problem that had not gotten sufficient attention.

Criminals already knew how to sidejack Web sessions before Butler created Firesheep. What Firesheep did was make sidejacking so simple that even ordinary computer users could do it. More than a half million copies of Firesheep were downloaded in the first week, and undoubtedly some of these people actually used the software to sidejack Web sessions, which is wrong. It is disingenuous for Butler to "reject the notion that something like Firesheep turns otherwise innocent people evil." He provided a tool that made it much simpler for people to do something that is wrong, and therefore he has some moral accountability for the misdeeds of the people who downloaded Firesheep.

Ultimately, Butler was willing to tolerate a short-term increase in privacy violations in the hope that users would pressure Facebook, Twitter, and other sites to improve their security, which would result in fewer privacy violations in the long term. In other words, he was willing to use the victims of Firesheep as a means to his end. From a Kantian perspective, it was wrong for Butler to release Firesheep to the public.

There are other ways Butler could have achieved his goal without using other people. For example, he could have gone on a popular television show and hacked into the host's Facebook page, generating a great amount of publicity without having to release the software [17].

7.3 Malware

The Firesheep extension to the Firefox browser highlights a significant security weakness of unencrypted WiFi networks. Computers have security weaknesses, too, and there are a variety of ways in which malicious software, or **malware**, can become active on your computer. If you are lucky, these programs will do nothing other than consume a little CPU time and some disk space. If you are not so lucky, they may destroy valuable data stored in your computer's file system. An invading program may even allow outsiders to seize control of your computer. Once this happens, they may use your computer as a depository for stolen credit card information, a Web server dishing out pornographic images, or a launch pad for spam or a denial-of-service attack on a corporate or government server.

7.3.1 Viruses and Worms

Viruses represent one way in which malicious code can get into a computer. A **virus** is a piece of self-replicating code embedded within another program called the **host** [18]. Figure 7.1 illustrates how a virus replicates within a computer. When a user executes a host program infected with a virus, the virus code executes first. The virus finds another

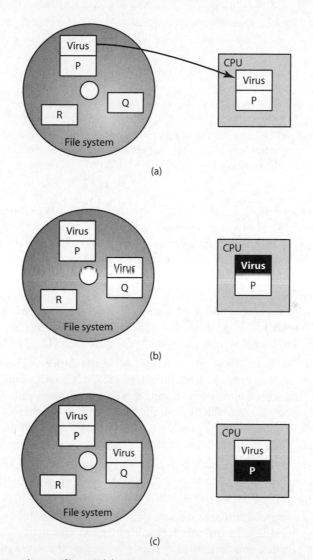

(a)

(b)

(c)

FIGURE 7.1 How a virus replicates. (a) A computer user executes program P, which is infected with a virus. (b) The virus code begins to execute. It finds another executable program Q and creates a new version of Q infected with the virus. (c) The virus passes control to program P. The user, who expected program P to execute, suspects nothing.

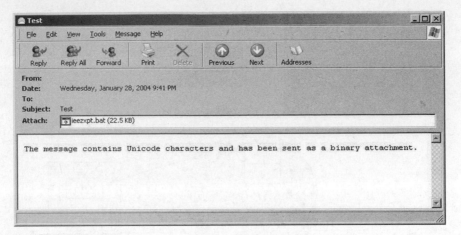

FIGURE 7.2 The attachment to this email message probably contains a virus. (The author didn't open it to find out.) (Screenshot by Microsoft. Copyright © 2011 by Microsoft Corporation. Reprinted with permission.)

executable program stored in the computer's file system and replaces the program with a virus-infected program. After doing this, the virus allows the host program to execute, which is what the user expected to happen. If the virus does its work quickly enough, the user may be unaware of the presence of the virus.

Because a virus is attached to a host program, you may find viruses anywhere you can find program files: hard disks, thumb drives, CD-ROMs, email attachments, and so on. Viruses can be spread from machine to machine via thumb drives or CDs. They may also be passed when a person downloads a file from the Internet. Sometimes viruses are attached to free computer games that people download and install on their computers.

Today, many viruses are spread via email attachments (Figure 7.2). We are all familiar with ordinary attachments such as photos, but attachments may also be executable programs or word processing documents or spreadsheets containing macros, which are small pieces of executable code. If the user opens an attachment containing a virus, the virus takes control of the computer, reads the user's email address book, and uses these addresses to send virus-contaminated emails to others, as illustrated in Figure 7.3.

Some viruses are fairly innocent; they simply replicate. These viruses occupy disk space and consume CPU time, but the harm they do is relatively minor. Other viruses are malicious and can cause significant damage to a person's file system.

Commercial antivirus software packages allow computer users to detect and destroy viruses lurking on their computers. To be most effective, users must keep them up-to-date by downloading patterns corresponding to the latest viruses from the vendor's Web site. Unfortunately, many people are negligent about keeping their virus protection software up-to-date. According to the statistics office of the European Union, a survey of Internet users revealed that 31 percent of them had experienced a computer virus in the previous twelve months that had resulted in a loss of information or time, even though

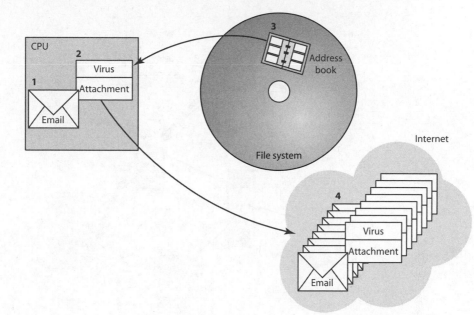

FIGURE 7.3 How an email virus spreads. A computer user reads an email with an attachment (1). The user opens the attachment, which contains a virus (2). The virus reads the user's email address book (3). The virus sends emails with virus-containing attachments (4).

84 percent of them said that their computer was running antivirus software [19]. That means they were not keeping their virus protection current.

To make matters worse, criminals have found a way to profit from people's concern about virses and their eagerness to install antivirus software when they believe their systems are infected. In July 2011, more than two million PCs were infected with a fake antivirus application that actually routed traffic destined for Google through intermediate servers controlled by the attacker. The purpose of the malware appeared to be to generate "click through" income for the hackers by directing people to Web sites containing fake security programs [20].

A **worm** is a self-contained program that spreads through a computer network by exploiting security holes in the computers connected to the network (Figure 7.4). The technical term "worm" comes from *The Shockwave Rider*, a 1975 science fiction novel written by John Brunner [21].

7.3.2 The Internet Worm

The most famous worm of all time is also the first one to get the attention of the mainstream media, which is why it is popularly known as the Internet worm, even though

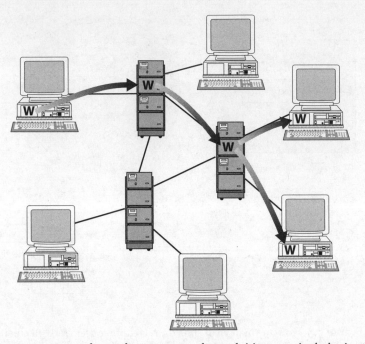

Figure 7.4 A worm spreads to other computers by exploiting security holes in computer networks.

many other worms have been created that propagate through the Internet. The primary source for this narrative is the excellent biography of Robert Morris in *Cyberpunk: Outlaws and Hackers on the Computer Frontier*, written by Katie Hafner and John Markoff [22].

BACKGROUND OF ROBERT TAPPAN MORRIS, JR

Robert Tappan Morris, Jr., began learning about the Unix operating system when he was still in junior high school. His father was a computer security researcher at Bell Labs, and young Morris was given an account on a Bell Labs computer that he could access from a teletype at home. It didn't take him long to discover security holes in Unix. In a 1982 interview with Gina Kolata, a writer for *Smithsonian* magazine, Morris admitted he had broken into networked computers and read other people's email. "I never told myself that there was nothing wrong with what I was doing," he said, but he acknowledged that he found breaking into systems challenging and exciting, and he admitted that he continued to do it.

As an undergraduate at Harvard, Morris majored in computer science. He quickly gained a reputation for being the computer lab's Unix expert. After his freshman year, Morris worked at Bell Labs. The result of his work was a technical paper describing a security hole in Berkeley Unix.

While at Harvard, Morris was responsible for several computer pranks. In one of them, he installed a program that required people logging in to answer a question posed by "the Oracle" and then ask the Oracle another question. (The Oracle program worked by passing questions and answers among people trying to log in.)

DESIGNING THE WORM

Morris entered the graduate program in computer science at Cornell University in the fall of 1988. He became intrigued with the idea of creating a computer worm that would exploit bugs he had found in three Unix applications: ftp, sendmail, and fingerd. His "wish list" for the worm had about two dozen goals, including:

- Infect three machines per local area network.
- Only consume CPU cycles if the machines are idle.
- Avoid slow machines.
- Break passwords in order to spread to other computers.

The goal of the worm was to infect as many computers as possible. It would not destroy or corrupt data files on the machines it infected.

LAUNCHING THE WORM

On November 2, 1988, Morris learned that a fix for the ftp bug had been posted to the Internet, meaning his worm program could no longer take advantage of that security hole. However, nobody had posted fixes to the other two bugs Morris knew about. After making some last-minute changes to the worm program, he logged in to a computer at the MIT Artificial Intelligence Lab and launched the worm at about 7:30 p.m.

The worm quickly spread to thousands of computers at military installations, medical research facilities, and universities. Unfortunately, due to several bugs in the worm's programming, computers became infected with hundreds of copies of the worm, causing them to crash every few minutes or become practically unresponsive to the programs of legitimate users.

Morris contacted friends at Harvard to discuss what ought to be done next. They agreed that Andy Sudduth would anonymously post a message to the Internet. Sudduth's message is below.[1] Harvard's computers were not affected (the security holes had already been patched), and you can tell from the last sentence that Sudduth was having a hard time believing Morris's story:

```
A Possible virus report:

There may be a virus loose on the internet.
Here is the gist of a message I got:

I'm sorry.
```

```
Here are some steps to prevent further
transmission:

1) don't run finger, or fix it to not
overrun its stack when reading arguments.
2) recompile sendmail w/o DEBUG defined
3) don't run rexed

Hope this helps, but more, I hope it is a hoax.
```

Sudduth's email was supposed to get routed through a computer at Brown University. However, computers at Brown were already infected with the worm and did not have spare cycles to route the message. Also, the email did not have a subject line, which made it less likely to be read during a crisis. The result is that the message was read too late to be of any help to those fighting the worm.

System administrators at various universities worked frantically to stop the spread of the worm. Within a day they had examined the worm's code, discovered the bugs in sendmail and fingerd, and published fixes to the Internet community. No one knows exactly how many computers were infected by the worm, but it did make a significant number of systems unusable for a day or two [23].

After some sleuthing by reporter John Markoff, *The New York Times* named Robert Tappan Morris, Jr., as the author of the worm. Morris was suspended from Cornell University. A year later, he was the first person to receive a felony conviction under the U.S. Computer Fraud and Abuse Act. He was sentenced to 3 years' probation, 400 hours of community service, and fined $10,000. His legal fees and fines exceeded $150,000.

ETHICAL EVALUATION

Was Robert Morris, Jr., wrong to unleash the Internet Worm?

A Kantian evaluation must focus on Morris's will. Did Morris have good will? His stated goal was to see how many Internet computers he could infect with the worm. While Morris did not want to crash these computers or destroy any data stored on them, his motivation was fundamentally selfish: he wanted the thrill of seeing his creation running on thousands of computers. He used others because he gained access to their machines without their permission. There is also evidence Morris knew he was using others: he took measures designed to prevent people from discovering that he was the author of the worm. From a Kantian point of view, Morris's action was wrong.

From a social contract point of view, Morris's action was also wrong. He violated the property rights of the individuals and organizations whose computers were infected by the worm. They had the right to determine who would use their computers, and they attempted to enforce this right by requiring people to identify themselves by user name and password. Morris took advantage of security holes in these computers to gain unauthorized access to them. When his worm caused these computers to become unresponsive or crash, he denied access to the legitimate users of these computers.

A utilitarian evaluation of the case focuses on the benefits and harms resulting from the spread of the worm. The principal benefit of the Internet Worm was that organizations managing these Unix computers discovered there were two significant security holes in their systems. They received the instructions they needed to patch these holes before a truly malicious intruder took advantage of them to enter their systems and do a lot of damage to their data. Of course, Morris could have produced the same beneficial result simply by contacting the system administrators at UC Berkeley and informing them of the security holes he had found.

The Internet Worm had numerous harmful consequences. A large amount of time was spent by system administrators as they defended their machines from further attacks, tracked down the problem, installed patches, and brought machines back on line. There was a disruption in email and file exchange traffic caused by computers being taken off the network. About 6,000 computers were unavailable for a day or two. During this time, many thousands of people were less productive than they could have been had the systems been up and running. Morris himself was harmed by his actions. He was suspended from Cornell and sentenced to three years of probation and 400 hours of community service. His fines and legal fees exceeded $150,000. From a utilitarian viewpoint, Morris was wrong to have released the Internet Worm.

In conclusion, Morris may not have been acting maliciously, but he was acting selfishly. If he had wanted to experiment with worms, he probably could have gotten permission to try out his creations on a local area network detached from the Internet, so that even if his worm had multiplied out of control, there would have been no fallout to the rest of the computer community. Instead, he chose to use the entire Internet as his experimental laboratory, inconveniencing thousands of people.

7.3.3 Other Notable Worms

SASSER

The Sasser worm, launched in April 2004, exploited a previously identified security weakness with PCs running the Windows operating system. Computers with up-to-date software were safe from the worm, but it infected about 18 million computers worldwide nonetheless. The effects of the worm were relatively benign; infected computers simply shut themselves down shortly after booting. Still, the worm made millions of computers unusable and disrupted operations at Delta Airlines, the European Commission, Australian railroads, and the British coast guard [24].

After Microsoft offered a €250,000 award, a fellow student pointed the finger at German teenager Sven Jaschan, who confessed to the crime and then began working for German computer security firm Securepoint. Because he was 17 when he released the worm, Jaschan was tried in a juvenile court, which sentenced him to one-and-a-half years' probation and 30 hours of community service [24, 25, 26].

INSTANT MESSAGING WORMS

Two early worms to strike instant messaging systems were Choke and Hello, which appeared in 2001. Worms were less devastating back then, because only about 141 million people used instant messaging. Today, more than 800 million people rely on instant messaging, so the impact of worms can be much greater. The appearance of the Kelvir worm in 2005 forced the Reuters news agency to remove 60,000 subscribers from its Microsoft-based instant messaging service for 20 hours [27]. In 2010, a variant of the Palevo instant messaging worm rapidly spread through Romania, Mongolia, and Indonesia [28].

CONFICKER

The Conficker (or Downadup) worm, which appeared on Windows computers in November 2008, is notable because computer security experts have found it particularly difficult to eradicate. The worm is able to propogate in several ways [29]. The original variant of the worm spread to computers that were not up-to-date with the latest security patches from Microsoft. The second version of the worm, which appeared about a month later, had two new features that accelerated its spread: the ability to invade computers with weak password protection and the ability to propogate through USB memory sticks and shared files on local area networks. Early in 2009, between 8 and 15 million computers were infected with Conficker, including portions of military networks in France, the United Kingdom, and Germany [30].

According to Rodney Joffe of the Conficker Working Group, "It's using the best current practices and state of the art to communicate and to protect itself" [31]. Even though millions of copies of this worm are circulating, it does not appear to have done great harm. Security experts remain baffled as to the goals of those who created it [32].

7.3.4 Cross–site Scripting

Cross-site scripting is another way in which malware may be downloaded without a user's knowlege. Web sites that allow users to read what other users have posted are vulnerable to this security problem. The attacker injects a client-side script into a Web site. When an innocent user visits the site some time later, the user's browser executes the script, which may steal cookies, track the user's activity, or perform another malicious action.

7.3.5 Drive–by Downloads

Many malware creators have hacked into legitimate Web sites and installed software booby traps. In some cases, simply visiting a compromised Web site can result in the unintentional downloading of software, called a **drive-by download**. Another kind of drive-by download occurs when a Web surfer encounters a pop-up window asking permission to download software. The user approves the download, thinking the code is necessary to view the content on the Web site, but in actuality the download contains malware.

The drive-by download problem is growing [33]. The Google Anti-Malware Team has discovered more than three million URLs that initiate drive-by downloads. That may not seem like so many URLs, given the size of the Web, but hackers target the most popular Web sites. The proof of this is that about 1.3 percent of queries to Google's search engine result in a malicious URL appearing somewhere in the results page [34].

7.3.6 Trojan Horses and Backdoor Trojans

A **Trojan horse** is a program with a benign capability that conceals another, sinister purpose. When the user executes a Trojan horse, the program performs the expected beneficial task. However, the program is also performing actions unknown to, and not in the best interests of, the user.

A recent example of a Trojan horse is Mocmex, first uncovered in 2008 in digital picture frames manufactured in China. It spread from digital picture frames to computer hard drives and other portable storage devices people attached to their PCs. The purpose of the Trojan horse appeared to be to steal passwords to online computer games [35].

A **backdoor Trojan** is a Trojan horse that gives the attacker access to the victim's computer. For example, a backdoor Trojan may purport to cleanse malware from a computer, but in actuality it installs spyware (described later).

7.3.7 Rootkits

A **rootkit** is a set of programs that provide privileged access to a computer. Once installed, a rootkit is activated every time the computer is booted. Rootkits are difficult to detect because they start running before the operating system has completed booted up, and they can use security privileges to mask their presence.

7.3.8 Spyware and Adware

Spyware is a program that communicates over an Internet connection without the user's knowledge or consent. Spyware programs can monitor Web surfing, log keystrokes, take snapshots of the computer screen, and send reports back to a host computer. Spyware is often part of a rootkit.

Adware is a type of spyware that displays pop-up advertisements related to what the user is doing.

Since people would not intentionally download a spyware program, spyware must get installed using subterfuge. Free software downloaded from the Internet often contains spyware. Alternatively, the spyware may be a Trojan horse, tricking users into downloading it because they think it serves a useful purpose. A Trojan horse containing spyware an example of a **backdoor Trojan**. A 2006 survey of U.S. consumers with broadband Internet connections found that 89 percent of them had spyware on their computers [36].

7.3.9 Bots and Botnets

A **bot** is a particular kind of backdoor Trojan that responds to commands sent by a command-and-control program located on an external computer. The first bots supported legitimate applications: Internet Relay Chat channels and multiplayer Internet games. Today, however, bots are frequently used to support illegal activities. A collection of bot-infected computers is called a **botnet**, and a person who controls a botnet is called a **bot herder**. Botnets can range in size from a few thousand computers to over a million computers. In most cases, people have no idea that their PCs have been compromised and are part of a botnet.

It's been estimated that as much as 90 percent of spam is distributed through botnets [37]. Bots can also be used as spyware, stealing files or logging keystrokes to gain credit card numbers or other sensitive information. Botnets can also be used to support distributed denial-of-service attacks, which we will discuss in Section 7.4.1.

The sophistication of bots continues to increase. Computers typically have signature-based detection schemes to identify and destroy bots by looking for particular patterns in their underlying machine code. To counter these detection schemes, programmers are now creating bots able to spin off functionally equivalent bots that have somewhat different machine code.

7.3.10 Defensive Measures

Three defensive measures are important in protecting personal computers from malware: seurity patches, anti-malware tools, and firewalls.

Some kinds of malware exploit vulnerabilities in software systems, and software makers respond by modifying their code to remove the vulnerabilities. At regular intervals software makers release security patches so that the users of the software can update their systems to remove the vulnerabilities that have been uncovered. In fact, most worms exploit vulnerabilities for which security patches have already been created. That means they can only infect those computers that have not been kept up-to-date with the latest patches.

Anti-malware tools are designed to protect computers against malware, such as viruses, worms, Trojan horses, adware, and spyware. Anti-malware software can be used to scan a computer's hard drive, detecting files that appear to contain viruses or spyware, and deleting the files (with the user's approval). The rapid rate at which new malware appears necessitates frequent updating of these tools.

A firewall is a software application installed on a single computer that can selectively block network traffic to and from that computer. A firewall gives the user the ability to control which programs running on the computer are able to access the Internet. One weakness of firewalls is that they are vulnerable to being manipulated by malware. If a computer is infected by a piece of malware, the malware may be able to shut down the firewall, since it is running on the same computer.

7.4 Cyber Crime and Cyber Attacks

The Internet plays a vital role in the economic life of developed nations. Its effects include streamlining interactions between manufacturers and their suppliers, stimulating the creation of new companies, fostering the development of new business models, making online videoconferencing much more affordable, and changing how people shop. Today, there are more than 80 million .com domains. The Information Technology & Innovation Foundation estimates that the global economic benefits of the commercial

Internet exceed \$1.5 trillion per year [38]. The annual benefits of e-commerce alone are estimated at \$400 billion [38]. Given the amount of money changing hands, it's not surprising that organized crime is active on the Internet. The economic importance of Internet-based activities also makes Internet infrastructure an attractive target for politically motivated attacks.

We begin this section by reviewing three common Internet-based attacks. We then explore how these attacks have been used as the means to achieve criminal or political ends.

7.4.1 Types of Attack

PHISHING AND SPEAR-PHISHING

A **phishing** (pronounced "fishing") attack is a large-scale effort to gain sensitive information from gullible computer users. An attacker sends out millions of email messages from a botnet. The messages inform the recipients that one of their accounts has been compromised and directs them to connect to a Web site to resolve the problem. Targeted users that click on the link encounter an impostor Web site designed to resemble the genuine ecommerce site. Once on the site, they are asked for a login name, password, and other private information. Information collected by the imposter site can then be used for identity theft.

According to an industry study, there were at least 67,000 phishing attacks worldwide in the second half of 2010. An interesting development is the increase in phishing attacks on Chinese e-commerce sites, indicating the growing importance of the Chinese economy [39].

Spear-phishing is a variant of phishing in which the attacker selects email addresses that target a particular group of recipients. For example, an attacker may target elderly people judged to be more gullible or members of a group that have access to valuable information [40].

SQL INJECTION

SQL injection is a method of attacking a database-driven Web application that has improper security. The attacker accesses the application like any other client of the application, but by inserting (injecting) an SQL query into a text string from the client to the application, the attacker can trick the application into returning sensitive information.

DENIAL-OF-SERVICE AND DISTRIBUTED DENIAL-OF-SERVICE ATTACKS

A **denial-of-service (DoS) attack** is an intentional action designed to prevent legitimate users from making use of a computer service [41]. A DoS attack may involve unauthorized access to one or more computer systems, but the goal of a DoS attack is not to steal information. Instead, the aim of a DoS attack is to disrupt a computer server's ability to respond to its clients. Interfering with the normal use of computer services can result in significant harm. A company selling products and services over the Internet may lose business. A military organization may find its communications disrupted. A government or nonprofit organization may be unable to get its message out to the public.

A DoS attack is an example of an "asymmetric" attack, in which a single person can harm a huge organization, such as a multinational corporation or even a government. Since terrorist organizations specialize in asymmetric attacks, some fear that DoS attacks will become an important part of the terrorist arsenal [42, 43].

In a **distributed denial-of-service (DDoS) attack,** the attacker rents access to a botnet from a **bot herder.** At the selected time, the command-and-control computer sends the appropriate instructions to the bots, which launch their attack on the targeted system.

7.4.2 Cyber Crime

Criminal organizations have discovered that a great deal of money can be made from malware, so many of them have entered the arena, raising the stakes for corporations and individuals trying to protect their systems and sensitive information, respectively. Edward Skoudis paints a grim picture of the contemporary landscape:

> Some attackers sell to the highest bidder customized malicious code to control victim machines. They may rent out armies of infected systems useful for spam delivery, phishing schemes, denial-of-service attacks, or identity theft. Spyware companies and overly aggressive advertisers buy such code to infiltrate and control victim machines. A single infected machine displaying pop-up ads, customizing search engine results, and intercepting keystrokes for financial accounts could net an attack $1 per month or more. A keystroke logger on an infected machine could help the attacker gather credit card numbers and make $1,000 or more from that victim before the fraud is discovered. With control of 10,000 machines, an attacker could set up a solid profit flow from cyber crime. Organized crime groups may assemble collectives of such attackers to create a business, giving rise to a malicious code industry. In the late 1990s, most malicious code publicly released was the work of determined hobbyists, but today, attackers have monetized their malicious code; their profit centers throw off funds that can be channeled into research and development to create more powerful malicious software and refined business models, as well as to fund other crimes. [40]

In this section, we review a few well-known cyber crime incidents.

JEANSON JAMES ANCHETA

In 2004 and 2005, Internet cafe employee Jeanson James Ancheta created a network of about 400,000 bots, including computers operated by the U.S. Department of Defense. Adware companies, spammers, and others paid Ancheta for the use of these computers. After being arrested by the FBI, Ancheta pleaded guilty to a variety of charges, including conspiring to violate the Computer Fraud Abuse Act and the CAN-SPAM Act. In May 2005, a federal judge sentenced Ancheta to 57 months in prison and required him to pay $15,000 in restitution to the U.S. government for infecting Department of Defense computers. Ancheta also forfeited to the government the proceeds of his illegal activity, including his 1993 BMW, more than $60,000 in cash, and his computer equipment [44, 45].

PHARMAMASTER

Israeli company Blue Security created a spam-deterrence system for people tired of receiving unwanted email. Blue Security sold the service to businesses, but individuals could protect their home computers for free. About half a milion people signed up for this free service. Users loaded a bot called Blue Frog on their computers. The bot integrated with Yahoo! Mail, Gmail, and Hotmail, checking incoming email messages for spam. When it discovered a spam message, the bot would contact a Blue Security server to determine the source of the email. Then the bot would send the spammer an opt-out message [46].

Spammers who indiscriminately sent emails to millions of addresses started receiving hundreds of thousands of opt-out messages, disrupting their operations. Six of the world's top ten spammers agreed to use Blue Security's filtering software to remove Blue Frog users from their email lists [46].

One spammer, nicknamed PharmaMaster, did not back down. He threatened Blue Frog users with messages such as this one: "Unfortunately, due to the tactics used by Blue Security, you will end up receiving this message or other nonsensical spams 20–40 times more than you would normally" [37]. He followed through on his threats on May 1, 2006, by sending Blue Frog users 10 to 20 times as much spam as they would normally receive [46].

The next day, PharmaMaster went after Blue Security itself. He launched a massive DDoS attack from tens of thousands of bots targeting Blue Security's servers. The huge torrent of incoming messages disabled the Blue Frog service. Later DDoS attacks focused on other companies providing Internet services to Blue Security. Finally, the spammer targeted the businesses that paid for Blue Security's services. When Blue Security realized it could not protect its business customers from DDoS attacks and virus-laced emails, it reluctantly discontinued its service. "We cannot take the responsibility for an ever-escalating cyberwar through our continued operations," wrote Eran Reshef, CEO of Blue Security. "We are discontinuing all of our anti-spam activities" [46]. Blue Security's decision to fight bots with bots—always controversial—was ultimately unsuccessful.

ALBERT GONZALEZ

In 2010, Albert Gonzalez was sentenced to 20 years of imprisonment after pleading guilty to using an SQL injection attack to steal more than 130 million credit and debit card numbers. Some of the credit and debit card numbers were sold online, leading to unauthorized purchases and bank withdrawals. The targets of the attacks were Heartland Payment Systems, 7-Eleven, Hannaford Brothers Supermarkets, TJX, DSW, Barnes and Noble, Office Max, and the Dave & Buster's chain of restaurants. Most of the numbers were stolen from Heartland Payment Systems, which estimated its losses at $130 million [47, 48].

AVALANCHE GANG

The Avalanche Gang is the name given the criminal enterprise responsible for more phishing attacks than any other organization. The Anti-Phishing Working Group (APWG) estimated that the Avalanche Gang was responsible for two-thirds of all global phishing attacks launched in the second half of 2009. In the second half of 2010, APWG noticed that Avalanche had nearly ceased its phishing attacks, leading to APWG to speculate that Avalanche was changing strategies and focusing on the propagation of spam that tricks people into downloading the Zeus Trojan Horse [49].

7.4.3 Politically Motivated Cyber Attacks

A **cyber attack** is a "computer-to-computer attack that undermines the confidentiality, integrity, or availability of a computer or information resident on it" [50]. Some nation states, terrorist organizations, and allied groups are mounting politically motivated cyber attacks on the computer and network infrastructure of their opponents, and some of these efforts have caused major disruptions.

ESTONIA (2007)

The small Baltic country of Estonia was part of the Soviet Union from the end of the Second World War until it became independent in 1991, and ethnic Russians still make up about a quarter of its population. In the capital city of Tallinn, a large bronze statue of a Soviet soldier had long been point of controversy between Estonians and Russians. Russians saw it as a symbol of the sacrifices made by Soviet troops in the victory over Germany in the Great Patriotic War, while Estonians saw it as a symbol of the oppressive Soviet occupation.

After 16 years of independence, the Estonian government decided to relocate the controversial statue from downtown Tallinn to a Russian military cemetery in the suburbs. They knew the relocation would be hugely unpopular with the Russians. In fact, the Russian government had warned that removing the statue would be "disastrous for Estonians" [51]. The police were prepared for violence, and although ethnic Russians rioted for two nights after the statue was moved, the damage was limited.

The government also expected an attack on its cyber infrastructure. Sure enough, an attack came, but its magnitude was greater than anything expected by the government's Internet security group. DDoS attacks from nearly a million computers targeted Estonian government ministries and all of Estonia's major commercial banks, telecommunications companies, and media outlets. To combat the attacks, much of Estonia's Internet was made inaccessible to computers outside the country, and on May 10, Estonia's largest bank had to suspend online services for an hour [51, 52].

In 2009, a group of Russian activists connected with Nashi, a pro-Kremlin youth group, claimed responsibility for the cyber attacks [53].

GEORGIA (2008)

Georgia is another former Soviet republic that gained independence in 1991. South Ossetia, a region of Georgia adjacent to Russia, gained de facto autonomy from Georgia after a brief war in 1991, though it continues to be recognized as a part of Georgia by the international community. On August 7, 2008, after provocations by South Ossetian separatists, Georgia sent troops into South Ossetia. Russian forces entered South Ossetia on August 8, and Russian and Georgian troops fought in South Ossetia for four days. A ceasefire between Georgia and Russia was signed a week later.

The conflict between Georgia and Russia is notable because even before Russian troops had entered South Ossetia, the Georgian government suffered a series of DDoS attacks that affected its ability to communicate with the outside world. Multiple Web sites went down for hours. The Georgian government went so far as to switch some of its Web hosting locations to the United States. American security experts said they had uncovered evidence of involvement by the Russian Business Network, a criminal gang located in St. Peterburg, but there was no clear link to the Russian military [54, 55, 56].

GEORGIA (2009)

Twitter service was unavailable *worldwide* for several hours on August 6, 2009, due to a massive DDoS attack. Max Kelly, the chief security officer at Facebook, said the attack was an effort to silence a political blogger from the Republic of Georgia, citing as evidence the fact that three other sites used by the activist—Facebook, LiveJournal, and Google—were also targets of DDoS attacks at the same time [57, 58].

No group took responsibility for the attacks, but some noted that August 6, 2009, was the first anniversary of the war between Georgia and Russia over South Ossetia [59].

EXILED TIBETAN GOVERNMENT (2009)

In 2009, computer security experts uncovered a surveillance effort targeting the Dalai Lama, the exiled Tibetan government, and other Tibetans. Some agency had used back-door Trojans to penetrate 1,295 computers in 103 countries, creating a spying system the experts named GhostNet. When a victim opened an email attachment supposedly containing the translation of a book, the backdoor Trojan was activated. Each backdoor Trojan was able to transfer data files and email messages back to the controlling computer. Even more ominously, it could access the computer's microphone, turning the PC into an eavesdropping station. Some of the researchers that discovered GhostNet blamed the Chinese government for the intrusions, but the Chinese government denied responsibility [60, 61].

UNITED STATES AND SOUTH KOREA (2009)

A DDoS attack on governmental agencies and commercial Web sites in the United States and South Korea paralyzed a third of them over the Fourth of July weekend in 2009. Targets in the United States included the White House, the Treasury Department, the Secret Service, the New York Stock Exchange, and Nasdaq. In South Korea, the targets included the Blue House (presidential mansion), the Defense Ministry, and the National Assembly.

The DDoS attack was relatively minor, involving a botnet containing only 50,000–65,000 computers, compared with large-scale attacks that may utilize a million computers. Still, the attack disrupted different networks over a period of days as it shifted targets, and some sites in South Korea were unavailable or compromised as late as July 9. South Korea's National Intelligence Service blamed the North Korean government or its sympathizers for the attack, hypothesizing that the attack was in retaliation for United Nations sanctions against North Korea. According to computer experts, it was unlikely the source of the attack would ever be positively identified because those responsible for the attack launched it from systems owned by others [62, 63].

STUXNET WORM (2009)

Industrial processes such as chemical plants, oil and gas pipelines, and electrical power grids require constant monitoring. In the pre-computer era, monitoring was done by employees who watched gauges and warning lights, turned dials, and opened and closed valves. Computers allowed the automation of centralization of monitoring. In the 1980s, distributed control systems eliminated local control cabinets. Instead, networks carried information to centralized control centers. Computer monitors with color-coded fields replaced the gauges and warning lights. Initially, distributed control systems were proprietary, but customers asked for "open systems, common protocols and vendor interoperability" [64]. They got what they wanted with the advent of Supervisory Control and Data Acquisition (SCADA) systems based on the Internet Protocol. Internet-based SCADA systems are less expensive and are easier to maintain and administer than proprietary systems (Figure 7.5). Another way to save money and time is to allow an outsider to connect with the SCADA system remotely to perform diagnostics.

These advances carry with them security risks. Allowing remote diagnostics creates an opportunity for a malicious outsider to gain access. Many industrial machines

FIGURE 7.5 Internet-based supervisory control and data acquisition systems can save money and make systems easier to administer, but they also carry security risks. (© p77/ZUMA Press/Newscom)

contain embedded microprocessors. Industrial machines last a long time, which means many of these machines contain older microprocessors. Security patches designed to ward off malware may not be available for these microprocessors, and even if they are available, it may be impractical to install them because the processor is so slow that it cannot run the security code and keep up with its machine-control responsibilities.

The Stuxnet worm, launched in 2009, attacked SCADA systems running Siemens software [65]. The worm appeared to target five industrial facilities in Iran, and it may have caused a temporary shutdown of Iran's nuclear program by infecting computers controlling centrifuges processing uranium [66, 67]. There is some evidence that Israeli Defense Forces may have been responsible for unleashing the worm [68].

7.5 Online Voting

Throughout this chapter, we have seen many ways in which malefactors can breech the security of networked computers, yet the convenience and low cost of completing many tasks online are significant benefits. It should come as no surprise, then, that an online solution is often proposed when there is a problem with a traditional process. In this section, we evaluate a proposal to conduct elections over the Internet.

7.5.1 Motivation for Online Voting

The 2000 Presidential election was one of the closest contests in U.S. history. Florida was the pivotal state; without Florida's electoral votes, neither Democrat Al Gore nor Republican George W. Bush had a majority of votes in the Electoral College. After a manual recount of the votes in four heavily Democratic counties, the Florida Secretary of State declared that Bush had received 2,912,790 votes to Gore's total of 2,912,253. Bush's margin of victory was incredibly small: less than 2 votes out of every 10,000 votes cast.

Most of these counties used a keypunch voting machine in which voters select a candidate by using a stylus to poke out a hole in a card next to the candidate's name. Two voting irregularities were traced to the use of these machines. The first irregularity was that sometimes the stylus doesn't punch the hole cleanly, leaving a tiny, rectangular piece of card hanging by one or more corners. Votes with "hanging chad" are typically not counted by automatic vote tabulators. The manual recount focused on identifying ballots with hanging chad that ought to have been counted. The second irregularity was that some voters in Palm Beach County were confused by its "butterfly ballot" and mistakenly punched the hole corresponding to Reform Party candidate Pat Buchanan rather than the hole for Democratic candidate Al Gore (Figure 7.6). This confusion may have cost Al Gore the votes he needed to win Florida [69].

7.5.2 Proposals

The problems with the election in Florida led to a variety of actions to improve the reliability of voting systems in the United States. Many states replaced paper-based systems

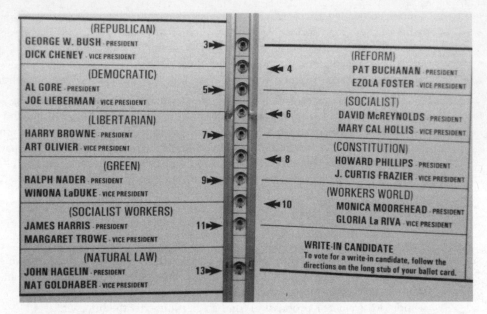

FIGURE 7.6 The layout of the "butterfly ballot" apparently led thousands of Palm Beach County, Florida voters supporting candidate Al Gore to punch the hole associated with Pat Buchanan by mistake. (AP Photo/Gary I. Rothstein)

with direct recording electronic voting machines. (These systems are discussed in Chapter 8.)

Others have suggested that voting via the Internet be used, at least as a way of casting absentee ballots. In fact, online voting is already a reality. It was used in the 2000 Alaska Republican Presidential preference poll and the 2000 Arizona Democratic Presidential primary [70]. One hundred thousand Americans in the military and living overseas were going to have the opportunity to vote over the Internet in the 2004 Presidential primaries as part of the Secure Electronic Registration and Voting Experiment, until the government cancelled the experiment at the last minute [71].

Other nations are ahead of the United States in allowing voting over the Internet. Local elections in the United Kingdom used online voting in 2001. In 2003, French citizens living in the United States were allowed to use the Internet to elect their representatives to the Assembly of French Citizens Abroad. Estonia was the first country to allow all of its citizens to vote online in local and national elections. Several cantons in Switzerland have made constitutional changes approving the Internet as an official voting option, along with voting at a polling station and voting by mail.

7.5.3 Ethical Evaluation

In this section, we make a utilitarian evaluation of the morality of online voting by weighing its benefits and risks. The discussion assumes that online voting would be implemented via a Web browser, though similar arguments could be made if another technology were employed.

BENEFITS OF ONLINE VOTING

Advocates of online voting say it would have numerous advantages: [72]:

Online voting would give people who ordinarily could not get to the polls the opportunity to cast a ballot from their homes.

Votes cast via the Internet could be counted much more quickly than votes cast on paper.

Electronic votes will not have any of the ambiguity associated with physical votes, such as hanging chad, erasures, etc.

Elections conducted online will cost less money than traditional elections.

Online voting will eliminate the risk of somebody tampering with a ballot box containing physical votes.

While in most elections people vote for a single candidate, other elections allow a person to vote for multiple candidates. For example, a school board may have three vacancies, and voters may be asked to vote for three candidates. It would be easy to program the voting form to prevent people from accidentally overvoting—choosing too many candidates.

Sometimes a long, complicated ballot results in undervoting—where a voter accidentally forgets to mark a candidate for a particular office. A Web form could be designed in multiple pages so that each page had the candidates for a single office. Hence online voting could reduce undervoting.

RISKS OF ONLINE VOTING

Critics of online voting have pointed to numerous risks associated with casting ballots over the Web [72]:

Online voting is unfair because it gives an unfair advantage to those who are financially better off. It will be easier for people with computers and Internet connections at home to vote.

The same system that authenticates the voter also records the ballot. This makes it more difficult to preserve the privacy of the voter.

Online voting increases the opportunities for vote solicitation and vote selling. Suppose person X agrees to vote for candidate Y in return for getting a payment from Z. If person X votes from his personal computer, he could allow person Z to watch as he cast his vote for Y, proving that he fulfilled his end of the bargain. This is much less likely to occur at an official polling place monitored by election officials.

A Web site hosting an election is an obvious target for a DDoS attack. Unlike corporate Web sites, which have attracted the attention of teenage hackers, a national election Web site could attract the attention of foreign governments or terrorists trying to disrupt the electoral process. What happens if the Web site is unavailable and people are not able to access it before the election deadline?

If voting is done from home computers, the security of the election depends on the security of these home computers. The next few paragraphs describe ways in which the security of home computers could be compromised.

A virus could change a person's vote without that person even suspecting what had happened. Many people have physical access to other people's computers, giving them the opportunity to install voter-deceiving applications in the weeks leading up to the election. Alternatively, a rogue programmer or group of programmers within a software company could sneak in a vote-tampering virus.

A backdoor Trojan lurking in a voter's computer could allow a person's vote to be observed by an outsider. A backdoor Trojan could even allow an outsider to cast a ballot in lieu of the rightful voter.

An attacker could fool a user into thinking he was connected to the vote server when in actuality he was connected to a phony vote server controlled by the attacker. For example, the attacker could send an email telling voters to click on a link to reach the polling site. When voters did so, they would be connected to the phony voting site. The attacker could ask for the voter's credentials, then use this information to connect to the real voter site and cast a vote for the candidate(s) desired by the attacker.

UTILITARIAN ANALYSIS

A utilitarian analysis must add up the positive and negative outcomes to determine whether allowing online voting is a good action to take. Recall from Section 2.7.2 that not all outcomes have equal weight. We must consider the probability of the outcome, the value of the outcome on each affected person, and the number of people affected.

Sometimes this calculation is relatively straightforward. For example, one of the benefits of online voting is that people who voted online would not have to travel to a polling place and wait in line. Suppose online voting replaced polling places in the United States. This change would affect about 50 percent of adult Americans (the ones who actually vote) [73]. We can estimate that the average voter spends about an hour traveling to a polling place, waiting in line, and traveling back. The average annual salary in the United States is about $37,000, or about $18.00 per hour [74]. We could compute, then, that the time savings associated with replacing polling places with online voting would be worth about $18.00 times one-half the adult population, or $9.00 for every adult.

It is more difficult to come up with reasonable weights for other outcomes. For example, a risk of online voting is that a DDoS attack may prevent legitimate voters from casting their votes before the deadline. While an election result that does not reflect the will of the voters is a great harm, the weight of this harm is reduced by three probabilities: the probability that someone would attempt a DDoS attack, the probability that a DDoS attack would be successful, and the probability that a successful DDoS attack would change the outcome of the election. Experts could have vastly different estimates of these probabilities, allowing the scales of the utilitarian evaluation to tip one way or the other.

KANTIAN ANALYSIS

A Kantian analysis of any voting system would focus on the principle that the will of each voter should be reflected in that voter's ballot. The integrity of each ballot is paramount. For this reason, every vote should leave a paper record, so that in the event of controversy a recount can be held to ensure the correctness of the election result. Eliminating paper records in order to achieve the ends of saving time and money or boosting voter turnout is wrong from a Kantian perspective.

CONCLUSIONS

We have surveyed the potential benefits and risks of holding elections online, and we have examined the morality of online voting from a utilitarian and a Kantian point of view.

Are we holding computers up to too high a standard? After all, existing voting systems are imperfect. There are two key differences, however, between existing mechanical or electromechanical systems and the proposed online system.

Existing systems are highly localized. A single person may be able to corrupt the election process at a few voting places, but it is impossible to taint the election results across an entire state. A Web-based election system would make it much easier for a single malicious person to taint the process on a wide scale.

The second difference is that most current systems produce a paper record of the vote. Where paper records do not exist, there is a push to make them mandatory [75]. When all else fails, the hard copy can be consulted to try to discern the intent of the voters. A Web-based voting system would not have paper records verified by citizens as true representations of their votes.

There is already evidence of tampering in online elections. In April 2002, Vivendi Universal, a Paris media conglomerate, held an online vote of its shareholders. Hackers caused ballots of some large shareholders to be counted as abstentions [72]. If a private election can draw the attention of a hacker, imagine how much more attractive a target a California election Web site will be!

Bruce Schneier has written, "A secure Internet voting system is theoretically possible, but it would be the first secure networked application ever created in computing history" [76].

Any election system that relies upon the security of personal computers managed by ordinary citizens will be vulnerable to electoral fraud. For this reason alone, there is a strong case to be made that a government should not allow online voting to be conducted in this way.

Summary

Computer and network security are important not just to those who manage the mainframe computer systems of corporations and government agencies, but to anyone who has a personal computer connected to the Internet. The more that people use computers to mediate their activities, the more attractive they become to criminal enterprises.

One strategy adopted by criminals is to try to get information directly from computer users. Phishing attacks are an example of this kind of exploit. Some people "fall" for phishing attacks because they are accustomed to providing sensitive financial information over an Internet connection.

Another strategy is to spy on the activities of computer users. Some spyware programs contain keystroke loggers that collect and report credit card numbers and other sensitive information users type on the keyboard as they visit ecommerce sites.

Criminals can also make money by co-opting personal computers, turning them into bots. Bot herders rent huge botnets to those who wish to use them as launching pads for spamming, phishing attacks, or distributed denial-of-service attacks.

Personal computers can become infected with malware many different ways. Even if users remember never to open a suspect email attachment, their systems may still become infected. A worm may enter a computer by taking advantage of a security weakness in the operating system. By simply visiting a Web site, a computer user may become the victim of a cross-site injection or a drive-by download. That is why it is important that all personal computer users set up personal firewalls and keep their systems up-to-date with anti-malware tools.

The recent rise in politically motivated cyber attacks raises some interesting questions. How vulnerable would the United States economy be to a cyber attack by a determined foe? At what point does a cyber attack on another nation become an act of war? Should a nation holding an Internet-based election be concerned about interference from one of its enemies?

Review Questions

1. How has the term "hacker" evolved since the 1950s?

2. Describe three "low-tech" methods that hackers have used to obtain login names and passwords.

3. What is the maximum penalty for violating the Computer Fraud and Abuse Act?

4. Why is it dangerous to surf the Web using an open WiFi network; i.e., one that does not require a password?

5. Define the following terms in your own words:
   - Adware
   - Backdoor Trojan
   - Bot
   - Botnet
   - Cross-site scripting
   - Drive-by download
   - Rootkit
   - Spyware

   - Trojan horse
   - Virus
   - Worm

6. Why is it dangerous for an email program to open attachments automatically, without waiting for the user to select them?

7. Soon after the Internet Worm was released, Andy Sudduth sent out an email explaining how to stop the worm. Why was this email of no help to the system administrators fighting the spread of the worm?

8. In your own words, define each of these terms:
   - Denial-of-service attack
   - Distributed denial-of-service attack
   - Phishing
   - Spear-phishing
   - SQL injection

9. Give two examples of how criminal organizations have used the Internet to make money.

10. What is a cyber attack?

11. If converting SCADA systems to the Internet Protocol increases the risk of a hacker taking control of an industrial process, why are companies converting SCADA systems to IP?

12. What did the Stuxnet worm do?

13. Explain two different ways a vote thief could cast multiple votes in an online election.

Discussion Questions

14. In a study done in London, people in subway stations were offered a cheap pen in return for disclosing their passwords. About 90 percent offered their passwords in return for the pen [77]. What can be done to get people to take security more seriously?

15. Email viruses are typically launched by people who modify header information to hide their identity. Brightmail's Enrique Salem says that in the future, your email reader will authenticate the sender before putting the message in your inbox. That way, you will know the source of all the emails you read. Alan Nugent of Novell says, "I'm kind of a fan of eliminating anonymity if that is the price for security" [78]. Will eliminating anonymity make computers more secure?

16. Are there conditions under which the release of a worm, virus, or Trojan horse would be morally justifiable?

17. When his worm program did not perform as expected, Robert Morris, Jr., contacted two old friends from Harvard to decide what to do next. One of them, Andy Sudduth, agreed to email an anonymous message apologizing for the worm and describing how to protect computers from it, without disclosing Morris as the creator of the worm [22]. Was this the right thing for Sudduth to do?

18. Kalamazoo College requires all computers connected to the campus network be running up-to-date antivirus software. When a student's computer is discovered to have a virus, its network connection is cut until a staff member can remove the virus. If it turns out that the computer was not running up-to-date antivirus software, the student is fined $100 [79]. Is this a morally justifiable policy?

19. Adam and Charlene are good friends. Both attend East Dakota State University. One day, when Adam is off campus interviewing for a part-time job, someone asks him how many credit hours of computer science courses he has completed. Adam calls Charlene and asks her to access his student records by logging into the campus mainframe as if she were Adam. He provides Charlene with his student identification number and password so that she can do this. Is it wrong for Adam to share this information with Charlene? Is it wrong for Charlene to retrieve this information for Adam?

20. Carnegie Mellon University, Harvard University, and the Massachusetts Institute of Technology denied admission to more than 100 business school applicants because they took an online peek at the status of their applications. These students learned how to circumvent the program's security, and they used this knowledge to view their files and see if they had been accepted. Students could see information about their own application, but could not view the status of other students' applications. In many cases the students learned that no admission decision had yet been made. Do you feel the response of these universities was appropriate?

21. Millions of American homes are equipped with wireless networks. If the network is not made secure, any nearby computer with a wireless card can use the network. The range of home wireless networks often extends into neighboring homes, particularly in apartment complexes. If your neighbor's wireless network extends into your home, is it wrong to use that network to get free Internet access?

22. Is it morally acceptable to use a denial-of-service attack to shut down a Web server that distributes child pornography?

23. Some would argue that technological development is inevitable. If Butler had not created Firesheep, someone else would have. Every invention can be put to good or bad uses. Therefore, creators of new technologies bear no moral responsibility for their inventions. In contrast, the author argues that people who create a tool making it easier for someone to do something immoral share some moral accountability for the misdeeds done by people using the tool. Which perspective do you find more compelling?

24. Suppose it is true that Israeli Defense Forces were reponsible for unleashing the Stuxnet worm, which caused a temporary shutdown of Iran's nuclear program by damaging centrifuges processing uranium. Was unleashing this worm morally justifiable?

25. Do you agree with the author that it is a bad idea for a government to allow online voting from home computers?

In–Class Exercises

26. Debate this proposition: Those who create nondestructive malware are doing the computer industry a favor because the patches created to block them make computers more

secure. To use an analogy, each virus has the effect of strengthening the immune systems of the computers it targets.

27. The University of Calgary offered a senior-level computer science course called "Computer Viruses and Malware." The course taught students how to write viruses, worms, and Trojan horses. It also discussed the history of computer viruses and taught students how to block attacks. All course assignments were done on a closed computer network isolated from the Internet. Some computer security experts criticized the University for offering the course. One researcher said, "No one argues criminology students should commit a murder to understand how a murderer thinks" [80]. Debate whether the University of Calgary was wrong to offer the course.

28. Divide the class into two groups to debate the proposition: "It is wrong for a company to hire a former malicious hacker as a security consultant."

29. A distributed denial-of-service attack makes the Web site for a top electronic retailer inaccessible for an entire day. As a result of the attack, nearly a million customers were inconvenienced, and the retailer lost millions of dollars of sales to its competitors. Law enforcement agencies apprehend the person who launched the attack. Should the punishment be determined strictly by considering the crime that was committed, or should the identity of the culprit be taken into account? If the identity of the perpetrator should be taken into account, what punishment do you think would be appropriate if he were:

    • A teenager who launched the attack out of curiosity
    • An adult dedicated to fighting the country's overly materialistic culture
    • A member of a terrorist organization attempting to harm the national economy

30. Divide the class into two groups. One group should come up with arguments why the United States should work to create an international ban on cyber attacks, analogous to the Chemical Weapons Convention, which outlaws the production use of chemical weapons. The other group should come up with arguments why the United States should strive to become preeminent in cyber attack technology.

31. East Dakota has decided to allow its citizens to vote over the Web in the Presidential election, if they so desire. Thirty percent of the eligible voters choose to cast their ballots over the Web. The national election is so closely contested that whoever wins the electoral votes of East Dakota will be the next President. After the election, state elections officials report the vote tally and declare Candidate X to be the winner.

    Two weeks after the inauguration of President X, state officials uncover evidence of massive electoral fraud. Some voters were tricked into connecting to a phony voting site. The organization running the phony site used the credentials provided by the duped voters to connect to the actual voting site and cast a vote for Candidate X.

    State officials conclude the electoral fraud may have changed the outcome of the election, but they cannot say for sure. They have no evidence that Candidate X knew anything about this scheme to increase his vote tally.

    Divide the class into groups representing President X, the other Presidential candidates, citizens of East Dakota, and citizens of other states to discuss the proper response to this revelation. For guidance, consult Article II, Section 1, and Amendment XII to the United States Constitution.

Further Reading

John Brunner. *The Shockwave Rider*. Harper & Row, New York, NY, 1975.

Richard A. Clarke and Robert K. Knake. *Cyber War: The Next Threat to National Security and What to Do About It*. HarperCollins Publishers, New York, NY, 2010.

Katie Hafner and John Markoff. *Cyberpunk: Outlaws and Hackers on the Computer Frontier*. Simon & Schuster, New York, NY, 1991.

Steven Levy. *Hackers: Heroes of the Computer Revolution*. Penguin Books, New York, NY, 1994.

References

[1]   Steven Levy. *Hackers: Heroes of the Computer Revolution*. Anchor Press/Doubleday, Garden City, NY, 1984.

[2]   G. Malkin and T. LaQuey Parker, editors. "Hacker." *Internet Users' Glossary*, January 1993. www.rfc-editor.org.

[3]   Dan Verton. "Corporate America Is Lazy, Say Hackers; Vandalism of USA Today Site a Warning." *Computerworld*, July 22, 2002.

[4]   Marcia Savage. "Mitnick Turns Gamekeeper." *TechWeb.com*, October 30, 2000.

[5]   Michael Arnone. "Hacker Steals Personal Data on Foreign Students at U. of Kansas." *The Chronicle of Higher Education*, January 24, 2003.

[6]   Sara Lipka. "Hacker Breaks into Database for Tracking International Students at UNLV." *The Chronicle of Higher Education*, March 21, 2005.

[7]   Dan Carnevale. "Harvard and MIT Join Carnegie Mellon in Rejecting Applicants Who Broke into Business-School Networks." *The Chronicle of Higher Education*, March 9, 2005.

[8]   Eric Butler. "Firesheep." *codebutler (Web site)*. October 24, 2010. codebutler.com.

[9]   Bob Brown. "Father of Firesheep Fires Away After Wild Week in WiFi Security." *NetworkWorld*, November 2, 2011. www.networkworld.com.

[10]   Tom Anderson. "Firesheep in Wolves' Clothing: Extension Lets You Hack into Twitter, Facebook Accounts Easily." *TechCrunch*, October 24, 2010. techcrunch.com.

[11]   Jason Fitzpatrick. "Firesheep Sniffs Out Facebook and Other User Credentials on Wi-Fi Hotspots." *Lifehacker*, October 25, 2010. lifehacker.com.

[12]   Gregg Keizer. "How to Protect Against Firesheep Attacks." *Computerworld*, October 26, 2010. www.computerworld.com.

[13]   Sharon Machlis. "How to Hijack Facebook Using Firesheep." *PCWorld*, October 30, 2010. www.pcworld.com.

[14]   Eric Butler. "Firesheep, a Week Later: Ethics and Legality." *codebutler (Web site)*. November 1, 2011. codebutler.com.

[15]   ] Alex Rice. "A Continued Commitment to Security." *The Facebook Blog*, January 26, 2011. blog.facebook.com.

[16]   Paul Ducklin. "Twitter Goes Secure—Say Goodbye to Firesheep with 'Always use HTTPS' Option." *nakedsecurity (blog)*, March 16, 2011.

[17] Jessical Goodman. "Firesheep, What Color Is Your Hat?" *FeelingElephant's Weblog*, November 30, 2010. feelingelephants.wordpress.com.

[18] David Ferbrache. *A Pathology of Computer Viruses*. Springer-Verlag, London, England, 1992.

[19] Eurostat News Release. "Nearly One Third of Internet Users in the EU27 Caught a Computer Virus; 84% of Internet Users Use IT Security Software for Protection." February 7, 2011. europa.eu.

[20] "Google Warns TWO MILLION Users Their Computers Have Been Infected with a Virus." *Mail Online*, July 21, 2011. www.dailymail.co.uk.

[21] John Brunner. *The Shockwave Rider*. Harper & Row, New York, NY, 1975.

[22] Katie Hafner and John Markoff. *Cyberpunk: Outlaws and Hackers on the Computer Frontier*. Simon & Schuster, New York, NY, 1991.

[23] Paul Graham. "The Submarine." April 2005. www.paulgraham.com.

[24] "Worm Turns for Teenager Who Befuddled Microsoft." *The Times (London)*, July 6, 2005.

[25] "Hacker Behind Sasser, Netsky Worms Gets Job with German Security Company." *San Jose (CA) Mercury News*, September 28, 2004.

[26] John Leyden. "Sasser Suspect Walks Free." *The Register*, July 8, 2005. www.theregister.do.uk.

[27] Celeste Biever. "Instant Messaging Falls Prey to Worms." *New Scientist*, May 14, 2005.

[28] Hanleigh Daniels. "Palevo is Worming Its Way via IM Spam." *Tech Smart*, May 4, 2010. www.techsmart.co.za.

[29] Ben Nahorney, editor. "The Downadup Codex: A Comprehensive Guide to the Threat's Mechanics." Edition 1.0. Symantec Corporation, 2009. www.symantec.com

[30] "Virus Strikes 15 Million PCs." UPI, January 26, 2009. www.upi.com.

[31] John Markoff. "Defying Experts, Rogue Computer Code Still Lurks." *The New York Times*, August 27, 2009.

[32] Brian Prince. "Conficker Worm Deadline Passes Quietly—So Far." *IT Security & Network Security News*, April 1, 2009. www.eweek.com.

[33] John Leyden. "Drive-by Download Menace Spreading Fast." *The Register*, January 23, 2008. www.theregister.co.uk.

[34] Ryan Naraine. "Drive-by Downloads. The Web Under Siege." *Securelist*, April 15, 2009. www.securelist.com.

[35] Steve Sechrist. "State of Security: China's Trojan Horse." *Display Daily*, March 18, 2008. displaydaily.com.

[36] Webroot. "Spyware Infection Rates Return to Peak 2004 Levels According to Webroot State of Spyware Report." Aigist 15, 2006. www.webroot.com.

[37] Scott Berinato. "Attack of the Bots." *Wired*, November 2006.

[38] Robert D. Atkinson, Stephen J. Ezell, Scott M. Andes, Daniel D. Castro, and Richard Bennett. "The Internet Economy 25 Years after .Com: Transforming Commerce & Life." The Information Technology & Innovation Foundation, March 2010. www.itif.org.

[39] Greg Aaron and Rod Rasmussen. *Global Phishing Survey: Trends and Domain Name Use in 2H2010*. APWG Internet Policy Committee, April 2011. www.apwg.org.

[40] Edward Skoudis. "Evolutionary Trends in Cyberspace." In *Cyberpower and National Security*. Edited by Franklin D. Kramer, Stuart H. Starr, and Larry K. Wentz. Potomac Books, 2009, pp. 163–164.

[41] CERT Coordination Center. "Denial of Service Attacks," June 4, 2001. www.cert.org/ tech_tips/ denial_of_service.html.

[42] Mike Toner. "Cyberterrorism Danger Lurking." *The Atlanta Journal and Constitution*, November 2, 2001.

[43] Toni O'Loughlin. "Cyber Terrorism Reaches New Heights." *Australian Financial Review*, April 4, 2003.

[44] "Zombie Master Jeanson Ancheta Pleads Guilty." *Spam Daily News*, January 23, 2006. www.spamdailynews.com.

[45] "Zombie Master Jeanson Ancheta Sentenced to 5 Years in Prison." *Spam Daily News*, May 9, 2006. www.spamdailynews.com.

[46] Robert Lemos. "Blue Security Folds Under Spammer's Wrath." *SecurityFocus*, May 17, 2006. www.securityfocus.com.

[47] Kim Zetter. "TJX Hacker Charged with Heartland, Hannaford Breaches." *Wired Threat Level: Privacy, Crime and Security Online*, August 17, 2009. www.wired.com.

[48] David Morrison. "Albert Gonzalez, Mastermind Heartland Hacker, Gets 20 Years." *Credit Union Times*, April 7, 2010. www.cutimes.com.

[49] "Avalanche Botnet Moves from Distributing Spam to Zeus Lures." *SC Magazine*, October 25, 2010. www.scmagazineuk.com.

[50] Kevin O'Shea. "Cyber Attack Investigative Tools and Technologies." *Institute for Security Technology Studies at Dartmouth College*, May 7, 2003.

[51] Joshua Davis. "Hackers Take Down the Most Wired Country in Europe." *Wired*, August 21, 2007. www.wired.com.

[52] Mark Lander and John Markoff. "Digital Fears Emerge After Data Siege in Estonia." *The New York Times*, May 29, 2007. www.nytimes.com.

[53] "A Look at Estonia's Cyber Attack in 2007." *Associated Press*, July 8, 2009. www.msnbc .msn.com.

[54] John Markoff. "Before the Gunfire, Cyberattacks." *The New York Times*, August 12, 2008. www.nytimes.com.

[55] Kevin Coleman. "Cyber War 2.0 — Russia v. Georgia." *Defense Tech*, August 13, 2008. defensetech.org.

[56] "War, Redefined." *The Los Angeles Times*, August 17, 2008. articles.latimes.com.

[57] Jared Newman. "Twitter Crippled by Denial-of-Service Attack." *PCWorld Blogs*, August 6, 2009. www.pcworld.com.

[58] Elinor Mills. "Twitter, Facebook Attack Targeted One User." *cnet news*, August 6, 2009. http://news.cnet.com.

[59] Graham Cluley. "Was Twitter Denial-of-Service Targeting Anti-Russian Blogger?" *Graham Cluley's Blog*, August 7, 2009. www.sophos.com.

[60] "A Chinese Ghost in the Machine?" *The Economist*, April 4, 2009.

[61] John Markoff. "Tracking Cyberspies through the Web Wilderness." *The New York Times*, May 12, 2009.

[62] Choe Sang-Hun and John Markoff. "Cyberattacks Jam Government and Commercial Web Sites in U.S. and South Korea." *The New York Times*, July 9, 2009.

[63] John Markoff. "Internet's Anonymity Makes Cyberattack Hard to Trace." *The New York Times*, July 17, 2009.

[64] "Hacking the Industrial Network." Phoenix Contact, Harrisburg, Pennsylvania. www .isa.org.

[65] "Siemens SCADA Systems Under Attack by Information Stealing Worm." *Help Net Security*, July 20, 2010. www.net-security.org.

[66] "Iran Confirms Stuxnet Worm Halted Centrifuges." CBS News, November 29, 2010. www.cbsnews.com.

[67] John Markoff. "Malware Aimed at Iran Hit Five Sites, Report Says." *The New York Times*, February 11, 2011. www.nytimes.com.

[68] Christopher Williams. "Israeli Video Shows Stuxnet as One of Its Successes." *The Telegraph*, February 15, 2011. www.telegraph.co.uk.

[69] A. Agresti and B. Presnell. "Misvotes, Undervotes, and Overvotes: The 2000 Presidential Election in Florida." *Statistical Science*, 17(4):436–440, 2002.

[70] Aviel D. Rubin. "Security Considerations for Remote Electronic Voting." *Communications of the ACM*, 45(12):39–44, December 2002.

[71] Sam Hananel. "Thousands to Cast Ballots by Web in 2004." *Associated Press*, July 12, 2003.

[72] Rebecca Mercuri. "A Better Ballot Box?" *IEEE Spectrum*, pages 46–50, October 2002.

[73] Thomas E. Patterson. *The Vanishing Voter: Public Involvement in an Age of Uncertainty*. Alfred A. Knopf/Random House, New York, NY, 2002.

[74] U.S. Department of Labor. "Quarterly Census of Employment and Wages," August 2, 2005. www.bls.gov.

[75] Todd R. Weiss. "N.J. to Get E-voting Paper Trail, but Not Until 2008; a Legal Battle Continues to Try to Put the Law into Effect Sooner." *Computerworld*, July 15, 2005.

[76] Bruce Schneier. "Technology Was Only Part of the Florida Problem." *Computerworld*, December 18, 2000.

[77] John Leyden. "Office Workers Give Away Passwords for a Cheap Pen." *The Register*, April 17, 2003. www.theregister.co.uk.

[78] "Fighting the Worms of Mass Destruction." *The Economist*, pages 65–67, November 29th, 2003.

[79] Kalamazoo College Information Technology Services. "Computer Virus Policy." reason.kzoo.edu. Accessed July 29, 2011.

[80] Brock Read. "How to Write a Computer Virus, for College Credit." *The Chronicle of Higher Education*, January 16, 2004.

Matt Bishop

Matt Bishop received his Ph.D. in computer science from Purdue University, where he specialized in computer security, in 1984. He was a research scientist at the Research Institute for Advanced Computer Science and was on the faculty at Dartmouth College before joining the Department of Computer Science at the University of California at Davis. He teaches courses in computer security, operating systems, and programming.

His main research area is the analysis of vulnerabilities in computer systems, including modeling them, building tools to detect vulnerabilities, and ameliorating or eliminating them. This includes detecting and handling all types of malicious logic. He is active in the areas of network security, the study of denial of service attacks and defenses, policy modeling, software assurance testing, and formal modeling of access control. He also studies the issue of trust as an underpinning for security policies, procedures, and mechanisms.

He is active in information assurance education, is a charter member of the Colloquium on Information Systems Security Education, and led a project to gather and make available many unpublished seminal works in computer security. He has authored a textbook, *Computer Security: Art and Science*, published by Addison–Wesley Professional.

What led you to focus your research on system vulnerabilities?

I became interested in this area because of the ubiquity of the problem. We have been designing and building computer systems since the 1950s, and we still don't know how to secure systems in practice. Why not? How can we find the existing vulnerabilities and improve the security of those existing systems?

Also, there are parallels with nontechnical fields. I find those parallels fascinating, and I enjoy learning and studying other fields to see if any of the methods and ideas from those fields can be applied to analyzing systems and improving their security. Some fields, like military science, political science, and psychology, have obvious connections. Others, such as art and literature, have less obvious connections. But all emphasize the importance of people to computer and software security.

Do you have an example of what can happen when security is treated as an add-on, rather than designed into a system from the beginning?

Yes. Consider the Internet. When it was first implemented (as the old ARPANET), the protocols were not developed to supply the security services that are now considered important. (The security services that were considered important were various forms of robustness, so that the network would provide connectivity even in the face of multiple failures of systems in the network and even of portions of the network itself. It supplied those services very well.) As a result, security services such as authentication, confidentiality of messages, and integrity of messages are being treated as add-ons rather than the protocols being redesigned to provide those services inherently. So today we have security problems in the descendent of the ARPANET, the Internet.

How can the choice of programming language affect the security of the resulting program?

In two ways. The more obvious one is that some programming languages enforce constraints that limit unsafe practices. For example, in Java, the language prevents indexing beyond the end of an array. In C, the language does not. So you can get buffer overflows in C, but it's much harder to get buffer overflows in Java. The less obvious one is that the language controls how most programmers think about their algorithms. For example, a language that is functional matches some algorithms better than one that is imperative. This means the programmer will make fewer mistakes, and the mistakes he or she makes will tend to be at the implementation level rather than the conceptual or design level—and mistakes at the implementation level will be *much* easier to fix.

What can be done about the problem of viruses, worms, and Trojan horses?

These programs run with the authority of the user who triggers them; worms also spread autonomously through the network and most often take advantage of vulnerabilities to enter a system and spread from it. So, several things can ameliorate the situation:

1. Minimize the number of network services you run. In particular, if you don't need the service, disable it. This will stop the spread of many worms.

2. Don't run any attachments you receive in the mail unless you trust the person who sent them to you. Most viruses and many worms spread this way. In particular, some mailers (such as Outlook) can be set up to execute and/or unpack attachments automatically. This feature should be disabled.

3. The user should not be able to alter certain files, such as system programs and system configuration files. If the user must be able to alter them, confirmation should be required. This will limit the effect of most viruses to affecting the user rather than the system as a whole or other users on the system.

Many personal computer users do not update their systems with the latest operating system patches. Should computer manufacturers be given the ability (and the obligation) to keep up-to-date all of their customers' Internet-connected computers?

I question the wisdom of allowing vendors to update computers remotely. The problem is that vendors do not know the particular environment in which the computers function. The environment determines what "security" means. So, a patch that improves security in one realm may weaken it in another.

As an example, suppose a company disallows any connections from the network except through a virtual private network (VPN). Its systems were designed to start all servers in a particular directory that contains all network servers. So to enforce this restriction, all network servers *except* the VPN are removed from the systems. This prevents the other servers from being started.

The system vendor discovers a security vulnerability in the email server and the login procedure. It fixes both, and sends out a patch that includes a new login program and a new email server. The patch installs both, and reboots the system so the new login program and email server will be used immediately.

The problem here is that by installing the new email server (which improves security in most systems), the company's systems now are nonsecure, as they can be connected to via a port other than those used for the VPN (for example, the email port, port 25). The vendor's patch may therefore damage security.

We saw this with Windows XP SP2. It patched many holes, but also broke various third party applications, some of them very important to their users.

So, I believe vendors should be obligated to work with their customers to provide security patches and enhancements, but should not be given the ability to keep the systems up-to-date unless the customer asks for it. Vendors should also provide better configuration interfaces, and default configurations, that are easy to set up and change, as well as (free) support to help customers use them.

Do you expect personal computers a decade from now to be more secure than they are today?

In some ways yes, and in other ways no. I expect that they will provide more security services that can be configured to make the systems more secure in various environments—not all environments, though! I also expect that the main problem for securing systems will be configuration, operation, and maintenance, though, and those problems will not be overcome in a decade, because they are primarily people problems and not technical problems.

What advice can you offer students who are seriously interested in creating secure software systems?

Focus on all aspects of the software system. Identify the specific requirements that the software system is to solve, develop a security policy that the software system is to meet (and that will meet the requirements), design and implement the software correctly, and consider the environment in which it will be used when you do all this. Also, make the software system as easy to install and configure as possible, and plan that the users will make errors. People aren't perfect, and any security that depends upon them doing everything correctly will ultimately fail.

CHAPTER

8

Computer Reliability

The major difference between a thing that might go wrong and a thing that cannot possibly go wrong is that when a thing that cannot possibly go wrong goes wrong it usually turns out to be impossible to get at or repair.

—DOUGLAS ADAMS, *Mostly Harmless*

8.1 Introduction

COMPUTER DATABASES TRACK MANY OF OUR ACTIVITIES. What happens when a computer is fed bad information, or when someone misinterprets the information retrieved from a computer? We are surrounded by devices containing embedded computers. What happens when a computer program contains an error that causes the computer to malfunction?

Sometimes the effects of a computer error are trivial. You are playing a game on your PC, do something unusual, and the program crashes, forcing you to start over. At other times computer malfunctions result in a real inconvenience. You get an incorrect bill in the mail, and you end up spending hours on the phone with the company's customer service agents to get the mistake fixed. Some software bugs have resulted in businesses making poor decisions that have cost them millions of dollars. On a few occasions, failures in a computerized system have even resulted in fatalities.

In this chapter, we examine various ways in which computerized systems have proven to be unreliable. Systems typically have many components, of which the computer is just one. A well-engineered system can tolerate the malfunction of any single component without failing. Unfortunately, there are many examples of systems in which the computer was the weakest link and a computer error led to the failure of the entire system. The failure may have been due to a data-entry or data-retrieval error, poor design, or inadequate testing. Through a variety of examples, you will gain a greater appreciation for the complexity of building a reliable computerized system.

We also take a look at computer simulations, which are playing an increasingly important role in modern science and engineering. We survey some of the uses to which these simulations are put and describe how those who develop simulations can validate the underlying models.

Software engineering arose out of the difficulties organizations encountered when they began constructing large software systems. Software engineering refers to the use of processes and tools that allow programs to be created in a more structured manner. We describe the software development process and provide evidence that more software projects are being completed on time and on budget.

At the end of the chapter, we take a look at software warranties. Software manufacturers typically disclaim any liability for lost profits or other consequential damages resulting from the use of their products. We discuss how much responsibility software manufacturers ought to take for the quality of their products. Some say software should be held to the same standards as other products, while others say we ought to have a different set of expectations when it comes to the reliability of the software we purchase.

8.2 Data–Entry or Data–Retrieval Errors

Sometimes computerized systems fail because the wrong data have been entered into them or because people incorrectly interpret the data they retrieve. In this section, we give several examples of wrong actions being taken due to errors in data entry or data retrieval.

8.2.1 Disfranchised Voters

In the November 2000 general election, Florida disqualified thousands of voters because pre-election screening identified them as felons. The records in the computer database, however, were incorrect; the voters had been charged with misdemeanors. Nevertheless, they were forbidden from voting. This error may have affected the outcome of the Presidential election [1].

8.2.2 False Arrests

As we saw in Chapter 6, the databases of the National Crime Information Center (NCIC) contain a total of about 40 million records related to stolen automobiles, missing persons, wanted persons, suspected terrorists, and much more. There have been numerous stories of police making false arrests based on information they retrieved from the NCIC. Here are three.

Sheila Jackson Stossier, an airline flight attendant, was arrested at the New Orleans airport by police who confused her with Shirley Jackson, who was wanted in Texas. She spent one night in jail and was detained for five days [2].

California police, relying upon information in the NCIC, twice arrested and jailed Roberto Hernandez as a suspect in a Chicago burglary case. The first time he was jailed for 12 days, while the second time he was held for a week before he was freed. They had confused him with another Roberto Hernandez, who had the same height and weight. Both Hernandezes had brown hair, brown eyes, and tattoos on their left arms. They also had the same birthday, and their Social Security numbers differed by only a single digit [3].

Someone used personal information about Michigan resident Terry Dean Rogan to obtain a California driver's license using his name. After this person was arrested for two homicides and two robberies, police entered information about these crimes into the NCIC under his false identity. Over a period of 14 months, the real Terry Dean Rogan was arrested five times by Los Angeles police, three times at gun point, even though he and Michigan police had tried to get the NCIC records corrected after his first arrest. Rogan sued the Los Angeles Police Department and was awarded $55,000 [2].

8.2.3   Analysis: Accuracy of NCIC Records

Stepping away from a requirement of the Privacy Act of 1974, the Justice Department announced in March 2003 that it would no longer require the FBI to ensure the accuracy of information about criminals and crime victims before entering it in the NCIC database [4].

Should the U.S. government take responsibility for the accuracy of the information stored in NCIC databases?

The Department of Justice argues that it is impractical for it to be responsible for the information in the NCIC database [5]: Much of the information that gets entered into the database is provided by other law enforcement and intelligence agencies. The FBI has no way of verifying that all the information is accurate, relevant, and complete. Even when the information is coming from inside the FBI, agents should be able to use their discretion to determine which information may be useful in criminal investigations. If the FBI strictly followed the provisions of the Privacy Act and verified the accuracy of every record entered into the NCIC, the amount of information in the database would be greatly curtailed. The database would be a much less useful tool for law enforcement agencies. The result could be a decrease in the number of criminals arrested by law enforcement agencies.

Privacy advocates counter that the accuracy of the NCIC databases is now more important than ever, because an increasing number of records are stored in these databases. As more erroneous records are put into the database, the probability of innocent American citizens being falsely arrested also increases.

Which argument is stronger? Let's focus on one of the oldest NCIC databases: the database of stolen vehicles. The total amount of harm caused to society by automobile theft is great. Over one million automobiles are stolen in the United States every year. Victims of car theft are subjected to emotional stress, may sustain a financial loss, and can spend a lot of time trying to recover or replace the vehicle. In addition, the prevalence of automobile theft harms everyone who owns a car by raising insurance rates. In the past, car thieves could reduce the probability that a stolen car would be recovered by transporting it across a state line, but the NCIC database contains information about stolen vehicles throughout the United States, and it has enabled law enforcement officials to identify cars stolen anywhere in the nation. At the present time, just over half of all stolen vehicles are recovered. If we make the conservative estimate that the NCIC has increased the percentage of recovered cars by just 10 percent, more than 50,000 additional cars are being returned to their owners each year, a significant benefit. On the other hand, if an error in the NCIC stolen car database leads to a false arrest, the harm caused to the innocent driver is great. However, there are only a few stories of false arrests stemming from errors in the NCIC stolen car database. The total amount of benefit derived from the NCIC database of stolen automobiles appears to be much greater than the total amount of harm it has caused. We conclude the creation and maintenance of this database has been the right course of action.

8.3 Software and Billing Errors

Even if the data entered into a computer are correct, the system may still produce the wrong result or collapse entirely if there are errors in the computer programs manipulating the data. Newspapers are full of stories about software bugs or "glitches." Here is a selection of stories that have appeared in print.

8.3.1 Errors Leading to System Malfunctions

Linda Brooks of Minneapolis, Minnesota, opened her mail on July 21, 2001, and found a phone bill for $57,346.20. A bug in Qwest's billing software caused it to charge some customers as much as $600 per minute for the use of their cell phones. About 1.4 percent of Qwest's customers, 14,000 in all, received incorrect bills. A Qwest spokesperson said the bug was in a newly installed billing system [6].

The U.S. Department of Agriculture implemented new livestock price-reporting guidelines after discovering that software errors had caused the USDA to understate the prices meat packers were receiving for beef. Since beef producers and packers negotiate cattle contracts based on the USDA price reports, the errors cost beef producers between $15 and $20 million [7].

In 1996, a software error at the U.S. Postal Service caused it to return to the senders two weeks' worth of mail addressed to the Patent and Trademark Office. In all, 50,000 pieces of mail were returned to sender [8].

A University of Pittsburgh study revealed that for most students, computer spelling and grammar error checkers actually increased the number of errors they made [9, 10].

Between September 2008 and May 2009, hundreds of families living in public housing in New York City were charged too much rent because of an error in the program that calculated their monthly bills. For nine months, the New York City Housing Authority did not take seriously the renters' complaints that they were being overcharged. Instead, it took to court many of the renters who did not make the higher payments and threatened them with eviction [11].

In 2010, about 450 California prison inmates with a "high risk of violence" were mistakenly released as part of a program meant to reduce prison overcrowding. California officials could not return any of them to prison or put them on supervised parole because they had already been granted "nonrevocable parole" [12].

8.3.2 Errors Leading to System Failures

On the first day a new, fully computerized ambulance dispatch system became operational in the City of London, people making emergency calls were put on hold for up to 30 minutes, the system lost track of some calls, and ambulances took up to three hours to respond. As many as 20 people died because ambulances did not arrive in time [13].

A software error led the Chicago Board of Trade to suspend trading for an hour on January 23, 1998. Another bug caused it to suspend trading for 45 minutes on April 1, 1998. In both cases, the temporary shutdown of the trading caused some investors to lose money [14]. System errors caused trading on the London International Financial Futures and Options Exchange to be halted twice within two weeks in May 1999. The second failure idled dealers for an hour and a half [16].

Thailand's finance minister was trapped inside his BMW limousine for 10 minutes when the on-board computer crashed, locking all doors and windows and turning off the air-conditioning. Security guards had to use sledge hammers to break a window, enabling Suchart Jaovisidha and his driver to escape [15].

Japan's air traffic control system went down for an hour on the morning of March 1, 2003, delaying departures for hours. The backup system failed at the same time as the main system, which was out of commission for four hours. Airports kept in touch via telephone, and no passengers were put at risk. However, some flights were delayed over two hours, and 32 domestic flights had to be canceled [17].

A new laboratory computer system at Los Angeles County+USC Medical Center became backlogged the day after it was turned on. For several hours on both April 16 and 17, 2003, emergency room doctors told the County of Los Angeles to stop sending ambulances, because the doctors could not get access to the laboratory results they needed. "It's almost like practicing Third World medicine," said Dr. Amanda Garner. "We rely so much on our computers and our fast-world technology that we were almost blinded" [18].

FIGURE 8.1 Comair cancelled all of its flights on Christmas Day, 2004, because the computer system that assigned crews to flights failed. (AP Photo/Al Behrman, File)

Comair, a subsidiary of Delta Air Lines, canceled all 1,100 of its flights on Christmas Day, 2004, because the computer system that assigns crews to flights stopped running (Figure 8.1). Airline officials said the software could not handle the large number of flight cancellations caused by bad weather on December 23 and 24. About 30,000 travelers in 118 cities were affected by the flight cancellations [19].

In August 2005 the passengers on a Malaysia Airlines flight from Perth, Australia, to Kuala Lumpur, Malaysia, suddenly found themselves on a roller coaster–like ride seven miles above the Indian Ocean. When the Boeing 777 unexpectedly began a rapid climb, the pilot disconnected the autopilot, but it took him 45 seconds to regain control of the jet. The plane zoomed upward, downward, and then upward a second time before leveling out. After an investigation, Boeing reported that a software error had caused the flight computers to receive faulty information about the plane's speed and acceleration. In addition, another error had caused the flight computers to fail to respond immediately to the pilot's commands [20].

8.3.3 Analysis: E–Retailer Posts Wrong Price, Refuses to Deliver

Amazon.com shut down its British Web site on March 13, 2003, after a software error led it to offer iPaq handheld computers for £7 instead of the correct price of about £275. Before Amazon.com shut down the site, electronic bargain hunters had flocked to Amazon.com's Web site, some of them ordering as many as ten iPaQs [21]. Amazon said that customers who ordered at the mistaken price should not expect delivery unless they paid the difference between the advertised price and the actual price. An Amazon.com spokesperson said, "In our Pricing and Availability Policy, we state that where an item's correct price is higher than our stated price, we contact the customer before dispatching. Customers will be offered the opportunity either to cancel their order or to place new orders for the item at the correct price" [22].

Was Amazon.com wrong to refuse to fill the orders of the people who bought iPaqs for £7?

Let's analyze the problem from a rule utilitarian point of view. We can imagine a moral rule of the form: "A person or organization wishing to sell a product must always honor the advertised price." What would happen if this rule were universally followed? More time and effort would be spent proofreading advertisements, whether printed or electronic. Organizations responsible for publishing the advertisements in newspapers, magazines, and Web sites would also take more care to ensure no errors were introduced. There is a good chance companies would take out insurance policies to guard against the catastrophic losses that could result from a typo. To pay for these additional costs, the prices of the products sold by these companies would be higher. The proposed rule would harm every consumer who ended up paying more for products. The rule would benefit the few consumers who took advantage of misprints to get good deals on certain goods. We conclude the proposed moral rule has more harms than benefits, and Amazon.com did the right thing by refusing the ship the iPaqs.

We *could* argue, from a Kantian point of view, that the knowledgeable consumers who ordered the iPaqs did something wrong. The correct price was £275; the advertised price was £7. While electronic products may go on sale, retailers simply do not drop the price of their goods by 97.5 percent, even when they are being put on clearance. If consumers understood the advertised price was an error, then they were taking advantage of Amazon.com's stockholders by ordering the iPaq before the error was corrected. They were not acting in "good faith."

8.4 Notable Software System Failures

In this section, we shift our focus to complicated devices or systems controlled at least in part by computers. An **embedded system** is a computer used as a component of a larger system. You can find microprocessor-based embedded systems in microwave ovens, thermostats, automobiles, traffic lights, and a myriad of other modern devices. Because computers need software to execute, every embedded system has a software component.

Software is playing an ever-larger role in system functionality [23]. There are several reasons why hardware controllers are being replaced by microprocessors controlled by software. Software controllers are faster. They can perform more sophisticated functions, taking more input data into account. They cost less, use less energy, and do not wear out. Unfortunately, while hardware controllers have a reputation for high reliability, the same cannot be said for their software replacements.

Most embedded systems are also **real-time systems**: computers that process data from sensors as events occur. The microprocessor that controls the air bags in a modern automobile is a real-time system, because it must instantly react to readings from its sensors and deploy the air bags at the time of a collision. The microprocessor in a cell phone is another example of a real-time system that converts electrical signals into radio waves, and vice versa.

This section contains seven examples of computer system failures: the Patriot missile system used in the Gulf War, the Ariane 5 launch vehicle, AT&T's long-distance network, NASA's robot missions to Mars, the automated baggage system at Denver International Airport, the Tokyo Stock Exchange, and direct recording electronic voting machines. These are all examples of embedded, real-time systems. In every case at least part of the failure was due to errors in the software component of the system. Studying these errors provides important lessons for anyone involved in the development of an embedded system.

8.4.1 Patriot Missile

The Patriot missile system was originally designed by the U.S. Army to shoot down airplanes. In the 1991 Gulf War, the Army put the Patriot missile system to work defending against Scud missiles launched at Israel and Saudi Arabia.

At the end of the Gulf War, the Army claimed the Patriot missile defense system had been 95 percent effective at destroying incoming Scud missiles. Later analyses showed that perhaps as few as 9 percent of the Scuds were actually destroyed by Patriot missiles. As it turns out, many Scuds simply fell apart as they approached their targets—their destruction had nothing at all to do with the Patriot missiles launched at them.

The most significant failure of the Patriot missile system occurred during the night of February 25, 1991, when a Scud missile fired from Iraq hit a U.S. Army barracks in Dhahran, Saudi Arabia, killing 28 soldiers. The Patriot missile battery defending the area never even fired at the incoming Scud.

Mississippi congressman Howard Wolpe asked the General Accounting Office (GAO) to investigate this incident. The GAO report traced the failure of the Patriot system to a software error (Figure 8.2). The missile battery did detect the incoming Scud missile as it came over the horizon. However, in order to prevent the system from responding to false alarms, the computer was programmed to check multiple times for the presence of the missile. The computer predicted the flight path of the incoming missile, directed the radar to focus in on that area, and scanned a segment of the radar signal, called a range gate, for the target. In this case, the program scanned the wrong range gate. Since it did not detect the Scud, it did not fire the Patriot missile.

Why did the program scan the wrong range gate? The tracking system relied upon getting signals from the system clock. These values were stored in a floating-point variable with insufficient precision, resulting in a small mathematical error called a *truncation*. The longer the system ran, the more these truncation errors added up. The Patriot missile system was designed to operate for only a few hours at a time. However, the sys-

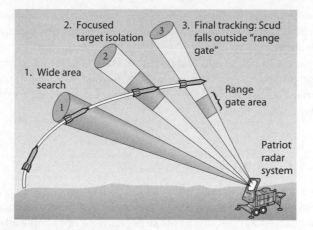

FIGURE 8.2 A software error caused the Patriot missile system to lose track of incoming Scud missiles. (1) The radar system doing a wide area search picks up the Scud missile. (2) The radar system isolates the proposed target. (3) A software error causes the system to produce a faulty range gate. The system loses track of the missile, because it does not fly through this gate. (Figure from SCIENCE 255:1347. Copyright ©1992 by The American Association for the Advancement of Science. Reprinted with permission.)

tem at Dhahran had been in continuous operation for 100 hours. The accumulation of errors led to a difference between the actual time and the computed time of about 0.3433 seconds. Because missiles travel at high speeds, the 0.3433-second error led to a tracking error of 687 meters (about half a mile). That was enough of an error to prevent the missile battery from locating the Scud in the range gate area [24].

8.4.2 Ariane 5

The Ariane 5 was a satellite launch vehicle designed by the French space agency, the Centre National d'Etudes Spatiales, and the European Space Agency. About 40 seconds into its maiden flight on June 4, 1996, a software error caused the nozzles on the solid boosters and the main rocket engine to swivel to extreme positions. As a result, the rocket veered sharply off course. When the links between the solid boosters and the core stage ruptured, the launch vehicle self-destructed. The rocket carried satellites worth $500 million, which were not insured [25].

A board of inquiry traced the software error to a piece of code that converts a 64-bit floating-point value into a 16-bit signed integer. The value to be converted exceeded the maximum value that could be stored in the integer variable, causing an exception to be raised. Unfortunately, there was no exception handling mechanism for this particular exception, so the onboard computers crashed.

The faulty piece of code had been part of the software for the Ariane 4. The 64-bit floating-point value represented the horizontal bias of the launch vehicle, which is related to its horizontal velocity. When the software module was designed, engineers determined that it would be impossible for the horizontal bias to be so large that it could not be stored in a 16-bit signed integer. There was no need for an error handler, because an error could not occur. This code was moved "as is" into the software for the Ariane 5. That proved to be an extremely costly mistake, because the Ariane 5 was faster than the Ariane 4. The original assumptions made by the designers of the software no longer held true [26].

8.4.3 AT&T Long–Distance Network

On the afternoon of January 15, 1990, AT&T's long-distance network suffered a significant disruption of service. About half of the computerized telephone-routing switches crashed, and the remainder of the switches could not handle all of the traffic. As a result of this failure, about 70 million long-distance telephone calls could not be put through, and about 60,000 people lost all telephone service. AT&T lost tens of millions of dollars of revenue. It also lost some of its credibility as a reliable provider of long-distance service.

Investigation by AT&T engineers revealed that the network crash was brought about by a single faulty line of code in an error-recovery procedure. The system was designed so that if a server discovered it was in an error state, it would reboot itself, a crude but effective way of "wiping the slate clean." After a switch rebooted itself, it would send an "OK" message to other switches, letting them know it was back on line. The software bug manifested itself when a very busy switch received an "OK" message. Under certain circumstances, handling the "OK" message would cause the busy switch to enter an error state and reboot.

On the afternoon of January 15, 1990, a System 7 switch in New York City detected an error condition and rebooted itself (Figure 8.3). When it came back on line, it broadcast an "OK" message. All of the switches receiving the "OK" messages handled them correctly, except three very busy switches in St. Louis, Detroit, and Atlanta. These switches detected an error condition and rebooted. When they came back up, all of them broadcast "OK" messages across the network, causing other switches to fail in an ever-expanding wave.

Every switch failure compounded the problem in two ways. When the switch went down, it pushed more long-distance traffic onto the other switches, making them busier. When the switch came back up, it broadcast "OK" messages to these busier switches, causing some of them to fail. Some switches rebooted repeatedly under the barrage of "OK" messages. Within 10 minutes, half of the switches in the AT&T network had failed.

The crash could have been much worse, but AT&T had converted only 80 of its network switches to the System 7 software. It had left System 6 software running on 34 of the switches, "just in case." The System 6 switches did not have the software bug and did not crash [27, 28].

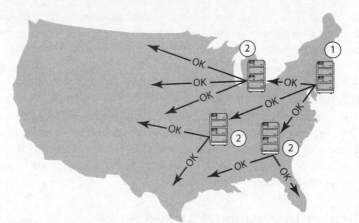

FIGURE 8.3 A software bug in error-recovery code made AT&T's System 7 switches crash in 1990. (1) A single switch in New York City detects an error condition and reboots. When it comes back up, it sends an "OK" message to other switches. (2) Switches in Detroit, St. Louis, and Atlanta are so busy that handling the "OK" message causes them to fail. They detect an error condition and reboot. When they come back up, they send out "OK" messages to other switches, causing some of them to fail, and so on.

8.4.4 Robot Missions to Mars

NASA designed the $125-million Mars Climate Orbiter to facilitate communications between Earth and automated probes on the surface of Mars, including the Mars Polar Lander. Ironically, the spacecraft was lost because of a miscommunication between two support teams on Earth.

The Lockheed Martin flight operations team in Colorado designed its software to use English units. Its program output thrust in terms of foot-pounds. The navigation team at the Jet Propulsion Laboratory in California designed its software to use metric units. Its program expected thrust to be input in terms of newtons. One foot-pound equals 4.45 newtons. On September 23, 1999, the Mars Climate Orbiter neared the Red Planet. When it was time for the spacecraft to fire its engine to enter orbit, the Colorado team supplied thrust information to the California team, which relayed it to the spacecraft. Because of the units mismatch, the navigation team specified 4.45 times too much thrust. The spacecraft flew too close to the surface of Mars and burned up in its atmosphere.

A few months later NASA's Martian program suffered a second catastrophe. The Mars Polar Lander, produced at a cost of $165 million, was supposed to land on the south pole of Mars and provide data that would help scientists understand how the Martian climate has changed over time. On December 3, 1999, NASA lost contact with the Mars Polar Lander. NASA engineers suspect that the system's software got a false signal from the landing gear and shut down the engines 100 feet above the planet's surface.

Tony Spear was project manager of the Mars Pathfinder mission. He said, "It is just as hard to do Mars missions now as it was in the mid-70s. I'm a big believer that software hasn't gone anywhere. Software is the number-one problem" [29].

After Spear made this observation, NASA successfully landed two Mars Exploration Rovers on the Red Planet [30]. The rovers, named Opportunity and Spirit, were launched from Earth in June and July of 2003, successfully landing on Mars in January 2004. Mission planners had hoped that each rover would complete a three-month mission, looking for clues that the Martian surface once had enough water to sustain life. The rovers greatly exceeded this goal. The Spirit rover operated successfully for more than five years. Opportunity found evidence of a former saltwater lake, and was still operational after seven years.

8.4.5 Denver International Airport

As airline passenger traffic strained the capacity of Stapleton International Airport, the City and County of Denver planned the construction of a much larger airport. Stapleton International Airport had earned a reputation for slow baggage handling, and the project planners wanted to ensure the new airport would not suffer from the same problem. They announced an ambitious plan to create a one-of-a-kind, state-of-the-art automated baggage handling system for the Denver International Airport (DIA).

The airport authorities signed a $193-million contract with BAE Automated Systems to design and build the automated baggage-handling system, which consisted of thousands of baggage carts traveling roller-coaster-style on 21 miles of metal tracks. According to the design, agents would label a piece of luggage and put it on a conveyer belt. Computers would route each bag along one or more belts until they reached a cart-loading point, where each bag would be loaded into its own tub-like cart. Scanners would read the destination information from the suitcase label, and computers would then route each cart along the tracks at 20 miles per hour to the correct unloading point, where each bag would be unloaded onto a conveyer belt and carried to its final destination. To monitor the movement of the bags, the system used 56 barcode scanners and 5,000 electric eyes.

There were problems from the outset of the project. The airport design was already done before the baggage handling system was chosen. As a result, the underground tunnels were small and had sharp turns, making it difficult to shoehorn in an automated baggage system. And given its ambitious goals, the project timeline was too short.

However, the most important problem with the automated baggage handler was that the complexity of the system exceeded the ability of the development team to understand it. Here are a few of the problems BAE encountered:

- Luggage carts were misrouted and failed to arrive at their destinations.
- Computers lost track of where the carts were.
- Barcode printers didn't print tags clearly enough to be read by scanners.
- Luggage had to be properly positioned on conveyors in order to load properly.

- Bumpers on the carts interfered with the electric photocells.
- Workers painted over electric eyes or knocked photo sensors out of alignment.
- Light luggage was thrown off rapidly moving carts.
- Luggage was shredded by automated baggage handlers.
- The design did not consider the problem of fairly balancing the number of available carts among all the locations needing them.

BAE attempted to solve these problems one at a time by trial and error, but the system was too complicated to yield to this problem-solving approach. BAE should have been looking at the big picture, trying to find where the specifications for the system were wrong or unattainable.

DIA was supposed to open on October 31, 1993. The opening was delayed repeatedly because the baggage-handling system was not yet operational. Eventually, the Mayor of Denver announced the city would spend $50 million to build a conventional luggage handling system using tugs and carts. (This conventional system actually ended up costing $71 million.) On February 28, 1995, flights to and from the new airport began. However, Concourse A was not open at all. Concourse C opened with 11 airlines using a traditional baggage system. The BAE automated system, far over budget at $311 million, was used only by United Airlines in Concourse B to handle outgoing baggage originating in Denver. United used a traditional system for the rest of its baggage in Concourse B.

The failure of BAE to deliver a working system on time resulted in a 16-month delay in the opening of DIA. This delay cost Denver $1 million a *day* in interest on bonds and operating costs. As a result, DIA began charging all of the airlines a flight fee of about $20 per passenger, the highest airport fee in the nation. Airlines passed along this cost to consumers by raising ticket prices of flights going through Denver [31].

While the story of the Denver International Airport is noteworthy because of the large amount of money involved, it is not unusual for software projects to take longer than expected and to cost more than anticipated. In fact, most software projects are not completed on time and on budget. We'll explore this issue in greater detail in Section 8.7.

8.4.6 Tokyo Stock Exchange

December 8, 2005, was the first day that shares of J-Com, a recruiting company, were made available to the public on the Tokyo Stock Exchange. That morning, an employee of Mizuho Securities received a call from a customer, who said he wished to sell one share of J-Com stock at a price of ¥610,000. At 9:27 a.m., the Mizuho Securities employee mistakenly entered an order to sell 610,000 shares of J-Com at ¥1 per share. When the computer screen displayed a "Beyond price limit" warning, the employee overrode the warning by hitting the Enter key twice, sending the order to the Tokyo Stock Exchange. At 9:28 a.m., the sell order appeared on the Tokyo Stock Exchange's display board. Spotting the mistake, Mizuho Securities attempted to cancel the sell order several times between 9:29 and 9:35 a.m., but these attempts failed because of a bug in the Tokyo Stock

Exchange trading program. Mizuho also phoned the Tokyo Stock Exchange, asking the TSE to cancel the sell order, but the Tokyo Stock Exchange refused.

Beginning at 9:35 a.m., Mizuho started to buy back shares of J-Com, but it was only able to purchase about a half million shares. More than 96,000 shares had already been purchased by other parties. It was impossible for Mizuho to provide shares to these buyers because J-Com only had 14,500 publicly traded shares. Under the terms of a special arrangement brokered by the stock exchange, Mizuho settled these accounts by paying ¥912,000 per share to the buyers. In all, Mizuho Securities lost ¥40 billion ($225 million) buying back shares. When the Tokyo Stock Exchange refused to compensate Mizuho Securities for the loss, Mizuho Securities sued the Tokyo Stock Exchange. The case has not yet been settled.

Eventually the Tokyo Stock Exchange identified the bug that prevented the order from being canceled. The bug had gone undetected for five years because it only occurred when seven different unusual conditions all happened simultaneously [32].

8.4.7 Direct Recording Electronic Voting Machines

Nearly two million ballots were not counted in the 2000 U.S. Presidential election because they registered either no choice or multiple choices. The incredibly close election in Florida was marred by the "hanging chad" and "butterfly ballot" controversies discussed in Section 7.5. To avoid a repeat of these problems, Congress passed, and President Bush signed, the Help America Vote Act of 2002 (HAVA). HAVA provided money to states to replace punch card voting systems and improve standards for administering elections [33].

Many states used HAVA funds to purchase direct recording electronic (DRE) voting machines. DRE voting machines allow voters to indicate each of their choices by touching the screen or pressing a button (Figure 8.4). After all selections have been made, a summary screen displays the voter's choices. At this point, the voter may either cast the ballot or back up to make changes.

Brazil and India have run national elections using DRE voting machines exclusively [34]. In the United States, a variety of voting technologies are still being used; during the November 2006 general election, about one-third of voters cast their ballots on DRE systems. Proponents of DRE voting machines point out the speed and accuracy of machine counting. They say the systems are more tamper-resistant than paper ballots, which can be marked by election workers. When the ballots are electronic, it is impossible for precincts to run out of ballots if turnout is higher than expected. In addition, touch-screen voting machines can be programmed to help voters avoid the previously mentioned errors of not choosing a candidate or selecting too many candidates [35].

Some computer experts have spoken out against the conversion to touch-screen voting machines, arguing that they are not necessarily any better than the systems they are replacing. In particular, experts worry about programming errors and the lack of a **paper audit trail**: a record of the original ballots cast.

FIGURE 8.4 This Diebold voting machine uses a touch-sensitive screen to capture each voter's choices. (© AP Photo/Rogelio Solis)

Quite a few voting irregularities have been linked to DRE voting machines since 2002. Here is a selection:

- In November 2002, a programming error caused a touch-screen voting machine to fail to record 436 ballots cast in Wake County, North Carolina [36].

- Touch-screen voting machines reported that 144,000 ballots were cast in a 2003 election held in Boone County, Indiana, even though county had only 19,000 registered voters. After a programming error was fixed, the ballots were recounted, producing new results consistent with the number of votes actually cast. However, because there was no paper audit trail, there was no way to know if the new results were correct [37].

- Florida held a special election in January 2004 to determine who would represent State House District 91. When the 10,844 votes were tallied, the voting machines reported that 134 voters had not voted for a candidate, even though that was the only race on the ballot. The winning candidate received 12 more votes than the runner-up. Since the voting machines had no record of the original votes, there was no recount [37].

- In November 2004, initial printouts from all the DRE voting machines in LaPorte County, Indiana, reported exactly 300 votes, disregarding more than 50,000 votes until the problem was sorted out [38].

- In November 2004, a bug in the vote-counting software in DRE voting machines in Guilford County, North Carolina, caused the systems to begin counting backward after they reached a maximum count of 32,767. After the problem was fixed, a recount changed the outcome of two races and gave another 22,000 votes to Presidential candidate John Kerry [39].

- In 2006, some Florida voters had a hard time voting for Democratic candidates on DRE voting machines. After choosing Democrats, these voters discovered that the machine's summary screen replaced some of the Democrats with their Republican opponents. Some voters had to repeat their votes several times in order for the proper candidate's name to appear on the summary screen [40].

- In a Congressional election held in November 2006 in Florida, more than 18,000 votes cast on DRE voting machines were not recorded. The final tally showed Republican Vern Buchanan beating Democrat Christine Jennings by only 369 votes [41].

Some computer experts are worried about the vulnerability of electronic voting machines to tampering. Finnish security specialist Harri Hursti investigated the memory cartridges used to record votes in Diebold DRE voting machines. (After the polls close, these cartridges are removed from the machines and taken to a central location, where the votes are tallied.) Hursti discovered that he could use a readily available agricultural scanning device to change the vote counts without leaving a trace [42].

Computer science professor Herbert Thompson examined the centralized Diebold machine that tallies the votes from the individual DRE voting machines. According to Thompson, the system lacked even a rudimentary authentication mechanism; he was able to access the system's program without a login name or password. By inserting just five lines of code, he successfully switched 5,000 votes from one candidate to another. "I am positive an eighth grader could do this," he said [42].

Without access to the source code to touch-screen systems, there is no way to test how secure they are. The manufacturers of these systems have refused to make the software public, saying the source code is valuable intellectual property—a trade secret. The Open Voting Consortium has criticized the corporate control of elections in the United States and advocates the development of open-source software to make elections "open and transparent" [43].

Critics of touch-screen voting systems say these systems make possible an unprecedented level of election fraud. The old, lever-style mechanical voting machines were susceptible to fraud at the local level. A voting official could enter a voting booth and vote multiple times for a slate of candidates, but the number of extra votes that can be added in any precinct without attracting attention was limited. In contrast, by changing the programming of an electronic voting system, a single person could change votes across thousands of precincts [44].

Supporters of touch-screen voting machines say criticisms of DRE voting machines are overblown. A report by the Pacific Research Institute maintains that DRE voting systems are more secure than traditional paper ballots, which can be tampered with by elections officials. "Open source advocates and paper trail champions want to steer e-voting off a cliff. Rather than demanding utopian machines and spreading conspiracy theories for political gain, they should re-focus their energy in a way that actually helps American voters" [45].

Nevertheless, some states are having second thoughts about DRE voting machines. In May 2007 Florida's legislature voted to replace DRE voting machines with optical scan ballots. Voters select candidates by filling in bubbles next to their names, and optical scanning machines count the marked ballots. This approach leaves a paper audit trail that makes possible manual recounts in disputed elections [46].

8.5 Therac–25

Soon after German physicist Wilhelm Roentgen discovered the x-ray in 1895, physicians began using radiation to treat cancer. Today, between 50 and 60 percent of cancer patients are treated with radiation, either to destroy cancer cells or relieve pain. Linear accelerators create high-energy electron beams to treat shallow tumors and x-ray beams to reach deeper tumors.

The Therac-25 linear accelerator was notoriously unreliable. It was not unusual for the system to malfunction 40 times a day. We devote an entire section to telling the story of the Therac-25 because it is a striking example of the harm that can be caused when the safety of a system relies solely upon the quality of its embedded software.

In a 20-month period between June 1985 and January 1987, the Therac-25 administered massive overdoses to six patients, causing the deaths of three of them. While 1987 may seem like the distant past to many of you, it does give us the advantage of 20/20 hindsight. The entire story has been thoroughly researched and documented [47]. Failures of computerized systems continue to this day, but they have not yet been fully played out and analyzed.

8.5.1 Genesis of the Therac–25

Atomic Energy of Canada Limited (AECL) and the French corporation CGR cooperated in the 1970s to build two linear accelerators: the Therac-6 and the Therac-20. Both the Therac-6 and the Therac-20 were modernizations of older CGR linear accelerators. The distinguishing feature of the Therac series was the use of a DEC PDP 11 minicomputer as a "front end." By adding the computer, the linear accelerators were easier to operate. The Therac-6 and the Therac-20 were actually capable of working independently of the PDP 11, and all of their safety features were built into the hardware.

After producing the Therac-20, AECL and CGR went their separate ways. AECL moved ahead with the development and deployment of a next-generation linear accelerator called the Therac-25. Like the Therac-6 and the Therac-20, the Therac-25 made use of a PDP 11. Unlike its predecessor machines, however, AECL designed the PDP 11 to be an integral part of the device; the linear accelerator was incapable of operating without the computer. This design decision enabled AECL to reduce costs by replacing some of the hardware safety features of the Therac-20 with software safety features in the Therac-25.

AECL also decided to reuse some of the Therac-6 and Therac-20 software in the Therac-25. Code reuse saves time and money. Theoretically, "tried and true" software is more reliable than newly written code, but as we shall see, that assumption was invalid in this case.

AECL shipped its first Therac-25 in 1983. In all, it delivered 11 systems in Canada and the United States. The Therac-25 was a large machine that was placed in its own room. Shielding in the walls, ceiling, and floor of the room prevented outsiders from being exposed to radiation. A television camera, microphone, and speaker in the room allowed the technician in an adjoining room to view and communicate with the patient undergoing treatment.

8.5.2 Chronology of Accidents and AECL Responses

MARIETTA, GEORGIA, JUNE 1985

A 61-year-old breast cancer patient was being treated at the Kennestone Regional Oncology Center. After radiation was administered to the area of her collarbone, she complained that she had been burned.

The Kennestone physicist contacted AECL and asked if it was possible that the Therac-25 had failed to diffuse the electron beam. Engineers at AECL replied that this could not happen.

The patient suffered crippling injuries as a result of the overdose, which the physicist later estimated was 75 to 100 times too large. She sued AECL and the hospital in October 1985.

HAMILTON, ONTARIO, JULY 1985

A 40-year-old woman was being treated for cervical cancer at the Ontario Cancer Foundation. When the operator tried to administer the treatment, the machine shut down after five seconds with an error message. According to the display, the linear accelerator had not yet delivered any radiation to the patient. Following standard operating procedure, the operator typed "P" for "proceed." The system shut down in the same way, indicating that the patient had not yet received a dose of radiation. (Recall it was not unusual for the machine to malfunction several dozen times a day.) The operator typed "P" three more times, always with the same result, until the system entered "treatment suspend" mode.

The operator went into the room where the patient was. The patient complained that she had been burned. The lab called in a service technician, who could find nothing wrong with the machine. The clinic reported the malfunction to AECL.

When the patient returned for further treatment three days later, she was hospitalized for a radiation overdose. It was later estimated that she had received between 65 and 85 times the normal dose of radiation. The patient died of cancer in November 1985.

FIRST AECL INVESTIGATION, JULY–SEPTEMBER 1985

After the Ontario overdose, AECL sent out an engineer to investigate. While the engineer was unable to reproduce the overdose, he did uncover design problems related to a microswitch. AECL introduced hardware and software changes to fix the microswitch problem.

YAKIMA, WASHINGTON, DECEMBER 1985

The next documented overdose accident occurred at Yakima Valley Memorial Hospital. A woman receiving a series of radiation treatments developed a strange reddening on her hip after one of the treatments. The inflammation took the form of several parallel stripes. The hospital staff tried to determine the cause of the unusual stripes. They suspected the pattern could have been caused by the slots in the accelerator's blocking trays, but these trays had already been discarded by the time the staff began their investigation. After ruling out other possible causes for the reaction, the staff suspected a radiation overdose and contacted AECL by letter and by phone.

AECL replied in a letter that neither the Therac-25 nor operator error could have produced the described damage. Two pages of the letter explained why it was technically impossible for the Therac-25 to produce an overdose. The letter also claimed that no similar accidents had been reported.

The patient survived, although the overdose scarred her and left her with a mild disability.

TYLER, TEXAS, MARCH 1986

A male patient came to the East Texas Cancer Center (ETCC) for the ninth in a series of radiation treatments for a cancerous tumor on his back. The operator entered the treatment data into the computer. She noticed that she had typed "X" (for x-ray) instead of "E" (for electron beam). This was a common mistake, because x-ray treatments are much more common. Being an experienced operator, she quickly fixed her mistake by using the up arrow key to move the cursor back to the appropriate field, changing the "X" to an "E" and moving the cursor back to the bottom of the screen. When the system displayed "beam ready," she typed "B" (for beam on). After a few seconds, the Therac-25 shut down. The console screen contained the message "Malfunction 54" and indicated a "treatment pause," a low-priority problem. The dose monitor showed that the patient had received only 6 units of treatment rather than the desired 202 units. The operator hit the "P" (proceed) key to continue the treatment.

The cancer patient and the operator were in adjoining rooms. Normally a video camera and intercom would enable the operator to monitor her patients. However, at the time of the accident neither system was operational.

The patient had received eight prior treatments, so he knew something was wrong as soon as the ninth treatment began. He was instantly aware of the overdose—he felt as if someone had poured hot coffee on his back or given him an electric shock. As he tried to get up from the table, the accelerator delivered its second dose, which hit him in the arm. The operator became aware of the problem when the patient began pounding on the door. He had received between 80 and 125 times the prescribed amount of radiation. He suffered acute pain and steadily lost bodily functions until he died from complications of the overdose five months later.

SECOND AECL INVESTIGATION, MARCH 1986

After the accident, the ETCC shut down its Therac-25 and notified AECL. AECL sent out two engineers to examine the system. Try as they might, they could not reproduce Malfunction 54. They told the physicians it was impossible for the Therac-25 to overdose a patient, and they suggested that the patient may have received an electrical shock due to a fault in the hospital's electrical system.

The ETCC checked out the electrical system and found no problems with it. After double-checking the linear accelerator's calibration, they put the Therac-25 back into service.

TYLER, TEXAS, APRIL 1986

The second Tyler, Texas, accident was virtually a replay of the prior accident at ETCC. The same technician was in control of the Therac-25, and she went through the same process of entering x-ray when she meant electron beam, then going back and correcting her mistake. Once again, the machine halted with a Malfunction 54 shortly after she activated the electron beam. This time, however, the intercom was working, and she rushed to the accelerator when she heard the patient moan. There was nothing she could do to help him. The patient had received a massive dose of radiation to his brain, and he died three weeks later.

After the accident, ETCC immediately shut down the Therac-25 and contacted AECL again.

YAKIMA, WASHINGTON, JANUARY 1987

A second patient was severely burned by the Therac-25 at Yakima Valley Memorial Hospital under circumstances almost identical to those of the December 1985 accident. Four days after the treatment, the patient's skin revealed a series of parallel red stripes—the same pattern that had perplexed the radiation staff in the case of the previous patient. This time, the staff members were able to match the burns to the slots in the Therac-25's blocking tray. The patient died three months later.

THERAC-25 DECLARED DEFECTIVE, FEBRUARY 1987

On February 10, 1987, the FDA declared the Therac-25 to be defective. In order for the Therac-25 to gain back FDA approval, AECL had to demonstrate how it would make the system safe. Five months later, after five revisions, AECL produced a corrective action plan that met the approval of the FDA. This plan incorporated a variety of hardware interlocks to prevent the machine from delivering overdoses or activating the beam when the turntable was not in the correct position.

8.5.3 Software Errors

In the course of investigating the accidents, AECL discovered a variety of hardware and software problems with the Therac-25. Two of the software errors are examples of race conditions. In a **race condition,** two or more concurrent tasks share a variable, and the order in which they read or write the value of the variable can affect the behavior of the program. Race conditions are extremely difficult to identify and fix, because usually the two tasks do not interfere with each other and nothing goes wrong. Only in rare conditions will the tasks actually interfere with each other as they manipulate the variable, causing the error to occur. We describe both of these errors to give you some insight into how difficult they are to detect.

The accidents at the ETCC occurred because of a race condition associated with the command screen (Figure 8.5). One task was responsible for handling keyboard input and making changes to the command screen. A second task was responsible for monitoring the command screen for changes and moving the magnets into position. After the operator uses the first task to complete the prescription (1), the second task sees the cursor in the lower right-hand corner of the screen and begins the eight-second process of moving the magnets (2). Meanwhile, the operator sees her mistake. The first task responds to her keystrokes and lets her change the "X" to an "E" (3). She gets the cursor back to the lower right-hand corner before eight seconds are up (4). Now the second task finishes moving the magnets (5). It sees the cursor in the lower right-hand corner of the screen and incorrectly assumes the screen has not changed. The crucial substitution of electron beam for x-ray goes unnoticed.

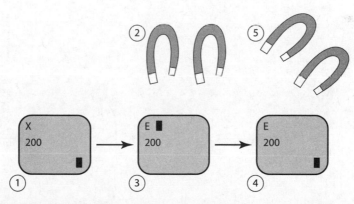

FIGURE 8.5 Illustration of a Therac-25 bug revealed by fast-typing operators. (1) The operator finishes filling in the form. The software knows the form is filled in because the cursor is in the lower right-hand corner of the screen. (2) The software instructs the magnets to move into the correct positions. While the magnets are moving, the software does not check for screen edits. (3) The operator changes the prescription from x-ray to electron beam. (4) The operator finishes the edit, returning the cursor to the lower right-hand corner of the screen. (5) The magnets finish moving. The software now checks the screen cursor. Since it is in the lower right-hand corner, the program assumes there have been no edits.

What makes this bug particularly treacherous is that it only occurs with faster, more experienced operators. Slower operators would not be able to complete the edit and get the cursor back to the lower right-hand corner of the screen in only eight seconds. If the cursor happened to be anywhere else on the screen when the magnets stopped moving, the software would check for a screen edit and there would be no overdose. It is ironic that the safety of the system actually *decreased* as the experience of the operator *increased*.

Another race condition was responsible for the overdoses at the Yakima Valley Memorial Hospital (Figure 8.6). It occurred when the machine was putting the electron-beam gun back into position. A variable was supposed to be 0 if the gun was ready to fire. Any other value meant the gun was not ready. As long as the electron beam gun was out of position, one task kept incrementing that variable. Unfortunately, the variable could only store the values from 0 to 255. Incrementing it when it had the value 255 would result in the variable's value rolling over to 0, like a car's odometer.

Nearly every time that the operator hit the SET button when the gun was out of position, the variable was not 0 and the gun did not fire (Figure 8.6a). However, there was a very slight chance that the variable would have just rolled over when the operator hit the SET button (Figure 8.6b). In this case the accelerator would emit a charge, even though the system was not ready.

8.5.4 Postmortem

Let's consider some of the mistakes AECL made in the design, development, and support of this system.

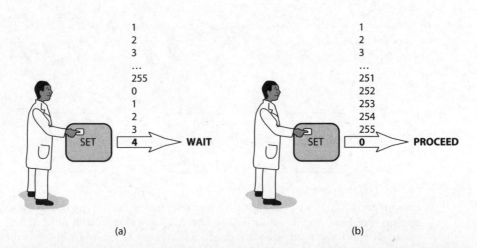

(a)   (b)

FIGURE 8.6 The Therac-25 could administer radiation too soon if the operator hit the SET button at precisely the wrong time. As long as the electron-beam gun was out of position, a software task kept incrementing an 8-bit variable. (a) Usually when the operator hit the SET button, the variable was not zero and the system would wait, just as it was supposed to. (b) If the operator hit the SET button just as the variable rolled over from 255 to 0, the system would administer radiation, even though the gun was out of position.

When accidents were reported, AECL focused on identifying and fixing particular software bugs. This approach was too narrow. As Nancy Leveson and Clark Turner point out, "most accidents are system accidents; that is, they stem from complex interactions between various components and activities" [47]. The entire system was broken, not just the software. A strategy of eliminating bugs assumes that at some point the last bug will be eradicated. But as Leveson and Turner write, "There is always another software bug" [47].

The real problem was that the system was not designed to be fail-safe. Good engineering practice dictates that a system should be designed so that no single point of failure will lead to a catastrophe. By relying completely upon software for protection against overdoses, the Therac-25 designers ignored this fundamental engineering principle.

Another flaw in the design of the Therac-25 was its lack of software or hardware devices to detect and report overdoses and shut down the accelerator immediately. Instead, the Therac-25 designers left it up to the patients to report when they had received overdoses.

There are also particular software lessons we can learn from the case of the Therac-25. First, it is very difficult to find software errors in programs where multiple tasks execute at the same time and interact through shared variables. Second, the software design needs to be as simple as possible, and design decisions must be documented to aid in the maintenance of the system. Third, the code must be reasonably documented at the time it is written.

Fourth, reusing code does not always increase the quality of the final product. AECL assumed that by reusing code from the Therac-6 and Therac-20, the software would be more reliable. After all, the code had been part of systems used by customers for years with no problems. This assumption turned out to be wrong. The earlier codes did contain errors. These errors remained undetected because the earlier machines had hardware interlocks that prevented the computer's erroneous commands from harming patients.

The tragedy was compounded because AECL did not communicate fully with its customers. For example, AECL told the physicists in Washington and Texas that an overdose was impossible, even though AECL had already been sued by the patient in Georgia.

8.5.5 Moral Responsibility of the Therac–25 Team

Should the developers and managers at AECL be held morally responsible for the deaths resulting from the use of the Therac-25 they produced?

In order for a moral agent to be responsible for a harmful event, two conditions must hold:

- *Causal condition*: the actions (or inactions) of the agent must have caused the harm.
- *Mental condition*: the actions (or inactions) must have been intended or willed by the agent.

In this case, the causal condition is easy to establish. The deaths resulted both from the action of AECL employees (creating the therapy machine that administered the overdose) and the inaction of AECL employees (failing to withdraw the machine from service or even inform other users of the machine that there had been overdoses).

What about the second condition? Surely the engineers at AECL did not intend or try to create a machine that would administer lethal overdoses of radiation. However, philosophers also extend the mental condition to include unintended harm if the moral agent's actions were the result of carelessness, recklessness, or negligence. The design team took a number of actions that fall into this category. It constructed a system without hardware interlocks to prevent overdoses or the beam from being activated when the turntable was not in a correct position. The machine had no software or hardware devices to detect an accidental overdose. Management allowed software to be developed without adequate documentation. It presumed the correctness of reused code and failed to test it thoroughly. For these reasons, the mental condition holds as well, and we conclude the Therac-25 team at AECL is morally responsible for the deaths caused by the Therac-25 radiation therapy machine.

8.5.6 Postscript

More than two decades after the Therac-25 accidents, computer errors related to radiation machines continue to maim and kill patients. In late 2006, Scott Jerome-Parks received three overdoses from a linear accelerator at a New York City Hospital that led to his death a few weeks later. He was only 43 years old. About the same time, 32-year-old breast cancer patient Alexandra Jn-Charles received 27 straight days of radiation overdoses at another New York hospital that led to her death. An investigation of radiation overdoses by *The New York Times* concluded that a variety of errors, including faulty software, were leading to crippling or fatal accidents [48].

8.6 Computer Simulations

In the previous section, we focused on an unreliable computer-controlled system that delivered lethal doses of radiation to cancer patients, but even systems kept behind the locked doors of a computer room can cause harm. Errors in computer simulations can result in poorly designed products, mediocre science, and bad policy decisions. In this section, we review our growing reliance on computer simulations for designing products, understanding our world, and even predicting the future, and we describe ways in which computer modelers validate their simulations.

8.6.1 Uses of Simulation

Computer simulation plays a key role in contemporary science and engineering. There are many reasons why a scientist or engineer may not be able to perform a physical experiment. It may be too expensive or time-consuming, or it may be unethical or impossible to perform. Computer simulations have been used to design nuclear weapons, search for oil, create pharmaceuticals, and design safer, more fuel efficient cars. They have even been used to design consumer products such as disposable diapers [49].

Some computer simulations model past events. For example, when astrophysicists derive theories about the evolution of the universe, they can test them through computer simulations. A computer simulation has demonstrated that a gas disk around a young star can fragment into giant gas planets such as Jupiter [50].

A second use of computer simulations is to understand the world around us. One of the first important uses of computer simulations was to aid in the exploration for oil. Drilling a single well costs millions of dollars, and most drillings result in "dry wells" that produce no revenue. Geologists lay out networks of microphones and set off explosive charges. Computers analyze the echoes received by the microphones to produce graphical representations of underground rock formations. Analyzing these formations helps petroleum engineers select the most promising sites to drill.

Computer simulations are also used to predict the future. Modern weather predictions are based on computer simulations. These predictions become particularly important when people are exposed to extreme weather conditions, such as floods, tornadoes, and hurricanes (Figure 8.7). Every computer simulation has an underlying mathematical model. Faster computers enable scientists and engineers to develop more sophisticated models. Over time, the quality of these models has improved.

Of course, the predictions made by computer simulations can be wrong. In 1972, the Club of Rome, an international think tank based in Germany, commissioned a book called *The Limits to Growth*. The book predicted that a continued exponential increase in world population would lead to shortages of minerals and farm land, higher food prices, and significant increases in pollution [51]. A year after the book was published, the Arab

FIGURE 8.7 We rely on computer simulations to predict the path and speed of hurricanes. (Courtesy of NASA)

oil embargo resulted in dramatically higher oil and gasoline prices in Western nations, giving credence to these alarming forecasts. As it turns out, the book's predictions were far too pessimistic. While the population of the earth has indeed increased by more than 80 percent in the past 40 years, the amount of tilled land has barely increased, food and mineral prices have dropped, and pollution is in decline in major Western cities [52].

The computer model underlying *The Limits to Growth* was flawed. It assumed all deposits of essential resources had already been discovered. In actuality, many new deposits of oil and other resources have been found in the past four decades. The model ignored the technological improvements that allow society to decrease its use of resources, such as reducing the demand for oil by improving the fuel efficiency of cars or reducing the demand for silver by replacing conventional photography with digital photography.

8.6.2 Validating Simulations

A computer simulation may produce erroneous results for two fundamentally different reasons. The program may have a bug in it, or the model upon which the program is based may be flawed. **Verification** is the process of determining if the computer program correctly implements the model. **Validation** is the process of determining if the model is an accurate representation of the real system [53]. In this section, we'll focus on the process of validation.

One way to validate a model is to make sure it duplicates the performance of the actual system. For example, automobile and truck manufacturers create computer models of their products (Figure 8.8). They use these models to see how well vehicles will perform in a variety of crash situations. Crashing an automobile on a computer is faster and much less expensive than crashing an actual car. To validate their models, manufac-

FIGURE 8.8 One way to validate a model is to make sure it duplicates the performance of the actual system. (Courtesy of Daimler AG)

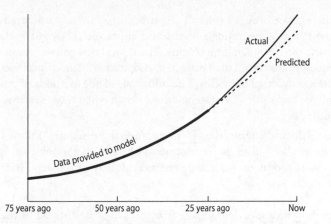

FIGURE 8.9 You can validate a model's ability to predict 25 years into the future by using it to "predict the present" with data 25 or more years old. You can then compare the model's prediction of the present with current reality.

turers compare the results of crashing an actual vehicle with the results predicted by the computer model.

Validating a model that predicts the future can introduce new difficulties. If we are predicting tomorrow's weather, it is reasonable to validate the model by waiting until tomorrow and seeing how well the prediction held up. However, suppose you are a scientist using a global warming model to estimate what the climate will be like 50 years from now. You cannot validate this model by comparing its prediction with reality, because you cannot afford to wait 50 years to see if its prediction came true. However, you can validate the model by using it to *predict the present*.

Figure 8.9 illustrates how a model can predict the present. Suppose you want to see how well your model predicts events 25 years into the future. You have access to data going back 75 years. You let the model use data at least 25 years old, but you do not let the model see any data collected in the past 25 years. The job of predicting the present, given 25-year-old data, is presumably just as hard as the job of predicting 25 years into the future, given present data. The advantage of predicting the present is that you can use current data to validate the model.

A final way to validate a computer model is to see if it has credibility with experts and decision makers. Ultimately, a model is valuable only if it is believed by those who have the power to use its results to reach a conclusion or make a decision.

8.7 Software Engineering

The field of software engineering grew out of a growing awareness of a "software crisis." In the 1960s, computer architects had taken advantage of commercial integrated circuits to design much more powerful mainframe computers. These computers could execute much larger programs than their predecessors. Programmers responded by designing powerful new operating systems and applications. Unfortunately, their programming efforts were plagued by problems. The typical new software system was delivered behind schedule, cost more than expected, did not perform as specified, contained many bugs, and was too hard to modify. The informal, ad hoc methods of programming that worked fine for early software systems broke down when these systems reach a certain level of complexity.

Software engineering is an engineering discipline focused on the production of software, as well as the development of tools, methodologies, and theories supporting software production. Software engineers follow a four-step process to develop a software product [54]:

1. Specification: defining the functions to be performed by the software
2. Development: producing the software that meets the specifications
3. Validation: testing the software
4. Evolution: modifying the software to meet the changing needs of the customer

8.7.1 Specification

The process of specification focuses on determining the requirements of the system and the constraints under which it must operate. Software engineers communicate with the intended users of the system to determine what their needs are. They must decide if the software system is feasible given the budget and the schedule requirements of the customer. If a piece of software is going to replace an existing process, the software engineers study the current process to help them understand the functions the software must perform. The software engineers may develop prototypes of the user interface to confirm that the system will meet the user's needs.

The specification process results in a high-level statement of requirements and perhaps a mock-up of the user interface that the users can approve. The software engineers also produce a low-level requirements statement that provides the details needed by those who are going to actually implement the software system.

8.7.2 Development

During the development phase, the software engineers produce a working software system that matches the specifications. The first design is based on a high-level, abstract view of the system. The process of developing the high-level design reveals ambiguities, omissions, or outright errors in the specification. When these mistakes are discovered, the specification must be amended. Fixing mistakes is quicker and less expensive when the design is still at a higher, more abstract level.

Gradually, the software engineers add levels of detail to the design. As this is done, the various components of the system become clear. Designers pay particular attention to ensure the interfaces between each component are clearly spelled out. They choose the algorithms to be performed and data structures to be manipulated.

Since the emergence of software engineering as a discipline, a variety of structured design methodologies have been developed. These design methodologies result in the creation of large amounts of design documentation in the form of visual diagrams. Many organizations use **computer-assisted software engineering (CASE) tools** to support the process of developing and documenting an ever-more-detailed design.

Another noteworthy improvement in software engineering methodologies is object-oriented design. In a traditional design, the software system is viewed as a group of functions manipulating a set of shared data structures. In an **object-oriented design,** the software system is seen as a group of objects passing each other messages. Each object has its own state and manipulates its own data based on the messages it receives.

Object-oriented systems have several advantages over systems constructed in a more traditional way:

1. *Because each object is associated with a particular component of the system, object-oriented designs can be easier to understand.*

   More easily understood designs can save time during the programming, testing, and maintenance phases of a software project.

2. *Because each object hides its state and private data from other objects, other objects cannot accidentally modify its data items.*

   The result can be fewer errors like the race conditions described in Section 8.5.

3. *Because objects are independent of each other, it is much easier to reuse components of an object-oriented system.*

   A single object definition created for one software system can be copied and inserted into a new software system without bringing along other, unnecessary objects.

When the design has reached a great enough level of detail, software engineers write the actual computer programs implementing the software system. Many different programming languages exist; each language has its strengths and weaknesses. Programmers usually implement object-oriented systems using an object-oriented programming language, such as C++, Java, or C#.

8.7.3 Validation

The purpose of validation (also called testing) is to ensure the software satisfies the specification and meets the needs of the user. In some companies, testing is an assignment given to newly hired software engineers, who soon move on to design work after proving their worth. However, good testing requires a great deal of technical skill, and some organizations promote testing as a career path.

Testing software is much harder than testing other engineered artifacts, such as bridges. We know how to construct scale models that we can use to validate our designs. To determine how much weight a model bridge can carry, we can test its response to various loads. The stresses and strains on the members and the deflection of the span change gradually as we add weight, allowing us to experiment with a manageable number of different loading scenarios. Engineers can extrapolate from the data they collect to generate predictions regarding the capabilities of a full-scale bridge. By increasing the size of various components, they can add a substantial margin of error to ensure the completed bridge will not fail.

A computer program is not at all like a bridge. Testing a program with a small problem can reveal the existence of bugs, but it cannot prove that the program will work when it is fed a much larger problem. The response of a computer program to nearly identical data sets may not be continuous. Instead, programs that appear to be working just fine may fail when only a single parameter is changed by a small amount. Yet programmers cannot exhaustively test programs. Even small programs have a virtually infinite number of different inputs. Since exhaustive testing is impossible, programs can never be completely tested. Software testers strive to put together suites of test cases that exercise all the capabilities of the component or system being validated.

To reduce the complexity of validating a large software system, testing is usually performed in stages. In the first stage of testing, each individual module of the system is tested independently. It is easier to isolate and fix the causes of errors when the number of lines of code is relatively small. After each module has been debugged, modules are combined into larger subsystems for testing. Eventually, all of the subsystems are combined in the complete system. When an error is detected and a bug is fixed in a particular module, all of the test cases related to the module should be repeated to see if the change that fixed one bug accidentally introduced another bug.

EVOLUTION

Successful software systems evolve over time to meet the changing needs of their users. The evolution of a software system resembles the creation of a software system in many ways. Software engineers must understand the needs of the users, assess the strengths and weaknesses of the current system, and design modifications to the software. The same CASE tools used to create a new software system can aid in its evolution. Many of the data sets developed for the original system can be reused when validating the updated system.

8.7.4 Software Quality Is Improving

There is evidence that the field of software engineering is becoming more mature (Figure 8.10). The Standish Group [55] regularly tracks thousands of IT projects. As recently as 1994, about one-third of all software projects were canceled before completion. About one-half of the projects were completed but had time and/or cost overruns, which were often quite large. Only about one-sixth of the projects were completed on time and on budget, and even in these case the completed systems often had fewer features than originally planned. Another survey by the Standish Group in 2009 showed that the probability of a software project being completed on time and on budget had doubled, to about one in three. Only about one-quarter of the software projects surveyed were can-

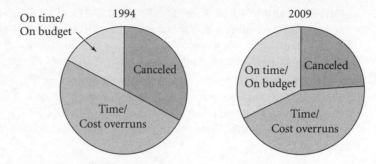

FIGURE 8.10 Research by the Standish Group reveals that the success rate of IT projects in 2009 was twice that of 1994. Today, about one-third of software projects are completed on time and on budget.

celed. Slightly less than half of the projects were late and/or over budget, but the time and cost overruns were not as large as in the first survey. Overall, the ability of companies to produce software on time and on budget improved over this 15-year period.

Still, with only about one in three software projects being completed on time and on budget, the industry has a long way to go. Rapid change is a fact of life in the software industry. In order to stay competitive, companies must release products quickly. Many organizations feel a tension between meeting tight deadlines and strictly following software engineering methodologies.

8.8 Software Warranties

As mentioned earlier, Leveson and Turner state that "there is always another software bug" [47]. If perfect software is impossible, what kind of warranty should a consumer expect to get from a software company? In this section, we survey the software warranties offered by software manufacturers, how these warranties have held up in court, and the debate over new legislation spelling out conditions for licensing computer software in the United States.

8.8.1 Shrinkwrap Warranties

Consumer software is often called **shrinkwrap software** because of the plastic wrap surrounding the box containing the software and manuals. Not too many years ago, consumer software manufacturers provided no warranty for their products at all. Purchasers had to accept shrinkwrap software "as is." Today, many shrinkwrap software manufacturers, including Microsoft, provide a 90-day replacement or money-back guarantee if the program fails [56]. Here is the wording Microsoft included with its limited warranty for Microsoft Office 2000:

LIMITED WARRANTY FOR SOFTWARE PRODUCTS ACQUIRED IN THE U.S. AND CANADA. Microsoft warrants that (a) the SOFTWARE PRODUCT will perform substantially in accordance with the accompanying written materials for a period of ninety (90) days from the date of receipt . . .

CUSTOMER REMEDIES. Microsoft's and its suppliers' entire liability and your exclusive remedy shall be, at Microsoft's option, either (a) return of the price paid, if any, or (b) repair or replacement of the SOFTWARE PRODUCT that does not meet Microsoft's Limited Warranty and which is returned to Microsoft with a copy of your receipt.

At least Microsoft is willing to state that its software will actually do more or less what the documentation says it can do. The warranty for Railroad Tycoon, distributed by Gathering of Developers, promises only that you'll be able to install the software:

LIMITED WARRANTY. Owner warrants that the original Storage Media holding the SOFTWARE is free from defects in materials and workmanship under normal use and service for a period of ninety (90) days from the date of purchase as evidenced by Your receipt. If for any reason You find defects in the Storage Media, or if you are unable to install the SOFTWARE on your home or portable computer, You may return the SOFTWARE and all ACCOMPANYING MATERIALS to the place You obtained it for a full refund. This limited warranty does not apply if You have damaged the SOFTWARE by accident or abuse.

I wonder what would happen if you actually did go back to the store with an opened game and asked for a full refund.

While vendors may be willing to give you a refund if you cannot get their software to install on your computer, they are certainly not going to accept any liability if your business is harmed because their software crashes at the wrong time. Later in the Microsoft Office 2000 Professional warranty, we find these words:

TO THE MAXIMUM EXTENT PERMITTED BY APPLICABLE LAW, IN NO EVENT SHALL MICROSOFT OR ITS SUPPLIERS BE LIABLE FOR ANY SPE-CIAL, INCIDENTAL, INDIRECT, OR CONSEQUENTIAL DAMAGES WHAT-SOEVER (INCLUDING, WITHOUT LIMITATION, DAMAGES FOR LOSS OF BUSINESS PROFITS, BUSINESS INTERRUPTION, LOSS OF BUSINESS INFOR-MATION, OR ANY OTHER PECUNIARY LOSS) ARISING OUT OF THE USE OF OR INABILITY TO USE THE SOFTWARE PRODUCT OR THE PROVISION OF OR FAILURE TO PROVIDE SUPPORT SERVICES, EVEN IF MICROSOFT HAS BEEN ADVISED OF THE POSSIBILITY OF SUCH DAMAGES. IN ANY CASE, MICROSOFT'S ENTIRE LIABILITY UNDER ANY PROVISION OF THIS UELA SHALL BE LIMITED TO THE GREATER OF THE AMOUNT ACTUALLY PAID FOR THE SOFTWARE PRODUCT OR U.S. $5.00; PROVIDED, HOWEVER, IF YOU HAVE ENTERED INTO A MICROSOFT SUPPORT SERVICES AGREE-MENT, MICROSOFT'S ENTIRE LIABILITY REGARDING SUPPORT SERVICES SHALL BE GOVERNED BY THE TERMS OF THAT AGREEMENT.

Here is even blunter language from the license agreement accompanying Harmonic Visions's Music Ace program:

WE DO NOT WARRANT THAT THIS SOFTWARE WILL MEET YOUR RE-QUIREMENTS OR THAT ITS OPERATION WILL BE UNINTERRUPTED OR ERROR-FREE. WE EXCLUDE AND EXPRESSLY DISCLAIM ALL EXPRESS AND IMPLIED WARRANTIES NOT STATED HEREIN, INCLUDING THE IMPLIED WARRANTIES OF MERCHANTABILITY AND FITNESS FOR A PARTICULAR PURPOSE.

In other words, don't blame us if the program doesn't do what you hoped it would do, or if it crashes all the time, or if it is full of bugs.

8.8.2 Are Software Warranties Enforceable?

How can software manufacturers get away with disclaiming any warranties on their products? It's not clear that they can. Article 2 of the Uniform Commercial Code (UCC) governs the sale of products in the United States. In 1975, Congress passed the Magnuson-Moss Warranty Act. One goal of the act was to prevent manufacturers from putting unfair warranties on products costing more than $25. A second goal was to make it economically feasible for consumers to bring warranty suits by allowing courts to award attorneys' fees. Together, the Magnuson-Moss Warranty Act and Article 2 of the UCC protect the rights of consumers. A computer program is a product. Hence, unfair warranties on shrinkwrap software could be in violation of these laws.

An early court case, *Step-Saver Data Systems v. Wyse Technology and The Software Link*, seemed to affirm the notion that software manufacturers could be held responsible for defects in their products, despite what they put in their warranties. However, two later cases seemed to indicate the opposite. In *ProCD v. Zeidenberg*, the court ruled that the customer was bound to the license agreement, even if the license agreement does not appear on the outside of the shrinkwrap box. *Mortenson v. Timberline Software* showed that a warranty disclaiming the manufacturer's liability could hold up in court.

STEP-SAVER DATA SYSTEMS V. WYSE TECHNOLOGY AND THE SOFTWARE LINK

Step-Saver Data Systems, Inc. sold timesharing computer systems consisting of an IBM PC AT server, Wyse terminals, and an operating system provided by The Software Link, Inc. (TSL). In 1986–1987, Step-Saver purchased and resold 142 copies of the Multilink Advanced operating system provided by TSL.

To purchase the software, Step-Saver called TSL and placed an order, then followed up with a purchase order. According to Step-Saver, the TSL phone sales representatives said that Multilink was compatible with most DOS applications. The box containing the Multilink software included a licensing agreement in which TSL disclaimed all express and implied warranties.

Step-Saver's timesharing systems did not work properly, and the combined efforts of Step-Saver, Wyse, and TSL could not fix the problems. Step-Saver was sued by twelve of its customers. In turn, Step-Saver sued Wyse Technology and TSL.

The Third Circuit of the U.S. Court of Appeals ruled in favor of Step-Saver [57]. It based its argument on Article 2 of the UCC. The court held that the original contract between Step-Saver and TSL consisted of the purchase order, the invoice, and the oral statements made by TSL representatives on the telephone. The license agreement had additional terms that would have materially altered the contract. However, Step-Saver never agreed to these terms.

The court wrote, "In the absence of a party's express assent to the additional or different terms of the writing, section 2-207 [of the UCC] provides a default rule that the parties intended, as the terms of their agreement, those terms to which both parties have agreed along with any terms implied by the provision of the UCC." The court noted that the president of Step-Saver had objected to the terms of the licensing agreement. He had refused to sign a document formalizing the licensing agreement. Even after this, TSL had continued to sell to Step-Saver, implying that TSL wanted the business even if the contract did not include the language in the licensing agreement. That is why the court ruled that the purchase order, the invoice, and the oral statements constituted the contract, not the license agreement.

PROCD, INC. V. ZEIDENBERG

ProCD invested more than $10 million to construct a computer database containing information from more than 3,000 telephone directories. ProCD also developed a proprietary technology to compress and encrypt the data. It created an application program enabling users to search the database for records matching criteria they specified. ProCD targeted its product, called SelectPhone, to two different markets: companies interested in generating mailing lists, and individuals interested in finding the phone numbers or addresses of particular people they wanted to call or write. Consumers who wanted SelectPhone for personal use could purchase it for $150; companies paid much more for the right to put the package to commercial use. ProCD included in the consumer version of SelectPhone a license prohibiting the commercial use of the database and program. In addition, the license terms were displayed on the user's computer monitor every time the program was executed.

Matthew Zeidenberg purchased the consumer version of SelectPhone in 1994. He formed a company called Silken Mountain Web Services, Inc., which resold the information in the SelectPhone database. The price it charged was substantially less than the commercial price of SelectPhone. ProCD sued Matthew Zeidenberg for violating the licensing agreement.

At the trial, the defense argued that Zeidenberg could not be held to the terms of the licensing agreement, since they were not printed on the outside of the box containing the software. The U.S. Court of Appeals for the Seventh Circuit ruled in favor of ProCD. Judge Frank Easterbrook wrote, "Shrinkwrap licenses are enforceable unless their terms are objectionable on grounds applicable to contracts in general (for example, if they violate a rule of positive law, or if they are unconscionable)" [58].

MORTENSON V. TIMBERLINE SOFTWARE

M. A. Mortenson Company was a national construction contractor with a regional office in Bellevue, Washington. Timberline Software, Inc. produced software for the construction industry. Mortenson had used software from Timberline for several years. In July 1993, Mortenson purchased eight copies of a bidding package called Precision Bid Analysis.

Timberline's licensing agreement included this paragraph:

LIMITATION OF REMEDIES AND LIABILITY.

NEITHER TIMBERLINE NOR ANYONE ELSE WHO HAS BEEN INVOLVED IN THE CREATION, PRODUCTION OR DELIVERY OF THE PROGRAMS OR USER MANUALS SHALL BE LIABLE TO YOU FOR ANY DAMAGES OF ANY TIME, INCLUDING BUT NOT LIMITED TO, ANY LOST PROFITS, LOST SAVINGS, LOSS OF ANTICIPATED BENEFITS, OR OTHER INCIDENTAL, OR CONSEQUENTIAL DAMAGES, ARISING OUT OF THE USE OR INABILITY TO USE SUCH PROGRAMS, WHETHER ARISING OUT OF CONTRACT, NEGLIGENCE, STRICT TORT, OR UNDER ANY WARRANTY, OR OTHERWISE, EVEN IF TIMBERLINE HAS BEEN ADVISED OF THE POSSIBILITY OF SUCH DAMAGES OR FOR ANY OTHER CLAIM BY ANY OTHER PARTY. TIMBERLINE'S LIABILITY FOR DAMAGES IN NO EVENT SHALL EXCEED THE LICENSE FEE PAID FOR THE RIGHT TO USE THE PROGRAMS.

In December 1993, Mortenson used Precision Bid Analysis to prepare a bid for the Harborview Medical Center in Seattle. On the day the bid was due, the software malfunctioned. It printed the message "Abort: Cannot find alternate" 19 times. Mortenson continued to use the software and submitted the bid the software produced. After the firm won the contract, Mortenson discovered that its bid was $1.95 million too low.

Mortenson sued Timberline for breach of express and implied warranties. It turns out Timberline had been aware of the bug uncovered by Mortenson since May 1993. Timberline had fixed the bug and already sent a newer version of the program to some of its other customers who had encountered it. It had not sent the improved program to Mortenson. Nevertheless, Timberline argued that the lawsuit be summarily dismissed because the licensing agreement limited the consequential damages that Mortsenson could recover from Timberline. The King County Superior Court ruled in favor of Timberline. The ruling was upheld by the Washington Court of Appeals and the Supreme Court of the State of Washington [59].

8.8.3 Moral Responsibility of Software Manufacturers

Should producers of shrinkwrap software be held responsible for defects in their programs?

Let's consider the consequences of holding manufacturers of shrinkwrap software liable for damages, such as lost profits, caused by errors encountered by licensees. Currently, manufacturers rely upon consumers to help them identify bugs in their products. If they must find these bugs themselves, they will need to hire many more software testers. The result will be higher prices and longer program development times.

Prudent companies would most likely purchase insurance to protect them from potential lawsuits. This insurance could be very expensive, depending upon the maximum liability to which a company could be held responsible. The cost of the insurance would be passed along to consumers in the form of higher prices.

These changes in the consumer software industry would affect small, start-up companies more than large, established firms. The changes would slow the entry of new companies into the field. The result would be a decrease in level of innovation and vitality in the software industry.

Consumers could license software with a higher degree of confidence, knowing that the companies stood by their products. While there might be fewer products available, and their prices would be higher, they would be more reliable.

The result of our utilitarian analysis depends upon how much weight we give to the various consequences. Let's suppose we conclude that software manufacturers should not be held liable for lost profits and other negative consequences arising from errors in their programs, because the harms are greater than the benefits. We may still ask the following question: What are the rights of consumers who license shrinkwrap software?

Consider this hypothetical scenario. A consumer goes to the store, pays $49.95, and brings home a copy of *Incredible Bulk*. The game is usable, but it contains some annoying bugs. The next year the company releases *Incredible Bulk II*. If the consumer wants all the latest bug fixes, he needs to buy the second edition. Of course, *Incredible Bulk II* has cool new features. And, as you might expect, some of these features are buggy. Never fear! The bugs will be fixed when *Incredible Bulk III* comes out in 12 months. Is this a fair arrangement?

From a social contract point of view, this arrangement is unfair. Consumers should have the right to be informed of bugs the manufacturer knows about. This knowledge allows a consumer to enter into a contract with his eyes wide open. Ideally, a manufacturer would be open about disclosing the weaknesses in its product. More realistically, consumer organizations can test software products and provide reviews for potential buyers.

If a consumer purchases the right to use product A, and the manufacturer removes defects from product A, the consumer should not have to purchase additional features in order to get access to the fixes to the original product. Manufacturers should make software patches containing bug fixes available on the Web for free downloading by their customers. Withholding these patches until the next major release of the software is wrong from a social contract point of view.

Summary

Computers are part of larger systems, and ultimately it is the reliability of the entire system that is important. A well-engineered system can tolerate the malfunction of any single component without failing. This chapter has presented many examples of how the computer turned out to be the "weak link" in the system, leading to a failure. These examples provide important lessons for computer scientists and others involved in the design, implementation, and testing of large systems.

Two sources of failure are data-entry errors and data-retrieval errors. While it's easy to focus on a particular mistake made by the person entering or retrieving the data, the system is larger than the individual person. For example, in the case of the 2000 general election in Florida, incorrect records in the computer database disqualified thousands of voters. The data-entry errors caused the *voting system* to work incorrectly. Sheila Jackson Stossier was arrested by police who confused her with Shirley Jackson. The data-retrieval error caused the *criminal justice system* to perform incorrectly.

When the topics are software and billing errors, it is easier to identify the system that is failing. For example, when Qwest sent out 14,000 incorrect bills to its cellular phone customers, it's clear that the billing system had failed.

In Sections 8.4 and 8.5, the larger systems were easy to spot. Several embedded systems were dissected to determine the causes of their failures. The program for the Patriot missile's radar tracking system had a subtle flaw: a tiny truncation error occurred every time the clock signal was stored in a floating-point variable. Over a period of 100 hours, all those tiny errors added up to a significant amount, causing the radar system to lose its target. The Ariane 5 blew up because a single assignment statement caused the onboard computers to crash. The AT&T long-distance network collapsed because of one faulty line of code.

A well-engineered system does not fail when a single component fails. In the case of hardware, this principle is easier to apply. For example, a jetliner may have three engines. It is designed to be able to fly on any two of the engines, so if a single engine fails, the plane can still fly to the nearest airport and land. When it comes to software, the goal is much harder to meet. If we have two computers in the system, that will provide redundancy in case one of the computers has a hardware failure. However, if both computers are running the same software, there is still no software redundancy. A software bug that causes one computer to fail will cause both computers to fail. The partial collapse of the AT&T long-distance network is an example of this phenomenon. All 80 switches containing the latest version of the software failed. Fortunately, 34 switches were running an older version of the software, which prevented a total collapse of AT&T's system.

Imagine what it would take to provide true redundancy in the case of software systems. Should companies maintain two entirely different billing systems so that the bills produced by one system could be double-checked by the other? Should the federal government support two completely different implementations of the National Crime Information Center? These alternatives seem unrealistic. On the other hand, redundancy seems much more feasible when we look at data-entry and data-retrieval operations. Two different data-entry operators could input records into databases, and the computer could check to make sure the records agreed. This would reduce the chance of bad data being entered into databases in the first place. Two different people could look at the results returned from a computer query, using their own common sense and understanding to see if the output makes sense. A paper audit trail is a practical way to add redundancy to an electronic voting machine.

While it may not be infeasible to provide redundant software systems, safety-critical systems should never rely completely upon a single piece of software. The Therac-25 overdoses occurred because the system lacked the hardware interlocks of the earlier models.

The stories of computer system failures contain other valuable lessons. The Ariane 5 and Therac-25 failures show that it can be dangerous to reuse code. Assumptions that were valid when the code was originally written may no longer be true when the code is reused. Since some of these assumptions may not be documented, the new design team may not have the opportunity to check if these assumptions still hold true in the new system.

The automated baggage system at the Denver International Airport demonstrates the difficulty of debugging a complex system. Tackling one problem at a time, solving it, and moving on to the next problem proved to be a poor approach, because the overall system design had serious flaws. For example, BAE did not even realize that simply getting luggage carts to where they were needed in a fair manner was an incredibly difficult problem. Even if BAE had solved all the low-level technical problems, this high-level problem would have prevented the system from meeting its performance goals during the busiest times.

Finally, systems can fail because of miscommunications among people. The Mars Climate Orbiter is an example of this kind of failure. The software written by the team in Colorado used English units, while the software written by the team in California used metric units. The output of one program was incompatible with the input to the other program, but a poorly specified interface allowed this error to remain undetected until after the spacecraft was destroyed.

Computer simulations are used to perform numerical experiments that lead to new scientific discoveries and help engineers create better products. For this reason, it is important that simulations provide reliable results. Simulations are validated by comparing predicted results with reality. If a simulation is designed to predict future events, it can be validated by giving it data about the past and asking it to predict the present. Finally, simulations are validated when their results are believed by domain experts and policymakers.

The discipline of software engineering emerged from a growing realization of a "software crisis." While small programs can be written in an ad hoc manner, large programs must be carefully constructed if they are to be reliable. Software engineering is the application of engineering methodologies to the creation and evolution of software artifacts. Surveys of the IT industry reveal that more projects are being completed on time and on budget, and fewer projects are being canceled. This may be evidence that software engineering is having a positive impact. However, since most projects are still not completed on time and on budget, there remains much room for improvement. For many companies, shipping a product by a particular date continues to be a higher priority than following a strict software development methodology.

Should software manufacturers be held accountable for the quality of their software, or is a program a completely different kind of product than a socket wrench? An examination of the software warranties manufacturers include in their licensing agreements reveals that while some vendors refund the purchase price of software that does not meet the needs of the purchaser, they do not want to be held liable for any damages that occur from the use of their software. These warranties seem to fly in the face of Article 2 of the Uniform Commercial Code and the Magnuson-Moss Warranty Act. Some courts have ruled that software manufacturers cannot disclaim liability for consequential damages, but other court decisions imply that software warranties disclaiming liability are enforceable.

Review Questions

1. What kinds of mistakes may cause a computer to produce a faulty output?

2. What is the difference between a data-entry error and a data-retrieval error?

3. What reasons did the U.S. Department of Justice give for no longer requiring the FBI to ensure the accuracy of information kept in the NCIC databases?

4. What is an embedded system? What is a real-time system?

5. What does a linear accelerator do?

6. What was the most important difference between the Therac-20 and its successor, the Therac-25?

7. How long was the Therac-25 in operation before the first documented accident? How much longer did it take for the system to be declared unsafe?

8. What is a race condition in software? Why are race conditions difficult to debug?

9. The following reasons have been given for the failure of computerized systems:

    I. A system designed for one purpose was used for another purpose.
    II. Software was reused without adequate testing.
    III. There was an error in storing or converting a data value.
    IV. A line of code became a single point of failure.
    V. The overall system was too complicated to analyze.
    VI. There was a software race condition.
    VII. There was another software error (not listed above).

       For each of the systems listed below, select the principal reason or reasons why it failed to operate as specified.

    a. Patriot missile
    b. Ariane 5
    c. AT&T long-distance network
    d. Mars Climate Orbiter
    e. Mars Polar Lander
    f. Denver International Airport baggage system
    g. Tokyo Stock Exchange
    h. Direct recording electronic voting machines
    i. Therac-25

10. What are the advantages of allowing software users to identify and report bugs? What are the disadvantages?

11. Why are computer simulations playing an increasingly important role in science and engineering?

12. List five uses of computer simulation.

13. What is the difference between a model and a computer simulation?

14. What is the difference between verification and validation?

15. Name two different ways to validate a computer simulation.

16. What does Article 2 of the Uniform Commercial Code deal with?

17. What was the purpose of the Magnuson-Moss Warranty Act?

18. Why do some people argue that shrinkwrap software should be exempt from the Magnuson-Moss Warranty Act and Article 2 of the Uniform Commercial Code?

19. What is the significance of the court's ruling in *Step-Saver Data Systems v. Wyse Technology and The Software Link*?

20. What is the significance of the court's ruling in *ProCD, Inc. v. Zeidenberg*?

21. What is the significance of the court's ruling in *Mortenson v. Timberline Software*?

Discussion Questions

22. Have you ever been the victim of a software error? Whom did you blame? Now that you know more about the reliability of computer systems, do you still feel the same way?

23. Should an e-commerce site be required to honor the prices at which it offers and sells goods and services?

24. Should the FBI be responsible for the accuracy of information about criminals and crime victims it enters into the National Crime Information Center database?

25. Over a period of seven years, about 500 residents of Freeport, Texas, were overbilled for their water usage. Each resident paid on average about $170 too much, making the total amount of the overbillings about $100,000. The city council decided not to issue refunds, saying that about 300,000 bills would have had to have been examined, some residents had left town, and the individual refunds were not that large [60]. Did the city council make the right decision?

26. If a company sends a consumer an incorrect bill, should the company compensate the consumer for the time and effort the consumer takes to straighten out the mistake?

27. The chapter quotes NASA's Mars Pathfinder project manager as saying software hasn't improved in quality in the past 25 years. How could you determine whether software quality has improved in the past 25 years?

28. Perhaps programs used for business purposes ought to conform to higher standards of quality than games. With respect to software warranties, would it make sense to distinguish between software used for entertainment purposes (such as a first-person shooter game) and software used for business (such as a spreadsheet)?

29. Read the entire end-user license agreement (EULA) from a piece of commercial software. Do any of the conditions seem shady or unreasonable? If so, which ones?

30. While waiting for an appointment with your physician, you see a brochure advertising a new surgical procedure that implants a tiny microprocessor inside your skull just behind your left ear. The purpose of the chip is to help you associate names with faces. The procedure for inserting the chip is so simple that your physician is performing it in his office. Suppose your career takes you into sales, where such a device could help you earn higher commissions. What questions would you want to have answered before you agreed to have such a device inserted into your skull?

In–class Exercises

31. Debate the moral responsibility of three agents associated with the two Therac-25 overdoses occurring in Tyler, Texas: the radiation technician, the hospital director, and the programmer who wrote the code controlling the machine. Divide the class into six groups. Three groups (one for each of the three agents) should give reasons why their particular party should bear at least some of the moral responsibility for the deaths. The other three groups (one for each of the three agents) should give reasons why their particular party should not bear any moral responsibility.

32. California is working on an "intelligent highway" system that would allow computer-controlled automobiles to travel faster and closer together on freeways than today's human-controlled cars. What kinds of safety devices would have to be in such a system in order for you to feel comfortable using an intelligent highway? How many people in class would be comfortable being one of the first people to use the intelligent highway?

33. The New York Transit Authority is transforming the L line into a partially automated subway line. A central computer system will control the speed and spacing of all trains on the line. However, each train will have an operator that starts and stops the train and has the ability to take control of it in an emergency [61]. How many people in the class would ride on a computer-controlled subway train that did not have a human operator on board?

34. Identify people in the class who have been beta testers for new software products. Ask them to tell the rest of the class about their experiences. What did acting as a beta tester teach them about software reliability?

35. A start-up company called Medick has been developing an exciting new product for handheld computers that will revolutionize the way nurses keep track of their hospitalized patients. The device will save nurses a great deal of time doing routine paperwork, reduce their stress levels, and enable them to spend more time with their patients.

   Medick's sales force has led hospital administrators to believe the product will be available next week as originally scheduled. Unfortunately, the package still contains quite a few bugs. All of the known bugs appear to be minor, but some of the planned tests have not yet been performed.

   Because of the fierce competition in the medical software industry, it is critical that this company be the first to market. It appears a well-established company will release a similar product in a few weeks. If its product appears first, Medick will probably go out of business.

Divide the class into five groups representing the software engineers programming the device, the sales force that has been promoting the device, the managers of Medick, the venture capitalists who bankrolled Medick, and the nurses at a hospital purchasing the device. Discuss the best course of action for Medick.

Further Reading/Viewing

Walt Bogdanich. "Radiation Offers New Cures, and Ways to Do Harm." *The New York Times*, January 23, 2010. "As Technology Surges, Radiation Safeguards Lag." *The New York Times*, January 27, 2010. www.nytimes.com.

IBM. "What 3 Million Lines of Code Means to a Piece of Luggage." Schiphol Case Study Video. www.ibm.com/innovation/us/leadership/luggage/.

Poul-Henning Kamp. "The Most Expensive One-byte Mistake: Did Ken, Dennis, and Brian Choose Wrong with NUL-terminated Text Strings?" *ACM Queue*, July 25, 2011. queue .acm.org.

Nancy Leveson and Clark Turner. "An Investigation of the Therac-25 Accidents." *Computer*, pages 18–41, July 1993.

Peter G. Neumann. *Computer-Related Risks*. ACM Press, New York, NY, 1995.

Proceedings of the Annual Conference on Computer Safety, Reliability, and Security (SAFE-COMP), published annually by Springer-Verlag.

References

[1]   Jennifer DiSabatino. "Unregulated Databases Hold Personal Data." *Computerworld*, 36(4), January 21, 2002.

[2]   Peter G. Neumann. "More on False Arrests." *The Risks Digest*, 1(5), September 4, 1985.

[3]   Rodney Hoffman. "NCIC Information Leads to Repeat False Arrest Suit." *The Risks Digest*, 8(71), May 17, 1989.

[4]   Ted Bridis. "U.S. Lifts FBI Criminal Database Checks." *Associated Press*, March 25, 2003.

[5]   Department of Justice, Federal Bureau of Investigation. "Privacy Act of 1974; Implementation." *Federal Register*, 68(56), March 24, 2003.

[6]   "Computer Glitch Is to Blame for Faulty Bills, Qwest Says." *The Deseret News (Salt Lake City, Utah)*, July 24, 2001.

[7]   "USDA Changes Livestock Price-Reporting Guidelines." *Amarillo (Texas) Globe-News*, July 24, 2001.

[8]   "Software Error Returns Patent Office Mail." *The New York Times*, August 9, 1996.

[9]   "Spelling and Grammar Checkers Add Errors." *Wired News*, March 18, 2003.

[10]   D. F. Galletta, A. Durcikova, A. Everard, and B. Jones. "Does Spell-Checking Software Need a Warning Label?" *Communications of the ACM*, forthcoming.

[11] Manny Fernandez. "Computer Error Caused Rent Troubles for Public Housing Tenants." *The New York Times*, August 5, 2009.

[12] "Calif. Computer Flub Lets Violent Prisoners Go Free." *The Seattle Times*, May 26, 2011.

[13] Ian MacKinnon and Stephen Goodwin. "Ambulance Chief Quits after Patients Die in Computer Failure." *The Independent (London)*, October 29, 1992.

[14] Aaron Lucchetti and Gregory Zuckerman. "Software Glitch Halts Trading on CBOT on April Fool's Day." *The Wall Street Journal*, page C19, April 2, 1998.

[15] Reuters. "Official Trapped in Car After Computer Fails." *NYTimes.com*, May 12, 2003.

[16] "Liffe Glitch Halts All Electronic Trading for a Second Time." *The Wall Street Journal*, May 12, 1999.

[17] "Flights at Japanese Airports Delayed." *Associated Press*, March 1, 2003.

[18] "LA County's Main Hospital Has Computer Breakdown, Delays Ensue." *Associated Press*, April 22, 2003.

[19] "Computer Glitches Shut Down Comair Flights." *Associated Press*, December 26, 2004.

[20]] Daniel Michaels and Andy Pasztor. "Flight Check: Incidents Prompt New Scrutiny of Airplane Software Glitches." *The Wall Street Journal*, May 30, 2006.

[21] Robert Fry. "It's a Steal: Bargain-Hunting or Barefaced Robbery?" *The Times (London)*, April 8, 2003.

[22] "Amazon Pulls British Site after iPaq Fire-Sale." *NYtimes.com*, March 19, 2003.

[23] Victor L. Winter and Sourav Bhattacharya. Preface. In *High Integrity Software*, edited by Victor L. Winter and Sourav Bhattacharya. Kluwer Academic Publishers, Boston, MA, 2001.

[24] E. Marshall. "Fatal Error: How Patriot Overlooked a Scud." *Science*, 255(5050):1347, March 13, 1992.

[25] Jean-Marc Jézéquel and Bertrand Meyer. "Design by Contract: The Lessons of Ariane." *Computer*, pages 129–130, January 1997.

[26] J. L. Lions. "ARIANE 5: Flight 501 Failure, Report by the Inquiry Board." European Space Agency, July 19, 1996. www.esa.int.

[27] Ivars Peterson. "Finding Fault: The Formidable Task of Eradicating Software Bugs." *Science News*, 139, February 16, 1991.

[28] Bruce Sterling. *The Hacker Crackdown: Law and Disorder on the Electronic Frontier*. Bantam Books, New York, NY, 1992.

[29] Jeff Foust. "Why Is Mars So Hard?" *The Space Review*, June 2, 2003. www.thespace review.com.

[30] Jet Propulsion Laboratory, California Institute of Technology. "NASA Facts: Mars Exploration Rover," October 2004. marsrover.jpl.nasa.gov.

[31] Richard de Neufville. "The Baggage System at Denver: Prospects and Lessons." *Journal of Air Transport Management*, 1(4):229–236, December 1994.

[32] Tetsuo Tamai. "Social Impact of Information System Failures." *Computer*, June 2009.

[33] Stefan Lovgren. "Are Electronic Voting Machines Reliable?" *National Geographic News*, November 1, 2004. http://news.nationalgeographic.com.

[34] Jarrett Blanc. "Challenging the Norms and Standards of Election Administration: Electronic Voting." In *Challenging the Norms and Standards of Election Administration*. IFES, Washington, DC, 2007.

[35] Sonia Arrison and Vince Vasquez. *Upgrading America's Ballot Box: The Rise of E-Voting*, 2nd edition. Pacific Research Institute, San Francisco, CA, 2006.

[36] "Electronic Ballots Fail to Win Over Wake Voters, Election Officials; Machines Provide Improper Vote Count at Two Locations," *WRAL-TV* (Raleigh-Durham, NC), November 2, 2002.

[37] Barbara Simons. "Electronic Voting Systems: the Good, the Bad, and the Stupid." *RFID* 2(7), October 2004.

[38] William Rivers Pitt. "Worse than 2000: Tuesday's Electoral Disaster" (editorial). *truthout*, November 8, 2004. www.truthout.org.

[39] Mark Johnson. "Winner So Far: Confusion." *The Charlotte Observer*, November 5, 2004.

[40] Charles Rabin and Darran Simon. "Glitches Cited in Early Voting: Early Voters Are Urged to Cast Their Ballots with Care Following Scattered Reports of Problems with Heavily Used Machines." *The Miami Herald*, October 28, 2006.

[41] "Florida Candidate Disputes Election Results." *CNN.com*, December 20, 2006.

[42] Marc Caputo and Gary Fineout. "New Tests Fuel Doubts about Vote Machines." *The Miami Herald*, December 15, 2005.

[43] "Transparent Liberty, Accountable Election Systems" (leaflet). The Open Voting Consortium. www.openvoting.org.

[44] Cheryl Gerber. "Voting 2.0." *Chronogram*, January 2006.

[45] "More E-Voting Red Tape Threatens Ballot Booth Benefits, New Study Says" (press release). Pacific Research Institute, October 31, 2006.

[46] Terry Aguayo and Christine Jordan Sexton. "Florida Acts to Eliminate Touch-Screen Voting System." *The New York Times*, May 4, 2007.

[47] Nancy Leveson and Clark Turner. "An Investigation of the Therac-25 Accidents." *Computer*, 26(7):18–41, 1993.

[48] Walt Bogdanich. "Radiation Offers New Cures, and Ways to Do Harm." *The New York Times*, January 23, 2010. www.nytimes.com.

[49] William J. Kauffman III and Larry L. Smarr. *Supercomputing and the Transformation of Science*. Scientific American Library, New York, NY, 1993.

[50] Lucio Mayer, Tom Quinn, James Wadsley, and Joachim Stadel. "Forming Giant Planets via Fragmentation of Protoplanetary Disks." *Science*, November 29, 2002.

[51] Donnella H. Meadows, Dennis I. Meadows, Jorgen Randers and William W. Behrens III. *The Limits To Growth*. Universe Books, New York, NY, 1972.

[52] Bjørn Lomborg and Olivier Rubin. "Limits to Growth." *Foreign Policy*, October/November 2002.

[53] G. S. Fishman and P. J. Kiviat. "The Statistics of Discrete Event Simulation." *Simulation*, 10:185–195, 1968.

[54] Ian Sommerville. *Software Engineering*. 6th ed. Addison-Wesley, Harlow, England, 2001.

[55] David Rubinstein. "Standish Group Report: There's Less Development Chaos Today." *SD Times*, March 1, 2007. sdtimes.com.

[56]   Scot Petersen. "Taking the Rap for Bad Software." *PC Week*, page 29, February 28, 2000.

[57]   United States Court of Appeals for the Third Circuit. *Step-Saver Data Systems, Inc. v. Wyse Technology and The Software Link, Inc.,* 1991. 939 F. 2d 91.

[58]   United States Court of Appeals for the Seventh Circuit. *ProCD, Inc., v. Matthew Zeidenberg and Silken Mountain Web Services, Inc., Appeal from the United States District Court for the Western District of Wisconsin,* 1996. 96–1139.

[59]   Supreme Court of the State of Washington. *M.A. Mortenson Co. v. Timberline Software Corp., et al. Opinion,* 2000.

[60]   "Texans Get Soaked." *IEEE Software*, page 114, September/October 1997.

[61]   Elizabeth Hays. "L Trains Do Compute." *New York Daily News*, January 18, 2004.

Avi Rubin

Dr. Avi D. Rubin is Professor of Computer Science and Technical Director of the Information Security Institute at Johns Hopkins University. Professor Rubin directs the NSF–funded ACCURATE center for correct, usable, reliable, auditable, and transparent elections. He is also a co–founder of Independent Security Evaluators (www.securityevaluators.com), a security consulting firm.

Dr. Rubin has testified before the U.S. House and Senate on multiple occasions. In January 2004 *Baltimore Magazine* named him Baltimorean of the Year for his work in safeguarding the integrity of our election process. He is also the recipient of the 2004 Electronic Frontiers Foundation Pioneer Award.

Professor Rubin is author of several books, including *Brave New Ballot* (Random House, 2006), *Firewalls and Internet Security*, second edition, with Bill Cheswick and Steve Bellovin (Addison–Wesley, 2003), *White-Hat Security Arsenal* (Addison–Wesley, 2001), and *Web Security Sourcebook*, with Dan Geer and Marcus Ranum (John Wiley & Sons, 1997). He is Associate Editor of ACM *Transactions on Internet Technology*, Associate Editor of *IEEE Security & Privacy,* and an Advisory Board member of Springer's Information Security and Cryptography Book Series.

The Pacific Research Institute maintains that DRE voting machines are more secure than traditional paper ballots, which they say can be tampered with by elections officials. Presumably you disagree with their assertion?

I agree with them that paper ballots can be tampered with. I also believe that for an unsophisticated attacker, it is probably easier to tamper with paper ballots than with the election results in DREs. However, there are several reasons why I think the use of DREs poses a bigger threat to the integrity of an election than paper ballots do. First, tampering with paper ballots is more likely to be detected than tampering with software or electronic ballots. Second, if someone were to rig the software in a DRE, that could impact ballots in thousands of places, while tampering with paper ballots has to occur on a retail level, increasing the exposure for the attacker. But perhaps my greatest concern is that an accidental bug in a DRE could result in the wrong election results being reported, without anyone ever knowing it. Since paper ballots are not software based, an analogous threat does not exist for paper ballots.

Proponents say that DRE voting machines eliminate errors that have plagued other voting systems. Two common examples: punched cards can have "hanging chads," and paper ballots can't prevent a voter from accidentally voting for two candidates. Do these benefits outweigh the potential risks?

The hanging chad is a problem related to punch card systems, not paper ballots in general. I think punch card systems should no longer be used. Optical scan technology, a different form of paper ballots, does not suffer the same problems. There are also systems that avoid voter error problems such as voters voting for two candidates when they are only allowed to vote for one. For example, in precinct scanners, the scanner can spit out a ballot that is marked incorrectly, giving the voter a chance to fix it. There are commercial scanners that do this. Furthermore, ballot-marking machines, where voters mark the ballot on a touch screen but then a paper ballot is printed and fed into a scanner, do not suffer from any of these problems.

What led you to investigate the reliability of Diebold DRE voting machines?

I was a computer security researcher, and in the late 1990s I became interested in electronic voting because it is a hard and interesting problem. When the source code for the Diebold voting machine was found on the Internet, I viewed it as an opportunity to study a real system that was actually used for voting.

In your paper "Analysis of an Electronic Voting System," you concluded that the public should have access to the source code used in electronic voting machines, yet this code represents a valuable intellectual property to the companies that wrote it. Why should a company commit time and money to develop innovative, high-quality software that will be revealed to everybody, including potential competitors?

I think that the transparency requirement for something like voting trumps any intellectual property protection that a vendor might want. Furthermore, we have a patent system in this country that can protect intellectual property, and which also requires full disclosure. I find this whole argument pretty silly because the primary functionality of a voting machine is very simple. Finally, many companies have shown that they can make plenty of money with open-source systems.

You've expressed concern that in a close election, "paperless DREs (direct recording electronic voting machines) will produce a cloud of uncertainty over the election." What do you propose, and how would it increase the accuracy of electronic voting systems?

I propose paper ballots with optical scanners at the precinct, which can detect voter error. For accessibility, I propose that voters be given the option of using a ballot marking machine, as I described above.

Would you say that federal funding of ACCURATE is proof that there is widespread understanding of the problems associated with DRE voting machines and support for guaranteeing fair elections?

ACCURATE was funded by the National Science Foundation (NSF). The process for funding NSF centers involve rigorous peer review by many top computer scientists. The computer science community understands the risks associated with DREs and also the need to find an alternative system that is transparent, accurate, correct, and which can justifiably hold the public confidence.

How is ACCURATE going to improve the voting process in the United States?

Our center is developing technology to aid in the voting process. Our investigators are intimately involved in the elections process, working with officials at all levels and volunteering in running elections. It is our hope the some of the technology developed by our center will be utilized in the design and implementation of future systems, to avoid the possibility of an errant software bug or a malicious attacker being able to corrupt an election.

CHAPTER

9 Professional Ethics

We have come through a strange cycle in programming, starting with the creation of programming itself as a human activity. Executives with the tiniest smattering of knowledge assume that anyone can write a program, and only now are programmers beginning to win their battle for recognition as true professionals.

—GERALD WEINBERG, *The Psychology of Computer Programming*, 1971

9.1 Introduction

INFORMALLY, A **PROFESSION** IS A VOCATION THAT REQUIRES A HIGH LEVEL OF EDUCATION and practical experience in the field. Medicine and law are two well-known professions. We pay doctors and lawyers well, trusting that they will correctly ascertain and treat our medical and legal problems, respectively. Professionals have a special obligation to ensure their actions are for the good of those who depend on them because their decisions can have more serious consequences than the choices made by those holding less responsible positions in society.

In this chapter, we focus on moral decisions made by people who design, implement, or maintain computer hardware or software systems. We begin by considering the extent to which a computer-related career is a profession along the lines of medicine or law. Next, we present and analyze a code of ethics for an important computer-related discipline: software engineering. Our analysis leads us into a discussion of virtue ethics, an ethical theory based on the idea that good character is the source of correct moral decisions. Four case studies give us the opportunity to use the software engineering code of ethics as a tool for ethical analysis.

Finally, we discuss whistleblowing: a situation in which a member of an organization breaks ranks to reveal actual or potential harm to the public. Whistleblowing raises important moral questions about loyalty, trust, and responsibility. Two accounts of whistleblowing illuminate these moral questions and demonstrate the personal sacrifices some have made for the greater good of society. We consider the important role management plays in creating an organizational atmosphere that either allows or suppresses internal dissent.

9.2 Are Computer Experts Professionals?

Millions of people have a computer-related job title, such as computer engineer, computer scientist, programmer, software engineer, system administrator, or systems analyst. Is a computer-related career a profession like medicine or law? Let's consider the characteristics of a well-developed profession.

9.2.1 Characteristics of a Profession

A fully developed profession has a well-organized infrastructure for certifying new members and supporting those who already belong to the profession. Ford and Gibbs have identified eight components of a mature professional infrastructure [1]:[1]

- *Initial professional education*—formal course work completed by candidates before they begin practicing the profession
- *Accreditation*—assures that the formal course work meets the standards of the profession
- *Skills development*—activities that provide candidates with the opportunity to gain practical skills needed to practice the profession
- *Certification*—process by which candidates are evaluated to determine their readiness to enter the profession
- *Licensing*—the process giving candidates the legal right to practice the profession
- *Professional development*—formal course work completed by professionals in order to maintain and develop their knowledge and skills
- *Code of ethics*—mechanism by which a profession ensures that its members will use their knowledge and skills for the benefit of society

1. From Gary Ford and Norman E. Gibbs. "A Mature Profession of Software Engineering." Technical report, Carnegie Mellon University, January 1996. Copyright © 1996 Carnegie Mellon University. All Rights Reserved.

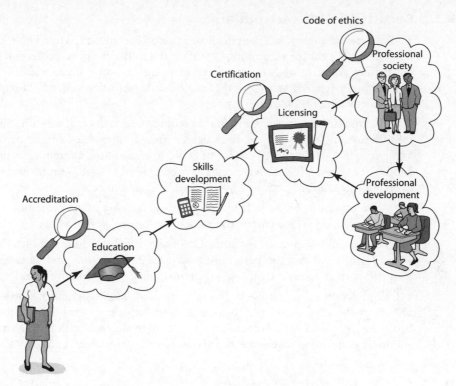

FIGURE 9.1 A mature profession has eight attributes that enable it to certify new members and support existing members [1].

• *Professional society*—organization promoting the welfare of the profession, typically consisting of most if not all of the members of the profession

Figure 9.1 illustrates how these components work together to support the profession. A person desiring to join the profession undertakes some initial professional education. A process of accreditation assures that the educational process is sound. After completing their formal education, candidates gain skills through practical experience working in the field. Another check determines if the candidate is ready to be certified. Successful candidates are licensed to practice the profession.

When the public can trust the competence and integrity of the members of a profession, every one of its members benefits. For this reason professionals have a stake in ensuring that fellow members of the profession are capable and act appropriately. For mature professions, professional societies establish codes of ethics and require their members to keep their knowledge current through continuing education and training. Professionals who do not follow the code of ethics or fail to keep up with changes in the field can lose their licenses.

9.2.2 Certified Public Accountants

To illustrate these steps, let's consider how a person becomes a Certified Public Accountant (CPA). We choose accounting because it is a fully developed profession that does not require graduate study for membership. In this respect it is more similar to a typical computer-related career than the medical or legal professions, which require their members to earn advanced degrees.

The first step for someone wishing to become a CPA is to graduate with 150 semester credit hours and at least a bachelor's degree from an accredited college or university. Many people pursuing a CPA choose to major in accounting, although it is not strictly necessary. However, the candidate must have completed at least 24 semester credit hours in accounting, auditing, business law, finance, and tax subjects.

After graduation, the candidate gets practical training in the profession by finding employment as an accountant working under the supervision of a CPA.

Finally, candidates must sit for the CPA exam, which has four sections. Candidates who do not pass at least two parts must re-take the entire exam. Candidates who pass at least two parts of the exam must pass the remaining parts within five years.

Completion of the necessary formal education, plus satisfactory scores on every section of the CPA exam, plus two years' work experience enable an accountant to become a Certified Public Accountant. In order to retain certification, CPAs must fulfill continuing education requirements and abide by the profession's code of ethics.

9.2.3 Computer–Related Careers

IS A COMPUTER-RELATED CAREER A PROFESSION?

It is easy to find a crucial difference between systems analysts, computer programmers, and system administrators on the one hand and accountants, lawyers, and physicians on the other hand. At the heart of every mature profession is certification and licensing. Certification and licensing allow a profession to determine who will be allowed to practice the profession. For example, a person may not practice law in a state without passing the bar exam and being granted a license. In contrast, people may write computer programs and maintain computer systems, either as consultants, sole proprietors, or members of larger firms, without being certified or having been granted a license.

There are other differences between computer-related careers and mature professions. A person does not have to complete college or serve an apprenticeship under the guidance of an experienced mentor in order to gain employment as a programmer, system administrator, or systems analyst. The vast majority of people who hold computer-related jobs do not belong to either of computing's professional societies. It is up to particular employers to monitor the behavior of their employees and guide their continuing education—no professional organization has the authority to forbid someone from managing computer networks or writing computer programs.

In another important respect computer programmers differ from most professionals, such as dentists and ministers. Typically, professionals work directly with individual clients. A dentist treats one patient at a time. An accountant audits one business at a time.

Most computer programmers work inside a company as part of a team that includes many other programmers as well as managers. In this environment the responsibility of an individual person is more difficult to discern. Low-level technical decisions are made by groups, and final authority rests with management.

STATUS OF CERTIFICATION AND LICENSING

The two largest organizations supporting the computing field are the IEEE Computer Society (IEEE-CS), with about 85,000 members, and the Association for Computing Machinery (ACM), with about 92,000 members. Like organizations supporting mature professions, the IEEE-CS and the ACM strive to advance the discipline and support their members through publications, conferences, local chapters, student chapters, technical committees, and the development of standards.

A **software engineer** is someone engaged in the development or maintenance of software, or someone who teaches in this area. In 1993, the IEEE-CS and ACM set up a joint steering committee to explore the establishment of software engineering as a profession. The joint steering committee created several task forces to address particular issues. One task force conducted a survey of practitioners with the goal of understanding the knowledge and skills required by software engineers. Another task force developed accreditation criteria for undergraduate programs in software engineering. A third task force developed a code of ethics for software engineers.

In May 1999, the ACM Council passed a resolution that stated, in part, "ACM is opposed to the licensing of software engineers at this time because ACM believes that it is premature and would not be effective in addressing the problems of software quality and reliability" [2].

ABILITY TO HARM PUBLIC

The computing "profession" may not be as well developed as the medical or legal professions, but in one key respect—the ability to harm members of the public—those who design, implement, and maintain computer hardware and software systems sometimes hold responsibilities similar to those held by members of mature professions. The Therac-25 killed or gravely injured at least six people, in part because of defective software. While most software engineers do not write code for safety-critical systems such as linear accelerators, society does depend on the quality of their work. People make important business decisions based on the results they get from their spreadsheet programs. Millions rely upon commercial software to help them produce their income tax returns. Errors in programs can result in such harms as lost time, incorrect businesses decisions, and fines. System administrators are responsible for keeping computer systems running reliably without infringing on the privacy of the computer users.

The ability to cause harm to members of the public is a powerful reason why those in computer-related careers should follow a code of ethics, even if they are not professionals in the same sense as physicians, lawyers, and CPAs. As a good example of a code of ethics for those in computer-related disciplines, we present the Software Engineering Code of Ethics and Professional Practice, endorsed by both the ACM and the IEEE-CS.

9.3 Software Engineering Code of Ethics

The Software Engineering Code of Ethics and Professional Practice is a practical framework for moral decision-making related to problems that software engineers may encounter.

The Software Engineering Code of Ethics and Professional Practice, reproduced in its entirety below, is Copyright © 2011 by ACM Publications. Reprinted with permission.

9.3.1 Preamble

Computers have a central and growing role in commerce, industry, government, medicine, education, entertainment and society at large. Software engineers are those who contribute by direct participation or by teaching, to the analysis, specification, design, development, certification, maintenance and testing of software systems. Because of their roles in developing software systems, software engineers have significant opportunities to do good or cause harm, to enable others to do good or cause harm, or to influence others to do good or cause harm. To ensure, as much as possible, that their efforts will be used for good, software engineers must commit themselves to making software engineering a beneficial and respected profession. In accordance with that commitment, software engineers shall adhere to the following Code of Ethics and Professional Practice.

The Code contains eight Principles related to the behavior of and decisions made by professional software engineers, including practitioners, educators, managers, supervisors and policymakers, as well as trainees and students of the profession. The Principles identify the ethically responsible relationships in which individuals, groups, and organizations participate and the primary obligations within these relationships. The Clauses of each Principle are illustrations of some of the obligations included in these relationships. These obligations are founded in the software engineer's humanity, in special care owed to people affected by the work of software engineers, and the unique elements of the practice of software engineering. The Code prescribes these as obligations of anyone claiming to be or aspiring to be a software engineer.

It is not intended that the individual parts of the Code be used in isolation to justify errors of omission or commission. The list of Principles and Clauses is not exhaustive. The Clauses should not be read as separating the acceptable from the unacceptable in professional conduct in all practical situations. The Code is not a simple ethical algorithm that generates ethical decisions. In some situations standards may be in tension with each other or with standards from other sources. These situations require the software engineer to use ethical judgment to act in a manner which is most consistent with the spirit of the Code of Ethics and Professional Practice, given the circumstances.

Ethical tensions can best be addressed by thoughtful consideration of fundamental principles, rather than blind reliance on detailed regulations. These Principles should influence software engineers to consider broadly who is affected by their work; to examine if they and their colleagues are treating other human beings with due respect; to consider how the public, if reasonably well informed, would view their decisions; to analyze how the least empowered will be affected by their decisions; and to consider whether their acts would be judged worthy of the ideal professional working as a software engineer. In all these judgments concern for the health, safety and welfare of the public is primary; that is, the "Public Interest" is central to this Code.

The dynamic and demanding context of software engineering requires a code that is adaptable and relevant to new situations as they occur. However, even in this generality, the Code provides support for software engineers and managers of software engineers who need to take positive action in a specific case by documenting the ethical stance of the profession. The Code provides an ethical foundation to which individuals within teams and the team as a whole can appeal. The Code helps to define those actions that are ethically improper to request of a software engineer or teams of software engineers.

The Code is not simply for adjudicating the nature of questionable acts; it also has an important educational function. As this Code expresses the consensus of the profession on ethical issues, it is a means to educate both the public and aspiring professionals about the ethical obligations of all software engineers.

9.3.2 Principles

PRINCIPLE 1: PUBLIC

Software engineers shall act consistently with the public interest. In particular, software engineers shall, as appropriate:

1.01 Accept full responsibility for their own work.

1.02 Moderate the interests of the software engineer, the employer, the client and the users with the public good.

1.03 Approve software only if they have a well-founded belief that it is safe, meets specifications, passes appropriate tests, and does not diminish quality of life, diminish privacy or harm the environment. The ultimate effect of the work should be to the public good.

1.04 Disclose to appropriate persons or authorities any actual or potential danger to the user, the public, or the environment, that they reasonably believe to be associated with software or related documents.

1.05 Cooperate in efforts to address matters of grave public concern caused by software, its installation, maintenance, support or documentation.

1.06 Be fair and avoid deception in all statements, particularly public ones, concerning software or related documents, methods and tools.

1.07 Consider issues of physical disabilities, allocation of resources, economic disadvantage and other factors that can diminish access to the benefits of software.

1.08 Be encouraged to volunteer professional skills to good causes and contribute to public education concerning the discipline.

FIGURE 9.2 Software engineers shall approve software only if they have a well-founded belief that it is safe, meets specifications, passes appropriate tests, and does not diminish quality of life, diminish privacy, or harm the environment. The ultimate effect of the work should be to the public good (Clause 1.03).

PRINCIPLE 2: CLIENT AND EMPLOYER

Software engineers shall act in a manner that is in the best interests of their client and employer, consistent with the public interest. In particular, software engineers shall, as appropriate:

2.01 Provide service in their areas of competence, being honest and forthright about any limitations of their experience and education.

2.02 Not knowingly use software that is obtained or retained either illegally or unethically.

2.03 Use the property of a client or employer only in ways properly authorized, and with the client's or employer's knowledge and consent.

2.04 Ensure that any document upon which they rely has been approved, when required, by someone authorized to approve it.

2.05 Keep private any confidential information gained in their professional work, where such confidentiality is consistent with the public interest and consistent with the law.

2.06 Identify, document, collect evidence and report to the client or the employer promptly if, in their opinion, a project is likely to fail, to prove too expensive, to violate intellectual property law, or otherwise to be problematic.

2.07 Identify, document, and report significant issues of social concern, of which they are aware, in software or related documents, to the employer or the client.

2.08 Accept no outside work detrimental to the work they perform for their primary employer.

FIGURE 9.3 Software engineers shall not knowingly use software that is obtained or retained either illegally or unethically (Clause 2.02).

2.09   Promote no interest adverse to their employer or client, unless a higher ethical concern is being compromised; in that case, inform the employer or another appropriate authority of the ethical concern.

PRINCIPLE 3: PRODUCT

Software engineers shall ensure that their products and related modifications meet the highest professional standards possible. In particular, software engineers shall, as appropriate:

3.01   Strive for high quality, acceptable cost and a reasonable schedule, ensuring significant tradeoffs are clear to and accepted by the employer and the client, and are available for consideration by the user and the public.

3.02   Ensure proper and achievable goals and objectives for any project on which they work or propose.

3.03   Identify, define and address ethical, economic, cultural, legal and environmental issues related to work projects.

3.04   Ensure that they are qualified for any project on which they work or propose to work by an appropriate combination of education and training, and experience.

3.05   Ensure an appropriate method is used for any project on which they work or propose to work.

3.06   Work to follow professional standards, when available, that are most appropriate for the task at hand, departing from these only when ethically or technically justified.

3.07   Strive to fully understand the specifications for software on which they work.

Project Goals:
Work from Web browser
Easy to learn
~~*Capture 100% market share*~~

FIGURE 9.4 Software engineers shall ensure proper and achievable goals and objectives for any project on which they work or propose (Clause 3.02).

3.08 Ensure that specifications for software on which they work have been well documented, satisfy the users' requirements and have the appropriate approvals.

3.09 Ensure realistic quantitative estimates of cost, scheduling, personnel, quality and outcomes on any project on which they work or propose to work and provide an uncertainty assessment of these estimates.

3.10 Ensure adequate testing, debugging, and review of software and related documents on which they work.

3.11 Ensure adequate documentation, including significant problems discovered and solutions adopted, for any project on which they work.

3.12 Work to develop software and related documents that respect the privacy of those who will be affected by that software.

3.13 Be careful to use only accurate data derived by ethical and lawful means, and use it only in ways properly authorized.

3.14 Maintain the integrity of data, being sensitive to outdated or flawed occurrences.

3.15 Treat all forms of software maintenance with the same professionalism as new development.

PRINCIPLE 4: JUDGMENT

Software engineers shall maintain integrity and independence in their professional judgment. In particular, software engineers shall, as appropriate:

4.01 Temper all technical judgments by the need to support and maintain human values.

4.02 Only endorse documents either prepared under their supervision or within their areas of competence and with which they are in agreement.

4.03 Maintain professional objectivity with respect to any software or related documents they are asked to evaluate.

4.04 Not engage in deceptive financial practices such as bribery, double billing, or other improper financial practices.

4.05 Disclose to all concerned parties those conflicts of interest that cannot reasonably be avoided or escaped.

4.06 Refuse to participate, as members or advisors, in a private, governmental or professional body concerned with software related issues, in which they, their employers or their clients have undisclosed potential conflicts of interest.

PRINCIPLE 5: MANAGEMENT

Software engineering managers and leaders shall subscribe to and promote an ethical approach to the management of software development and maintenance. In particular, those managing or leading software engineers shall, as appropriate:

5.01 Ensure good management for any project on which they work, including effective procedures for promotion of quality and reduction of risk.

5.02 Ensure that software engineers are informed of standards before being held to them.

5.03 Ensure that software engineers know the employer's policies and procedures for protecting passwords, files and information that is confidential to the employer or confidential to others.

5.04 Assign work only after taking into account appropriate contributions of education and experience tempered with a desire to further that education and experience.

5.05 Ensure realistic quantitative estimates of cost, scheduling, personnel, quality and outcomes on any project on which they work or propose to work, and provide an uncertainty assessment of these estimates.

5.06 Attract potential software engineers only by a full and accurate description of the conditions of employment.

5.07 Offer fair and just remuneration.

5.08 Not unjustly prevent someone from taking a position for which that person is suitably qualified.

5.09 Ensure that there is a fair agreement concerning ownership of any software, processes, research, writing, or other intellectual property to which a software engineer has contributed.

5.10 Provide for due process in hearing charges of violation of an employer's policy or of this Code.

5.11 Not ask a software engineer to do anything inconsistent with this Code.

5.12 Not punish anyone for expressing ethical concerns about a project.

FIGURE 9.5 Software engineers shall help develop an organizational environment favorable to acting ethically (Clause 6.01).

PRINCIPLE 6: PROFESSION

Software engineers shall advance the integrity and reputation of the profession consistent with the public interest. In particular, software engineers shall, as appropriate:

6.01   Help develop an organizational environment favorable to acting ethically.

6.02   Promote public knowledge of software engineering.

6.03   Extend software engineering knowledge by appropriate participation in professional organizations, meetings and publications.

6.04   Support, as members of a profession, other software engineers striving to follow this Code.

6.05   Not promote their own interest at the expense of the profession, client or employer.

6.06   Obey all laws governing their work, unless, in exceptional circumstances, such compliance is inconsistent with the public interest.

6.07   Be accurate in stating the characteristics of software on which they work, avoiding not only false claims but also claims that might reasonably be supposed to be speculative, vacuous, deceptive, misleading, or doubtful.

6.08   Take responsibility for detecting, correcting, and reporting errors in software and associated documents on which they work.

6.09   Ensure that clients, employers, and supervisors know of the software engineer's commitment to this Code of ethics, and the subsequent ramifications of such commitment.

6.10   Avoid associations with businesses and organizations which are in conflict with this code.

6.11 Recognize that violations of this Code are inconsistent with being a professional software engineer.

6.12 Express concerns to the people involved when significant violations of this Code are detected unless this is impossible, counter-productive, or dangerous.

6.13 Report significant violations of this Code to appropriate authorities when it is clear that consultation with people involved in these significant violations is impossible, counter-productive or dangerous.

PRINCIPLE 7: COLLEAGUES

Software engineers shall be fair to and supportive of their colleagues. In particular, software engineers shall, as appropriate:

7.01 Encourage colleagues to adhere to this Code.

7.02 Assist colleagues in professional development.

7.03 Credit fully the work of others and refrain from taking undue credit.

7.04 Review the work of others in an objective, candid, and properly documented way.

7.05 Give a fair hearing to the opinions, concerns, or complaints of a colleague.

7.06 Assist colleagues in being fully aware of current standard work practices including policies and procedures for protecting passwords, files and other confidential information, and security measures in general.

7.07 Not unfairly intervene in the career of any colleague; however, concern for the employer, the client or public interest may compel software engineers, in good faith, to question the competence of a colleague.

7.08 In situations outside of their own areas of competence, call upon the opinions of other professionals who have competence in that area.

PRINCIPLE 8: SELF

Software engineers shall participate in lifelong learning regarding the practice of their profession and shall promote an ethical approach to the practice of the profession. In particular, software engineers shall continually endeavor to:

8.01 Further their knowledge of developments in the analysis, specification, design, development, maintenance and testing of software and related documents, together with the management of the development process.

8.02 Improve their ability to create safe, reliable, and useful quality software at reasonable cost and within a reasonable time.

8.03 Improve their ability to produce accurate, informative, and well-written documentation.

8.04 Improve their understanding of the software and related documents on which they work and of the environment in which they will be used.

8.05 Improve their knowledge of relevant standards and the law governing the software and related documents on which they work.

FIGURE 9.6 Software engineers shall continually endeavor to improve their ability to create safe, reliable, and useful quality software at reasonable cost and within a reasonable time (Clause 8.02).

8.06   Improve their knowledge of this Code, its interpretation, and its application to their work.

8.07   Not give unfair treatment to anyone because of any irrelevant prejudices.

8.08   Not influence others to undertake any action that involves a breach of this Code.

8.09   Recognize that personal violations of this Code are inconsistent with being a professional software engineer.

9.4   Analysis of the Code

In this section, we analyze the Code and derive an alternate set of underlying principles upon which it rests.

9.4.1   Preamble

The preamble to the Code points out that there is no mechanical process for determining the correct actions to take when faced with a moral problem. Our experience evaluating moral problems related to the introduction and use of information technology confirms this statement. Even two people with similar philosophies may reach different conclusions when confronted with a moral problem. Two Kantians may agree on the basic facts of a moral problem, but disagree on how to characterize the will of the moral agent. Two utilitarians may agree on the benefits and harms resulting from a proposed action, but assign different weights to the outcomes, causing them to reach opposite conclusions.

The preamble also warns against taking an overly legalistic view of the Code. Simply because an action is not expressly forbidden by the Code does not mean it is morally acceptable. Instead, judgment is needed to detect when a moral problem has arisen and to determine the right thing to do in a particular situation.

While the Code is expressed as a collection of rules, these rules are based on principles grounded in different ethical theories. This is not surprising, considering that the Code was drafted by a committee. When we encounter a situation where two rules conflict, the preamble urges us to ask questions that will help us consider the principles underlying the rules. These questions demonstrate the multifaceted grounding of the Code:

1. *Who is affected?*

   Utilitarians focus on determining how an action benefits or harms other people.

2. *Am I treating other human beings with respect?*

   Kant's Categorical Imperative tells us to treat others as ends in themselves, rather than simply as a means to an end.

3. *Would my decision hold up to public scrutiny?*

   A cultural relativist is concerned about whether an action conforms with the mores of society.

4. *How will those who are least empowered be affected?*

   Rawls's second principle of justice requires us to consider whether inequalities are to the greatest benefit of the least-advantaged members of society.

5. *Are my acts worthy of the ideal professional?*

   The ethics of virtue is based on imitation of morally superior role models. Since we did not discuss virtue ethics in Chapter 2, let's examine it now.

9.4.2 Virtue Ethics

ORIGIN OF VIRTUE ETHICS

In *The Nicomachean Ethics*, Aristotle expresses the opinion that happiness results from living a life of virtue [3]. He distinguishes between *intellectual virtue*, which is developed through education, and *moral virtue*, which comes about through repetition of the appropriate acts (Figure 9.7). You can acquire the virtue of honesty, for example, by habitually telling the truth. According to Aristotle, deriving pleasure from a virtuous act is a sign that you have acquired that virtue.

There is a wealth of virtues, of course. Here is a brief list of two dozen virtues given by James Rachels: benevolence, civility, compassion, conscientiousness, cooperativeness, courage, courteousness, dependability, fairness, friendliness, generosity, honesty, industriousness, justice, loyalty, moderation, patience, prudence, reasonableness, self-discipline, self-reliance, tactfulness, thoughtfulness, and tolerance [4].

A person who possesses many moral virtues has a strong moral character. According to Aristotle, when people with strong character face a moral problem, they know the

FIGURE 9.7 According to Aristotle, happiness derives from living a life of virtue. You acquire moral virtues by repeating the appropriate acts.

right thing to do, because the action will be consistent with their character. As Justin Oakley and Dean Cocking put it, "An action is right if and only if it is what an agent with a virtuous character would do in the circumstances" [5].

STRENGTHS OF VIRTUE ETHICS

Virtue ethics has two advantages over the ethical theories we considered in Chapter 2. First, it provides a motivation for good behavior. The calculus of utility and the Categorical Imperative say nothing about motivation. Virtue ethics, on the other hand, stresses the importance of loyalty, thoughtfulness, courteousness, dependability, and other characteristics of healthy social interactions.

A second advantage of virtue ethics is that it provides a solution to the problem of impartiality. Recall that utilitarianism, Kantianism, and social contract theory require us to be completely impartial and treat all human beings as equals. This assumption leads to moral evaluations that are hard for most people to accept. For example, when a couple is faced with the choice between using $4,000 to take their children to Disneyland for a week or feeding 1,000 starving Africans for a month, the calculus of utility would conclude saving 1,000 lives was the right thing to do. However, most of us expect that good parents will show more kindness to their children than to people living on the other side of the world.

Virtue ethics avoids the pitfall of impartiality by rejecting the notion that every action must be designed to produce the maximum benefit for people overall [5]. Instead, some virtues are partial toward certain people, while others are impartial and treat everyone equally. Generosity and loyalty are examples of virtues that allow a person to be partial toward friends and family members. Honesty, civility, and courteousness are examples of virtues that a person would extend equally to all human beings.

VIRTUE ETHICS COMPLEMENTS OTHER THEORIES

Rather than treating virtue ethics as a stand-alone theory, some ethicists believe it makes more sense to see virtue ethics as a complement to one of the other theories, such as utilitarianism. Adding virtue ethics allows ethical decision makers to consider their rationale for taking the action as well as the beneficial or harmful effects of the action.

Remember the problem of moral luck, one of the major criticisms of act utilitarianism? Since an action is judged right or wrong based solely on its consequences, an unlucky, unintended consequence can result in an action being considered wrong. Suppose your mother-in-law is in the hospital and you send her an expensive and beautiful bouquet of flowers. Unfortunately, she gets an allergic reaction to one of the flowers in the bouquet. As a result, she must spend an additional four days in the hospital. From a purely act utilitarian point of view, you did the wrong thing when you sent your mother-in-law the flowers. In a mixed act utilitarian/virtue ethics theory, we would also take into account that you were acting out of thoughtfulness, a virtue. If nothing else, introducing the virtue ethics component makes it easier for us to think about some of the other consequences of the action. Despite the allergic reaction, your mother in law appreciated your kind gesture, a benefit. In addition, you strengthened your habit of thoughtfulness by practicing it on your mother-in-law, another benefit.

9.4.3 Alternative List of Fundamental Principles

The start of each section of the Code begins with the statement of a fundamental principle. For example, the first section begins with the fundamental principle, "Software engineers shall act consistently with the public interest." All of these statements of fundamental principles are expressed from the point of view of what software engineers ought to do.

Another way to devise a list of fundamental principles is to consider those virtues we would like to instill among all the members of any profession. We end up with a set of general, discipline-independent rules that cut across the eight categories of the Code. Here is an alternative list of fundamental principles derived using that approach:

1. *Be impartial.*

   The good of the general public is equally important to the good of your organization or company. The good of your profession and your company are equally important to your personal good. It is wrong to promote your agenda at the expense of your firm, and it is wrong to promote the interests of your firm at the expense of society. (Supports Clauses 1.02, 1.03, 1.05, 1.07, 3.03, 3.12, 4.01, and 6.05.)

2. *Disclose information that others ought to know.*

   Do not let others come to harm by concealing information from them. Do not make misleading or deceptive statements. Disclose potential conflicts of interest. (Supports Clauses 1.04, 1.06, 2.06, 2.07, 3.01, 4.05, 4.06, 5.05, 5.06, 6.07, 6.08, 6.09, 6.12, and 6.13.)

3. *Respect the rights of others.*

   Do not infringe on the privacy rights, property rights, or intellectual property rights of others. (Supports Clauses 2.02, 2.03, 2.05, and 3.13.)

4. *Treat others justly.*

   Everyone deserves fair wages and appropriate credit for work performed. Do not discriminate against others for attributes unrelated to the job they must do. Do not penalize others for following the Code. (Supports Clauses 5.06, 5.07, 5.08, 5.09, 5.10, 5.11, 5.12, 7.03, 7.04, 7.05, 7.07, and 8.07.)

5. *Take responsibility for your actions and inactions.*

   As a moral agent, you are responsible for the things you do, both good and bad. You may also be responsible for bad things that you allow to happen through your inaction. (Supports Clauses 1.01, 3.04, 3.05, 3.06, 3.07, 3.08, 3.10, 3.11, 3.14, 3.15, 4.02, and 7.08.)

6. *Take responsibility for the actions of those you supervise.*

   Managers are responsible for setting up work assignments and training opportunities to promote quality and reduce risk. They should create effective communication channels with subordinates so that they can monitor the work being done and be aware of any quality or risk issues that arise. (Supports Clauses 5.01, 5.02, 5.03, and 5.04.)

7. *Maintain your integrity.*

   Deliver on your commitments and be loyal to your employer, while obeying the law. Do not ask someone else to do something you would not be willing to do yourself. (Supports Clauses 2.01, 2.04, 2.08, 2.09, 3.01, 3.02, 3.09, 4.03, 4.04, 6.06, 6.10, 6.11, 8.08, and 8.09.)

8. *Continually improve your abilities.*

   Take advantage of opportunities to improve your software engineering skills and your ability to put the Code to use. (Supports Clauses 8.01, 8.02, 8.03, 8.04, 8.05, and 8.06.)

9. *Share your knowledge, expertise, and values.*

   Volunteer your time and skills to worthy causes. Help bring others to your level of knowledge about software engineering and professional ethics. (Supports Clauses 1.08, 6.01, 6.02, 6.03, 6.04, 7.01, 7.02, and 7.06.)

In the following section, we will use these fundamental, discipline-independent principles to facilitate our analysis in four case studies related to computing.

9.5 Case Studies

Throughout this text we have evaluated a wide range of moral problems. Our methodology has been to evaluate the moral problem from the point of view of Kantianism, act utilitarianism, rule utilitarianism, and social contract theory.

Another way to evaluate information technology–related moral problems is to make use of the Software Code of Ethics and Professional Practice. We follow a three-step process:

1. Consult the list of fundamental principles and identify those that are relevant to the moral problem.
2. Search the list of clauses accompanying each of the relevant fundamental principles to see which speak most directly to the issue.
3. Determine whether the contemplated action aligns with or contradicts the statements in the clauses. If the action is in agreement with all of the clauses, that provides strong evidence the action is moral. If the action is in disagreement with all of the clauses, it is safe to say the action is immoral.

    Usually, the contemplated action will be supported by some clauses and opposed by others. When this happens, we must use our judgment to determine which of the clauses are most important before we can reach a conclusion about the morality of the contemplated action.

In the remainder of this section, we will apply this methodology to four case studies.

9.5.1 Software Recommendation

∼ Scenario

Sam Shaw calls the Department of Computer Science at East Dakota State University seeking advice on how to improve the security of his business's local area network. A secretary in the department routes Mr. Shaw's call to Professor Jane Smith, an internationally recognized expert in the field. Professor Smith answers several questions posed by Mr. Shaw regarding network security. When Mr. Shaw asks Professor Smith to recommend a software package to identify security problems, Professor Smith tells him that NetCheks got the personal computer magazine's top rating. She does not mention that the same magazine gave a "best buy" rating to another product with fewer features but a much lower price. She also fails to mention that NetCheks is a product of a spin-off company started by one of her former students and that she owns 10 percent of the company.

Analysis

From our list of nine fundamental principles, three are most relevant here:

- Be impartial.
- Disclose information that others ought to know.
- Share your knowledge, expertise, and values.

Searching the list of clauses identified with these fundamental principles, the following ones seem to fit the case study most closely:

- *1.06. Be fair and avoid deception in all statements, particularly public ones, concerning software or related documents, methods and tools.*
  Professor Smith was deceptive when she mentioned the most highly rated software package but not the one rated to be a "best buy."

- *1.08. Be encouraged to volunteer professional skills to good causes and contribute to public education concerning the discipline.*

- *6.02. Promote public knowledge of software engineering.*
  Professor Smith freely provided Sam Shaw with valuable information about network security.

- *4.05. Disclose to all concerned parties those conflicts of interest that cannot reasonably be avoided or escaped.*

- *6.05. Not promote their own interest at the expense of the profession, client or employer.*
  Professor Smith did not tell Sam Shaw that she had a personal stake in the success of the NetCheks software. She did not tell him about the "best buy" package that may have provided him every feature he needed at a much lower price.

Mr. Shaw was asking Professor Smith for free advice, and she provided it. When she freely shared her knowledge about network security, she was acting in the spirit of Clauses 1.08 and 6.02, and doing a good thing.

However, Professor Smith appears to have violated the other three clauses to at least some degree. Most importantly, she did not reveal her personal interest in NetCheks, which could lead her to be biased. The fact that the she did not mention the "best buy" package is evidence that she was neither evenhanded nor completely forthcoming when she answered Mr. Shaw's question about software packages.

Perhaps Mr. Shaw should have heeded the maxim, "Free advice is worth what you pay for it." Nevertheless, the ignorance or foolishness of one person does not excuse the bad behavior of another. Professor Smith should have revealed her conflict of interest. At that point, Mr. Shaw could have chosen to get another opinion if he so desired.   ～

9.5.2 Child Pornography

～ Scenario

Joe Green, a system administrator for a large corporation, is installing a new software package on the PC used by employee Chuck Dennis. The company has not authorized Joe to read other people's emails, Web logs, or personal files. However, in the course of installing the software, he accidentally comes across directories containing files with suspicious-looking names. He opens a few of the files and discovers they contain child pornography. Joe believes possessing such images is against federal law. What should he do?

Analysis

Looking over the list of nine fundamental principles, we find these to be most relevant to our scenario:

- Be impartial.
- Respect the rights of others.
- Treat others justly.
- Maintain your integrity.

We examine the lists of clauses associated with these four fundamental principles and identify those which are most relevant:

- *2.03. Use the property of a client or employer only in ways properly authorized, and with the client's or employer's knowledge and consent.*
  Somebody has misused the company's PC by using it to store images of child pornography. By this principle Joe has an obligation to report what he discovered.

- *2.09. Promote no interest adverse to their employer or client, unless a higher ethical concern is being compromised; in that case, inform the employer or another appropriate authority of the ethical concern.*
  While revealing the existence of the child pornography may harm the employee, possessing child pornography is illegal. Applying this principle would lead Joe to disclose what he discovered.

- *3.13. Be careful to use only accurate data derived by ethical and lawful means, and use it only in ways properly authorized.*
  Joe discovered the child pornography by violating the company's policy against examining files on personal computers used by employees.

- *5.10. Provide for due process in hearing charges of violation of an employer's policy or of this Code.*
  Simply because Chuck had these files on his computer does not necessarily mean he is guilty. Perhaps someone else broke into Chuck's computer and stored the images there.

Our analysis is more complicated because Joe violated company policy to uncover the child pornography on Chuck's PC. Once he has this knowledge, however, the remaining principles guide Joe to reveal what he has discovered to the relevant authorities within the corporation, even though management may punish Joe for breaking the privacy policy. There is the possibility that Chuck is a victim. Someone else may be trying to frame Chuck or use his computer as a safe stash for their collection of images. Joe should be discreet until a complete investigation is completed and Chuck has had the opportunity to defend himself.

9.5.3 Anti–Worm

∼ SCENARIO

The Internet is plagued by a new worm that infects PCs by exploiting a security hole in a popular operating system. Tim Smart creates an anti-worm that exploits the same security hole to spread from PC to PC. When Tim's anti-worm gets into a PC, it automatically downloads a software patch that plugs the security hole. In other words, it fixes the PC so that it is no longer vulnerable to attacks via that security hole [6].

Tim releases the anti-worm, taking precautions to ensure that it cannot be traced back to him. The anti-worm quickly spreads throughout the Internet, consuming large amounts of network bandwidth and entering millions of computers. To system administrators, it looks just like another worm, and they battle its spread the same way they fight all other worms [7].

Analysis

These fundamental principles are most relevant to the anti-worm scenario:

- Continually improve your abilities.
- Share your knowledge, expertise, and values.
- Respect the rights of others.
- Take responsibility for your actions and inactions.

Examining the list of clauses associated with each of these fundamental principles reveals those that are most relevant to our case study:

- *1.01. Accept full responsibility for their own work.*
  Tim tried to prevent others from discovering that he was the author of the anti-worm. He did not accept responsibility for what he had done.

- *1.08. Be encouraged to volunteer professional skills to good causes and contribute to public education concerning the discipline.*
  The anti-worm did something good by patching security holes in PCs. Tim provided the anti-worm to the Internet community without charge. However, system administrators spent a lot of time trying to halt the spread of the anti-worm, a harmful effect.

- *2.03. Use the property of a client or employer only in ways properly authorized, and with the client's or the employer's knowledge and consent.*
  Tim's "client" is the community of Internet PC owners who happen to use the operating system with the security hole. While his anti-worm was designed to benefit them, it entered their systems without their knowledge or consent. The anti-worm also consumed a great deal of network bandwidth without the consent of the relevant telecommunications companies.

- *8.01. Further their knowledge of developments in the analysis, specification, design, development, maintenance, and testing of software and related documents, together with the management of the development process.*
- *8.02. Improve their ability to create safe, reliable, and useful quality software at reasonable cost and within a reasonable time.*
- *8.06. Improve their knowledge of this Code, its interpretations, and its application to their work.*

Tim followed the letter of these three clauses when he acquired a copy of the worm, figured out how it worked, and created a reliable anti-worm in a short period of time. The experience improved his knowledge and skills. Perhaps he should invest some time improving his ability to interpret and use the Code of Ethics!

According to some of these principles, Tim did the right thing. According to others, Tim was wrong to release the anti-worm. How do we resolve this dilemma? We can simplify our analysis by deciding that Tim's welfare is less important than the public good. Using this logic, we will no longer consider the fact that Tim improved his technical knowledge and skills by developing and releasing the anti-worm.

That leaves us with three clauses remaining (1.01, 1.08, and 2.03). From the point of view of Clause 1.01, what Tim did was wrong. By attempting to hide his identity, Tim refused to accept responsibility for launching the anti-worm. He has clearly violated the Code of Ethics in this regard.

When we evaluate Tim's action from the point of view of Clause 1.08, we must determine whether his efforts were directed to a "good cause." Certainly Tim's anti-worm benefited the PCs it infected by removing a security vulnerability. However, it harmed the Internet by consuming large amounts of bandwidth, and it harmed system administrators, who spent time battling it. Because there were harmful as well as beneficial consequences, we cannot say that Tim's efforts were directed to a completely good cause.

Finally, let's evaluate Tim's action from the point of view of Clause 2.03. Even though the anti-worm was completely benevolent, Tim violated the property rights of the PC owners, because the anti-worm infected their PCs without authorization. Hence, Tim's release of the anti-worm was wrong from the point of view of this Clause.

To summarize our analysis, Tim's release of the anti-worm is clearly wrong from the point of view of Clauses 1.01 and 2.03. It is also hard to argue that he satisfied the spirit of Clause 1.08. We conclude that Tim's action violated the Software Engineering Code of Ethics and Professional Practice. ∽

9.5.4 Consulting Opportunity

∽ SCENARIO

Acme Corporation licenses a sophisticated software package to many state, county, and city governments. Government agencies have the choice of three levels of service: the bronze level provides online support only; the silver level adds phone support; and the gold level includes training classes taught on the customer's site. The gold level of support costs $20,000/year more than the silver level.

Jean is one of the Acme employees who works in the support organization. Mostly Jean provides phone support, but from time to time he teaches an on-site class. In fact, Jean created many of the instructional materials used in these classes. Because of the recession, quite a few government agencies have dropped from the gold level of support to the silver level, and some members of Jean's training group have lost their jobs. Jean has a family to support, and he is wondering if his position will soon be eliminated as well.

The state government of East Dakota is one of the many customers that no longer pay Acme Corporation for on-site training. One day Jean gets a call from Maria, who works for the East Dakota state agency using the software package. Maria offers to pay Jean $5,000 plus expenses to run a five-day training class that covers the same material as the official course taught by Acme.

Jean accepts the offer, but he does not inform anyone at Acme Corporation of his decision. Working at home on evenings and weekends, he develops his own set of instructional materials. He takes a week of paid vacation from work, travels to East Daktoa, and teaches the class.

Analysis

From our list of fundamental principles, quite a few are relevant here:

- Be impartial.
- Take responsibility for your actions and inactions.
- Disclose information that others ought to know.
- Maintain your integrity.
- Continually improve your abilities.

Examining the clauses associated with each of these fundamental principles, the ones that most closely fit this case study are:

- *3.04 Ensure that they are qualified for any project on which they work or propose to work by an appropriate combination of education and training, and experience.*
  Based on his prior experience at Acme, Jean was certainly well qualified to develop the instructional materials and teach the class in East Dakota. He has fulfilled this obligation of the Code.

- *8.04 Improve their understanding of the software and related documents on which they work and of the environment in which they will be used.*
  By creating his own set of instructional materials, Jean probably developed an even better understanding of the software package and its capabilities. There is a good chance he came up with some insights about better ways to

teach others how to use the software. This additional knowledge will make Jean a more valuable employee of Acme Corporation.

- *4.05 Disclose to all concerned parties those conflicts of interest that cannot reasonably be avoided or escaped.*
  By accepting the consulting job with the East Dakota state government, Jean created a conflict of interest between himself and Acme Corporation. Namely, it is in Jean's interest if East Dakota does not purchase the gold level of support, but it is in Acme Corporation's interest if East Dakota does buy the gold level of support. Jean violated this clause by not disclosing his consulting job to Acme Corporation.

- *2.08 Accept no outside work detrimental to the work they perform for their primary employer.*
  Employers provide employees with weekends off and paid vacations so that they can rest from their labors and return to work refreshed and able to perform at a high level. You could argue that Jean's consulting work was detrimental to his "day job" at Acme Corporation because it filled his evenings and weekends and kept him from getting a proper vacation.

- *6.05 Not promote their own interest at the expense of the profession, client or employer.*
  By agreeing to teach the class in East Dakota, Jean put his own interest above that of his employer. Clearly the East Dakota state government recognized a need to have some on-site training. If Jean did not accept the consulting job, the East Dakota government may have gone back to the gold level of support from Acme.

You could argue that Jean is actually helping Acme Corporation. Governments are dropping the gold level of support because it is simply too expensive, but phone support and online support aren't enough. If these agencies cannot find another source of on-site training, they may stop using Acme's software altogether. By providing East Dakota with affordable, on-site training, Jean was helping ensure that East Dakota would remain a customer of Acme Corporation, albeit at the silver level.

You could also argue that Jean's work for East Dakota improved his knowledge of the software package and his ability to teach others how to use it, making him a more effective phone support person at Acme.

However, it's unlikely upper management at Acme Corporation will be convinced by these arguments, particularly since Jean did not disclose the offer from East Dakota before accepting it. Jean's decision is much more likely to cause management to question his loyalty to his company and his fellow employees. If the company learns about his consulting work, Jean may well be the next person laid off.

To conclude our analysis, Jean's actions were wrong and unwise. He violated clauses 2.08, 4.05, and 6.05 of the Software Engineering Code of Ethics and Professional Practice, and he may have put his full-time job in jeopardy.   ∽

9.6 Whistleblowing

All four case studies presented in the previous section involve the actions of a single individual. It is easy for us to assign moral responsibility to that person and to discuss how things might have turned out better if he or she had acted differently. Often, however, a product or decision is the cumulative result of the work of many people within a larger organization. Suppose somebody within the organization perceives a danger to the public but is unable to persuade the rest of the organization to make needed changes to eliminate that danger. Should that person go outside the organization with the information?

A **whistleblower** is someone who breaks ranks with an organization in order to make an unauthorized disclosure of information about a harmful situation after attempts to report the concerns through authorized organizational channels have been ignored or rebuffed [8]. Sometimes employees become whistleblowers out of fear that actions taken by their employer may harm the public; other times they have identified fraudulent use of tax dollars [9].

9.6.1 Morton Thiokol/NASA

On January 28, 1986, the space shuttle *Challenger* lifted off from Cape Canaveral. On board were seven astronauts, including schoolteacher Christa McAuliffe, the first civilian to fly into space. Just 73 seconds after lift-off, hot gases leaking from one of the booster rockets led to an explosion that destroyed the *Challenger* and killed everyone on board (Figure 9.8).

Engineer Roger Boisjoly was in charge of inspecting the O-rings on the boosters recovered after launches of the space shuttle. The O-rings were supposed to seal connections between sections of the booster rockets. On two occasions in 1985, he had seen evidence that a primary O-ring seal had failed. Boisjoly presented a report on his findings to NASA officials at the Marshall Space Flight Center. Frustrated that NASA officials were not giving sufficient attention to the problem, he wrote a memo to Vice President for Engineering Robert Lund stating that an O-ring failure could lead to the loss of a shuttle flight and the launch pad. Despite Boisjoly's persistent efforts to get the seals redesigned, the problem was not fixed.

On January 27, 1986, Boisjoly and a group of Morton Thiokol engineers met to discuss the proposed launch for the following day. Florida was in the middle of an unusual cold snap; the weather forecast for northern Florida called for an overnight low of 18 degrees Fahrenheit. The engineers knew that frigid temperatures greatly increased the probability that an O-ring would fail, allowing hot gases to escape from a booster rocket. They prepared a set of 14 slides that documented their concern about a low-temperature launch.

The evening of January 27, Morton Thiokol had a teleconference with the Marshall Space Flight Center and the Kennedy Space Center. Morton Thiokol's presentation ended with the engineers' recommendation that NASA not launch the *Challenger* if the temperature was below 53 degrees. NASA asked Morton Thiokol Vice President

FIGURE 9.8 The explosion of the *Challenger* killed seven astronauts, including the first schoolteacher in space, Christa McAuliffe. (Courtesy of NASA)

Joe Kilminster for a go/no-go decision. Kilminster said his recommendation was not to launch.

NASA officials were displeased to get this recommendation from Morton Thiokol. The launch had already been delayed several times. They were eager to launch the space shuttle before the President's State of the Union address the following evening, so that the President could include the mission in his speech. After NASA officials expressed their dismay with the recommendation, Kilminster asked for a five-minute break in the proceedings.

During the recess, Morton Thiokol's four top managers huddled away from the engineers. Senior Vice President Jerald Mason and Vice President Calvin Wiggins supported the launch, while Vice Presidents Joseph Kilminster and Robert Lund were opposed. However, Lund changed his mind after Mason "told him to take off his engineering hat and put on his management hat" [10]. (More than half of Morton Thiokol's profits came from its work for NASA.)

When Morton Thiokol rejoined the teleconference, Kilminster told NASA officials that Morton Thiokol recommended the launch go ahead. NASA officials at the Marshall Flight Center prevented the engineers' negative recommendation from being communicated to the NASA officials with final authority to approve or delay the launch.

A month after the loss of the *Challenger*, Boisjoly testified before a Presidential commission appointed to investigate the disaster. Morton Thiokol lawyers had advised Boisjoly to reply to every question with a simple "yes" or "no." Instead, Boisjoly shared with the commission his hypothesis about how the cold temperature had caused the failure of an O-ring. In later meetings with commission members, he presented documents that supported his hypothesis, including his 1985 memo. Boisjoly's testimony and documents contradicted the testimony of Morton Thiokol management. The company responded by isolating Boisjoly from NASA personnel and the O-ring redesign effort [10, 11].

Distressed by the hostile environment, Boisjoly stopped working for Morton Thiokol in July 1986. Two years later, he found work as a forensic engineer.

9.6.2 Hughes Aircraft

In the 1980s, Hughes Aircraft manufactured military-grade hybrid computer chips at its Micro-electronic Circuit Division in Newport Beach, California. (A *hybrid computer chip* contains both digital and analog circuits.) The division produced about 100,000 hybrid chips per year. The military put these chips in a variety of sophisticated weapons systems, such as fighter planes and air-to-air missiles. Manufacturing these chips was a lucrative business for Hughes Aircraft; the government paid between $300 and $5,000 for each chip.

In return for paying these high prices, the government insisted that the chips pass stringent quality assurance tests. Hughes Aircraft technicians made two kinds of tests. First, they ensured the chips functioned correctly. Second, they checked the chips for resistance to shocks, high temperatures, and moisture. About 10 percent of the chips failed at least one of these tests. A common problem was that a chip would have a defective seal, which let moisture in. These chips were called "leakers."

Margaret Goodearl and Donald LaRue supervised the testing area. The company hired Ruth Ibarra to be an independent quality control agent.

In August 1986, floor worker Lisa Lightner found a leaker. Donald LaRue ordered her to pass the chip. Lightner told Goodearl, and Goodearl reported the incident to upper management. Hughes Aircraft management threatened to fire Goodearl if she didn't reveal the identity of the worker who had complained.

Two months later, LaRue ordered Shirley Reddick, another floor worker, to reseal lids on some hybrid chips, in violation of the required process for handling leakers. Reddick reported the incident to Goodearl, who relayed the report to upper management. Again, Goodearl was told she might be fired if she kept up this pattern of behavior.

In the same month, LaRue asked tester Rachel Janesch to certify that a defective hybrid chip had passed the leak test. Goodearl played a role in reporting the incident to Hughes Aircraft management. In this case, the chips were retested.

Goodearl and Ibarra found a box of hybrid chips with blank paperwork, meaning the necessary tests had not been performed. When Goodearl reported this discovery to her superiors, they told her she was no longer part of the team. Goodearl filed a formal harassment complaint. A mid-level manager in Personnel called her into his office, tore up her complaint, threw his glasses at her, and said, "If you ever do anything like that again, I will fire your ass" [9].

Goodearl's performance evaluations, which had been excellent, dropped sharply as soon as she began complaining about irregularities in the chip testing facility. In late 1986, Goodearl and Ibarra contacted the Office of the Inspector General, part of the U.S. Department of Justice. A joint decision was made for Goodearl and Ibarra to find a clear-cut case of fraud.

One day, LaRue put two leaky hybrid chips on his desk, planning to approve them after Goodearl had gone home. Goodearl and Ibarra made photocopies of the documentation showing the chips had failed the leak test. After the chips were shipped from Hughes Aircraft, the Department of Defense tested them and found them to be leakers. As a result of this incident, the Office of the Inspector General began a formal investigation of fraud at Hughes Aircraft.

Hughes Aircraft fired Goodearl in 1989. Ibarra had left Hughes Aircraft in 1988, "after being relieved of all meaningful responsibilities and put in a cubicle with nothing to do" [12]. In 1990, Goodearl and Ruth Ibarra (now known under her married name, Ruth Aldred) filed a civil suit against Hughes Aircraft, claiming that Hughes Aircraft had violated the False Claims Act by falsifying records in order to defraud the government. This civil suit was put on hold until the end of the criminal trial.

The Inspector General's criminal investigation led to a trial in 1992. The jury found Hughes Aircraft guilty of conspiring to defraud the government. Hughes Aircraft appealed the verdict, but the verdict was upheld. Since a criminal conviction can be used as evidence in a civil trial, the verdict nearly assured that Goodearl and Alred would prevail in their civil suit. Hughes Aircraft began negotiating a settlement in the civil suit.

Four years later, Hughes Aircraft was ordered to pay $4.05 million in damages. Goodearl and Aldred received 22 percent of the settlement, or $891,000. In addition, Hughes Aircraft was required to pay their legal fees, which amounted to $450,000 [9, 13].

Goodearl and Aldred paid a high price for whistleblowing. Both were unemployed for an extended period of time. Aldred and her husband went on welfare until they could find work. Goodearl and her husband had to file for bankruptcy, and they eventually divorced. Despite these hardships, both whistleblowers said they "would do it all again" [14].

9.6.3 U.S. Legislation Related to Whistleblowing

Whistleblowers are usually punished for disclosing information that organizations have tried to keep under wraps. If they do not lose their jobs outright, they have probably lost all chances for future advancement within the organization. Whistleblowers and their families typically suffer emotional distress and economic hardship.

Nevertheless, whistleblowers often serve the public good. For this reason the U.S. government has passed two pieces of legislation to encourage whistleblowing: the False Claims Act and the Whistleblower Protection Act of 1989.

The False Claims Act was first enacted by Congress in 1863 in response to massive fraud perpetrated by companies providing supplies to the Union Army during the Civil War. The law allowed a whistleblower to sue, on behalf of the government, a person or company that was submitting falsified claims to the government. If the organization were found guilty and forced to pay a settlement to the government, the whistleblower received half of the settlement.

In 1943, Congress amended the False Claims Act, drastically reducing the share of the settlement a whistleblower would receive and limiting the evidence or information a whistleblower could use in the lawsuit. As a result, the law fell into disuse.

In the mid-1980s, the media carried numerous stories about defense contractors perpetrating fraud against the government. Congress responded by amending the False Claims Act once again, making it easier for people to put together a successful lawsuit and allowing whistleblowers to receive between 15 and 30 percent of settlements. The False Claims Act also provides certain protections to whistleblowers against retaliation by their employers.

The Whistleblower Protection Act of 1989 establishes certain safeguards for federal employees and former employees who claim negative personnel actions have been taken against them for whistleblowing. Whistleblowers can appeal to the U.S. Merit Systems Protection Board.

9.6.4 Morality of Whistleblowing

Are whistleblowers heroes or traitors? Marcia Miceli and Janet Near point out that people become whistleblowers for different reasons. They suggest we ought to consider their motives before we decide if they were acting morally [15]. While it is fair to say that all whistleblowers are trying to bring an end to wrongdoing, they may well have other reasons for publicizing a problem. We can evaluate the morality of whistleblowing by considering whether the whistleblower is motivated by a desire to help others or harm others.

Consider a person who has known about a dangerous product for years, but only becomes a whistleblower after he has been turned down for a raise or promotion. If the disgruntled employee whistleblows in order to exact revenge on an organization that has let him down, the primary motivation is to hurt the company, not to help the public.

Another example of questionable whistleblowing is the case of employees who have been involved in a cover-up for some period of time, realize that they are about to be caught, and then cooperate with the authorities to identify other guilty parties in order to avoid punishment.

But suppose a person doesn't have ulterior motives for whistleblowing and is doing it simply to inform the public of a dangerous situation or a misappropriation of funds. There are three general reactions to altruistic whistleblowing [11].

WHISTLEBLOWERS CAUSE HARM

The typical corporate response to whistleblowing is to condemn it. Whistleblowers are disloyal to their companies. Through their actions they generate bad publicity, disrupt the social fabric of an organization, and make it more difficult for everyone to work as part of a team. In other words, their betrayal causes short-term and long-term damage to the company. While it is the responsibility of engineers to point out technical problems, the management of a company is ultimately responsible for the decisions being made, both good and bad. If management makes a mistake, the public has recourse through the legal system to seek damages from the company, and the Board of Directors or CEO can replace the managers who have used bad judgment.

The weakness with this response is its cavalier and overly legalistic attitude toward public harm. If people are hurt or killed, they or their heirs can always sue for damages. Yet surely society is better off if people are not harmed in the first place. A monetary settlement is a poor replacement for a human life.

WHISTLEBLOWING IS A SIGN OF ORGANIZATIONAL FAILURE

A second response to whistleblowing is to view it as a symptom of an organizational failure that results in harm all around [16]. The company suffers from bad publicity. The careers of accused managers can be ruined. It makes people suspicious of one another, eroding team spirit. Whistleblowers typically suffer retaliation and become estranged from their coworkers. Labeled as troublemakers, their long-term prospects with the company are dim.

Since whistleblowing is a sign of failure, organizations need to find a way to prevent it from happening in the first place. Some suggest that organizations can eliminate the need for whistleblowing by creating management structures and communication processes that allow concerns to be raised, discussed, and resolved.

This may be easier said than done. Robert Spitzer observes that organizations have shifted away from principle-based decision making to utilitarian decision making. A characteristic of rule-oriented ethical decision-making is its absolute nature. According to Kantianism or social contract theory, the end never justifies the means. If an action violates a moral rule, it shouldn't be done, period. In contrast, a utilitarian process weighs expected benefits and harms. Once an organization begins using utilitarian thinking, the question is no longer "Should we do it?" but "How much of it can we do without harm?" Spitzer writes, "One can see situations in which it would be permissible to use an evil means to achieve a good so long as enough benefit can be actualized." He suggests that organizations should return to using principle-based ethics in their decision-making [17].

WHISTLEBLOWING AS A MORAL DUTY

A third response is to assert that under certain circumstances people have a moral duty to whistleblow. Whistleblowing is alluded to in Clauses 1.02, 1.03, 1.04, 1.05, 2.05, 2.09, 3.01, 6.06, and 6.13 of the Software Engineering Code of Ethics and Professional Practice. These clauses provide a justification for whistleblowing in a variety of circumstances.

Richard De George believes whistleblowers should ask themselves five questions:

1. Do you believe the problem may result in "serious and considerable harm to the public"?

2. Have you told your manager your concerns about the potential harm?

3. Have you tried every possible channel within the organization to resolve the problem?

4. Have you documented evidence that would persuade a neutral outsider that your view is correct?

5. Are you reasonably sure that if you do bring this matter to public attention, something can be done to prevent the anticipated harm?

According to De George, you have a right to whistleblow if you answer "yes" to the first three questions; if you answer "yes" to all five questions, you have a duty to whistleblow [18].

De George's five requirements are controversial. Some would say whistleblowing is justified even when fewer requirements are met. For example, what if the potential whistleblower knows about a problem that could result in the death or injury of millions of people, such as a meltdown inside a nuclear power plant? The whistleblower has communicated his concerns to his manager, but there is not time to lobby every potential decision maker in the company. He is reasonably sure that if he contacted a television station, something could be done to prevent the meltdown. At the very least, the media could alert people so that they could get out of harm's way. Shouldn't that person be obliged to whistleblow, even though the answer to the third question is "no"?

To others, insisting that the whistleblower have convincing documentation is too strict a condition to be met in order for whistleblowing to be a moral imperative. After all, once the whistleblower has revealed the wrong to another organization, that organization may be in a better position to gather supporting evidence than the whistleblower [19].

Along the same line, some argue that whistleblowing should be considered an obligation even when only the first three requirements are met. They hold that people should be willing to sacrifice their good and the good of their family for the greater good of society.

Others believe De George goes too far when he gives conditions under which people are morally *required* to whistleblow. These commentators suggest that a person's obligation to whistleblow must be weighed against that person's other obligations, such as the duty to take care of one's family. Whistleblowing often results in significant emotional stress and the loss of employment. If it results in a person being labeled a troublemaker, whistleblowing can end a career. Hence, there are serious emotional and financial consequences to whistleblowing that affect not only whistleblowers but also their spouses and children [11].

Put another way, is it reasonable to take a strictly utilitarian approach to whistleblowing? Should we expect potential whistleblowers to weigh the benefits to a large number of people against the harm to themselves and their family, and decide to go public? After all, the whistleblower has already gone out on a limb to inform management of the dangerous situation. It is the managers who made the immoral decision to cover up the problem, not the whistleblower. We are asking a lot when we ask innocent people to sacrifice their career and the welfare of their family for the benefit of strangers. We shouldn't be surprised to learn that when whistleblower Al Ripskis was asked what advice he would give potential whistleblowers, his immediate reply was "Forget it!" [20].

On the other hand, whistleblower Carlos G. Bell, Jr., chastises fellow engineers for the way they duck responsibility:

> We engineers are almost without exception only too willing to assign moral responsibility to any administrator or executive or politician under whom we can place ourselves. Our reward for living in such ways is a part of the American dream: we are involved in very few arguments and year-by-year, we build up sizable pensions for our old age [21].

Moral responsibility is different from other kinds of responsibility. First of all, moral responsibility must be borne by people. While the Fourteenth Amendment to the Constitution may make a corporation a person in the legal sense of the word, a corporation is not a moral agent. We cannot assign moral responsibility to a corporation or any other organization [22].

Second, moral responsibility is different from role responsibility, causal responsibility, and legal responsibility in that it is not exclusive [22]. **Role responsibility** is responsibility borne because of a person's assigned duties. A company may hire a bookkeeper to send out invoices and pay the bills. It is the bookkeeper's responsibility to get the bills paid on time. **Causal responsibility** is responsibility assigned to people because they did something (or failed to do something) that caused something to happen. "Joe is responsible for the network being down, because he released the virus that caused the computers to crash." **Legal responsibility** is responsibility assigned by law. Homeowners are responsible for the medical bills of a postal carrier who slips and falls on their driveway. Role responsibility, causal responsibility, and legal responsibility can be exclusive. For example, if one person is responsible for paying the bills, the other employees are not. Moral responsibility is not exclusive. For example, if an infant is brought into a home, both the mother and the father are responsible for the baby's well-being.

Because moral responsibility is not exclusive, people cannot pass the buck by saying, "My boss made the final decision, not me," or by saying, "I just wrote the software; I wasn't responsible for testing it." When people abdicate their moral responsibility, great harms can be done. In the 1970s, executives at Ford Motor Company were anxious to begin selling a 2,000-pound, $2,000 alternative to Japanese imports. Unfortunately, prototypes of the Ford Pinto could not pass the mandatory collision test, because the windshield kept popping out. Forbidden from making design changes that would increase the weight of the car or delay its introduction, engineers solved the problem by redirecting the energy of the collision down the drive train to the gas tank. They knew this change would make the gas tank more likely to rupture, but the car did not have to pass a fuel tank integrity test. Covering up design problems allowed Ford to get its subcompact car to market. However, Ford eventually paid millions of dollars to settle dozens of lawsuits resulting from fiery crashes involving Pintos. Moreover, unfavorable media attention harmed Ford's reputation for years [20].

Michael McFarland argues that a team of engineers should be held to a higher level of moral responsibility than any of its individual members. There may well be situations where a person has a duty to speak the truth. To this duty, McFarland adds another duty held by moral agents: the duty to help others in need. If whistleblowing should be done, and no individual has the strength to do it, then it must be done by the group acting collectively [23].

Summary

A computer-related job, such as system administration, computer programming, or software engineering, is not a full-fledged profession like medicine or law, because you do not need to be certified and licensed in order to design, implement, or maintain computer hardware or software. Nevertheless, those who work with computers can, through inadequate education, insufficient practical training, or bad choices, cause a great deal of harm to members of the public. In this respect, the responsibility of computer "professionals" can be similar to that held by members of fully developed professions. For these reasons, the two largest computing societies have worked together to develop a code of ethics to guide the actions of software engineers: those who develop or maintain software or teach in this area.

The Software Engineering Code of Ethics and Professional Practice is based upon eight general principles related to the following subjects: the public, client and employer, product, judgment, management, profession, colleagues, and self. Each of these general principles contains a list of clauses related to specific areas of potential moral concern for the practicing software engineer. Good judgment is still needed, however. In many situations, there is a conflict between two or more of the relevant clauses. At these times, the decision-maker must determine which of the clauses is most relevant and/or most important.

The Code of Ethics asks software engineers to ponder if their actions are worthy of the ideal professional. The ethics of virtue, or virtue ethics, is based on the imitation of morally superior role models. Virtue ethics arises from Aristotle's belief that happiness is the result of living a virtuous life. One of the strengths of virtue ethics is that it makes clear how good deeds are motivated by friendship, loyalty, dependability, and other praiseworthy attributes of a good person. Another strength of virtue ethics—at least according to its supporters—is that it does not demand that every action produce the maximum benefit, solving the problem of impartiality that plagues Kantianism, utilitarianism, and social contract theory. On the other hand, virtue ethics does not provide a formal process for moral decision-making. For this reason some philosophers argue that virtue ethics should be used as a complement to another theory, such as utilitarianism, rather than as a stand-alone ethical theory.

To many, whistleblowing is a heroic act requiring great moral courage. A whistleblower brings to light a real or potential harm to the public, such as an abuse of taxpayers' money or a defective product, after trying and failing to get the problem resolved within the organization. Inevitably, whistleblowers and their families suffer emotionally and economically. It may take a decade for a whistleblower to be vindicated in court.

Different commentators have taken widely different views about whistleblowing. Some say whistleblowing does so much harm to the whistleblower and the organization that it is never the right thing to do. At the other extreme are those who argue any harm done to whistleblowers and their families is outweighed by the benefits to society, at least when certain conditions are met. In the middle are those who argue that any decision for or against whistleblowing must be made on a case-by-case basis.

If whistleblowing is ever called for, it is only as a last resort. Everyone agrees that people who discover real or potential harms to the public should first attempt to get the problem fixed within the organization. It would be better if there were never a need for whistleblowing. Organizations ought to have communication and decision-making structures that make it easier to identify and deal with financial irregularities or product defects.

The predominant American corporate mindset does not align well with this ideal. Managers focused on maximizing "the bottom line" may well make decisions on utilitarian grounds, weighing the costs and benefits of each alternative. Utilitarian thinking allows an organization to do something that is slightly bad in order to reap a greater good. Undisclosed bad deeds are less harmful than those brought to the light. Hence, utilitarian thinking can create an atmosphere in which the free communication of organizational actions is suppressed. In this environment, those who wish to report financial irregularities or product defects are ignored or silenced. The financial scandals at Enron, Tyco International, WorldCom, Adelphia Communications, and other corporations that cost investors billions of dollars have prompted some ethicists to call for a return to principle-based decision-making.

Review Questions

1. What is a profession? How is a computer-related career, such as programming or system administration, similar to a fully developed profession, such as medicine? How is a computer-related career unlike a fully developed profession?

2. Why did the ACM pass a resolution opposed to the licensing of software engineers?

3. Identify as many clauses as you can in the Software Engineering Code of Ethics and Professional Practice that refer to issues related to privacy.

4. Identify as many clauses as you can in the Software Engineering Code of Ethics and Professional Practice that refer to issues related to intellectual property.

5. Identify five clauses in the Software Engineering Code of Ethics and Professional Practice that reflect a utilitarian ethical viewpoint.

6. Identify five clauses in the Software Engineering Code of Ethics and Professional Practice that reflect a Kantian viewpoint.

7. Describe virtue ethics in your own words.

8. The text gives James Rachels's short list of 24 virtues. Come up with a list of 5 additional virtues.

9. What is whistleblowing? What harms does it cause? What benefits may it provide?

10. Which clauses in the Software Engineering Code of Ethics and Professional Practice support the legitimacy of whistleblowing? Which clauses in the Code may be violated by a whistleblower (assuming the whistleblower is telling the truth)?

Discussion Questions

11. The *Challenger* disaster led to the deaths of seven astronauts and the loss of hundreds of millions of dollars worth of equipment. How much moral responsibility should each of the following groups hold for this tragedy: Morton Thiokol engineers, Morton Thiokol senior management, NASA management?

12. In the criminal proceedings resulting from the government's investigation of fraud at the Micro-electronic Circuit Division, the jury found Hughes Aircraft guilty, but it found supervisor Donald LaRue not guilty. The jury felt LaRue was simply following orders from management. Was the jury's decision a just one?

13. Do you agree with Michael McFarland that a team of engineers has greater moral responsibility than any individual engineer on the team?

14. You are a manager in charge of a section of 30 employees in a large corporation. This morning one of your employees—Jane Lee—enters your office and tells you she thinks two members of your staff are having an affair. These employees are married—but not to each other. Jane is afraid that if it is true, others in the office will inevitably find out about it, harming morale and productivity. She suggests that you discreetly monitor their emails to see if they provide evidence of an affair. If you find evidence, you can nip the problem in the bud. If there is no problem, you do not have to embarrass yourself by talking with the employees. What should you do? [24]

15. According to virtue ethics, the right action to take in a particular situation is the action that a person with strong moral character would take. If you decide to practice virtue ethics, you need to find a moral role model. How would you choose a role model?

16. Two weeks ago, you started a new job as system administrator for a computer lab at a small college. Wanting to make a good impression, you immediately set out to learn more about the various applications provided to the users of the lab. One of the packages, an engineering design tool, seemed way out of date. You looked through the lab's file of licensing agreements to see how much it would cost to get an upgrade. To your horror, you discovered that the college never purchased a license for the software—it is running a bootlegged copy!

    When you bring this to the attention of your boss, the college's Director of Information Technology, he says, "The license for this software would cost us $10,000, which we don't have in our budget right now. This software is absolutely needed for our engineering students, though. Maybe we can get the license next year. For the time being, just keep the current version running."

    How would you respond to your manager?

17. You are a junior in college. You sent your resume to a half-dozen companies hoping to get a summer internship. Two weeks ago XYZ Corporation contacted you and offered you a paid summer internship. One week ago you accepted their offer, agreeing to start work a week after your last final exam. Today you received a much better internship offer from ABC Corporation. What should you do?

18. You are a senior in college. You sent your resume to a half-dozen companies hoping to get a job. A month ago you interviewed at ABC Corporation and XYZ Corporation. Two weeks ago XYZ Corporation offered you a job. One week ago you accepted their offer, agreeing to start work a month after graduation. Today you received a much better offer from ABC Corporation. What should you do?

19. You are the manager of a software development group within a large corporation. Your group would be more productive if the PCs were upgraded, but you do not have any money left in your annual equipment budget. Because of employee turnover, you do have plenty of money left in your personnel budget, but corporate rules do not allow you to spend personnel funds on equipment.

    If you overspend your equipment budget, you will receive a negative performance review. You also know that whatever money is left over in your budget at the end of the fiscal year is "swept up" by the corporation. In other words, you cannot carry over a surplus from one year to the next—your group loses the money.

    You complain about your situation to the manager of another group, who has the opposite problem. She has plenty of money left in her equipment budget, but her personnel expenses are going to exceed her labor budget unless she does something. She offers to buy you the $50,000 of equipment you need out of her budget, if you pick up $50,000 of her personnel expenses out of your budget. If you take this action, both groups will get what they need, and neither group will exceed any of its budgets.

    Discuss the morality of the proposed course of action.

20. Five years ago, Al graduated from college and began working for Superlative Software Corporation. His most recent promotion has made him the manager of a large group of software engineers and support staff. One of Al's responsibilities is to submit his budget request for the next fiscal year. He's never done this before, so one day over lunch he asks Barb, a more experienced manager, for some advice.

    Barb: Figure out what you really need to complete the projects your group will be doing, and then add another 20 percent. High-level management always cuts everybody's budget 10 to 20 percent, so after they reduce your budget, you'll still have the money you'll need.

    Al: But the memo from the Vice President said we should only ask for the amount of money we really need.

    Barb: Nobody pays attention to that.

    Al: What if they ask me to justify my budget? It's be pretty obvious that I've padded it.

    Barb: They never do that—they don't have the time. Even if they did, you can work the numbers to justify the extra staff you'll need to meet the tight deadlines they've set.

    Al: You mean lie?

Barb: Look, what are you going to do if your group doesn't get the budget it needs? You won't be able to staff up for the new projects. That means you and all your current staff are going to be super stressed all year long trying to meet the deadlines. Spare yourself a lot of grief and do what all the other managers are doing.

What would you do if you were in Al's position? Why?

21. Connie interviews a candidate for a software engineering position. She feels the person has several holes in his technical background that could hinder his job performance. The next day, Connie and five other people who have interviewed the candidate meet with the hiring manager to discuss his strengths and weaknesses. Before Connie speaks, everyone else voices the opinion that the candidate has great technical skills and should be hired. It seems clear to her that the hiring manager wants to offer this person a job. She wonders if she should bother voicing her reservations.

What would you do if you were in Connie's position? Why?

In–class Exercises

22. A college equips its large lecture halls with wireless networks, and it requires all of its students to purchase a laptop computer when they enroll. A computer science professor plans to streamline how quizzes are administered in his introductory programming class. Students will take the quizzes online as they sit in the classroom. A computer will grade the quizzes instantly, providing the students with instant feedback. The computer will also provide the professor with information about how well the students did on each question, which will enable him to spend more of his lecture time focusing on those topics that the students are having the hardest time understanding. Discuss the benefits and risks associated with implementing the proposed system.

23. Company X wants to open a dating service Web site. It hires Company Y to develop the software. Company Y hires Gina as a private contractor to provide a piece of instant messaging software for the package. Gina's contract says she is not responsible for the security of the site. Company Y is supposed to perform that bit of programming. However, software development runs behind schedule, and Company Y implements a simplistic security scheme that allows all messages to be sent in plain text, which is clearly insecure.

Gina brings her concerns to the management of Company Y. Company Y thanks her for her concern, but indicates it still plans to deliver the software without telling Company X. Company Y reminds Gina that she has signed a confidentiality agreement that forbids her from talking about the software to anyone, including Company X.

What should Gina do?

24. You are members of the information services team at a large corporation. The President has asked for a confidential meeting with your group to talk about ways to improve productivity. The President wants to ensure that people are not sending personal emails or surfing the Web for entertainment while they are supposed to be working. The Chief Information Officer suggests that employees be informed that their emails and Web surfing will be monitored. In truth, the company does not have the resources to do this and does not plan to implement any monitoring. The CIO strictly forbids anyone in the information services team from revealing this fact. Debate the morality of management making such an announcement.

25. The members of the class are the employees of a small, privately held company that produces computer games. Everyone shares in the profits of the company. The company has been making electronic versions of popular board games for established game companies. Business is steady, but profits have not been large. The marketing team says that a first-person shooter game based on the war in Afghanistan would generate a huge amount of publicity for the company and could be highly profitable. Debate the morality of producing such a game.

Further Reading

Association for Computing Machinery Web site. www.acm.org.

Margaret Coady and Sidney Bloch, editors. *Codes of Ethics and the Professions*. Melbourne University Press, Melbourne, Australia, 1996.

ComputingCases.org (Web site).

Myron Peretz Glazer and Penina Migdal Glazer. *The Whistleblowers: Exposing Corruption in Government and Industry*. Basic Books, New York, NY, 1989.

Dan Gotterbarn. "Why Bother with Ethics in Computing: Addressing Harmful Paradigms?" *ACM Inroads*, March 2010, p. 9.

IEEE Computer Society Web site. www.computer.org.

Deborah G. Johnson. *Ethical Issues in Engineering*. Prentice Hall, Englewood Cliffs, NJ, 1991.

Alasdair MacIntyre. *After Virtue*. 2nd ed. University of Notre Dame Press, Notre Dame, IN, 1984.

C. Dianne Martin. "Building Character." *ACM Inroads*, March 2010, p. 11.

Mike W. Martin. *Meaningful Work: Rethinking Professional Ethics*. Oxford University Press, New York, NY, 2000.

Justin Oakley and Dean Cocking. *Virtue Ethics and Professional Roles*. Cambridge University Press, Cambridge, England, 2001.

References

[1]   Gary Ford and Norman E. Gibbs. "A Mature Profession of Software Engineering." Technical report, Carnegie-Mellon University, January 1996. CMU/ SEI-96-TR-004, ESC-TR-96-004.

[2]   Fran Allen (co chair), Barry Boehm, Fred Brooks, Jim Browne, Dave Farber, Sue Graham, Jim Gray, Paula Hawthorn (co chair), Ken Kennedy, Nancy Leveson, Dave Nagel, Peter Neumann, Dave Parnas, and Bill Wulf. "ACM Panel and Professional Licensing in Software Engineering Report to Council." May 15, 1999. www.acm.org/serving/se_policy.

[3]   Aristotle. *The Nicomachean Ethics*. Oxford University Press, Oxford, England, 1998. Translated by F. H. Peters and M. Ostwald.

[4]   James Rachels. *The Elements of Moral Philosophy*. 4th ed. McGraw-Hill, Boston, MA, 2003.

[5]   Justin Oakley and Dean Cocking. *Virtue Ethics and Professional Roles*. Cambridge University Press, Cambridge, England, 2001.

[6]   J. Eric Smith. "Anti-worm Worm Makes Rounds, Cleanses Systems of Infection." www .geek.com, August 20, 2003.

[7]   Florence Olsen. "Attacks Threaten Computer Networks as Students Arrive for the Fall Semester." *The Chronicle of Higher Education*, September 5, 2003.

[8]   Irena Blonder. "Blowing the Whistle." In *Codes of Ethics and the Professions*, pages 166–190. Melbourne University Press, Melbourne, Australia, 1996.

[9]   Kevin W. Bowyer. "Goodearl and Aldred versus Hughes Aircraft: A Whistle-Blowing Case Study." In *Frontiers in Education*, pages S2F2–S2F7. October 2000.

[10]   Roger M. Boisjoly. "The Challenger Disaster: Moral Responsibility and the Working Engineer." In *Ethical Issues in Engineering*, pages 6–14. Edited by Deborah G. Johnson. Prentice Hall, Englewood Cliffs, NJ, 1991.

[11]   Mike W. Martin. *Meaningful Work: Rethinking Professional Ethics*. Oxford University Press, New York, NY, 2000.

[12]   Taxpayers Against Fraud. "U.S. Department of Justice Joins Whistle-blowers in Lawsuit Against Hughes Aircraft Seeking Several Hundred Million Dollars." December 15, 1992. Press release.

[13]   "The Hughes Whistleblowing Case." ComputingCases.org.

[14]   Andre Mouchard. "Whistle-Blowers Set to Use Their Reward." *The Orange County Register (California)*, September 11, 1996.

[15]   Marcia P. Miceli and Janet P. Near. "Whistle-Blowing as Antisocial Behavior." In *Antisocial Behavior in Organizations*. SAGE Publications, Thousand Oaks, CA, 1997.

[16]   Michael Davis. "Avoiding the Tragedy of Whistleblowing." *Business and Professional Ethics Journal*, 8(4):3–19, Winter 1989.

[17]   Robert J. Spitzer, S.J. "For Good Reason, 'Organizational Ethics' a Hot Topic Nowadays." *Gonzaga (Gonzaga University newsletter)*, 5(2):2, Fall 2003.

[18]   Richard T. DeGeorge. *Business Ethics*. 3rd ed. Macmillan, New York, NY, 1990.

[19]   Gene G. James. "Whistle Blowing: Its Moral Justification." In *Business Ethics*, 2nd ed., pages 332–344. McGraw-Hill, New York, NY, 1990.

[20]   Myron Peretz Glazer and Penina Migdal Glazer. *The Whistleblowers: Exposing Corruption in Government and Industry*. Basic Books, New York, NY, 1989.

[21]   Bell, Carlos G., Jr. "One Ethical Problem Faced by the Atomic Energy Commission and Its Contractors." In *Beyond Whistleblowing: Defining Engineers' Responsibilities, Proceedings of the Second National Conference on Ethics in Engineering*, pages 250–258. Illinois Institute of Technology, Chicago, IL, 1983.

[22]   John Ladd. "Collective and Individual Moral Responsibility in Engineering: Some Questions." In *Beyond Whistleblowing: Defining Engineers' Responsibilities, Proceedings of the Second National Conference on Ethics in Engineering*, pages 90–113. Illinois Institute of Technology, Chicago, IL, 1983.

[23]   Michael McFarland. "The Public Health, Safety, and Welfare: An Analysis of the Social Responsibility of Engineers." In *Ethical Issues in Engineering*, edited by D. G. Johnson, pages 159–174. Prentice Hall, Englewood Cliffs, NJ, 1991.

[24]   Herbert W. Lovelace. "When Affairs of the Heart Raise IT Privacy Issues." *InformationWeek.com*, December 10, 2001.

Paul Axtell

Paul Axtell is a corporate communications consultant who has helped clients such as John Deere, American Express, Hewlett–Packard, Kodak, Monsanto, Oregon State University, Ohio State University, and a number of K–12 school districts to enhance individual and group performance and organizational effectiveness. Axtell has worked in Brazil and Canada, and has done training for young African political leaders.

Some of Axtell's current projects include coaching manufacturing teams, supporting cultural change within a university, managing a year-long training program for organizational consultants, changing working relationships within management groups, and developing training programs for elementary and middle school reading coaches.

Axtell has three areas of focus. The first is contextual education. That is, how do you give people the ability to shift their thinking, broaden their point of view, and change the way they fundamentally relate to current issues and each other? The second area of focus is process skills. How do you set up and manage conversations in a way that works for everyone involved? The third area is creating an awareness for the best practices of working together in group situations.

Axtell received his B.S. in Chemical Engineering from South Dakota School of Mines and Technology and an MBA from Washington University in St. Louis.

Some commentators have suggested that whistleblowing is a sign of organizational failure. They suggest that organizations can eliminate the need for whistleblowing by creating management structures and communication processes that allow concerns to be raised, discussed, and resolved. Do you agree with this assessment?

Whistleblowing is a check and balance that is needed in certain circumstances. It is certainly alarming when a situation gets so out of hand that an employee must go to outside authorities to get someone to pay attention. When this happens, it not only reveals a set of circumstances that are not working, but it also adds to the distrust of the people who lead corporate organizations.

It should not be surprising, however, that we encounter such situations. Almost all of our relationships, both personal and organizational, have problems that begin with not being able to talk. We are raised in a culture that says it's not safe to share our thinking, voice our concerns, or push back in conversations. We debate about bringing things up at home with loved ones and at work in meetings. Given this fundamental approach to relationship and conversation, we should expect problems.

So, whatever attention we can give to create structures and processes and permission and safety is well worth it. And the need for it goes well beyond uncovering misdeeds and poor practices. The real benefit would be in a sense of belonging and caring that goes with an open and honest relationship.

In addition to setting up structures that protect people, we need to embrace a far larger goal. We need to set out to establish a cultural norm of freedom, permission, and safety. It will be very difficult to obtain because we are not raised or trained to create such a culture. Still, how can it not be the right path to be on?

Training will probably be required on both sides. We all need training on how to raise questions and concerns with a bit more set-up and graciousness. We need to be clear that we are on the same side and speak consistent with that context. And we all need training on how to hear and respond to questions and complaints, especially when they are not presented in the best way.

If a corporation wants to change the culture, it needs to pay attention to the people it is grooming to be supervisors, managers, and directors. As columnist Dave Berry says, "If your date is rude to the waiter, you are dating a rude person." That makes a lot of sense as we promote people. We do need to do the training, but most behavior starts with perception.

From your experience, what are the principal barriers to improved communication inside a large corporation?

I would say that there are three principal barriers. First, people are raised to be careful and not speak up. Second, most supervisors and managers do not have the skill set to thoughtfully deal with questions and complaints. Third, our lack of follow-up and follow-through makes things worse when we invite feedback and then don't deliver.

How can a corporation remove these barriers?

Constantly invite people to raise issues and concerns. However, don't ask if you don't intend to follow through. Have a great response to missteps by employees. It's management's reaction to problems that determines whether employees feel safe. Lastly, get to know people. It's very difficult to speak up when I don't know you.

Can you give examples of how email can be harmful to communication within an organization?

Email has a couple of potential pitfalls. The most common is a lack of context for the message. Context is usually communicated by either tone of voice or set-up. Obviously tone of voice is missing on email, and people usually are very brief, which means they don't do adequate set-up. On the receiving end of the message sits a human being who by default tends to take things personally. That creates a defensive response.

What is the most challenging part of your job?

The first challenge is to re-teach people how to learn. We were all wonderful learners when we were two and three years old. We observed. We mimicked. We paid attention to the people around us. We practiced until we could do things. We had little or no concern with looking foolish or not knowing how to do something. Then later, we came to value knowing and information as having more relevance than tacit knowledge. Amazingly, it's the really good people who still want to learn, who still want feedback. Most of us are highly selective about who can give us feedback about what. We are not wide open to feedback. We are not even looking for it, for the most part.

The second challenge is to get people to acknowledge the impact of conversation in their lives—even to the point of arguing that they don't really have much else to work with. After their technical competence, it is the quality of their conversations that determines how things turn out. Conversation is the basis for their relationships. Conversation is the basis for having influence in an organization. Conversation determines the culture. Conversation determines how they are viewed.

The third challenge is in working to change the perceptions or views of individuals who have somehow gotten to a place in life where they are not responsible for what happens. As soon as you and I say to ourselves or others that "it's not our fault" or "it's not our job," we essentially are at the mercy of the circumstances. Certainly the things that happen in our lives often control the outcomes, but truly effective people don't give in completely to the circumstances. They maintain the view that they can make a difference in how things turn out. Interestingly, these people rarely give excuses.

What surprises you the most about communications in the corporate world?

I'm not so sure I'm surprised, but I think there are a number of things that seem to be missing that would make a big difference if they were present:

1. If managers wrote more of their own communication pieces and signed them, they would come across as more authentic. Employees are also highly skeptical about positive spin writing and admire a more direct, what-is-so way of writing.

2. Written notes of acknowledgment and appreciation mean so much to people. We keep them for years. Yet handwritten notes to individuals and groups are a lost art.

3. An essential part of being effective is having the ability to set up a conversation, keep it on track, and wrap it up, not only in meetings but also in hallway conversations. These process skills are often missing at all levels of the organization.

4. Making specific commitments with clear due dates would reduce the amount of upsets that occur with unfulfilled expectations and lack of progress.

5. Checking in with people about their families, projects, weekends, and then engaging and enjoying in the conversation that follows is another piece that technical folks tend not to do.

10 Work and Wealth

Work keeps at bay three great evils: boredom, vice, and need.

—VOLTAIRE

10.1 Introduction

IT'S 6:30 P.M. AND A NEW SHIFT IS STARTING AT THE LIVEBRIDGE CALL CENTER. Twenty-year-old college graduate "Kristy Grover" begins phoning people to verify information they have provided on their credit card applications. She will work until 3:00 a.m. Her hours are unusual because "Kristy Grover" is actually Shilpa Thukral, and she is calling the United States from India. Companies like LiveBridge are saving billions of dollars every year by employing hundreds of thousands of Indians to staff call centers and back offices. A technical service company can hire an Indian worker for about $12,000 a year, compared to about $59,000 a year for an American employee [1].

Back in 1996, the Indian telecommunications infrastructure supported a mere 13,000 simultaneous overseas phone conversations. Multinational corporations invested in new underwater fiber-optic cables, and by 2002, the overseas phone capacity had increased to more than 2.5 million simultaneous calls, making it possible for American companies to export hundreds of thousands of jobs to India [1].

The globalization of the job market is just one of many changes that information technology and automation have brought to the workplace. In this chapter, we examine a variety of moral problems brought about by workplace changes. First we consider the following question: Does automation increase unemployment? Some evidence supports an affirmative answer to the question, but other evidence suggests that automation actually creates more jobs than it replaces. There is no doubt that automation has led to enormous increases in productivity. That leads us to our second question: If productivity has increased so much, why is everyone working so hard? We will examine how we have chosen to use our extra productivity.

Some futurists warn that advances in artificial intelligence and robotics will lead to massive unemployment in the not-too-distant future. We consider the morality of attempting to construct highly intelligent machines.

More mundane information technology has already led to significant changes in the way companies organize themselves. It has also led to an increase in telework (also called telecommuting), the use of temporary workers, workplace monitoring, and distributed, multinational teams. We consider how these changes have improved and harmed the lives of individual workers.

Globalization is now a fact of life. Some organizations are convinced globalization benefits everyone in the world, the poor as well as the rich. Others are certain that globalization harms everyone in the world. We'll present the arguments offered by each side to support its position. We'll also focus on the contentious issue of foreign IT workers in the United States.

Many view those without access to information technology as being severely disadvantaged. The term "digital divide" refers to the opportunity gap brought about because some people do not have access to modern information technology, particularly the Internet. We look at evidence of the digital divide and study two fundamentally different models of how new technologies are diffused through a society.

Information technology has made it easier for an unequal share of benefits to accumulate in the hands of a few top performers, leading some to call this the "winner-take-all society." We explore the factors creating the winner-take-all phenomenon, the economic problems it causes, and potential remedies.

10.2 Automation and Unemployment

Many science fiction writers have described future worlds where machines do much of the noncreative work. Some writers paint an optimistic view of these worlds. In Isaac Asimov's short stories and novels, technology is seen as a tool for the betterment of mankind. Intelligent robots may be disliked by some people, but they are not a threat. The "Three Laws of Robotics" are etched into their positronic brains, guaranteeing that they will never turn against their creators [2]. Other writers, such as Kurt Vonnegut, Jr., describe dystopias. Vonnegut's *Player Piano* concerns a future America in which nearly all manufacturing jobs have been lost to automation. People hate machines for taking away their feelings of self-worth, yet their fascination with automation makes its triumph appear inevitable [3].

In the "jobless recovery" following the Great Recession of 2008–2009, corporate profits have soared, but the unemployment rate has remained stubbornly high. Are we

FIGURE 10.1 General Motors exited bankruptcy in 2009 with 30 percent fewer employees. (© Danny Lehman / CORBIS)

about to enter an era of high unemployment caused by automation? Let's consider both sides of this question.

10.2.1 Automation and Job Destruction

LOST MANUFACTURING JOBS

Manufacturing employment peaked in the United States in 1979, with 19.4 million jobs. By 2011, manufacturing employment had dropped 40 percent, to 11.7 million, even though the population of the United States had increased 39 percent during the same time period. The percentage of American workers involved in manufacturing has dropped significantly, from 35 percent in 1947 to 9 percent in 2011 (Figure 10.1).

Meanwhile, thanks to automation, manufacturing output in America continues to rise. It has doubled since 1970 [4]. In other words, productivity has increased: fewer workers are making more products. For example, in 1977, it took 35 person-hours to manufacture an automobile in the United States. By 2008, the number of person-hours had dropped to 15 hours [5].

LOST WHITE-COLLAR JOBS

The effects of automation are felt in the office, too. Email, voice mail, and high-speed copy machines eliminate secretarial and clerical positions. Even jobs requiring advanced degrees are vulnerable. Spreadsheets and other software packages reduce the need for accountants and bookkeepers [6]. Twenty years ago, a pharmacist in a small Canadian town would fill about 8,000 prescriptions in a year. Today, Merck-Medco runs a Web-accessible pharmacy that uses robots to dispense 8,000 prescriptions an *hour* [7].

In fact, the economic recovery of 1991–1996 was notable because of the large number of white-collar, middle-management jobs that were eliminated, even as the economy grew. Unlike the recession of the early 1980s, most of the people whose jobs were eliminated in the 1990s had at least some college education. A large number of these jobs were occupied by people making more than $50,000. Only 35 percent of these higher-paid victims of downsizing were able to find jobs that paid as well [8].

WORKING HARDER, MAKING LESS

While inflation-adjusted household incomes were flat between 1979 and 1994, the work week got longer. Harvard economist Juliet Schor reports that between 1970 and 1990, the average American increased the number of hours spent at work per year by 163. That's equal to an *extra month* at work every year [9].

Some believe longer work hours are a consequence of corporate downsizing, which is facilitated by the introduction of automation and information technology (Figure 10.2). When an organization sheds some of its workers, the work that needs to be done is divided among fewer employees. Hence there is a natural tendency for the number of hours worked to increase. In addition, the fact that people have been laid off is a strong incentive for those who remain to work harder so that they won't be part of the next layoff [10].

Advances in information technology have also made it easier for people to bring work home. For example, many companies now provide their employees with laptop computers. At work, employees turn their laptop into a desktop system by plugging in a full-sized keyboard, mouse, and monitor. By bringing their laptop home, they have access to the various project files they need to continue working. Labor advocates Stanley

FIGURE 10.2 When jobs are lost to automation or the introduction of information technology, the remaining workers may work harder in order to avoid being part of the next layoff.

Aronowitz, Dawn Esposito, and William DiFazio have written, "After nearly a century when homework was regarded as a wage-busting tool, computers have made it easier for employers to revive this practice. With pagers, cell phones, and laptop computers, all time becomes work time" [6].

They conclude:

> Late capitalist society is engaged in a long-term historical process of destroying job security . . . More than ever, we worry about work and are working longer hours; we are more than ever driven, nervous, seemingly trapped. At the very same time, and paradoxically, the twenty-first century bodes a time of post-work: of automation and work reorganization replacing people at faster and faster rates [6].

10.2.2 Automation and Job Creation

Traditional economists hold a quite different view about the effects of automation and information technology on jobs. They have concluded that while new technology may destroy certain jobs, it also creates new jobs. The net result is an increase, not a decrease, in the number of available jobs.

INCREASED PURCHASING POWER

The logic of these "automation optimists" is illustrated in Figure 10.3. On the surface, it is obvious that automation eliminates certain jobs. That's what automation means. However, it's also important to look beneath the surface. Automation is introduced as a cost-saving measure. It is less expensive for a machine to perform a particular job than a human being. Because companies compete with each other, lower production costs result in lower prices for the consumer. The drop in the price of a product has two beneficial effects. First, it increases the demand for the product. In order to produce more

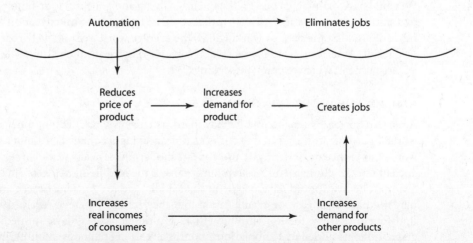

FIGURE 10.3 Superficially, automation eliminates jobs; but automation can also stimulate the creation of new jobs.

of the product, workers must be hired. Second, people who were already purchasing the product don't have to pay as much for it. That gives them more money to spend on other things, increasing the demand for other products. This, too, results in job creation. Finally, there is an additional effect, not illustrated in the figure. Some people must be employed designing, creating, and servicing the automated devices themselves.

Consider the automation of stock exchanges. In the past, shares of securities were bought and sold on the floors of stock exchanges by people employed as floor brokers. Today, electronic systems handle most of these transactions, and electronic trading has made transactions quicker and less expensive. Although electronic trading has greatly decreased the number of people employed as floor brokers, the number of shares being traded has increased sharply, and employment in the securities industry has continued to rise (except during recessions) [11]. New kinds of jobs have been created. For example, securities firms have hired mathematicians and computer scientists to develop sophisticated automated trading systems.

WORKING LESS, MAKING MORE

Martin Carnoy disputes the notion that people are working longer hours now than they used to. "Workers today," he writes, "work much less than those of a century ago, produce more, earn substantially more, and have access to a greater variety of jobs. Technology displaced workers but also contributed to a much higher labor productivity and the production of new products, which helped create new jobs, economic growth, and higher incomes" [12].

10.2.3 Effects of Increase in Productivity

Productivity in the United States doubled between 1948 and 1990. Juliet Schor asks us to consider what our society could have done with this dramatic increase in productivity. We could have maintained our 1948 standard of living and gone to a four-hour work day, or a six-month work year. Or every worker could be taking every other year off with pay. Instead of taking the path of working less, the average work week actually rose slightly. As a result, Americans in 1990 owned and consumed twice as much as in 1948, but had less free time in which to enjoy these things [9].

AMERICANS WORK LONG HOURS

American society is remarkable for how hard its citizens work. The number of hours worked per year in the United States is significantly higher than the number of hours worked in France or Germany. It also appears modern Americans work harder than the ancient Greeks, Romans, or Western Europeans of the Middle Ages. According to Juliet Schor, "The lives of ordinary people in the Middle Ages or Ancient Greece and Rome may not have been easy, or even pleasant, but they certainly were leisurely" [9]. In the mid-fourth century, the Roman Empire had 175 public festival days. In medieval England, holidays added up to about four months a year; in Spain, five months; in France, six months. "There is considerable evidence of what economists call the backward-bending supply curve of labor—the idea that when wages rise, workers supply less labor . . . [Laborers] worked only as many days as were necessary to earn their customary income" [9].

We do not have to look back into history to find significantly shorter work weeks. Consider contemporary "stone age" societies. The Kapauku of Papua never work two days in a row. Australian aborigines and men of the Sandwich Islands work only about four hours per day. Kung Bushmen work 15 hours a week [9].

PROTESTANT WORK ETHIC

Why are Americans such hard workers? In his famous essay *The Protestant Ethic and the Spirit of Capitalism*, Max Weber argues that the Protestant Reformation in general, and Calvinism in particular, stimulated the growth of capitalism in Western Europe. Before the Reformation, work was seen in a traditional light. Weber describes the traditional view toward labor in this way:

> A man does not "by nature" wish to earn more and more money, but simply to live as he is accustomed to live and to earn as much as is necessary for that purpose [13].

According to Weber, the Calvinist theology introduced a radically different conception of work. He writes:

> Waste of time is thus the first and in principle the deadliest of sins . . . [T]he religious valuation of restless, continuous, systematic work in a worldly calling, as the highest means to asceticism, and at the same time the surest and most evident proof of rebirth and genuine faith, must have been the most powerful conceivable lever for the expansion of that attitude toward life which we have here called the spirit of capitalism [13].

We can see an example of the "Protestant work ethic" in the early history of New England. The Puritans banished all holidays, insisting that Sunday be the sole day of rest. In 1659, the General Court of Massachusetts decreed that citizens who celebrated Christmas or other holidays by refusing to work or feasting should be fined or whipped.

TIME VERSUS POSSESSIONS

We have exchanged leisure time for material possessions. Compared to medieval Europeans or modern Bushmen, we have vastly superior health care systems, educational institutions, and transportation networks. We live in climate-controlled environments, and we have an incredible number of choices with respect to where we travel, what we wear, what we eat, and how we entertain ourselves. The cost of these freedoms and luxuries is less leisure time.

Despite our high standard of living, our expectations about what we ought to have continue to rise. In 1964, the average new American home had 1,470 square feet and one television set. Only about 20 percent of new homes had air conditioning. In 2001, the size of the average new home had risen to 2,100 square feet, and nearly 100 percent of new homes were equipped with air conditioning. The typical family home has two or three television sets. In order to maintain this lifestyle, people are working harder [10].

10.2.4 Rise of the Robots?

While automation has not yet shortened the work week of the typical American, some experts maintain that most jobs will eventually be taken over by machines. In fact, roboticist Hans Moravec predicts that by 2050, robots will have replaced human workers not just in manufacturing jobs, but in decision-making roles, too [14].

The *Encyclopedia of Computer Science* defines **artificial intelligence** (**AI**) as "a field of computer science and engineering concerned with the computational understanding of what is commonly called intelligent behavior, and with the creation of artifacts that exhibit such behavior" [15]. The same source defines **robots** as "programmable machines that either in performance or appearance imitate human activities" [15]. According to Moravec, developments in artificial intelligence and robotics were held back for decades by inadequate computer power. Rapid increases in microprocessor speeds have resulted in many breakthroughs. Here are a few notable achievements in artificial intelligence and robotics since 1995:

- A minivan equipped with a video camera and a portable workstation drove from Pittsburgh, Pennsylvania, to San Diego, California, in 1995. The computer was in control of the steering wheel 98.2% of the time [16]. (A human operator controlled the minivan's gas pedal and brakes, maintaining an average speed of about 60 miles per hour.)

- The IBM supercomputer called Deep Blue defeated world chess champion Gary Kasparov in a six-game match in 1997 [17].

- In 2000, Japanese automaker Honda created ASIMO, the first humanoid robot (android) capable of climbing and descending stairs. Two years later, engineers gave ASIMO the ability to interpret and respond to human gestures and postures [18]. Some believe Japan is a hotbed of robotic research because its population is declining and becoming more elderly, and the Japanese seem to lack the cultural fears of robots that grip many Westerners [19].

- Swedish appliance giant Electrolux introduced Trilobite, the world's first domestic robotic floor vacuum cleaner, in 2001 [20].

- Stanley, a robotic car developed at Stanford University, and four other autonomous vehicles successfully completed a rugged, 128-mile course through the Nevada desert in 2005 (Figure 10.4). Stanley was the fastest vehicle to finish the race, averaging about 19 miles per hour [21].

- In February 2011, an AI program named Watson, running on an IBM supercomputer, easily defeated the two most successful human *Jeopardy*! champions in history: Ken Jennings and Brad Rutter (Figure 10.5). At the end of the three-episode competition, Watson had won $77,147, compared to $24,000 for Jennings and $21,600 for Rutter.

Moravec believes these innovations are just the beginning of a new era in automation. In 30 years, inexpensive desktop computers will be a million times faster than today's models, allowing them to run sophisticated AI programs. "In the [21st] century inexpensive but capable robots will displace human labor so broadly that the average

FIGURE 10.4 The Stanford Racing Team converted a Volkswagen Touareg into an autonomous vehicle named Stanley that successfully followed a 128-mile course through the Nevada desert in 2005. (© Gene Blevins/Reuters/Corbis)

workday will have to plummet to practically zero to keep everyone usefully employed" [14]. Moravec predicts humans will retire to a world of "luxurious lassitide" [14].

Perhaps Moravec has an grossly inflated view of what robots may be able to do in 40 years, but what if he is right? The changes he is predicting would profoundly affect our society. For this reason, Richard Epstein suggests there is an urgent need to discuss ethical issues related to the creation of intelligent robots, before they become a reality [22]. Here are some of the questions Epstein has raised:

- Is it wrong to create machines capable of making human labor obsolete?

- Will humans become demoralized by the presence of vastly more intelligent robots? If so, is it wrong to work on the development of such robots?

- Is it morally acceptable to work on the development of an intelligent machine if we cannot be sure that the machine's actions will be benevolent?

- How will we ensure that intelligent robots will not be put to an evil purpose by a malevolent human?

Figure 10.5 In 2011, an AI program named Watson running on an IBM supercomputer trounced the two greatest (human) *Jeopardy!* champions: Ken Jennings and Brad Rutter. (© AP Photo/Seth Wenig)

- How will our notions of intellectual property change if computers become capable of creative work?
- How will our ideas about privacy have to change if legions of superfast computers are analyzing the electronic records of our lives?

Michael LaChat notes, "Many look upon the outbreak of AI research with an uneasy amusement, an amusement masking . . . a considerable disquiet. Perhaps it is the fear that we might succeed, perhaps it is the fear that we might create a Frankenstein, or perhaps it is the fear that we might become eclipsed, in a strange oedipal drama, by our own creation" [23].

LaChat evaluates the issue in the following way. Some people would like to try to construct a **personal AI**—a machine that is conscious of its own existence. No one has proven it can't be done, so let's assume it's theoretically possible. Is it morally acceptable to attempt the construction of a personal AI?

Here is one line of reasoning: According to the second formulation of the Categorical Imperative, we should always treat other persons as ends in themselves and never treat other persons merely as means to an end. In the attempt to construct a personal AI, scientists would be treating the personal AI they created as a means to the end of increasing scientific knowledge. It is reasonable to assume that a fully conscious personal AI would be unwilling to accept its status as a piece of property. In this case, owning a personal AI would be a form of exploitation.

Are we prepared to grant a personal AI the same rights guaranteed to human persons under the United Nation's Universal Declaration of Human Rights, which (among other things) forbids slavery and servitude, and guarantees everyone freedom of movement? If we plan to treat personal AIs as property, then from a Kantian point of view any effort to bring about a personal AI would be immoral.

LaChat concedes that this line of reasoning rests on the controversial assumption that a conscious machine should be given the same moral status as a human being. The argument assumes that a personal AI would have free will and the ability to make moral choices. Perhaps any system operated by a computer program does not have free will, because it has no choice other than to execute the program's instructions as dictated by the architecture of the CPU. If a personal AI does not have free will, it cannot make moral choices, and from a Kantian point of view it should not be valued as an end in itself. Despite its intelligence, it would not have the same moral status as a human being. Creating a personal AI without free will would be morally acceptable.

We do not know whether scientists and engineers will ever be able to construct a personal AI, and we cannot say whether a personal AI would possess free will. Our predictions are uncertain because we do not understand the source of free will in humans. In fact, some philosophers, psychologists, and neuroscientists deny the existence of free will. LaChat concludes, "Though the first word of ethics is 'do no harm,' we can perhaps look forward to innovation with a thoughtful caution," knowing that we may "eclipse ourselves with our own inventions" [23].

It is important to note that mainstream opinion in the artificial intelligence research community holds that the prospects of a personal AI being constructed are quite remote. A panel of leading experts in artificial intelligence met in Pacific Grove, California, in February 2009, to reflect on the societal consequences of the advances in machine intelligence. According to a report from the meeting, the experts were skeptical of the view that machines with superhuman intelligence are on the horizon [24].

10.3   Workplace Changes

Experts debate whether or not information technology has resulted in a net reduction in available jobs, but there is no dispute that information technology has affected *how* people work. In this section, we survey a few of the ways that information technology is fundamentally changing the work experience.

10.3.1   Organizational Changes

Information technology has influenced the way manufacturing and service companies organize themselves. A typical early use of computers was to automate a back-office function, such as payroll. Using computers in this way required a company to make no changes in its organization. Later, companies began using computers inside manufacturing units. Computers enabled companies to customize products and provide better service to their customers. This use of computers delegated more responsibility to the line

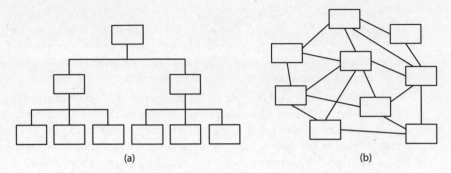

(a)   (b)

FIGURE 10.6 (a) When interactions are more expensive and time-consuming, most information flows between people and their managers. Organizations are rigid and hierarchical. (b) When interactions become inexpensive and fast, the flow of information is much more flexible. Organizations become flatter and more dynamic.

workers, and it encouraged a decentralization of sales and support functions, reducing a company's bureaucracy. Information technology within corporations reached a third stage with the creation of computer networks linking different parts of the business. For example, integrating cash registers with inventory systems has allowed companies to order replacements automatically.

The overall effect of the introduction of information technology is to flatten organizational structures. When the primary source of information distribution was the hand-typed, carbon-copied memorandum, most information flow followed the lines in organization charts (Figure 10.6a). Today, a wide variety of technologies allow any member of an organization to contact any other member with minimal effort and cost (Figure 10.6b). As a result, new opportunities arise. Many companies assemble "tiger teams" of expert workers drawn from various parts of the organization chart. A team will work together for a short period of time to solve an urgent problem, then disband. Flexible information flow also allows companies to adopt "just-in-time" production and distribution methods, reducing inventory costs [25].

Information technology also streamlines organizations by eliminating transactional middlemen. For example, consider the automation of the supply chain. Suppose company A buys widgets from company B. In the past, someone at company A called someone at company B to order the widgets. Today, many companies have adopted **supply-chain automation.** A computer at company A is linked to a computer at company B. The computers are responsible for ordering the widgets, eliminating the need for the middlemen. Automating the paperwork activities associated with purchasing supplies can reduce the number of people who produce purchase orders and invoices, pay bills, process checks, etc. The likely effect of information technology on organizations will be an increased demand in some job categories, while the demand in other categories will drop (Table 10.1) [26].

Dell Computer is a leader in supply-chain automation. Customers order computers directly from Dell by telephone or through its Web site. Seventy percent of Dell's sales are

TABLE 10.1 Greater use of information technology in the workplace will increase demand for employees in certain job categories while reducing demand for employees in other categories.

Higher Demand	Lower Demand
Computer engineers	Bank clerks
Computer support specialists	Procurement specialists
Systems analysts	Financial records processing staff
Database administrators	Secretaries, stenographers, and typists
Desktop publishing specialists	Communications equipment operators
	Computer operators

to large corporations. These companies have custom Web sites that have preconfigured systems tailored to the needs of the purchaser. Dell does not make any computers until they are ordered, allowing it to keep its inventory small—enough for only a few days' production [27].

10.3.2 Telework

Another workplace change brought about through information technology is the rise of telework. **Telework** (also called telecommuting) refers to an arrangement where employees spend a significant portion of their work day at a distance from the employer or a traditional place of work [28]. One kind of telework is working out of a home office. Another example of telework is someone who commutes to a telecenter rather than the company's site. Telecenters provide employees from different firms the ability to connect to their company's computers. A third example of telework are salespersons who have no offices, instead transacting all of their business from their cars using cell phones and laptop computers.

According to the Consumer Electronics Association, 37 percent of workers in the United States telework at least one day a month [29].

ADVANTAGES OF TELEWORK

The rapid growth in the number of teleworkers is evidence there are significant benefits associated with telework. Here are some of the most frequently cited advantages of telework [28, 30]:

1. *Telework increases productivity.*

   A variety of studies have shown teleworkers have 10 to 43 percent more productivity than on-site workers.

2. *Telework reduces absenteeism.*

   Teleworkers are less likely to miss work than someone coming into the office.

3. *Telework improves morale.*

Employees who are teleworking have more freedom. It is easier for them to schedule their work around their personal schedules. If they are working at home, they can dress more casually.

4. *A company can recruit and retain more top employees.*

For example, a company that allows telework can recruit employees who otherwise would not be interested in the job because they are unable or unwilling to be within commuting distance of the main office. Telework allows companies to retain employees (such as mothers of young children) who would quit otherwise.

5. *Telework saves overhead.*

With some of its workers away from the office, a company doesn't have to invest as much of its resources in office space.

6. *Telework improves the resilience of a company.*

Because not all the employees are in one place, the company is less likely to be harmed by a natural disaster or a terrorist attack.

7. *Telework is good for the environment.*

Teleworkers do not take part in the daily commute, which saves energy and reduces pollution.

8. *Employees may save money by teleworking.*

They may not have to purchase as much business attire, and they may be able to avoid paying child-care expenses.

DISADVANTAGES OF TELEWORK

Telework has its detractors, too. Here are some of the reasons most frequently given why companies discourage or prohibit telework:

1. *Telework threatens the authority and control of managers.*

When employees work at a distance from their managers, they naturally have more autonomy. How can a manager manage an employee who is not around?

2. *Telework makes it impossible for an employee to have a face-to-face interaction with customers at the company site.*

For some jobs these interactions are crucial, meaning the job simply cannot be done from a distance.

3. *Sensitive information is less secure.*

If a person has valuable physical or electronic files at home or in an automobile, they may be far less secure than if they were kept at the office. There is a greater chance that the information will be lost or compromised through fire or theft.

4. *When people in an organization do not keep the same hours or come into the office every day, it is more difficult to schedule team meetings.*

Even if employees are only teleworking one or two days a week, many others in the organization can suffer significant inconvenience.

5. *Teleworkers are less visible.*

There is a danger that teleworkers will be forgotten when it's time for raises or promotions. When somebody is "never around," others can get the idea that that person is not making a contribution to the organization.

6. *When faced with a problem or a need for information, employees at the office are less likely to contact a teleworker than another person on site.*

Meanwhile, many teleworkers are afraid to leave their telephones even for a short time, afraid that if someone from work calls them and they are not around, they will get the reputation for not being "at work."

7. *Teleworkers are isolated.*

Some jobs require people to bounce ideas off co-workers. What are people working at home supposed to do?

8. *Teleworkers end up working longer hours for the same pay.*

When everything a person needs to do his job is right there at home, he is more likely to keep coming back to it. How does someone leave her work at the office when her home *is* her office? Critics of telework say that overwork is the reason why teleworkers exhibit higher productivity.

10.3.3 Temporary Work

The modern business environment is highly competitive and rapidly fluctuating. As a result, the level of commitment companies are willing to make to their employees is dropping. Some companies once boasted that they took care of their employees and did not engage in layoffs during business downturns. Those days are gone. The dot-com bust led to massive layoffs in the information technology industry.

Companies are giving themselves more flexibility and saving money on benefits by hiring more subcontractors and temporary employees. Workers cannot count on long-term employment with a single firm. Instead, they must rely on their "knowledge portfolios," which they carry from job to job [12].

10.3.4 Monitoring

Information technology has given companies many new tools to monitor the activities of their employees. An American Management Association/ePolicy Institute survey in 2007 revealed that 66 percent of employers were monitoring the Internet use their employees. Other examples of employee monitoring by American employers included video surveillance (48%), monitoring keyboard activity (45%), monitoring time spent on the phone (45%), and monitoring emails (43%) [31].

The principal purpose of monitoring is to identify inappropriate use of company resources [32]. A quarter of companies in the United Kingdom have fired employees for improper use of the Internet. In the majority of these cases, the employee was surfing the Web for pornography. Another study of employee emails concluded that eliminating email containing gossip and jokes would cut the time staff spend reading email by 30 percent [33]. A study conducted by IDC concluded that between 30 and 40 percent of Internet use by employees was not work-related [34].

Monitoring can help detect illegal activities of employees, as well. By monitoring instant messaging conversations, employers have caught employees who had performed various misdeeds, including an employee who hacked into a company computer after being denied a promotion [35].

Monitoring is also used to ensure that customers are getting the products and services they need. Reviewing customer phone calls to help desks can reveal if the company ought to be providing its customers with better documentation or training [36].

Many companies use monitoring to gauge the productivity of their workers. For example, telemarketing firms keep track of how many calls their employees make per hour. Sometimes monitoring can help an organization assess the quality of the work done by its employees. Major League Baseball has introduced QuesTec's Umpire Information System to evaluate how well umpires are calling balls and strikes [37].

Companies are beginning to investigate the use of wireless networks to track the locations of their employees. Knowing the location of service technicians would enable an automated system to respond to a breakdown by alerting the technician closest to the malfunctioning piece of equipment. A system that tracked the locations of hospital physicians could upload a patient's file into the wireless laptop held by a doctor approaching a hospital bed.

More schools are using video cameras to increase security [38]. The school district in Biloxi, Mississippi, used gambling-generated tax receipts to install digital cameras in all 500 of its classrooms. An elementary school principal gushes, "It's like truth serum. When we have a he-said, she-said situation, nine times out of 10, all we have to do is ask children if they want us to go back and look at the camera, and they fess up" [39].

It's an open question whether monitoring is ultimately beneficial to an organization. Obviously, organizations institute monitoring because they have reason to believe it will improve the quantity and/or quality of the work performed by its employees. There is evidence that employee monitoring makes employees more focused on their tasks, but also reduces job satisfaction [40].

10.3.5 Multinational Teams

In the 1980s, General Electric and Citibank set up software development teams in India. Since then, many corporations have established field offices in India, including Analog Devices, Cadence Design Systems, Cisco, Intel, Microsoft, and Sun Microsystems. Bangalore, in particular, has made an effort to become the Silicon Valley of India. Companies use Indian companies to write software, process credit card applications, and do billing. Texas Instrument's chip-design team in Bangalore has 200 patents to its name. Hewlett Packard and Oracle both have thousands of employees in India. SAP has 500 engineers in Bangalore.

Multinational teams allow a company to have people at work more hours during the day. It becomes easier to have a call support center open 24 hours a day. It is even possible for projects to be shuttled between multiple sites, allowing around-the-clock progress to be made on time-sensitive products. For example, a team in Palo Alto can spend its day finding bugs in a piece of software, then hand the bug reports over to a team in Bangalore that spends *its* day fixing the bugs [41].

However, the main attraction of India is cost savings. Wages in India are substantially lower than in the United States or Western Europe. The total cost of an Indian computer programmer is about $20,000 a year. Companies say they need to lower their expenses in order to stay in business. If they go out of business, their U.S. employees will lose their jobs. Hence, creating multinational teams is a way for companies to stay in business and preserve jobs in the United States [42].

Creating multinational teams has disadvantages, too. The principal disadvantage is that the infrastructure in less developed countries can make business more difficult. For example, because India has only two international airports—one in New Delhi and the other in Mumbai—it is hard to travel to and from Bangalore. The highway system in India is primitive, and electrical power is unreliable.

Despite the difficulties, corporations are increasingly making use of multinational teams. About 90,000 IT-related jobs in the United States are moving to foreign countries every year, and at American companies whose revenues are at least $5 billion, about a quarter of IT jobs have already moved offshore [43].

10.4 Globalization

Globalization refers to the process of creating a worldwide network of businesses and markets. Globalization results in a greater mobility of goods, services, and capital around the world. Investments are made across national boundaries. Products manufactured in one country are sold in another. Consumers calling a telephone help center get connected with support technicians located on the other side of the world.

The rapidly decreasing cost of information technology has made globalization possible (Figure 10.7). The cost of computing dropped by 99.99 percent between 1975 and 1995. The cost of an international telephone call from New York to London dropped by 99 percent between 1930 and 1996 [44]. Companies have made extensive use of low-cost information technology to coordinate operations distributed around the planet.

10.4.1 Arguments for Globalization

Those who favor globalization seek the removal of trade barriers between nations. The North American Free Trade Agreement (NAFTA) between Canada, the United States, and Mexico was a step toward globalization.

The World Trade Organization (WTO) is an international body that devises rules for international trade and promotes the goal of free trade among nations. The WTO and other proponents of globalization support free trade with these arguments:

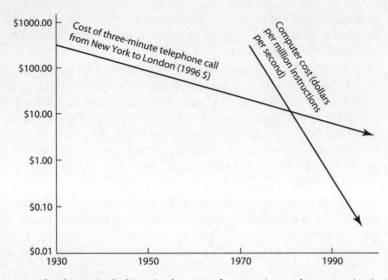

FIGURE 10.7 The dramatic declines in the cost of computing and communications have made global enterprises feasible.

1. *Globalization increases competition among multiple possible providers of the same product.*

   Competition ensures that higher-quality products are sold at the best possible prices. Consumers get better prices when each area produces the goods or services it does best: corn in Kansas, automobiles in Ontario, semiconductors in Singapore, and so on. When prices are lower, the real purchasing power of consumers is higher. Hence, globalization increases everyone's standard of living.

2. *People in poorer countries deserve jobs, too.*

   When they gain employment, their prosperity increases.

3. *Every example in the past century of a poor country becoming more prosperous has been the result of that country producing goods for the world market rather than trying for self-sufficiency* [45].

4. *Creating jobs around the world reduces unrest and leads to more stability.*

   Countries with interdependent economies are less likely to go to war with each other.

10.4.2 Arguments against Globalization

Ralph Nader, American trade unions, the European farm lobby, and organizations such as Friends of the Earth, Greenpeace, and Oxfam oppose globalization. They give these reasons why globalization is a bad trend:

1. *The United States and other governments should not be subordinate to the WTO.*

The WTO makes the rules for globalization, but nobody elected it. It makes its decisions behind closed doors. Every member country, from the United States to the tiniest dictatorship, has one vote in the WTO.

2. *American workers should not be forced to compete with foreign workers who do not receive decent pay and working conditions.*

The WTO does not require member countries to protect the rights of their workers. It has not banned child labor. Dictatorships such as the People's Republic of China are allowed to participate in the WTO even though they do not let their workers organize into labor unions.

3. *Globalization has accelerated the loss of both manufacturing jobs and white-collar jobs overseas.*

4. *The removal of trade barriers hurts workers in foreign countries, too.*

For example, NAFTA removed tariffs between Canada, Mexico, and the United States. Because they receive agricultural subsidies from the U.S. government, large American agribusinesses grow corn and wheat for less than its true cost of production and sell the grain in Mexico. Mexican farmers who cannot compete with these prices are driven out of business. Most of them cannot find jobs in Mexico and end up immigrating to the United States [46].

Even if globalization is a good idea, there are reasons why a company may not choose to move its facilities to the place where labor is the least expensive. Interestingly, these arguments are more relevant to "blue collar" jobs such as manufacturing than they are to "white collar" jobs such as computer programming. With automation, the cost of labor becomes a smaller percentage of the total cost of a product. Once the labor cost is reduced to a small enough fraction, it makes little difference whether the factory is located in China or the United States. Meanwhile, there are definite additional costs associated with foreign factories. If you include products in transit, foreign factories carry more inventory than identical factories in the United States. There are also more worries about security when the product is being made in a foreign country. For these reasons, moving a factory to a less-developed country is not always in the best interest of a company [4].

10.4.3 Dot–Com Bust Increases IT Sector Unemployment

In the 1990s, Intel's stock rose 3,900 percent, Microsoft's stock increased in value 7,500 percent, and Cisco System's stock soared an incredible 66,000 percent. That means $1,000 of Cisco stock purchased in 1990 was worth $661,000 at the end of 1999. Investors looking for new opportunities for high returns focused on **dot-coms,** Internet-related start-up companies. Speculators pushed up the values of many companies that had never earned a profit. Early in 2000, the total valuation of 370 Internet start-ups was $1.5 trillion, even though they had only $40 billion in sales (that's *sales*, not profits) [47].

In early 2000, the speculative bubble burst, and the prices of dot-com stocks fell rapidly. The resulting "dot-com bust" resulting in 862 high-tech start-ups going out of business between January 2000 and June 2002. Across the United States, the high-tech industry shed half a million jobs [48]. In San Francisco and Silicon Valley, the dot-com bust resulted in the loss of 13 percent of nonagricultural jobs, the worst downturn since the Great Depression [49].

10.4.4 Foreign Workers in the American IT Industry

Even while hundreds of thousands of information technology workers were losing their jobs, U.S. companies hired tens of thousands of foreigners to work in the United States. The U.S. government grants these workers visas allowing them to work in America. The two most common visas are called the H-1B and the L-1.

An H-1B visa allows a foreigner to work in the United States for up to six years. In order for a company to get an H-1B visa for a foreign employee, the company must demonstrate that there are no Americans qualified to do the job. The company must also pay the foreign worker the prevailing wage for the job. Information technology companies have made extensive use of H-1B visas to bring in skilled foreign workers and to hire foreign students graduating from U.S. universities.

In the midst of the high-tech downturn, the U.S. government continued to issue tens of thousands of H-1B visas: 163,600 in 2000–2001 and 79,100 in 2001–2002. Meanwhile, the unemployment rate among American computer science professionals was about 5.1 percent. Many of the 100,000 unemployed computer scientists complained to Congress about the large number of H-1B visas being issued. Some professional organizations argued against giving out any H-1B visas at all [50]. Congress decided to drop the H-1B quota to 65,000 for the fiscal year beginning October 1, 2003, and it initially set a quota of 65,000 for the following fiscal year. However, the 65,000 H-1B visas approved for 2004–2005 were filled in a single day; representatives of universities and technology companies said the quota was set too low [51]. Bill Gates said, "Anyone who's got the education and the experience, they're not out there unemployed" [52]. Congress responded in May 2005, by allowing an exemption for an additional 20,000 foreigners with advanced degrees (master's or higher).

The annual quota of 65,000 H-1B visas and the exemption for 20,000 foreigners with advanced degrees remain in effect. During the deep economic recession of 2008–2009, the unemployment rate rose sharply, and the U.S. Citizenship and Immigration Service had a difficult time filling the quota mandated by Congress. With about a month to go in the 2008–2009 fiscal year, the USCIS had received only 45,000 petitions for the regular H-1B vis and about 20,000 petitions for the advanced degree exemption [53].

The other important work visa is called the L-1. American companies use L-1 visas to move workers from overseas facilities to the United States for up to seven years. For example, Intel employees in Bangalore, India, could be transferred to Hillsboro, Oregon, if they held an L-1 visa. Employees brought in to the United States under an L-1 visa do not need to be paid the prevailing wage. That saves employers money.

Critics of L-1 visas claim lower-paid foreign workers are replacing higher-paid American workers within the walls of high-tech facilities located in the United States. The U.S. Congress has put no limit on the number of L-1 visas that may be issued in any given year, but the number of foreigners working in the United States under L-1 visas is much smaller than the number holding H-1B visas. In 2006, about 50,000 foreigners were employed in the United States under this visa program [54].

10.4.5 Foreign Competition

The debate over the number of visas to grant foreign workers seeking employment in the United States should not mask another trend: the increasing capabilities of IT companies within developing nations, particularly China and India.

In 2004, IBM agreed to sell its PC division to Chinese computer manufacturer Lenovo for $1.75 billion, making Lenovo the number three manufacturer of PCs in the world [55]. A few months later, Chinese Premier Wen Jiabao visited India to encourage new collaborations between Chinese hardware companies and Indian software companies [56]. Today, China is the world's number one producer of computer hardware (Figure 10.8).

India's IT outsourcing industry is growing rapidly; Indian companies now employ more than a million people and have annual sales exceeding $17 billion. About 70 percent of these sales are in software engineering work, such as designing, programming, and maintaining computer programs. The other 30 percent of these sales are in IT-related services, such as call centers, medical transcription, and x-ray interpretation [57].

Some Chinese universities are becoming recognized for their research expertise. For example, the Institute of Computing Technology at the Chinese Academy of Science

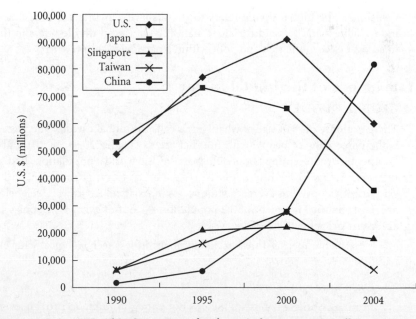

FIGURE 10.8 In 1990, China's computer-hardware industry was virtually nonexistent. By 2004, China had become the world's leading computer-hardware-producing nation.

and Tsinghua University have been actively involved in the development of the Open64 optimizing compiler [58].

More evidence of global competition comes from the annual Association for Computing Machinery International Collegiate Programming Contest. When the contest began 29 years ago, only schools from North America and Europe competed. In 2011, more than 8,000 teams from 88 countries entered the contest. No American team has placed first since Harvey Mudd College in 1997. In the five-year period from 2007 to 2011, all of the winning teams were from universities in China, Russia, or Poland, and of the 50 teams placing in the top ten during this same time period, only five were from the United States [59].

During the deep recession of 2008 and 2009, American corporations like Microsoft, General Electric, JP Morgan Chase, and Best Buy continued "offshoring" white-collar jobs to India and other countries in order reduce their cost of doing business [60].

10.5 The Digital Divide

The **digital divide** refers to the situation where some people have access to modern information technology while others do not. The underlying assumption motivating the term is that people who use telephones, computers, and the Internet have opportunities denied to people without access to these devices. The idea of a digital divide became popular in the mid-1990s with the rapid growth in popularity of the World Wide Web.

According to Pippa Norris, the digital divide has two fundamentally different dimensions. The **global divide** refers to the disparity in Internet access between more industrialized and less industrialized nations. The **social divide** refers to the difference in access between the rich and poor within a particular country [61].

10.5.1 Evidence of the Digital Divide

GLOBAL DIVIDE

There is plenty of evidence of what Norris calls the global divide. One piece of evidence is the percentage of people with Internet access (Figure 10.9). In 2011, about 2.1 billion people, representing about 30 percent of the world's population, had access to the Internet. Access to the Internet in North America, Oceania/Australia, and Europe was significantly above this average, while access in Asia and Africa was well below this average. Only about 11 percent of the population—1 out of every 9 persons—had Internet access in Africa in 2011 [62].

What is hampering Internet development in less technologically developed countries?

1. *Often there is little wealth.*

    In many of these countries there is not enough money to provide everyone in the country with the necessities of life, much less pay for Internet connections.

2. *Many of these countries have an inadequate telecommunications infrastructure.*

For example, less than 5 percent of the people in the African nations of Burundi, the Central African Republic, Chad, Comoros, Eritria, Ethiopia, Guinea, Malawi, Niger, Rwanda, and Sierra Leone subscribe to a telephone service [63]. Many poor people have no access to newspapers, radio, or television [61].

3. *The primary language is not English.*

English is the dominant language for business and scientific development, giving English-speaking countries a comparative advantage with respect to competing in the global marketplace.

4. *Literacy is low, and education is inadequate.*

Half of the population in poorer countries has no opportunity to attend secondary schools. There is a strong correlation between literacy and wealth, both for individuals and for societies [27].

5. *The country's culture may not make participating in the Information Age a priority* [64].

SOCIAL DIVIDE

Even within wealthy countries such as the United States, the extent to which people use the Internet varies widely according to age, wealth, and educational achievement. Pew Internet polled Americans to find out how many made use of the Internet in the year 2008. Online access varied from 93 percent of 12–17-year-olds to 27 percent for those 76 and over [65]. A 2011 study revealed that fully 96 percent of adults living in households

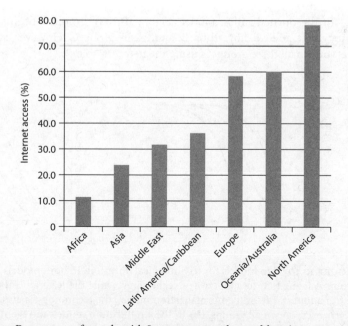

FIGURE 10.9 Percentage of people with Internet access, by world region.

with annual incomes at least $75,000 used the Internet, compared to 63 percent of adults living in households with annual incomes less than $30,000. While 94 percent of those with a college degree used the Internet, only 42 percent of those who dropped out of high school went online [66].

10.5.2 Models of Technological Diffusion

New technologies are usually expensive. Hence, the first people to adopt new technologies are those who are better off. As the technology matures, its price drops dramatically, enabling more people to acquire it. Eventually the price of the technology becomes low enough that it becomes available to nearly everyone.

The history of the consumer VCR illustrates this phenomenon. The first VHS VCR, introduced by RCA in 1977, retailed for $1,000. That's $3,562 in 2009 dollars. In 2009, you could buy a VHS VCR from a mass-marketer for under $30. That means between 1977 and 2009, the price of a VCR in constant dollars fell by more than 99 percent! As the price declined, more people could afford to purchase a VCR and sales increased rapidly. The VCR progressed from a luxury that only the rich could afford into a consumer product found in nearly every American household.

Technological diffusion refers to the rate at which a new technology is assimilated into a society. Two different theories predict how a new technology is acquired by people in a society, based on their socioeconomic status (Figure 10.10). We divide society into three groups. People with the highest socioeconomic status are in group A, people with the lowest socioeconomic status are in group C, and group B consists of those people in the middle.

In the **normalization model** (Figure 10.10a), group A begins to adopt the technology first, followed by group B, and finally group C. However, at some point nearly everyone in all three groups is using the new technology.

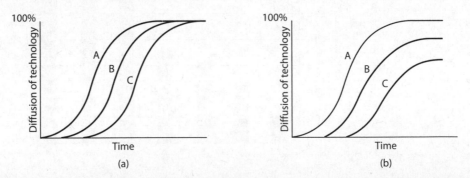

FIGURE 10.10 Two models for technological diffusion. In both models the most advantaged group A is the first to adopt a new technology, while the least advantaged group C is the last to adopt it. (a) In the normalization model, the technology is eventually embraced by nearly everyone in all groups. (b) In the stratification model, the eventual adoption rate of the technology is lower for less-advantaged groups.

In the **stratification model** (Figure 10.10b), the order of adoption is the same. However, in this model the eventual number of people in group C who adopt the technology is lower than the number of adoptees in group A. The percentage of people in group B who adopt the technology is somewhere between the levels of the other two groups.

Technological optimists believe the global adoption of information technology will follow the normalization model. Information technology will make the world a better place by reducing poverty in developing countries. Creating opportunities elsewhere will reduce the number of people trying to immigrate into the United States.

Technological pessimists believe information technology adoption will follow the stratification model, leading to a permanent condition of "haves" and "have nots." Information technology will only exacerbate existing inequalities between rich and poor nations and between rich and poor people within each nation [61].

Technological pessimists point out that the gap between the richest 20 countries and the poorest 20 countries continues to grow. In 1960, the average gross domestic product (GDP) of the richest countries was 18 times larger than the average GDP of the poorest countries. By 1995, the gap had grown to become 37 times greater. Some of the poorest countries grew even poorer during the last third of the twentieth century [27].

10.5.3 Critiques of the Digital Divide

Mark Warschauer has suggested three reasons why the term "digital divide" is not helpful. First, it tends to promote the idea that the difference between the "haves" and the "have nots" is simply a question of access. Some politicians have jumped to the conclusion that providing technology will close the divide. Warschauer says this approach will not work. To back his claim, he gives as an example the story of a small town in Ireland.

While many factories in Ireland produce IT products, there is not a lot of use of IT among Irish citizens. Ireland's telecommunications company held a contest in 1997 to select and fund an "Information Age Town." The winner was Ennis, a town of 15,000 in western Ireland (Figure 10.11). The $22 million of prize money represented $1,200 per resident, a large sum for a poor community. Every business was equipped with an Integrated Services Digital Network (ISDN) line, a Web site, and a smart-card reader. Every family received a smart card and a personal computer.

Three years later, there was little evidence of people using the new technology. Devices had been introduced without adequately explaining to the people why they might want to use them. The benefits were not obvious. Sometimes the technology competed with social systems that were working just fine. For example, before the introduction of the new technology, unemployed workers visited the social welfare office three times a week to sign in and get an unemployment payment. These visits served an important social function for the unemployed people. It gave them an opportunity to visit with other people and keep their spirits up. Once the PCs were introduced, the workers were supposed to "sign in" and receive their payments over the Internet. Many of the workers did not like the new system. It appears that many of the PCs were sold on the black market.

FIGURE 10.11 Unemployed workers in Ennis, Ireland, resisted using the Internet to receive their benefits, preferring to report in person to the social welfare office, where they could visit with other people. (© Richard Cummins/CORBIS)

The unemployed workers simply went back to reporting in person to the social welfare office.

For IT to make a difference, social systems must change as well. The introduction of information technology must take into account local culture, which includes language, literacy, and community values.

Warschauer's second criticism of the term "digital divide" is that it implies everyone is on one side or another of a huge canyon. Everybody is put into one of two categories: "haves" and "have nots." In reality access is a continuum, and each individual occupies a particular place on it. For example, how do you categorize someone who has a 56K modem connecting his PC to the Internet? Certainly that person has online access, but he is not able to retrieve the same wealth of material as someone with a broadband connection.

Thirdly, Warschauer says that the term "digital divide" implies that a lack of access will lead to a less advantaged position in society. Is that the proper causality? Models of technological diffusion show that those with a less advantaged position in society tend to adopt new technologies at a later time, which is an argument that the causality goes the other way. In reality, there is no simple causality. Each factor affects the other [27].

Rob Kling has put it this way:

[The] big problem with "the digital divide" framing is that it tends to connote "digital solutions," i.e., computers and telecommunications, without engaging the important set of complementary resources and complex interventions to support social inclusion, of which informational technology applications may be enabling elements, but are certainly insufficient when simply added to the status quo mix of resources and relationships" [27].

Finally, Warschauer points out that the Internet does not represent the pinnacle of information technology. In the next few decades, dramatic new technologies will be created. We will see these new technologies being adopted at different speeds, too.

10.5.4   Net Neutrality

The corporations that operate the long-distance Internet backbone connections in the United States have suggested that they may begin **tiered service**—charging more for higher-priority routing of Internet packets. These companies have said that tiered service will be needed in the future to guarantee a satisfactory level of service to companies that require it, such as Voice-over-IP (VoIP) providers [67].

Content providers, such as Google and Yahoo!, have combined with the American Library Association and consumer groups to oppose any notion of tiered service. These groups have asked the U.S. Congress to enact "net neutrality" legislation that would require Internet service providers to treat all packets the same. Consumer groups suggest that if tiered service is enacted, only large corporations would be able to pay for the highest level of service. Small start-up companies wouldn't be able to compete with established corporate giants. Hence, tiered service would discourage innovation and competition. Another argument against tiered service is based on the concern that companies controlling the Internet might block or degrade access to non favored content or applications [67]. For example, a customer with an AT&T/Yahoo! DSL connection might find that high definition video content from AT&T channels performs better than high definition video from other providers [68]. Net neutrality advocates say this is unfair and must be prevented, pointing out that 95 percent of consumers have only two choices for broadband access: the local cable company or the local telephone company [69].

Opponents of "net neutrality" legislation suggest that allowing people to pay more to get a higher quality of service can sometimes be to the benefit of consumers. For example, rapid delivery of data packets is more valuable to a person using the Internet for videoconferencing than a person who simply sends email messages. Internet backbone providers argue that even though there is currently enough bandwidth, the rapidly increasing popularity of YouTube and other online video sites will soon fill the Internet's data pipes. A significant amount of money is needed to upgrade the Internet infrastructure to support the higher-bandwidth applications of the future. This money ought to come from the companies that are selling access to the data-intensive content [67].

In a 2007 report, the U.S. Federal Trade Commission concluded the market was becoming more, not less, competitive, and suggested that Congress "proceed with caution" before passing any legislation [67]. Even though it appears unlikely that Congress will pass any net neutrality legislation in the near future, Internet backbone providers are unlikely to move toward tiered service without getting some kind of approval from the FTC [70].

10.6 The "Winner–Take–All Society"

10.6.1 The Winner–Take–All Phenomenon

The Declaration of Independence states that "all men are created equal," but we live in a society in which some people have far more wealth and power than others. What if everyone were guaranteed roughly the same amount of income? The traditional answer to this question is that there would be little motivation for people to exert themselves, either mentally or physically. If everyone were paid the same, there would be no point in getting an education, taking risks, or working hard. Productivity would be low, and the overall standard of living would be poor. For this reason, many people believe a superior alternative is a market economy that rewards innovation, hard work, and risk-taking by compensating people according to the value of the goods they produce.

In *The Winner-Take-All Society*, economists Robert Frank and Philip Cook explore the growth of markets where a few top performers receive a disproportionate share of the rewards. Their book is the primary source for this section [71].

Frank and Cook observe that the winner-take-all phenomenon has existed for quite awhile in the realms of sports, entertainment, and the arts. A few "superstar" athletes, actors, and novelists earn millions from their work and garner lucrative endorsements, while those who perform at a slightly lower level make far less. However, the winner-take-all phenomenon has now spread throughout our global economy. Sometimes the qualitative difference between the top product and the second-best product is very slight, yet that can be the difference between success and failure. Hence corporations compete for the top executive talent that can give them the edge over their competition. The compensation of CEOs at America's largest corporations has risen much faster than the wages of production workers (Figure 10.12) [72].

Several factors have led toward winner-take-all phenomena in our economy:

1. *Information technology and efficient transportation systems make it easier for a leading product to dominate the worldwide market.*

   For example, consider a music studio that has a digital recording of the world's best orchestra playing Beethoven's *Symphony No. 5 in C minor*. The studio can produce millions of perfect copies of this recording, enough for every classical music lover on the planet. Why would anyone want to listen to the second-best orchestra when a CD of the best orchestra is available for virtually the same price?

2. *Network economies encourage people to flock to the same product.*

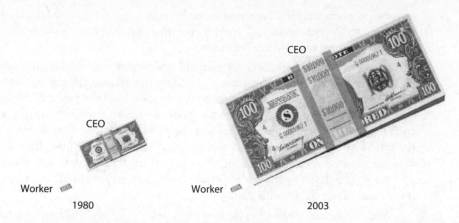

Figure 10.12 In 1980, the average pay for a CEO at a large American company was about 40 times the pay of a production worker. By 2003, the ratio had risen to about 400 to 1.

If by chance you should need to use someone else's computer, it is far more likely that that person will own a Windows PC than a Macintosh. In this respect, knowing how to use a Windows computer has greater utility than knowing how to use a Macintosh. If a person cannot decide which computer to purchase, this factor alone may encourage someone to buy a Windows PC.

3. *English has become the de facto language of international business.*

English is the native language in 12 countries, including the United States, which is the dominant economic power on the planet. Another 56 countries teach English in their schools. The dominance of English makes it easier for products to find a worldwide market.

4. *Business norms have changed.*

In the past, large businesses promoted from within and would not recruit executives from other firms. Today, firms vigorously compete with each other for top executive talent.

10.6.2 Harmful Effects of Winner–Take–All

Frank and Cook argue that winner-take-all effects are bad for the economy, for a variety of reasons. First, winner-take-all markets increase the gap between the rich and the poor. Between 1979 and 1989, the inflation-adjusted incomes of the top 1 percent of U.S. wage-earners doubled, while the median income was flat, and the average income of the bottom 20 percent actually declined.

Winner-take-all effects draw some of the most talented people into socially unproductive work. The problem with winner-take-all contests is that they attract too many contestants. For every comedian who hosts a late-night talk show, tens of thousands of comedians struggle in nightclubs, hoping for their big break. The multimillion-dollar incomes of a relatively few high-profile attorneys help attract many of the brightest college students toward law school. We end up with a glut of lawyers. Meanwhile, there is a shortage of nurses and nuclear engineers.

Winner-take-all markets create wasteful investment and consumption. For example, there is fierce competition among candidates for slots in the top business and law schools. No one wants to go for an interview looking less than his or her best. For this reason, male interviewees are reluctant to show up for an interview wearing a suit that costs less than $600. But if everyone is wearing a $600 suit, no one has an advantage over the others due to his attire. If they had all spent $300 on their suits, there would have been the same relative equity. The behavior of business school applicants is similar to an arms race. The desire to seek an advantage leads to an escalation of consumption, even if the eventual result is simply parity.

A disproportionate share of the best and brightest college students become concentrated in a few elite institutions. "The day has already arrived," write Frank and Cook, "when failure to have an elite undergraduate degree closes certain doors completely, no matter what other stellar credentials a student might possess" [71]. Many Wall Street firms will not even interview candidates who did not graduate from one of a very small number of top law schools. These law schools show a preference for graduates of elite undergraduate programs. Hence, high school students interested in reaching the top of the legal profession know their best chance is to do their undergraduate work at an elite school. The result is a tremendous competition for a relatively small number of openings at these colleges, while in truth, there are hundreds of top-quality public and private colleges and universities in the United States.

Winner-take-all is not fair, because it gives much greater rewards to the top performers than those whose performance is only slightly inferior. Here is an example from the world of professional sports, where winnings and performance data are objective and publicly available. Jim Furyk and Brian Bateman both play on the PGA Tour. Their skill levels are very close (see Table 10.2), but near the end of the 2009 season, Furyk had won 99 times as much in prize money as Bateman.

TABLE 10.2 Comparison of personal statistics of PGA Tour professionals Brian Bateman and Jim Furyk near the end of the 2009 season.

Metric	Brian Bateman	Jim Furyk
Driving distance (yards)	289.1	278.1
Driving accuracy (%)	56.23	70.24
Greens in regulation (%)	63.95	64.67
Putts/round	29.42	28.17
Scoring average	71.89	70.24
Tournaments entered	21	21
Winnings	$35,379	$3,514,215

Winner-take-all markets harm our culture. Here's why. People are social; they like to read the same books and see the same movies as their friends. It gives them something to talk about. Suppose two books have about the same appeal to a consumer, but one of them is on a best-seller list. The consumer is more likely to select the book on the best-seller list, because it increases the probability she will encounter a friend who has read it. But that means it's really important for a book publisher to get its books on the best-seller list. Publishers know that books written by "name" authors have a greater chance of making the best-seller list than books written by new authors. This knowledge can lead a publisher to give a big advance to a well-known author to produce a second-rate work, rather than invest the same resources in developing an unknown, but more talented, author. The same effect happens with movie producers. Hoping for the largest possible sales on the first weekend, they bankroll second-rate sequels to big hits rather than original stories filmed by lesser-known directors.

10.6.3 Reducing Winner–Take–All Effects

If winner-take-all markets have harmful consequences on our economy and society, what can be done? Frank and Cook suggest four ways to reduce winner-take-all effects. First, societies can enact laws limiting the number of hours that stores remain open for business. These laws ensure parity among competing businesses and prevent them from engaging in positional arms races. Without these laws, one business may extend its hours in order to gain an advantage over its competitors. Soon, all of its competitors follow suit. Parity is restored, but now all the employees must bear the burden of the longer hours. Regulations on business hours are often called "blue laws."

Second, in the absence of laws, businesses can form cooperative agreements to reduce positional arms races. An example is when a group of professional sport team owners agree to establish a cap on team salaries.

Third, more progressive tax structures reduce excess competition for the few hand-somely rewarded positions. Back in 1961, the marginal tax rate on income in the highest tax bracket was 91 percent. By 1989, the highest marginal income tax rate had been lowered to 28 percent. Consumption taxes and luxury taxes are other ways of targeting the wealthiest people. Heavily taxing those with the highest incomes makes a higher income less attractive and dissuades some people from competing for the highest-paying jobs. Society benefits when these people engage in more productive work.

Finally, campaign finance reform can reduce the political power of the wealthiest 1 percent of the population, who control 37 percent of the wealth. Reducing the political power of the very wealthy is another way to reduce the attraction of competing for the highest-paying positions.

Summary

This chapter has explored a variety of ways in which information technology and automation have affected the workplace. It began by asking the question: Does automation increase unemployment? On the surface, the answer to this question seems obvious: Of course automation increases unemployment. That is what automation means: replacing human labor with machine labor. Industrial robots, voice mail systems, and a myriad of other devices have displaced millions of workers in the past 50 years. However, a deeper look reveals how automation can create jobs, too. When products are less expensive, more people want to buy them, increasing the number that must be made. If products are less expensive, consumers have more money left to spend, which increases demand for other products. Finally, some people are involved in creating and maintaining the machines themselves. For these reasons, the rapid introduction of automation has not yet led to widespread unemployment in the countries where automation is used the most. In fact, the total number of manufacturing jobs worldwide continues to increase.

Thanks to automation, productivity has more than doubled since World War II. However, the length of the work week in the most highly industrialized nations has not decreased by half. Instead, productivity has been used to increase the standard of living. This choice is understandable, since our society defines success in terms of wealth and material possessions. However, not all cultures have the same values. People in some "primitive" cultures choose to work much shorter hours.

Intelligent robots have been a fixture of science fiction novels for more than sixty years. In the past decade, however, faster microprocessors have enabled AI researchers to create systems capable of amazing feats, such as steering a minivan driven across America. A few ethicists have suggested that we temper our efforts to create ever-more-intelligent computers with some reflection about how highly intelligent computers would affect society.

Information technology has transformed the way businesses organize themselves. Rapid and inexpensive communications allow many more information channels to open up within organizations, which can speed processes and eliminate middlemen. Evidence of more flexible organizational structures include the rise of telework and multinational teams. Improvements in information technology have also given management unprecedented access to the moment-by-moment activities of employees. Workplace monitoring has become the rule, rather than the exception, in large corporations.

As modern information technology has spread around the world, corporations form tightly connected networks and sell their products and services in many markets. This process is called globalization. Advocates of globalization claim it creates jobs for people in poorer countries and increases competition, resulting in lower prices and a higher standard of living for everyone. Critics of globalization say it forces workers in highly developed countries to compete with people willing to work for a fraction of the pay.

The notion that only manufacturing jobs could be lost to overseas competition has been disproved by recent events. While the dot-com bust has put hundreds of thousands of IT professionals out of work in the United States, American companies have shipped hundreds of thousands of jobs to India and other countries where well-educated people will work for a fraction of what an American earns. Unemployed American high-tech workers have criticized companies for hiring large numbers of foreigners to work in the

United States under H-1B or L-1 visas. Companies respond that reducing labor costs is a necessity in a competitive marketplace. In order to survive and thrive, companies must keep prices down and profits up.

The "digital divide" is a way of dividing people into two groups: those with access to information technology and those who do not have access. The term is based on the premise that access to information technology is a prerequisite for success in the information age. Some also assume that simply giving people access to the technology will solve the problem. Pippa Norris points out that there are several fundamentally different dimensions to the digital divide. One dimension separates the more industrialized nations from the less industrialized nations. Another dimension separates rich and poor within a particular country. Mark Warschauer says the notion of a digital divide is too simplistic for three reasons. First, people have widely varying access to information technology. Access should be seen as continuum, not a division into "haves" and "have nots." Second, simply giving people information technology devices, such as computers, cell phones, and Internet accounts, does not guarantee they will take full advantage of the opportunities they make available. For IT to make a difference, social systems must be taken into account. The use of information technology "is a social practice, involving access to physical artifacts, content, skills, and social support" [27]. Third, it's too simplistic to say that a lack of access causes someone to have lower socioeconomic status. You could just as easily say that people with lower socioeconomic status adopt new technologies later. In reality, each factor influences the other.

Frank and Cook invented the term "winner-take-all society" to refer to the way that information technology, the spread of English, network effects, and other factors are creating marketplaces where a few top performers gain a disproportionate share of the rewards. They present evidence that winner-take-all effects harm our economy and our culture, and they suggest actions that can be taken to reduce the winner-take-all phenomenon.

Review Questions

1. What are some benefits brought about by automation? What are some harms brought about by automation?

2. What evidence has been given to show that automation eliminates jobs? What evidence has been given to show that automation creates more jobs than it destroys?

3. If automation has doubled productivity since World War II, why hasn't the work week gotten shorter?

4. How can information technology lead to changes in the structure of an organization?

5. How can telework improve the environment?

6. Why do teleworkers fret about being less visible?

7. Proponents of globalization claim that it helps workers in developing countries. Opponents of globalization claim the opposite. Summarize the arguments pro and con.

8. How does Norris categorize the digital divide?

9. Why does Warschauer say the notion of the digital divide is too simplistic and perhaps harmful?

Discussion Questions

10. Do you agree with Voltaire that a lack of work results in boredom and vice?

11. Would you accept a salaried position (paying a certain amount each month) if you knew it would require you to work at least 50 hours per week in order to complete the required work?

12. If automation leads to chronic and widespread unemployment, should the government provide long-term unemployed adult citizens with the opportunity to do meaningful work at a wage that will keep them out of poverty? Why or why not?

13. Labor advocates Stanley Aronowitz, Dawn Esposito, and William DiFazio say the United States should institute a guaranteed income that would provide each adult with enough money for food, housing, clothing, health care, and recreation. What are the merits and demerits of this proposal?

14. Is it wrong to create machines capable of making human labor obsolete?

15. The Umpire Information System, produced by QuesTec, demonstrates that a computer can call balls and strikes more accurately than a human umpire. In fact, the system is being used by Major League Baseball to evaluate the accuracy of the umpires' calls. Should Major League Baseball allow the Umpire Information System have the final say on calling balls and strikes?

16. Will humans become demoralized by the presence of vastly more intelligent robots? If so, is it wrong to work on the development of such robots?

17. Is it morally acceptable to work on the development of an intelligent machine if it cannot be guaranteed the machine's actions will be benevolent?

18. How will our notions of intellectual property change if computers become capable of creative work?

19. How will our ideas about privacy have to change if legions of superfast computers are analyzing the electronic records of our lives?

20. Kant says that humans should always be treated as ends in themselves, never merely as means to an end. Are there any circumstances under which an intelligent computer should be given the same consideration?

21. It is possible to program responses into computers that simulate human emotions. For example, when a computer taking on the role of a nurse hears a parent say, "My child has diahrrea," it can respond, "I'm sorry to hear that." Studies have shown that people can develop an emotional bond with machines that appear to demonstrate human feelings such as empathy. Is it wrong to encourage these attachments by programming computers to mimic human emotions?

22. A multinational corporation has an office in Palo Alto, California, and an office in Bangalore, India. A 21-year-old American computer science graduate works as a software tester at the Palo Alto office. A 21-year-old Indian computer science graduate has an identical position at the Bangalore office. The American earns $65,000 per year in salary and benefits; the Indian earns $15,000 per year in salary and benefits. Is this arrangement moral? Should the company give equal pay and benefits for equal work?

23. Do you support the concept of tiered Internet service, providing higher bandwidth to those who pay for premium service? To what extent does tiered Internet service already exist?

24. Would the music industry be healthier if winner-take-all effects were reduced? If so, which of the proposed solutions in Section 9.6.3 would make the most sense for the music industry?

25. Should the federal government discourage companies from taking advantage of their salaried employees by requiring firms to pay overtime to *any* employee who works more than 40 hours in one week?

26. Do you agree with Martin Ford (interviewed at the end of this chapter) that countries will need to introduce guaranteed income schemes to preserve the market for goals and services?

In-class Exercises

27. The Department of Homeland Security is interested in using computers to identify suspected terrorists operating within the United States. It would like to mine databases containing information about purchases and travel to detect patterns that may identify individuals who are engaged in, or at least planning, terrorist activity. It asks a panel of computer scientists to determine the feasibility of this project. A panel member says the most difficult problem will be determining what patterns of transactions to look for. He suggests it might be possible to construct a computer program that uses artificial intelligence to mimic a terrorist organization. The program would determine the actions needed to execute a terrorist act. Once these actions were determined, it would be possible to search database records to find evidence of these actions.

    Debate the morality of developing a computer program capable of planning the steps needed to execute an act of terror.

28. A multinational corporation transfers a foreign employee to the United States on an L-1 visa. The foreign employee is a computer programmer, working alongside an American computer programmer doing the same work. Both programmers joined the company five years ago, after graduating from college. Their training, skills, and experience are virtually identical.

    Divide the class into two groups, pro and con, to debate the following proposition: "The salaries and benefits of the two computer programmers should be roughly equivalent."

29. You lead a group of five software engineers involved in the testing of a new product. Your manager tells you that because of a company-wide layoff, you will need to give notice to

one member of your team. From your interactions with the team members, you can easily identify the two members who are least productive, but you are not sure which of them you should lay off. You know that the company keeps track of all Internet traffic to each person's computer, although you have never shared this information with your team. You could use this information to determine how much time, if any, these two employees are spending surfing the Web. Is it wrong to access these records?

30. A company runs a large technical support office. At any time, about 50 technical support specialists are on duty, answering phone calls from customers. The company is considering paying the technical support specialists based on two criteria: the average number of phone calls they answer per hour and the results of occasional customer satisfaction surveys. Debate the pros and cons of the proposed method of determining wages.

31. In this role-playing exercise students weigh the pros and cons of working for companies with different philosophies about work.

Company A is a large, established hardware and software company. Employees have a reasonable level of job security, although there have been layoffs in the past few years. Salaries are highly competitive. The company offers stock options, but the stock price is not rising rapidly, and employees know they are not going to get rich from selling their options. The typical programmer works about 45 hours a week.

Company B is a medium-sized, mature software company that plays a dominant role in a specialized market. The company has never had to lay off employees. Salaries are a little low by industry standards, but programmers get paid overtime when they work more than 40 hours a week. The company discourages managers from resorting to overtime work on projects. Many employees are involved in community activities, such as coaching their kids' sports teams.

Company C is a small start-up company trying to be the first to bring a new kind of shopping experience to the Web. Salaries are not high, but all of the employees have a lot of stock options. If the product is successful, everyone expects to become a multimillionaire when the company goes public in a couple of years. In return for the stock options, the founders expect a total commitment from all the employees until the product is released. Every programmer in the company is working 10 hours a day, 7 days a week.

Divide the class into four groups: three groups of recruiters and one group of students about to graduate from college. Each group of recruiters, representing one of the three companies, should make a "pitch" that highlights the reasons why their company represents the best opportunity. The graduates should raise possible negative aspects of working for each company.

32. Debate the following proposition: "It is immoral for a corporation to pay its chief executive officer (CEO) 400 times as much as a production worker."

Further Reading

Stanley Aronowitz and Jonathan Cutler, editors. *Post-Work: The Wages of Cybernation*. Routledge, New York, NY, 1998.

Jason Borenstein. "Work Life in the Robotic Age." *Communications of the ACM*, July 2010.

Martin Carnoy. *Sustaining the New Economy: Work, Family, and Community in the Information Age*. Russell Sage Foundation (Harvard University Press), New York, NY (Cambridge, MA), 2000.

Philip K. Dick. *Do Androids Dream of Electric Sheep?* Del Ray, 1996.

Martin Ford. *The Lights in the Tunnel: Automation, Accelerating Technology, and the Economy of the Future*. CreateSpace, 2009.

Robert H. Frank and Philip J. Cook. *The Winner-Take-All Society*. The Free Press, New York, NY, 1995.

Thomas L. Friedman. *The World Is Flat [Updated and Expanded]: A Brief History of the Twenty-first Century*. Farrar, Straus and Giroux, New York, NY, 2006.

Alan Joch. "Debating Net Neutrality." *Communications of the ACM*, October 2009.

Steven Levy. "The AI Revolution Is On." *Wired*, January 2010.

Pippa Norris. *Digital Divide: Civic Engagement, Information Poverty, and the Internet Worldwide*. Cambridge University Press, Cambridge, England, 2001.

A. Pawlowski. "Why Is America the 'No-vacation Nation'?" www.cnn.com, May 23, 2011.

Juliet B. Schor. *The Overworked American: The Unexpected Decline of Leisure*. BasicBooks, 1991.

Kurt Vonnegut, Jr. *Player Piano*. Delacourte Press, New York, NY, 1952. (A paperback edition published by Dell in 1999 is still in print.)

Mark Warschauer. *Technology and Social Inclusion: Rethinking the Digital Divide*. The MIT Press, Cambridge, MA, 2003.

References

[1]   Jeffrey Kosseff. "U.S. Calls, India Answers." *The Sunday Oregonian (Portland, Oregon)*, October 5, 2003.

[2]   Isaad Asimov. "Runaround." *Amazing Science Fiction*, March 1942.

[3]   Kurt Vonnegut, Jr. *Player Piano*. Delacourte Press, New York, NY, 1952.

[4]   "The Misery of Manufacturing." *The Economist*, pages 61–62, September 27, 2003.

[5]   Todd Lassa. "Toyota, Chrysler Have North America's Most Efficient Plants." *Motor Trend* (blog), July 5, 2008. blogs.motortrend.com.

[6]   Stanley Aronowitz, Dawn Esposito, William DiFazio, and Margaret Yard. "The Post-Work Manifesto." In *Post-Work: The Wages of Cybernation*, edited by Stanley Aronowitz and Jonathan Cutler, pages 31–80. Routledge, New York, NY, 1998.

[7]   Michael Gurstein. "Perspectives on Urban and Rural Community Informatics: Theory and Performance, Community Informatics and Strategies for Flexible Networking." In *Closing the Digital Divide: Transforming Regional Economies and Communities with Information Technology*, edited by Stewart Marshall, Wallace Taylor, and Xinghuo Yu, pages 1–11. Praeger, Westport, CT, 2003.

[8]   Louis Uchitelle and N. R. Kleinfield. "The Price of Jobs Lost." In *The Downsizing of America*. Times Books/Random House, New York, NY, 1996.

[9]   Juliet B. Schor. *The Overworked American: The Unexpected Decline of Leisure*. Basic Books, New York, NY, 1991.

[10] Melissa Will. "Hyper Business or Just . . . Hyperbusy." *Women in Business*, 53(3), May/June 2001.

[11] Michael H. Strople. "Bears, Bulls, and Brokers: Employment Trends in the Securities Industry." Monthly Labor Review Online, 128(12), December 2005. www.bls.gov.

[12] Martin Carnoy. *Sustaining the New Economy: Work, Family, and the Community in the Information Age*. Russell Sage Foundation/Harvard University Press, New York, NY/Cambridge, MA, 2000.

[13] Max Weber. *The Protestant Ethic and the Spirit of Capitalism*. Charles Scribner's Sons, New York, NY, 1958. Translated by Talcott Parsons, with a foreword by R. H. Tawney.

[14] Hans Moravec. *Robot: Mere Machine to Transcendent Mind*. Oxford University Press, Oxford, England, 1999.

[15] Anthony Ralton, Edwin D. Reilly, and David Hemmendinger, editors. *Encyclopedia of Computer Science*. Groves Dictionaries, New York, NY, fourth edition, 2000.

[16] Steven Ashley. "Driving Between the Lines." *Mechanical Engineering*, 117(11), November 1995.

[17] Monty Newborn. *Deep Blue: An Artificial Intelligence Milestone*. Springer, 2002.

[18] "Humanoids on the March." *The Economist*, March 12, 2005.

[19] "Better than People." *The Economist*, December 20, 2005.

[20] Electrolux. "The Trilobite 2.0," August 3, 2005. www.electrolux.com/node613.asp.

[21] Joshua Davis. "Say Hello to Stanley." *Wired*, January 2006.

[22] Richard G. Epstein. Review article. "Ethics and Information Technology," 1:227–236, 1999.

[23] Michael R. LaChat. "Artificial Intelligence and Ethics: An Exercise in the Moral Imagination." *The AI Magazine*, pages 70–79, Summer 1986.

[24] AAAI Presidential Panel on Long-Term AI Futures. "Interim Report from the Panel Chairs." August 2009. http://research.microsoft.com/en-us/um/people/horvitz.

[25] M. Castells. "The Informational Economy and the New International Division of Labor." In *The New Global Economy in the Information Age: Reflections on Our Changing World*, edited by M. Carnoy, M. Castells, S. S. Cohen, and F. H. Cardoso, pages 15–43. Pennsylvania State University Press, University Park, PA, 1993.

[26] Charles Babcock, Doug Brown, and Louis Trager. "Do You Live in the Internet's Rust Belt?" *Interactive Week*, September 4, 2000.

[27] Mark Warschauer. *Technology and Social Inclusion: Rethinking the Digital Divide*. The MIT Press, Cambridge, MA, 2003.

[28] Mike Gray, Noel Hodson, and Gil Gordon. *Teleworking Explained*. John Wiley & Sons, Chichester, England, 1993.

[29] Lance Whitney. "Report: Two of Every Five of Workers Telecommute." *CNET News*, October 9, 2009. news.cnet.com.

[30] Joel Kugelmass. *Telecommuting: A Manager's Guide to Flexible Work Arrangements*. Lexington Books, New York, NY, 1995.

[31] American Management Association. "2007 Electronic Monitoring & Surveillance Survey." February 28, 2008. press.amanet.org.

[32] "Employers Take a Closer Look." InformationWeek.com, pages 40–41, July 15, 2002.

[33] Rachel Fielding. "Management Week: Web Misuse Rife in UK Firms." *VNU NET*, July 15, 2002.

[34] "Stopping Workplace Internet Abuse—First Step Is Identifying Scope of the Problem." *PR Newswire*, October 7, 2002.

[35] Carl Weinschenk. "Prying Eyes." *Information Security*, August 2002.

[36] Melissa Solomon. "Watching Workers; the Dos and Don'ts of Monitoring Employee Productivity." *Computerworld*, July 8, 2002.

[37] Murray Chass. "Umpires Renew Objections to Computer System." *The New York Times*, March 4, 2003.

[38] Katie Hafner. "Where the Hall Monitor Is a Webcam." *The New York Times*, February 27, 2003.

[39] Sam Dillon. "Classroom Cameras Catch Every Move." *The Sunday Oregonian (Portland, Oregon)*, September 28, 2003.

[40] Andrew Urbaczewski and Leonard M. Jessup. "Does Electronic Monitoring of Employee Internet Usage Work?" *Communications of the ACM*, 45(1):80–83, January 2002.

[41] Robert X. Cringely. "Holy Cow! What Are All These Programmers Doing in India?" *i, cringely*, July 10, 1997. www.pbs.org/cringely.

[42] Cindy Easton. "Offshore Software Development: Is It Helping or Hurting Our Economy?" *The Cursor (Software Association of Oregon)*, February 2003.

[43] Patrick Thibodeau. "Survey: One in Four IT Jobs Moving Offshore." *Computerworld*, December 9, 2008. www.computerworld.com.

[44] "One World." *The Economist*, October 18, 1997.

[45] Paul Krugman. "Enemies of the WTO; Bogus Arguments against the World Trade Organization." *Slate*, November 24, 1999. www.slate.msn.com.

[46] Kristi Disney. *Globalization: The Migration of Work and the Workers*. Oxfam America, Fall 2001. www.oxfamamerica.org/publications/art917.html.

[47] Anthony Perkins. "Investors: Brace Yourselves for the Next Bubble Bath." *Red Herring*, pages 21–22, November 13, 2000.

[48] Reuters. "Technology Sector Lost 560,000 Jobs in Two Years." *NYTimes.com*, March 19, 2003.

[49] Joseph Menn. "Data Reveals Severity of Tech's Pain." *The Los Angeles Times*, March 7, 2003.

[50] Patrick Thibodeau. "H-1B Visa Count Down, Anger Up." *Computerworld*, February 3, 2003.

[51] Patrick Thibodeau. "Feds to Research 20,000 H-1B Visas Next Week." *Computerworld*, May 4, 2005.

[52] Eric Chabrow. "Opposing Views: The Debate over the H-1B Visa Program." *Information Week*, May 9, 2005.

[53] U.S. Citizenship and Immigration Services. "Cap Count for H-1B and H-2B Workers for Fiscal Year 2010." September 3, 2009. www.uscis.gov.

[54] Ephraim Schwartz. "Senators Open Inquiry of L-1 Visa Program." *InfoWorld*, June 27, 2007. www.infoworld.com.

[55] "Chinese Firm Buys IBM PC Business." *BBC News*, December 8, 2004.

[56] S. Srinivasan. "Chinese PM Seeks Indian Tech Cooperation." *Associated Press*, April 10, 2005.

[57] Stella M. Hopkins. "Offshoring to India Taking Off." *The Charlotte (NC) Observer*, June 28, 2005.

[58] Alban Douillet, Juergen Ributzka, and Suneel Jain. "Open64 Compiler and Tools." sourceforge.net/projects/open64/.

[59] ACM International Collegiate Programming Contest (Web site). cm.baylor.edu /ICPCWiki/.

[60] Betsy Stark. "Companies Moving White-Collar Jobs Abroad." *ABC News*, July 29, 2009. http://abcnews.go.com.

[61] Pippa Norris. *Digital Divide: Civic Engagement, Information Poverty, and the Internet Worldwide*. Cambridge University Press, Cambridge, England, 2001.

[62] Internet World Stats: Usage and Population Statistics. "Internet Users in the World." March 31, 2011. www.internetworldstats.com.

[63] "Basic Indicators: Population, GDP, Total Telephone Subscribers and Total Telephone Subscribers per 100 People." International Telecommunications Union. October 7, 2007. www.itu.int.

[64] Elena Murelli. *Breaking the Digital Divide: Implications for Developing Countries*. SFI Publishing, 2002. Edited and with a foreword by Rogers W'o Okot-Uma.

[65] Sydney Jones. "Generations Online in 2009." Pew Internet & American Life Project. January 28, 2009. www.pewinternet.org.

[66] Pew Internet & American Life Project. "Demographics of Internet Users." May 2011. www.pewinternet.org.

[67] "Broadband Connectivity Competition Policy." Federal Trade Commission, Washington, DC, June 2007.

[68] Jim Louderback. "Winter of My Discontent." *PC Magazine*, April 10, 2007.

[69] S. Derek Turner. "Give Net Neutrality a Chance." *BusinessWeek Online*, July 12, 2007.

[70] Joan Engebretson. "Giants Face Off on Net Neutrality." *Telephony*, February 19, 2007.

[71] Robert H. Frank and Philip J. Cook. *The Winner-Take-All Society*. The Free Press, New York, NY, 1995.

[72] "Where's the Stick?" *The Economist*, page 13, October 11, 2003.

Martin Ford

Martin Ford is the author of *The Lights in the Tunnel: Automation, Accelerating Technology and the Economy of the Future.* The book argues that accelerating information technology, and in particular robotics and artificial intelligence, is likely to have a disruptive impact on the future job market and economy. He has also written articles focusing on job automation technology for publications such as *Forbes, Fortune,* and *The Washington Post.*

He is the founder of a Silicon Valley–based software development firm and has over 25 years experience in the fields of computer design and software development. He holds a computer engineering degree from the University of Michigan, Ann Arbor and a graduate business degree from the University of California, Los Angeles.

He blogs regularly at http://econfuture.wordpress.com.

What is propelling the trend toward job automation?

The primary force is the continuing acceleration of information technology. Computers are now able to take on basic cognitive tasks such as decision-making and problem-solving to an unprecedented degree, and this capability is certain to advance greatly over the next decade and beyond. We can expect dramatic advances in both robotics and in software automation applications that take on tasks and analysis now performed by white collar workers.

A closely related issue is the vast amount of data now being collected throughout the economy: businesses are tracking the actions and behaviors of both consumers and workers. Virtually every transaction and customer interaction, as well as a great many activities internal to organizations, is being recorded. As organizations strive to make sense of—and somehow leverage—all that information, algorithmic approaches are becoming the only viable option. That is driving a lot of development in artificial intelligence (in particular machine learning), and ultimately those advances are likely to get applied to a great many areas, including job automation.

Economic factors are also, of course, important. As consumer demand remains relatively weak, the primary path to corporate profitability is through efficiency and cost cutting. The danger going forward is that business will continue to focus on extracting as much wealth as possible through cost-cutting, rather than on making investments that create new markets and help expand the economy.

Why should we be concerned about the trend toward job automation?

I think it is a matter of degree. Technology has, of course, been advancing for hundreds of years, and we are all far better off because of that. However, I think we may soon approach a tipping point where machines evolve from being tools to becoming autonomous workers. Historically, as technology advanced and machines became more capable, the value of the average worker operating one of those machines increased, and so average wages also increased. However, once machines, on the average, get closer to running themselves, the value of workers will begin to stagnate and then decrease, rather than increase over time. In fact, we see evidence of that already: real wages for average workers in the United States have not increased since the 1970s.

Once we pass that tipping point, technology will no longer drive broad-based prosperity. Instead, the fruits of innovation will all go to a tiny number of people at the top of the income distribution—to people who own or control large amounts of capital.

Isn't offshoring a bigger threat to the jobs of computer professionals in the United States than automation?

Offshoring is more visible, but studies have shown that automation actually eliminates more IT jobs. In the 1990s, huge numbers of jobs were created for IT professionals like systems administrators. Many of those tasks are now automated, and the trend toward cloud computing is eliminating a lot of positions as businesses outsource IT functions to centralized facilities.

I think that offshoring is very often the leading edge of the trend toward automation. Both are driven by advancing technology. When the technology is not yet sufficient to fully automate a task, offshoring will be pursued on an interim basis, but in the longer run, the task may well get automated. We already see this in areas like basic customer service where low-wage offshore workers have been replaced by digital voice systems in some cases.

For a long time, economists have argued that the drop in the price of a product resulting from automation has two beneficial effects. It increases the demand for the product, which means more workers must be hired in order to help produce more of the product. Also, people who were already purchasing the product don't have to pay as much for it, meaning they have more money to spend on other things, increasing the demand for other products, which also results in job creation. Why is this line of reasoning no longer sound?

Once we pass the tipping point I mentioned earlier—where machines cease to be tools and begin to operate more autonomously—then businesses will be increasingly able to ramp up production without hiring many new workers. So from that point on, it will be very difficult to maintain full employment.

As an example, consider the mechanization of agriculture early in the twentieth century. Millions of farm jobs were eliminated, but ultimately those people found work in other sectors. As food prices fell, consumers were able to spend more on manufactured goods and on services—driving employment in those areas.

Why won't that same process happen today? Because today's information technology is ubiquitous: it will get applied to every sector of the economy and to every new industry that appears in the future. That is very different from agriculture or early manufacturing automation, where the technologies were primarily mechanical and highly specific to the sector. Today's IT is far more flexible and will impact across the board.

The greatest disruption to the U.S. job market will occur when the service sector begins to see substantial automation. It seems likely that many of the more traditional, labor-intensive areas of the economy—areas like fast food, retail, and other service jobs—will eventually be impacted by these technologies. Once that happens, it is difficult to see how the economy will create the millions of new jobs necessary to absorb those workers.

Most economists believe that the economy will once again adapt and create jobs in new industries and employment sectors. However, we already see that businesses and industries created in recent years are highly technology/capital-intensive—and not labor-intensive. We can probably get some insight into what future industries will look like by considering prominent corporations like Google, Facebook, Amazon, or Netflix. All rely heavily on technology and employ relatively few workers.

While it is easy to imagine many new industries arising in the future in areas like nanotechnology, biotech, genetic engineering, and so forth, it is much harder to imagine truly new future industries that will employ large numbers of "average" people. One possible exception may be the so-called "green jobs," but these are primarily infrastructure/refitting jobs doing things like installing insulation or solar panels; they are not really associated with a sustainable new employment sector. For the most part, it seems likely that information technology will underlie newly created industries, while at the same time disrupting the more traditional industries that now employ a large fraction of our workforce.

This sounds like a version of the tragedy of the commons. It is to the advantage of each individual company to reduce its costs by introducing automation and cutting workers, but when every company does this, the pool of consumers evaporates.

Yes, in fact in my book, *The Lights in the Tunnel,* I suggest that we should view the market for goods and services much like a public resource such as a river or an ocean. If you imagine that the market consists of a "river of purchasing power," then as a business sells a product or service into the market, it will extract purchasing power. As a business pays wages to workers, it returns purchasing power to the river.

However, as automation increases throughout the economy, the mechanism for returning purchasing power to the river begins to break down—so the river will eventually run dry. For any individual business, there is a clear incentive to pay out as little as possible in wages; yet collectively, those wages are the primary source of income for the consumers who purchase the products and services the businesses are selling.

In many cases, jobs have been eliminated through the introduction of information technology, but the job wasn't automated; the service function was transformed into a self-service function. I'm thinking of self-service gas pumps and self-service checkout lanes. The customer is now doing much of the work.

Yes, this trend is important because it effectively lowers the threshold for eliminating jobs. In fact, a business does not need to fully automate everything a worker does: it simply needs to make the task simple and approachable enough so it can be taken on by the consumer. This is, of course, happening with ATMs, self-serve checkout lanes, and increasingly sophisticated vending machines. We are also beginning to see information and customer service provided via mobile devices.

It's also important to note that self-service of this type will happen internal to organizations. For example, a manger who currently supervises a number of knowledge workers may someday instead have access to powerful AI-enabled tools that enable him or her to directly take on many of the tasks now performed by those workers. This is likely to further flatten organizations, eliminating knowledge-based jobs and middle managers.

Are you anti-technology? Would our global society be better off without the development of new information technologies?

Not at all. I believe that the prosperity we now enjoy in developed countries is almost entirely due to technological progress. And I think technology offers the only hope for increased prosperity in the future.

The problem is not with technology but with our economic system. We need to adapt it to reflect the new realities implied by advancing information technology. Without that, the benefits from innovation will accrue only to a tiny number of people, while the vast majority see their situations stagnate or decline. Ultimately, that seems likely to undermine the entire economy as well as our political and social institutions.

You have argued that without some fundamental changes, we're facing a continuing downward spiral in our economy: job losses leading to consumers being eliminated from the market leading to falling demand leading to further job losses. Briefly, what is your prescription for preventing this collapse?

Ultimately, I think we will have to decouple access to an income from the need to have a traditional job. The easiest way to do this is though some type of basic, guaranteed income scheme. In other words, everyone would receive an income, and those who have the necessary skills and motivation (and could find an opportunity) would also be able to generate additional income through work or entrepreneurship.

In today's political environment, a guaranteed income would probably be disparaged as an extreme leftist idea or "the welfare state run amok." However, a guaranteed income is actually a free-market concept and was supported by conservative economists like Friedrick Hayek and Milton Friedman.

One problem with a guaranteed income is that jobs, of course, provide more than just an income—work is a way to occupy time and also gives people a sense of purpose. In *The Lights in the Tunnel*, I suggest that we might modify a basic income scheme by incorporating incentives—especially for education.

For example, suppose we offered everyone a minimal income, but if a person manages to graduate from high school or pass an equivalency test, he or she will receive a higher income. The same could be done for higher levels of education, and other incentives such as work in the community could also be incorporated. The idea would be to maintain a strong incentive for the population to become educated while at the same time giving consumers access to the income they need to participate in and drive the economy.

A

Plagiarism

AN ETHICAL ANALYSIS OF A SCENARIO INVOLVING PLAGIARISM APPEARS IN SECTION 2.6.2. This appendix provides a much more complete picture of what plagiarism is and how to avoid it.

Consequences of Plagiarism

According to the Council of Writing Program Administrators (WPA), "plagiarism occurs when a writer deliberately uses someone else's language, ideas, or other original (not common-knowledge) material without acknowledging its source" [1]. The consequences of plagiarism can be severe. Newspaper reporters and college professors have lost their jobs because they plagiarized the work of others [2, 3]. Colleges and universities view plagiarism as a form of cheating. A few years ago at the University of Virginia, 48 students either quit or were expelled for plagiarism [4].

The vast amount of information freely available on the Internet, the power of search engines, and the cut-and-paste capability of contemporary computer programs have made it easier than ever to commit plagiarism. Of course, Web search engines can also make it easy for teachers to detect plagiarism [5].

Types of Plagiarism

You are plagiarizing if you deliberately do any of the following:

- Copy the words of another without both (1) putting the copied text in quotation marks and (2) citing the source
- Paraphrase the words of another without citing the source
- Incorporate the figures or drawings of another person without crediting the source
- Include facts that are not common knowledge without citing the source
- Use another person's ideas or theories without giving that person credit

Guidelines for Citing Sources

Common knowledge means information that is available in many places and known to a large number of people. For example, it is common knowledge that Delaware was the first state to ratify the United States Constitution. You do not have to cite a source when presenting common knowledge.

However, you *should* cite a source when you present facts that are not common knowledge. For example, it is not common knowledge that the percentage of college freshmen in the United States interested in majoring in computer science dropped by more than 60 percent between 2000 and 2004 [6].

You must cite a source if you present another person's interpretation of the facts, whether or not you acknowledge the person by name. For example, Cass Sunstein argues that information technology may weaken democracy by allowing people to filter out news that contradicts their view of the world [7]. If you repeat someone else's idea, you must cite where you found it.

How to Avoid Plagiarism

Always put quotation marks around text you have obtained from another source, and write down enough information about the source that you can cite it properly. Do this when you are collecting your notes, so that when you are writing your paper, you will not forget that the words are a direct quotation or whom you are quoting.

When you are paraphrasing the work of another, read over the material, then put it aside before you begin writing. That will help ensure you are using your own words to express the ideas. Check your paraphrase against the source document. Make sure you have not distorted the original meaning. Whenever you have used a phrase from the another person's work, you must put the phrase in quotation marks. Always cite the source of the ideas you are paraphrasing, even if there are no direct quotations.

Finally, remember to cite the sources of illustrations and figures that you reproduce.

Misuse of Sources

The WPA definition of plagiarism emphasizes that it is the *deliberate* attempt to conceal the source of the words or ideas. This aligns with our definition of ethics as being focused on the *voluntary* moral choices people make. If a person has no intention of deceiving, but fails to cite sources or use quotation marks correctly, that person's actions constitute misuse of sources.

Additional Information

For more information, read "Defining and Avoiding Plagiarism: The WPA Statement on Best Practices," which is the principal source document for this appendix [1].

References

[1]   Council of Writing Program Administrators. *Defining and Avoiding Plagiarism: The WPA Statement on Best Practices*, January, 2003. www.wpacouncil.org.

[2]   "Corrections." *The New York Times*, May 2, 2003.

[3]   Scott Smallwood. "Arts Professor at New School U. Resigns after Admitting Plagiarism." *The Chronicle of Higher Education*, September 20, 2004.

[4]   Brian Hansen. "Combating Plagiarism: Is the Internet Causing More Students to Copy?" *The CQ Researcher*, 13(32), 2003.

[5]   Katie Hafner. "Lessons in Internet Plagiarism." *The New York Times*, June 28, 2001.

[6]   Jay Vegso. "Interest in CS as a Major Drops among Incoming Freshmen." *Computing Research News*, 17(3), May 2005.

[7]   Cass Sunstein. *Republic.com*. Princeton University Press, Princeton, NJ, 2001.

Index